WITCHES, DRUIDS AND KING ARTHUR

Witches, Druids
and King Arthur

Ronald Hutton

**hambledon
continuum**

Hambledon Continuum

The Tower Building
11 York Road,
London, SE1 7NX

80 Maiden Lane,
Suite 704,
New York NY 10038

First Published 2003 in hardback

This edition published 2006

ISBN 1 85285 397 2 (hardback)
ISBN 1 85285 555 X (paperback)

A description of this book is available from the
British Library and from the Library of Congress.

Contents

Illustrations   vii

Introduction   ix

Acknowledgements   xvii

1   How Myths are Made   1

2   Arthur and the Academics   39

3   Glastonbury: Alternative Histories   59

4   The New Old Paganism   87

5   Paganism in the Missing Centuries   137

6   A Modest Look at Ritual Nudity   193

7   The Inklings and the Gods   215

8   The New Druidry   239

9   Living with Witchcraft   259

Notes   295

Index   351

Illustrations

Between Pages 142 and 143

1 The Round Table in the Great Hall of Winchester Castle

2 'Camelot, from the east and west', located at South Cadbury (Somerset)

3 The 'Sorcerer' of the Trois-Frères Cave.

4 Glastonbury Abbey

5 Merlin building Stonehenge

6 A Mythological Trilithon, from William Blake's *Jerusalem*

7 Wicker figure, from Aylett Sammes, *Britannia antiqua illustrata* (1676)

8 Winston Churchill and the Ancient Order of Druids

In Memory of

Hugh Trevor-Roper

*For having set me the example of ranging widely in time
and subject matter, along with so much else*

Introduction

A short while before sending this book to press, I stopped off to collect some clothes from a local dry-cleaning firm. It was a cold morning, and I was the only customer present and probably the first for some time, to judge from the fact that the counter was deserted, but I could hear sounds of raucous merriment proceeding from an inner room, where the staff were gathered. After a time I attracted attention by coughing politely, and a woman emerged into the public area, looking embarrassed to see me. 'I expect that you think we're all mad in there', she said. With perfect sincerity, I replied that I did not, and that it was good to hear people enjoying themselves on a grey and cheerless weekday morning. She gave me a look that seemed to convey disappointment and incomprehension, and took the ticket for my cleaned items. As she went into the inner room to fetch them, I heard her remarking to her companions: 'That fellow out there thinks that we're all mad.' I then heard an explosion of indignation from the others, indicating their feelings regarding what a stuck-up sort of person I must be. When she reappeared with my things, I paid up without a word save of gratitude and departed with a feeling of complete resignation. This trivial episode had brought home to me, more vividly than any text of postmodernist philosophy, the manner in which human beings filter their 'actual' experiences of life through a set of preoccupations that determine the manner in which they wish to perceive it, and so mould it for others in turn. Only the accident that one of the people involved in the encounter happened to be about to complete a book has resulted in this particular incident becoming 'historical', but – more to the present point – only circumstance has resulted in it being recorded with anything like objective truth.

Or did I just invent the whole story myself, to illustrate an argument more neatly than any actual experience had done, and to make myself out to be a nicer sort of person than I really am?

There are three issues involved in that question, and in the tale attached to it, which are going to be reflected and considered constantly in the book that follows. Each one represents a stage in the transmission of a history: an alleged original incident or situation; a record made of it in a particular source; and the credit that is given to the source by the various readers of it. To deal effectively with each is the challenge that faces virtually any historian. What enhances the difficulty of the problems considered in this book is that they are in addition concerned with elements in history that have traditionally been grouped under the headings of the irrational and insubstantial: with mythology, legend, and the dealings of humans with what modern Europeans have termed the supernatural. In the process I confront a number of issues and questions that were left over for me from my previous books on paganism, witchcraft and magic.

The work is divided into three sections, corresponding to the three components of the subtitle. The order in which they are considered is slightly different from that given on the cover, simply because the latter sounded easier on the ear but the former makes a more logical progression. The first third of the book is devoted to different aspects of myth. Its first chapter provides a definition of what the latter is commonly taken to be, and then makes a general survey of different ways in which it is created and manifests itself to a historian. The remaining two parts of that section consider major case studies of the ways in which history and archaeology have coped with personalities and places that exist on the boundary between fact and fiction. The personality chosen is that of King Arthur, the place is Glastonbury.

The central section of the book is devoted to paganism, and specifically to one particular problem in the history of it. In my previous books on the subject I have drawn strong distinctions between the ancient religions of Europe and the Near East and the varieties of modern Paganism that are partly based on images and ideas drawn from them. I suggested that, although there are particular streams of transmission between them, such as ritual magic, seasonal customs, and artistic and literary traditions, there had been no continuous survival of pagan religions through Europe's Christian centuries. In this reading, the Paganism of today is a set of entirely valid religions developed in response to modern needs and having a history stretching back a couple of hundred years, even though (as stated) they draw heavily on ancient material. What is attempted in this book is a pair of additional enterprises, which operate together to plug the gap between the ancient and modern forms of pagan religion. The first is to examine those strains of ancient pagan belief that appeared towards the very end of the ancient world, which bore the strongest resemblance to present-day Paganism, and which have exerted the strongest influence upon it. The second is to look at ways in which a place was retained for the ancient deities within a structure of Christian belief during the medieval and early modern periods, and to seek an answer to the question of whether these traditions could amount to a survival of ancient paganism in a different form.

The last third of the book is placed under the general heading of 'magic', and is the most disparate in its nature. What unifies it is that all its four chapters examine ways in which twentieth-century British people have reworked the religious and magical inheritance of the European ancient world for present-day needs: all are in their way case studies of re-enchantment, although of very different kind. The first looks at the practice of ritual nudity, across human space and time, and relates it to the prominence of this practice in some forms of modern Paganism. The second argues for the powerful influence of pagan images and themes in the work of two very popular twentieth-century authors who have commonly been characterised as exemplars of Christian writing. The third seeks to understand contemporary English Druidry. The last looks at the personal pleasures and pitfalls of making an academic study of modern Pagan witchcraft.

The strongest link within the whole collection of studies is the interplay between fact and fiction in the making and the analysis of history: as has been stated, this is a perennial concern for historians, but one raised in particularly acute form in the chapters of this book. It is signalled by the title, for there are actually two King Arthurs considered in the contents, one of them the historical or mythical monarch of international renown, and the other a modern English Druid chieftain who has achieved a great deal of counter-cultural celebrity and whose assumed, or realised, identity is directly inspired by the traditions of the first Arthur. Which, however, is the more 'real' of the two? The 'historical' leader, who is the one whom everybody recognises but who may never have existed? Or the modern man whose existence is undoubted and whose actions may be securely documented and studied, but whose role depends on the acting out of a set of myths?

My own answer to that question is that the question itself is both valuable and ultimately insoluble: valuable because it does raise important issues about our relationship with the past and our concepts of what is real; insoluble because the answer must depend so much on individual viewpoint. The fact that I can make such suggestions, and that many readers are likely to disagree with them and in different ways, illustrates one of the difficulties posed by the writing of this book. Another derives from the fact that the latter draws on material more commonly associated with disciplines other than my own, such as anthropology, classics, religious studies and English literature, as well as with historians expert in fields in which I have never carried out primary research. Some of the work is explicitly historiographical, and much of its leans more heavily on the published conclusions of others than has been my habit hitherto. The scholarly project behind it remains my own, and so does the attitude to the writing of history – essentially a pluralist and open-ended one – and the set of tools and methods, which are those of somebody trained as an empiricist historian. There is always a danger, however, in encroaching on the traditional subject matter of other academic disciplines without also adopting the conceptual models and approaches associated with them: I highlight it particularly at the close of the sixth chapter. At best it is possible by working in this manner to make friends and collaborators in many different fields; at worst, it runs the risk of having no friends in any.

To be aware of a broad range of scholarly traditions, and of modern subcultures, also serves to bring home the fact that even apparently routine matters such as dating and labelling are now fraught with tough choices rooted in different ideologies. Like everybody in my society, I use the system of dates, first proposed by the monk Dennis the Short in the sixth century, which divides human time into two spheres leading up to, and away from, the presumed birth of Jesus Christ. This got built into western culture and has now become more or less universal; there seem to be no alternatives with a realistic chance of general acceptance. Dennis labelled each twelve-month period of the current epoch *Anno Domini* (in the Year of the Lord), to emphasise that the most important aspect of that epoch was that it followed the unique, and cosmos-changing, incarnation of the one true deity. This was subsequently shortened to AD, and later still the preceding period acquired the shorthand label BC (Before Christ).

Very recently, and following the globalisation of the system, it has been proposed that these traditional names should be adapted, because they so plainly reflect the claims of a particular religion, the Christian one. In this new reckoning the period long known as AD becomes the Common Era, and that preceding it is Before the Common Era; thus, in abbreviation, they are successively BCE and CE. The logical objection to this change is, plainly enough, that it makes little practical difference because the whole system still derives from the Christian claim of the Incarnation. The answer to this objection is that to use the term AD, even reduced to capitals, is implicitly to recognise the truth of that claim. In practice, the introduction of the new labels has been patchy, even within the academic world. The scholars who have most often to cope with the two-period system, archaeologists and ancient historians, have generally stuck to the traditional terms. This is not because they are a Christian group, but because they tend most often to be personally indifferent to religion. Their unthinking employment of the familiar system is in most cases simply a suggestion that no important issues are at stake in using it. It is proportionately logical that BCE and CE have appeared most frequently in the writings of specialists in religious studies, who cannot avoid spotting the implications of Anno Domini, and among them it is now more or less an orthodoxy. The new terms have so far made no discernible impression on public life, and appear to be almost unknown among people at large, with the important exception of those religious groups who have an interest in signalling their difference from Christianity, such as Pagans. To the latter, of course, they can be very important.

I confess that my own instincts in this regard lie with the archaeologists and ancient historians, my natural kin in my workplace. I don't feel that to retain the well-known terms is to make an affirmation of support for the Christian religion, when they are used so routinely by people who are plainly not committed Christians. The underlying system is, as said, im-mutably based on Christian claims and the term 'Common Era' is itself questionable because it has not been common (in the sense of being rec-ognised by most humans) for most of its span. Nor, as also suggested, does it yet mean anything to most of the general public, and will not without a lengthy period of re-education. None the less I have taken a political decision, in this book as in my last two, to use the labels BCE and CE instead of the customary pair. This is because I have a regard for the sensibilities of those who object to them, which I think to be wholly understandable. If the liberal core to my being shrinks from any spirit of evangelism, it recoils more vehemently from the notion of imposing terms on readers who will automatically be uncomfortable with them. I have never yet, by contrast, encountered anybody who has expressed discomfort or offence at my abandonment of the accustomed shorthand. This decision has, however, automatically set me on a course of public education that can in itself look remarkably evangelical. By using the new terms in print, I feel also obliged to employ them to audiences encountered in my own teaching, and in the round of talks to local history and archaeological societies, and to schools and colleges, in which most historians engage. It seems that, if this process continues, the manner in which we label time will alter from an unthinking and accepted system, familiar to our whole society and those with which it has most commonly dealt, to a pair of choices that will reflect personal religious, cultural and political positions. If so, then I am happy with that, as it represents the kind of culture in which I am personally most at ease; but not everybody will have the same feelings.

If such a case of conscience may hang on a chronological code, the same sensitivities now attend the presence or absence of a capital letter. They have been signalled already, in the use of the words 'pagan' and 'Pagan'. Throughout this book, I apply the terms 'Pagan' and 'Paganism' specifically to people who now self-consciously identify with the cluster of religions which have made up modern Paganism, and have appeared since the middle of the twentieth century. By contrast, I always speak of ancient paganism in the lower case, and use the term 'pagan' when referring to images and ideas recycled from it in later centuries. Left to my own devices I would not bother with capital letters at all, but simply distinguish ancient and modern forms of paganism. Ancient paganism was not a religion, but a spectrum of different religions which were never brought together into a single system. In the United Kingdom, and some other states, modern Pagan religions have been brought, since the end of the 1980s, into a conceptual and organisational network, but I still do not think that a capital letter is necessary to make a religion. My problem is that other people do. Since 1990 the term Pagan has been used with increasing frequency as a means of self-description by individuals who earlier would have defined themselves according to the particular tradition inside the cluster to which they be-longed: Wiccan, Druid, shamanic, Odinist, and so forth. Furthermore, the Pagan movement includes an increasing number of people who do not identify with any of those groupings, and hold simply to the Pagan label. To most of these the capital letter is important, because they are used to a society in which 'real' religions have capitals – Christianity, Islam, Budd-hism, Hinduism, and so forth. To deny a capital, in this mindset, is to belittle and diminish the tradition being described. Again, this has no instinctual resonance with me. There are sound linguistic grounds for the use of capitals in these other cases, in that they derive from proper nouns, and I would prefer to educate my society into taking something seriously irrespective of whether or not it has a large letter. To describe as Pagans members of a religion such as Wicca in the 1950s and 1960s is to back-project a later terminology and context upon them. As hinted above, I tend to be impatient of gesture politics. What makes me set aside my own impulses, and adopt the capitalised form for the modern religions, is partly a wish to show courtesy to those of my contemporaries to whom that alteration is significant. It is also, however, a suspicion that they may actually be right and that – however much I may regret and resent it – to put something under a larger letter actually will increase the respect of the average person in our society for it. To a great extent gesture politics may in fact work. The problem is now whether, for the sake of consistency, I should capitalise ancient paganism as well and, as said, I have decided firmly not to do so. This has the effect, emphasised above, of drawing attention to the facts that the pre-Christian religions of the European world never possessed a common theology or structure, and that we should try to avoid imposing on them Christian concepts of what a religion ought to be. It also draws a firm distinction between ancient paganism and modern Paganism and stresses the identity of the latter as a modern recreation of old religious forms. All these results suit my own attitudes and purposes perfectly well, but they will run counter to those of many Pagans in the recent past, and a fair number at the present day, who would prefer to view the ancient world in terms of modern identities and assumptions, and stress the continuities. In this situation, I find again that a more limited set of intellectual horizons, and tighter disciplinary boundaries, would have rescued me from difficulty. Ancient historians and classicists habitually refer to pre-Christian religions as paganism without the capital, while specialists in religious studies – or at least the few who take any notice of the subject – give it to modern Paganism. By retaining the dual system I am at least speaking a language that both sets of experts ought therefore to understand. Even here, however, the precedents are not entirely neat, because C. S. Lewis, a leading scholar of the past as well as a mighty pugilist in religious debate, gave the old religions the capital letter; but then he was not a specialist in antiquity.

A final dilemma through which I had to negotiate my way when preparing this book was the tone at which to pitch it. For all my life as an author, I have tried to write in a way in which I would be intelligible to, and give pleasure to, both professional colleagues and the general public. In this I am fairly typical of my discipline; indeed, the most respected and honoured of academic historians tend to be those who have managed the balancing act with the greatest flair. Of late, however, it has become more difficult. This is partly because the non-academic audience for my work has become more divided and sectarian: Pagans, modern ritual magicians and members of the New Age movement, for example, form a very particular readership, with prior knowledge, wishes and reactions very different from those of the public in general and to some extent from each other. American readers are developing markedly different priorities and assumptions from those in the United Kingdom.

The work of writing for specialist and general readers has, however, been made more still problematic by an increasing tendency for both constituencies to pull in opposite directions, and for those who serve them to exert greater pressure on university-based historians. It will be clear from the first words of the introduction that this book has been written in a manner accessible to virtually any reader; which certainly pleases my publisher. At the same time I am aware that the pressure to write primarily for professional colleagues has never been as intense as it is now. Since the 1990s university departments have been graded, and their funding alotted, according to their performance in the Research Assessment Exercise. As the latter is necessarily carried out by national teams of academic experts in the respective disciplines, university-based historians now have the crudest and most obvious incentive to package work in ways that are most meaningful and admirable to their professional peers. As before, the most talented will succeed in achieving success both with their colleagues and a wide and varied readership, so automatically pleasing their publishers; but the achievement is getting harder to make.

These comments may cumulatively build up an impression of difficulties and anxieties, but they should also be taken as a sign of challenges and excitements. As the pace and volume of academic publication has increased, as the pressures on the profession have become much greater, and as the number of fields populated by historians have multiplied, so the nature of the job has altered. Careers that thirty years ago may have been likened (according to the energy of the practitioner) to drifting or sculling downstream now commonly bear more resemblance to a continuous shooting of rapids, often in unfamiliar terrain. The process may be exhausting, and battering, but it is also exhilarating, and I hope that the scope and the tone of the following essays reflect both its problems and its joys.

Acknowledgements

The shadow of Glastonbury hangs over all of the first three essays in this collection. 'How Myths Are Made' was originally written as a talk for a camp of the Oak Dragon Project, an outgrowth from the Glastonbury Camps, back in 1990. Its first delivery was to an audience seated on hay bales in a meadow, a situation carrying echoes of the origins of the whole academic tradition. Since then it has been through many versions and been delivered many times, the most moving occasion being its reworking as the first David Lunn Memorial Lecture at Bristol Grammar School. 'Arthur and the Academics' was born out of a public debate over the human ability to recover the past, staged at Glastonbury a couple of months after I was lecturing in that meadow. One of the participants was Geoffrey Ashe, who subsequently recommended me to the University of Southern Mississippi as a speaker on the historiography of Arthur; and so that essay began to take shape. The successive summer schools of that same American university honed some of my perceptions, and an early version of them, entitled 'The Second Romantic Movement and the Arthurian Age', was published in a journal edited out of the University of Montana, *The Year's Work in Medievalism*, in 1994. The enthusiasm of Stanley Hauer for the summer schools, and of Gwendolyn Morgan for the journal, made both experiences possible. Debts to interviewees for the finished piece are recorded in its source references. The third piece, on Glastonbury itself, had its roots in a section excised from my book *The Pagan Religions of the Ancient British Isles*, worked up into a talk for the Isle of Avalon Foundation in 1993, and subsequently published by the latter as a cassette tape. The final version has been read by Philip Rahtz, and revised in accordance with his suggestions.

The fourth and fifth essays represent a book in miniature, which may well later be filled out and published in its own right. Such a volume was in my mind since conversations with Richard Buxton and Jan Bremmer in the mid 1990s, which are mentioned in a note, and much of the material for it was collected in 1995–96, when I was considering the writing of a history of ritual magic in Europe for a series then being launched by Blackwell. The series was discontinued before I committed myself to it, but I remain grateful to John Davey for the encouragement that led me to stockpile data for the book, and I have continued to do so. Both pieces were read in manuscript by my own colleague at Bristol, 'Tony' Antonovics, by an American academic expert in modern Paganism, Chas Clifton, and by an independent writer based in New York, John Yohalem, who all aided me with criticisms.

Earlier versions of the sixth chapter, 'A Modest Look at Ritual Nudity', were published in two journals, *Dragon's Blood*, edited out of Cardiff, in 1994, and *The Pomegranate*, edited out of British Columbia, in 2000. I am grateful to my colleague in the Department of Classics and Ancient History at Bristol, Richard Buxton, for commenting on the final draft. The contribution of Ana Adnan to 'The Inklings and the Gods' is obvious in the endnotes, but the whole thing would probably not have been written without the inspiration of her invitation to speak at the gathering devoted to Lewis and Tolkien that she hosted in the Gower Peninsula in 2001. The result was read by two masters of the subject, Tom Shippey and Patrick Curry, who were lavish in assistance and support. 'The New Druidry' was read in earlier versions, of necessity, by almost everybody described in it: Caitlín and John Matthews, Philip Carr-Gomm, Philip Shallcrass, Tim Sebastian, Rollo Maughfling, Arthur Pendragon, and Caroline Wise of the Fellowship of Isis. All replied helpfully and generously. The last essay, 'Living with Witchcraft', caused me the most nerves, and was given the toothcomb treatment by Joanne Pearson, James Sharpe, Sabina Magliocco and Diarmaid MacCulloch, all of whom I knew to be painstaking scholars and who represented between them a range of instinctual, disciplinary and religious positions. I was correct in my expectations: of the four, two urged me to be more candid, one warned me to be more reticent, and one advised me not to publish the piece at all. I doubt that I have got the final balance right, but the effort that these four friends put into it between them justifies to me in itself the fact that something of it should emerge into print

Bibliographical Note

As a balance between style and needs, full publication details are given for all books produced after 1950: for those before then, only the place and date of publication are provided.

How Myths are Made

A few decades ago, a young anthropologist called Nigel Barley was working among the Dowayo tribe of Cameroon. One day he had the following exchange, beginning when he asked the question

> Who organised this festival?'
> The man with the porcupine quills in his hair.'
> I can't see anyone with porcupine quills in his hair.'
> No, he's not wearing them.'

Barley used this example to illustrate his observation that tribal peoples tend to describe things as they should be, not as they actually are. The man concerned was associated with wearing porcupine quills, and so the person talking to Barley saw them there, even when they were not really present.[1] It is not just tribal peoples, however, who have this way of seeing the world.

Between 1881 and 1884 a conscientious antiquarian called the Abbé Cau-Durban excavated the floor of the cave of Marsoulas in the Pyrenean foothills of France. He was looking for Old Stone Age remains, and found them, but never once in the months which he devoted to this task did he seem to notice that the walls of the cave are covered on both sides by paintings from the same period. Marsoulas is a short, low-vaulted grotto, and so the artwork would have been in full and easy view of Cau-Durban each time that he looked up. He did not, however, expect to see it, because at that period Palaeolithic cave art was not yet recognised as existing; and, because it was not intellectually recognised, it was physically of no interest to him. To later prehistorians it was the most obvious feature of the cave.[2]

Much of what follows is going to be concerned with such phenomena: with human beings literally or figuratively seeing things that aren't there or not seeing things that are. It is also concerned with the way in which these effects are used in the development of myth, in the sense of a means of containing and transmitting cultural messages which has itself either no basis in reality or else transforms reality. This sense directly echoes the meaning of the original Greek word *muthos*, which signified a story told to entertain or to play upon emotion rather than a logical discourse. Anthropologists were deeply interested in myths all through the twentieth century, an interest which reached its apogee among the mid century structuralists. This chapter is concerned not so much with the structure and function of the phenomenon as with the means and mechanisms by which it is created and sustained.

The first area of concern is with national myths, and the symbols which embody and sustain them. It is perfectly obvious that nations are entities created by shared experiences, memories and symbolism, rather than geography, ethnicity or language. Some of the most successful nations, such as the United States, have been among the most ethnically diverse. North-eastern Europe has no natural frontiers while south-eastern Europe is a maze of mountains, peninsulas and islands, and yet firmly-defined national states have appeared in both. Switzerland was arguably one of the first such states to emerge in European history, and contains four different linguistic groups. The study of the manner in which nationality comes to be 'imagined' has been a growth area in recent historiography;[3] in this period of devolution within the United Kingdom, the case studies here will all be drawn from the non- English portions of the British Isles, from Scotland, Wales, Ireland, and Cornwall.

In the case of Scotland, the most instantly recognisable symbol of modern nationalism is the kilt, and the story of its development was given its most celebrated, and mischievous, telling by Hugh Trevor-Roper in the 1980s.[4] In its retelling here, the focus will be firmly upon the four men who were the principal creative agents in the adoption of the symbol. The first was its inventor, a Lancashire Quaker called Thomas Rawlinson. He was not interested in creating nationalism but in making money, specifically by smelting iron. It was the family business, and he formed the plan, with nine partners, of exploiting the forests of the Highlands as fuel for iron ore shipped up from England. In 1727 he leased a plot of land in Glengarry from the local chief, Ian Macdonnell, and established a furnace there under his personal direction. The project was a failure, as the cost of getting the ore in and the iron out exceeded the advantages of the supply of fuel. Rawlinson's stay also had its traumatic moments, the worst being when a party of Macdonnells tried to murder him for apparently usurping the local authority of their chief. It is not surprising that he gave up and pulled out after just nine of the thirty-one years of the lease had expired, but he left behind him a perpetual bequest of his stay. His chief concern was to get trees cut down as efficiently as possible and converted into charcoal, and the traditional Highland dress, the belted plaid, was not suited to the work. To speed it up, he devised a new garment for his workmen, of the skirt of the plaid, detached from the remainder of the garment which had been thrown over the shoulder. The convenience of the new form of dress soon recommended itself to the Macdonnells, and spread from Glengarry across the Highlands and northern Lowlands within a few years under the name of *feileadh-beg*. The agility which it gave the wearer also caused it to be preferred for the Highland regiments raised for the British army between 1740 and 1760. The ban on the traditional dress of the Highlanders following the rebellion of 1745, which lasted until 1782, made those regiments, in their new-style kilts, the legal expression of a distinctive Highland pride and costume.[5]

This ends the first stage in the development of the symbol, the functional one. The second was carried forward by a member of three of those regiments in succession, David Stewart of Garth, Perthshire, who joined the army at the age of thirteen in 1783 and thereafter made it his home. Between 1794 and 1814 he served in the Netherlands, Mediterranean and West Indies, rising to command the West India Rangers. He might never have given thought to his homeland at all had the end of the Napoleonic Wars not left him retired on half-pay, and had the colonel of the famous Highland regiment nicknamed the Black Watch not asked him to write its history. He commenced the work in 1817, and soon extended it to cover every regiment from the region, and to include a survey of the society which had produced them. This was the period in which Highlanders were starting to be romanticised, most notably in the novels of the Lowlander Sir Walter Scott, and Stewart turned them into the ideal of all that he felt that British soldiers should be: fiercely brave, loyal to their chiefs and their Crown, and filled with a collective pride in their military unit, whether clan or regiment. Much of his research was conducted not in the region itself, but in army mess-halls where he talked to elderly officers and drew on their memories of the previous century. The crux of his case was that the traditional spirit of the Highlands had to be renewed in order to provide Britain with a first-class pool of military manpower. The result, his two-volume study *Sketches of the Character, Manners and Present State of the Highlanders of Scotland*, was published in 1822.

The moment was perfect, because in that year George IV was making his state visit to Scotland, the first appearance in the country by a reigning monarch since the seventeenth century. In 1820 Stewart had founded a Celtic Society of Edinburgh, to promote the celebration of Highland ways and the readoption of Highland dress; by which he meant the kilt devised by Rawlinson and now long associated with the regiments. Its members were mostly young civilians inspired by the novels of Scott, who himself accepted the post of its president. He was duly chosen as master of ceremonies for the royal visit. Stewart, however, acted as his adviser, and was

'accepted as virtual dictator on all matters concerned with discipline, costume, and precedence'. He made sure that the guard of honour for the
king was comprised of members of the Celtic Society, wearing the kilt, and
that George himself sported the same costume. It was this event, more
than anything else, which made the ironmaster's garment the definitive
item of Scottish national dress. It also remade Stewart's own career, for in
1825 he was promoted to major-general, and four years later appointed to
govern the West Indian island of St Lucia. The appointment was his death
warrant, for St Lucia was notoriously unhealthy, and he died almost immediately of fever.[6]

One further step was yet to be taken. In his book, Stewart had propagated
the idea that Highland clans had worn distinctive patterns (or 'setts') of
tartan. It was wrong, and represented one of the classic moments when he
projected the recently-developed traditions of Highland regiments onto the
society which had produced them. He himself fully believed it, however,
and there was no alternative body of research then available to contradict
him. When the royal visit of 1822 occurred, he therefore required Highland
chiefs to turn up to greet their monarch, wearing the setts of their clan.
There ensued a desperate scramble among the chiefs concerned, both to
acquire tartan and to acquire information as to which setts should rightfully
be theirs. In this they received much assistance from two charming young
English brothers called Ian and Charles Hay Allen. They were the grandsons
of an admiral, and the sons of a clergyman's daughter and a rather mysterious
dilettante who had retired from the navy to divide his time between London
and Italy. King George's visit seems to have been a turning-point in their
lives as in so much else, for they appointed themselves as experts in the
traditional setts of clan tartans and got to work providing the requisite data
to the anxious chiefs. It is not certain how long they had been in Scotland
before 1822, but thereafter they made it the centre of their ambitions, and
of their fantasies, which developed along two parallel courses during the
rest of the 1820s. They began to suggest that they had documentary evidence
to prove that many Highland and Lowland names had distinctive setts since
the late middle ages. They also changed their name to 'Stuart Hay' and
began to hint that they were descended from Bonnie Prince Charlie.

In the former claim they gained some support from Scottish gentry keen
to possess family setts, and from a firm of tartan manufacturers keen to
pick up sales now that the market for military kilts was depressed in
peacetime. In the latter, they gained the patronage of the chief of the
Frasers, so that by the 1830s they were sporting the royal arms and styling
themselves 'the Princes', with a further change of family name to 'Stuart'.
More public progress was blocked in 1829 by Scott, who cast doubt upon

the evidence which they had attested for historic setts, and thought the young men concerned to be too fond of sporting fake orders of knighthood. After another ten years, Scott was safely dead, and the brothers made a bid for national acceptance between 1842 and 1844 by publishing two successive lavishly-illustrated books on Highland costume. The second in particular was an adroit mixture of genuine research, half-truth and outright invention. The Allens were ruined in 1847, when their claims to royal blood were attacked so savagely that they deemed it expedient to remove to the Austrian Empire. Their setts, however, were adopted as the basis for what was becoming the recognised range of clan and family tartans to match the new national costume of the kilt. The standard modern tourist map of Scottish tartans consists in essence of that of clan territories provided in Stewart's *Sketches*, combined with the setts developed ultimately from the work of the Allen brothers.[7] The process was completed during the revival of 'Celtic' cultural and political nationalisms from the late nineteenth century, when it became widely believed that Rawlinson's invention was not only the national dress of Scotland but had once been common to all countries to which the label of 'Celtic' was now applied. The garment was adopted by nationalists in Ireland, Brittany and Cornwall, with their own distinctive setts.[8]

What is so striking about this story, from the present point of enquiry, is the decisive part played by both of two classic forms of personality who make national myths and charge their symbols with emotion. In this case the symbol itself was a technological invention produced by a hard-headed foreign entrepreneur for a practical end, to maximise profit. It was then made symbolic by the two great varieties of myth-maker: a child of the nation itself, who departed to exile in a foreign land and then returned to his own to commence a love affair with it and redeem it, and by two foreigners who fell in love with a land not their own, came to identify it with themselves and gave themselves a new identity in the process, and in so doing reshaped the land itself. Both are also present in the second example, of Wales.

The Welsh in the late eighteenth and nineteenth centuries had in common with the Scots the experience of having been absorbed into a larger, and very successful, national unit dominated by the English. Their problem was therefore to ensure the maintenance of both the union and its advantages, and of their own historic national and cultural distinction which was the basis of their communal pride. This need helps to explain the general Welsh cultural revival of the late eighteenth century, represented most obviously by the reappearance of *eisteddfodau*, competitions of the performing arts.

These wholly lacked, however, an instantly recognisable national symbolism. It was provided by individuals who were not merely liminal in themselves, like those so prominent in the story of the kilt, but drawn from or active within a literal borderland, that region where the relatively Anglicised Welsh counties of Glamorgan and Breconshire met the English one of Monmouthshire.

The process was commenced by a figure who combined the charateristics of David Stewart and the Allens, a stonemason from Glamorgan called Edward Williams who took the name of Iolo Morganwg. Like Stewart, he had parted from his homeland, having emigrated to London and become part of the homesick and patriotic Welsh community there which played a large part in sponsoring the national revival. It was on Primrose Hill, north London, in 1792, that Williams first staged a ritual opening for an *eisteddfod* which he termed a *gorsedd*. It made an immediate impression on the London Welsh, but took considerably longer to be accepted in their homeland. Eventually it was incorporated into an *eisteddfod* at Carmarthen in 1819, and thereafter became standard at such events. Like the Allens, Williams passed off his compositions as a rediscovery of old tradition, in his case the tradition concerned being that of the ancient Druids. Like them, also, his work consisted of an ingenious mixture of genuine research, misrepresentation and forgery.[9]

If the *gorsedd* provided a set of actions proclaiming and embodying a distinctive Welsh identity, the next step was to find a costume, an object and a body of national literature to reinforce that identity. All these were furnished directly or indirectly by Augusta Hall, daughter of a London merchant called Waddington who had made a fortune in the American trade and retired first to Berkshire and then to the point in Monmouthshire where the rich Vale of Usk prepares to meet the Black Mountains, and England (until 1974) approached its border with Wales. She lived there for the rest of her life. Having inherited serious new money, she married more in the shape of Benjamin Hall, heir of the founder of one of Monmouthshire's main ironworks, Their wealth allowed the couple lives of leisured gentility. Benjamin achieved distinction in national politics, becoming ennobled as Baron Llanover and having Britain's most famous bell, 'Big Ben', named after him. Augusta acquired two evangelical passions. One was for Christianity, the other for Welsh cultural nationalism, to which she was thoroughly converted after attending an *eisteddfod* at Brecon in 1826. Thereafter she and her husband sponsored regular *eisteddfodau* at Abergavenny, the nearest town to their seat.

In the course of this work she encouraged two other remarkable individuals. One was Thomas Jeffrey Llewelyn Prichard, a travelling actor, journalist and author from Brecon who made a speciality of writing guide-books to encourage the swelling number of English tourists visiting Wales. In the late 1820s Augusta Hall employed him to catalogue her library. It was during these years that he published the assertion that each county of south Wales had its own traditional female costume. The idea was good for tourist business, although it has been rejected by historians of Welsh culture. It clearly made an impression on Augusta, who proposed to an *eisteddfod* at Cardiff in 1834 that a national costume be developed for Wales, as distinctive as that now claimed by the Scots. From 1836 onward she ensured that she and her female friends appeared at the *eisteddfodau* that she sponsored attired in such an outfit, and by mid century its red cloak, gown and petticoat, and tall black hat (none of these things particularly Welsh) had indeed been generally accepted as the national dress. The absence of any male equivalent has been put down to the disinclination of Benjamin Hall to take any interest in one. At the same time Augusta was providing her adopted country with a musical symbol, the triple harp. This was actually an Italian invention which had become popular in England in the seventeenth century and reached most of Wales in the course of the eighteenth. By the early nineteenth century it was commonly accepted there as both native and ancient. Augusta's enthusiasm for it, supported by her ample funds, helped to establish it as the national instrument *par excellence.*

Among the female friends who helped her to promote the costume was an aristocrat from the English midlands, Lady Charlotte Guest. Like Augusta she had married a rich ironmaster from the Anglo-Welsh borderland, in her case Sir Josiah Guest. Sadly, whereas the Halls' union was a conspicuous success, that of the Guests was not, and a recent scholar, Marion Wynne-Davies, has suggested that Charlotte fell in love with Wales to compensate for the lack of affection in her marriage. Whether or not this is true, her enthusiasm for Welsh culture was powerfully reinforced, if not actually engendered, by Augusta. The latter introduced her to a local minister, John Jones, who taught her the Welsh language and encouraged her in a project to translate the medieval tales contained in a manuscript preserved in an Oxford college, the Red Book of Hergest. The Red Book was written in medieval Welsh, while Charlotte had learned the modern kind, but Jones gallantly agreed to translate it from the former to the latter so that she could have the glory of rendering it into English. He had chosen his agent well, for she possessed both the social cachet and the literary flair to ensure the success of the resulting publication. It was produced between 1838 and 1849 by another of Augusta's projects, the Welsh Manuscripts Society, and represented the best of the stories from the Red Book, with others from different sources. Guest gave them the inaccurate but ringing collective name of *The Mabinogion,* and so furnished the Welsh with their classic body of epic national literature. The two English ladies had between them done more than anybody else to provide their adopted nation with a self-image.[10]

It is not surprising to find the same pattern at work in the much more tragic and bloody history of Irish nationalism. A recent historian of that nationalism has suggested that its popular appeal was derived from a myth, 'describing the struggle of an Irish race to free itself from the wrongs and oppressions of the English and Scots'. That race was characterised as having a distinctive, Gaelic, language and culture to fit its distinctive ethnicity, and a defining form of Christian religion, the Roman Catholic.[11] In reality, the most Gaelic and Catholic province of Ireland, and the most remote from England, is Connacht, and that was always the one most tractable to English rule. In the period of the Tudor and Stuart conquest its greatest medieval family, the Macwilliam, was conspicuously loyal to the English Crown (in its dual capacity as Crown of Ireland) and rewarded with the title of earls of Clanricarde. The greatest Gaelic family of Munster, the O'Briens, showed a similar loyalty, and was rewarded, in its different branches, with the titles of earls of Thomond and Inchiquin. During the great war of the 1640s, when most of the Catholics of Ireland rose in rebellion to gain home rule and security for their religion, their most terrible enemy in Munster was Murrough O'Brien of Inchiquin, who defended the causes of Protestantism and English rule with such savagery that the Catholics gave him the nickname of Murrough of the Burnings.

So who, then, were the main opponents of the English monarchy, who raised the standards of Irish independence and the Catholic faith? For most of the sixteenth century they were the Fitzgeralds, earls of Kildare and Desmond, the most powerful magnates in Leinster and Munster respectively. The Fitzgeralds were Normans, who had arrived in the land to help conquer it on behalf of the English Crown during the high middle ages, and acted as viceroys on behalf of it, ruling the half of the island under English control for most of the fifteenth and early sixteenth centuries. They turned upon their sovereigns only when ousted from power by a new succession of English adventurers. Similarly, what made the rebellion of the 1640s so serious was that the medieval English settlers rose en masse against the latest waves of newcomers from England, making common cause against them with native Irish. The main exception to this rule is the one that actually proves it: the events in Ulster where resistance to the English was led by the main Gaelic chief, Hugh O'Neill. The O'Neills had bid fair to match the example set by the MacWilliams and O'Briens, accepting the title of earls of Tyrone and showing every willingness to run their province on behalf of the Crown. What altered this apparently natural course of events was a pair of accidents. One was of personality, that Hugh O'Neill was an exceptionally sophisticated and cosmopolitan chief, brought up by an English family near Dublin and introducing the latest techniques of European warfare to his clansmen. For most of his life his ambition was to be an exceptionally capable local ruler on behalf of Queen Elizabeth. The other was of mortality, that all of his allies and supporters at Elizabeth's court died within a few years of each other, leaving his opponents temporarily in the ascendant and determined to truncate his power. It was then that he made the decision to play the Catholic and nationalist card and go into rebellion in alliance with the Spanish.[12]

Modern Irish nationalist myth has none of this; instead, it concentrates overwhelmingly on the figure of the English general Oliver Cromwell, and conveys a powerful impression that it was he who was responsible for imposing English and Protestant rule upon Ireland. There is some symbolic truth in this, as Cromwell's army brought to an end the rebellion of the 1640s, and the confiscations which followed shifted the bulk of the island from Catholic to Protestant ownership for the first time. On the other hand, there is a very different perspective on the picture; that Cromwell represented not so much the English as such as a newly-founded and deeply unpopular revolutionary republic, which was as much the enemy of English royalists, Irish Protestant royalists and Presbyterian Scots, as of Irish Catholics. The myth goes further, however, to assert that Cromwell's conquest was an unusually brutal and bloody affair, summed up most of all by the massacres which he perpetrated when he captured the towns of Drogheda and Wexford. In the 1980s the Irish Tourist Board ran a promotional video intended to introduce visitors to the regions of the modern Irish Republic. When it came to portray Drogheda it spoke of 'one of the blackest days in Irish history', when Cromwell had every man, woman and child in the town put to death.

The truth is very different. Not a single woman or child is known to have died at Drogheda when it fell, and those who perished at the storming of Wexford were drowned when the boats in which they were trying to flee capsized. Cromwell's orders were to kill the garrisons of the towns as an object lesson for refusing to surrender, and in both cases some male civilians got cut down in the confusion of the fighting. In neither, and especially in that of Wexford, was the design to kill the soldiers inside the towns itself completely carried out. To slaughter most of a garrison was harsh by English standards, but not by those of this war in Ireland, where earlier the Anglo-Irishman Sir Charles Coote and the Gaelic chief Murrough of the Burnings had both carried out atrocities after storming towns which exceeded any of those perpetrated by Cromwell. Furthermore, the whole rebellion of the 1640s had begun with a slaughter of Protestant settlers, by the Catholic rebels, which may well rank as the worst massacre of civilians in the whole history of the British Isles. After his two brutal episodes at Drogheda and Wexford, Cromwell himself treated four more towns with notable clemency, and after he returned to England his successor in the Irish command, Henry Ireton, became praised by the Catholic population as the most gentle and just general they had known. All this, however, is expunged from the nationalist myth. When and how then did the myth develop? The answer has recently been provided by Toby Barnard: that it was a concoction of the late nineteenth century, when both Irish nationalists and their opponents found Cromwell a convenient symbol around or against whom to rally emotion. For both the convenience lay in the way in which it got rid of a much more complex, and less tractable, reality.[13]

In large part, the exercise was needed because the reality was still too messy, and paradoxical, for comfort. The great Irish constitutional nationalists of the eighteenth century, such as Henry Grattan and Edmund Burke, were all members of just that Protestant Ascendancy which had been first installed by the Cromwellian conquest. Like the Fitzgeralds before them, they had turned. The first modern organisation dedicated to both a political and military struggle for Irish independence, the United Irishmen, was founded by Protestants at Belfast, then as now the greatest single stronghold of Irish Protestantism. Its main hero, Wolfe Tone, the founder of Irish republican nationalism, was the descendant of French Protestant refugees from Catholic persecution and rejected revealed Christianity. Irish Catholicism was one of the main forces opposed to republican revolution until well into the nineteenth century. Even in that latter century the centre of the movement for repeal of the union with England was Dublin, the seat of English rule. The Gaelic and Catholic west gave little support to it until Anglicisation began to reach it in the 1880s. The Home Rule party of that period was founded by Isaac Butt, son of a Protestant rector who experienced a conversion to Irish nationalism in the 1860s, and its most famous leader was another scion of the Ascendancy, Charles Stewart Parnell.[14]

The same pattern holds good for the century's revival of Irish cultural nationalism. Its founders were Thomas Davis, Standish O'Grady and Douglas Hyde, all members of the Protestant elite and graduates of its main educational institution, Trinity College Dublin. Davis was the figure who inspired the others, and was himself influenced by the example of German Romanticism. Its most celebrated figures, William Butler Yeats, John Millington Synge, George Moore, George Russell and James Joyce, were all of

English settler stock and all save Joyce were Protestants. All, furthermore, were as much international as nationalist figures. Moore had to live in Paris and read French realist novels before he became interested in social issues, and then it was the English poor about whom he wrote first. Synge also served his literary apprenticeship in Paris, and Joyce came to settle there. Yeats's first major literary work was set in Morocco, while Russell drew inspiration from Hindu and Buddhist ideas mediated through Theosophy. Most of them found a major influence in Russian writers. The national theatre which Yeats and Synge founded in Dublin was most savagely criticized by nationalist and Catholic commentators. A generation later, the man who devotedly collected the Gaelic tales of the Blasket Islands and made them a central part of modern Irish consciousness, Robin Flower, was a Keeper of Manuscripts at the British Museum.[15]

All this might suggest that Ireland is like India, a country that seduces all those who think they have conquered it, but such a conclusion would ignore the evidence of the same patterns at work in the gentler modern nationalisms of Scotland and Wales. The parallel becomes particularly significant when considering two of the key figures who came to dominate Irish nationalist politics in the early twentieth century, by which time they had at last become identified with with Gaelicism and Catholicism. Eamon De Valera was half Spanish, born in New York, and first named Edward. He would have remained an American had his father not died and his mother sent him back to her family in Ireland, where he stayed after an attempt to return to the United States had failed. Michael Collins certainly came from native Irish farming stock, but his formative years were spent in London, working first for the British Post Office and then for an American financial company. He acquired his militant nationalism among the expatriate Irish community, and took his oath to fight for independence in a hall in Islington. The first leader of an Irish republic, Patrick Pearse, was the son of a London stonemason. His political career was largely a result of the way in which, amid the tensions between his parents, he came to side with his mother, a Catholic Dubliner. The most famous of those who were executed with him after the Easter Rising was James Connolly, a man born and raised in Edinburgh. He left Scotland only because of unemployment, and the chance offer of a job took him to Dublin after he had contemplated emigration to Chile. The point is worth driving home, that people caught up in a struggle to fashion themselves will commonly fashion nations in the process. Nationalists, like other dream-makers, are usually walkers between worlds. Ernie O'Malley was a physical force Irish republican who fought the British until 1921, and the Free State after that, but retained a lifelong love of English literature. Pearse himself adored and emulated Wordsworth. In 1916 Thomas MacDonagh, a university lecturer at Dublin, devoted his last class to Jane Austen. He ended with the words 'Ah, there's nobody like Jane, lads', and then went off to fight alongside Pearse and Connolly in the Easter Rising, and die with them. The tensions involved in such schizophrenia serve generally just to give a sharper edge to militancy.[16]

Modern Cornish nationalism has a much shorter, calmer and simpler history, focused above all upon the process of reviving the Cornish language; but here again the same pattern obtains. The revival was essentially the work of three men. The first, Henry Jenner, was born and bred in Cornwall, but his interest in linguistics derived from his job in London, as Assistant Keeper of Manuscripts at the British Museum (a generation before Flower worked there). He was converted to the idea of reviving Cornish after learning about revivals of other Celtic languages. The second man was Robert Morton Nance, who was born and grew up in Wales, of Cornish parents. He returned to his ancestral land in 1906, met Jenner three years later, and got swept up in the cause. The third was A. S. D. Smith, a school-teacher from Sussex who moved to Cornwall and made the land and its identity his own. Together they established a visible expression of national pride in 1928 by founding a Cornish Gorsedd (or, in the Cornish version, Gorseth), copying the ceremonies which Edward Williams had invented in London over a hundred years before.[17] The expatriate, the returning son, and the outsider seeking a new home and role; all were as potent in this story as in the others. Recent investigations of nationalism have laid emphasis upon the importance of medium (such as print), experience (such as revolution) and rallying points (flags or songs) in creating a sense of nationhood. It is argued here that an equal stress should be laid upon the special sorts of human being who act as the dynamic agents in bringing that creation into being.

Implicit at moments in the analysis above is a different theme: the power of literary fiction over fact. It has often been said that an inspiring fiction is usually preferred to a dull fact; the point might be pushed further to suggest that once a fiction is crafted cleverly enough to provide an enter-taining story, it has the capacity to overpower virtually *any* facts given sufficient time. To say this is not to deny that facts are deeply problematic and elusive entities in themselves. It is just to assert that a wildly and patently inaccurate account of events will be preferred to more objective accounts if it is packaged attractively enough, for the simple reason that it will be remembered and retold longer.

There is an island in eastern Polynesia called Nuku-Hiva, the most important of the Marquesa archipelago, and one of its valleys is called Taipi–vai. This has a prominent place in western literature, because the American author Herman Melville made it the setting for the book which first established his reputation, *Typee*, published in 1846. The work was represented as an authentic account of a stay which he had made in the valley five years before, and indeed it incorporated some of his own observations and experiences. He also, however, made sure that before he wrote the book he read every account of the South Pacific upon which he could lay his hands, and added to his narrative whole sections lifted from these other works. On top of these interpolations he invented entire episodes, which can be identified because they are geographically impossible or else violate all that is known of the social customs of the Marquesans. At times we have a direct means of checking his assertions, most spectacularly in the case of his description of his entry into the main port of Nuku-Hiva on a whaling ship. His portrait of the beautiful young native girls, swimming out to offer themselves to the sailors, is one of the most famous in the whole of literature about Polynesia, and has recurred in later literary and cinematic representations of that culture. There also survives, however, a private account of the same entry by Melville's own best friend aboard his ship, which records only the empty beauty of the bay. The spectacular scene in *Typee* seems to represent an ironic rewriting of one found in an earlier book, Charles Stewart's *A Visit to the South Seas* (1831).[18]

These considerations make it impossible to accept more than a small proportion of Melville's book as a representation of actual events and a first-hand ethnographic record; much of it is a beautifully crafted work of fiction. The major point here is that not only is it commonly taken as literal truth, but that it is the only story about nineteenth-century Taipi–vai which anybody now seems to know. Throughout the twentieth century visitors to the valley have seen it almost wholly in Melville's terms, eagerly matching incidents which he recounts to specific points of its scenery. The few remaining inhabitants assist them, and have no alternative accounts of their history during that century to provide; there are materials for such a history lying in western archives and libraries, but as far as memory is concerned – whether of visitors or of locals – only the fiction remains.[19]

The Marquesas might be accounted an extreme case, a society so traumatised by the experience of colonialism that it is not surprising that it became severed from its own past. The same pattern, however, is found in a larger island; that of Britain. When I was collecting folklore in west Wales during the 1960s and 1970s, the traditional stories which I heard most commonly in the region concerned a much-loved character called Twm Sion Cati. He certainly existed, being a gentleman seated near Tregaron,

Cardiganshire, in the late sixteenth and early seventeenth century. His reputation during his lifetime was as a deeply respected antiquarian and poet, the region's leading expert in genealogy. He may have had a wild youth, for in 1559 the newly-crowned Elizabeth I issued a pardon to him, but the Latin text of this document seems to refer to fines and debts rather than crimes. It is possible that all it signifies is a willingness by the new queen to help a useful Protestant subject out of financial trouble at a time when her regime was seeking support in the provinces. For whatever reason, by the late eighteenth century Twm Sion Cati was remembered in folk tales as a cunning and unscrupulous robber, with a famous wit, almost unrecognisable as the learned gentleman in the historical records. Some specific claims of the legend – that he married a rich heiress at Brecon and became a high sheriff – are certainly false. All of it may be so.[20]

His story took a new twist from 1823, when a Londoner called William Deacon published a collection of tales set in South Wales. He had taken a long holiday in the region when convalescing from an illness, and entertained himself by gathering folk traditions there. Deacon hoped that Wales might be a means to recover his career as well as his health. Hitherto he had been a not very successful journalist; now he tried to emulate his literary hero, Sir Walter Scott, by turning Welsh history and folklore into popular romances to duplicate Scott's work in Scotland. One of his stories concerned Twm Sion Cati, whom he relocated in the years around 1400 and refashioned as the outlaw hero of a melodrama, explicitly comparing him to Scott's famous Scottish outlaw, Rob Roy. The result was only a modest success, even when Deacon turned it into a play in 1824, but it inspired another struggling author of the decade who hoped to bring Welsh material to an English audience. This was none other than Llewelyn Prichard, then engaged in cataloguing Augusta Hall's library, and the result was a bestseller, *The Adventures and Vagaries of Twm Sion Catti* (sic), which appeared in 1828. Whereas Deacon had transplanted the hero to the middle ages, Prichard located him in a Wales with eighteenth-century society and seventeenth-century characters, and turned him into a mighty trickster and social rebel who stole from the rich and gave to the poor. This character was so engaging that he seized the popular imagination, and the adventures which Prichard invented for him passed into oral tradition among both English- and Welsh-speaking communities. By the twentieth century not merely the historic facts about Twm Sion Cati but the eighteenth-century legend of him had been more or less forgotten; it was Prichard's literary fiction that lived on.[21]

The English in general, and their intelligensia in particular, are no more immune to the same pattern. In 1819 Sir Walter Scott's novel *Ivanhoe* depended for much of its plot on the notion that ethnic rivalry between

Normans and Anglo-Saxons remained strong until the end of the twelfth century. The book was a fiction, based on minimal research, and in historical terms this aspect of it was utterly wrong. Its imagery was, however, so compelling that it influenced the view of the middle ages of not only a string of playwrights and novelists up to the mid twentieth century but some of the greatest Victorian historians, such as Lord Macaulay and Thomas Carlyle, and some of their most eminent French counterparts, such as Augustin Thierry and Jules Michelet.[22] In the formative decades of my own study of history, the 1960s and 1970s, I became aware that the impressions which most people had of the English Civil War derived from the novels of Captain Marryat, while those of Charles Dickens and Baroness Orczy had produced the commonly held images of the French Revolution, and those of Edgar Allen Poe and Dostoyevsky had produced the popular image of the Spanish Inquisition.

Very often, when dealing with major historical figures, the image is a single one. Anybody who has carried out any study of the individuals concerned will know that Alfred the Great never burned any cakes, that Marie-Antoinette never said 'If they have no bread, let them eat cake', and that the native American Chief Seattle never said 'How can you buy or sell the sky, the warmth of the land? ... The idea is strange to us, The earth does not belong to man. Man belongs to the earth'. It is very unlikely that Sir Francis Drake ever played bowls on Plymouth Hoe as the Spanish Armada was approaching, or that Sir Walter Raleigh ever spread his cloak over a puddle before Queen Elizabeth.[23] All these tales were spread about the people concerned long after their own time; but they are very often all that a modern person knows about them. Each represented the essence of what the teller believed *should* be known about the figure concerned: Alfred's humility, Marie-Antoinette's cruel ignorance, the native American relationship with the land, Drake's cool courage, and Raleigh's flamboyant gallantry.

Sometimes the process of creation is well documented, and results from a deliberate act of deception. The most popular story associated with Wales in the past two hundred years has probably been that of Prince Llewelyn and his dog Gelert. The dog killed a wolf which had got into the chamber where the prince's baby son was sleeping, overturning the cradle in the struggle. The prince came in, and saw the signs of the struggle and the bloodstains, but not the live child or dead wolf, both of whom were concealed by overturned furniture. He assumed that his dog had killed his child, and slew the animal himself in a fury, only then discovering his tragic mistake and erecting a memorial to the faithful pet. This is still to be seen at Beddgelert – Gelert's grave – in north Wales, where the headstone left by the prince for his dog is one of the tourist attractions of the region. In fact the story appears to come from India, where it was told in a fifth-century Buddhist work, the *Pancha Tantra*. By the end of the middle ages it had been retold in various books all over Europe and the Middle East. Nobody associated it with north Wales until the end of the eighteenth century, and then it was transplanted thither by an enterprising businessman.

He was David Pritchard, who arrived in Beddgelert from South Wales in about 1793 and decided to build a hotel there to cater for the growing tourist traffic to the locality, drawn by the majestic beauties of the Snowdon massif. Those visitors still lacked an incentive to stop in the little town, rather than pass through it, and so he decided to provide one, while his hotel was still under construction. The name of the settlement derives from an obscure early medieval saint. It was Pritchard who had the brainwave of locating the tearjerking old Indian story there, identifying the prince with the historic local hero Llewelyn the Great, and making Gelert the name of the dog. Realising that a physical monument would greatly increase its impact, he set to work with two friends to raise a gravestone. The first boulder which they tried to shift from the nearby hillside proved to be too heavy for them, and so a second and lighter one became the definitive marker. The Royal Goat Hotel opened in 1801, and within a decade the story had become peculiarly identified with the town and started to acquire an international association with it. It entered the oral repertoire of Welsh-speakers, and within a couple of generations was repeated by them as an authentic tradition.[24]

This episode also functions as an illustration of another major theme, the power of a good story to transcend geographical, political and cultural boundaries, taking on local trappings each time it is carried into a new region. This phenomenon was confronted at the opening of the 1960s by the distinguished scholar of Celtic literatures, Kenneth Hurlstone Jackson, when he considered the composition of the earliest known Welsh stories. His inspection of folklore collections came up with such basic plots as the tale of twin brothers, one of whom travels to a foreign land and is killed there by an evil woman, only for the other, sensing his fate, to travel there, thwart the murderess, and restore his twin to life. The oldest known example of it is contained in an Egyptian papyrus dated to around 1250 BCE, but by Jackson's time it was recorded in nearly 800 folk versions, sixty-six in Danish, sixty-five in German, twenty-eight in Czech, twenty-seven in Italian, and so forth. Another very popular plot concerned a witty servant or younger brother who rescues his master or sibling from the clutches of a king who has condemned him to death, by answering a set series of riddles. This is also first known from an Egyptian source, this time a Coptic manuscript of *c.* 850 CE, and was exceptionally popular in Europe during the middle ages. It has since been recorded in almost 600 folk versions.

Some well-known stories had more remote points of apparent origin. That of Cinderella is first recorded in ninth-century China, and appears in Europe 800 years later. It is probably impossible to locate the birthplace of the tale of a hero cornered by an ogre, who escapes by deceiving the monster into thinking that his name is 'Nobody'. It is most famous in the west from its appearance in Homer's *Odyssey*, but is also found in *The Arabian Nights*, and in popular versions collected by folklorists from Scotland to China. A similar range was achieved by the motif of the ring lost in a river or sea, which turns up in the belly of a fish, just in time to save the life or reputation of the person who had lost it. This tale is told by the ancient Greek historian Herodotus (in a context which suggests that it came to him from Egypt), but also in the lives of thirteen Christian saints, in an old Sanskrit text, in *The Arabian Nights*, and in a set of medieval Hebrew rabbinical writings. The problem which preoccupied Kenneth Jackson was that when he came to analyse the stories which made up the earliest and best-known Welsh literature, those forming the bulk of Charlotte Guest's *Mabinogion*, it turned out that many of the components of them could be found in older literary works from Rome to India. There was nothing specifically Welsh about them at all.[25]

This pattern does present a large problem for historians who try to use imaginative literature as a means of reconstructing the actual natures of past societies. Jackson may have fallen foul of it himself in a different work, when he was putting a case for the existence of a fairly uniform Iron Age 'Celtic' culture which covered the whole area represented by Celtic languages. A prime example which he used was that medieval Irish stories contain the motif of the 'champion's portion', the right of the best warrior at a feast to demand and receive the first and finest cut of meat. He pointed out that this also appears in Greek and Roman sources describing tribal customs in the south of what is now France, at the other end of the putative Celtic world. This is certainly so; but the problem is that it is now recognised that the Irish stories were composed by highly literate authors, who read Greek and Roman texts. They could easily have taken ideas from these to spice up native tales.[26]

Such a phenomenon may provide a solution to a puzzle that has vexed scholars of early Irish literature ever since archaeology began to furnish sufficient physical material to provide comparison with the portraits made in the stories; the heroes depicted in the medieval Irish stories ride and fight in chariots, but none of the harness associated with chariots has turned up in Iron Age Irish deposits. This gave pause to those who had assumed, like

Jackson himself, that the Irish myths and sagas represented an authentic memory of life in pre-Christian Ireland. The problem may be removed if it is remembered that in the greatest and most widely-read, of all ancient Greek literature, the *Iliad* of Homer, heroes use chariots; and early medieval Irish scholars were avid readers of Greek.[27] A parallel difficulty attends experts in Anglo-Saxon culture, who have long noticed that early English literature is marked by a brooding sense of fate – *Wyrd* – and the rule which it exerts over the destinies of mortals. This may well represent a continuation of tradition from a pagan past, and furnish an insight into a pre-Christian English mentality; but one of the most popular books in Anglo-Saxon England was the *Consolations of Philosophy* by the late Roman writer Boethius, which propagates just such a view of the cosmos.[28] An anthropologist investigating tribal magic in the Andes came to the realisation that it had been transformed by ritual texts and practices contained in European grimoires smuggled in by members of the colonial Spanish population.[29]

Good storytellers will lift material from any source in order to embellish local landmarks. In nineteenth-century Cornwall, it was said that a prophet had lived on Bodmin Moor, refreshing hunters who ventured onto it with draughts of a marvellous drink held in a golden goblet. One day a braggart among them vowed to his friends to drain the goblet; on failing in this he threw the drink into the face of the sage, and rode off clutching the vessel. His horse threw him, and he was killed, leaving his companions to bury him under a cairn of rocks, the goblet still clutched in his hand. The apparently remarkable feature of this story is that when the cairn associated with the tale was excavated, in 1837, the skeleton of a man was found beneath it, with a splendid golden goblet. He had been buried in the early Bronze Age, and his grave not disturbed until the excavators dug into it.

This assemblage of facts has been used to illustrate the extraordinary range and accuracy of British folk memory, which had apparently preserved a record of a particular burial for almost four thousand years. It was cited as such as recently as 1981, by a very prominent and justly respected prehistorian.[30] The problem with it was spotted by another archaeologist, Leslie Grinsell; that the legend of the prophet, the goblet and the braggart is not recorded as associated with the cairn until 1899. It was also, moreover, told of a mound in Yorkshire and ten different places in Norway, and seems to be a Scandinavian legend which has been carried to Britain. When the news of the finding of the Bronze Age goblet spread, some enterprising storyteller seems to have attached it to Bodmin Moor.[31]

Clear in that last example, and implicit in many of those before, is another major theme of myth-making: the role of collective memory. Until the

1960s 'oral tradition' was taken very seriously by many historians and folk-lorists as an authentic record of past events, even if in an embroidered and symbolic form. It was used to supplement written sources, and sometimes to replace them if none existed. Two caveats need to be entered against this statement. The first is that there were always members of both disci-plines who expressed strong reservations concerning this tendency, or even opposition to it. The second is that 'oral tradition' needs to be dis-tinguished from 'oral history' or 'spoken history', although the two clearly overlap and scholars do not always use the terms with precision. The former denotes a body of belief held collectively by a whole society or by groups within it, and apparently passed down to them by word of mouth. The latter denotes personal experience, usually of the person making the statement, described directly to a researcher in conversation. Oral history is a category of primary source material as important and viable as any other, and one relatively neglected until the late twentieth century. My concern here is with the former phenomenon, of beliefs about the past held collectively by people who had no direct experience of what they were describing.

The decisive re-evaluation of oral tradition came about in studies of African peoples, and because of a division which had long existed between historians and anthropologists in that field. The former had tended to take literally the traditional histories told by tribes about their own past, while the latter tended to see them as symbolic constructions of considerable cultural importance but very little direct connection with real events. In the 1960s the two views collided with each other, and the anthropologists won. A few specific cases became celebrated in assisting the swing of opinion. One concerned the Lotuko of the upper Nile, who were visited by the explorer Samuel Baker in the 1860s. A subsequent English visitor to them in the 1900s found that they could recall none of the personalities and events encountered among them by Baker during his stay; their memory for either stretched back for no more than a couple of decades. Another case referred to the Tiv of northern Nigeria. British administrators there in the early years of the twentieth century carefully wrote down the oral genealogies upon which local rights and duties were based. Forty years later the Tiv began to claim that these recorded genealogies were incorrect, because they were no longer convenient to the obligations which the tribe, in changing circumstances, wished to recognise. As such obligations were always sanctioned by immemorial tradition, any alteration in them had to be brought about by changing the memory of that tradition. A third example was that of the Gonja state in northern Ghana. The legend of its founder was noted by British observers as having been changed over the period of sixty years since they had first recorded it, to take account of the transformation in the number of local chiefdoms.[32]

The mounting compilation of evidence such as this led Africanists to conclude that oral traditions served more to sanction arrangements in the present than to provide a faithful record of previous times; indeed, that they left people with little perception of the past other than in terms of the present. This did not mean that such traditions were useless to scholars, for they sometimes contained information about genuine events which could be used to complement written records, and at all times they provided invaluable insights into the ways in which traditional societies remade their perceptions of the past to serve present needs. They simply could no longer be taken on face value; even where memories of the past were supposed to be preserved carefully by specialists – tribal bards and genealogists – the practical limit of accuracy was about 120 years. That was when it ceased to be possible to remember conversations with people who had actually once lived through the time being recalled. Traditions concerning more remote occurrences could sometimes be very accurate, but most were not, and without independent corroboration, from written records, archaeology or linguistics, it was impossible to tell which stories belonged to each category. Oral tradition could therefore not be ignored whenever it was available to scholars, but could only be used in combination with other sorts of evidence.[33]

These insights were applied by historians of Europe, with exactly similar results. A comparison of written records, oral traditions and archaeo- logical evidence in ancient Athens revealed that the family memories of aristocrats were fairly accurate up to the time of grandparents; effectively about a hundred years. Beyond that, they passed into the nebulous realm of 'ancestors' and became dramatically inaccurate. Indeed, they were steadily – sometimes flagrantly – reworked to take account of changing circumstances. Political memories were even briefer and less reliable, having an effective range of about fifty years. Even at the space of a century, events were remembered in sparse and simple terms, with few individuals identified and mythological elements creeping in.[34] The records of early modern England are studded with similar evidence. To cite a fairly standard example, in 1613 a jury at a court of survey in Monmouthshire reported the medieval fortress at Caldicot to be 'an old ancient castle ... in ruin and decay, but the cause of the decay thereof they cannot present, for it was before the memory of this jury or any of them'. 'Them' in this context meant the elderly people of the local community. Historians know that Caldicot Castle was in fact dismantled soon after the attainder of its last owner, the Duke of Buckingham, in 1521. To the people of Jacobean Monmouthshire, the early Tudor period, less than a hundred years before, had effectively become prehistoric.[35]

There seem to be two different, if intertwined, forces at work in the fashioning of memory into mythology. One is the conscious or unconscious transformation of the past into an artefact of maximum significance and utility to the present. A three-dimensional example of this was encountered by three archaeologists in 1988, when they were excavating a medieval village at Faris in Jordan. The local tribe, thinking that what they were uncovering might be valuable property, came to stake claims to it. Every day, the excavators had to cope with a string of visitors, each with a vivid and contradictory account of how they, or their father or grandfather, had been brought up in the house currently being studied. Some of the claims incorporated memories of deeds achieved when fighting the Turks in the First World War. It was quite obvious to the archaeologists that none of the buildings had been occupied since the middle ages, and, when they checked the stories of wartime heroics against contemporary written records of the war in that district; they found them to be impossible. An oral mythology was being constructed on the spot.[36]

The other force is in many respects an opposite one; the reshaping of memories of the past as a result of later experiences which have transformed the people who had the memories. An especially striking experience of this can be found by returning to the Marquesas. When western scholars began to collect folklore and oral traditions from the native islanders, in the late nineteenth and early twentieth centuries, they were told firmly that the archipelago had first been settled from the east. They were also informed that the monumental temple platforms and carved statues now lying abandoned in the interior of the islands had been the work of an earlier race, who were destroyed or absorbed by the ancestors of the modern Marquesans. These stories were accompanied by names of leading individuals and occasional circumstantial detail, and it is not surprising that they were believed by some scholars. The Norwegian Thor Heyerdahl sailed a balsa-wood raft, the *Kon-Tiki*, from Peru to Polynesia to demonstrate how the earlier migration would have occurred. Archaeologists and historians have now, however, established beyond doubt that the truth was the exact opposite of the story asserted by the Marquesans. The temples and statues had been built by their own ancestors, who were, indeed, still building them during the early nineteenth century when contact with Europeans had become regular. Those ancestors had been the first and only settlers of the islands before European contact, and they had arrived from the western Pacific. What the oral tradition of the early twentieth century actually teaches, therefore, is a valuable lesson in how completely a bruising experience of colonialism can cut a people off from its past. One specialist in Marquesan studies, Greg Dening, has commented on the fact that the Marquesans are now totally reliant on white scholars, who are equipped with the necessary archives and archaeological techniques, to regain any sense of what their own history and prehistory actually were.[37]

Once more, a leap from Nuku-Hiva to Britain can be instructive. From the early middle ages to the Tudor period, the land of Cornwall intermittently caused the English Crown serious trouble, by rising first against its rule and latterly against its policies. The Cornish allied with Viking bands to fight English kings, and were crushed alongside their enemies. In 1497 they rose against taxation, and were bloodily defeated at Blackheath. In 1549 they rebelled to defend traditional religion against the Protestantism of the Edwardian Reformation, and three pitched battles were needed to quell them. When W. S. Lack-Szyrma came to collect Cornish popular traditions of historical events in the early nineteenth century, however, he found that they had been recast in a thoroughly Anglocentric and Protestant form. The Vikings were now seen as savage enemies, and folk tales celebrated resistance to the Spanish Armada and to the Catholic Counter-Reformation of Mary Tudor, which took place after the reign of Edward VI, and before Elizabeth made Protestantism dominant for good. Folk memory had taken on the prejudices of its conquerors. It was not until the resurgence of Cornish nationalism in the twentieth century that a heritage of separatism and resistance began to be eulogised again, and that was based firmly upon information regained from books.[38]

Two personal experiences of disillusion with the literal truth of oral tradition may reinforce the problems discussed above. One was that of my late colleague at Bristol, the archaeologist Leslie Grinsell, who began his career in the 1920s with the conviction that a systematic study of folklore connected with prehistoric monuments in Britain would furnish authentic memories of the purposes for which those structures had been designed. In holding this view, he was simply repeating a truism among many archaeologists at that time, absorbed in turn from the attitudes of folklorists. What distinguished Leslie was that he actually made such a survey. When it was complete, in the 1970s, he concluded that folklore had no utility for the prehistorian whatsoever, other than as a revelation of much later attitudes to, and treatment of, the sites.[39]

The single apparent exception to this pattern of utter irrelevance was Bryn yr Ellyllon, the Hill of the Goblins, a Bronze Age burial mound which once existed near Mold, in north-east Wales. It was levelled by a farmer in 1833, and in its burial chamber was found a magnificent gold cape. This discovery was linked to a tradition that a giant ghost in golden armour was sometimes seen at the mound, and in this case the pattern obtaining at the Bodmin burial was reversed, for the folk tale apparently preceded the excavation.[40] In the opinion of Jeremy Harte, author of one of the liveliest recent considerations of the pitfalls of folk memory, this sequence of events still does nothing to prove the ability of that memory to retain accurate information from the remote past. As he points out, hundreds of prehistoric mounds have gathered to them tales of buried treasure, and of ghosts associated with it. In virtually all cases these tales proved false when they were opened, but the law of averages makes it likely that sooner or later one would actually prove to have something golden inside.[41] In fact the example of Bryn yr Ellyllon is even less secure than that. The only source for the prior existence of the ghost story is a lady who wrote two years after the discovery. Among the two informants whom she cited for it was the farmer who had found the cape; but, in his own detailed account of the event, he made no mention of a ghost. It is not easy to conclude, from this material, to what extent – if any – she embroidered a folk tradition to take account of the sensational find.[42]

The other case study of disillusion is my own, and relates to folk memories of the English Civil War. When working upon my doctoral thesis on the royalist war effort, during the 1970s, I was still deeply influenced by the earlier folklorist orthodoxy that such memories had real utility for the historian; and it was true that a few pieces of oral testimony seemed accurate and valuable. One was that of a Herefordshire man who was conscripted into a royalist army in his youth, and escaped by knocking down a guard; he told the story to his grand-daughter, who lived long enough to impart it to a nineteenth-century antiquarian. In 1839 an old man told of how his grandfather had served in the parliamentarian garrison of Barthomley church, Cheshire, most of whom was slaughtered by royalists in 1643. His grandfather had been one of the few survivors, and recalled that the atrocity had occurred because the attackers were avenging one of their number who had been shot dead by one of the garrison before it surrendered.[43] In 1870 a family at Brecon was still able to provide a circumstantial account of a visit by Charles I to their house in the course of the war, linked to a jug from which he had drunk and which was preserved as an heirloom.[44] All of these cases accord well with contemporary records. The first two are effectively oral history, and the last was tied to a physical object which would have helped the transmission of the account. I was also impressed to be told at Dudley Castle, in the Black Country of the west midlands, that the ghost of the Civil War governor still haunted the ruins. This would make a good fit with the historical figure, Thomas Leveson, who was particularly feared and hated in the locality.[45] Since then, however, I have wondered whether the story might not itself have been a result of more recent antiquarianism. At any rate, it matches the known facts.

Against these droplets must be set an ocean of misinformation. In the three counties of Kent, Lincolnshire and Yorkshire alone, local tradition held that fourteen fortresses had been besieged and left scarred or in ruins by Oliver Cromwell. Cromwell in fact was present at the siege of none of them, and five of them played no part in the war at all. The only castle which he did beleaguer in any of the three counties was Pontefract, where no folklore seems to identify him. At Ely it was confidently said that he had battered down the cathedral tower with two heavy guns which still stood on the nearby green. The tower in fact fell in the fifteenth century, and the guns were from the nineteenth. In Hampshire it was told how Cromwell had been shot dead in the pulpit of Alton church, and how he had hidden his treasure in a well at Merdon. At Norton Conyers, Yorkshire, the tale ran that he had chased the royalist Sir Richard Graham back to the manor house after the battle of Marston Moor, and killed him there, leaving the prints of his horse's hoofs on the landing. The real Sir Richard Graham died peacefully nine years after the battle.[46]

These examples are just a selection of the false tales told about Oliver, especially in the eastern counties, and reflect both the dominance in national life which he came to achieve in the decade after the Civil War, and the cult of him as a national hero in Victorian England. Other folklore about the war seems to be just badly-remembered schoolbook history, mixed up with local landmarks. Into this category would fall the farmer in Huntingdonshire in the 1970s who asserted that Charles II had hidden in a certain tree at Steeple Gidding until the 'Roundheads' pulled him down and cut off his head; this confused Charles I with Charles II, and Huntingdonshire with Shropshire.[47] In other cases real memories had become distorted. Somebody was shot dead in Alton church during the war, but it was a royalist colonel, not Cromwell. At Scropton, Staffordshire, the story was told in the nineteenth century of how Cromwell destroyed the nearby royalist castle of Tutbury. The villagers of Scropton had rung their bells in joy, whereupon Cromwell rewarded them by giving each freeholder land in Needwood Forest. Tutbury had indeed been a royalist stronghold, reduced and dismantled in 1646; but not by Cromwell. In 1654 the former royal forest of Needwood was sold off by Cromwell's government to pay its soldiers, and in 1658 local villagers were compensated for the loss of their grazing rights there. These are the genuine events which underlie the story, but the latter is worse than useless as a means of retrieving the former.[48]

At times local memory lost the plot altogether. In 1643 there was a bloody skirmish near Farleigh Wick in Somerset, between the armies of Sir Ralph

Hopton and Sir William Waller. In 1902 this was still dramatically apparent as the debris of war was being dug up there, and holes made by musket and cannon shot were visible in the walls of a lane. Local people, however, had no idea of when the fighting had taken place. One said that it had been against the French. Another told of how 'the king' had been staying at a local manor house when a cannonball had burst through the walls and almost killed him. He had heard this from his grandmother, who said it was 'common talk'.[49]

The vivid detail of the cannonball is typical of this sort of false history. A marble hearth-stone at Combe Manor, Berkshire, bears an indelible stain. This was said in modern times to be the blood of the royalist Colonel Rawlinson, flying from the second battle of Newbury. He hid in the chimney, hanging on to the top, but an enemy trooper on the roof saw his fingers and chopped them off, so that he fell down the shaft and was killed. The king's men were not routed at that battle, however, and there was no Colonel Rawlinson recorded among them. At Packwood House, Warwickshire, it was told how the famous parliamentarian Henry Ireton had stayed there in 1642. He had seen a young man lurking in the grounds, a royalist courting his daughter, and had him caught, taken to Kenilworth Castle and shot. Ireton had no daughter in 1642, and no royalist martyr is recorded at that date, when such an execution would have been sensational. At Duddon, Cheshire, folk memory celebrated Grace Trigg, a servant at nearby Hockenhull Hall, who was found hiding in a cellar there by parliamentarian soldiers after the royalist owners had fled. They tortured her to force her to reveal where the family valuables were hidden, and when she would not tell them they beheaded her on the back stairs. Jacqueline Simpson, who investigated this story, concluded that it was a fiction inspired by the sign of a pub in the village, showing a headless woman. In reality, this was a local representative of a pub sign fairly common in the nineteenth century, 'The Silent Woman', which was itself a nasty misogynist joke, suggesting that only a headless woman could be silent.[50]

In the early twentieth century a ghostly scream was heard regularly by policemen patrolling the Digbeth district of Birmingham. Some locals were of the opinion that it was caused by a railway engine in nearby sidings, but others believed that it was spectral in origin. One of these recalled the phenomenon when talking to the folklorist Roy Palmer in 1973, and ascribed it to the murder of an entire family in Milk Street when Prince Rupert's royalist army had stormed Birmingham in 1643. According to the old man concerned, Rupert's troopers had beheaded their victims one after the other, including five children. Such an appalling incident is not, however, mentioned in any contemporary source, including two pamphlets turned out by the parliamentarian press in an attempt to make capital out of the sack of Birmingham. They itemised every misdeed alleged against Rupert's men, but not this multiple murder which would have been the greatest propaganda gift of all.[51]

One of the most colourful and well-loved stories connected with the war is told of Goodrich Castle in Herefordshire, which stands in impressive rose-red ruin above the River Wye. The fortress was held for the king until 1646, when it was reduced in a long siege mounted by the parliamentarian commander John Birch. The story concerns the love between Birch's niece Alice and one of the garrison, Charles Clifford. She eloped to join her lover in the castle, and when it became obvious that it could not hold out, they attempted to escape under cover of darkness, crossing the Wye on a horse. They failed to complete the crossing and drowned, leaving their ghosts to haunt the ruins and their cries to be heard in every storm. It is an affecting tale, but not one found in any of the contemporary records of Birch's career, including two different accounts of the siege. Nor was it collected by the two scholars who diligently sought out written and oral evidence of the war in the county during the mid nineteenth century. It seems to have been invented between 1880 and 1910.[52]

One further example must suffice. Not far from Goodrich was an even more famous royalist stronghold, Raglan Castle, which was also reduced in 1646. Around 1800 a local antiquary made strenuous efforts to discover oral traditions concerning the siege, and failed. By the early twentieth century, however, it was confidently reported that Lady Fairfax, the wife of the besieging general, had slipped out of a house in the village below to warn the garrison of an impending attack. As a striking piece of visual corroboration, visitors were shown the very window from which she had climbed to give the warning. Alas! The anecdote never explained why Lady Fairfax should have thus wished to betray both her cause and her husband when in historical fact she dearly loved both. A man who had grown up in the house during the nineteenth century had never heard it; and the window concerned had been constructed in 1860.[53]

These tales are wholly representative illustrations of the mass of bogus or distorted tradition about the war. They are still useful to a historian, for they reveal much of how popular memory actually functions; for example, they testify amply to the enduring appetite of the English public for horror stories. What is undeniable is that they are misleading to somebody interested in the history of the war itself. This matters in much more than a personal sense, because the Civil War was one of the most traumatic and divisive experiences which the English have ever undergone, touching every part of the realm, furnishing a succession of dramatic episodes, and provoking strong feeling at every level of society. Its impact upon folklore is proportionately heavy, and it is very significant that such lore should have preserved so very little of what actually happened.

It is yet more striking to realise that the amnesia and confusion represented by popular tradition began to set in within twenty years of the events. In 1661 a Dutch visitor to England, William Schellinks, kept a journal of what he saw, heard and surmised upon his travels. At Canterbury he noted that Cromwell had been responsible for the destruction of all the stained glass, statues and crosses in English churches. This work had in fact been carried out by order of Parliament between 1641 and 1645, before Cromwell held any power at all. A while later, the Dutchman recorded that Archbishop William Laud had been beheaded in Cromwell's 'reign'. Now, that 'reign', a word only appropriate to his period as Lord Protector, had commenced in 1654. Laud had been beheaded nine years before that, on the orders of the same Parliament, and Cromwell had not been involved in the process. Only three years after the death of the Protector himself, therefore, an intelligent and attentive foreign visitor was picking up an impression of the Civil Wars and Interregnum which was already almost as garbled as that revealed by later folklore collections.[54] The sense of the past displayed by the early modern English seems, on the whole, to have compared unfavourably even with that of the Lotuko.

The vagaries of folk memory are associated with defects in another presumed entity much beloved of the Edwardians: folk wisdom. There is no doubt that many of the sayings, remedies and topographical beliefs credited to common and traditional peoples embody a great deal of good sense and practical efficacy. On the other hand, some clearly do not. They are wrong in every straightforward sense, even harmfully so, and represent a different sort of myth-making: the preference of the traditional reputation of a thing over its actual and discernible nature. Nigel Barley's Dowayo firmly believed that chameleons were poisonous, despite a total lack of any objective evidence for that opinion and fairly regular contact with the animal concerned; the belief was accepted because it had always been accepted. Once again a leap from a tribal society to the British Isles reveals a parallel rather than a contrast, for the Manx have always dreaded the pygmy shrew as venomous. Now, it is logical to assume that at some point in the past a person was bitten by one of these little rodents and exhibited symptoms of poisoning resulting from some other cause but reasonably enough blamed on the animal. It is also, however, logical to suppose that at some point in the five thousand years in which human beings have inhabited the Isle of Man, somebody might have worked out that the shrew is not in fact poisonous. Apparently nobody did; and once the belief was adopted, it could not be eradicated by empirical reasoning.[55]

Beliefs that are not empirically valid can, of course, have deep and cogent symbolic significance, and most structures of religion, magic and old-fashioned science include such symbolic conceptions of reality. Within their own parameters, they are entirely sensible and logical. Having said that, there are traditional beliefs which lack both any practical value and any discernible framework of logic. Jacqueline Simpson, collecting information on folk medicine in the border counties of England and Wales, started to boggle at some of the remedies confidently reported to her:

> to carry the mossy ball from a rose bush prevents toothache; to cut one's toe-nails while sitting under an ash tree cures it; to carry a potato or a mole's paw cures rheumatism; if you apply nine linen bandages smeared with a mixture of powdered garlic and lard to a child with measles or scarlet fever and then bury them, this will draw the fever out of him; 'a fine fat spider, all alive and kicking', eaten with butter will cure ague; woodlice make good pills; powdered cockroaches cure dropsy; cooked hedgehog cures epilepsy; mouse pie or roast mice cure bed-wetting; eelskin garters prevent cramp; to tie a sheep's lungs or a bullock's melt to the soles of a patient with pneumonia will draw the infection out of him; live woodlice hung in a bag round a baby's neck will cure him of thrush; an onion on a mantelpiece will draw infections into it.

It is not surprising that she concluded that such beliefs seem 'so very odd and arbitrary that they defy all attempts at explanation'.[56]

If traditional beliefs do not need to have either empirical truth or symbolic logic, then it is not actually necessary for events to occur to make their impact on contemporary politics. I am not speaking here of the public fraud, the deliberate manufacturing of misinformation by governments to deceive their subjects or foreign powers, so much as of the casual generation of major non-events by ordinary people. The most extreme example of this is the mass hallucination, and two examples may serve to illustrate this phenomenon. In the autumn of 1678 a panic broke across England which has become known as the Popish Plot, started by unscrupulous charlatans and based on a tale that Roman Catholics had conspired to murder the king, Charles II, and seize power. As news of this spread, people began to see mysterious bands of armed horsemen abroad in the centre of the night. They were reported at Whitby on 15 November, when somebody claimed that forty riders had marched through local villages in the darkest hours. Within eleven days, such bands had been sighted in every county in England, roaming between midnight and dawn. Their timing, numbers, equipment and routes were often noted with great precision. Royal garrisons all over the nation were placed on alert and ordered to mount night patrols. None of them caught sight of any of the reported horsemen, and as the years passed government enquiries revealed what historians have amply confirmed; that the plot was a hoax. There never were any armed riders roving by night in November 1678. Hundreds of people, however, were sure that they had seen them.[57]

The other case study concerns England in late 1914, when a rumour swept through the nation that Russian soldiers were passing through it to reinforce the Western Front of the First World War. An official investigation of the stories revealed that they had been produced by three successive misunderstandings. The first was the arrival of a telegram which announced the unloading of a large number of 'Russians' at a British port. The reference was to a shipment of Russian eggs. Once that had started the rumour, it was compounded by a bearded Scotsman on a train, who was asked by excited English on the platform where he came from. He shouted through the window that it was from Ross-shire, which was indeed a Scottish county. Those on the platform, of course, misheard him. Finally, the tale was apparently confirmed by some French officers anxious for the transmission of supplies to the front, who kept demanding of Englishmen when 'ze rations' were going to arrive.

These three developments were sufficient; soon Russians were not only expected to be crossing England, but were seen to be doing so, all over the country. They were reported as crowding out railway carriages, the window blinds drawn down to conceal them. They were glimpsed on station platforms, stamping the snow from their boots. They were heard calling for vodka at Carlisle and Berwick on Tweed. One of them jammed a slot machine with a rouble at Durham. Thousands of them were reported, by hundreds of witnesses; but not a single one was ever actually there.[58]

It is a proverb that there is no smoke without fire. Clearly so, but it is equally clear that the human race is capable of seeing huge clouds of smoke without a single spark ever having been struck, save in the overheating furnace of the imagination.

A final category of myth to be considered here is that of the Bold Fact, a confident and striking piece of information produced by a pioneering scholar, which is accepted uncritically by successors for long after its appearance. Of course, many Bold Facts are subsequently proved to be wholly accurate, and worthy of the weight of extrapolation based upon them. Others are subject only to those alterations of perception and preoccupation which are part of the ongoing process of enquiry. Others, however, turn out to be wholly or partially wrong, and in that sense belong to the category of myth. Three examples will be considered here.

The first concerns the presumed number of victims of the early modern witch trials. During the eighteenth century, it became generally accepted by the ruling elites of Europe that witchcraft did not exist, and therefore that people executed for the alleged crime of it during the past three hundred years had all been innocent as charged. As such, the trials became a powerful polemical weapon of liberals attacking traditional structures of authority in church and state. No more than anybody else, however, did those liberals have any notion of how many executions had actually been carried out, for the research needed to provide anything like a reasonable guess had not yet begun to be undertaken. Early estimates therefore varied widely. Voltaire guessed at 100,000, while later in the eighteenth century a Catholic scholar, Jakob Anton Kollman, came up with 30,000. Ninteenth-century computations varied even more wildly. To the German folklorist Jakob Grimm the death toll had simply been 'countless'. To the famous British liberal W. E. H. Lecky it comprised 'a few thousand', while another British writer, Charles Mackay, talked of 'thousands upon thousands', and a Dutch antiquarian, Jacobus Scheltema, of 100,000.

It was to be an eighteenth-century calculation which was to achieve the status of perceived orthodoxy, produced by a local historian living in the north German town of Quedlinburg. In 1793 he published an article aimed at the anticlerical intellectuals of Berlin, and which gave the remarkably precise figure of 9,442,994 executions for the crime of witchcraft in Christendom. He had arrived at this simply by discovering records of the burning of thirty witches at Quedlinburg itself between 1569 amd 1583 and assuming that these were normative for every equivalent period of time as long as the laws against witchcraft were in operation. This multiplication meant that 866 people would have been executed as witches in the town over that whole period, and he simply kept on multiplying the figure in relation to the presumed population of other Christian countries. The exercise was based on a false assumption, for in fact his records reflected not a chronic situation, but the main period of witch trials in the town. For those who did not know or suspect this, however, it had a formidable air of exact calculation about it.

Its other unusual feature, of course, was that it was extremely large, and this proved to be the more enduring asset, as it got taken up during the late nineteenth century by intellectuals bent on questioning traditional forms of Christianity. A Viennese professor of Old Testament studies, Gustav Roskoff, rounded it down to a handier nine million, and this figure was used with particular energy by German Protestant writers to attack the Catholic Church in particular. In 1893 it reached a popular audience in the English-speaking world, when it was quoted by an American writer,

Matilda Joslyn Gage. Her work was to campaign for the political and social rights of women, and the book which contained the figure, *Woman, Church and State*, was an early classic of reimagined women's history, and based upon existing polemical publications. To Gage, the women prosecuted for witchcraft had been pagan priestesses, especially skilled in healing, and their deaths had been contrived by churchmen not just to wipe out their religion but to break any spirit of female independence. The immensity of this German estimate of executions underscored the enormity of the crime involved. It was the single precise, confidently declared and repeatedly quoted figure which scholarship had provided. Cultural changes gave it new force in the late twentieth century. It was taken up and repeated in the 1950s by the books of Gerald Gardner, the man who certainly publicised and possibly founded the modern pagan witch religion of Wicca. His texts were read by American feminists towards the end of the 1960s, when the figure of the witch was again being viewed as an image of independent female power, and the same readers soon rediscovered Gage herself. As a result, the classic American radical feminist works of the 1970s, most of all those of Mary Daly and Andrea Dworkin, gave full prominence to the estimate of nine million deaths; as a proven fact it served to establish the status of women as the most persecuted group in European history, outweighing even the victims of the twentieth-century genocidal campaigns. As such, it passed into the liberal and radical culture of the period, celebrated in folksong, poem and liturgy, and re-exported to Britain where politicians such as Ken Livingstone quoted it in newspaper articles and speeches in the 1980s. During those same years, however, sustained and systematic academic research was at last under way into the early modern trials and the social context in which they had been set. By the 1990s enough detailed local studies had been produced, spanning Europe, to make a rationally-calculated overall estimate possible; and that most commonly accepted consists of a range between 40,000 and 50,000 executions. It will take years for this to filter through to most areas of contemporary popular culture, and only then will the century-long reign of a wild guess be over.[59]

The second case study concerns another American author, of much greater academic repute than Matilda Gage: the anthropologist Margaret Mead. In 1928 she published *Coming of Age in Samoa*, her most famous book and the most popular piece of anthropological fieldwork ever written. Samoa is an archipelago in Polynesia, west of the Marquesas, and the revelation which Mead offered to western readers was that its society was unusually peaceful, well-balanced, non-competitive and irreligious, and offered a joyous sexual freedom to its young people. As a result, adolescence in Samoa was an easy and pleasant time of life, devoid of the emotional stresses with which it was associated in Europe and North America. The message was clear: that human behaviour is culturally produced, that western culture inflicts unnecessary guilt and suffering upon its people, and especially upon its young people; and that a study of tribal societies can serve to provide better models for ways in which Europeans and Americans can exist in the future. The power of these arguments must be obvious, and they made a proportionately profound impact upon twentieth-century liberal thought. It was sustained until 1983, when another specialist in Samoan anthropology, a New Zealander called Derek Freeman, published a sensational attack upon Mead's work, claiming that it was faulty in every respect and had been the product of wish-fulfilment. He insisted that actual Samoan society, since the time of first contact with Europeans, had been very different from that which she had represented, and that her portrait was therefore invalid.[60]

If that were all that was involved in the matter, then it would be a simple case of the vaporisation of a scholarly error, the replacement of a badly flawed representation of truth with another and better one. Things are, however, not that simple. Mead's image of Samoa certainly qualifies as a Bold Fact, in the terms of the present discussion, but Freeman's challenge did not result in a straightforward invalidation of it. What ensued instead was a hectic debate among anthropologists, virtually all North American, in which most of the certainties of the discipline got laid in ruin. In their tussles with each other, the participants called into question all the means by which authenticity and viability could be established in ethnographic research. Never before had it been made so painfully obvious to an observer how much that research is conditioned by the resources, interests, identity, personality and prejudices of the researcher; how complex and heterogeneous native cultures can be, not merely different age groups and social levels but even different individuals within them having widely disparate views of the world and behaving in different ways; that native informants can deceive visiting scholars, either deliberately or unconsciously; that anthropological statistics can be plausibly compiled in a range of ways, to give radically different results; and that comparatively little fieldwork is ever tested or checked by independent researchers. In the particular case of Samoa, the reports of twentieth-century anthropologists could be rejected asreferring to a society tainted by westernisation. The reports of nineteenth-century visitors, however, could be regarded as blinded by common cultural prejudices when they agreed with each other, and accused of being obviously unreliable when they disagreed. The end result of the debate was a complete absence of positive consensus. It was now obvious that Mead's research could no longer be accepted on face value, but neither could that of Freeman, and it was far from clear which of them was the more correct, as both the discipline and the evidence upon which they had depended were so badly flawed.[61]

My third example is a visual image, that of the best-known human figure from the whole extant catalogue of European Old Stone Age art, the co-called Sorcerer of Trois-Frères. The latter is a cave system in southern France discovered in 1916, which contains some of the finest and most elaborate known Palaeolithic paintings and engravings. As such, it represented a scholarly windfall for the owner of the land on which it lay, Count Napoléon Henri Bégouen, who was himself a distinguished prehistorian specializing in the Old Stone Age. To assist in inspecting and evaluating the find he called in a friend of even greater distinction in the field, the Abbé Henri Breuil, 'The Father of Prehistory'. Breuil worked at the cave on and off for the next ten years, engaged above all in the work of drawing the various pieces of artwork.[62] His enthusiasm and stamina for this pursuit had been one of his many claims to fame, and he produced many of the standard images of Stone Age art which have illustrated textbooks upon the subject. So it was with the painting which was to become his favourite in the Trois-Frères cave, isolated in a high alcove. In his drawing of it, reproduced many times over, it appears as a dancing male human figure, body in half profile and face turned towards the viewer. It has the eyes of an owl, the tail of a horse, the body of a horse or deer, a long beard, the ears of a deer, animal forepaws, and tall spreading stag's antlers. It was to this that he and Begouen gave the name of 'The Sorcerer'.

The choice of name was itself a significant gesture of interpretation, for at that period both men were inclined to the view that Palaeolithic cave art was linked to hunting magic, by which the artists hoped to gain greater power over the animals who were their prey or their rivals by representing them and working rites with the images. According to this notion, the strange composite figure of Trois-Frères was a magician-priest, similar to historic tribal shamans or medicine people, who conducted the rites and represented in his own body aspects of the natural world over which humans hoped to gain greater control, either as an imaginary and symbolic image or as an actual costume donned for ceremonies.[63]

Breuil himself, however, came to change his mind about the image, and the context in which he did so raises fascinating questions about the manner in which scholarly ideas are formed and mutated. In 1931 the British author Margaret Murray published *The God of the Witches*, the second of three books in which she defended the theory – propounded before her by Matilda Joslyn Gage among others – that the people tried as witches in early modern Europe had been practitioners of a surviving pagan religion. This one was devoted to the image of the horned god whom she held to have been the principal deity of the religion. She commenced her survey of the apparent iconography of this deity with the 'Sorcerer', employing Breuil's drawing. Upon the basis of this she declared that this was 'the earliest known representation of a deity' on earth, and that fairly certainly it represented 'the incarnate god' who was believed to preside over the fertility of the animal kingdom. When Breuil himself published general surveys of Palaeolithic art and culture during the following decades, it was Murray's interpretation of the figure which he adopted, overturning the earlier characterisation of it as a human magician to declare that it depicted the dominant deity of the painters, the god of fertility. In other words, Breuil had passed an image to Murray, who had passed back to him a belief about it.[64] Both of them may have been correct in this belief, or alternatively the older assumption that it was intended to be a human might also be right; but there is one major problem. The figure drawn by Breuil is not the same as the one actually painted on the cave wall.

The cave of Trois-Frères has remained in private hands and closed to visitors except in exceptional circumstances, a situation which is no doubt propitious to the preservation of the art. It seems that nobody has been able to work there for as long as Breuil did, and so that is why his drawings are generally used as the basis for discussions of its contents. In one of his later books, the abbé published a photograph of 'The Sorcerer' alongside his famous drawing, and felt compelled to comment that the latter had been traced 'after deciphering some parts invisible at a distance'. Indeed the contrast between the two is immediately obvious, the photograph showing a figure which lacks some of the most prominent and celebrated features of the drawing. The difference does beg the question why, as the art in the cave does not seem to be faded or damaged, some parts of this painting should be so bold, and some so faint, effectively to invisibility.[65]

In 1967, after Breuil's death, Peter Ucko and André Rosenfeld published their survey of Palaeolithic cave art, and had more recent photographs upon which to comment. They noted, cautiously, that 'many of the details shown in Breuil's drawings are not visible'. The original apparently lacked the front paws, the beard, the owl eyes, the ears and at least one antler; most of the features, in fact, which had made the portrait in the drawing so striking. These two authors suggested that these might have been Breuil's 'interpretation of faint scratches on the rock', or else that the figure had been damaged since his study; although they added that it did seem hard to imagine how damage might have occurred.[66] Later and better photographs reinforce these doubts;[67] none of the features which Breuil drew upon or round the head, and some of those on the body, can certainly be seen to be present. It is still possible that scratches or carvings on the cave surface might be interpreted as extensions of the painting, but there is as yet no scholarly consensus on the matter. All that seems definite is that the figure would never have excited so much interest without the very firm and striking image which the abbé 'reconstructed' from it.

How could this discrepancy have occurred? One explanation may simply be that the physical conditions in which he was operating were not conducive to high standards of certainty. He complained himself about the inaccessibility of 'The Sorcerer', and how when working on the latter it was 'difficult to hold at the same time a lamp, one's paper and pencil, and a drawing board for the retouching of a tracing, taking care at the same time not to slide downwards'.[68] In these circumstances nobody should be surprised if his tracing had taken in features of the wall which have only doubtful relationship with the figure. It may be added, however, that the presence of these extra features upon the latter fitted very well with the current theory supported by Breuil, that the art was connected to hunting magic. Furthermore, the abbé was at other times, and in easier circumstances, capable of producing copies of ancient art which also bore out his ideas and which differ markedly from the impressions of other observers. In 1920 he visited Ireland, and made drawings of the spiral designs carved in some of its Neolithic passage tombs. His theory was that they represented beings, and in his enthusiasm he touched them up to show them very clearly to contain human faces. When these drawings of his are contrasted with those of other scholars, and with photographs, it is very obvious how much he has transformed them into different images.[69] 'The Sorcerer' seems to have undergone the same process.

It should be emphasised that none of these examples should be taken to belittle Gage, Mead or Breuil. The first was never a scholar, let alone a historian, but a political activist and polemicist, and should be acknowledged and honoured as that, while the contribution of the other two to anthropology and prehistory was tremendous, and obvious, and not contingent on the aspects of their work discussed here. It may well be that the sort of bold, creative and imaginative personality which pioneers new areas of knowledge or activity is precisely the kind which will also at times be too assertive and imaginative in interpretation, and that the Bold Fact is one mechanism by which this effect can operate. The finest scholars can also be the most potent makers of myth. If so, any responsibility and culpability for error is shared by colleagues and successors, whose duty it is to check and evaluate the information and ideas which they have provided. Any bitterness or blame expressed on the part of those who had believed the latter, and later found them wanting, can only belong to a context in which leaders in scholarly disciplines are regarded as charismatic semi-sacred figures who provide others with a better and more truthful way of perceiving the world. In the opinion of the present writer, that is not a healthy way in which to treat scholarship. The latter is both a cooperative venture and, inevitably, a flawed one.

During the past three decades academic scholarship has taken two different attitudes to the element of myth in its work. On the one hand, the healthy iconoclasm that has swept the profession since the 1960s has resulted in an unprecedented quantity and breadth of attacks upon received orthodoxies, and of revelations of the subjective and sometimes erroneous way in which the latter had been developed. A common subtitle of works of this period which evaluated past research has been 'the making of a myth'. This attitude has generally implied that by sweeping away such myths, a closer approximation to the truth is obtained. At the same time there has been a growing sense that this does not necessarily follow, and that – as in the case of the Samoan controversy among anthropologists – the destruction of a former certainty does not automatically result in a few and better-founded one, but in doubts as to how the truth may ever be attained.

There appear to be four different processes of recognition in operation here. The first is that research which is carried out systematically, and with especial emphasis upon records contemporary to the events described, or careful excavation, or trained fieldwork, will almost inevitably produce a more accurate impression of past or present than that furnished by more informal and impressionistic means. Left to its own devices, much of the latter would effectively belong to the category of myth; the discussion of the shortcomings of popular memory, made above, should have pointed up this lesson. That is why modern societies find it worthwhile to maintain professional scholars in relatively large numbers, although non-professional work, carried out to the same systematic standards, can be just as good. The second recognition is that by the most recent standards a great deal of previous scholarship, including that from inside the academy, has been so imperfect in its methods and limited in its perceptions that it has contained a very large mythological element. The third is that recent scholars have become very good at myth-busting, at pointing out the inadequacies and mistakes of previous research and how these came about. The fourth is that objective truth is so hard to ascertain that even the best and most rigorous research is likely to produce conclusions which are still to some extent myths. Each of these perceptions seems to be equally valid, but the relationship between them is complex and can be confusing.

The implications for a historian are that the discipline of history operates like a science in its negative aspects, of testing and evaluating assertions, and like an art in its positive respects, of advancing opinions about the nature of the past. Specifically, it is a bardic art, as the historian is expected to address the society within which she or he is operating and to hold up to it images of the past. During the past couple of decades doubts have often been aired concerning the response of the public to historical revisionism, with the argument that most societies want histories which provide positive information and appear to explain, helpfully and persuasively, features of the present which are most apparent, and intriguing or disturbing, to those living in it. This is, runs the argument, what most people believe that they are paying the professionals to do. While that view is clearly accurate in many respects, my own experience of the public – whether encountered as pupils, neighbours, correspondents, lecture-hall audiences, tour-groups, mass-media personnel or members of social groupings whom I have studied in the course of my own research – is that it enjoys the spectacle of myth-busting just as much as the revelation of positive new information about the past. It still wants from historians above all what it has always wanted since the first bard tuned an instrument to sing of days of old: to be edified and to be entertained, and of the two the latter is the more important. In that sense the present-day historian faces a pair of constant, tremendous, challenges. One is to strive for methods and attitudes which embody the best chance of recovering as much knowledge of the past as possible, from as many different viewpoints as can be attained. The second is to craft that information for an audience in such a way as to turn it into stories with the carrying power of myth.

2

Arthur and the Academics

Many people have studied, and continue to study, the impact of the Arthurian legend upon the imagination of poets, novelists and artists. Less frequently discussed is the impact of that legend upon the minds of modern historians and archaeologists.[1] The reason is obvious enough: that in the later two-thirds of this century these professional scholars are generally supposed to have been immune to the lure of romance, confining themselves to the pragmatic evaluation of objective data. Such a view tends to be associated with a concept of the academy as essentially a sealed community, immune to influence from enthusiasts outside it and having in turn a minimal effect upon the creative imagination of the wider society; it is supposed to educate with fact, not to inspire with myth. This, at least, is the ideal to which it aspires. Had that ideal been even remotely attainable then the story of modern scholarly attitudes to the historical Arthur would be infinitely less engrossing, less endearing, and less sad.

It must be admitted at once that Arthur has always caused problems to historians, for ever since his legend became internationally renowned, over eight hundred years ago, there have been writers to cast doubt on his very existence. The list of such sceptics stretches from William of Newburgh in the twelfth century, through Sir Walter Raleigh in the sixteenth and John Milton in the seventeenth, to a clutch of respected authors around 1900. What rescued him from them in earlier periods was mostly blind faith, but for the past hundred years he has depended almost wholly upon two documents. Their importance to the subject is so obvious that, at the risk of trying the patience of anybody already acquainted with it, they must be summarised here. One is a section of the *Historia Brittonum*, a Latin work completed in the years 829 or 830 by somebody working in the kingdom of Gwynedd, in north-west Wales, who also knew the south-eastern parts of Wales extremely well. At present about thirty-five medieval copies of it survive. Five attribute the authorship to 'Ninnius', apparently on the basis of a guess made by somebody in the eleventh or twelfth centuries, who thought that it could have been composed by a scholar (actually called Nemnius and often called Nennius) who lived at about the right time. Whoever wrote it was intent upon assembling materials to tell the story of how the Anglo-Saxons came to dispossess the native British (the later Welsh) of most of their island. This story was presented in a manner designed to reassure readers that the British and their descendants were still a people marked out by particular divine favour and a heroic tradition, that they had thus far been defeated by treachery and weight of numbers, that they would one day repossess their lost lands, and that the rulers of Gwynedd were their natural leaders.

The 'Arthurian' section is provided to foster the image of the British as a godly and martial race with a glorious past, and consists of a list of twelve of Arthur's victories. Two are singled out for special notice: Castle Guinnion, where Arthur carried the image of the Virgin on his shoulders or shield, and Badon Hill (or Mountain), where he killed 960 enemies. None of these battles can be attributed with confidence to any other leader and only one can be located with any degree of confidence: Celidon Wood, a name used in other early Welsh sources for a forest in what is now southern Scotland. The list is prefaced with the statement that Arthur fought against the Anglo-Saxons, and was *dux bellorum*, commander in the battles, even though he was not by birth of the first rank. It was possibly adapted for the *Historia* from a praise-poem in Welsh, boasting of the victories, a genre well recorded in the seventh and eighth centuries. This would accord with the usual practice of the author – wherever it can be tested against older material – of remodelling data from existing texts and traditions. Whatever its origins, it seems to have been all that he could find as evidence for the historical Arthur, although by the time at which he wrote legends about the hero's exploits were already circulating. In a catalogue of 'marvels' appended to his work, he included two sites in south-east Wales and its border, a footprint and a cairn, associated with these tales. The context of the battle-list in the *Historia* is itself a little unclear, for it forms a piece by itself following a section upon events in Kent and preceding one upon northern England.[2]

The other document is the *Annales Cambriae*, a chronicle of events from the fifth century onward, put together from older materials in the kingdom of Dyfed (south-west Wales). It seems most likely to have been written at St David's in the years 953–54. For the years up to 613 the main source was a set of Irish annals, but these were interleaved with seven entries of unknown provenance which refer, wherever they can be located, to events in northern Britain and north Wales. The first of these is '516: the battle of Badon in which Arthur carried the cross of Our Lord Jesus Christ upon his shoulders three days and nights and the British were victorious'. The date may alternatively be 518, and 'shoulders' may actually be 'shield'. The second is '537: the strife of Camlann in which Arthur and Medraut perished; and there was death in England and Ireland'. The date may be 539 instead, and an alternative reading of the battle's name is Camlaun. The uncertainty about the dating is due to the fact that Year One of the *Annales* is not precisely fixed, and neither of the dates given for the 'Arthurian' entries can be corroborated from any other evidence. The site of Camlann is uncertain, and it may be noted that the sentence does not indicate who Medraut was, whether he and Arthur were allies or enemies, and who if anybody won the battle. Some slight indication that the two entries were originally from different sources is given by the fact that 'battle of Badon' is given in Latin and 'strife of Camlann' in Welsh.[3]

No reference to Arthur is definitely earlier than those in the *Historia* and the *Annales*, but there is one which has often been taken as such, in the famous early Welsh poem *Y Gododdin*. The poem tells of how a force of British warriors from what is now south-eastern Scotland was almost annihilated at Catraeth, probably Catterick in Yorkshire. One of them, Gwawrddur, is described as achieving mighty deeds in the battle, 'although he was not Arthur'. The problem with the Gododdin is that it could have been composed at any time between *c.* 600 and *c.* 1100, although its orthography perhaps makes a date before 1000 more likely. Furthermore, while it might have been the work of a poet from the region in which it is set, it might also have been produced in Wales, by somebody using or even inventing a tradition of northern events. It worsens the problem for historians of Arthur that the reference to him appears in only one of the two surviving versions of the text, and may have been added after the year 1100.[4]

There is, notoriously, one surviving source from the Britain of the time to which Arthur may be assigned; the *De excidio* of Gildas. It is not certain who Gildas was or where he lived, and he may have written this work at any time between *c.* 450 and *c.* 560, although a date in the second half of that span seems more likely. His purpose at least is clear: to castigate the sins of contemporary British society, exemplified by five rulers. The kingdoms of four of them have been located, and all are in what is now Wales, Devon and Cornwall. As part of his denunciation, Gildas provided a summary history of British affairs during the previous few hundred years, although for most of the fifth century he seems to have had no native written sources and to have filled the gap with tradition. This told him of how a 'proud tyrant' had invited Saxons to settle in the east of the island to defend it against the attacks of other enemies. These eventually turned upon their paymasters and ravaged Britain as far as the western sea. Resistance to them was rallied by a noble Briton called Ambrosius Aurelianus, and a war ensued in which fortune favoured first one side and then the other in a series of clashes. 'Almost the last' and 'not the least' of these was 'the siege of Badon Hill', at which the Saxons were defeated, although Gildas does not say who commanded the British there. The result of these campaigns was to confine the Saxons to part of the island and to re-establish peace, which by Gildas's own time was threatened by the crimes and feuds of the British rulers themselves.[5]

It has always been noticed that Gildas does not apparently mention Arthur, and various explanations have been advanced to prevent this from hampering belief in the latter's historical reality. One is that Ambrosius actually *was* Arthur, the latter being a nickname derived from the Celtic word 'arth', meaning a bear. It is true that the *Historia* also mentions Ambrosius, as a separate individual, but its compiler may have been confused. Alternatively, one of the kings abused by Gildas, Cuneglasus, is described as 'charioteer of the Bear's Stronghold', and the Bear in question may, again, be Arthur. Philologically, the name Arthur can itself be much more easily derived from the Latin 'Artorius' than the Welsh 'arth', but the resemblance between the two was close enough to allow of puns and associations. Another argument is that Gildas names very few individuals anyway, and may not have bothered to tell an audience who won at Badon when it would have known perfectly well that Arthur did. Yet another possibility is that he had a grudge against the hero (as against so many other rulers) and chose to ignore him. The same sort of reasoning can dispose of the related problem that Arthur does not feature in the Anglo-Saxon sources. The standard reply is that neither does Ambrosius, for the earliest of these sources was compiled in the early eighth century. As the early English seem to have been illiterate until *c.* 600, the only material which might have survived from before then would have been poems and other pieces of oral tradition. These would naturally record victories rather than defeats, and the relative silence of the Anglo-Saxon documents with regard to the early sixth century would very credibly reflect the British resurgence described in different ways by Gildas and the *Historia Brittonum.*[6]

This, then, is all the evidence, and knowledge of it has remained virtually unchanged in the course of this century even though study of the various documents has revealed a little more about their place, dates and modes of composition. The most rational conclusion to be drawn from them, perhaps, is that there is some slight reason to believe in a historical Arthur even if very little can be said about him. If there were one region rather than another in which to commence a search for further information, then the documents would seem to point towards the north. British society of the relevant period was not, after all, illiterate. Several hundred of its memorial stones have been identified, one of them apparently belonging to one of the monarchs denounced by Gildas, and there is a real chance that archaeology will turn up more. Such, at any rate, seems to be what the stock of information suggests. The most influential historians and arch-aeologists ignored it. Instead, they chose to follow the legend, and in the process created an enormous bubble of mythologizing. When this burst it was replaced by a triumphant scepticism which itself looks suspiciously like an emotional reaction.

For the first third of the twentieth century, at least, the approach was indeed relatively cautious and pragmatic, as may be demonstrated from four differ-ent sorts of work published between 1929 and 1935. A famous scholar of medieval literature, Sir Edmund Chambers, made a survey of that dealing with Arthur which commenced by describing the supposedly historical references in detail and inviting readers to draw conclusions from them. A poet and novelist, Gilbert Sheldon, wrote a popular history of early medieval England in which he synthesised Gildas, the *Historia Brittonum* and the Anglo-Saxon sources and suggested that Arthur was real but 'shadowy'; the result was respectable enough to be bought by universities. A historian, W. G. Collingwood, argued that, since the early English texts tended to locate most of the initial fighting between Briton and Saxon in south-eastern England, the sites of Arthur's battles should be sought in that region. The archaeologist O. G. S. Crawford riposted by pointing out that Celidon Wood was certainly in the north, that the 'Arthurian' sources seemed to be asso-ciated with that area more than any other, and that there was in fact some evidence for early Anglo-Saxon activity there.[7] He went on to suggest a set of archaeological features in it which might repay investigation by scholars interested in the question.[8]

The spiral of dreams began in 1936, when Oxford University Press pub-lished the first volume of a new, authoritative, history of England, written by acclaimed experts in the respective periods. The section on Roman Britain was entrusted to Professor R. G. Collingwood, who was also asked to deal with the post-Roman British and seems to have taken an emotional holiday when he did so. He proposed that Arthur's title in the *Historia*, of *dux bellorum*, meant that he was the successor of the Roman *comes*, or supreme commander, of the province. He would therefore have led a crack mobile force, and the ideal one to have used against the Anglo-Saxons would have been one of armoured cavalry, like the *cataphractarii* deployed by the eastern Roman emperors against Germanic enemies. Thus he would have ranged all over Britain with his body of knights behind him and been 'a great champion of the British people'. His betrayal and death would have occurred when the knights, victorious and therefore now redundant, turned on each other.[9] There was not a shred of evidence for any of this, being simply an imposition of the medieval Arthurian legend upon a fifth-century setting.

That, of course, was what made it immediately attractive to the modern British public, and it was after all offered to them in a work intended to form the basis of future educational texts. From now on Collingwood's ghostly cataphracts were to gallop through the popular imagination, their hoof prints being found in historical novels,[10] amateur works of history [11] and school textbooks.[12]

They did not, however, make much of an impact within the academy itself. There the lead in study of the 'Arthurian' documents during the next two decades was taken not by historians or archaeologists but by specialists in early Welsh literature. Their opinions were summed up in the years between 1954 and 1963, when three of the most notable pronounced on the matter. All agreed that Collingwood's picture was mere fantasy. Rachel Bromwich pointed out that many of the main characters in the development of the Arthurian legend, including Merlin, Peredur, Owain and Tristan, were found first in texts concerning northern England and southern Scotland, either produced there or concerning that region. As indicated, the earliest references to Arthur themselves pointed faintly in that direction. She therefore endorsed Crawford's opinion that he was a northern hero.[13] Nora Chadwick called the evidence for his existence 'at least highly unsatisfactory', but thought that the cumulative amount of tradition could not altogether be ignored. She therefore endorsed Bromwich's view, although she suggested that Arthur might have been Gildas's Ambrosius.[14] Most widely read was Kenneth Jackson, who declared that Arthur 'may well have existed' but that proof was impossible.

He did, however, encourage belief by assigning the earliest possible date to the *Gododdin* and the putative poem listing the battles, and pointed out the existence of Arthur or variants of it as a fashionable name among royalty in Celtic Britain in the late sixth century. He therefore indicated that Arthur's reputation was already well established before 600, virtually within living memory of his probable time.[15] None of these guesses were, in fact, secure. The literary works could both be much later and the names all occurred in kingdoms with strong Irish connections and could just be versions of the well-known Irish royal name of Art or Airt. Jackson also broke ranks with his companions by suggesting that Arthur's principal exploits were in southern England, for no other reason than that 'tradition', meaning medieval legend, put them there. Still, adventurous though his comments were, they fell far short of Collingwood and far below the hopes of Britain's most famous amateur historian at the time, Sir Winston Churchill. Hearing of the tentative pronouncements of the literary scholars, he snorted 'This is not much to show after so much toil and learning'.[16] The invitation was open to historians and archaeologists to try to show more.

It was taken, dramatically, and the origins of this process lay long before, in 1929. It was then that the public Commissioners of Works acquired the ruined castle of Tintagel in Cornwall, reputedly Arthur's birthplace. They instructed one of their archaeologists, C. A. Ralegh Radford, to examine the site, and he did so in 1933–34, finding various structures and a large quantity of pottery imported from the Mediterranean in the period c. 450 to c. 600. In the bold manner of excavators of his time, he confidently pronounced it to have been a Celtic monastery, and in subsequent decades repeated this opinion with imaginative reconstructions of the buildings. He found nothing to link it directly to the Arthurian legend, and so did not attempt to do this.[17] He was, however, encouraged to turn his attention in 1936 to another Cornish monument, the prehistoric fort of Castle Dore. Twelfth-century literature had made the nearby manor of Lantyne the setting for the story of King Mark, Tristan and Iseult. South of the earthwork stood the Long Stone, an inscribed megalith of the fifth or sixth century. The lettering begins with a now illegible name and continues 'lies here, son of Cunomorus'. In the sixteenth and seventeenth centuries, the first name was read as Cirusius. In the twentieth century one scholar made out Drustagni, another, working with utmost care, Cirusinius.[18] Cunomorus at least is plain, and a Welsh genealogy recorded a king of that name in south-west Britain in the appropriate period. More to Radford's point, a ninth-century text identified a ruler in Brittany, called both Cunomorus and Marcus. To Radford this was enough to indicate that the man on the Cornish stone could be the legendary King Mark, and he declared the name of his son, on the stone, to be Drustaus, near enough to Tristan (in the tale, Mark's nephew) to suggest a connection. Using this exciting information, he and friends called a public meeting to raise funds for a dig. The result was a sample excavation in which, among a 'maze of postholes', Radford discerned the outline of a palace with two halls, one ninety feet long. He decided that this seemed to date somewhere in the early medieval period and declared that he had found the residence of King Mark, the setting for the famous story.[19]

He was, however, unable to publish his conclusions until 1951, and two years later the expert on Welsh literature, Rachel Bromwich, brought out a study of the Tristan legend which argued that it was a compound of Scottish, Irish and Welsh tales, located in Cornwall only in the twelfth century.[20] Radford's response to this inconvenient information was to ignore it. Subsequently archaeologists tended to read him, literary scholars read Bromwich, and historians read either or neither. Certainly as the decade progressed Radford's own cumulative achievements in archaeology became all the more impressive, and so did the importance of the imported ceramics which he had identified at Tintagel. By 1959 the same sorts of pottery had been found on twelve other sites in Cornwall, Devon, Somerset and Wales, indicating that at some stage between 450 and 600 they had all been occupied by people wealthy and important enough to exchange products with the Mediterranean world.[21] This increased interest among archaeologists in what might have been Arthur's time, and provided a powerful incentive for somebody with sufficient enthusiasm to use excavation to test the truth of his legend further.

Such a figure had appeared in 1957, with the publication of Geoffrey Ashe's luminously beautiful book *King Arthur's Avalon*. Ashe stood in a tradition of early twentieth-century Christian mystics who had fallen in love with Glastonbury, the fabled Isle of Avalon, and this work was his tribute to it. He employed his broad knowledge of medieval literature and history to suggest that all the traditional legends about it might have been true, including the claim that Arthur had been buried in the abbey. His purpose was to establish Glastonbury as 'England's New Jerusalem' and to inspire its 'rebirth'.[22] To this end his technique was simple: to show that the old stories could not conclusively be disproved and to argue from this that there was every reason to believe in them, especially as they were magnificent in themselves and part of the heritage of the nation. He could never quite free himself from the feeling that there was something morally reprehensible about a scholar who demanded absolute proof before belief and took pleasure in debunking beloved old tales. Though he was no academic himself, his book was quite plausible enough to win a place on university library shelves.

By the end of the 1950s Radford and Ashe were acquainted, and one of the fruits of that acquaintance was the former's excavation of part of Glastonbury Abbey in 1962–63. The result was, as he initially recorded, disappointing: he found a bank, ditch, cemetery and post-holes apparently older than *c.* 700, but no evidence that they had not been made by the Anglo-Saxons who had arrived there about forty years before. He could only cite the fact that Celtic saints (among others) were venerated at the monastery in the tenth century as a rather lame indication that it was already there in Arthur's presumed time.[23] Ashe, however, was already cherishing a plan for a much bigger project, the excavation of the hill-fort near South Cadbury in the same county of Somerset. Since the sixteenth century local tradition had held that this had once been Camelot, Arthur's favourite residence, and in the 1950s field-walking there had turned up shreds of the Mediterranean pottery which indicated a high-status site of the right age. A dig of that size would, however, be extremely expensive, requiring a major exercise in fund-raising. In 1965 Ashe and Radford began the process by forming the Camelot Research Committee, justifying the name with the fact that (because of the legend) the Ordnance Survey Map already attached it to South Cadbury Castle. It included another archaeologist working in Somerset, Philip Rahtz, and one then operating in Wales, Leslie Alcock, who was invited to supervise the prospective excavation.

Alcock was the obvious choice, having more experience in working on post-Roman sites than any other archaeologist at the time, and having in addition been trained as a historian.[24] He found himself sharing this committee with members of groups such as the Knights of the Round Table and the Pendragon Society, whom Ashe had brought in to add their enthusiasm and resources. The presidency was offered to Britain's most famous living archaeologist, Sir Mortimer Wheeler, friend to both Radford and Alcock and voted Television Personality of the Year in 1954. Wheeler accepted it cheerfully and used his enormous influence to help win money from institutions such as the British Academy for a trial excavation in 1966. It revealed that South Cadbury Castle, though an Iron Age structure, had indeed been refortified in the post-Roman period. A kindly providence ordained that during the same summer the musical *Camelot* was playing to packed cinemas, and popular interest in Arthur was running high. Press reporters and television cameras were called to Cadbury, where they found Sir Mortimer declaring that Britain could be on the brink of a discovery to rank with those of Heinrich Schliemann. He did not apparently recognise the irony of this remark. Schliemann, determined to prove the reality of the Trojan War, had certainly uncovered splendid civilisations on sites associated with its heroes. He had never, however, actually achieved his dream, for the remains which he had linked to those heroes had all turned out to be of the wrong date.

Nevertheless, the declaration had an impressive effect. Money now poured into the committee's funds, especially from the *Observer* newspaper which bought exclusive rights to further discoveries. In the next summer five thousand visitors turned up to view the work. That autumn Ashe whipped up interest still further by editing a volume of essays entitled *The Quest for Arthur's Britain*. He collaborated with Alcock in one which dealt with the finds at Cadbury and wrote four more of the essays himself, grouping the traditional literary sources for a historical Arthur with medieval Welsh tales and archaeological finds to suggest that the evidence in favour of the hero's existence was now much enhanced. He held Arthur up as a focus for a 'new and acceptable patriotism'. Alcock added a piece upon Wales, announcing that every time a site associated in story with characters from the 'Arthurian' age had been excavated, it had proved to have been occupied at that period; he did not draw the same attention to the fact that so had places without any legendary associations. Radford indulged in a little myth-enhancement by writing of his finds at Tintagel and Castle Dore. He added an extra letter to the first name which he had read upon the Long Stone, so that it now became 'Drustanus', even closer to the Tristan of legend. The impact upon the Cornish Tourist Board was certainly dramatic, for the monolith was henceforth labelled 'The Tristan Stone'.

Radford also contributed a chapter on Glastonbury Abbey, in which the chance that the earliest features there were pre-Saxon was restated as a probability. He also started another imaginary hare running by suggesting that the Isle of Avalon had been not merely a Celtic but a pagan holy place, and that the earthwork known as Ponter's Ball had defined its sacred precinct (Philip Rahtz dug into it soon after and found that its earliest certain date was twelfth century). Rahtz himself added another essay on Glastonbury in which, rather unhelpfully to Radford, he stressed that not a fragment of evidence had been found on the abbey site which indicated occupation before the Saxons arrived. He also reported that he had dug in other places in the Isle with strong mystical associations, to no other result. Yet on Glastonbury Tor, the hill above the abbey, he had indeed found a small settlement with pottery from the fifth or sixth century. He could not tell whether it had been secular or religious, but Ashe linked it to a twelfth-century legend in which the Isle of Avalon was made the stronghold of King Melwas, abductor of Arthur's queen Guinevere. The collection, published in 1968, made a favourable impact upon academe and became a bestseller among the public. Ashe followed it in 1969 with a full-length book upon the figure of Arthur, redeploying the same data.[25]

Meanwhile, up on the hill of South Cadbury, Leslie Alcock was struggling to justify all this excitement. The new funding allowed him three more seasons, ending in 1970. He made many finds of value to scholars of the Iron Age and Roman and Saxon periods and, mercifully, found one internal structure which seemed to date from that of Arthur, with a pattern of post-holes which he interpreted as a feasting-hall sixty feet long. He had not, however, discovered anything which directly linked the place to the hero himself. Baulked of this, the *Observer* and his other sponsors hoped that subsequent analysis of the data would somehow provide the connection. Geoffrey Ashe strove to satisfy the popular readership with a book entitled *Camelot and the Vision of Albion*, in which he treated Cadbury as he had done Glastonbury, recounting all the traditions about it and summarising what was known to be fact and showing that there was nothing to refute the identification with Arthur's court. In the same year, 1971, Alcock supplied a fat textbook, *Arthur's Britain*, to the academic world and more learned public. He expertly summarised all the archaeological evidence for the fifth- and sixth-century British, and also made a thorough examination of the literary evidence for the historical Arthur. He agreed that the battle-list might not have derived from the hero's own time but suggested that the two crucial entries in the *Annales Cambriae* were taken from a sixth-century 'Easter table', a list of dates for the Easter feast next to which records of contemporary events were jotted. Upon this notion he based a claim that he had provided 'acceptable historical evidence that Arthur was a genuine historical figure'.[26] Thus bolstered, he brought out his account of the Cad- bury dig in 1972. One difficulty with it was that, after all the publicity which had funded it, he had to put the name 'Camelot' in the title, whereas inside he pointed out (quite correctly) that Camelot was an invention of twelfth- century troubadours. Alcock solved the problem by using for the title a quotation linking South Cadbury and Camelot which, contracted, enabled the publishers to put the words 'Cadbury-Camelot' on the spine. He con- cluded his survey of his discoveries with the observation that nowhere else had a sub-Roman fortification been discovered that extended round such a wide area. He argued from this that it was intended to shelter a British war-band of record size – if not certainly of Arthur then of a figure just like him. Sir Mortimer Wheeler added a foreword mocking 'those earnest scholars' who had doubted the value of the dig, evoking again the ghost of Schliemann and proclaiming that 'there is now at last an indubitable "Arthur" and his ilk'; though the inverted commas could make a reader wonder what was indubitable.[27]

Sir Mortimer's jibes at other scholars were the more triumphant in that the immediate impact of Alcock's books upon academe was very favourable and earned him a professorial chair. A textbook published in 1973 could state that there was now 'general agreement' that Arthur was 'a genuinely historical figure'.[28] The bubble of enthusiasm for this view indeed reached its widest extent that year, with the appearance of two more books. One was the paperback edition of *King Arthur's Avalon* in which Ashe claimed that archaeology had now lent substance to the traditions of Arthur's grave and Melwas's fortress, and that 'we' could now say that Cadbury was 'quite probably' Camelot. The other was a huge history of the British Isles between 350 and 650 by a respected academic, John Morris of University College London. He entitled it *The Age of Arthur* and provided a detailed narrative of the hero's career based on medieval documents from many periods, pounded together with a confidence and ruthlessness at least as great as that which any amateur devotee had shown. Whereas Alcock had regarded Arthur as a war chief, curiously inconsequential in his impact on events,

Morris called him the last Roman emperor of Britain and asserted that his rule had formed the identities of the English and Welsh nations.

The impact of all this upon the public imagination was tremendous. The success of *The Quest for Arthur's Britain* encouraged a set of writers to rush out coffee-table books on the same theme.[29] A television series, *Arthur of the Britons*, was rapidly launched and enjoyed considerable success, portraying him as leading a Celtic war-band against the Saxons from a timber fort in the manner described by Alcock. Furthermore, as well as being a genuinely national hero, he also became one for a counter-culture. The years around 1970 were also those of what I have elsewhere termed the Second Romantic Movement. One aspect of this was a profound desire to reinvest the world with magic and mystery, often partnered with a determination to challenge social norms. For a hundred years English intellectuals had turned to Celtic literature and art as an alternative tradition to their own culture. As a Celt himself, Arthur could now be made into an embodiment of that challenge. Many critics at the time of its release noticed that the British fort in *Arthur of the Britons* looked very like a hippy camp; indeed the lead actor had in fact just been prominent in a production of *Hair*. The face of Arthur on the jacket of Ashe's *Camelot*, with its streaming locks and moustache and head-band, might have been seen that year at many a demonstration or rock concert. The book made a quite deliberate appeal to this audience, calling for a spiritual renewal of Britain and praising the visions of counter-cultural heroes such as Blake, Shelley and Gandhi. Glastonbury began to fill up with young dreamers in jeans, kaftans and Afghan coats, drawn there partly by its traditional reputation for enchantment but also by the books of Geoffrey Ashe himself. It was not exactly the New Jerusalem which he had visualised in 1957, but he was touched and delighted by it.[30]

Very few voices were raised in criticism of the new confidence in a 'real' Arthur, and those were all in academic journals. Much of Sir Mortimer Wheeler's sarcasm may have been directed at another archaeologist who worked on West Country sites, Charles Thomas. He greeted *The Quest for Arthur's Britain* with the accusation that the excitement over Cadbury was draining support away from the investigation of other promising monuments.[31] His feelings came to be shared by one of the Camelot Research Committee, Philip Rahtz. The latter was digging another Cadbury Castle, this time near Bristol. Although it was smaller than the now celebrated one, it turned out not only to have also been refortified in the post-Roman period but to yield a much richer assemblage of finds from that age. It had clearly been occupied by people of very high status, but there was no sixteenth-century legend attached to it and so no Geoffrey Ashe to argue for it. The excavation took place with minimal public interest and financial support, and twenty years passed before a report could be published; there was never any question of a popular book.[32] In 1972 Rahtz openly broke ranks with his former colleagues on the committee, publishing an essay written with another friend, Peter Fowler. This, like Thomas, suggested that it was absurd to label the whole period from 400 to 700 'the Arthurian Age' as people were starting to do. It also suggested that strongholds such as South Cadbury could as easily have been refuges for local populations as bases for war bands led by 'Arthur-type figures'. The next year Rahtz reviewed Alcock's book on South Cadbury, making the damning suggestion that the works from the so-called Arthurian period were not in fact securely enough dated to attribute them to it. He had also, more gently, re-examined the report on Castle Dore. While he still thought it possible that Radford had found a palace, he reminded readers that no material at all had been found there from the period of the newly-renamed Tristan Stone.[33] Rahtz was, however, an archaeologist not a historian. Arthur was a literary figure, and it was in the field of literary evidence that his reputation as a historical fact had to be made or broken.

The group which had made the running in that field during the 1950s had been the experts in early Welsh texts, and it was this which had been most thrust to the side by the hyperbole created by South Cadbury. It had the greatest possible incentive to puncture the latter. Yet two of its leading figures in that earlier period, Chadwick and Jackson, were now dead, and the survivors were not by nature very combative. Rachel Bromwich mildly repeated her former assertion that if the documents pointed to one region it was to the north. Kathleen Hughes, in what became the definitive study of the *Annales Cambriae*, showed that there was in fact no evidence that the 'Arthurian' entries derived from an Easter table as Alcock had suggested, and that they could have come from a number of other sources, including legend. Yet she allowed that Alcock's theory was 'not impossible'.[34] More astringent were the reviews of Morris's *Age of Arthur*, which had so far outrun the evidence, and with such confidence, that scholars felt the need to pulverise its assertions at length and in detail.[35] These reactions were none the less limited and defensive. A more deliberate and comprehensive challenge required a new generation with a different mentality, and one was in the process of emergence. Part of the legacy of the Second Romantic Movement had been a novel disrespect for orthodoxy and tradition on the part of the young, and it affected the academy as much as the wider society. By the mid 1970s the scholars just starting to make reputations in universities were systematically attacking established ideas in an unprecedented manner, a phenomenon which acquired the label of 'revisionism'. The English

Reformation, the English Civil War, the Industrial Revolution and the whole character of the Neolithic were all re-evaluated in this way, and to this mentality the 'Arthurian Age' represented a sitting target. Ironically, many of the young iconoclasts had been drawn to their subjects by the very glamour cast over them by their predecessors, and so it was with the one who was to be Arthur's executioner, David Dumville. He had emerged from the established tradition of Welsh textual scholarship, having been a pupil of Rachel Bromwich, but his own research, into the *Historia Brittonum* and related documents, was encouraged in large part by the contemporary fascination with Arthur and his presumed time. Having won respect with his close evaluations of certain key texts, he felt ready to launch a systematic atttack on some assumptions which had been underpinned by those texts. He wrote a seminar paper to this end, and, having tested it in various universities, published it in a journal in 1977. It pointed out, simply and crushingly, that there was virtually no firm evidence for any of the political personalities of Britain from *c.* 420 to *c.* 540, and certainly none whatsoever for Arthur. If Alcock's argument had hung upon an Easter table which had probably never existed, then it all fell to pieces at a glance. There was therefore no proof that Arthur had ever been more than a mythical figure.[36]

The effect of this short piece upon academics was immediate and tremendous. This was not merely because of its relentless analysis of the sources but because it so perfectly caught the mood of the moment. It was cited with admiration on many high tables and in many common rooms, often by scholars who had no direct concern with history, let alone the period concerned, and often none too accurately; I frequently heard it said that Dumville had proved that Arthur never existed, which was patently not the case. The consensus among historians shifted at once. From then until the end of the century most works dealing with post-Roman Britain have either ignored the subject of Arthur, derided it or suggested that it was somebody else's problem.[37] The longest statement upon it since Morris's book was made by Thomas Charles-Edwards in 1991, in an essay modelled upon that by Kenneth Jackson over thirty years before. The difference was that he struck away all the hope that Jackson had held out and expanded the criticisms which Dumville had made, concluding that nothing of value could be said about an 'Arthur of history'.[38] At the same time the youth culture had shifted again; the Year of Dumville had also been the Year of Punk Rock. The 1970s had brought Britain not a spiritual rebirth but inflation, unemployment, energy crises, industrial unrest and an increasing extremism in street politics. The mood of optimistic idealism among the young in the first years of the decade had given way to an exuberant nihilism. To those who embraced the latter, Arthur was yet another despised authority figure or part of the childlike romanticism associated with the now even more despised hippies. When Arthur returned to the screen, in John Boorman's film *Excalibur*, it was once again in the glamour and melodrama of medieval legend. In place of the earnest hippiedom of *Arthur of the Britons*, the grotesque armour and brutal ways of Boorman's knights were the chivalric equivalents of Punk.

There remained many people who clung to the earlier counter-culture, especially around Glastonbury, but they too were acquiring a harder edge, produced by radical feminism. Radford's suggestion that Glastonbury had been a pagan holy place had been avidly embraced by those who associated Christianity with a discarded parental civilisation. Some of the most avid were those who believed that prehistoric society had been matriarchal and its religion centred upon a Great Goddess, both being destroyed by warlike patriarchal brutes who had laid the foundation of all the ills of modern society. To such thinkers Arthur could look suspiciously like a patriarch. So, for that matter, could Geoffrey Ashe. Instead, they declared that the whole Isle of Avalon was in the shape of The Goddess, that the terraces on the Tor were a prehistoric processional way in Her honour and that the medieval abbey's dedication to the Virgin Mary had been an echo of Her worship. The most celebrated Arthurian novel of the 1980s, *Mists of Avalon* by the American Marion Zimmer Bradley, was based upon these beliefs. In terms of hard evidence they were even less susceptible of proof (or disproof) than the older legends about Glastonbury. As an exercise in consciousness-raising, however, they were brilliant; one of the most celebrated shrines of an all-powerful male god, associated in legend with a warrior king, had been captured for feminism.

In this climate, those who had been the proponents of the historical Arthur were suddenly left isolated. By a cruel trick of fate the most pugnacious of them, John Morris, died suddenly on the day upon which Dumville's attack was published. The book which he had been promising to explain his interpretation of the sources perished with him. Radford was long in retirement. Alcock found himself completely without answers to Dumville's charges and henceforth declared himself an 'agnostic' where Arthur was concerned. He did reply to Rahtz about South Cadbury in 1982, when he pointed out that his interpretation of it as a uniquely large military and administrative centre had never been disproved. He also, although with less conviction, defended his interpretation of the set of post-holes inside which he had called a hall. What he did not do was to reassert any likely connection with Arthur.[39]

Bereft of his academic allies in Britain, Geoffrey Ashe now stood alone. He had to continue to defend the historical Arthur for the simple reason that the success of his early books had led him to become a professional writer and lecturer. He had to publish to survive, and Arthur and Glastonbury were his principal subjects. Furthermore it had been his own passion for them which had driven him to write in the first place, and this had not waned with time. To the beliefs of the radical feminists he accorded the same privilege which he had given to all others, saying that, as they could not postively be disproved, they deserved to be treated as true. He duly incorporated them into new books on the Isle of Avalon.[40] The historians were a harder matter. Dumville had destroyed Alcock's one piece of evidence, and so Ashe now set himself to find another. He noted that his well-loved medieval tales had set some of Arthur's most important accomplishments in France. He accordingly looked at continental sources and in three of them he found an account of how in about 470 a 'king of the Britons' called Riothamus or Riotimus brought a big army to help the Romans against the Goths in Berry, France, only to be betrayed by his allies and defeated. As the name just meant 'high king', Ashe argued that it was a title and that in fact he could have been Arthur.[41] There were obvious objections to the theory. 'Britons' in this context could more easily mean the people of Brittany than Britain, and the fact that one source describes them as coming by sea to Berry could just signify that they sailed up the Loire. It was still not real evidence. Nevertheless, it was an interesting addition to the list of possibilities, it was published in a learned journal (in 1981), and one cannot help feeling that if it had appeared ten years before then it would have been discussed with excitement in British universities. Now it was almost totally ignored there. For the rest of the 1980s Ashe continued to turn out popular books on Arthur, dealing with the lack of interest in his theory by declaring that he had won the debate by default.[42] His works were no longer read by British academics, for the simple reason that since the Dumville article most university libraries had ceased to buy them. The nation which he had hailed with such patriotic fervour had never paid him honour. By way of compensation, American institutions, attracted by the exciting subjects and accessible style of his books, began to invite him to visiting professorships. In 1992, when this pattern was compounded by personal links, he moved his main residence to the United States. He was not the first person to discover that, whether or not the New Jerusalem is easier to find in the New World than the Old, it is certainly easier to market there.

To an impartial observer, there was perhaps something slightly unbalanced in the attitude of British academe towards the subject in the late 1970s and the 1980s. In 1979 Charles Thomas's contempt for the notion of a historical Arthur was so profound that he could only refer to the hero in inverted commas, a privilege which he did not extend to any of the other figures associated with the fifth and sixth centuries. His principal concern at that time was with St Patrick, a genuine fifth-century personality attested by contemporary documents. Yet his reconstruction of the chronology and events of Patrick's life voyaged so much beyond these that it made his absolute scepticism in the matter of Arthur seem a little odd.[43] In 1986 J. N. L. Myres published a textbook in which he spoke sarcastically of the 'waste of the historian's time' represented by previous interest in Arthur, and dismissed him. In the same work he went on to take for granted the existence of a string of early Anglo-Saxon heroes and battles, the evidence for which would not have satisfied a Dumville.[44] It could appear that some scholars were continuing to apply the more generous frame of reference of an earlier age in every case except that of Arthur.

Archaeologists, who were reacting against the traditional picture of heroes, war-bands and savage fighting between Saxon and Briton, tended to emphasise the lack of any sign of social stratification in fifth-century Anglo-Saxon cemeteries or of destruction upon settlement sites. They presented a picture of slow and peaceful infiltration of a stable rural society by early English settlers.[45] While this may possibly been true of Kent and East Anglia, in general it makes nonsense of the testimony of Gildas (who in this case was referring to events in his parents' lifetime) and of the large number of defensive earthworks, roughly dateable to this period, in southern England. One, the Wansdyke, is the largest in the British Isles and argues for either a mighty communal effort or a powerful kingdom in that region. As for the north, where after all the documentary evidence has arguably always located Arthur, it has still thousands of miles of earthwork and thousands of enclosures left unexamined. The relative lack of interest in its post-Roman archaeology is partly a result of the diversion of attention to the west country by the Arthurian enthusiasts there, and it is the west which has produced the most remarkable example of a determined reaction against such enthusiasm in the face of a considerable incentive to it.

In the 1980s the last faith in Ralegh Radford's identification of Castle Dore as King Mark's palace was shaken: Rahtz's hint was made explicit and it was observed that Radford may have joined up the post-holes of a collection of small huts to make the outlines of larger buildings.[46] The scholar who spelled this out was a young Cornishman, Oliver Padel, who was very proud of his county and would certainly have given full credence to better evidence. Ironically, while Radford seemed to have been wrong about Castle Dore, he also appeared to have been wrong about Tintagel, with precisely opposite implications. In the course of the 1970s a set of scholars, including Thomas and Padel, came to realise that there was in fact nothing to indicate that it had been a monastery; it had instead every sign of having been a very important royal or princely residence of the fifth and sixth century, exactly as legend had always made it to be. Further excavation by Thomas in the 1980s seemed to confirm this impression. What was remarkable was the spectacle of all involved bending over backwards to avoid appearing to give any credence to the medieval tradition. Thomas took the opportunity for another sneer at 'that arch-shadow Arthur', and suggested that the place had been the home of a 'regional chieftain' rather than even one of 'the shadowy kings' of south-west Britain. This was despite the fact that one of those kings, Gildas's 'Constantine, tyrant whelp of the filthy lioness', was clearly a powerful ruler and that Tintagel was the most important site of his time yet found in his dominions. Padel, faced with the fact that the place had been deserted from the seventh to the twelfth centuries and yet tradition had accurately recorded its nature, admitted that 'one hardly dares to make such a suggestion for fear of what may be made of it in some circles'. He hastily added that Arthur was not involved in the matter as legend had never called it his residence (as opposed to his birthplace). Padel's study of place-names seemed to prove that the Tristan legend was already known in Cornwall by 967, long before Bromwich had believed that it could have arrived there and perhaps earlier than it can be found anywhere else. Yet he carefully avoided asserting that it had originated there.[47] There is no doubt that had these discoveries been made at any time up to 1977 then they would have caused considerable romantic excitement and been communicated to the public in this spirit. Now the scholars concerned were doing their utmost to keep excitement, speculation and public interest to a minimum. In 1991 the director of a television programme about archaeology described to me how he had struggled for an hour at Tintagel to persuade one of those scholars to make any comment whatsoever upon the possible relationship between the finds and the legends, and had failed completely.

In his concern for his audience, the director too had his point. Right up to the present, visitors to public libraries, Glastonbury and Tintagel, looking for information upon King Arthur, will find the books of Ashe, and that of Alcock which is in a new paperback edition. Dumville has never addressed the general public on the matter, preferring so far to write only for his colleagues. None of the textbook-writers who have followed him have provided any full explanation for the academic rejection of the historical Arthur. Yet public interest in the issue remains high. Much of it is simply traditional, built into the culture of the land, but one of the enduring results of the Second Romantic Movement has been to replace the detective story with the fantasy novel as the most popular literary genre. Enchanted swords, magicians, wise women and armoured warriors have never been more popular, in books, films and role-playing games. In 1991 a public day-school was held by Bristol archaeologists to celebrate the seventieth birthday of Philip Rahtz, on the subject of 'Somerset in the Age of King Arthur'. The title attracted a huge audience, and the appearance of Rahtz himself, Thomas, Fowler and an Anglo-Saxon specialist, Martin Carver, ensured splendid lectures. The only problem, from the point of view of those listening, was that they had paid to hear about Arthur, and each of the speakers remarked in a few seconds that he had no interest in him and then proceeded with his slides of post-Roman sites. Towards the end one of the audience was bold enough to ask about current attitudes towards the hero. Rahtz asked if any of his fellow-archaeologists were willing to summarise the views of 'the new historians'. There was complete silence. None of the speakers felt able to explain why the political and military history of Britain during an important two centuries had suddenly become unwritable, and why thirty years of intensive work by professional scholars had succeeded in making what were traditionally known as the Dark Ages even darker than before.

The remainder of the 1990s and the opening of the new century have sustained the same pattern. When Leslie Alcock produced his latest review of the evidence from Cadbury in 1995, he did not mention Arthur at all; instead he argued that it had been the fortress of a local king, with a full awareness that even this interpretation was insecure. His attitude was general among his fellow academics. Michael Costen's history of early medieval Somerset opened its chapter on the sub-Roman period with the words 'We can begin by dismissing King Arthur'. N. J. Higham considered that the latter was a myth imposed by later Welsh writers, and K. R. Dark managed to produce a long and careful study of Britain between 300 and 800 while ignoring him. Oliver Padel attempted to provide his own death-blow to the king by arguing that the folkloric elements in the Arthurian legend preceded the historical, and that he was the Brittonic-speaking peoples' equivalent to Fionn Mac Cumhail among the Gaelic-speakers; a purely mythical figure who was later given a pseudo-historical context. Once more a further possible interpretation of the material was added, without the certainty suggested by the author; for since the 'historical' and the 'folkloric' Arthur appear together in the oldest surviving accounts, it is still possible that the first was the original. The origins of stories in Celtic literatures are so utterly unknown that it is just possible that the Fenian cycle was actually influenced by the Arthurian legend, or indeed that Fionn himself was once a real person.

There were also a few exceptions to the pattern of rejection. The most prominent was probably Eric John, a historian conscious of his status as a maverick, who remarked that the ascription to the hero of a genuine late

Roman military office, and the precision with which his battles were re-membered, made him sound like somebody who had once had a genuine identity. Even he, however, prefaced these thoughts with the qualification that only a romantic novelist would try to find 'the real Arthur', and the prevailing attitude among experts at the opening of the new century was summed up in a textbook by Edward James: 'proof in these matters is an impossible dream'.[48]

The place where enduring public interest and assumed academic indi-fference most obviously met continued to be Tintagel, which had become the sixth most-visited site in the custody of the government agency for the care of monuments. In 1993 that body published a standard history of it, commissioned from Charles Thomas, who now suggested that it was not only an important seasonal residence for the region's royalty but the place for the inauguration of its kings. From 1990 the government employed Christopher Morris to renew excavation there, and by the end of the decade he had confirmed its status as a major royal centre, one of the most important sites of the sub-Roman period in the whole of Britain.

Throughout all this work Arthur was either ignored or dismissed, but he intruded into it anyway in 1998, when an engraved slate was found in the lower terrace of the castle. In lettering which appeared to be sixth-century, it had the deeply incised word 'AKE', and under it the scrawled graffito 'Pater Coliavificit Artognou'. This could, perhaps, be translated as 'Artognou Father of a descendent of Coll had made ...' The artefact caused an im-mediate stir in the mass media, because of the perceived similarity between the names Artognou and Arthur, but that similarity is a slight one, and the lack of any willingness on the part of experts to fan the excitement caused it to die down almost as fast as it had arisen.[49]

Eric John was correct to feel uneasy about the current tendency among specialists to write off Arthur altogether. It begs the enormous question of how a character who may never have existed came, within three hundred years of his presumed lifetime, to be the greatest hero of his people. The traditional sources for his career have not been exposed as forgeries or errors, but left without a context. Essentially all that has changed since 1960 is that experts were inclined then to stress the earliest possible date for their origin and are determined now to emphasise the latest possible one. This shift has been one result of the activities of the Camelot Research Committee. Another has been a widening of the gap between the academy and the public which ultimately supports it and which it serves. The tragedy of this situation is that both achievements are directly contrary to everything for which the members of that committee strove.

3

Glastonbury: Alternative Histories

The small Somerset town of Glastonbury is currently the principal British centre of the New Age, that late twentieth-century western movement which holds that modern civilisation values the material over the spiritual and that a revival of spirituality, drawing on many different cultural models, is needed to redress an unhealthy imbalance. As such, it has effectively become the British capital of dreams. The visitor wanders through the shops lining the two main streets and the courtyards and alleyways beyond them, brushing against Indian shawls and Peruvian silver jewellery, and locally made images of Green Men and pregnant goddesses, hearing the cool voices of women sing from compact discs about queens and wizards and earth magic, passing stands of cards decorated with native Americans, animal spirits, witches and zodiacs, and browsing through bookshelves in which characters from early Celtic literature rub shoulders with shamans, dowsers and The Goddess.

There are three monuments about which all these wares are assembled, and which attract the tourists and pilgrims before whom they are displayed. One is entirely human, and is most prominent in conventional guidebooks: the extensive ruins of the medieval abbey. The others consist of natural features embellished by human hands. One dominates the entire landscape, towering over the town and the whole complex of hills upon the side of which the latter is built and which collectively bears the traditional name of the Isle of Avalon. It is the tallest of those summits, Glastonbury Tor, a pinnacle of limestone and clay capped with hard sandstone, 522 feet tall and further extended by the late medieval tower of a vanished church dedicated to St Michael. Restored on successive occasions in the nineteenth and twentieth centuries, this tower looms at the top of the Tor like an upraised finger, making a dramatic silhouette from the flat lands around the Isle. The hardness of the sandstone cap is partly due to its impregnation with the iron carried by the water of a spring which once issued from the summit. Erosion has meant that during all human time the spring has flowed from the foot of the Tor instead. Its mineral compounds cause its water to stain all that it soaks a livid orange in colour, and it is now set in a landscaped garden crafted with considerable beauty and esoteric symbolism. Known as the Chalice Well, it represents the third of the principal sights of Glastonbury for visitors, and the most beloved of mystics.

A pilgrim arriving in 1520 would have encountered some similarities and differences. The most obvious of the latter would have been that the abbey was still intact; indeed, it was at the peak of its development. It was the second richest in England, and its abbot sat in the House of Lords, yielding precedence only to the abbot of St Albans, shrine of the land's first Christian martyr. It church was probably the longest ecclesiastical building of the English, and its interior would have been a marvel of carved stonework illuminated by stained glass and candlelight and rich with incense. Near the end of the nave, the visitor would have encountered a black marble tomb with a lion at each corner and an effigy of a king at its foot. This was the resting place of the bones of King Arthur and his queen Guinevere. Beyond was the high altar, with a silver and gilt antipendium set before it. In front of it also were three shrines containing the relics of saints. The greatest, covered in gold and silver, was that of St Patrick, the apostle of Ireland, while two other Irishmen, Benignus and Indract, were lodged in the other reliquaries. If any pilgrim needed a potted history of the monastery – the equivalent of a guidebook – one had been provided since the late fourteenth century. It took the form of a large six-leaf manuscript, written in handsome Gothic lettering, mounted on a wooden frame, and displayed in the church so that anybody might read it. Within it was a digest of what the monks now claimed to be the early story of their foundation.

It told of how Joseph of Arimathea, the man who had given his family tomb to hold the body of Christ after the Crucifixion, subsequently became a Christian missionary working under the apostle Philip in what is now France. Philip eventually decided to make him the leader of a mission to Britain, and sent him thither with a group of followers. Three local kings combined to grant him the twelve hides of land which were to form the core of the abbey's medieval estate, centred on the later Isle of Avalon, then known by its native British name of Ynyswitrin, the Glass Island. Upon the Isle Joseph built the first Christian church in Britain, of wattle, and settled there with eleven companions. After the last of them died, the site was deserted until the year 166, when the British king Lucius asked Pope Eleutherius to send missionaries to his people. Two duly arrived, SS Phagan and Deruvian, and discovered the wattle church, refounding a community of twelve hermits around it and building a second church, of stone. This religious settlement survived until the fifth century, when St Patrick arrived from Ireland and turned it into a regular monastery with himself at its head.

An erudite pilgrim would also be aware of two other stories concerning the early history of the Isle, contained in the lives of two Welsh saints who had allegedly operated in the fifth or sixth centuries. In one, concerning Gildas, Glastonbury was the stronghold of Melwas, king of Somerset, who had abducted Arthur's wife Guinevere. Arthur had besieged it, but had been hampered by the marshes which then surrounded the Isle. Peace was made, and the queen returned, through the mediation of the saint, who brought the two kings together in the abbey church. Gildas himself then retired to a hermitage nearby, and was buried in the same church when he died. The other story is found in the Life of Collen, and describes how this holy man encountered the castle of Gwyn ap Nudd, lord of the Underworld in Welsh myth, on the summit of Glastonbury Tor. By sprinkling it with holy water, he caused the fortress, Gwyn and all his attendant spirits to vanish.

The visitor in 1520 would have seen various physical associations of these stories. The reigning abbot, Richard Beere, was very anxious to promote the cult of Joseph of Arimathea, and had made a new crypt beneath the Lady Chapel of the abbey, reputedly the site of the wattle church, as a shrine to the saint. An image of the Virgin Mary, kept in the Lady Chapel, was said to have been made by Joseph himself, and in that very year a verse life of Joseph had been printed to reinforce his connection with Glastonbury. Apart from the shrine and the image, it mentioned some botanical wonders, a walnut tree in the old cemetery of the abbey which never came into leaf till June, and three hawthorns on Wirrall Hill ('the hill of the bog-myrtles'), the south-western corner of the Isle, which were in leaf, and blossomed, at Christmas. The Tor was, then as now, the second sacred focus of Glaston-bury, with its church of St Michael still in good repair and functioning as a small monastery in its own right, dependent on the abbey. The third focus was not, however, the Chalice Well, but another daughter house at Beckery in the south west of the Isle. It displayed a wallet, necklace, bell, and weaving implements, all allegedly left there by the Mother Saint of Ireland, Bridget, on a visit to Glastonbury in the fifth or sixth century.[1]

Within twenty years, all this complex of sacred institutions had been swept away as part of Henry VIII's general dissolution of the monasteries. The last abbot, Richard Whiting, had been hanged on the Tor between two of his monks and his severed head stuck over the abbey gateway. The shrines had all been destroyed and a process of despoilation commenced upon the buildings which was to continue for almost three hundred years and remove the house at Beckery altogether, reduce that on the Tor to the ruined tower, and leave only shells and fragments of the main abbey. It is noteworthy how little popular commotion or resistance this process caused. In 1536 large areas of the north of England exploded into the great popular rebellion of the Pilgrimage of Grace, intended (amongst other things) to save some religious houses. In 1549 Devon and Cornwall rebelled in an attempt to preserve the traditional church service. Central Somerset remained quiet throughout both years. It is possible that the abbey's record as a landlord and a dispenser of local justice had been heavy-handed enough to make many local people glad to see it go. It is also possible that the ideas which drove on the religious changes had found early adherents in the county. Certainly, Somerset soon turned into a shire with fewer Catholics and more radical Protestants than most others. When a Catholic monarch succeeded to the English throne in 1685 it became the centre of a popular uprising to unseat him, which was crushed by the royal army in the famous battle at Sedgemoor, to the west of Glastonbury.

Glastonbury itself became in these years a notable centre of radical Protestantism. It was a regular matter for comment in the eighteenth century that the progressive demolition of the abbey was due in part to the exceptional hostility felt by some townspeople towards these relics of popery.[2] The only one of its buildings to survive more or less intact to the present is the abbot's kitchen, and that owed its preservation largely to the fact that it was used as a Quaker meeting house. Some local pride and devotion remained attached to the survivor of the three hawthorn trees on Wirrall Hill, which flowered in midwinter, and the sprigs which later grew from it. By 1677 the tree was said to have been brought by Joseph of Arimathea himself, and this had grown by 1715 into a local legend that it had sprouted miraculously from his staff, stuck into the ground when he first reached the Isle. The name of the hill itself was becoming corrupted to Wearyall, and said to commemorate the fatigue of the saint and his party at their moment of arrival.[3] In general, however, the attitude of local people to the medieval remains was at best dismissive. After the passage of the first national legislation to protect ancient and medieval monuments in 1882, the owner of the site on which the shards of abbey stood is said to have remarked: 'Well, they are ruins now, and if they fall down they will be ruins still, won't they, what do you want more?'[4]

In fact, attitudes were already changing by that date, and would produce not merely a long process of investigation into the early history and pre-history of the Isle, but a considerable augmentation of the claims made about them. At base these developments were part of the general disposition of the nineteenth-century British to study their past in a systematic fashion never attempted before. The specific context for the investigation of Glastonbury, however, consisted of that burgeoning of interest in, and admiration of, the middle ages, and of the Arthurian legends in particular, which commenced at the end of the eighteenth century and became a major part of British culture in the late nineteenth. It was under Victoria that restoration work began upon the Tor tower, and excavations, badly conducted and worse recorded, commenced among the ruins of the abbey.[5] By 1886, also, a significant further accretion had taken place to the local stories of Joseph of Arimathea. It was now claimed that he had buried the chalice used at the Last Supper, commonly identified with the Holy Grail, in the Isle. As he did so a spring of water had sprung from the spot, staining all that it flowed over red in memory of the blood of Christ; and this had become the Chalice Well. The main piece of evidence advanced for this claim was the name of the well, and its appearance may (or may not) have had something to do with the fact that the well had become owned by a Roman Catholic seminary, the principal of which was an antiquarian.[6]

From 1886 events began to pick up speed. In that year a local museum was established in the town and a Glastonbury Antiquarian Society founded to maintain it and to encourage research.[7] In 1892 the society sponsored excavations in a field on the levels north west of the Isle. These continued until 1908 and revealed what was intepreted as an Iron Age lake village of the sort previously discovered in Switzerland. The site plan published at the end of the work, and the drawing of a reconstructed village inspired by it, showed a very substantial settlement, of ninety houses. When exacavation was completed at that site, it commenced at another near Meare, further out in the same former marshland. Work went on there until 1924, and the structures uncovered were considered to be a second lake village. These discoveries were of national importance, for the boggy conditions preserved artefacts so well that the Glastonbury 'village' became the classic British Iron Age settlement site from which interpretations of the whole period were derived.[8] The richness of the finds caused some historians by the mid twentieth century to declare that 'Glastonbury was the Bristol of the day', the point at which trade-routes of all central and western England, and Wales, converged.[9]

These finds, and the continuing public enthusiasm for the middle ages and for Arthurian themes, stimulated further interest in the Isle and its remains. In 1907 the ruins of the abbey were purchased by the Church of England, and systematic excavation commenced under the direction of the Somerset Archaeological Society, while restoration work was undertaken by the Church Commissioners. In 1912 a Christian socialist writer from London, Alice Buckton, purchased the Chalice Well and began to promote it as a place of sanctity and pilgrimage. She also established a centre of traditional crafts there, and founded a theatre troupe, the Guild of Glastonbury and Street Festival Players. In 1914 the composer Rutland Boughton established an annual Glastonbury Festival of performing arts, which reached its peak of activity between 1919 and 1926.[10]

The reputation of the town developed accordingly. By the early 1900s it had become a place of pilgrimage for Christian mystics, and the excavation and restoration of the abbey had more than physical effects upon the site. By 1911 people were hearing ghostly bells in the ruins at night, and smelling incense there, phenomena which nobody could remember being reported during the long years when the remains were in private ownership.[11] Their numinous atmosphere was supercharged in 1918, when the Bristol architect who was directing the excavations, Frederick Bligh Bond, published a claim that his work had been aided by communications from the spirits of medieval and Tudor monks, left in the field of cosmic memory. Bond went on to write a series of further books to develop the idea that Glastonbury lay under the special protection of a body of elevated souls, and to advance the theory that the sacred and esoteric science of gematria (holy numbers) underpinned the planning of the abbey. Specifically, the whole complex of buildings was contained within a regular grid of squares, each with a side of 74 feet, the magic unit of the sun.[12]

It was not merely Christian associations which were being invoked in the developing spiritual profile of the place. The decades around 1900 were marked by a powerful tendency on the part of the English to search for a timeless and organic relationship with their country. Part of this took the form of a yearning to view Christian sacred sites as natural developments from pre-Christian religions, so that the two formed a continuum rooted in the land itself.[13] The discovery of the 'lake village' projected the past of Glastonbury back into the pagan Iron Age, the time of the Druids. By 1909 a correspondent of the *Spectator*, writing from Hampshire, could advance as fact the opinion that the Isle had been a pilgrimage centre for Druids from all over Europe. In his scheme it had been served by priestesses, and marked by the huge figure of a salmon, traced out in the contours of the landscape. The origins of this idea are as yet obscure; there is an apparent harmony with the medieval Irish legend of the Salmon of Wisdom, but this may be misleading. Certainly the concept was already around five years earlier, when two of the visionary writers of the contemporary 'Celtic Renaissance', John Goodchild and William Sharp, visited Glastonbury and the former showed the latter what he took to be the form of the giant fish below Wirrall Hill. The writer in 1909 declared, in a manner wholly characteristic of the time, that such ancient remains proved 'that at no time in the history of the human race has God left Himself without witness, even if that witness be of the nature we call pagan'.[14]

The relationship between Glastonbury, paganism and Christianity was

treated in different ways in subsequent years. At the height of the festivals
coordinated by Boughton, rumour in the town held that the young actresses
and actors who performed in them (mostly coming from London) 'were
given to running to the top of the Glastonbury Tor in order to greet the
dawn in a state of pagan undress'.[15] In 1933 the novelist John Cowper Powys
made a character decry the trite romanticism which had become associated
with the place, 'like scented church-lamp oil'. At the same time he affirmed
his own belief in 'the immemorial Mystery of Glastonbury', a power 'older
than Christianity, older than the Druids, older than the gods of the Norse-
men or the Romans, older than the gods of the Neolithic men'. In his
view 'everyone who came to this spot seemed to draw something from it,
attracted by a magnetism too powerful for anyone to resist'.[16] Publishing
the next year, the ritual magician Dion Fortune saw the relationship as
more polarised, though complementary; the Tor and Chalice Well belonged
to the 'Old Gods', 'the fiery pagan forces that make the heart leap and
burn', while the abbey ruins embodied the Christian faith. 'And some love
one, and some the other.' In her vision (or as she put it, her tradition)
there was once a prehistoric stone circle, dedicated to the sun, upon the
Tor. A processional way climbed up to it, by which the priests of the sun
ascended from 'the Blood Well of sacrifice' at the foot.[17]

Dion Fortune was a Londoner with a second home in Glastonbury, and
it was to be another Londoner on holiday who was to provide the period's
single greatest contribution to the claims regarding the past of the place.
This was Katherine Maltwood, wife of a very rich industrialist who owned
a summer home on the Polden Hills to the south west. In 1929 she was
spending time there while engaged in the work of providing illustrations
for one of the medieval Arthurian romances, *The High History of the Holy
Grail*. Viewed from the tower of her house, the Glastonbury landscape
seemed to her to provide the setting for the tale, and to have been shaped
in ancient times into huge figures, visible from above and representing a
zodiac which evoked the primal forces of life.[18] It has been noted above
that by 1904 people were already seeing such shapes in the Isle, and in
1574 the scholar and magician John Dee had made a map of the district
in which he claimed to have found heavenly constellations plotted out
upon the ground.[19] Maltwood drew also upon the theories of nineteenth-
century authors such as Godfrey Higgins and Iolo Morganwg to expound
her system of thirteen signs, delineated by old roads, streams and earthworks, and echoed in place-names and local legends. To her they formed
a sacred mystery so old that it predated the Druids, but which had now been
revealed by the modern devices of aerial photography and the Ordnance
Survey map.[20]

With the work of Maltwood, Powys and Fortune the first period of the revival of Glastonbury as a holy place may said to have been completed. Between the mid 1930s and the mid 1950s the process marked time, little being written about it and little done there. It was only in the late 1950s that the second wave of revival began, gathering a momentum which has continued to the present.

That second wave was precipitated in 1957 by the publication of Geoffrey Ashe's book, *King Arthur's Avalon*. It collated all the evidence for Glaston-bury as successively a major holy centre of the pagan Celts, one of Celtic Christianity, and one of medieval English and Roman Catholic Christianity. It did so in exciting and beautiful prose, and made a claim for Glastonbury as a place of unique sanctity in Britain. In 1959 a Chalice Well Trust was formed to administer and maintain the spring as a place of pilgrimage.[21] An exceptionally lovely garden was landscaped around it, which is main-tained to the present. At the opening of the 1960s the archaeologist Ralegh Radford conducted his excavations in the abbey precinct, and in 1968 his contribution to Ashe's edition of essays, *The Quest for Arthur's Britain*, pressed the claims of Glastonbury to have been an ancient pagan holy place with all the authority of his standing as a respected archaeologist.

In particular, Radford cited three pieces of evidence. The first consisted of the earthwork known as Ponter's Ball. The Isle of Avalon was never a true island, but a peninsula jutting out from the limestone hills of east Somerset. It has always been thrown into dramatic relief by the flatness of the marshes, now drained but still prone to winter flooding, which sur-rounded it on three sides. The ridge which connects it to the eastern hills is itself narrow and relatively low, and the single ditch and bank of Ponter's Ball stretches across most of it. To Radford the fact that they did not bisect the whole ridge suggested that they were not intended for defence, and that they were 'best explained as the *temenos* or enclosure of a great pagan Celtic sanctuary'. His second piece of evidence was that 'St Indracht and St Patrick are Celtic saints, and it is difficult to believe that their cult was introduced at Glastonbury after the Saxon conquest'. His third was that the earliest remains of the abbey were in form very like those of early Irish monasteries.[22]

At the same time writers from outside the world of formal scholarship were once again making contributions to the subject. One was Geoffrey Russell, who had worked in Ceylon for most of his life, had received a mystical vision of a spiral, and had returned to the British Isles with an interest in mazes and labyrinths. Dion Fortune, it may be remembered, had spoken of a prehistoric processional way mounting the Tor. In 1969 Russell drew attention to the curious terracing of the hill, hitherto usually interpreted as field systems created for medieval agriculture, and suggested that they were the remains of a spiral maze by which worshippers once climbed to the summit. He considered that it might have been 'Celtic' in origin.[23] In 1969 also John Michell published his book *The View Over Atlantis*, probably the most influential single text of the late twentieth-century interest in 'earth mysteries'. In it he proposed that the Tor was one of the major markers upon the most impressive of all the channels of natural energy flowing across the surface of the planet, which are known to believers as leys. In this case the line concerned ran from the huge prehistoric temple at Avebury to the dramatic natural rock of St Michael's Mount in Cornwall. He also took up Bond's idea of mystical mathematics underlying the site of the abbey, and extended it. In the new scheme the town and abbey together were laid out 'according to the magic square of the Sun, with exactly the same numbers and patterns as those that determined the form of Stonehenge'. The town lay under two interlinked circles with radii of 660 feet, the 'cabbalistic number of earth', and the axis of the abbey pointed directly to Stonehenge. The core estate of the abbey contained the same quantity of land as that of the New Jerusalem in the biblical book of Revelation. All this, to John Michell, suggested a secret system of wisdom uniting the medieval monks and their architects with the builders of prehistoric monuments and spanning at least four thousand years.[24]

In the 1960s and 1970s, other writers took up Katherine Maltwood's idea of the Glastonbury Zodiac, reshaping and reinforcing it.[25] In the following two decades feminists declared that as the Isle had once been a pagan sanctuary, it would have to have honoured the Great Goddess who, in their view of prehistory, had been the deity universally venerated before the coming of patriarchy. Once again, it was Geoffrey Ashe who produced the initial vision, in a novel published in 1973 when a character sees the whole Isle of Avalon becoming a living divine woman, her body fashioned from its contours.[26] Subsequently the most consistent writer to promote the concept of the Isle as a centre of ancient Goddess-worship, Kathy Jones, produced three different schemes whereby the clutch of hills represented the body of the divine feminine, so that mysteries could be enacted upon them.[27]

Such assertions and suggestions were both a cause and a product of that phenomenon whereby from the late 1960s onward the town and its outlying villages filled up with newcomers characterised by counter-cultural views and lifestyles. The transformation of Glastonbury into the New Age capital of Britain was complete by 1980, and has been sustained. One of the arrivals was a Londoner called Anthony Roberts, who produced in 1977 the neatest synthesis of the various accretions to ideas of the place's past which had been made since the century began. In this, the first monument to be constructed was the zodiac, laid out at any time between 10,000 and 2700 BCE. Then came astronomer priests, who around 2000 BCE dug Ponter's Ball, put up standing stones, and developed the Chalice Well. Druids followed, making the spiral maze around the Tor and the nodal points for the ley system. Last was Christianity, 'which came late to the area, first as an inheritor, then as a usurper, finally as a destroyer'.[28]

These, then, are the claims that have been made regarding the past of Glastonbury, from the late middle ages until the present. What *is* the documentary and material evidence by which they can be judged?

Of all the legendary associations of Glastonbury, the most heavily investigated have been those regarding King Arthur and Joseph of Arimathea. There is general agreement that the linkage between Arthur and the abbey took place relatively late in the history of the latter, and that its context was a disastrous fire in 1184, which completely destroyed the wooden church that was the oldest and most sacred part of the complex. The monastery thereby suffered a serious blow to its prestige, and was also left with an expensive programme of rebuilding. The reigning king, Henry II, promised funds to assist this, but the work had hardly begun when Henry died in 1189, and the new monarch, Richard I, cut off the money in order to finance his own plans for a crusade. It was in this crisis that the monks of Glastonbury announced, in 1191, that they had discovered the bodies of Arthur and Guinevere in the old cemetery of their abbey. The political circumstances were exceptionally propitious for such a find, consisting of the struggle of the reigning Plantagenet royal family to consolidate an empire which covered most of the British Isles and about half of France. Their title to these lands would be strengthened if they could claim to be the natural heirs of Arthur, portrayed in Geoffrey of Monmouth's celebrated recent history as the sovereign of all north-western Europe. It could be especially potent in marginal areas of the Plantagenet domain such as Wales and Brittany, where Arthur was a national hero. The discovery of his bones in England, the heartland of that domain, was a significant endorsement of that claim.

This sequence of events has caused several writers to suggest that the discovery was a hoax concocted to provide a way out of a crisis in the abbey's fortunes.[29] The monks' evidence for identifying the bodies consisted of a lead cross a foot tall, found with them and stating that the male corpse was that of King Arthur, buried in the Isle of Avalon. It has twice been pointed out that this characterisation of Arthur has such a close fit with that made by Geoffrey of Monmouth, but not with that of older writers (who neither automatically gave Arthur the royal title nor related him to Avalon), that it strengthens the suspicion of fraud.[30] The lettering on the cross (which is now lost but is depicted in a sixteenth-century drawing) is more that of the tenth than of the twelfth century; but it was used in some twelfth-century inscriptions, and in any case the monks were quite capable of imitating an earlier script. Comparisons of the first accounts of the find suggest that the story of it was altered in order to arrive at the formulation most likely to command widest acceptance. Initially it seems to have been announced that the body of Mordred had been found with those of the king and queen, and that Guinevere also was named upon the cross.[31] It is possible that these discrepancies are the result of confusion in the reports rather than changes in the official story; but even without them it is impossible to give much credit to the latter. The linkage between Arthur and Glastonbury therefore remains at best very doubtful, and its most enduring legacy has been the identification of the group of hills upon which Glastonbury stands with the mythical Isle of Avalon of the Arthurian romances; a name which has been followed in the present chapter for lack of any alternative.

The association of Joseph with the abbey came even later, and apparently as a result of the growing importance of the saint in romantic literature. Before 1200 Robert de Boron had declared that Joseph had brought the Holy Grail to the 'Vales of Avaron' in the west of Britain. This garbled identification of its destination with the fabulous Avalon of the Arthurian legend, and the new claim of Glastonbury to be the latter, made a convergence between the abbey and Joseph inevitable, and before 1250 the saint had been added to the official history of the monastery, as its founder. Not much was made of the claim for another hundred years, until the late fourteenth century when a new need to increase pilgrimage revenue provided a practical incentive for developing it. A political incentive was added in the early fifteenth, with the inception of regular Church councils in which the antiquity, and precedence, of the divisions of the western Church rooted in the various nations became an issue of pride and rivalry. The status of Joseph at Glastonbury rose accordingly, and reached its apogee in the early sixteenth century. As said above, the link between the saint and the 'holy thorn' which flowers at Christmas was not made for almost two hundred years after that; the tree itself is a fairly common Levantine species, *Cratagus Oxyacantha Praecox*, which is not recorded at Glastonbury before the reference of 1520 cited earlier. Specimens were presumably brought there by a pilgrim returning from the Middle East.

In view of all this, most historians to have written on the subject have treated the association between Joseph and Glastonbury as a medieval fiction.[32] James Carley, one of those who have been kindest towards the possibility that the abbey's medieval traditions might contain truth, actually used it to defend the monks against the charge that they had faked the discovery of Arthur's body. He wrote in 1988 that the fact that they never claimed to have found the body of Joseph, despite strong incentives and repeated searches, strongly suggests that they believed the burials uncovered in 1191 to be genuinely those of Arthur and Guinevere, whether or not they actually were. With admirable probity, he himself announced six years later that new evidence proved that in 1419, when the claims of the English to precedence in Church councils made proof of a very early Christian foundation in England especially desirable, the monks of Glastonbury were preparing to announce that they had found the bodies of Joseph and all his followers. Official disclosure of the discovery was delayed until the king, Henry V, returned from fighting in France. Instead he died there, and meanwhile the question of precedence in councils became less pressing, and so the scheme was called off.[33] Knowledge of it does now weaken faith further in the sincerity of the abbey's claims both to an association with Joseph and to contain the grave of Arthur.

In the 1990s a rescue attempt was mounted upon the claim to Joseph by Deborah Crawford, who has argued that oral traditions, which have left no trace in the written record, may have underpinned the later documented linkage of the saint and Glastonbury.[34] Even she, however, could do no better than to try to have the historicity of the legend declared 'an open question'. This is probably its true status, but her argument as it stands possesses two defects. The first is that there is no evidence that such oral traditions ever existed. The second is that she infers the possible existence of them by using Jan Vansina's techniques for recognising oral components in texts of African traditions. In doing so she has discounted the cautions voiced by Vansina and other scholars of African history concerning the limitations of treating oral tradition as historical evidence.

A further inspection of the high and later medieval sources prunes away other texts and issues from the category of good evidence. One is the story of St Gildas and the contest between Arthur and Melwas at Glastonbury. The *Life* concerned is a twelfth-century work, probably by the respected Welsh author Caradoc of Llancarfan. It draws in part upon an earlier Breton text, but adds several episodes of its own, and that referring to Glastonbury is one of these.[35] That story may derive from a separate, and older, tradition, but there is no evidence of this and it may well have been a product of the writer's imagination. Antonia Gransden has suggested that the monks of Glastonbury themselves hired Caradoc to write the work to boost their reputation, much as at the same time they commissioned a history of the abbey from another celebrated author, William of Malmesbury.[36] This is possible, but there is absolutely no proof of it. All that can be said is that this *Vita Gildae* is not good source material for events in Glastonbury six centuries before. The same is even more true of the other Welsh saint's life, *Buchedd Collen*. It survives only in a sixteenth-century version, and the style is that of the high medieval romances, not of earlier hagiography.[37] It therefore seems to be a very late composition, of the thirteenth or fourteenth century, and can be taken even less seriously as a reflection of very early medieval history.

What both works do reflect is the impression which Glastonbury was making upon the imagination of the Welsh from the twelfth century onward, greatly enhanced by royal recognition of it as the burial place of Arthur. Ceridwen Lloyd-Morgan has studied the relevant sources and found no mention of Glastonbury at all in any Welsh text before the twelfth century. After 1191, such texts most commonly called it 'Ynys Afallach', accepting its new claim to have been the Isle of Avalon. She could find no mention of the term 'Ynyswitrin' before the early thirteenth century and it remained rare; her opinion was that it was simply a Welsh rendering of the name Glastonbury. Had it been prevalent in Welsh sources from earlier medieval periods, the case that it was the original, British, term for the place, and that the abbey was a pre-Saxon foundation, would have been much strengthened. As things stand, it cannot be used to support that case at all, and it seems that he earliest known name for the foundation was the English one, Glastonbury, which is itself susceptible of different interpretation but may simply mean the settlement of the *glastan*, Anglo-Saxon for oak trees.[38]

The round-up of high medieval sources for the early history of the abbey can be completed by looking at the work of William of Malmesbury, who was commissioned by the monks to write upon the subject in the mid twelfth century. His original text is best preserved in his *De gestis regum Angliae*, and makes some interesting contrasts with the later, fully developed, foundation legend. It does not of course mention St Joseph. Instead, it comments that 'documents of no meagre credit' said that the old wattle church of the abbey (the one about to be destroyed in the fire of 1184) was built by Christ's own disciples. It also stated the different tradition that 'annals of good credit' asserted that this church was constructed by the missionaries sent by Pope Eleutherius in response to the request from Lucius, cited above. William, like the admirable scholar that he was, added that neither tale represented 'facts of solid truth'. Indeed they do not, and his courtesy to his sources cannot conceal this fact. The one concerning Christ's disciples seems to have rested on nothing but vague assertion, while the precise story about Eleutherius's missionaries derives from Bede's famous eighth-century *Ecclesiastical History*. It had a respectable pedigree by William's time, but this does not rescue it from being a pious fantasy, for there never was a second-century ruler of Britain called Lucius.[39]

In this manner, the written traditions regarding the history of Glastonbury before the fifth century evaporate into intangibility. To consider whether those which remain supply any better evidence for a 'Celtic' origin to the abbey, it is necessary next to concentrate upon the sources surviving from the centuries before the Norman Conquest.

What is perfectly obvious from the Anglo-Saxon records for Glastonbury is that the abbey was one of the favourite religious houses of the early English rulers of Wessex. As the royal family of Wessex came to take over the whole of England in the tenth century, the position of the abbey rose in proportion, until by the time that the Normans invaded it was the richest in the realm. In many ways, the quest of the house for its historical roots during the twelfth century represented a series of attempts to regain its pre-eminent position under the less favourable rule of Norman and Plantagenet newcomers.

The Anglo-Saxon sources also make plain the phenomenon to which Ralegh Radford drew attention as evidence for the pre-Saxon origin of the abbey: that for an English institution it venerated an unusually large number of Irish saints. To recapitulate, it claimed to possess the bones of Patrick, Benignus and Indract, and personal effects of Bridget. A closer look at each, however, reveals serious problems with Radford's suggestion. Benignus turns out probably have started his career as a local Anglo-Saxon holy man, Beonna, whose shrine was at Meare in the marshes to the north. Benignus was the Latin form of his name, and by coincidence also the Latinisation of the name of the much more famous Irish saint Benen, which is why the two became confused. Eventually Benen eclipsed Beonna, whose relics were translated from Meare to Glastonbury in 1091 and identified wholly with the Irishman. This sequence of events is not absolutely certain, but is does seem likely, and is now commonly accepted.[40] Indract (or in Radford's version, Indracht) is not recorded as identified with Glastonbury until the eleventh century. It is important for our present purposes that neither of the two extant versions of his life make any connection between him and the pre-Saxon history of the abbey. Instead, his legend told that he was an Irish pilgrim murdered near Glastonbury in the reign of the eighth-century Saxon king Ine. His name is certainly an Anglicisation of a fairly common Irish name, Indrechtach, and he may perhaps be identified with an abbot of Iona who was called that and was murdered in England in 854.[41] This is uncertain, but the traditions concerning him seem in any case to be irrelevant to a quest for the origins of the abbey.

The associations with Bridget and Patrick are more complex. No Irish life of Bridget mentions a visit to Britain. Nor do any of the hagiographies of Patrick mention a return by him to Britain, although like those of Bridget they begin relatively soon after the saint's death. Doubt is further increased by the fact that the Irish have always claimed that his body is buried at Downpatrick in Ulster, not at Glastonbury. Moreover, writings of Patrick himself exist, being some of the very few genuine fifth-century texts which survive for the British Isles, and in one (the *Confessio*) he states clearly that he will never return to Britain, but intends to devote the rest of his life to his Irish ministry.[42] The Glastonbury tradition was based firmly on the insistence that he did indeed make such a return. The problem might be resolved by the possibility – itself aired for over a thousand years – that there were two missionaries to the Irish called Patrick, who became blended in the later figure of the saint. This has never, however, been proven, and probably never will be. The monks of Glastonbury were themselves aware of the chance that there might be two men involved. Documents associated with Glastonbury in the tenth and eleventh centuries show a state of confusion as the prevailing story was successively amended to distinguish between the two, and to determine which was claimed by the abbey, until the attempt was abandoned at the end of the Anglo-Saxon period. One historian, H. P. R. Finberg, has justly remarked that such confusion bears 'all the marks of an uncertain and insecurely founded tradition'.[43]

What does seem certain is that there was a colony of Irish monks at Glastonbury in the early tenth century. Its existence is established by the testimonies of biographers of that century's greatest English saint, Dunstan, who grew up in the district and came to lead the abbey. One, writing around the year 1000, says that these Irishmen were there to honour the burial place of Patrick. Another, working about a hundred years later, added that they had gone into voluntary exile to win religious merit; which was certainly in accord with Irish practice at the time. Their presence provides a context for the growth of cults of Irish saints at the abbey, but how they got there in the first place is a matter for speculation. Finberg suggested that they were invited over by Alfred the Great, who fostered links with Ireland as part of his efforts to re-establish learning in England after the disruption of the Viking invasions.[44] It can only be said that this is possible.

As the state of evidence exists – and it is unlikely to alter – there is no trace of an association between Patrick and Glastonbury before the tenth century, about half a millennium after the lifetime of the saint. This leaves us with two possible conclusions. One is that St Patrick (or one of two men with that name) really did live and die at a pre-Saxon monastery at Glastonbury. The other is that he never did, and that his cult there is based upon a legend. In the latter case, there are a number of putative explanations for the appearance of the belief, most of which have been proposed already by Finberg. One is that the colony of Irish monks established there by the opening of the tenth century brought some relics of Patrick (and Bridget) with them from Ireland. Another is that what was commemorated in Somerset was not Patrick's burial place but his birthplace; of which more later. A third is that the cult was based upon a confusion between Patrick and the Cornish saint Petroc, of whom the abbey also claimed a bone and some clothing; such confusion certainly occurred at times in Devon and Cornwall. A fourth is that the word *patricius* was both a name and a title, used in both sub-Roman Britain and Anglo-Saxon England to indicate a high-ranking office-holder. A grave-marker bearing this title might have existed at Glastonbury and misled later readers.[45] Amid such a gaggle of possibilities, the truth may be for ever lost.

The only other literary evidence consists of the first charters of the abbey, designating grants of land to it, and here again possibilities rather than certainties are provided. By the thirteenth century Glastonbury proudly claimed one from Patrick himself, which is clearly a forgery made around 1220. Another, only existing in a high medieval copy, purported to be a grant made in 601 by a local British king, and used the Welsh form of the name of Glastonbury, Ynyswitrin. A scholar in 1960 thought that it could be genuine, and thus evidence of the existence of the abbey before the Saxons arrived. More recently, the formidable David Dumville has termed it a 'rank forgery'. His view is echoed by Lesley Abrams in her study of the Anglo-Saxon endowments of the abbey: to her it 'is singularly unconvincing as a document'.[46]

Sarah Foot, who has made the most systematic attempt so far to rescue the early history of the abbey from later additions and interpolations to documents, has come up with the following conclusions. An Anglo-Saxon list of the earliest set of dignitaries associated with Glastonbury survives, and identifies an abbot called Haemgils as the first of all. Haemgils was the recipient of three charters which are only documented in later copies but seem from their style to be based on genuine seventh-century originals. He was also named in the grants which head the list of apparently genuine royal charters in a thirteenth-century compilation. According to another charter, he had a prominent tomb in the abbey church. The charters mentioned above date from the years 680–82, shortly after the West Saxon conquest of the region from the native British. No foundation document survives for the monastery, to clinch our knowledge of when it came into existence. Lesley Abrams has suggested that there is no great significance to this absence, because the writing of charters itself only came to be a routine procedure in the course of the late seventh century. Alternatively, she adds, it may be that a foundation charter did exist but that the monks later decided to scrap it, in order to claim a greater antiquity for their house. Upon this evidence, Sarah Foot suggested that Glastonbury was established in the late seventh century, by the rulers of Wessex who had just conquered the district, and that 'there seems no reason to doubt' that Haemgils was indeed the very first abbot. Lesley Abrams has declared, more cautiously, that 'the evidence for the early history of the Anglo-Saxon community on the site is so poor and doubtful that it cannot even be suggested with confidence which king – if it was a king – was responsible for its foundation'. She adds that 'the hard evidence is lacking' for any pre-Saxon establishment.[47]

This is as far as documentary evidence can take us, and the result has been inconclusive if at times suggestive. The only hope now for a clear resolution of the question of Glastonbury's origins lies in the province of material remains, and with the discipline of archaeology.

As mentioned above, antiquaries began to dig among the ruins of the abbey in the nineteenth century, and work there has been systematic since the 1900s, joined by excavations of high quality into other parts of the Isle of Avalon since the opening of the 1960s. The result, however, is very patchy and the record of the many explorations of the abbey precinct itself is especially poor. None of the results of thirty-four seasons of excavation of the abbey between the 1900s and the 1960s has been fully published, and less than a dozen finds have been illustrated.[48] What does seem to remain true is what Philip Rahtz pointed out in 1968; that so far not a single feature has been discovered in the whole area covered by the fully-developed medieval abbey which can be securely dated to a period before the Anglo-Saxon. None of the characteristic deposits of Iron Age, Roman or sub-Roman sites are present, and this would appear to support Sarah Foot's suggestion from the documents that the house was a Saxon foundation. At the opening of the 1980s Ralegh Radford was still declaring confidently that a still visible bank and ditch marked the limit of 'the British monastic enclosure', but in 1984 he made a brave retraction of his former view, stating that 'no physical evidence of a British monastery has survived the analysis of those results which are available'. One development which had influenced this change had been the results of the excavation of the bank and ditch, published in 1982. Timber stakes at the ditch's bottom yielded dates of 670 plus 100 or minus 30 years, and 610 plus 50 or minus 70 years. The former seemed to make the boundary precinct Anglo-Saxon. On the other hand, the variation just about allowed for a pre-Saxon construction, and a large structure was located nearby with wood in it dated to 590 plus 60 or minus 160 years. The wood might, of course, have been older than the structure, and the latter need not have been monastic anyway, and so positive proof of a British monastery on the site is indeed still missing; but the results hold open the chance.[49]

Similar blanks were drawn at other celebrated sites in the Isle. That of the daughter house at Beckery was excavated extensively by Philip Rahtz in 1967–68, and no structures found which could be dated earlier than the Anglo-Saxon period.[50] In 1961 Rahtz had dug at the Chalice Well, and found that the stonework surrounding it dated from the late twelfth century. No traces of earlier building were found, and none of the votive deposits associated with pagan sacred springs such as those at nearby Bath and at Carrawburgh in Northumberland. A hole near the well might have been made by a yew which had grown there in Roman times, and this in turn could have been a sacred tree; but there is a lot of speculation here. The name of the well, so suggestive to modern ears, is a recent corruption of the medieval 'Chalkwell', simply indicating a limestone spring.[51] There is no evidence that it was regarded as holy during the time when the abbey was functional. It is often said that it became celebrated as a healing spring in the mid eighteenth century, after one Matthew Chancellor claimed to have been cured of asthma by drinking its waters. Chancellor himself, however, declared that the well from which he drank was in the remains of the abbey, and it was this still extant spring, now commonly called St Joseph's Well, which was hailed as *the* 'Holy Well of Glastonbury' in 1806. It is true that as the fame of the cure spread, and the town developed into a spa, water was piped from the Chalice Well to baths lower down the valley. There is no sign, however, that the Chalice Well itself was viewed as having any sacred or legendary associations until the Catholic seminary took it over in the late nineteenth century.[52] Even then, it was not one of the sights of the Isle, and when the modern pilgrimages commenced at the opening of the twentieth, the three most-visited monuments were the abbey, the Tor and the spring once connected to the chapel at Beckery. The latter had replaced that in the abbey itself as the holy well of Glastonbury.[53] The present dominant status of the Chalice Well has been achieved mainly because of the enthusiasm of Alice Buckton and the later Chalice Well Trust.

More confusion surrounds the status of Ponter's Ball, the earthwork across the peninsula connecting the Isle to the eastern hills which featured so prominently in Ralegh Radford's vision of a huge pagan sacred enclosure. The problem with this vision is that when an excavation was made of the bank in 1909, pottery was found beneath it which could date from anywhere between the tenth and twelfth centuries. This suggests that it is a high medieval construction, and Radford's riposte, that it could be a pagan feature which was *redug* in the middle ages, must count as a heroic work of defence in its own right. Radford's other argument, that as the earthwork could be outflanked at either end it could hardly have been military in purpose, was answered by Philip Rahtz. He pointed out that a construction of that sort would have been quite sufficient to deter cattle-raiders. It would indeed; and any enemies bent on carrying off substantial plunder.[54] Rahtz himself wondered whether the high medieval context would have provided any occasion for the abbey to build such a defence, but here there is a clear affirmative answer. Between the 1190s and the 1320s, the abbey was engaged in a bitter struggle to keep its independence from the bishops of nearby Wells. Twice in 1199 armed bands were sent from Wells to take Glastonbury by force and punish its monks, so that this would be a very good context for the construction of a work to defend the only permanently accessible route into the isle. The same period was, moreover, a considerable one for building works on the part of the abbey, partly to assert its dignity against the bishops. Just one of the thirteenth-century abbots, Michael of Amesbury, supervised the extension of the abbey church and the erection of a sea wall at Brent Marsh, ten mills on monastery properties and a hundred new houses in the town; the construction of the earthwork would have fitted well into programmes like these.[55] On the other hand, there is no clear evidence that it did. The dig of 1909 has never been properly published, and at present Ponter's Ball remains an enigma.

Amid this general dearth of pre-Saxon structures in the isle there remains a resounding exception: the Tor itself, the summit of which was the setting in 1964–66 for the most famous of Philip Rahtz's Glastonbury excavations. He found no traces of any construction work of the prehistoric or Roman periods, but uncovered a settlement from the fifth or sixth centuries, the time traditionally associated with Arthur. It was relatively small, having wooden buildings into which a couple of dozen people might have crowded, and its purpose remains an open question. In the 1960s Rahtz was inclined to favour the idea that it was the stronghold of a petty chieftain, and related it to the medieval legend of Melwas. It did, however, lack any source of water closer than the foot of the hill, so was not designed to stand a siege. Moreover it showed none of the high-status glassware normally associated with royal or princely strongholds of the period. By the 1990s, therefore, Philip Rahtz was more inclined to view the structures as the remains of a religious community of the time.[56] The absence of water, again, would have made it difficult for monks to perform the ritual cleansings incumbent on their offices, but hermitages were sometimes founded in such high and lonely positions where the opportunities for withdrawal and contemplation outweighed the practical difficulties. If so, then the settlement on the Tor represents the only solid evidence yet found for the existence of a native British monastery at Glastonbury, predating the arrival of the kings of Wessex.

It is not, however, that solid, for not only does it remain possible that the site was a military stronghold, but there is a third interpretation of it which would fit the data as well as the religious one. The summit of the Tor is intervisible with two other prominent Somerset hills, Cadbury Castle (famed in the 1960s and 1970s as the putative Camelot) and Brent Knoll. From Brent Knoll it is possible to see across the Severn estuary to the Welsh coast, and the hill of Dinas Powys. All of these landmarks were occupied in the sub-Roman period. It is therefore legitimate to argue that they might have functioned as a chain of lookout posts, from which the whole tract of land and sea between the Blackdown Hills and the Black Mountains could have been surveyed, and between which alarm signals could pass. Such a function would have fitted the structures on the Tor very well, and the identity of the enemy against whom they would have been built at that period is very clear: the Irish.

Although overshadowed in English history by the Anglo-Saxon settle-ments, the importance of Irish raiding and occupation of the western coasts of Britain to the history of later Roman and sub-Roman Britain is well established. Apart from presenting a considerable general problem to the Roman province, the Irish established the permanent kingdoms of Dalriada in Scotland (the embryo of the future Scottish state) and Dyfed in Wales. Epigraphic evidence suggests that they had a strong if temporary presence in Devon and Cornwall, and they may even have settled in Somerset.[57] Whether or not St Patrick ever died there, this later English county remains one of the most likely areas to have contained his birthplace, from which he was taken to Ireland by slave-raiders. It fits well the description which Patrick himself provided of his native district, as a landscape of small towns and an enduring local government after the Roman pattern, and there is even a good match between the Bannventa Berniae which he mentioned as his family home and the Anglo-Saxon place-names of the Banwell area.[58] The Severn estuary represented a highway for Irish ships into some of the richest parts of the west country, and it has been suggested that three of the villas excavated along the Bristol Avon were burned out by a single raiding party working its way up that river.[59] The Britons of the west country eventually saw off this menace before succumbing to the Saxons instead, and a system of watchtowers and forts in which Glastonbury Tor played a part may have been one of the devices which enabled them to do so.

The question of a prehistoric spiral maze dug into the sides of the Tor represents a separate issue. In favour of such a structure it may be argued that the spiral walkway does exist, on the ground, and that there is no evidence that land hunger was ever so great in the Isle to make worthwhile the digging of agricultural terraces on such a steep hill. Against it may be put the points that Philip Rahtz did not find any trace of prehistoric or Roman structures on the top of the Tor, and that not a single maze or labyrinth, of all those built or portrayed in northern Europe, has securely been dated to a period before the Roman. Neither set of arguments, however, is as secure as it seems. We simply do not know enough about the history of land use in the environs of Glastonbury to tell how great a pressure on natural resources might have existed there in the middle ages. Administrative records from elsewhere in Somerset, such as the Vale of Taunton Deane, prove the existence of considerable land hunger during the maximum of medieval population growth, in the thirteenth and early fourteenth centuries. In the same period, agricultural land around Glastonbury itself was clearly becoming exhausted, as it was left fallow for longer and longer periods. Against the negative evidence, in turn, it may be argued that the construction of the monastery of St Michael involved the digging out of a large section of the summit of the Tor which might have contained the vital evidence for prehistoric structures. Although no mazes in northern Europe have yet been securely dated before the Roman period, a number may well be prehistoric, and the spiral was certainly a prominent motif in Neolithic art, found in widely dispersed parts of the British Isles.

A third interpretation of the terraces is that they do indeed represent a spiral walkway, but of medieval date and constructed for pilgrims ascending to the church on the summit; such ritual pathways, linked to the Stations of the Cross, are used to this day in Roman Catholic countries. Fairly similar concentric terraces may be detected around the famous Anglo-Saxon monastery at Whitby in Yorkshire. The only secure way to date the feature at Glastonbury Tor would be an extensive excavation of the hillside, and such a procedure would be very expensive indeed. The one certain conclusion to be drawn from the evidence is that the terraces were made by humans; differential erosion of the hill by natural forces could not have produced them.[60] Even more than Ponter's Ball, the Tor 'maze' remains a puzzle.

The 'maze' is at least a solid landscape feature. Whatever the debates over its nature, its existence itself is not in doubt. The same cannot be said of the other patterns and forms which have been perceived or sensed in the Glastonbury landscape in the course of the twentieth century. One, of course, is Katherine Maltwood's zodiac. Even such generous-hearted authors as Geoffrey Ashe and John Michell have experienced difficulty in accepting the literal truth of this phenomenon,[61] and those who have made such an acceptance have sometimes redrawn the lines of the figures to suit their own interpretations, to an extent which undermines faith in the original concept.[62] The landscape features which are supposed to delineate the zodiac are apparently of widely varying date, and there is no known archaeological concept into which the notion of a zodiac itself (developed in ancient Babylon and brought even as far west as Egypt only as late as the last centuries BCE) would fit. Similar difficulties attend John Michell's own elaboration of Bligh Bond's theory of gematria, that a system of mystical numbers underlies the ground plan of abbey, town and estates of Glastonbury. There is no inherent reason why a culture as preoccupied with God and geometry as the medieval church should not have employed such a system. What makes acceptance of this one difficult is that both abbey and town grew up slowly and haphazardly over hundreds of years and many changes of regime. It is hard to believe that their builders adhered to a grand plan throughout this period, without ever mentioning it in the various histories and chronicles produced at or for the monastery; especially as such a plan would have been a matter for pride rather than shame or fear. When it is stated that the same system underlies the plan of Stonehenge, another multi-period monument apparently abandoned more than a thousand years before Christianity reached Britain, credulity is stretched to breaking point.

Such issues can at least be discussed in terms of history and topography, but others lie beyond these spheres. One is the system of energy-bearing leys of which Glastonbury Tor is a nodal point. John Michell himself stated that like the zodiac these had to be 'accepted as a poetic rather than a scientific truth', and I endorse that. I have no problem either with his additional statement that the ley system 'may actually be invisible to those whose previous knowledge tells them that it cannot exist'.[63] I would only add the corollary, that it may only be visible to those who are previously disposed to believe that it does exist. The same remarks apply to the goddess-figures which Geoffrey Ashe and Kathy Jones have seen in the landscape of the Isle of Avalon. It would be seriously mistaken, however, to surmise from this that I therefore consider all this category of claims to be without merit. Whatever their status as scholarship, their power as poetic vision is tremendous; they are part of an impulse to re-enchant the landscape which was one of the themes of twentieth-century British culture.

When all this is said, therefore, the only unequivocal evidence of long-term occupation of the district containing the present Isle of Avalon before the sub-Roman period consists of the 'lake villages' described earlier. The status of these has been reviewed in turn, in recent years, and some of the earlier claims made for them revised. It was mentioned, for example, that the first reconstruction of the settlement near Glastonbury itself showed a substantial collection of some ninety buildings. Further consideration of the ground plans and finds has produced the conclusion that only some of these structures were in use at any one time, and that not all of them were dwellings. The largest actual size of the village is now reckoned at thirteen houses. Furthermore, the richness of the finds has been ever more clearly ascribed to the boggy conditions. for further archaeology has revealed that in both economic and technological respects it was overshadowed by several other centres of Iron Age occupation in northern and eastern Somerset. The 'Bristol of the Iron Age' has thus shrunk to a small and relatively unimportant settlement, built out in a marsh and perhaps only occupied in summer. As for the other putative village. at Meare, it was re-excavated in 1978–84 and is now considered to have been no settlement at all but the site of a seasonal fair, held in the wetland which bounded the territories of three local tribes.[64]

It needs to be emphasised that the Isle is not bare of prehistoric and Roman finds, for flints and Roman potsherds have been recovered from several sites. The problem here is that such scraps of artefact can be found at most places in England and only testify to the number of people who have walked over the land during the past few millennia. The Somerset Levels, Mendips and east Somerset hills were all centres of considerable human activity from the Neolithic onward, and the Isle of Avalon must have been constantly visited and crossed during the prehistoric and Roman periods. Thus, the Neolithic axe-head and flint blades found on the Tor by Philip Rahtz's excavation may have been deposited there as religious objects, or fallen out of the bags or pockets of individuals who had climbed the hill for practical purposes or for pleasure. The Roman potsherds and tile found in the same dig could indicate that significant activity occurred on the summit in Roman times themselves, but these objects could equally well have been taken up the Tor in the middle ages, in clay used for the building of the monastery. The large number of fossil ammonites which the excavators uncovered could have been collected there as votive offerings, valued for their spiral or ram's horn shape, or all have weathered out of the rock of the hilltop, in which they occur naturally.[65]

Roman brick, potsherds, glass and tiles have been found at points in the town, but as Ralegh Radford has recognised,[66] these could easily have been carted in from elsewhere in Somerset during the medieval period, trapped in the clay used for building projects or looted from ruined Roman buildings for reuse as construction materials. An early medieval brass censer made in the eastern Mediterranean and also dug up in the town could equally well have been employed by native British churchmen or their Anglo-Saxon equivalents.[67] There are prehistoric and Roman structures in the Isle; in 1998 some post-holes were discovered next to the Chalice Well gardens which were subsequently dated to the late Neolithic, and a Roman building existed on part of Wirrall Hill. Neither, however, may have amounted to more than a farmstead.[68] The failure so far to discover a single grave in the whole of the Isle of Avalon, dateable to any period before the middle ages, is a powerful argument against supposing the existence of any large-scale settlement in it, or any important religious site, until that time. There was talk in the late twentieth century of large stones existing till recently on its hills, and suggestions that they might once have formed the megaliths of a prehistoric sanctuary.[69] Against this it must be pointed out that Glastonbury was visited in 1723 by William Stukeley, the finest field antiquarian of the time, who had a proven expertise in locating and drawing prehistoric monuments. He mapped out the medieval antiquities of the town and its surroundings, but did not note anything which seemed to him to date from an earlier period.[70] It seems likely, therefore, that the stones were naturally occurring blocks.

None of this is conclusive negative evidence. Large areas of the Isle, and much of the town, remain unexcavated and may conceal the remains of a settlement, burials or ceremonial monuments. It is worthy of comment, however, how rich the surrounding areas of north Somerset are in sacred sites dating from the Neolithic, Bronze and Iron Ages, and the Romano-British period. Their remains have been clear enough in many cases on the ground, and aerial photography has detected many more. To cite the most important examples, Neolithic stone circles are represented by the spectacular complex at Stanton Drew and earthen circles by the huge specimens at Priddy and the smaller one at Gorsey Bigbury. Neolithic long barrows and Bronze Age round barrows are both scattered across the region. The remains of Romano-British pagan temples have been found at Brean Down, Pagans Hill, Henley Wood and Lamyatt Beacon, and suspected at Cadbury (Congresbury) Camp, Brent Knoll and Durston. Centres of early British Christianity have been suggested, from excavated evidence, at Cannington, Congresbury, Ilchester and Shepton Mallet. In comparison with all these, the paucity of hard data from Glastonbury is striking. The most compelling argument in favour of prehistoric or Roman activity in the Isle of Avalon is the dramatic physical presence of the hills, dominated by the sharp peak of the Tor. They draw the eye, and thus it may be supposed that they excited reverence in past ages. There is some danger, however, in assuming that ancient peoples had the same aesthetic reactions and emotional priorities as those today. What is awe-inspiring to us may have been forbidding to them.

It appears, moreover, as if Glastonbury might be fitted into a pattern of political reordering whereby, on conquering fresh land in the west country from native British rulers, the seventh-century kings of Wessex made a deliberate policy of creating new centres of power. Thus, fresh administrative bases were founded at Taunton and Somerton in preference to Roman towns such as Ilchester. New episcopal sees were established at Sherborne and Wells. To found a major new abbey at Glastonbury to accompany the episcopal seat at Wells would have made perfect sense in terms of such a policy, and the surviving documents offer a good candidate for the identity of the particular monarch who carried it out. The earliest of the charters which seem certainly to be copied from genuine originals were given by Centwine, a king of Wessex praised by his contemporary St Aldhelm for his energy in establishing monasteries.[71]

What ought to be obvious from the assessments made above is that the early history of Glastonbury – upon claims regarding which the whole reputation of the town and its monuments rests – can be plausibly written in a great many different ways. They occupy between them points extending across a large span between two extreme positions. One is that all of the visions which have been offered of the pre-Saxon story of the place are indeed true: that it was a great pagan sanctuary, that a huge zodiac was laid out around it, that Joseph of Arimathea founded the first church there, that King Arthur was buried there, and so forth. It must be stressed that this is still possible. The other extreme position is that there was no significant human activity at Glastonbury whatsoever before a watch-tower was built there in the course of a military emergency in the sub-Roman period, and no religious institution before a king of Wessex founded a monastery there. If the evidence for that case has been laid out here with exceptional care, this is because it has apparently never been represented before with the force that now seems to be due to it. This essay is not intended, however, to clinch that case. Its purpose is rather to illustrate the variety of cases that can now be made, with no decisive arguments for any.

In observing how the history and archaeology of Glastonbury have been represented, three important patterns are clearly discernible. The first is that the whole tremendous reputation of the place at the present day rests upon claims made for it by the Anglo-Saxons and the medieval church. Without these the later associations of it with pagan spirituality and 'Celtic' Christianity would never have developed, and yet the latter are, in the popular mind, the very phenomena most opposed to the English, Catholic, context within which the body of tradition first developed. The second is that the twentieth-century pattern of belief and disbelief in this tradition follows exactly the same trajectory as that regarding the historical status of Arthur. Thus a popular willingness to believe, based upon the Victorian cult of romantic medievalism, won growing support from archaeologists and historians which rose to a peak in the 1960s. Thereafter professional disillusion set in and resulted in a series of works which questioned the claims for the antiquity of the abbey.

The third observation reflects a major theme of the first chapter in this book: the role of the outsider in fostering self-images for communities. It must be obvious enough from the account above that immigrants and visitors from outside Glastonbury, above all from London, have played a major part in developing its twentieth-century traditions. What needs to be stressed now is the importance of its relationship with North America. Citizens of the United States were already taking a close interest in its monuments by the 1900s, inspired by their romantic associations, and only circumstance prevented them from playing a more prominent part. A coterie of them attempted to purchase the abbey ruins in 1907, intending to establish a 'chivalric college' for boys upon the site. Five years later one rich American lady made a determined effort to buy the Chalice Well, and would probably have succeeded had not her train broken down en route, allowing the poorer Alice Buckton to purchase it instead.[72] Here time has provided its compensations, for during the 1990s a pair of her compatriots took over the management of the well and its garden. Bligh Bond emigrated to the USA after his dismissal from the direction of the abbey excavations, and Katherine Maltwood moved to Canada. It has been told how Geoffrey Ashe followed them, and should be emphasised now that his original enthusiasm for Glastonbury was kindled while reading about it in libraries in Ottawa and Toronto during his youth.[73] His vision of it as the centre of a spiritually regenerated Britain was conceived before he had ever actually been there; this vision originated in the New World as well as finding its most sympathetic reception there.

The same considerations apply to academic studies. During the late twentieth century the more sceptical treatments of the Glastonbury traditions – by Philip Rahtz, R. F. Treharne, Antonia Gransden, H. P. R. Finberg, Richard Barber, S. C. Morland, Sarah Foot, Lesley Abrams and Ceridwen Lloyd-Morgan – have been the work of British scholars. The most sympathetic considerations of the same traditions, conversely, have been made by a Canadian, James Carley, and a Californian, Deborah Crawford. Both, interestingly, have adopted at times the tone of Geoffrey Ashe, of appearing to find an intrinsic moral failing in the sceptics. The former has spoken of his first visit to Glastonbury as a 'pilgrimage', and declared that the child in the fable, who pointed out that the Emperor's New Clothes were sham, was 'needlessly destructive', and should have been 'severely punished for interference and insubordination'![74] The latter has opined that 'discussion of the Glastonbury legendary construct has been haunted by an ungenerous and judgemental spirit'.[75] Dramatic and beautiful the Isle of Avalon may be, but it still seems that its enchantment increases as distance from it grows.

The twentieth century, indeed, restored Glastonbury to a position of spiritual power as great as that which it occupied in the middle ages, but with a significant difference. At that period it represented a single religion, and a single denomination within that. Now the monuments and the shops which flank them, and the people who frequent and serve both, embody between them the greatest diversity of faiths to be found visibly expressed in any comparably small area of Britain. In part this is simply an aspect of the New Age movement, that it depends upon the notion that participants effectively develop their own spiritualities from many different potential sources of inspiration. It is also, however, the result of the diversity of ways in which the history and prehistory of Glastonbury can be interpreted, and the many different beliefs and needs which they can serve. In this sense the enigmatic quality of some of the monuments, and the intangible nature of its medieval and modern traditions, represent the greatest gifts which it makes to modern religion.

4

The New Old Paganism

When I first considered the relationship between ancient European paganism and modern Paganism, at the opening of the 1990s, I stressed a number of contrasts. I identified the former as essentially polytheistic, venerating many different goddesses and gods, as making a sharp distinction between religion and magic, and as representing the old, respectable and dominant faith which Christianity was to challenge in the role of brash newcomer. Modern Paganism (and especially Wicca and the other forms of Pagan witchcraft which have generally served as its template) is mainly duotheistic, recognising a pairing of a goddess and god who between them represent the cosmos. It dissolves distinctions between religion and magic, and itself represents a newly-appeared and often pugnacious challenger to a long-established set of Christian religions. Added to lesser contrasts, this led me to conclude that 'the paganism of today has virtually nothing in common with that of the past except the name, which is itself of Christian coinage'. The 'past', in this context, was clearly that of Europe. I added one major qualification: that if the most important varieties of modern Paganism 'are viewed as a form of ritual magic, then they have a distinguished and very long pedigree, stretching back ... to the early modern and medieval texts which derived by many stages from those of Hellenistic Egypt'.[1]

Long before the end of the decade, it had become obvious to me that this model was inadequate. Although still true – as far as anybody could tell – for the ancient British Isles, and substantially so for the rest of Europe, it ignored the existence of certain types of ancient religion which far more closely resembled Paganism, had certainly influenced it, and had certain linear connections with it. They were in every sense marginal to my own preoccupations when I made the statements quoted above. They were overtly derived from the traditions of Egypt and the Near East, whereas I was concerned with those of the opposite corner of Europe, and they made little apparent impact on ancient European paganism outside parts of Greece. They appeared at the very end of the pagan ancient world, at and after the time at which Christianity became the official creed of the Roman Empire, and were arguably influenced by Christian thought. They were also very much the preserve of a self-conscious intellectual elite, detached from the masses and usually disempowered. None the less, the private and avant-garde nature of these ideas and practices gave them something else in common with those of modern pagans. It became clear to me that my work on the intellectual roots of modern Paganism would be incomplete unless I made a consideration of their nature and of their influence on the Pagan religions which reappeared in the twentieth century.[2] What follows represents an attempt to fulfil that project.

One conspicuous way in which the new kind of ancient paganism differed from the old was in denying or qualifying polytheism. The classic scholarly view of the pagan religions of the Roman Empire, was summed up by Ramsey MacMullen in 1981: they were essentially conservative, plural, ancestral and local. Their polytheism was one aspect of their pluralism; in MacMullen's characterisation, to the pagan inhabitants of that empire, 'monotheists counted as atheists'.[3] The same view was taken in the year 2000 by Ken Dowden in his survey of ancient religion across Europe.[4] During the 1990s another leading expert in the field, Garth Fowden, went further, to propose that the term 'pagan' should be dropped altogether when speaking of the pre-Christian religions of the European and Mediterranean worlds, because it was derived from Christian apologetics and could embody Christian stereotypes. In its place, he preferred to speak simply of 'polytheists'.[5]

During the same decade, however, a precisely opposite tendency set in among other ancient historians. They preferred to emphasise the tendency of late antique paganism to monotheism, in the sense provided earlier by John Peter Kennedy: that if 'polytheism may be stipulated as the view that there are many final principles of order, power and value', then 'monotheism would thus be the claim that there is one ultimate such principle'. Kennedy had pointed out that ancient Mediterranean polytheism could become pagan monotheism simply by a change of emphasis, by focusing on 'the ultimate unity of divinity behind its plural manifestations'.[6] In 1999 a group of scholars published a collection of essays to drive home the point that by the late Roman period such a change of emphasis was quite widespread, especially among educated people in the Greek-speaking east of the empire[7]

To support this claim they mustered a set of quotations from well-known pagan authors from the second century onward, including Apuleius, Celsus, Aelius Aristides and Maximus of Tyre. By the end of the fourth century some pagans could treat monotheism as an obvious feature of their creed, such as Maximus of Madaura, a correspondent of the great Christian bishop Augustine. A fellow inhabitant of North Africa, he wrote to the churchman 'that the supreme God is one, without offspring, as it were the great and august father of nature, what person is there so mad and totally deprived of sense as to wish to deny?'[8] Such quotations can easily be multiplied from other sources. In the mid fourth century the last pagan emperor, Julian, could close a letter by speaking repeatedly of 'God', as the master, guide and arbiter of the world. The recipient of the letter, the pagan orator Themistius, went on to inform Julian's Christian successor, Jovian, that the deities of polytheists were really only forms and aspects of the single God whom Christians also worshipped. One of Julian's friends, the philosopher and politician Salutius, declared that traditional goddesses and gods were as much parts of the single creator god as thoughts are of the mind. A generation later, the Roman senator Symmachus spoke for the pagans of his city by echoing both Salutius and Themistius. He added that 'whatever each person worships, it is reasonable to think of them as one. We see the same stars, the sky is shared by all, the same world surrounds us.'[9]

It may be suggested here that four different processes lay behind this development. One was the creation of the Roman Empire itself, a huge span of peoples, societies and local religious systems united under an efficient and well-centralised despotism. It seems natural that the minds of some at least of its citizens should start to conceive of the divine in the same manner, as a single controlling intelligence with local manifestations and representatives. Such a view was actively promoted by some of the last pagan emperors as a means of increasing the cohesion of the state. Famously, one of them, Aurelian, established an official cult of the sun as the presiding deity of the empire in 274, representing the solar force as the sum of all attributes belonging to other gods. This was continued until it slowly metamorphosed into an acceptance of Christianity by the emperor Constantine between forty and fifty years later. When Constantine's nephew Julian restored paganism as the imperial religion, and hailed the sun as the mightiest of gods, holding together the whole universe and acting as the immediate agent of the creator, he was in that respect merely reverting to Aurelian's system[10]

A second impulse behind the growth of pagan monotheism was the influence of Christianity itself. Jan Bremmer has noted how, from the second century onwards, apparently new mystery religions appeared, devoted to gods who die and resurrect, such as Atis, or act as personal saviours, such as Mithras.[11] One of the authors cited earlier as a proponent of belief in the unity of deity, Apuleius, was a professed initiate of one of these new mystery traditions, that of Isis. G. W. Bowersock has drawn attention to the fondness of late paganism for trinities – at least in Rome's Asian provinces – and the appearance in Syria and Egypt of virgin goddesses who give birth to saviour gods[12]

A third force leading to expressions of monotheism was the need to propitiate an increasingly dominant and intolerant Christianity, by arguing (in the event, vainly) that pagan and Christian honoured the same deity in different ways. This was certainly the context of the declarations quoted above from Themistius, Symmachus and Maximus of Madaura. Clifford Ando has analysed the manner in which many pagans during the fourth and fifth centuries attempted to appeal to Christians on their own terms by alluding to themes in contemporary Christian debate and adopting a Christian vocabulary. Maximus was not the only pagan correspondent of Augustine to use an affirmation of loyalty to a single creator god as a means of trying to assuage the hostility of this increasingly powerful bishop.[13]

It is the fourth force which is most important for the concerns of this chapter: the need of pagans, confronted with Christian attack, to construct a coherent theology capable of uniting the localised and disparate religions of the old polytheism and answering the challenge of the new religion. Traditional European paganism had no theology at all, and the nearest equivalent to it had been provided by the philosophers of the Greek-speaking world. Since their apperance in the sixth century BCE, those philosophers had spoken of a single entity from which the whole cosmos proceeded, and to which some attributed intelligence and purpose. By the time of the Roman Empire, all three of the major ancient schools of philosophy – Platonists, Peripatetics and Stoics – postulated the existence of a god who providentially ruled the universe and was the only absolutely divine being. This concept had a broader historic background, in that during the second millennium BCE Mesopotamian cultures were starting to speak of one ruling god whom all others obeyed. By the time of Homer and Hesiod, in the early first millennium BCE, the Greeks had taken over this idea. During the second half of that millennium assemblies of deities vanished from the Semitic inscriptions of the Near East, to be replaced by devotion to a supreme god and to lesser deities who had become specialised functionaries operating under his rule. By that last millennium BCE the Egyptians had gone further, to characterise their deities as proceeding from the subdivision of an original creator god. There were many different local accounts of how this creation occurred, which were never rationalised or standardised. One of the subsequently best-known, from Memphis, made the original deity a being both female and male, who gave birth to a goddess and god who then themselves became lovers to generate heaven and earth. It was these concepts which the Greek-speaking philosophers, often themselves subsequently operating out of Egypt and Rome's Asian provinces, refined into that of a primal creating and controlling god.[14]

In the fourth and fifth centuries of the Christian era it was one tradition of those philosophers, however, which was to make the running in the development of an all-embracing pagan theology which could be deployed against the rival claims of Christianity: that of Neoplatonism. As this matters greatly for what follows, and as many readers expert in other aspects of the present book may know little about late antiquity, a brief introduction to this school and its main exponents may be helpful. It is generally recognised as being founded in the third century by Plotinus, who taught that all existence emanates ultimately from a benevolent entity called the One, who is primal and limitless. This emanation represented a separation, regrettable in itself, and the goal of intelligent beings ought therefore to be reunion with the One. The latter's first emanation had been a divine Intelligence, which in turn had produced Soul, which was responsible for the formation of bodies in the visible world. Plotinus's thought was turned into a tradition during the later third century by his pupil Porphyry, who edited and propagated it as a rival system to Christianity, capable of rationalising the whole of ancient pagan culture. In his teaching, the One, the Intelligence and the Soul became more of a united trinity at the source of all being.[15]

The tradition was developed further by Iamblichus, in the late third and early fourth centuries. who turned it yet further into a cosmic umbrella under which all the traditional religions of the Near East could be gathered. He attached great worth to ritual observances as a means towards reunion with the divine, including all the long-established ceremonial practices of paganism, and represented the many deities of the old religions as a spreading cascade of emanations from the original triad of entities at the summit, all themselves grouped in threes and dedicated to assist humans in reconnecting themselves with the fount of existence.[16] Iamblichus provided an important source of inspiration to Julian in the mid fourth century, in the latter's brief career as an important author as well as emperor. Julian constructed his own view of the nature of supreme deity, in which, as described, all creation arose from a single entity, the King or One, on whose behalf the universe was ruled by the sun-god, Helios, whom he also identified with the saviour-god Mithras. It is not always clear when he referred to 'God' whether he intended to mean the original creator or the solar deity. In addition, Helios was the senior partner of another ruling triad, with Zeus and Hades, and Zeus was the son and spouse of Cybele, 'the Mother of the Gods', who was in some fashion the companion of the creator and had given birth to all the other higher deities. In Julian's cosmos, the heavens revolved in a circuit around the creator, who had assigned a range of tasks to local deities.[17]

Towards the end of the fourth century the teaching and writing of Neoplatonism became associated especially with what had been Plato's own academy at Athens, the masters of which saw themselves as being in an apostolic succession descending from Plotinus. The most famous was Proclus, whose career spanned the fifth century, a time when some pagans still nurtured hopes of recovering power in the eastern Roman Empire. Proclus elaborated the system of Iamblichus with greater coherence, to emphasise both the manner in which all the traditional deities and their cults could be comprehended within it and the interconnection of the whole cosmos with the One by whom it was conceived. As a result, in the words of H. D. Saffrey, 'this rich hierarchy of gods is a sort of ladder which allows the soul seeking the divine to ascend its rungs and unite itself at the top with the first god, the One Good'.[18]

It may thus be seen that at the end of antiquity Neoplatonism provided a means of reconciling polytheism with monotheism and of rationalising all the pre-Christian religions of the classical ancient world into a single system. It was not the only means of doing so; Themistius, Symmachus and the correspondents of Augustine were among those pagans who were not Neoplatonists, and yet spoke a language of monotheism with absolute confidence. It just happened to be the most coherent system to effect this work, the only one to produce a school and a tradition, and (above all) the one which established the texts and portraits of personalities best known to posterity. Three points need to be addressed now about the nature of late pagan monotheism in general and Neoplatonism in particular.

The first is that it represented in large part the explicit introduction of exotic elements into traditional Graeco-Roman culture. The general importance of Egyptian and Near Eastern ideas to the development of ancient monotheism has already been noted. It is true also that the civilisations of Egypt, Mesopotamia and Syria had long exerted an important influence on Greek thought and art, extending to the very beginnings of philosophy.[19] Conversely, even the Neoplatonists were anxious to situate themselves in the mainstream of Greek tradition, Iamblichus taking Pythagoras as his model, and Proclus identifying with Plato. None the less, they were also quite emphatic about the need to leaven that tradition by adopting or engaging with eastern ideas. Their own backgrounds reflected this emphasis. Plotinus taught in Italy but was reputed to be an Egyptian.[20] Porphyry was a Phoenician, and Iamblichus was a Syrian, based at Apamea near the desert interior. Proclus settled at Athens, but his family came from Lycia in Asia Minor.[21] More important is the attention drawn by them to the importance of the Near East as a source of spirituality. Aurelian's imperial cult of the sun was itself Syrian, shorn of some of its native trappings.[22] Porphyry invited his readers to revere the religious concepts of the Egyptians, Phoenicians, Assyrians, Babylonians and Hebrews,[23] while Iamblichus held up

Egypt and Assyria as the homelands of the finest spirituality. Both, and Proclus, drew heavily on specific Syrian texts which will be considered below. Polymnia Athanassiadi has summed up this pattern by stating that 'what *we* call Neoplatonism was the renovated paganism of the Hellenised Syrian, Egyptian or Arab'.[24] It all made perfect tactical sense, for the most successful religion to have emerged from the Near Eastern tendency to monotheism was Christianity, and one obvious way of reforming Mediterranean paganism to meet the challenge of the latter was to draw on other strains of that tendency.

The second major point to be raised about the process was that there remains considerable uncertainty as to how widespread it was, and how much it affected most late antique pagans. To these questions Ramsay MacMullen returned a robust answer, in his survey of the religions of the Roman Empire cited earlier. The Neoplatonist texts, and others associated with pagan monotheism, were by modern scholars 'given an importance quite out of scale with what contemporaries conceived their faith to be'. They were the ancient equivalent of 'higher criticism', confined to a few intellectuals out of touch with public or popular culture. The hundreds of inscriptions left to deities in the later Roman period, asserted MacMullen, continued to treat them as rulers, not as gradations of divine power, symbols, essences or emanations of the One. Pagan monotheism was 'all abstract doctrine, taught in universities'.[25] This view was given different support by Garth Fowden, who characterised the Neoplatonists and other late antique pagan sages as elitist, unworldly and socially incestuous, and thus both marginal and ineffectual in general terms.[26] It was these attitudes which the scholars who sought to highlight pagan monotheism were out to challenge. To Polymnia Athanassiadi, monotheism was simply 'the universal religious idiom of the men of late antiquity'. More modestly, she and Michael Frede stated elsewhere that it was quite widespread among pagans, especially in the eastern provinces of the empire.[27] How can these apparently conflicting assertions, made with equal confidence, be reconciled?

Evidence can be provided on both sides. In support of MacMullen, it can be stated that there is no evidence whatsoever of pagan monotheist ideas either north or west of Rome itself. Neither inscriptions nor literary sources reveal any trace of them in the provinces of Spain, Gaul or Britain. There is abundant evidence for syncretism, the identification of one particular deity with another, allowing the Roman goddesses and gods to be twinned with local equivalents. This might have provided a step towards monotheism, but it is not the same thing. It is also possible that the rural pilgrimage temples built in third- and fourth-century Roman Britain, in which a number of deities were apparently honoured under the same roof, may have been another movement towards a general unity of deity. There is, however, no evidence of this.[28] MacMullan's characterisation of the archaeological evidence for the Roman world in general seems to be a valid one; that it testifies overwhelmingly to a continuation of a wholly traditional localised polytheism. In support of the other case, it must be fairly obvious from the quotations given above that, from a mixture of tactical and evolutionary considerations, monotheism had become the dominant language of pagans negotiating with or opposing Christians by the middle of the fourth century. This meant effectively that it had turned into the self-image presented by them in public debate. How far it penetrated the attitudes and devotional practices of the majority of those who still adhered to the traditional cults and the mystery religions is very difficult to judge. As for the Neoplatonists in particular, the biographer of their leaders, Eunapius, recorded that by the end of the fourth century 'even great numbers of the vulgar' were 'swayed' by the doctrines of Plotinus. He did, however, add, without going into details, that they did not fully understand those doctrines, and he made the same claim for no other Neoplatonist teacher.[29]

The third point is that by the fifth century pagan and Christian languages of monotheism were converging to the point at which it is sometimes difficult to distinguish them, raising obvious difficulties for the manner in which historians can characterise paganism. The classic example of this is the *Saturnalia* of Macrobius, a series of fictitious conversations between members of Rome's cultural elite, some of them prominent pagans, who flourished between 370 and 410. One of the pagans expounds a view of the cosmos in which the latter is directed by a single divine power, identified with the sun, of which all individual deities are manifestations. It is very unlikely that the historical individual in question would actually have propounded such a scheme, but a much more serious problem with the text has been revealed since the 1960s. This is, that it has been identified as one written in the 430s, by a powerful noble who held the office of prefect of Italy in 431. To have held that post by that date he would have had to have been accepted as a Christian. This being so, either he was a pagan who concealed his religion to obtain power yet then proclaimed it in published writings (an unlikely juxtaposition), or else his book is not a pagan text. It certainly avoids any hint of anti-Christian sentiment, as does Macrobius's companion work, his *Commentary on the Dream of Scipio*, which also makes a profession of belief in an ultimate divine unity. The purpose of both books may well be to celebrate the cultural heritage of Rome in general, pagan and Christian, in an attempt to rally all parties and faiths to its defence at a time when the western Roman Empire was starting to disintegrate. The section of the *Saturnalia* which deals with divinity is not so much a theological exercise as a parade of literary erudition. As such, the work remains fascinating and significant, but cannot be treated in uncomplicated fashion as an example of late pagan belief.[30]

The equivalent case in the eastern empire is a long work by an Egyptian poet, Nonnus of Panopolis, written in the mid fifth century and celebrating the god Dionysus as a redeemer deity, embodying other gods, representing the directing intelligence of the world and shedding his tears to end the sorrows of mortals. The style seems too passionate to represent a mere literary exercise, but that is exactly what it may be, for Nonnus is a Christian name, and there also survives a verse paraphrase of St John's Gospel which was written at about the same time and in a manner close to his. As in the case of the work of Macrobius, the one element which would identify the text as firmly pagan, an open or veiled antipathy to Christianity, is missing. Further caution in the matter is suggested by the career of Nonnus's compatriot and fellow-author Cyril of Panopolis, who wrote with copious quotation from the pagan classics and often with a total absence of a sense of religion. We know, however, that he was a devout Christian who eventually became a bishop.[31]

These difficulties reflect a phenomenon which provides the critical context for any historian tracing the survival of ancient pagan ideas and images during the period from the fourth to the twentieth centuries: the enduring love affair of Europeans with the cultural heritage of Mediterranean antiquity. As Alan Cameron has established, the great movement to recover and copy classical texts in Italy during the later fourth century was carried on mainly, if not wholly, by Christians. It was Christian emperors who ordered the repair of (pagan) works in the public libraries of Rome, at state expense. The poet Claudian achieved great professional success by composing works for the Christian imperial court that were filled with references to pagan deities.[32] All this makes the recovery of late antique pagan thought all the more difficult, and tends to throw the later Neoplatonist school into greater prominence, as it acquired a corporate identity and distinguished itself so clearly from Christianity. That retrospective prominence may be misleading, and exaggerate the contemporary importance of the writers concerned; or it may not. What seems to be beyond argument is that among philosophers and intellectuals, and in public debate, a form of monotheism had come to dominate the paganism of the Roman Empire by the middle of the fourth century, in a fashion quite unknown before.

A second change was that pagans who still thought in terms of a plurality of deities were sometimes giving increased attention to divinities, or aspects of divinity, which had hitherto been relatively neglected, and which were to anticipate developments which would be very marked in modern Paganism. It is true that the traditional cults of goddesses and gods often remained very strong, and had to be eradicated in many places by direct Christian action supported by covert or open imperial sympathy. Literary sources and private dedications, however, show new developments running alongside them. One was a tendency, manifested in the poetry of the fourth and fifth centuries, for divine beings to become regarded as allegorical figures, and the stories about their actions to be treated as embodying veiled cosmic truths. This was accompanied by another, to honour beings who represented major natural forces rather than figures with human forms and actions and regional loyalties. A third was a new devotion to superhuman figures who were travellers or communicators, linking different worlds and repesenting the transcendental qualities of the divine. In all these, the solvent effect of imperial rule on old boundaries and loyalties is obvious.[33]

One of the gods to benefit from these processes was Dionysus, who became venerated in many parts of the Greek-speaking east as a serene figure representing the intelligence of the cosmos and an educator and redeemer of humanity. These qualities were linked with his earlier attributes as an embodiment of the animating forces of nature.[34] Another beneficiary was Pan, whose reputation in classical Greek literature had been, in the words of Patricia Merivale, that of 'a comic-grotesque godling who is a second-class citizen and a non-Homeric latecomer among the Olympians'. By the time of the Roman Empire he had become recognised by (mainly urban) writers of poetry, novels and satires as the patron deity of tranquil rural life. In the first century, however, the Stoic philosopher Cornutus drew attention to the coincidence of his name with the Greek word for 'all', and this was strongly developed by the learned authors of Rome in the early fifth century, above all Servius and Macrobius. In their works the horned god of the woods and pastures became the ruler and vivifying principle of the entire material world, and one of the great creative and recreative forces of nature.[35]

Images of goddesses developed on a parallel track. A brand new one had emerged by the fourth century in the shape of Natura (Nature), a female divinity embodying the life and fertility of the natural world. References to 'natura', as an abstract principle representing that world, appear in Roman literary works from the first century onward. This principle became blended with older Greek philosophical concepts of a primal divine creator and mover, and given feminine form. The first recorded appearance of the result seems to have been in an Orphic Hymn, composed in Greek at some point of the imperial period, and hailing 'all-parent Physis' (Physis being the Greek equivalent to Natura), as the maker, shaper and nourisher of living things. By the fourth century this concept was familiar enough for Christian writers, Lactantius and Prudentius, to denounce it and assert that Natura merely sustained the material world as the servant of their One God. In the poetry of Claudian, the Graeco-Egyptian serving the Christian imperial court in Italy at the end of the century, she appears as a mighty cosmic power standing between the supreme god, Zeus, and all other deities, and ruling over mating, conception and birth. It is significant that we cannot tell to which religion Claudian himself belonged. The readiness with which Natura could translate into the cosmology of the Christian one was confirmed by Augustine himself, who called her a teacher and guide of truth, appointed by the true deity to carry out his will. Neoplatonists likewise incorporated her into their systems. To Damascius, the greatest of that school in the early sixth century and the last leader of the academy at Athens, she was to be identified with Rhea, the mother of Zeus, as the provider of the path by which humanity could reunite with the one ultimate deity.[36]

Natura's success had a knock-on effect on the fortunes of a traditional goddess associated with flowering and generation: Venus. Her other association, with love in all forms, combined with these attributes to confirm her potency as a literary figure for fifth-century writers. The Gallic poet Sidonius Apollinaris gave her an earthly paradise in a cavern, from which she tamed the spirits of independent young men and turned them to thoughts of marriage. Another poet, Ennodius, celebrated her as the bringer of spring as well as patroness of weddings, dancing naked among the flowers. The seriousness with which Venus was treated as an allegorical force of nature may be indicated by the fact that neither of these authors was either a pagan or a libertine: Sidonius and Ennodius were both bishops.[37]

To some extent, the role of divine teacher and mediatrix given to Natura in the western provinces of the empire was taken in the eastern half by Hekate. The growth of the latter's reputation had been a long and complex process, commencing at the opening of Greek history with a position as the patron goddess of Caria in Asia Minor. She already enjoyed some reputation among the Greeks themselves, Hesiod hailing her as a bringer of prosperity, guardian of roads, gates and travellers, nurse of children and bringer of light to the eyes of the newborn. Another very early source, the 'Hymn to Demeter' probably dating from the seventh century BCE, calls her the companion to that goddess in the search for her daughter Kore. Later she became an attendant and guide to Kore (or Persephone) in the latter's role as queen of the underworld. This association with the uncanny was strengthened as, from the fifth century, her role as protectress of travellers and highways was given particular expression as the ruler of crossroads, traditionally haunted places. To match this her images became triple, her three forms being backed around a pillar and gazing out in different directions.

It was therefore logical that, from the fifth century also, writers began to regard her as a patroness of magicians, leading a nocturnal retinue of spirits, hounds and ghosts who could be lent to the service of those who invoked her power correctly. She was also made into an illuminatrix of darkness, and finder of lost things, and so associated with the moon. By the late imperial period poets and commentators were starting to use the names Hekate, Luna and Diana interchangeably for a goddess representing the three realms of heaven, earth and underworld, and the three phases of the moon. The Neoplatonist philosopher Porphyry was credited with the belief that Hekate's three aspects represented the new, waxing and full phases of the lunar orb. Servius, writing in Rome in the years around 400, noted that some people thought 'Triple Hekate' to be a moon goddess known as Luna above the earth, Diana upon it and Persephone below it. Her enduring characteristic as a deity of boundaries and pathways, coupled with her association with ghosts, demons and magic, made her an obvious patroness both of ritual magic and of the late antique yearning for a personal union with the divine. As such, she features prominently in handbooks of magic, and also in the mystical texts known as the Chaldean Oracles, both of which will be discussed below. The people who sought her aid in both contexts seem to have been few: in Prudence Jones's words, a 'tiny clique of active followers'. None the less, by the end of the fourth century the concept of a goddess representing three phases of the moon, and associated with magic, was fairly well known at least among the literary elites of the Roman Empire.[38]

The pattern here is clear. Alongside the traditional pagan deities, concerned with particular places, peoples, human activities and aspects of the natural world, were appearing or developing others who represented more general cosmic powers. Especially favoured were gods associated with the vitalising and regenerating forces of nature, and goddesses who either embodied the whole natural world or else were associated with the phases of the moon, a nocturnal spirit world, and magic. Both were to have a long history in subsequent western culture, and to feature as the main deities of modern Paganism.

The third great alteration in Mediterranean paganism at the end of antiquity, was that some forms of it dissolved a widespread and officially recognised distinction between religion and magic, using religious procedures for magical purposes, or vice-versa. To state this, however, is to wade directly into a major scholarly debate which demands some detailed consideration before an intervention in it can be made here. For the first two-thirds of the twentieth century such a statement would have been relatively unproblematic, for there was a broad spectrum of agreement over what the distinction between religion and magic actually was. In large part it was based upon one enunciated by the century's best-known anthropological writer, Sir James Frazer: that religion consists in essence of asking supernatural powers for favours or praising and honouring them, while magic contains the assumption that human beings can to some extent manipulate supernatural power for their own ends. This was subsequently reinforced by the formula provided by one of the most famed of early field anthropologists, Bronislaw Malinowski, who declared that religious rites are not usually directed to a specific purpose, whereas magic always is; the latter was therefore an attempt to control chance and circumstance where demonstrably practical measures ('science') were not sufficient.

By mid century, the working definitions had become more sophisticated than these, although derived from the same model, and it was on these more complex and sensitive formulations that the scholarly consensus was based. One was provided by Ruth Benedict in the 1930s, starting with the acknowledgement that magic and religion form a continuum, founded on the concept of supernatural power and not established in any evolutionary sequence. That got rid of Frazer's assumption that the two could be clearly separated and that magic represented a lower and more primitive set of beliefs. His basic definition, and that of Malinowski, was nevertheless preserved: magic was a body of formalised procedures by which supernatural power was controlled and utilised. In the years around 1950 William J. Goode reiterated it: magic was distinguished from religion by the concrete specificity of its goals, a manipulative attitude, an instrumental character, frequent practitioner-client relationships, frequent individualist voluntarism and ad hoc performance. At the same time he fully acknowledged that such definitions were of ideal types of behaviour, which in practice could often be hard to distinguish.[39]

Sustained challenges to the traditional definitions began in the 1960s. One of the most influential was made by the leading British anthropologist, E. E. Evans-Pritchard, who drew attention to the very diverse terminologies used by native cultures for attitudes to and transactions with the supernatural, and the difficulty of translating them into scholarly categories. He felt that, carelessly done, such a translation could create confusion; but he reiterated a belief that magic could be distinguished from religion. A more wide-reaching doubt was entered by Murray and Rosalie Wax, who suggested that the traditional distinction held up well within western culture but did not work so well for those of native peoples, who did not compartmentalise their activities as neatly. They suggested that the term 'magic' be abandoned in anthropology, or else that the range of its meanings and their place in processes of cross-cultural interaction be better appreciated. Dorothy Hammond suggested that magic be included within religion as one type of the practices of which religious ritual is composed. She recommended that it be contrasted not with religion itself but with prayer or sacrifice, magic consisting of ritual practices which 'express belief in human powers as effective forces' and assume that 'the gods do not rule alone'.[40]

These criticisms between them define the terms in which most of the debate over the traditional definition of magic was to be conducted among anthropologists during the following two decades. It may be noted that to a great extent they called for more sensitive use or finer tuning of that definition rather than its abandonment, and Hammond effectively restated it within a reordered framework. Some of the contributions to the debate argued for the merits of retaining it as a working model.[41] In general, however, they were more notable for discussing the shortcomings of it, a mood which very clearly corresponded to the dominant tendencies of the discipline in a post-colonial era: of avoiding the imposition of general classifications of human behaviour based on western conventions and assumptions, and the need to study particular societies in depth with full acknowledgement of their individuality and of the diversity of cultural belief.[42] By 1980 it was already possible for one onlooker to declare that 'modern anthropologists' had reached a consensus that the old dichotomy between magic and religion was totally unworkable, and that in terms of beliefs and practices there was no way of distinguishing magic from religious ritual. Eleven years later an equally well-informed observer concluded that what had resulted was not a consensus but 'a confusing spectrum of divergent theories', with a 'marked tendency' still 'to single out manipulative-coercive versus emotional-supplicatory attitudes as the essential distinction between magic and (other components of) religion'. This author also noted that the debate had been characterised more by attacks on the definitions of others than attempts to supply practical alternatives, and embodied a tendency to polarise theoretical extremes which represented ideal abstractions.[43]

Both of these commentators, with their very different perceptions, were scholars of the ancient Mediterranean world, and they were speaking of the debate because it had spilled over into their field. During the 1970s, works produced within it tended to repeat the traditional means of distinguishing magic from religion, as something accepted and not problematical.[44] During the 1980s the discussions among anthropologists began to have a knock-on effect in the disciplines of classical and biblical studies, and by the 1990s had generated a disruption of the traditional model in those fields as

complete as that in anthropology. It could produce some startling changes
of mind among established scholars, one of the most remarkable of which
was demonstrated by Ramsay MacMullen. In a major book published in
1981, he repeated the traditional distinction between religion and magic,
with absolute confidence. Sixteen years later, in another substantial work,
he pronounced that he intended to waste no time on 'the relationship
between religion and magic and the exact meaning of the two terms. For
historians of the west, knowing only their own discipline and only the one
Judaeo-Christian religious tradition, these matters used to be intellectually
as well as theologically indigestible. Now, the lessons of anthropology grown
familiar, it is common to accept the impossibility of separating magic from
religion and move on to more interesting subjects'.[45] The second statement,
with its reference to the 'Judaeo-Christian' tradition, illustrates neatly one
of the sub-texts of the debate among the author's colleagues. In large part
the struggle to redefine and reclassify practices which had hitherto been
labelled as magical represented a marked increase in the interest of ancient
historians in those practices, and a struggle to bring them into the mainstream of the writing of religious history. At times those engaged in this
struggle showed awareness that the traditional distinction and definition
had to some extent marginalised and denigrated what had been called magic
within the study of ancient civilisations, and that this pattern had reflected
Christian prejudices or modernist value-judgements.[46]

Certainly, the disintegration of the consensus over definitions among
ancient historians produced no agreement on a new working model. There
was a general shift from distinguishing religion from magic to distinguishing
the latter from other forms of religious or spiritual activity, but this was a
shift of degree rather than kind, and the traditional means of characterising
magic proved to have remarkable powers of survival. In 1991 the editors of
a collection of essays which addressed the issue commented (with regret)
that 'there cannot at present be said to exist anything like a consensus over
the deployment and definition of terms ... Many continue to cling, consciously or not, to the standard dichotomy.' One of the contributors to the
collection went further, to suggest that the 'standard' distinction remained
the most widespread in classical studies.[47] Indeed, some of their colleagues
were restating it against the new wave of criticism, such as H. S. Versnel in
the same year. He argued that magic could be a category within religion
or outside it, but needed to be distinguished from non-magic, and religion
represented an obvious model of contrast. He recommended an 'open'
definition, with characteristics being removed or added as tested against
particular cases: for the present, the obvious stock of characteristics were
that magic was instrumental, manipulative and coercive, with short-term,

concrete and often individual goals. The following year another scholar argued for the utility of the same approach in studies of ancient Greece, with the caution that anthropology suggested that the more 'primitive' a culture under study, the less likely it was to be meaningful.[48]

At the other end of the decade, much the same situation persisted. Of four contributors to a collection on witchcraft and magic in ancient Greece and Rome, published in 1999, two rejected outright the traditional distinction. One commented that definitions of magic and religion varied according to period, context and source, but added that the unifying theme of magic was the human location and manipulation of the secret forces in the cosmos. This was a very close approximation to the traditional formula, and the latter was endorsed by the fourth contributor, who commented that it 'was still much in vogue'.[49] In the same year another collection of essays was published, on ancient magical theory and practice. Of two contributors who directly addressed the debate, one roundly asserted that the traditional distinction 'may still be fundamental to the study of magic' and defended it as such. The second suggested that 'the most fruitful approach is neither to make an absolute distinction between religious ritual and magical practices, nor to pretend that there is no difference'. He added that magic was best distinguished as 'the appropriation of ritual power to personal ends', again a formula very close to the accustomed one. A third assumed that magic was a category distinct from religion.[50] A similar spectrum of opinion is revealed by sampling works by historians of the subsequent, medieval, period. In 1989 one expressed the opinion that the traditional distinction between religion and magic was unhelpful when dealing with material from the middle ages. Two years later another restated it, as the most useful when analysing the same material. In 1998 a collection of essays by different authors was published on 'medieval ritual magic', which consistently treated the definition of magic as traditional and unproblematic.[51] The last pronouncement on the subject read before completing the present essay was by Peter Green, who summed up the debate over definitions as having 'created almost unbelievable confusion through conflicting dogmatic pronouncements'. He proposed that the traditional working formulation was still the best, and could be applied throughout the ancient world: that magic concerns acts designed to tap into supernatural powers for the benefit of the humans who work them and directed at practical rather than symbolic objectives.[52]

It should be apparent, therefore, that the standard twentieth-century definition of magic, and contrast between it and religion, retained considerable vitality at the end of the century, despite attempts to reject and replace it. Indeed, some of the latter in themselves had obvious limitations.

Many of the criticisms of the traditional model consisted of an analysis of particular texts or categories of document, to demonstrate that the distinction did not work in these cases.[53] The problem here was that the traditional definition had portrayed religion and magic as a continuum, rather than two discrete and opposed categories, with the recognition that they overlapped. The scholars who concentrated on varieties of text as case-studies generally failed to attempt the work of proving why the latter should be regarded as normative rather than exemplars of the overlap in action. Nor did many of them suggest what should be substituted for the previous definition of magic once it had been rejected. Some of the critics of the traditional model, moreover, tended to slip into something approaching an acknowledgement of it. In 1991 Fritz Graf concluded that the familiar distinction between religion and magic was unworkable in the case of a particular group of texts. Three years later, he published a major study of 'magic in the ancient world', at one point of which he defined magicians as people who convince deities through a higher knowledge and coerce them through invocation: pretty well the classic formula. His one qualification was that coercion was only one of a range of strategies employed by magicians to achieve their ends; but then the achievement of an end was also part of the formerly established definition of magic.[54] Peter Kingsley declared in 1995 that the traditional distinction was 'impossible to sustain', but was then driven to speaking vaguely of 'magic as generally understood', without any further attempt to explain what that now was, and why.[55] One of the earliest attacks on the customary formulation among ancient historians was made by David Aune, who began by declaring that a dichotomy between magic and religion was impractical, then proceeded to suggest they differed in their means of achieving very similar goals, and finally that magic seemed to give humans methods of guaranteeing results which religion could not. A distinction had been restated, again, on very much the traditional lines.[56] By 1999 another scholar was driven to complain that 'there still is, it appears, something we want to call "magic", although we no longer have a clear idea of what it is'.[57]

This said, some critics of the traditional model have tried, coherently and consistently, to provide a replacement for it, and their proposals have taken three forms. One holds that the term 'magic' should be abandoned altogether and replaced with another. Richard Gordon has tentatively pointed out that a way to achieve this is to speak of 'ritual power', which is itself rooted in ancient usage and is based on the claim of practitioners to summon and realise internal and external powers for their own ends. Viewed from within this could be said to be religious, viewed from without as illicit. The problem with this formulation is that its definition is uncommonly close to that traditionally provided for magic itself, raising the question of why a change is necessary. The distinction drawn, that magic (when opposed to religion) carries connotations of the illicit, is itself specific to particular cultures. It becomes redundant if a more functional view of magic, embodied in the traditional definition, is taken. Given these difficulties, it is unlikely that such an alternative terminology will have a utility obvious enough to eclipse usage of the familiar word among scholars, let alone our wider society; it is significant that Gordon's comments themselves appeared in a collection entitled *Envisioning Magic*.[58] Two years later, Marvin Meyer and Richard Smith republished an edition of texts with the proposal that to speak of 'ritual power' enabled historians to escape from the difficulties now associated with the older terminology; but they still called their book *Ancient Christian Magic*. What they held to be the feature of the texts that they edited which distinguished the latter from other kinds of ritual was that they were 'overt in their manipulation of power and force'; again, a definition very close to the traditional way of delineating magic.[59]

The second major alternative to the traditional definition has been to abandon it in favour of those used by ancient cultures for the phenomena which have been classed together by modern writers under the label of magic. This process involved for some proponents the recognition that the label concerned has been used to cover a range of phenomena which the ancients distinguished under different names, and to which they took differing attitudes. In one form or another, this course has been propounded since 1990 by Mary Beard, John North, Simon Price, Alan Segal, Richard Gordon, Daniel Ogden, Matthew Dickie and John Gager; a formidable roll-call.[60] It has the merit of employing in ancient Mediterranean studies the caution entered by Evans-Pritchard for anthropology; of being careful to avoid the application of modern western terms, categories and concepts to other societies, without taking account of major cultural differences. It also draws attention to the complexity of historical attitudes, both at a given moment and in change over time. The very word 'magic' is derived from the Greek *mageia*, translated into Latin as *magia*, which appeared in these respective languages at particular times, carrying connotations which developed in subsequent periods, and representing only some aspects of the phenomenon which scholars would later call magic. No study of that phenomenon in the world of antiquity can indeed be responsibly undertaken without incorporating such insights. On the other hand, to proceed only by using (mutable) ancient terms and definitions for 'what we call magic' is to run the risk of a different sort of inconsistency and to sacrifice any hope of a rigorous and generally recognised terminology which can unite scholars of different periods, regions and disciplines. Furthermore, there is a tendency in the studies which have embraced this methodology for the twentieth-century model of magic to remain, in ghostly form, as the conceptual umbrella which defines the range of ancient activities and terminologies which are studied.

The third alternative approach has been to class as magic those ritual activities that a given society has defined as illicit and dangerous, and opposed to the communal and established religion. This has an academic pedigree almost as long and distinguished as the traditional scholarly definition, being suggested by Emile Durkheim in the early years of the twentieth century and restated by Marcel Mauss in 1950.[61] It can overlap with the second approach, in that some of the terms used for particular ritual practices in the ancient world opposed them to religious norms. The notion of magic as something defined and redefined by social interaction was advocated in the 1980s by Charles Robert Philips, and propounded in the 1990s by him and by Alan Segal, John North, Jonathan Z. Smith and Stephen Ricks; another impressive list of authorities.[62] Once again, it must be stated as an absolute that no study of the subject in any society should be divorced from its specific social and cultural context. In the case of the Mediterranean ancient world, it is beyond question that the Romans increasingly identified magic with any clandestine rites, and placed an unusually heavy stress on the centrality of public and communal religion. This tendency converged with that of Jewish and Christian tradition, to define magic as beliefs and practices which deviated sharply from dominant religious norms, to produce a powerful blend that was to determine official attitudes in Europe for the rest of the middle ages and beyond. The problem with taking this model as the basic interpretative framework is that a social manipulation of definitions is often only possible because definitions and categories existed anyway. What has commonly been called magic was condemned as unorthodox because it had certain features which marked it off from the official cult of deities. If those bore a correspondence to the twentieth-century category of magic, then the latter cannot so readily be discarded. It may be suggested that the acid test of the definition of magic as the religious Other is whether the practices and attitudes defined as that by Jews, Christians and Romans in the imperial period were found in other societies (and especially in other ancient, and neighbouring, societies) without such sanctions being applied to them. If they were, then the sociological definition becomes divisive and culturally specific, and a more functional way of looking at the subject can seem to have greater utility after all.

It must now be obvious that any considered statements upon the relationship between magic and religion in the ancient Mediterranean world must represent a contribution to a complex, continuing and not altogether coherent debate. During the past thirty years, this debate has trodden what had seemed a reasonable amount of scholarly common ground into a quagmire. To put things more positively, it has asked some hard and worthwhile questions of an accepted model and forced historians to consider the issues concerned with a much greater care and sensitivity, giving a new prominence and importance to the whole subject area. One difficulty of the debate is that there has been no general agreement on the terms in which it is conducted, and the chronological and geographical boundaries of its remit. Another has been that critics of the traditional distinction between religion and magic have tended to devote much effort to determining what magic is or should not be, while taking the nature of religion very much for granted. To a considerable extent, the attitudes of specialists have been determined largely by the utility of particular constructions to their own research, and by personal, institutional and national affinities; it is notable that the attack on the traditional definition has been largely inspired by American academics, and resisted mainly by their continental European counterparts. Attitudes may also have been shaped by cultural contexts; there are hints in the literature that some authors have personally encountered more scholarly prejudice against the study of what has been called magic than others, and associated this with the distinction between it and religion. All this strongly suggests that there can be no easy or rapid resolution to the controversy, and that further contributions to it will be kindly received only in those quarters already disposed to welcome them by existing stances. With all these difficulties in mind, such a contribution is now to be attempted.

The working definition of religion adopted here is broadly that established in the nineteenth century, most notably by Sir Edward Tylor: a belief in the existence of spiritual beings who are in some measure responsible for the cosmos, and in the need of humans to form relationships with them in which they are accorded some respect.[63] Magic is defined here as embracing any formalised practices by human beings designed to achieve particular ends by the manipulation and direction of supernatural power or of spiritual power concealed within the natural world. This formulation is essentially the traditional twentieth-century one as developed by Ruth Benedict and William Goody, and without any of the ideological baggage associated with it by Sir James Frazer and complained of by later criticis. It does not seek to order religion and magic in any evolutionary or hierarchical sequence, or attach any value judgements to them. It recognises that they form a continuum rather than separate and opposed phenomena, that the same functionaries can easily engage in and represent both, and that there are particular texts and activities which associate elements of the two so closely that there is little profit in attempting to distinguish them. It also recognises that at other times they can be sharply distinguished. When the two definitions adopted here are linked, it must be obvious that by them magic can exist as a category within religion but also outside it. A further addition to be made to them is that, whereas all magic involves a component of ritual, some term is still needed to distinguish those varieties which involve elaborate ceremonies, blending special words, actions and physical objects. Since the nineteenth century, these have been known variously as 'high', 'learned', 'ritual' or 'ceremonial' magic. The first two of those terms carry implicit value-judgements of a kind which may be unhelpful. The others involve a tautology, because, as said, all magical actions are to some extent rites. My own way of getting round these difficulties is to use the expression 'complex ritual magic' for these more elaborate varieties.

I have said that different definitions are convenient to scholars employed in different areas of research, and this one suits me because of my encounters with people in contemporary society who are self-consciously magicians, and indeed employ concepts and practices derived very plainly from the western tradition of what has been called magic. Their attitudes, however, are as clearly irreligious, as they profess no need to respect spiritual beings, and often no belief in such beings at all, but regard the arcane powers which they manipulate as existing in or emanating from themselves, or else as concealed within the natural order of the cosmos. Rather than seek to find another means of describing what they do which violates both their self-definition and their obvious connection to a tradition hitherto labelled magical, it makes sense to me to accept that magic can exist outside religion, at the present day. It remains now to see how well this pair of definitions can be applied to the ancient Mediterranean and Near Eastern worlds. Clearly, from the summary of the debate given above, there are others who still think that they can be, and what follows is a contribution to their position.

Although Tylor and Frazer were the academics most often associated with this definitional structure in the twentieth century, they were working with much older ideas. The concept of magic as differing from religion in its manipulative quality and its attempts to make change conform to human will is found in the writing of Christian apologists and evangelists from Augustine of Hippo to C. S. Lewis.[64] It is always worth remembering when dealing with Frazer, however, that he was a lapsed Christian but a professional classicist, and the same concept was found in the classical ancient world. Under the pagan Roman empire, it seems to have been a defence for people accused of practising magic to profess complete submission to the will of benevolent deities and insist that anything that they accomplished was only with the permission and assistance of these divinities. The holy man Apollonius of Tyana allegedly secured his acquittal on a charge of being a magician by claiming that he merely prayed to the god Heracles, who answered his plea. Apuleius, also in court on a similar charge, made a successful defence by contrasting those like himself, who obeyed deities, with genuine magicians, who were popularly believed to coerce them. The Neoplatonist sage Plotinus attacked Gnosticism by accusing its protagonists of preaching incantations designed to draw down the higher divine powers to serve them. His successor Iamblichus protected his own spiritual practices against the same charge by claiming that they were prescribed and assisted by benevolent divinities, unlike common magic which tried to impose human will on the divine. In the first century of the imperial period, the scholar Pliny and the playwright and philosopher Seneca both condemned magic as a wish to give orders to deities.[65]

Fritz Graf has demonstrated that in the earlier, classical Greek, period, commentators used words, later regarded as equivalent to 'magician' in a wider sense, to include anybody involved in religious or spiritual practices outside collective and public religion, including mystery cults.[66] None the less, it is possible to find authors articulating the same distinction between magic and religion (or at least normative religious practice) as that found in the Roman Empire. The most famous is Plato. who attacked those who, for financial reward, were 'promising to persuade the deities by bewitching them, as it were, with sacrifices, prayers and incantations'.[67] Plato's tremendous reputation in later periods doubtless helped to reinforce the importance of this distinction, but it is also found before he wrote, in the medical treatise entitled 'On the Sacred Disease'. Dated to the years around 400 BCE, it opposes the use of medicines and spells which seek to compel divine beings to those which supplicate for their aid and are therefore permissible.[68] This seems to be the earliest known usage of the distinction in Europe, and to be part of a process of closer definition of right and wrong spiritual practices which took place in Greek culture during the sixth and fifth centuries BCE as part of the development of its 'classical' period. The terms *mageia* (the ancestor of 'magic') and *magos* (the ancestor of 'magician') seem to appear as part of this process.[69] It remains possible, however, that our sources for the subject dating from before the sixth and fifth centuries are so few that the development may be illusory. There seems to be no Greek or Latin text extant in which the author argues against the notion that to attempt to manipulate or compel deities is a bad thing, and that notion therefore seems to reflect a general component of Graeco-Roman literary culture.

What needs to be confronted is the question of how far this translated into common attitudes and behaviour. The evidence suggests, as shown above, that it did so by the time of the Roman Empire. That for the classical Greek world is less straightforward. Much recent debate has concentrated on curse-tablets, items which appear in Greece from the early fifth century BCE onward and are especially common around Athens. In the imperial period they spread across much of the Graeco-Roman cultural province. They are objects inscribed with words designed to bind, punish or obstruct other humans, and then buried. Christopher Faraone and John Gager have used them as test cases of the need to abandon the concept of magic as a separate category of human activity when studying ancient history, asserting that they mix the characteristics of supplicatory prayer to deities and magical formulae intended to compel action. By contrast, H. S. Versnel has distinguished tablets which appeal for justice to deities against crimes and misdeeds from those which order divine powers around, deal mainly with those associated with the night and the underworld, and are inspired by motives of gain or jealousy. He has proposed that the former be termed 'judicial prayers' and belong to religion, while the latter, although embodying elements of prayer, are classic pieces of 'black' magic. Associated with controversy over the implications of the texts is doubt over their social respectability. Faraone has concluded that there is nothing to indicate that the making of them was regarded as an illicit or shameful activity. Gager has noted that classical Greek law-codes never mention the tablets as such, but that the latter might have been illegal under more general measures directed against the constraint or injury of other humans, or against impiety. Both he and Daniel Ogden have noticed that the texts on them have curiously counter-cultural features, such as the use of exotic names, the reckoning of descent through female lines and retrograde writing, which are not found in the normal religious practice of Greek society. These strongly suggest the identity of these tablets as things defined explicitly against religious norms. Matthew Dickie, looking at the wider problem of the acceptability and legality of magical acts, as defined above, has failed to reach a secure conclusion. It seems that we can neither assert that magic-working on its own was ever prosecuted as impiety, nor that the laws against impiety were never extended to cover the working of magic.[70] What must be clear from this summary of the debate is that curse-tablets do not provide clear evidence either to refute the utility of the definition of magic used here, when applied to ancient Mediterranean cultures, or to argue that texts commonly regarded as magical by earlier scholars (as these tablets have been) can now be relegated safely to an undifferentiated category of religion. They illustrate well the difficulty of determining whether or not the fear of compelling deities to the human will, plain in the literary sources, was reflected in at least the accepted and public face of popular belief. There seems to be no suggestion in the literature itself that it was not, and by imperial Roman times we have the public declaration of Apuleius that 'the common herd' both defined magic as the coercion of the gods, and condemned it as such. As early as the fourth century BCE, in Athens, there is a well-recorded case of a woman being executed on a charge of impiety, for using incantations to deflect the wrath of the deities from those who had apparently incurred it [71]

All this becomes more clearly important when Graeco-Roman cultural attitudes are contrasted with those of another major ancient civilisation: Egypt. Historians of the latter have long noticed, and emphasised, the differences between them. Ancient Egyptians believed that the cosmos was animated and controlled by spiritual power, *heka*, which was morally neutral. It was manipulated by the deities to regulate and maintain the natural order, but could also be used against them, and employed by humans for their own ends. It was especially associated with words and writing, but also with actions, and with particular stones, plants and varieties of incense. The mobilisation of it consisted of ritual, to unite words and materials through acts. As the deities were adept in it, so they were believed to be prepared to sanction its use in humans who paid them the necessary respect; but those humans, once empowered, were also seen as capable of using it to threaten and coerce deities to their own will. This procedure was regarded as perfectly respectable, and is found as far back in Egyptian history as the Pyramid Texts of the mid third millennium BCE. What appears in those inscriptions, and in the later Coffin Texts, Book of the Dead and writings in New Kingdom royal tombs, is a complete disregard for the later Graeco-Roman categories of religion and magic. Sources mingle praise and threats, prayers and demands, to divine beings, and the same text, such as a hymn, can appear in both magical and religious contexts. The usual authors and performers of magic were functionaries of the official and orthodox religion and attached to its temples, especially a category translated as the 'lector', who functioned both as priest and community magician. Its practice was quite legal, even when employed against public or private enemies, unless it were turned against the king himself. The category of behaviour which is known in English as 'witchcraft' was therefore both unknown and meaningless in Egyptian culture.[72] This is in sharp contrast to the situation in ancient Greece, where attempts to use magic against other humans were illegal, and even more to that at Rome, where two sets of mass trials in the early second century BCE resulted in the execution of 2000 and 3000 people respectively for the alleged crime of attempting to kill by uncanny means. These are body-counts surpassing anything achieved in the Christian witch-hunts of early modern Europe.[73]

Ancient Egyptian magic had particular features which, in combination, were to be significant for the subsequent histories of complex ritual magic and modern Paganism in Europe. One was that, although literature and art suggest that many commoners had specialised magical knowledge for specific purposes, the lector-priests depended on special books of rituals kept in the temple libraries and reserved for themselves. Another is the importance of forming a sacred space for the definition and control of spiritual power. Another was the emphasis on the need of human beings to prepare for magical operations by purifying their bodies and by sweeping the sacred space and sprinkling it with water. Another – which appeared by the early first millennium BCE – was the tradition that humans could summon supernatural beings and turn them into servitors, to carry out tasks at will. A fifth is the emphasis on 'authoritative utterance', on speaking invocations and evocations aloud. Many spells began with the calling of a divine being, who would be asked or required to intervene in the material world on behalf of the speaker. As part of this process, magicians sometimes took on and acted out in ritual the identities of deities especially famed for use of *heka*. A sixth feature – regarded throughout the ancient world as peculiarly Egyptian – is the belief that the power of divinities could be drawn by invocation into material objects, such as statues, and animate them. A seventh was a faith in the potency of secret names, representing the true identity of beings. A seventh is the increasing importance of the moon in magical operations from the first millennium BCE onward. An eighth is the use of consecrated working tools in those operations, notably staffs and wands, and the importance of combinations of particular colours to the rites[74]

All this makes it hardly surprising that, in the Graeco-Roman world, Egypt was famed as the pre-eminent land of magicians and of magical knowledge.[75] Given the current debate over terminology, it would be easy for a proponent of the abolition of any attempt to distinguish between religion and magic to use the Egyptian material as an exemplar of that case. As said, different scholars find different strategies convenient to particular ends, and I find the contrast and tension between Graeco-Roman and Egyptian attitudes which the distinction brings out to be especially useful for the investigation being made here. To cover my back, however, it is worth quoting the Egyptologists themselves on the terminology. All state that in Egypt magic was a part of orthodox religion, but persist in referring to 'magic' as a distinct phenomenon in their texts and commonly in their titles. Robert Ritner accepts a modern definition of it as 'any activity which seeks to obtain goals outside the simple laws of cause and effect'. He emphasises that this must not be confused with ancient attitudes and semantics, but acknowledges it as a viable scholarly framework. Dominic Montserrat states that Egyptian magic 'was about using complex rituals to manipulate other people or the gods in order to make something happen'. Geraldine Pinch suggests that magical texts are distinguished by their freedom from the constraints of the conventions of most Egyptian religion, of asking only for a limited number of gifts from the deities, allowing the practitioners to obtain power to effect specific ends.[76] All these opinions are obviously compatible with the working definitions used in the present essay.

It remains to see how Egyptian attitudes to magic compared with those of other civilisations of the ancient Near East. Those in the small Israelite kingdoms of Palestine during the early first millennium BCE seem to be fairly clear from analysis of the Old Testament: any operations to employ magical power outside the established religion and by other people than its representatives were condemned. Frederick Cryer has found plenty of evidence for magic, defined as procedures for producing action from extra-human sources in specific situations, in the official religion; but this only strengthened the hostility towards those attempting these procedures beyond the control of the religious hierarchy and official ideology. By imperial times Jewish thought had hardened into regarding most such attempts as inherently wicked, and assisted by demons, and these ideas fed directly into Christianity.[77] The contrast with Egypt is plain. The situation in the major states of Mesopotamia, the closest political and social comparisons with Egypt, was different again. The evidence is most abundant for the Assyrian Empire in the early first millennium BCE, although the texts concerned drew at times on material from the preceding superstate of Babylonia. Like the Egyptians, the Assyrians collected magical texts in temple libraries, for use by a specialist elite in a wide variety of contexts and for various needs; but with a number of differences. The Mesopotamian material shows no sign that human beings were believed to be capable of coercing deities, or even of commanding lesser spirits, without divine help. It also identified divinities far more closely with heavenly bodies, and made a practice of timing important actions in harmony with the movements of the moon, planets and stars. The texts show an acute fear of witchcraft, to judge from the number of spells in them designed to counteract magic employed secretly and maliciously by other human beings. There is no sign that they were translated into any other ancient languages before their script became forgotten in the third to first centuries BCE, and the great legacy of Mesopotamian magic to later cultures was astrology, filtered through Egypt.[78] None the less, this in itself, coupled with the earlier close association between state structures, religion and magic in the region, was enough to give

Mesopotamia a powerful reputation for arcane knowledge in the Graeco-Roman world. Known there as 'Chaldeans', its people had a reputation as magicians initially greater than those of Egypt, as they were identified with the great foreign menace to the Greek states, the Persian Empire. Only with the removal of that threat, and the absorption of Egypt into the Greek world, did the land of the Nile become pre-eminent as the home of magic. None the less, this spectrum of regional traditions does seem to make the Egyptian one all the more remarkable, and the more sharply distinct from the Hebrew, Christian and Graeco-Roman.

It was under Roman rule that Egypt made its greatest contributions to later western spirituality. These were directly influenced, and inspired, by the successive conquests of the land by European powers since the fourth century BCE. First the arrival of a Macedonian royal family opened the land up (to some extent) to Greek culture, while the establishment of Alexandria as the greatest city of the Levant put the kingdom's main political and social centre at a crossroads of peoples and ideas. Then incorporation into the Roman Empire involved it in the general decay of established religious cults which was one consequence of imperial rule; in the case of Egypt in particular, effected directly by cutting off the traditional state financial support for the temples. This practical alteration combined with the spiritual effects of the new mobility of peoples and the erosion of local loyalties and institutions that was an inevitable consequence of empire. These manifested, especially in the eastern provinces, as a desire for a direct relationship with a personal divine saviour, a single supreme god, or a single controlling divine power. Christianity was one expression of this, Neoplatonism another, and Mithraism and the other mystery religions a third: the Egyptian equivalents were Gnosticism and Hermetism.

Both of these were concerned with obtaining direct knowledge of a supreme god, based on a conviction of a fundamental identity between that divinity and the human mind and soul. Both were based on the aim of returning the souls of humans to their point of origin in the supreme deity, and both emerged in Egypt between the second and fourth centuries CE. Both speak to an elite, of spiritual teachers with small groups of followers. Both are loose categories of texts designated by later scholars, and extremely disparate. The Gnostic writings are united by a more negative view of the known cosmos and its creator, who is distinguished from the one great and good god. The Hermetic texts are most easily defined by their common attribution or reference to Hermes, the Greek equivalent of the Egyptian god of wisdom, Thoth. They tend to have a more positive view of the cosmos and place more emphasis on systematic instruction and the role of the intellect in reunion with the divine.[79]

The main interest of the present study, however, lies in a third loose grouping of documents defined by later scholars, the so-called Greek magical papyri and the few known related manuscripts in the native ('Demotic') language. Whereas the Hermetic texts were established as a category by the early middle ages, and the Gnostic in the eighteenth century, the Greek magical papyri were only discovered in the nineteenth, and not comprehensively edited and published until the 1980s;[80] this work was both a reflection of the enhanced academic interest in ancient magic and a further stimulus to it. The Demotic papyri are still being read. The magical rituals found in both were mainly a product of the period between the first and third centuries in which Gnosticism and Hermetism also appeared, though they exist in versions copied and amended during the succeeding three hundred years. Their contents were an even more varied phenomenon than the writings of the other two movements. Some were mixed up with other classes of document altogether, such as administrative records, financial accounts and treatises on practical medicine. Many were simple spells of a traditional type with brief and exact formulae, and the attitudes and techniques embodied in them were generally those familiar from earlier Egyptian magic. There were, however, important respects in which they represented something new.

One was that the operations that they prescribed were more elaborate and ambitious. The basic form of a working was to invite or summon a deity to a consecrated space and then state a request to her or him. Sometimes the divinity is clearly under compulsion, and dismissed as well as made to manifest by set procedures.[81] In a number of texts the deity is expected to be drawn by the magician into the living body of another human being, usually a young boy, and made to speak oracles or answer questions through it; a clear development of the earlier Egyptian practice of animating statues.[82] The earlier concept of arcane correspondences between various parts of the natural world was developed into very complex ritual combinations of speech, action, timing, colour, working tools, vegetable materials, incenses, beverages, animal products and animal sacrifices: one operation required unbaked bricks, 'Anubian head of wheat', a falcon-wood plant, the fibre of a male date palm, male frankincense, a choice of libations (wine, beer, honey or the milk of a black cow), grapevine wood and charcoal, wormwood, sesame seeds and black cumin.[83] Solid objects, such as rings, were ceremonially invested with a permanent divine power by deities invoked to perform this task. The native tradition that spirits and divinities could be made responsive or obedient to humans who had learned their secret and 'true' names was developed into the ritual recitation of lengthy formulae of apparently meaningless words, supposed to be loaded with magical power.[84] At times the worker of the rites was expected to perpetuate another older tradition, of assuming the identity of a deity, with the possible innovation that the personification was intended in some fashion to become for a moment magically real.[85]

The second novel feature of these texts was their cosmopolitan nature. They were, as their name suggests, mostly written in Greek, the common language of the educated in the whole eastern half of the Roman Empire. In addition, they incorporated Greek heroes and sages especially associated with occult knowledge, such as Orpheus and Apollonius of Tyana, and Graeco-Roman deities especially associated with supreme power and wisdom, such as Helios, Zeus and Mithras, or with magic itself, above all Hermes and Hekate, or with love spells (Aphrodite and Eros). From Jewish tradition was taken the concept of controlling demons with the names of Jehovah (mostly known as Iao), Moses or Solomon, and of angels. The result could be an exuberant eclecticism: one rite includes an invocation to Apollo, which identifies that god with the sun deity Helios, the archangel Raphael, the demon Abrasax, and the Hebrew titles Adonai and Sabaoth, and calls him 'flaming messenger of Zeus, divine Iao'. Another makes Helios the archangel of the One God.[86] One of the formulae used in the papyri is also recorded at Beirut and in the Rhineland, while another is exactly prefigured in an Assyrian text; in that sense they sucked in rites and ideas found throughout the Roman Empire and Mesopotamia.[87]

A further novel feature, which has been noted by several commentators, was a change in the social context in which Egyptian magic was worked.[88] Some historians have seen the papyri as products of a new and mobile kind of magician operating in society at large and resulting from the decay of the temple system and of the services which it had provided. Others see them as contents of an old-fashioned temple library and written by a lector priest, but now working privately within the changed circumstances of a Roman government that frowned on the traditional Egyptian legitimation of magic. The clash between the two cultures was summed up vividly in the year 199 when the Roman prefect of Egypt outlawed divination in general, and especially that by the animation of images, as 'charlatanry'. These changes are almost certainly related to the new eclecticism of the texts and to their unprecedentedly ambitious character. The lector-priests had traditionally been concerned with providing defensive magic, against illness or enemies. The papyri showed a new interest in enabling practitioners and clients to achieve power, knowledge and worldly desires. Some of them embodied an assumption that their skills would be passed on by the private training of pupils and the personal transmission of texts.[89]

Associated with all these developments was a fourth, also noted by a number of scholars;[90] the appropriation of the language and atmosphere of the late Roman mystery religions for the practical purposes of magic. One papyrus cheerfully endorses the most important of those purposes as being 'to persuade the gods and all the goddesses'. It then goes on to call the practitioner 'blessed initiate of the sacred magic', and fated to 'be worshipped as a god since you have a god as a friend'.[91] A 'charm of Hekate Ereschigal against fear of punishment' (twinning a Greek-Anatolian goddess with a Babylonian one) proclaims 'I have been initiated, and I went down into the underground chamber of the Dactyls, and I saw the other things below, virgin, bitch and all the rest.' A 'spell to establish a relationship with Helios' asks above all to be 'maintained in knowledge of you' (the god), although it makes clear that such knowledge opens the way to the attainment of all worldly desires.[92] A rite dedicated to Typhon, 'god of gods' is designed to 'attain both the ruler of the universe and whatever you [those who work the ritual] command', the latter being one of the perquisites of the 'godlike nature which is accomplished through this divine encounter'[93] The most famous of these texts is the so-called Mithras Liturgy, which describes how a practitioner may ascend into the realms of the celestial divinities, level by level, to obtain a vision of the supreme deity and come to the verge of immortality; during the ascent the celebrant pronounces himself or herself to be a star. It refers to those fitted to perform the rite as 'initiates'. The point of all this religious ecstasy, revelation and beatification, however, is to obtain a divine answer to any question posed about earthly as well as heavenly affairs.[94]

Because they were mostly written in Greek, these documents have become readily discussed by classicists, to whom texts recorded in the native Egyptian scripts of hieroglyphs, Demotic and Coptic are not as accessible; indeed, the magical papyri are sometimes treated as a manifestation of Greek culture. As such, they have inevitably become important counters in the debate among ancient historians over the relationship between religion and magic, with predictably inconclusive results. To Alan Segal, the mixture of elements within them presents a classic example of the futility of trying to distinguish the two: in these papyri 'magic was religion'.[95] Fritz Graf and Einar Thomassen both think that a distinction can still be made, while the recent translator of these texts, Hans Dieter Betz, has declared roundly of their authors: 'They lacked what we would call "religion". They themselves no doubt believed that they possessed a "religion that worked", but what they in fact had produced was magic.'[96] What can be said here is that, self-evidently, the Greek magical papyri represent a classic case of an area in the spectrum of religion and magic in which the two strongly overlap. None the less, according to the definitions provided in this chapter, the traditional name for them was well chosen, and Betz was right: most of the contents of the papyri are magical rites of an absolutely classic kind, while in the cases where clear religious elements are present they are employed for magical ends.

What seems especially striking, therefore, was that just at that period in which official and popular attitudes across much of the Roman Empire were hardening further against magic, as a means of manipulating divine power for selfish ends, Egypt was producing an unusually sophisticated and elaborate tradition, based on texts and teaching, dedicated to doing exactly that. Moreover it was one which in some cases was elevated by religious claims and techniques. Two sources from elsewhere in the empire indicate what public opinion there made of such operations. One is the epic poem *Pharsalia*, composed at Rome in the first century by Lucan. It includes a character called Erichtho, who summons deities with a knowledge of their true names, and compels them to her will using ritual techniques quite similar to those recommended in the papyri. Erichtho, however, is intended to embody absolute evil and arouse feelings of repulsion and loathing in the reader.[97] The other is the defence which Apuleius claimed to have made at his own trial for magic, in a town on the African coast westward from Egypt. One of the charges against him that he had put a boy into a trance in order to make the youngster the mouthpiece for a deity who could then be questioned, a process for which (as said) several rites were recommended in the papyri. He called it a lie, and airily declared that he did not know whether such an operation was possible at all; the court believed him.[98] As well as illustrating the disapproval with which such practices were regarded, these sources also indicate that they were fairly well known even in the non-Greek western half of the empire. By embracing them with such enthusiasm, and linking some of them explicitly with divine revelation, the authors of the texts in the papyri were posing a very considerable challenge to the norms of Graeco-Roman religion.

It has often been considered that a simultaneous attempt to combine traditional religious and magical forms was being made further north in the Greek-speaking world, in the region bounded by Greece itself, Asia Minor and Syria. It hinges on the concept of 'theurgy', a word variously translated as 'divine work', 'making things divine', 'making deities', 'making deities of humans', 'doing the work of deities', 'working on deities' and 'being worked on by deities';[99] it must be clear that these interpretations have very different implications. Whatever its precise meaning, it has generally been taken to signify a set of techniques recommended by late antique philosophers to bring individual human beings into direct communion, or union, with divinities. It was generally ignored, marginalised or derided by modern scholars until the mid twentieth century, when the great Oxford classicist E. R. Dodds (swayed by his own keen interest in psychical research) proposed it to be a significant subject for study.[100] During the last twenty years there has been a boom in such studies, as part of the general growth of scholarly interest in ancient concepts and practices of magic.

To Dodds himself, theurgy was 'magic applied to a religious purpose'. For R. T. Wallis, writing twenty years later, it was 'a system of ritual purification based on a magical view of the universe'. More recent commentators have come up with parallel formulations. Polymnia Athanassiadi has pronounced it to be 'not just a technique ... but rather a dynamic state of mind'. Alan Segal thought it to be the force which turned magic into a consistent religion in the late Roman Empire. Sarah Iles Johnston has called definitions of it 'problematic for ancient and modern scholars alike', and added that it is not clear how much it belongs to the realm of magic. She subsequently decided to define it herself as 'an esoteric, revelatory religion'. Gregory Shaw termed it simply an entry into communion with deities, a usage endorsed with more specificity by Georg Luck, who said that it was a technique to achieve such communion and represented the ultimate development of the ancient mystery religions. He also, however, called it 'a kind of higher magic' and as such 'a form of pressure' on demons and gods. Rowland Smith thought it a variety of sorcery, that differed from most magic in its aims, to secure the ascent of the human soul to the divine. Matthew Dickie thought that to 'most modern scholars magic and theurgy seem indistinguishable'.[101] Two things should be obvious from this cluster of quotations. One is that there is a fairly widespread opinion that theurgy represented an application of magical forms to religious purposes, just as the magical papyri included an application of religious forms to magical purposes. The other is that, despite a range of confident personal assertions on the part of individual specialists, there is no scholarly consensus either on what theurgy literally means or on what practices it signified. Why should this be?

That question can only be answered by picking a way through the evidence piece by piece, and such a process must begin with the texts universally recognised as the historical starting point for theurgy, the sayings known collectively as the Chaldean Oracles. The first point to be made about these is that they represent portions of a vanished work, surviving only as fragmentary quotations selected by later authors, often centuries after their composition. We have no certain idea of the order in which these fragments appeared in the original work, or of their context, or of how great a part of the lost book they represent. Nor is there any absolute agreement on the canon of material, some scholars including in it quotations which other consider to be doubtful or misattributed.[102] The second problem is that we do not know how or by whom the Oracles were composed. Strictly speaking, they were supposed to be the utterances of deities, but by the fourth century the writing of them was attributed to a father and son from Mesopotamia, both called Julian, who had lived two hundred years before. There is no way in which this tradition can be proved or disproved. On stylistic grounds they can indeed be dated to the second century, and they seem to have emerged as a collection in Syria, but there is no certainty that they were composed at one time and place.[103] Their name gave them an exotic gloss, linking them to the reputation of Mesopotamians ('Chaldeans') for occult wisdom. Experts have disagreed sharply over the actual origins of the thought systems embodied in them, variously finding elements from Persian, Meso-potamian, Platonic, Pythagorean, Stoic and Gnostic sources. There seems to be a recent agreement that the Platonic and Gnostic strands are the most important.[104]

The third problem in interpreting these texts is that they are oracular in the most inconvenient sense, privileging poetic utterance over clear expo-sition and shading from mysticism to mystification. Typical examples of their style (and therefore not the most opaque) are 'The centre of Hekate is borne along in the midst of the Fathers' or 'And he is called Twice Transcendent, because he is dyadic ... and the other is termed Once Tran-scendent because he is unitary, but Hekate is called transcendent alone'.[105] This sort of thing may have been ambiguous or obscure even to ancient readers. Modern scholars can interpret it only in the light of other texts, and differ over which texts should be used, whether Middle Platonic writings, the Greek magical papyri, oracles delivered by late antique shrines, or medieval Greek works. Inevitably, the result is a diversity of interpreta-tions: Hans Lewy, Ruth Majercik, Sarah Iles Johnston, Rowland Smith and Stephen Ronan have all come up with different expositions of the cosmology of the Oracles, each plausible in its own way.[106]

When all this is said, some aspects of that cosmology are fairly clear, and agreed. It depends on a single, supreme, creator god, from which everything proceeds and to which all returns: 'For all things which issue from the One and, conversely, go back to the One, are divided, so to speak intelligibly, into many bodies', and 'The Father created all things in conformity with perfection and he entrusted them to the Second Mind'.[107] This Second Mind or Intellect is one of two major divine beings operating between the supreme deity and the rest of creation, and dominating a large number of other spirits and divinities. The other is the goddess Hekate. She is not, however, the lunar goddess of late Graeco-Roman tradition, but a giver of life and abundance, associated, like the other two great beings, with primal fire. The relationship of the two with each other, and with the supreme being, is not made clear, and the great creator deity is mentioned more often than the others. The point of religious devotion is to achieve reunion with him by one's own efforts: 'to hasten towards the light and towards the rays of the Father'.[108]

It is this process to which the word 'theurgy' was applied, once in the Oracles themselves and more consistently by those who quoted them later. What is less obvious is its practical import. As Georg Luck has pointed out, no proper description of a means to effect this mystical union survives in the fragments, and any attempt to reconstruct one must be tentative: 'perhaps every practitioner had an individual technique'.[109] There are references to things called *iynges*, which at times seem to be metaphysical, 'thoughts of the Father', but may also have a physical representation.[110] Hints are apparently dropped about initiation, though not indicating whether this is a solitary or group experience, and one passage suggests the presence of a priest to guide at least one of the rites, though this may be a metaphor. There are brief references to passwords and magical names in 'barbaric' languages.[111] The practitioner is certainly expected to be granted dramatic visions of deities.[112] One fragment warns that an earthly (and therefore perhaps evil) spirit may appear instead, but can be warded off by the recitation of a charm and the display of a special sort of stone.[113] All this sounds very much like the techniques employed in the magical papyri, and indeed directed here to the purpose of union with the divine; but the details are lacking.

There is a clutch of fragments which seem to be more explicit. In one, Hekate says that the prayers of the practitioner have compelled and persuaded her to leave the home of God and come to earth; an apparent clear reference to an invocation being used to compel the manifestation of a deity. Another speaks likewise of summoning her by compulsion, and has her seem to complain that 'the wretched heart of the medium is too weak to bear me'; an apparent allusion to the magical practice of summoning a deity into the body of a child, who then acts as a mouthpiece. A third refers to the ability of humans using 'secret iynges' to draw unwilling deities to the terrestrial realm, and a fourth directs that a god be released from a mortal body. Finally, one gives instructions for the making of a statue of Hekate from particular plant and animal materials. The latter are fairly clearly based on the doctrine of mystical correspondences between substances, so important to Egyptian magic, and the statue is probably intended to be animated with an invoked spirit, in the classic Egyptian fashion, but this is not explicit.[114] The problem with these texts is that they fall into the category of those which can be only doubtfully and controversially be attributed to the lost Oracles. Ruth Majercik has rejected them altogether, on the grounds that their expressed willingness to compel deities violates the spirit of those fragments more confidently included in the canon.[115] This argument depends upon an equally speculative view of what the overall message of the lost work actually was, but there is a better reason for setting these fragments aside. They are found in the work of a hostile writer, the Christian apologist Eusebius, and it is possible that they derive from a different text or different texts of complex ritual magic, and were used by him (innocently or not) to smear the reputation of the Chaldean Oracles and confuse them with more straightfoward, and disreputable, magical practices. With their departure from the body of evidence, any modern certainty over the practical nature of the 'theurgy' embodied in parts of the Oracles probably becomes impossible. Sarah Iles Johnston, Georg Luck, Ruth Majercik and Rowland Smith have all suggested possible reconstructions of the system used, but which of them is closest to the truth, or whether indeed there ever was an established system, seems to be a matter incapable of resolution.[116]

What is certain is that the Oracles made an obvious potential fit with the evolving philosophical tradition of Neoplatonism. Both spoke of the need to reunite with the primal divine One, but whereas Plotinus had outlined this position as an intellectual hypothesis, the Oracles presented it as divine revelation. In a period in which Christians were increasingly active in preaching their holy texts as god-given scriptures, the supposedly Chaldean texts provided pagan mystics with a rival body of divine mandates. Porphyry was the first philosopher to promote them as such. How he did so is itself a matter for speculation, for much of what he wrote has itself been lost. What is clear is that he issued a tremendous warning over the techniques which might be used to achieve reunion with divinity. One of the most famous of his surviving works is his *Letter to Anebo*, a short treatise in the form of a remonstrance to an apparently fictional Egyptian priest, condemning any notion that deities could be compelled to human will and ridiculing the use of 'barbaric' names in invocations. This was both a very clear rejection of the methods represented in the Greek magical papyri and an indication of how far knowledge of them had spread from Egypt among intellectuals by about the year 300; it is an explicit appeal to Greek tradition against Egyptian contamination.[117] Porphyry's attitude to magic is not, however, quite that simple, as other passages in his extant works testify. On the one hand, he wrote that ritual practices, and those associated with magic in particular, could distract humans from the spiritual exercises, and commitment to a life of virtue, that alone purified souls and made reunion with divinity possible. He warned of the danger that those who tried to summon deities would call evil spirits instead. He described with apparent disgust a rite in which a statue of Apollo was placed in bonds, surrounded by blinding lights and assaulted by prayers and chants to force the god to provide an oracle through it; only for the deity to beg his worshippers to leave him alone. Again, this is an example, at the least, of the stories of coercive ritual practices which were circulating by that time. On the other hand, Porphyry also admitted that magic could be made into a means to communicate with the divine, even though it was not the best way. The consensus among experts seems to be that he approved of ritual techniques only as a method of improving the lower aspects of the human soul, and only if they avoided that element of compulsion and manipulation of divinity which commonly defined magic.[118]

In one of the most celebrated rejoinders of ancient intellectual history, Porphyry's fellow Neoplatonist, Iamblichus, replied to the *Letter to Anebo* in the work for which he is now best known: *On the Mysteries of the Egyptians, Chaldeans and Assyrians*. As its name suggests, this recommended these non-European traditions, and especially that of Egypt, as a means of revitalising Graeco-Roman paganism. Against Porphyry's warnings, he asserted that the deities themselves had revealed or prescribed to humans ritual practices, including those of theurgy, as a means of communing with the divine. He also declared that they cooperated actively with mortals in these rites of their own volition and that virtuous practitioners had nothing to fear from evil spirits.[119] That much is clear; but further interpretation of the text has to reckon with serious difficulties. One is by now a familiar one, that many of the other works of Iamblichus, which would provide a better context for understanding his thought, have been lost. Another problem is that Iamblichus himself is not easy to understand; it was as apparent to the scholars of antiquity as to those of modernity that he was a complex and often obscure writer.[120] He himself defined theurgy as the performance of 'ineffable actions beyond all understanding' and 'the power of utterable symbols understood by the deities alone'.[121] This was almost certainly intended to be as imposing and uninformative as it sounds, and nowhere does Iamblichus provide a practical exposition of how his concept of theurgy operates. None the less, his text contains some clues.

One of the more important is the passage in which he states that 'theurgy ... often brings together stones, herbs, animals, incenses and other sacred, perfect and deiform objects'. A single stone or plant could connect humans directly with the divine.[122] This is essentially a restatement of the Egyptian doctrine of mystical correspondences between material substances. The latter, in less developed form, was probably one common to many or most ancient cultures, and fitted well in the Graeco-Roman world with the

Stoic philosophical doctrine of the intrinsic unity and sympathy of the universe. By the time of Iamblichus, however, it was particularly well known in that world through the practical treatise of the Egyptian writer Bolus of Mendes, which listed the magical properties of animals, plants and stones.[123] Iamblichus empowered it further with Neoplatonic doctrine. If all things emanated from an original One, then they were all interconnected, and these connections provided humans with pathways or communication systems to divinity.[124] 'It is requisite, therefore, to understand that the universe is one animal; and that the parts in it are, indeed, separated by places, but through the possession of one nature hasten to each other.'[125] This in itself, to Iamblichus, justified the heavy investment in ritual, material trappings and sacrifice characteristic of traditional paganism, and which acted as part of a process of correspondence and reunion. The cannier pagan was distinguished by knowledge of the precise nature of the material substances, numbers and incantations which should be used to contact and work with particular deities.[126]

Even among canny pagans, however, to Iamblichus theurgists were definitely superior. He emphasised that they were quite distinct from regular magicians, who impiously attempted to manipulate the system of correspondences for their own material profit, and to control it.[127] Such transgressors, approaching divinities without due reverence, were likely to become possessed by the many evil spirits who ranged the earth like ravening beasts.[128] Not only were theurgists more respectful and aimed at reunion with divinity, but they took their time, working carefully and patiently towards this goal: Iamblichus warned his readers not to 'leap after the gods'.[129] He also advised them to work with lesser divinities – demigods, angels, benevolent daemons and the spirits of heroes – rather than with actual deities, and to avoid honouring some goddesses and gods and neglecting others. He emphasised that only the most experienced priests, and with great difficulty, achieved a mystical union with the celestial divinities, and that most theurgists should not even attempt this.[130]

None the less, the celestial powers could choose to call to themselves humans who seemed to merit it sufficiently: 'for the whole life of the soul and all the powers that are in it, being in subjection to the deities, are moved in such a way as the deities, the leaders of the soul, please.'[131] The 'deities, being benevolent and gracious, generously shine their light on theurgists, calling their souls up to themselves, habituating them – while still in their bodies – to be detached from their bodies.'[132] When those moments of union occur, the human soul 'takes on the shape of the gods'.[133] Iamblichus makes it fairly clear that those happy few who achieve such bliss are marked out by inborn talents, and long training in prayer and pious exercises; the mere deployment of ritual and corresponding material objects will not suffice.[134] None the less, the most powerful theurgists could prepare themselves for the ascent and even provoke it: by 'observation of the critical moment' they could rise 'even to the divine creator'. He also seems to recognise, with approval, that humans could draw down divine beings to possess them and speak through them, in the manner of the rites recorded in the papyri.[135] None of this suggests a set pattern of ritual practices: only a general admonition to an intense pagan piety coupled with a study of the occult lore associated with ritual magic of the Egyptian sort. The central problem of Iamblichus's treatise is that it does not quite make clear whether operations such as the deployment of stones and plants or invocation of spirits or demigods into humans were necessary components of his concept of theurgy or practices against which he was defining it, and which it transcended. Sometimes he appears to support the first position, at other times the second.[136]

The tiny amount that is recorded of Iamblichus outside his own words bears out this picture. The nearest thing to a biography of him by an ancient author is the sketch provided by Eunapius almost a hundred years after his death. This claimed that the one occasion on which Iamblichus had used his powers to cause divine beings to manifest before his followers was when he brought about the brief appearance of the spirits of two sacred springs. He did so to impress his pupils with what a theurgist could achieve, but it was a long way short of the summoning of deities promised by the magical papyri or the doubtful fragments often associated with the Chaldean Oracles. The story moreover includes a warning from him to his audience that even such a treatment of demigods was 'irreverent', and Eunapius added that it might itself have been a complete fiction invented by his admirers.[137]

Iamblichus established theurgy as a concept to be reckoned with in Neo-platonism, but the next generation of philosophers from that tradition, in the mid fourth century, divided over it. The geographical centre of the movement had now moved north from Iamblichus's Syria to western Asia Minor. There one position was expounded by Eusebius,[138] who taught that philosophy was the only true means of coming to know the deities, while 'witchcraft and magic' tied people to worldly concerns. The other was most prominently associated with Maximus, who held that it was the duty of the learned 'to wrestle with the heavenly powers till you make them incline to be your servant'. His own greatest reputed feat was to animate a statue (of Hekate) in classic Egyptian fashion.[139] Or so we are told. The problem here is that our only source for these developments consists of the history written by Eunapius. This has so often been treated as objective truth that it may be worth pointing out that it is a literary work crafted with clear prejudices.

Eunapius makes Maximus's career into a cautionary tale of the bad end that comes to philosophers seduced by worldly ambitions and pride, so he may not be wholly reliable as to the details of his teachings and actions. What is certain is that Maximus did indeed assert that theurgy had an important place in human relations with the divine. He was one of the favourite thinkers of the Emperor Julian, who recommended the theurgists in his own writings (without elucidating the nature of their operations).[140]

In the fifth century, as said before, the centre of Neoplatonic teaching moved to the academy at Athens, and a succession of exponents among whom Proclus was pre-eminent. Theurgy was part of their tradition. Proclus himself defined it as 'power higher than all human wisdom, embracing the blessings of divination, the purifying powers of initiation, and, in one word, all the operations of divine possession', which again seems to imply that no one system or set of rites was recommended. The work of his in which this definition appears suggests that the human soul could be awoken, and prepared for its ascent to reunite with the divine, by various combinations of contemplation, prayer, invocation and the use of magical letters and numbers. It also warns against attempts to compel or manipulate divine power, and states that the deities themselves enacted three stages in the ascent of a human to true reunion with them: initiation, consecration and vision. These correspond to the three levels of prayer delineated by Iamblichus. The implication of the text seems to be that the process is a solitary one, a transaction between the lone theurgist and the divinities, but this is nowhere made absolutely explicit.[141]

Comparisons with other works of Proclus are made difficult by the usual problem that so many have disappeared, including most of his commentaries on the Chaldean Oracles which would probably have clarified our knowledge of both him and them. Enough of his writings survive to provide only a few further hints as to his notion of theurgy. The most important is *Of the Priestly Art According to the Greeks*, which in its extant form is probably a medieval digest made of his original text. It is a restatement, as a Greek doctrine, of what Iamblichus (with more justice) ascribed to the Egyptians: that material things are connected by spiritual links to deities, all being ultimately emanations from the One. Therefore priests learn to mix together stones, plants and incenses that correspond to particular deities to call upon those deities, and can employ other mixtures to repel unwanted spirits.[142] From two of Proclus's other works, E. H. Dodds teased out apparent allusions to rites designed to call a deity into a human being through whom the divinity could speak, of the sort familiar from the magical papyri.[143] In a third of his treatises, Proclus seems to say that theurgy taught both to supplicate the deities in the traditional religious manner and to use special

invocations to summon divine beings, in the tradition of ritual magic.[144]
Matthew Dickie has also picked up two other apparent endorsements of
magic in his commentaries on Plato. One is a spell to assist births, that
manipulates correspondences between the planets, the vowels, letters and
the signs of the zodiac, the other the animation of statues of deities by a
'performer of initiations', using a combination of invocation and the drawing
of symbols on the statues.[145]

In his case, however, we also have an 'external' source for his thought
and actions, a biography (or hagiography) produced by his successor as
leader of the Athenian academy, Marinus. This portrays him as both a holy
man, of exemplary sobriety and piety, and an accomplished ritual magician.
It states that by study of the Chaldean Oracles he became a master of
theurgy. As such, he both directed his thoughts upward to the divine, and
cared for earthly things: using a 'Chaldean' rite, he obtained a vision of
Hekate, working another ritual, he brought rain to save Attica from drought,
he used forms of divination and he 'employed the art of moving the divine
tops'.[146] The meaning of this last comment was apparently explained by
another subsequent leader of the academy, Damascius, who stated that by
whirling a top in one direction a human could invoke supernatural beings,
and by whirling it in the other dismiss them.[147] Marinus also, however,
extends the label 'theurgic' to works which reflect a more conventional
religious piety, considering Proclus's greatest practical achievement having
been to obtain a miraculous cure of a dying child by offering prayers to
the god of healing, Asclepius.[148]

As in the case of Iamblichus, it is not easy to attribute to Proclus a coherent
and unequivocal statement of what theurgy was and what it involved. Anne
Sheppard has made the most detailed and direct recent consideration of
the matter, and concluded that, for the whole of the fifth-century Athenian
Neoplatonist school, ritual acts were only efficacious to obtain results in the
physical world, and as first steps on the ascent of a human soul towards
the One. On the higher levels ritual was useless and a different, more mystical,
sort of theurgy was needed. She also drew attention to the apparent
discrepancy between the portrait of Proclus drawn by Marinus, with its
emphasis on his acts of ritual magic, and the lack of importance attributed
to such acts in Proclus's own writings. Conversely, Marinus makes little
reference for the quest for ascent to mystical reunion with divinity which
is so prominent in Proclus's work. From this, she raised the possibility that
the biography represented an attempt to construct an image of a stereotypical
holy man, with the marvels commonly associated with that in late antiquity,
rather than an objective account of its subject's own attitudes. R. T. Wallis
had earlier drawn attention to passages in Proclus's commentaries which

seem to assert that ritual had only a limited role in the purification and ascent of the soul that was the essential work of human salvation to Neoplatonists. This reading has recently been endorsed by Lucas Siorvanes, who has interpreted Proclus as speaking of a shift from a physical to a non-physical theurgy as the practitioner becomes an adept.[149]

A few extracts from the works of two later authors have also been applied to the problem of defining theurgy. One is the Neoplatonist philosopher Damascius, who wrote in the early sixth century. He described it simply as 'the worship of the gods', which ensured 'heavenbound salvation'.[150] This reinforces the impression that it was a blanket term to cover a wide range of spiritual exercises to assist the ascent of the soul, applied according to the taste of individual practitioners. Such an interpretation is supported further by sketches of Neoplatonist philosophers from his own time and the previous generation, provided by Damascius in the work in which the definition is supplied. They display a considerable diversity of personal emphases in choices of key texts and activities. Iamblichus and the Chaldean Oracles feature prominently among the influences valued by some of these thinkers, but not all. Some prized prayer and contemplation, others placed a high value on traditional religious rites. It may be telling that none of them are credited with an interest in ritual magic. Asclepiodotus comes closest, for it is said of him that he studied the properties of stones and herbs, and once worked a spell to save a friend and himself from drowning, but Damascius adds that he knew nothing of 'Chaldean lore'.[151]

The other later writer is of very different kind and period, being the medieval Greek churchman Michael Psellus, who lived half a millennium later. He was deeply interested in the history of theurgy, and recorded information about it from texts that have since vanished. He stated that theurgists animated statues and themselves became mouthpieces for divine beings, and employed inscribed gems and magical names. He described the magical top alluded to by Marinus and Damascius as a golden sphere inscribed with symbols and spun by a leather thong as the theurgist invoked. He also provided details of a particular 'Chaldean' rite, in which the operator consecrated a working space by inscribing a circle in the ground and burying in it a mixture of burnt spices, stones, herbs, leaves and flowers. On the next day these were dug up and the practitioner raised them in the left hand and invoked 'the teacher of the lifted-up sacrifice, the masters of the hylic substances, the ruler of the day, the lord of time and the demon lord of the Four'. The problem with all this is the obvious one; that we do not know how good Psellus's sources of information were, and whether he was recording fantasies, or the workings of magicians of a more straightforward sort, under the general heading of theurgy.[152]

The import of all this data seems to be that what late antique writers meant by theurgy signified a wide range of spiritual practices and exercises united by the aim of enabling the practitioner to commune directly with divinities and eventually to reunite with the divine. Rituals and knowledge of the arcane properties of the natural world were recognised as having their value for this process, but there is some doubt as to whether they were regarded as efficacious beyond its initial levels. There seem to have been no particular methods taught or prescribed, theurgists making their own choices from a range of possibilities, and on the whole the practice seems to have been a solitary one, perhaps with a companion, assistant or pupil for some workings, as in the case of the magic recorded in the papyri.[153] Theurgy certainly borrowed from the new, highly developed, form of ritual magic which those papyri embody, but only as one of the means utilised and perhaps not ultimately the most important. None the less, the borrowing was significant enough for the formula to be upheld, that if the magical papyri sometimes represented an application of religious forms to magical ends, so theurgy did indeed sometimes represent the reverse process.

One last question needs to be asked about it: how widespread a practice it actually was in late antiquity. Here the original texts themselves point all in one direction, by associating it with the most pronounced and exclusive intellectual snobbery. The Chaldean Oracles set the tone, declaring that 'theurgists do not fall into the herd' and 'must flee the mass of men who "are going about in herds"'.[154] They were echoed by Iamblichus, who made it plain that the higher grades of spiritual experience were attainable only by 'extremely rare' individuals, quite distinct from 'the great herd' which was forever trapped in earthly things.[155] No wonder that when Julian came to praise theurgists he called their teachings 'unknown, especially to the mob'.[156] The world of later Neoplatonism, as revealed in Marinus's biography of Proclus, is that of a small, defensive and socially isolated spiritual elite. Historically, Neoplatonic theurgy matters because of its impact on Julian and the later influence of its texts. Intellectually, it matters because it is a perfect illustration of the way in which Greek philosophy and religion could assimilate the challenges and opportunities posed by the sophisticated new ritual magic which had developed in Egypt. In the social context of its time, however, it was a very marginal phenomenon; one of the least popular and influential expressions of the late antique yearning for a human relationship with supreme divinity.

It is therefore beyond doubt that from the second century onward forms of paganism developed in the central and eastern Mediterranean world which differed in crucial aspects from those traditionally found in the regions covered by the Roman Empire. The main work of this essay, to suggest why they did develop in that form, and how much can be known of them, is now accomplished. It remains now to undertake its secondary purpose, of exploring the links and similarities between them and modern Paganism.

There can be no doubt that in several respects they bore a much closer resemblance to modern varieties of Paganism than the traditional religions of the pre-Christian ancient world. The resemblance is especially marked to Wicca, the longest-established and most influential of the modern traditions. It has always been noted that Wicca and other group-based forms of Pagan witchcraft resemble the mystery religions of late antiquity: relatively small numbers of people meeting in private to celebrate rites to particular deities and to progress through successive grades of initiation. The fact that the modern system is much more obviously derived from early modern Freemasonry than ancient religious societies does not weaken the force of the comparison. Another similarity between the late antique and the modern developments is that both venerate goddesses and gods associated with mighty forces of the natural world, and especially its vivifying and generative forces. There are very clear parallels between the rituals embodied in the Greek magical papyri and those of modern Pagan witchcraft: the careful preparation of a consecrated space; the emphasis on working tools; the employment of a religious context for operative magic; and (above all) the concept that divine energy can be drawn into solid objects and divine beings invoked into human beings to empower and inspire them. At times, also, the aims and methods of modern Pagan witchcraft seem close to those of theurgy (in the very general form in which the latter can be reconstructed): to use practices of ritual magic in order to assist a communion with the divine.

The question of whether any direct line of transmission exists between the two is large and difficult enough to require a wholly separate treatment; which will be attempted below. That of how far and how explicitly late antique texts exerted an influence on the modern development of Paganism also deserves a full-length study; but a brief preliminary sketch of one will be made now. If there was a single body of people which exerted an overwhelming influence on modern Paganism and ritual magic, it was the network of late Victorian occultists who formed themselves into the Hermetic Society and then the Hermetic Order of the Golden Dawn. It is not known that the former body, founded in the 1880s, worked any ritual magic. It was established, however, for the study of the European mystical inheritance, and its founder, Anna Kingsford, showed apparent signs in her (avowedly Christian) writings of the influence of Neoplatonism.

They preached the central importance of attempts to lead human souls back to union with the divine, leaving the limitations of the material world, and ascribed magic to a harmony of human and divine wills.[157] These passages sound very much like Iamblichus, though it is probable that also or instead they were influenced by the Hermetic texts after which her society was named, or even by oriental ideas filtered through theosophy.

The works of the leading members of the Golden Dawn show the same remarkable eclecticism as the order's rituals, and elements of late antique paganism appear in the resulting cocktail. Their importance varied tremendously with the individual concerned. The teachings of one of the most important founder-members, William Wynn Westcott, paid lip-service to the traditions that connected Freemasonry to the ancient mystery religions, but otherwise were almost wholly devoid of interest in paganism: their preoccupation was with masonic symbolism, the Cabbala, alchemy, astrology, divination and Rosicrucianism.[158] His partner and protégé in founding the order, Samuel Liddell Mathers, followed a different trajectory. His own initial enthusiasm was for the same subjects, but he displayed an increasing interest in complex ritual magic, and the texts historically associated with it. Although the most important of these were early modern, he drew also on those of the Greek magical papyri which had been edited by his time: the invocation that he prescribed for trainees to call on their Higher Genius or Holy Guardian Angel was taken straight from one of them.[159] As the 1890s progressed, and Mathers's leadership of the order became firmer, he and his wife Moina committed themselves to rites centred on deities and ritual trappings associated with late antique Egypt. As part of these they came to believe that divine force could be drawn into statues of deities, in the classic Egyptian manner, and that a single supreme god manifested in the form of individual deities charged with responsibility for different aspects of the universe. This also could be ascribed to Egyptian cosmology, although it has of course resonances with a much broader spectrum of later pagan monotheism.[160] In parallel with the Matherses, another leading member of the order, Florence Farr, was pursuing her own love affair with Egypt. Her concept of its magical traditions was based on an explicit blending of Iamblichus, the magical papyri and a Gnostic text, *Pistis Sophia*, which provided a developed version of the Memphite creation myth. In this, a Supreme Divine Essence had divided itself into a Great Father and Great Mother, whose children were the other deities and through whom emanated the rest of the universe. This system Farr termed 'Philosophical Christianity'.[161]

Neoplatonist influences became more obvious in the writings of a few prominent members of the successor orders of the Golden Dawn, in the 1930s. One of these was Israel Regardie, who extolled the work of Iamblichus,[162] He did so, however, in a work which was in general devoted to an exposition of Cabbala. A much more thoroughgoing recommendation of Neoplatonism as the key to magic was made by Charles Seymour. He was the leading intellectual influence on Dion Fortune's order of ritual magicians, the Fraternity of the Inner Light, between 1934 and 1938, and had made a first-hand study of Iamblichus, Proclus, Damascius and Psellus. From them he held up Neoplatonic theurgy as an ideal training for a magician, defining it as 'the combination of ritual and meditation in a properly prepared sanctuary, for the attainment of certain particular religious ends'. The actual system that he taught under this label was much more eclectic, reflecting the tradition of attempting to merge Greek, Egyptian, Hebrew and Indian religious motifs that was one of the main legacies of nineteenth-century occultism. None the less, he was exceptional in the prominence that he gave to Neoplatonists in his scheme, and the erudition with which he did so.[163] Very little of it seems to have rubbed off on his much more famous working partner, Dion Fortune herself, although he arguably had a great influence on her growing regard for ancient paganism. She did come to acknowledge the ancient deities as good and valid aspects of the One God. She also stated that the three most important of those aspects were Zeus, Pan and Helios, in a thoroughly late antique manner, and came close to a duotheism of the sort found in the Memphite cosmology by declaring that all gods are one god and all goddesses are one goddess, both produced by the 'one initiator'. She later shifted to terming a great goddess, called Isis or Nature, the ruler and giver of life to the material world under the One God. All this seems to be derived ultimately from late Graeco-Roman or Graeco-Egyptian sources, through Seymour or not, but it has none of his precise recommendation of the Neoplatonists.[164]

Traces of the latter are rare in Wicca itself. A few appear in the books of Gerald Gardner, the person who first publicised the religion and may have been the leading figure in its development. In the one that comprehensively announced the existence of Wicca, *Witchcraft Today*, he refers to Porphyry, Iamblichus and Proclus, but only glancingly, and cites Iamblichus's work in the bibliography without quoting it.[165] More important is his quotation of a section of Salutius in his last book, *The Meaning of Witchcraft*, which he uses to answer charges that witches are or were Satanists. By deploying Salutius's explanation for the existence of evil in the cosmos, as a wilful turning away by humans from a divinity that was essentially good, he denied that there was any need to believe in a cosmic force of evil at all. He also praised Salutius for his affirmation of belief in reincarnation and in an equivalent to the Hindu law of karma, and declared that his writings might be taken as 'a general statement' of the creed of Wicca.[166] Whether Salutius himself was a Neoplatonist is a matter for debate, and Gardner's use of his work was directed to the specific end of finding an alternative to the dualistic view of the universe, as a battleground between good and bad supernatural entities. None the less, it is an impressive and forceful use of a late antique author in a Wiccan text. It is also unique. In general, the thrust of Gardner's writing was to situate Pagan witchcraft at the centre of a new sort of eclecticism. Instead of the mixture of classical Mediterranean, ancient Near Eastern and Indian traditions familiar in modern ritual magic, he claimed for Wicca a thoroughly European heritage in which Graeco-Roman mystery religions had been blended with tribal rites from the north and west of the continent dating back to the Palaeolithic.

The lack of a clear theology for Wicca, and the diversity of influences present in the work of its adherents, make it hardly surprising that elements of Neoplatonism appear in a few of its liturgical texts, together with echoes of a huge range of other traditions. When Doreen Valiente wrote its most famous representation of female divinity, the Charge of the Goddess, in the 1950s, she made this deity one from whom 'all things proceed', and to whom 'all things must return'.[167] This is a Neoplatonic deity, and also a Hermetic one, clearly recognisable from a range of late classical texts. A later and less ubiquitous Wiccan text, the Dryghtyn or Dryghton Prayer, expresses belief in a single, genderless, eternal divinity which is the original source of all things. It goes on to refer to the more familiar deities and elemental spirits of the religion, and the implication seems to be that they have emanated from or been created by the primal entity, to which is given an Anglo-Saxon term, the Dryghtyn or 'dread lord'. How this occurred, and what the present relationship of humans to the supreme being should be, is not made clear, and – at least in its British homeland – the prayer never became a standard component of Wiccan liturgy. It seems to have the status of an optional extra, and appeared in the 1960s.[168]

Against these points of contact between Wicca and varieties of ancient pagan monotheism can be set a range of contrasts and differences. Gardner established one, resoundingly, in the same book as that in which he praised Salutius. He stated that witches 'quite realise that there must be some great "Prime Mover", some Supreme Deity; but they think that if It gives them no means of knowing It, it is because It does not want to be known; also, possibly, at our present stage of evolution we are incapable of understanding It. So It has appointed what might be called various Under-Gods, who manifest as the tribal gods of different peoples.' He listed a selection of these from the ancient world, culminating in 'the Horned God and the Goddess of the witches', and added that the latter 'can see no reason why each people should not worship their national gods'. At another point of the same work, he commented that other groups of occultists worked with Egyptian or Greek deities, 'but I cannot think that these contacts are as powerful here as they would be on their native soil; whereas the divinities of the Craft of the Wica [Gardner's spelling] are the Ancient Ones of Britain, part of the land itself'.169 This pays lip-service to an ultimate monotheism of the fourth-century kind, only to dismiss it as of no practical value and to enjoin what amounts in practice to a radical polytheism, in which people venerate deities traditionally associated with their own lands and cultures. It makes a very striking rejection of the Neoplatonist and Hermetic yearning for reunion with the One.

In 1989 Vivianne Crowley published an account of Wicca that included the first attempt since Gardner to relate its view of divinity to ancient philosophy. This recognised an overlap between its concept of the divine and that of Neoplatonism, but also registered two major differences. The first was that more Wiccans regarded divinity as being immanent throughout the universe and within human beings than something existing outside the created world; in this sense they were closer to the ancient Stoics than to Neoplatonists. She identified herself as finding that the inner human self was both immanent and transcendent, as it inhabited the material world and transcended it by reincarnation; but this was only a compromise with Neoplatonism. The other difference was that, although some Wiccans 'may see the divine as ultimately one, within the divine consciousness we see a duality'.170 This last point is crucial: the concept of a supreme and primal entity, central to Neoplatonism and other pagan monotheisms, was an optional one for Wicca, and perhaps a minority opinion, while the recognition of the cosmos as flowing between the complementary polarity of a goddess and a god was fundamental. Monotheism has been far more obvious in modern pagan witchcraft in its feminist form than in Wicca. The most celebrated exponent of feminist witchcraft is the Californian witch, Starhawk, whose view of the nature of deity received its fullest expression in 1987: 'To Witches, the cosmos is the living body of the Goddess, in whose being we all partake, who encompasses us and is immanent within us. We call her Goddess not to narrowly define her gender, but as a continual reminder that what we value is life brought into the world ... She has infinite names and guises, many of them male.' 171

Even this concept of the divine and its place in the cosmos, however, has a considerable difference from that of the monotheists of the late ancient world, and the distinction is founded in their attitudes to the material universe. The defining tenet of Gnosticism was that the visible world had been created by an inferior or evil deity, and that a tragic event had trapped humans within material bodies. The whole point of its revelation was to provide a means of escape to the world of spirit. The Hermetic texts differed over whether the earthly world was good or bad, but were united in claiming to show a way by which human souls could leave it, to return to their true home in the divine realm of the One God, beyond the stars.[172] The same pattern is found in the writings of the Neoplatonists. To Plotinus the visible world was the creation of a lesser deity, a place where goodness mingled with the evil of matter, which hindered the self-realisation of the soul. He too thought that the latter should seek an ascent to the heavens, and the One.[173] The Chaldean Oracles, likewise, represented matter as something that contaminated the soul, and had to be left behind for the upper worlds of pure light.[174] Iamblichus struggled to deny that matter was automatically bad or ugly, but consistently stated that evil and ugliness could occur only on the material plane, and joined the chorus of advice to quit it.[175] Such attitudes inevitably rubbed off on the lifestyles of believers. The theurgist emperor Julian chose a life of chastity.[176] The atmosphere of the fifth- and sixth-century Athenian academy is generally recognised as being that of a pagan monastery, characterised by sobriety and prayer, a simple diet and a view of sexual intercourse that legitimised it only for purposes of procreation and admired those who rejected it altogether.[177] Nothing could be further from the modern Pagan celebration of the physical world and its pleasures as a manifestation of divinity.

This contrast is linked to another: that not only are modern Pagans inclined to find the natural world of matter to be beautiful and sacred, but they tend to credit spiritual, supernatural and divine entities of all kinds with being either morally neutral or actively benevolent. To Iamblichus and the authors of the magical papyri, as to all or almost all the people of the ancient world, the earth and its underworld teemed with spirits that were at best dangerous and at worst actively malevolent. Salutius may have rejected the concept of a major divine principle of evil in the cosmos, but he certainly believed in demons, to whom the deities abandoned humans who committed evil.[178] Modern Paganism seems to have no concept of an innate malevolence in the natural world, and little sense of serious danger from the supernatural. Gardner prescribed a view of deities as beings who are themselves given form and power by human believers, and who need to work actively with the latter in order to maintain that power. The relationship between human and divine in ritual is therefore a reciprocal one.[179] This view illustrates vividly the almost incomparably greater confidence of twentieth-century people when dealing with the cosmos. No wonder Wiccans routinely ignore the warnings of Iamblichus, and invoke major deities into each other's bodies. No wonder, also, modern paganism is almost wholly lacking in any sense of a need to propitiate the divine, a need expressed in the universal ancient pagan custom of sacrifice. One of the purposes of the works of Iamblichus and Salutius was to defend this, even in its most controversial form, of offering up the life-blood of animals.[180]

The flow of religious transaction in modern Paganism is therefore exactly opposite to that of Gnosticism, Hermetism and Neoplatonism – and Christianity, which shares with them important aspects of the late antique thought-world. The aim in all of the latter was to free the human soul from a contaminated and dangerous earthly realm and enable it to ascend to the heavens and the realm of the one primal and original deity. The aim of modern Pagan witchcraft is to draw down divine power from the heavens, and from other parts of the cosmos, to enrich and improve existence in an earthly realm which is in essence beautiful and good and itself saturated in divinity, and within which humans may be indefinitely reborn.

In this, when all the reservations are made about differences of practice and of attitude, Wicca and its relations still bear more resemblance to the rites of the Greek magical papyri than to anything else in the ancient world. It is to them, and the Hellenised Egyptians who produced them, that modern Pagan witchcraft may look for its nearest ancient kin; as I suggested a dozen years ago. In that sense one of the clearest-sighted observers of the late antique world was not a pagan but one of the most vehement and venerated of its Christian churchmen, John Chrysostom. In one of his invectives, he summed up Egypt as 'mother of magicians, who discovered and passed on to others every kind of witchcraft'.[181]

5

Paganism in the Lost Centuries

In 1991 Ludo Milis edited a collection of essays by continental European scholars entitled *The Pagan Middle Ages*.[1] In his introduction, he suggested that the title might be taken as a contradiction in terms; the solution to this apparent problem, as clear to him as to any scholar of the period, was that it depends on what terms you adopt. During the late twentieth century it gradually became apparent that, all over Europe, the conversion of the rulers of a medieval state to Christianity was followed within a relatively short time by the formal acceptance of the new religion by their subjects. There is no evidence of the long-term persistence of paganism as an organised religion of resistance, meeting in secret or associated with military or political rebellion, once the ruling family of a particular kingdom had accepted the Christian faith and outlawed the traditional ways. This effectively means that paganism as a formal system of religion vanished from Mediterranean Europe after the sixth century, from the western and northern parts of the continent after the eleventh, and from the north-eastern portions after the fourteenth. Among the Saami nomads of the north-eastern regions of Scandinavia, it may have lingered into the seventeenth.

Milis and his collaborators, however, used the term in a different sense. Their preoccupation – and that of several other historians of the middle ages during the 1990s – was with the manner in which its society assimilated, rejected or disputed the cultural heritage of pagan antiquity. All over Europe, the pre-Christian religions bequeathed a rich inheritance of beliefs, practices, remedies, stories, symbols, images, ideas and forms. At all social levels and both within and without the Christian Churches, a constant process of adaptation, negotiation, disputation, utilisation and condemnation took place, as different groups and different individuals among them made their own relationships with this inheritance. Intellectual, religious, political and social elites struggled to define and police what could be taken directly from the old paganism into a Christian faith and society, what could be absorbed after some remodelling and redefinition, and what should be rejected and proscribed outright. Having made these decisions, often with some inconsistencies and subsequent changes of attitude, the elites concerned had the problem of making them effective.

The purpose of this chapter is to trace this process in the case of those particular forms of paganism that appeared in the Roman Empire towards the end of the ancient world, and have been noted as bearing most resemblance to the religions of the modern Pagan revival. Between the early nineteenth and the mid twentieth centuries there was a significant scholarly tradition of belief that an active and organised paganism had survived in Europe throughout the Christian middle ages. It was conceived as having been essentially a resistance movement of the common people, especially in the countryside, and (as seen) was disproved by more thorough research since the 1960s.[2] The present investigation moves through a different world, that of the scholarly elites. Late pagan monotheism, Neoplatonism, theurgy and Graeco-Egyptian ritual magic were all cultural forms that were conveyed by texts and developed by intellectuals. It remains to be asked now what was made of them during the succeeding thousand years, by people operating within societies restructured by the new monotheistic faiths of Christianity and Islam. In the process, it may be possible to answer the larger question of whether they provided any continuity of tradition during this long period that opposed, challenged or compromised the norms of the dominant religions. Did they, to any extent, represent a 'survival' of ancient paganism?

One obvious place in which to begin such an analysis is that in which historians have often identified a unique example of ancient paganism persisting long into the medieval period as an organised and self-conscious religion. It lies far beyond the boundaries of Europe, at the northern edge of the Fertile Crescent of the Middle East where Syria and Mesopotamia meet. It is the city of Carrhae, known in the middle ages as Harran, which in the classical period was an important eastern outpost of the Roman Empire and is now a ruin in the desert where the modern state of Turkey approaches its border with Syria. What is certain is that during the early middle ages it became the home of a religious sect that could be distinguished sharply from both Islam and Christianity, and drew explicitly on Hermetic and Platonic traditions. Beyond that, all is conjectural.

One of the enduring puzzles is how Harran developed into such a remarkable community in the first place. An answer that has recently acquired distinguished academic support is that it became the permanent refuge of the Neoplatonist academy of Athens. It is undisputed fact that in 529 the academy was closed by the Emperor Justinian, anxious to extinguish such a notable centre of surviving paganism. Led by Damascius, its members emigrated to Persia with other Neoplatonist scholars, but returned to the Roman Empire after a few years, under safe conduct. Where they went then is not known. In the 1980s a French academic, Michel Tardieu, suggested that they settled at Harran, and so established the city's tradition of tenacious, philosophically based paganism. His argument was founded partly on the later beliefs credited to the Harranians, and partly on the writings of one of the exiles, Simplicius, produced after the return from Persia. He detected in the latter references to calendar systems and religious beliefs that he felt could only be found together at Harran.[3] This idea was immediately adopted and amplified by a colleague of his at Paris, Ilstraut Hadot, and then by another French scholar, Pierre Chuvin. By the early 1990s it had secured enthusiastic support in the English-speaking world from Polymnia Athanassiadi and more measured acceptance by Garth Fowden.[4] It was then, however, subjected to serious criticism. The biggest objection to the theory was that Simplicius had depended for parts of his work on texts so scarce that they would only have been found in libraries as great as those of the main centres of the Greek-speaking world, such as Constantinople, Athens or Alexandria, and not in a frontier post like Harran. It was also pointed out that references to Syrian and Mesopotamian phenomena in the work of Simplicius could merely mean that he had travelled through those lands, not that he had settled there. More bluntly, it was declared that Tardieu had just misread him.[5] By the end of the decade even Athanassiadi could admit that the theory that the Neoplatonists settled at Harran was 'controversial'.[6] It seems to have acquired the status of an unverifiable hypothesis.

This result is bound up with the basic problem that very little is known about late antique Harran. It is certain that its native cults were of a range of deities identifiable from other parts of Syria and Mesopotamia, most of whom were related to planets: above all, the moon god Sin. It is certain also that by the sixth century it had acquired a reputation as a centre for surviving paganism, although it is not quite clear how much this was fostered by its traditional regional rival, the city of Edessa, as a means of disparaging it. Under Roman rule Edessa itself had a cultural life rich and complex enough to produce an original thinker, Bardaisan, who combined Christianity, Gnosticism, astrology, Greek philosophy, Hermetism and native paganism into a view of the cosmos in which a creator deity embodied lesser divinities as the heavenly bodies and sent out his Word to redeem humanity. If nearby Harran had an intelligensia as sophisticated, one need look no further for the roots of its medieval reputation; but no equivalent records survive from it in this period.[7] There were definitely many pagans left in Harran by the end of the sixth century, when the emperor Maurice ordered its bishop to conduct a savage persecution of them that resulted in a spate of executions and conversions.[8] Only about forty years later, the Arabs conquered the region.

This strongly suggests that there were still pagans present in or around the city when it became absorbed into the Arab Empire, and this is exactly what the Arab sources themselves say.[9] There is also an episode recorded at Harran in 737, that features the chief of the citizens as divining from the entrails of an animal in a thoroughly traditional pagan manner.[10] All these references, however, occur in texts dating from centuries after the events concerned, and may reflect either accurate tradition or back-projection of later beliefs concerning the city. A similar problem attends the single source extant that may date from the city in the early Arab period. This is a collection of prophecies credited to a Harranian called Baba. If he lived at all, it was well before the sixth century, when he is quoted as author of one of a list of pagan declarations allegedly predicting the coming of Christ. The collection, later compiled in his name, warns of the coming destruction of various cities to the benefit of Harran and its pagan deities. It survives apparently in two fragments, one in Arabic and one in Syriac, both dating from the twelfth and thirteenth centuries. The scholar who has carried out the most thorough analysis of them held out the hope that they reflected an original pagan text from the early Arab rule over Harran. He admitted, however, that this could never be 'fully certain', and that both fragments might be separate forgeries produced by later Muslim and Christian writers.[11]

The absence of contemporary evidence for the first two centuries of Arab rule over Harran exacerbates two related problems. One is that pagans should not have found their new Muslim masters any more tolerant than the Emperor Maurice, for the monotheism of Islam is even more insistent than that of Christianity. Polytheism is regarded by it as the greatest of all sins, and the Arabs outlawed it wherever they took power. On the other hand, certain forms of late paganism could be presented as monotheism, as described, and it is possible that their practitioners at Harran had greater success in pleading their case to the Arabs than their co-religionists elsewhere had achieved with Christians. Islam was predisposed to look favourably on the city because of its biblical association with Abraham, honoured as a prophet among Muslims, Christians and Jews; it is possible that its pagans may have traded on that link. The other problem is that we know very little about the early Arab Empire in general. Its imperial ruling family, the Umayyads, were the leaders of Islam, and yet archaeologists were surprised to excavate a bathhouse built by some of them at Qasr al-'Amra in Syria and find the walls painted with scenes from pagan Greek mythology.[12] It is possible that their attitude to Graeco-Syrian paganism itself was more tolerant than has been thought. Certainly they liked Harran. The last of their caliphs, Marwan II, actually made it the capital of the empire for six years, ended by the fall of his dynasty in 750. One of his predecessors, Umar II (682–720), is said to have transferred the medical school of Alexandria there. Around the end of his reign, the philosophical school of Alexandria apparently moved to Syria.[13] If the Umayyad caliphs were indeed transplanting Hellenistic philosophers and scientists to Harran, this would in itself suffice to account for the city's subsequent reputation as a centre for both.

That reputation is firmly recorded from the mid ninth century, when the Harranians who professed a religion different to Christianity, Judaism and Islam became known as 'Sabians'. This was a name with a considerable resonance among Muslims, for Muhammed himself had cited it in a list of faiths that, although not as pure in revelation as Islam, were sufficiently grounded in it to deserve toleration by true believers; the main others were, of course, those of Christians and Jews. By the ninth century, nobody seems to have been sure whom Muhammed had meant by this term, and scholars still debate the issue.[14] From the mid tenth century a story circulated that the pagan Harranians had adopted it deliberately in the year 830, to avoid persecution by the caliph Ma'mun. It was first found in the work of a hostile, Christian, source, and experts remain divided over whether it can be accepted.[15] What is certain is that, from the ninth century onwards, Arab scholars took a considerable interest in the so-called Sabians of Harran, which persisted for half a millennium. If their origins are mysterious, then so is their eventual fate. In 933 a decree was issued ordering them to convert to Islam, but a visitor to Harran in the following decade found that they survived as a community with recognised leaders and a single remaining public temple. Toleration of them was allegedly renewed in the late tenth century, when Harran became the capital of a petty Islamic state. Later medieval Arab writers agreed that it was finally revoked, and the last temple destroyed, at some point in the eleventh century. One said that it was in 1032, when Harran accepted Egyptian overlordship; another declared that it took place after a rebellion in 1083.[16] During the 1100s the city became a vital link in the Islamic resistance to the Crusades, joining Syrian to Mesopotamian Muslims, and as such was much favoured by the militantly Islamic Ayyubid dynasty that eventually ruled both regions. When a Spanish Muslim, ibn Jubayr, visited Harran in the 1180s, he found it devoted to his faith, without a physical trace or memory of the Sabians. Another visitor, in 1242, learned of the reputed sites of two of their former temples; but they themselves were long gone.[17]

The Sabians of Harran are therefore recorded as active in a period of just two hundred years, between the mid ninth and the mid eleventh centuries. Several sources for them survive from this span of time, and more from later periods when the accounts were presumably retrospective. Not one, however, was beyond doubt produced by a Sabian author. Most were the work of Christians or Muslims, and all may have been. The difficulties are typified by one of the most important bodies of evidence, the *Fihrist el-Ulum* of Muhammed ibn Ishaq ibn al-Nadim. This was a compendium of human knowledge, written in the 980s, and included a section on the Harran Sabians. Al-Nadim had no first-hand knowledge of them, but compiled his account from older sources which, like the good scholar that he was, he quoted entire and with attribution.[18] The first was taken from the work of a Muslim scholar, Ahmad ibn al-Tayyib al-Sarakhsi, who in turn quoted some material from the first Islamic philosopher, al-Kindi. In the mid ninth century the latter had seen one of their books, *Discourses of Hermes on Unity*, ostensibly written by Hermes for his son, which sounds exactly like one of the classic Hermetic tracts produced in late Roman Egypt. He thought it excellent, in that it testified to the essential unity of deity, with one eternal creator who had sent out apostles for the guidance of humanity, including Hermes and Aghathadimun (the latter a garbled name for a Graeco-Egyptian protective spirit). Al-Sarakhsi added that these people believed that salvation was provided for all humanity, although the wicked would have to endure a period of punishment. They all prayed towards the cardinal points of the compass, six times in each twenty-four hours, offered animal sacrifices to the planetary deities four times a month, and had a strict system of social and dietary taboos.

The second source was the Christian tale of how they had adopted the name 'Sabians' to avoid persecution in 830. The third was an extract from a book called *Al-Hatifi*, which was clearly a rather sensational account of the magic allegedly practised by them, including the making of pendants, signet stones, pictures, knots and incantations. It alleged that they regularly carried out the ritual murder of men who 'resembled Utarid' (Mercury), capturing their victims by deception and using their severed heads as oracles. Another of al-Nadim's sources was an anonymous list of Harranian deities, a curious mixture of recognisable ancient local goddesses and gods and Hebrew, Arab and other Semitic spirits. It culminated with a description of a religious festival, 'the return of the Idol to the Water'. He also had a set of notes on their alleged customs, including the assertion that the Harranians had formerly been divided into sects, one of which always remained indoors and shaved their heads and another of which would not wear gold, or red boots. He added a list of their headmen, from the late seventh to the early tenth centuries, giving the impression that they had formed a recognisable community during that span of time, but that its official status had been terminated around the 930s. He had also obtained

1. The Round Table in the Great Hall of Winchester Castle, with King Arthur surrounded by twenty-four knights. Rather than dating from the fifth century, it in fact dates from the reign of Henry III. The portrait of Arthur was added under Henry VIII. (*English Heritage*)

2. 'Camelot, from the east and west', located at South Cadbury (Somerset), in William Musgrave's *Antiquitates Britanno-Belgicae* (Exeter, 1719).

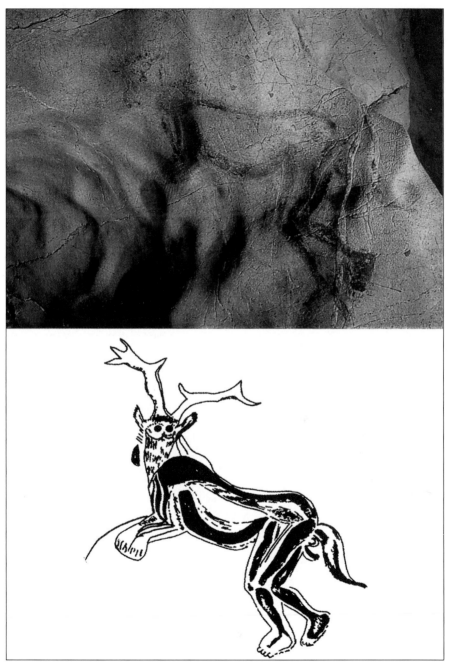

3. The eye of the beholder. Compare a recent photograph of the so-called 'Sorcerer' of the Trois-Frères cave with the constantly-reprinted drawing of it by the Abbé Breuil. (*R. Bégouën and H. Breuil*)

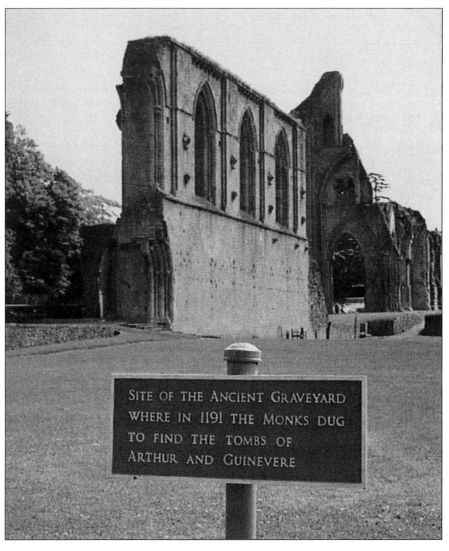

SITE OF THE ANCIENT GRAVEYARD
WHERE IN 1191 THE MONKS DUG
TO FIND THE TOMBS OF
ARTHUR AND GUINEVERE

4. Glastonbury Abbey, the site of the 'discovery' of the tombs of King Arthur and Queen Guinevere. In 1191.

5. Merlin building Stonehenge. (*British Library*)

And this the form of mighty Hand sitting on Albions cliffs
Before the face of Albion, a mighty threatning Form .
His bosom wide & shoulders huge overspreading wondrous
Bear Three strong sinewy Necks & Three awful & terrible Heads
Three Brains in contradictory council brooding incessantly.
Neither during to put in act its councils, fearing each other.
Therefore rejecting Ideas as nothing & holding all Wisdom
To consist. in the agreements & disagreents of Ideas.
Plotting to devour Albions Body of Humanity & Love .

Such Form the aggregate of the Twelve Sons of Albion took; & such
Their appearance when combind: but often by birth pangs & loud groans
They divide to Twelve: the key-bones & the chest dividing in pain
Disclose a hideous orifice: thence issuing the Giant-brood
Arise as the smoke of the furnace. shaking the rocks from sea to sea.
And there they combine into Three Forms. named Bacon & Newton & Locke.
In the Oak Groves of Albion which overspread all the Earth .

Imputing Sin & Righteousness to Individuals: Rahab
Sat deep within him hid: his Feminine Power unreveald
Brooding Abstract Philosophy. to destroy Imagination. the Divine-
Humanity A Three-fold Wonder: feminine: most beautiful: Three-fold
Each within other. On her white marble & even Neck. her Heart
Inorbd and bonified: with Locks of shadowing modesty. shining
Over her beautiful Female features. soft flourishing in beauty
Beams mild, all love and all perfection. that when the lips
Recieve a kiss from Gods or Men. a threefold kiss returns
From the pressd loveliness: so her whole immortal form three-fold
Three-fold embrace returns: consuming lives of Gods & Men
In fires of beauty melting them as gold & silver in the furnace
Her Brain enlabyrinths the whole heaven of her bosom & loins
To put in act what her Heart wills: O who can withstand her power
Her name is Vala in Eternity: in Time her name is Rahab
The Starry Heavens all were fled from the mighty limbs of Albion . His

6. A Mythological Trilithon, from William Blake's *Jerusalem*, which contains many references to Stonehenge and to Druids. The three figures are probably Bacon, Newton and Locke. (*British Library*)

The Wicker Image.

W. D. fe.

7. Wicker figure, from Aylett Sammes, *Britannia antiqua illustrata* (1676), associated the Druids with human sacrifice.

8. Winston Churchill at his induction into the Albion Lodge of the Ancient Order of Druids at Blenheim, 13 August 1908. (*Oxford Times*)

a mutilated extract allegedly translated into (bad) Arabic from one of their books and describing parts of the mysteries in which their priests initiated their young men into their religion. The rites are dedicated to 'the Lord', apparently the 'al-Bughadhariyuin' in whose shrine they are held, and consist of the exposition of (unspecified) allegories and the consumption of special food and drink. One of the rites is dedicated to 'the Seven', and another to 'the devil and idols', and celebrates 'the dogs, the ravens and the ants' as 'brothers'. The 'Seven' may be the planetary deities, but they may correspond to the seven evil spirits well known in ancient Mesopotamian magical tradition.[19] Likewise, ravens were an initiatory grade in the ancient mystery religion of Mithras, but with dogs and ants were commonly regarded with distaste in Middle Eastern cultures, so the reference may be part of a process of calumny intended by the whole text.

The most complex document copied into the Sabian section of the *Fihrist* is a list of the feasts allegedly celebrated at Harran, made by a Christian. It reveals an elaborate calendar of annual festivals, month by month, and adds the assertion that the Harranians believed that the seven main heavenly bodies (sun, moon and planets) were benevolent or malevolent deities who had emotions and amours equivalent to those of humans. Certainly the divinities named in the calendar correspond at times to planets, and to recognisable pre-Christian cults from the region. The cumulative effect of the list, however, is to portray a richness and flamboyance of pagan celebration remarkable for a city under Islamic rule, and especially one where a caliph himself had resided. Furthermore, it provides a very unpleasant overall impression of the religion concerned. Several of the feasts are in honour of evil spirits. At one the priest prays for the destruction of Islam and Christianity; in another he 'walks like a dog' to retrieve burning arrows in a rite of divination. There is regular animal sacrifice, something abominable to Christians and Muslims alike, including the burning alive of cattle and sheep hung up by clamps. One festival even insists on the ritual murder and consumption of a human child. It is impossible to tell how much of this is libel, and to what period of the city's history the calendar is supposed to refer. As has regularly been noticed by scholars, it can be compared with another ostensible list of Harranian festivals, copied into one of the books of the scientist Abu al-Rayhan Muhammed ibn Ahmad al-Biruni during the early eleventh century. It is credited to a different author, and although there is some overlap with that in al-Nadim there are also considerable differences. Once again the sequence of celebration is intensive and public, with plenty of sacrifice to a mixture of ancient pagan deities, demons and completely unidentifiable beings. Both lists have some correspondences to the festivals mentioned in another of al-Nadim's sources, though again there are differences, and neither of the others convey any better sense of the date at which all this activity was supposed to be carried on.[20] It may be a representation of Harran at a particular period of Islamic rule, or in a partly or wholly mythical past. None of these feasts, likewise, appear to reflect the Hermetic devotion to the supreme being and prophets mentioned by al-Kindi, the only author who explicitly used a Harranian text, although one that is cited in al-Nadim's pages at fourth hand. This hodge-podge of information, all suspect in different ways and often conflicting, is typical of our data for the Sabians of Harran, differing only from the norm in being so extensive and well recorded.

One of the most frustrating features of the evidence is the loss of testimony from individuals who were very well placed to provide it. One of these has already been mentioned: Abu Yusuf Ya'qub ibn Ishaq al-Kindi, who died in about the year 870, was based at Baghdad, and created the tradition of Muslim philosophy. He did so by setting his co-religionists the task of recovering the work of the Greek sages and then attempting to complete it. It has been mentioned that, as part of this work, he read a Hermetic text from Harran and thought it profound. He and his circle also translated works by Aristotle, Plato, Plotinus and Proclus, among other Greek and Hellenistic philosophers, and it seems that one of Plato's dialogues was also provided by a Harranian. One analysis of al-Kindi's main surviving exposition of philosophy emphasises, however, the almost complete lack of ideas in it taken from either Aristotle, Plotinus or Athenian Neoplatonism, and the considerable number that reflect instead concepts of Plato filtered through Hermetism and Gnosticism. Given his citation of a Harranian Hermetic treatise, this suggests again that Harran was a chief source of his ideas, but the matter cannot be determined.[21] In this respect, the most significant work attributed to al-Kindi may be one that combines the theory of innate sympathies within the cosmos – found in Egyptian magic, Bolus, Hermetism and late Neoplatonism – with the emphasis on heavenly bodies that was attributed to Harranian Sabianism. It suggests that all earthly affairs are influenced by stellar celestial rays that interact with mundane forms, sounds, images, gestures and fumigations; and that magicians could manipulate the world by producing such interactions. If al-Kindi took this idea from Harranians, then another clue is provided to the nature of the ideas peculiar to the city, but there is no evidence of this. Worse, there is actually no proof that he wrote the book concerned. It survives only in a thirteenth-century Latin translation that attributes authorship to him. The title corresponds to an Arabic one in a list of al-Kindi's works cited by al-Nadim, but there is no absolute proof that the extant manuscript was not produced by a later writer who credited it to the great philosopher.[22]

Another major scholar operating in Baghdad around the time of al-Kindi was Abu al-Hasan Tabith (or Thabit) ibn Qurrah (d. 901). He matters because he came from Harran himself, allegedly leaving the city because of sectarian disputes among the Sabians there. Once established in the imperial capital, he became a major influence on Arab science, achieving renown as a mathematician, logician, astronomer, astrologer and doctor, and founding a dynasty of scholars. Until his death he adhered to his native religion, and wrote five books on it. Had these survived, then we would probably be able to solve most of the puzzles hanging over the Sabians of Harran, but all have perished. It was known that one was on 'the laws of Hermes', which strengthens the probability that Hermetism represented a major strand in Harranian thought. He also, however, was credited with discussing Platonism.[23] Four centuries later, an author quoted from one of his books a ringing declaration that, despite much pressure, Harran had 'never been defiled with the error of Nazareth' (Christianity). He went on to call his people 'the heirs and transmitters of *hanputho*, which is honoured gloriously in this world. Lucky is he who bears the burden with a sure hope for the sake of *hanputho* ... Who has made manifest the secret sciences? On whom has dawned the divinity which gives divinations and teaches the knowledge of future events except the wise men of the *hanpe*?' The problem, here, of course, concerns the meaning of the Syriac terms *hanputho* and *hanpe*, which seem to convey a sense of 'pure religion'. They have been translated simply as 'paganism', but it has also been suggested that Thabit was associating Harran with the faith of its most revered resident, Abraham.[24] It may be suggested here that the most likely sense in which he employed the terms was to signify the cultural achievements of ancient Hellenistic civilisation in general, because he listed cities, harbours and the sciences among the creations for which *hanputho* was to be credited. This would fit neatly into the quest for the recovery of Greek learning that was the central intellectual programme in Baghdad at his time.

As well as his few books on religion and philosophy, Thabit wrote almost 170 on scientific subjects, which all may also be lost. The possible survivors are a group of tracts on astronomy, astrology and astral magic (that using the power of heavenly bodies), all translated from Arabic into Latin in the twelfth century. At that time they were attributed to Thabit, and one in particular, *De imaginibus*, was associated with him. This was a work devoted mainly to the fabrication and use of magical statuettes, using rings, seals and conjurations in harmony with the movements of planets and stars. Once empowered, the figures could be used for a range of purposes from driving away snakes and finding missing objects to destroying cities. The style has suggested to some a ninth-century date of composition, putting

it firmly in Thabit's own time, and the apparent match with al-Kindi's
reputed work on the effect of heavenly rays might strongly suggest a common
origin for both in a tradition of celestial magic special to Harran. The
modern editors, however, have declared that 'there is no test by which the
authorship can be determined'. The other tracts in the group also deal with
the effect of heavenly configurations on material objects and the means by
which they can be used to empower words and objects to achieve magical
ends. One, concerned with the making of seals and other engraved objects,
was specifically credited at times to Thabit, but it is not in the same style
as *De imaginibus*.[25] Certainly Thabit was just the most famous product of
a rich tradition of scientific teaching and learning at Harran, especially
devoted to mathematics, astronomy and medicine, which strengthens the
notion that the Umayyad caliphs had transplanted a school or schools there
from Alexandria. His own descendants were famous physicians at Baghdad.
In the tenth century other Harranians became respected doctors and historians in the imperial city, while Muslim scholars went to study at Harran.
In the early eleventh century, Spanish Muslims still visited the city to learn
medicine and mathematics there.[26]

The only one of these intellectual tourists to leave an account was Abu
al-Hasan ibn Husayn al-Mas'udi, a celebrated traveller and historian who
passed through Harran in the 940s. He spoke to a number of the learned
men of the Sabians and saw their last surviving temple. Frustratingly, he
recorded almost nothing of what he heard and saw. He did think it noteworthy to say that they vehemently denied making blood sacrifices or
practising divination, though he also divided the Harranian Sabians into
philosophers and a vulgar multitude who indeed may have engaged in such
practices; the scholars had their own meeting-house, a building distinct
from the temple. He noted a quotation from Plato on the door-knocker of
the meeting-house, translating either as 'who knows his own essence
becomes divine' or 'to know the divine is also to honour it'. The same
phrase was also quoted by two Neoplatonist philosophers from late antique
Alexandria, which might be taken to support further a connection between
Harran and that city. Al-Mas'udi also asserted that the Harranian philosophers honoured certain prophets, above all Hermes, whom they identified
with the Muslim Idris, the Hebrew Enoch and the Greek Orpheus. He
thought that they believed in the emanation of the cosmos from a creator
deity, and noted that they abstained from certain foods, such as pork,
chicken and beans.[27]

Once again, most of al-Mas'udi's works are lost, and it is possible that
he enlarged on what he found at Harran in some of those now missing.
In another sense, enough of what he wrote on the subject has survived to

confuse rather than clarify matters. He states that the Harranian Sabians had seven temples, each dedicated to a planetary deity who also represented an 'intellectual essence'. Each was in a different shape, associated with the deity concerned, and all contained mysteries and symbols that were hidden from outsiders.[28] The statement is in the present tense, suggesting that these places were in operation during his visit, yet conflicts directly with his other assertion that only one holy place of the Sabians remained operative by that time, with no particular dedication. It is hard to imagine the Umayyad caliphs or their provincial governors allowing the survival of such a large number of temples under their rule, representing between them a flagrant affirmation of polytheism, however covered by an assertion of ultimate monotheism and by a set of cosmic abstractions. Nor would such a situation have readily been tolerated in the pre-Islamic period by Justinian or Maurice. It is not clear, therefore, whether al-Mas'udi was describing actual structures or a system of buildings that had existed in a historical or mythical past. The issue is complicated still further by his quotation of a poem by a Harranian magistrate (apparently a Muslim), composed about forty years before his time and describing a temple that had stood near one of the city gates. This was dedicated to 'Azar, father of Abraham', linking Sabianism to Hebrew, Christian and Islamic tradition, but the poem asserted that it had underground chambers in which were placed idols of the planetary deities. Hidden human guardians made their voices seem to proceed from these during the initiation ceremonies of children, terrifying the latter and so confirming them in their faith.[29] Once again, this may be an objective account, or a libel against a rival religion.

Another much-quoted source from the period in which the Sabians of Harran flourished consists of the writings of a group known as the Ikhwan al-Safa, usually translated as 'the Pure Brethren' but rendered by some experts as 'the Faithful Companions'. They flourished in the tenth or eleventh centuries, probably at Basra in southern Iraq, at the opposite end of Meso-potamia from Harran. Together they attempted to produce a compendium of all human knowledge. The section on religion declares that all human doctrines have utility in teaching reason and imparting divine wisdom, and the system that it expounds is correspondingly eclectic. It is a compound of various mystical strains of Islam with Buddhism, Manicheanism and Greek philosophy, in which elements of Hermetism, Pythagoreanism, Aris-totle and Neoplatonism are apparently visible. In making this synthesis it explicitly acknowledges an intellectual debt to the Sabians, not merely as heirs to the Greeks but as their teachers. It declares Pythagoras himself to have been a native of Harran, and that the Greeks gained some ideas from the Syrians and Egyptians, naming Hermes, Homer and Agathodaimon among the great original thinkers. The French scholars Henry Corbin and Yves Marquet have gone on from this to argue that the Harranian Sabians were responsible for most of the philosophical concepts of the Ikhwan and transmitted to them most of their knowledge of Greek thought; a thesis that would be possible to confirm if only we knew more about what the Sabians actually believed.

The writings of the Ikhwan themselves seem to provide some insight into Harranian concepts. They apparently characterise them as belief in a creator god, who is one in essence but emanates into angels and human souls. Seven of its greater emanations were assigned the direction of the planets, which function as their temples and in turn guide the material universe, including humanity. Some of the divine souls are benevolent, and sacrifices need to be made to them to gain their favour; others are malevolent, and sacrifices are needed to avert their harm. Each planet has a sympathetic bond to terrestrial matter, especially specific metals and stones, which human beings can manipulate for their own benefit. According to this theology, humans can also return by huge spiritual efforts to their original homeland among the higher beings.

The Ikhwan recorded other details about the Sabians. They declared that they had erected eighty-seven temples to the planets and other higher powers, arranged in patterns to reflect those of the heavens. This contradicts al-Mas'udi's picture of a single temple left in tenth-century Harran, and may either reflect a remarkable Sabian revival in the late tenth century or (more probably) be a piece of pure imagination. There is also a detailed description of the initiation ceremony used for the young men of the Sabians, dedicated to 'Jurjas', 'greatest of the demons'. Elements of it echo rites and doctrines known from a variety of Greek, Egyptian and Near Eastern religions and mystical writings but correspond closely to none; like Jurjas himself, some remain unique. It is followed by a brief account of other Harranian deities, festivals and practices, loosely resembling one of those provided in the work of al-Nadim. All this has obvious correlations with earlier accounts of the Harranian Sabians, the passage on doctrine making a particularly good match with that supplied by Sarakhsi. This may reflect that the Muslim sources were simply repeating what was actually thought and done at Harran. It may, of course, also mean that they were drawing on a common body of Islamic tradition that was itself to some degree inaccurate.[30]

A few other writers provided accounts of the Sabians of Harran in the tenth century, and in the half a millennium that followed, a succession of others, mostly Muslim but sometimes Jewish, continued to do so. After year 1100, at latest, it is very unlikely that there were any actual Sabians left at Harran on whom they could base these judgements; they were therefore either repeating earlier accounts or making their own elaborations of or glosses on such accounts. These texts show general agreement on certain characteristics of the Harranian Sabians: that they believed in one primal deity, but also in lesser divinities embodied or dwelling in the planets. They also venerated certain prophets, of whom Hermes was the most commonly cited, and were identified with a system of ritual magic dependent on the correspondences between certain material substances and the nature and configurations of heavenly bodies; by the eleventh century, Harran had literally become a name to conjure with.[31] These later texts have commonly been added to the corpus of objective information on the subject, but the great problem with all of them, of course, is the reliability of the sources on which they were based, and the degree of fantasy with which they were constructed. The interpretation of the data has therefore tended in modern times to become an exercise in reconciliation, by which individual scholars compare the various different accounts and use their own judgement in deciding where they agree, and therefore constitute apparently solid evidence, and how the contradictions can be explained away in order to make the resulting reconstruction seem more plausible. Sometimes the work has been carried out crudely, by a process of scissors-and-paste treatment that leaves no room for doubt nor indicates the nature of the individual sources.[32] More recently it has tended to be carried out more carefully and thoroughly, but the essential nature of the technique is the same.[33]

This being so, it is possible in theory to produce interpretations of the evidence for the Sabians of Harran that span quite a broad spectrum between two extreme positions. One of the latter is to believe that their religious system can be confidently recovered from the extant data, without difficulty or necessary controversy; and this is well represented by the scissors-and-paste treatments mentioned above. The other is to conclude that the surviving sources are so defective, on so many grounds, that there is actually no real primary material, and therefore that nothing absolutely certain can ultimately be said about the subject. As far as I know, none of the specialists have advanced this argument, although Tamara Green has come close to it. Throughout the twentieth century, an impressive number of expert scholars and those working in related subjects have asserted that ancient paganism survived at Harran into the tenth and eleventh centuries, and most of them have also believed that it made a major contribution to Islamic culture.[34] The problem is that they have reached no agreement on what form that paganism took. To some it was the native religion of the city, a mixture of Syrian and Mesopotamian cults, to others it consisted of Neoplatonism and Hermetism brought from the

Greek cultural province, and to others it was a blend of the two, characterised according to the taste of the individual historian. This discordance naturally has serious implications for our ability to answer the related questions of how medieval Harranian paganism came to survive, and what its contribution to Islam actually was. Some scholars manipulate the language of scepticism in source analysis to support a position based on faith; thus, Francis Peters has declared that 'the Sabianism described in the Muslim sources was a myth'.[35] What he means by this, however, is that in his opinion the cult practices of ancient Mesopotamia survived at Harran but were disguised as Greek philosophy by the practitioners in order to win toleration from Islamic overlords. Only a glance at the characterisation of the evidence made above will indicate that this opinion is itself based on a selective – though perfectly credible – reading of the Muslim sources. If the Sabianism of Harran was a medieval religion, created by mixing ancient and late antique paganisms with elements taken in from Judaism, Christianity and Islam – a parallel to the Gnostic sect of Mandaeans who have existed to the present in southern Iraq by making a similar syncretism – then a straightforward characterisation of it as 'surviving paganism' becomes still more problematic.[36]

A still more vivid insight into the difficulties involved is provided by the work of Tamara Green, author of the most detailed and sensitive consideration of the subject yet to appear. She began it by stating that the identity and role of the Harranian Sabians 'have continued to be matters of sometimes acrimonious debate' since the ninth century, and that any study of them raises 'extraordinarily complex issues of historiographical methodology and ideological perspective'. In examining the Muslim texts she draws attention to their widely differing aims and absolute lack of first-hand knowledge of Harranian rites, and their tendency to shape their accounts with their own ideological concerns, which could have had little to do with the reality of what went on at Harran. In particular, she called into question whether al-Mas'udi could be regarded as an objective witness or the composer of an archetypal construct of what Harranians ought to do. She noted the almost total absence of 'any reliable information for the active continuity of ... earlier religious practices at Harran after the Muslim conquest' and called archaeological evidence 'non-existent' for the Islamic period. Her overall characterisation of the city was of one 'that had been constructed over and over again in the minds of succeeding generations ... every people who surveyed the city saw in its religious and intellectual fabric what they wanted and needed to see'. Despite all this, she felt able to conclude that a survival of ancient practices and rites into Muslim times at Harran was 'clearly possible'. This was her summary of the actual evidence; by the time that she reached her overall conclusion for her whole book on Harran, however, this survival had somehow become 'undoubted'.[37]

It is just possible that archaeology may resolve at least some of these problems, for Green's comment on the lack of evidence related to what we have, and not what may be obtained. Indeed, Harran's prospects in this regard may be exceptionally good. The Mongols depopulated and walled up the city in 1271, leaving it virtually intact until the present day. Surveys and trial excavations in the 1950s naturally enough revealed structures identifiable only with the final stage of the city's active history, as a bastion of Muslim orthodoxy. In 1983 a restoration and research programme began, but its published results have not yet revealed any material that can be related to the Sabians and it seems to have halted because of political unrest.[38] The site is now threatened by development of the region, and a thoroughly praiseworthy effort has now been launched in California to draw attention to its predicament and raise money for its exploration.[39] While such work is essential, it would be asking too much of archaeology in this case to expect it necessarily to solve the puzzles left by history. Some of the difficulties that may arise have been suggested by a site at Sumatar Harabesi in the mountains near Harran. Discovered in 1952 and explored further in 1971, it includes some of the earliest Syriac inscriptions ever recorded, carved images, and a group of ruined buildings. The carvings and inscriptions are dated to the second and third centuries, and their religious significance is still debated. Their discoverer suggested that the ruined buildings were planetary temples of the sort associated with the Sabians of Harran. This interpretation was, however, subsequently rejected by a colleague, who declared them to be tombs. The matter now seems open, and likely to remain so.[40]

It seems beyond dispute that Harran was a major centre of learning, and specifically of learning inspired by Greek texts, in the ninth and tenth centuries. It seems equally certain that as such it indeed made a contribution to the culture of the Islamic world, and through it to that of medieval Europe. It may be argued almost as strongly that this role was bound up with the existence within it of the Sabian community, practising a religion apparently unique for the time and still mysterious. Having said that, it may be wise not to overstate the importance of Harran in the transmission of knowledge from the ancient to the medieval worlds. The achievements of the school of Baghdad, in pioneering research into ancient philosophy and translating works from Greek to Arabic, rested overwhelmingly on the work of Christian scholars, not Harranians. Greek learning had become a feature of Syriac Christian culture from Edessa all the way across Mesopotamia to Marw in the north east of Persia, and their communities supplied the main conduit of it to Islam. They were also the main translators of Syriac works into Arabic. The Zoroastrians of Persia provided another route for Greek ideas into the Islamic world, as did the Jewish communities of the Middle East, who contributed especially to medical studies. Hermetism certainly reached Islam before the end of the eighth century, through Iranian astrologers, and had probably existed in Mesopotamian societies before the Arab conquest.[41] One of the main authorities on the Islamic absorption of Neoplatonism has suggested that it spread into the Arab world from three main points, of which Harran was one and Alexandria and Gondeshapur in southern Iraq the others, underpinned by lesser schools at Antioch, Edessa and Qinnesrin in Syria and Nisibis and Ras'aina in Iraq.[42] Another leading scholar has argued that the influence on Islamic thought of the Stoic school of Greek philosophy, with which Harran was never associated, may be greater than that of any other.[43] Mention of Alexandria drives home the point that, although the political centres of the Arab Empire lay successively in Arabia, Syria and Iraq, Egypt was a major part of it from an early stage and contributed its own tremendous heritage of culture directly, including Hermetism. In Roman times the land's major cult centre of Hermes (alias Thoth) was the city of Hermopolis. Towards the end of the eighth century, now named Akhmim, this produced the theologian Dhu al-Nun Abu'l-Faid Tauban ibn Ibrahim al-Misri, who preached the need for pious humans to break free of the flesh and ascend to reunion with the one supreme and good deity. This was a creed instantly recognisable from the Hermetic texts, and formed one of the foundations of the mystical Islamic tradition called Sufism.[44] By the tenth century Egypt had become the centre of a powerful breakaway Islamic state, which sponsored its own revival of Greek and Graeco-Egyptian studies.[45]

For the purposes of the present essay, it is fortunately not necessary to make the attempt to distinguish a specifically Harranian strain in medieval Islamic culture, let alone to suggest a solution to the mystery of what actually went on at Harran. It can treat the Arab spiritual matrix as a whole and, when sources attribute specific parts of it to the Harranians, to accept this as a contemporary belief rather than necessarily a statement of historical fact. With this position made clear, it is possible for the enquiry to get under way.

Neoplatonism was a philosophy developed by late antique pagans and subsequently adapted by some of them to justify and defend traditional pagan deities and rites. In its essence, however, it was compatible with virtually any monotheism, and so it is not surprising to find Islamic theologians from the ninth to the twelfth century blending it with their religion.

A concept of Allah as a transcendent deity who emanated the cosmos through a hierarchy of divine beings down to the material world became a distinctive strain in Muslim thought.[46] Likewise, al-Misri's adaptation of Hermetism to invite believers to a mystical reunion with Allah represented a use of Graeco-Egyptian ideas, stripped of their pagan associations, to enrich and reinforce the faith of Muhammed. The pre-Christian and pre-Islamic deities vanished from these models of the universe, to be replaced in the lower grades of the divine hierarchy by cosmic abstractions or angels, taken or developed from Hebrew, Christian or Islamic cosmology.

The only portion of Arabic culture in which honour to pagan goddesses and gods lingered was in the world of alternative spirituality represented by complex ritual magic. Orthodox Islamic attitudes to this were generally as hostile as those of Graeco-Roman paganism, late antique Judaism and Christianity. Any attempt by humans to exert an arcane influence over the material world, at will, was regarded as impious and forbidden by law to true believers. Equally, all educated medieval Muslims knew that these practices went on, and that there were sophisticated texts available that contained directions for them.[47] The earliest group of these were attributed to Abu Bakr Ahmed ibn Wahshiyya (or Wahshiyah or Wahshiyyah) al-Nabati, said to have flourished around the beginning of the tenth century. A corpus of works attributed to him survives, of which the most famous are devoted respectively to farming practices, alphabets associated with esoteric spirituality, astrology, toxicology and alchemy. They are written in an Arabic that strongly suggests that the author was not a native user of the language, and probably a Syriac Christian in origin. This would fit the expressed aim of the texts themselves, which is to make available to readers of Arabic the occult wisdom of the ancient peoples of Egypt, Syria and Mesopotamia.[48]

Having said this, all the usual trouble reappears. The identity of the true author has been controversial ever since the nineteenth century. It seems now unlikely that agreement will ever be reached on whether ibn Wahshiyya himself ever existed. There seems to be a large amount of current favour for the view that the works were produced by a convert to the Shiite branch of Islam, probably from Syrian Christianity and probably in the tenth century, but none of this may ever be certain. Evaluations of the quality of the contents have varied from an assertion that many of them are ancient texts from the great civilisations of the Near and Middle East, to a condemnation of most as outright forgeries. Again, since the mid twentieth century there seems to be a wary consensus that most of them are syncretic compilations in which genuinely ancient Greek, Egyptian, Mesopotamian, Persian and Indian ideas and practices are filtered through previous Syriac and Persian translations. The longest and most important of them, by far, is the compendium of magical and practical techniques to aid farming, the *Nabataean Agriculture.* It is united by that sense of mystical correspondences between spiritual and material phenomena that informed much Egyptian magic and influenced Stoicism, Neoplatonism and Hermetism. Like Iamblichus, it seeks to justify the use of magical techniques to the devout by insisting that they are divinely ordained, and distinguishing prophets and philosophers, who are vouchsafed visions of the future or of the nature of the cosmos by divinity, from common magicians, who are only effective in material matters. Some of the procedures in the book are devoted to summoning spirits, and obtaining divine responses to questions, in a manner familiar from the magical papyri. Unlike most of the magic of the papyri, but like that in the text credited to Thabit, some of the procedures involved coordination with the movements of the night sky.[49]

It was through these that the veneration of pre-Christian deities was most clearly to be preserved, and the point is made much more forcefully in the most famous of all Arabic works concerned with complex ritual magic. This is the *Ghayat al-hakim,* usually translated as 'the Aim of the Wise One', which was written in Islamic Spain in the mid eleventh century.[50] It was one result of that flowering of art and literature in which the many Muslim kingdoms of Spain followed up the programme commenced there in the previous century by a rival caliphate to that of Baghdad, established by a refugee branch of the Umayyad family: of collating and attempting to surpass the cultural achievements of the traditional centres of Islamic scholarship. The *Ghaya* attempted this enterprise in the field of magic. Geographically, it is therefore a European work, but its sources encompass the whole range of texts available in the Muslim world of the time. The author chose, because of the disreputable nature of much of his subject matter, to remain anonymous, but was justifiably proud of his industry and learning. He himself boasted of having read 224 books in the course of his research, and he can certainly be shown to have drawn material from most Arabic works on the esoteric sciences known to have been written in Syria and Mesopotamia during the ninth and tenth centuries. These in turn incorporated ideas drawn from Graeco-Roman, Graeco-Egyptian, Graeco-Syrian, Persian and Indian texts, with ancient Egyptian and Mesopotamian traditions standing in turn behind some of these. The author of the *Ghaya* himself credited three peoples above all with a reputation for learning in magical lore: the Sabians of Harran, the Greeks (signifying the whole Hellenised world of the Near East) and the Indians.

The book begins with a declaration of Islamic monotheism, blended with Neoplatonism by previous Arab works: that the whole cosmos proceeds from Allah, through a series of emanations, and therefore is based on divine unity and harmony. This is the philosophical basis for all that follows, for that unity is manifested in esoteric linkages and correspondences, the manipulation of which enables the magician to honour and fulfil the work of the One God. The status of the magician as a devout follower of divine will is emphasised by prescriptions for the need for piety and ritual and physical purity in the practice of magical operations. The ends sought are, however, resolutely practical: to prolong life, cure disease, escape prison, overcome enemies, attract love, succeed in business, politics and war, and so forth. The *Ghaya* therefore reflects the world of the Greek magical papyri, joining to it a cosmological justification taken from Muslim Neoplatonism but dispensing with interest in communion or union with the divine for its own sake. Its conception of magic is primarily as a craft of capturing and guiding the influence of spirit on matter, and is particularly concerned with the power exerted over the earth by celestial bodies, especially the seven planets (including sun and moon). The single most prominent magical technique recommended in the work is the making of talismans, physical objects created from the right materials at the right times and in the correct manner, into which the planetary rays can be directed and held ready for application. Their distinctive feature, separating them from other objects such as amulets, is the combination of the invocation of celestial power with the inscription of potent words, letters or symbols on them. Another technique important to the *Ghaya* is the invocation of the spirits ruling the planets to send out angels to do the magician's bidding. This is the theory embodied in the work attributed to al-Kindi, and the practice in that attributed to Thabit, employed on a grand magical scale.

David Pingree has produced a magisterial analysis of some of the sources on which the *Ghaya* drew.[51] He has demonstrated that the idea that stones, plants and animals have special relationships with the planets and the signs of the zodiac is found in a range of Greek and Graeco-Egyptian works from late antiquity. Associated with it in these works is the notion that a magician could use these substances to draw on their corresponding celestial powers. He suggested that this sort of magic originated in Mesopotamia, and that its reputation in the early medieval Near and Middle East was increased by the influence of Indian texts that were themselves partly inspired by a work from Greek-speaking Egypt. The concept that planets were embodied in or served by particular spirits – angels or demons – is found in compilations claiming to draw on Hebrew tradition, and dating anywhere between the fourth and the eleventh centuries. They contained directions for prayers to the planetary entity concerned, in particular ways and at particular times, to achieve the desires of magicians. Pingree suggests that they derive

ultimately from the prayers to planetary and stellar deities in ancient Mesopotamian texts, that have no parallels in Graeco-Roman or ancient Egyptian
sources. He made a further suggestion that, in his later work, became stated
as fact: that it was the Sabians of Harran who developed the idea of invoking
planetary powers into standardised material objects, and thereby gave the
Arab world its distinctive form of astral magic using talismans.

This may be the truth, and it is beyond doubt, as noted earlier, that Arab
writers themselves credited the Harranians with special veneration for planetary deities and expertise in a magic related to them. The problem here is
that stated above: whether we are to take Muslim, Christian and Jewish
perceptions of the Harranian Sabians as objective fact. David Pingree's
opinion is based partly on an acceptance of the texts of astral magic credited
to al-Kindi and Thabit as the works of those individuals; which, as shown,
is unproven. It also depends on the descriptions of the Sabian planetary
temples provided by al-Mas'udi, which have also been characterised as
problematic. It draws still more heavily on more elaborate accounts of the
same temples, differing in some details, furnished more than three centuries
later by the geographer Shams al-Din Muhammed al-Dimashqi.[52] By the
time that al-Dimashqi wrote, all Sabian activity had ceased at Harran for
about a couple of hundred years, so his information was derived from an
unknown source, referring to an unknown period. The latter might have
recorded objective data, or been a pure fantasy developed from the account
by al-Mas'udi. The planetary prayers in the *Ghaya* were taken from various
sources, two of them identified by Pingree as a Hermetic text translated
into or written in Arabic, and the *Nabataean Agriculture*. A third is attributed
by the author himself to an Indian source.

Most, however, were ostensibly taken by him from a lost text by an
otherwise unknown writer, al-Tabari, and purport to describe the private
rites of the Sabians of Harran. They prescribe the proper times, incenses,
garments and sacrifices necessary for the invocations of each planet and
the benefits that each bestow; thus, Saturn looks after political leaders, and
needs an incense containing opium and the ground skull of a black cat,
and the offering of a black he-goat. Most of the prayers call on both the
planet's ruling deity or spirit and the messenger or servitor angel associated
with it. The names are given in Arabic, Persian, Greek, Roman and Sanskrit
equivalents; all but the Roman are linguistically and culturally accurate.[53]
Pingree has accounted for the Indian elements, and for Indian parallels in
the descriptions of the Harranian temples, in terms of a direct influence
by the culture of India on the Sabians of Harran. This may be so; it may
also be that in imagining the magic with which the Sabians were credited
in reputation, Muslim writers drew on Indian texts and accounts of India

as one resource for the construction of a myth. There are a few other references to Harranian practices in the *Ghaya*, of the sort familiar from other Muslim texts of the time and before. They consist of two variants of the alleged Sabian custom of obtaining oracles from the head of a sacrificed man, one inserted into a discussion of Indian astrology and the other incorporating an important Harranian place-name; an account of child sacrifice and one of the offering of humans to Mars; another description of the initiation ceremony of young men into the Sabian religion (disagreeing in its details with those given in other Muslim texts); and one of a ceremony in honour of Saturn.[54] Once more, it is impossible to tell how much of this is reported fact, even at second or third hand, and how much is the product of gossip and fantasy.

As before, the present enquiry is not affected by that issue, for whether the concepts and practices credited to the Sabians of Harran were accurate or not, they formed part of the cultural repertoire of writers in Arabic during the tenth and eleventh centuries. The complexity and breadth of that repertoire is particularly well illustrated by the *Nabataean Agriculture* and the *Ghayat al-Hakim*, and David Pingree's careful researches have further reinforced our sense of those qualities. He is unquestionably correct, also, to draw attention to the practice of astral magic using talismans as the distinctive contribution of Arabic literature to esoteric tradition. Likewise, he is right to point to Mesopotamia as the ultimate homeland of astral magic, although here some qualifications of detail need to be made. The unusual interest in the movements of the heavens that characterised ancient Babylonian and Assyrian culture had developed by the fifth century BCE into exact observations of the moon and stars intended to help predict the future of individuals and states. By the end of that century the signs of the zodiac had also apparently appeared, although as a device for measuring time. These techniques reached Greece in the fourth century, and combined there with the interest in heavenly bodies that was one feature of the new Greek philosophy and science. One of its foremost protagonists, Plato, argued for the divinity of the planets and stars. The Stoics then worked astrology into their system, and from the second century it was strongly developed in Greek-speaking Egypt. There the zodiac was put into its enduring form, its twelve signs related to parts of the human body and joined with native star-deities known as 'decans', who ruled sections of the circle. It was there that most of the standard texts of astrology which circulated in later antiquity were produced, and it seems to have been there that particular stones, metals, plants and animals became associated with specific planets.[55] The latter development was the crucial one for the creation of medieval astral magic.

That magic, as found in medieval Arabic texts such as *De imaginibus* and the *Ghaya*,[56] was therefore based on a range of sources and influences spanning the arc of the globe from the Nile to the Ganges, with Mesopotamia and Egypt playing crucial roles in its development at different times. Scanning the religious and magical literature of late antique Egypt, it is apparent that all the materials for it are there already. The Greek magical papyri include a set invocation to the planet Venus, intended to attract a lover and made while offering a special incense and wearing a particular charm, and another to the angel of the sun to obtain a dream oracle, using laurel leaves inscribed with figures special to the signs of the zodiac.[57] As said earlier, they include a number of rites for the charging of material objects, such as rings, with divine power. While the seven planets are not prominent in the papyri, individually or collectively, they play a major part in some of the Hermetic texts, produced in Egypt at about the same time, functioning as the immediate agents of the one all-powerful creator deity.[58] Other Hermetic writings teach how to make amulets from mineral, vegetable and animal substances associated with particular planets or zodiacal signs, into which the power of those heavenly bodies could be drawn: the difference between these and talismans seems merely one of detail.[59] It may well be, as David Pingree suggests, that Mesopotamian tradition played a special part, once again, in turning these components into the developed form of astral magic found in the Arabic texts. There was, however, no necessity for it to do so, and there is no proof that it did.

One scholar of the *Ghaya* has characterised it as filled with 'the most flourishing paganism', signifying by this a total indifference to the governing religion and accepted moral standards.[60] This is only partly true, as the author made a direct attempt to assimilate his work to Islamic cosmology and justify it in terms of monotheistic piety, as has been seen. The comment has some justification in a different sense; that the prayers to the planetary deities treated them effectively as independent powers, and if they were described as emanations from Allah, then this still gave them the same status as the traditional deities in the system of the self-consciously pagan Neoplatonists. None the less, the legacy of ancient paganism to Islamic culture as a whole was a feeble one, containing few or no literary or artistic images of real familiarity or potency. It was otherwise in the Christian medieval world, where the tremendous legacy of Graeco-Roman civilisation made the old deities virtually inescapable. If the latter could become associated with astral magic, then their survival as beings regarded with respect and reverence, and approached with invocation, would be virtually certain. It was made easier, as things turned out, by the fact that Christianity had already sold this particular pass.

Most of the key antique texts on which medieval and early modern Christians relied for their concept of the universe taught them that the heavenly bodies were animate beings. Plato has been cited. Aristotle described the stars and planets as intermediaries between the one Prime Mover and inferior entities, responsible directly for all life and action in the material world. Cicero declared that they were divinities.[61] Some Christians had no difficulty in digesting this concept. One was a Roman called Julius Firmicus Maternus, who in the early fourth century wrote a ferocious attack on paganism as false religion.[62] He had also published a book in which he referred to the planets as deities, serving the supreme god and carrying out his will, and recommended astrology as a means of discovering that will.[63] This text was rediscovered in the eleventh century, and much copied and discussed thereafter.[64] Augustine condemned astrology with other forms of divination, but was uncertain of whether or not the planets were beings to be classed with angels.[65] This pattern seems to have signalled to some of the public at least that pagan deities associated with planets were immune from Christian censure, because in the 440s citizens of the western imperial capital of Ravenna were celebrating the New Year with parades of people costumed as these beings.[66]

During the great increase in theological writing in the early to mid twelfth century, the same issue was considered with the same results: a mixture of hesitation and positive recommendation. Pierre Abelard followed Augustine in being unable to reach a decision on whether the planets were animate beings. He did, however, quote Plato respectfully on the subject, agreed that heavenly bodies could control earthly phenomena, and accepted that human emotions could be influenced by forces hidden in plants and stones. William of Conches also used Plato, to argue that the supreme god had made the human soul but had entrusted the forming of the body to planets and stars. He then used Graeco-Roman mythology to associate deities with each planet and so delineate their respective qualities and influences. Bernard Silvester calmly called the planets 'gods who serve God in person', and who controlled the natural world while enjoying a beautific vision of the supreme deity. He also believed that they revealed the future and that pious humans could ascend to them after death and become celestial bodies in turn.[67] All this provided fertile ground for the reception of Muslim astral magic, but in addition Christianity was infused at its centre with a vivid sense of the power of ritual in drawing down celestial and divine power and investing it in material objects: in the rite of the mass. As the middle ages reached their centre, and western Christendom developed the doctrine of transubstantiation and of a Real Presence in the consecrated bread and wine, that sense would have intensified. For these reasons, a religion that had constructed itself on a rejection of both paganism and magic was in a position to make a number of possible compromises with both.

One of the most remarkable features of European humanity around the year 1100 was its physical mobility: of soldiers, pilgrims, merchants and scholars. This counted for much as, during that period, Latin Christianity set itself the project that had been undertaken by Islamic scholars during the past three centuries: of recovering all existing human knowledge and augmenting it. Adelard of Bath was born in Somerset in the late eleventh century, although his parents may have come from Lorraine. He commenced his teaching career at Bath Abbey, and then went on to study at Tours and Laon, in different parts of what is now France. He followed this with travels that certainly took him to Italy and Sicily and probably to Syria and Asia Minor as well, collecting Greek and Arabic texts. On his return, he seems to have worked at Bath, Hereford, Malvern and Worcester in England, and Bayeux and Chartres in what is now France, before his death in the 1150s. He became the first notable translator of works on mathematics, astronomy, astrology and astral magic from Arabic to Latin. Petrus Alfonsi was born a Jew in the Muslim kingdom of Saragossa, where he grew up reading Arabic. In 1106 he converted opportunely to Christianity as Christian armies closed in on Saragossa, and began travels that took him as far as Worcester. While staying there he made his own translation of a major Arab work on astronomy and gave lessons to English pupils, perhaps including Adelard.[68] By such means, over a hundred Arabic works were translated or paraphrased into Latin during the twelfth century, and more followed in the next. One of the latter was the *Ghaya*, translated into Spanish and then Latin in the mid thirteenth century. The Latin text, which was based on the Arab one but with many expansions and omissions, was given the name of *Picatrix*. This seems to have been a rendering of the name of an author identified by the Arab work as an expert on talismans, Bucratis. The most likely writer to stand behind this name is Harpokration, an Alexandrian of the fourth century, who adapted a Hermetic text concerned with the cure of illnesses by amulets engraved with signs manipulating the mystical correspondences of material things.[69] These were indeed proto-talismans, and if the origin of the name is indeed correctly identified it indicates how well the translators located the ultimate origin of this tradition, in late antique Egypt.

The translated texts on astrology told readers how they might learn the future course of events; those on astral magic told them how they might determine those events. In coming to terms with the challenges posed by the latter, Latin-reading Christians had to define their reactions to four different postulates. First, that the planets control earthly affairs. Second, that humans can work with them to exert some control of their own over those affairs. Third, that the planets are animate, being homes or bodies for divine beings who empower them. Fourth, that those beings can be identified with the Graeco-Roman deities whose names they bear. Anybody accepting the first and last of those postulates had effectively found a continuing and positive role for traditional deities in a Christian universe. Anybody accepting the second, and prepared to act on it, was engaging in complex ritual magic of a sort very similar to, and probably directly descended from, that of late antique Egypt.

The impact of these choices can be registered in the writings of intellectuals from the first half of the thirteenth century; and the most obvious feature of it was the diversity of the reactions provoked. Michael Scot, a clerical diplomat to whom one pope offered an archbishopric, declared that wise and powerful spirits ruled the planets in obedience to the creator god, and would respond to human wishes if invoked by name. He disassociated them from paganism, however, by giving them the names of Hebrew angels. William of Auvergne, archbishop of Paris from 1228 to 1249, opined that the heavenly bodies controlled material things, but not the human will or intellect, and condemned attempts to infuse their power into images. Thomas de Cantimpre, writing between 1228 and 1244, held that the planetary spirits controlled human behaviour in accordance with the will of the supreme god, and gave them their classical names. He thought it possible that all things on earth were generated by the influence of Venus. Robert Grosseteste (1175–1253), bishop of Lincoln, accepted the study of the heavens as the supreme science and believed that scarcely any human operation could be undertaken without taking the influence of planets and stars into account.[70]

These were the 'respectable' views on the subject. In the writings of the same churchmen appear glimpses of a flourishing intellectual underworld, in which the opportunities offered by the newly-translated texts were approved and perhaps attempted without inhibition. William of Auvergne claimed that in his youth, which would have been in the late twelfth century, he had read many books of magic. Among those that he identified specifically for condemnation were two that prescribed rites to tap into the power of the planet Venus, by 'Cocogrecus' and 'Tot grecus'.[71] It is interesting that the names of the alleged authors reflect a belief in the Greek-speaking world, again, as a major source of magical knowledge; and the second may echo the 'Tat' of the Hermetic texts, alias the Egyptian deity of wisdom, Thoth. This latter text has itself survived, also known as *Liber Veneris* and *De lapide Veneris*, and teaches how to make a talisman of Venus that may ultimately be endowed with the power of all seven planetary spirits by a mixture of fumigation, invocation and inscription.[72] William of Auvergne also labelled as dangerous the concept, which he held to have become widespread among otherwise pious Christians, that the power of divinity could be poured into human-made images of deities, using the aid of the planets and stars associated with them.[73] This was certainly one possible application of the *De imaginibus* credited to Thabit, which had been translated from Arabic twice over, in one case by Adelard of Bath himself. Another text that gave detailed instructions for the making of planetary talismans was the *Opus imaginum*, ascribed to the Graeco-Egyptian scholar Ptolemy, and this was also circulating in Latin by the early thirteenth century.[74]

By the second half of that century, Paris had become the centre of occult studies in western Europe, including planetary magic, and the latter was discussed by leading scholars with still greater interest and sympathy. The most respected of them, Albertus Magnus, openly endorsed the idea that marvels could be worked by carving the images of planetary and stellar spirits on metals at the correct moment. Roger Bacon agreed, holding that the spirits of the planets ruled human affairs between them and recognising them as the classical deities with whom those planets had been associated. Above all he honoured Mercury, as lord of wisdom and eloquence, and associated him with Christ. The anonymous *Speculum astronomiae* denied that the heavenly bodies were animate, and condemned the making of images of 'Venus, Belenus and Hermes', while commending the use of talismans empowered only by astrological conjunctions. Arnald of Villanova, who flourished between 1285 and 1311, argued that the one god alone could control spirits, and so humans could not master the power of the planets at all. He added, however, that they could accomplish great things by learning how heavenly bodies influenced earthly matter, and working with those influences. His contemporary, Peter of Abano, compromised by associating Christian angels with the planets, with whom humans might communicate. The debate continued at full pelt until the 1320s, when a learned astrologer called Cecco d'Ascoli was first dismissed from his chair at Bologna for his opinions and then actually burned at the stake by inquisitors at Florence for maintaining them. His writings had endorsed the by now familiar beliefs in the power of images fashioned to receive planetary influences. Cecco's execution in 1327 has always puzzled historians and been generally treated as an isolated and not very significant event; it has been assumed that he was unlucky enough to make exceptionally powerful and determined enemies.[75] Be that as it may, it is notable that, coincidentally or not, the public discussion of planetary magic came to an abrupt halt at that point, and was not resumed for most of the next hundred and fifty years.

Clearly consciousness of it and interest in it remained beneath the surface of theological publication. The manuscripts containing directions for it continued to be copied. In the late 1380s Antonious de Monte Ulmi broke the apparent public silence in his lectures on astronomy at the university of Bologna. He has left a book that both relates spirits to the planets and gives directions for the rites to invoke them into talismans. He commented that he himself had found the image of Hermes to be especially efficacious when used in conjunction with signs of the zodiac. As a sop to Christian anxieties, he recommended that the conscientious make confession to a priest before the magical operation, and have him bless the image to be used.[76] In 1419 the distinguished French theologian Jean Gerson attempted to place orthodox limits on the tradition, holding that the angels who ruled the planets did so only according to God's will and could be invoked only with devout prayer, making no use of magical characters or images.[77] The penetration of these concepts into lay culture is suggested by the survival of the occasional artefact, such as a tray made as a wedding gift in Florence in about 1420. It portrays a nude Venus, floating in the sky between two cupids and shedding her radiance over humans on the Earth below. The object was clearly intended as a symbol of good luck for the couple concerned, and neatly conflates the influence of the planet with the icon of the classical goddess, in a powerful image of divine benevolence.[78]

The interest in astral magic expressed by Latin Christendom was only one aspect of a general flowering of complex ritual magic within its culture. The phenomenon seems to have provided a parallel to that in Egypt during the Roman period, when a flourishing native tradition of magical operations was transformed into something much more elaborate, ambitious and cosmopolitan. Western Europe certainly possessed a rich heritage of magical practices during the early middle ages,[79] but it seems to have consisted mainly of relatively simple spells and charms designed for particular purposes. The new, sophisticated rituals appear in its records around the year 1200, and it may be assumed that they were inspired directly by the translation of Arabic texts and the assimilation of the late antique Hellenistic works that lay behind these. The process is, however, very hard to study because of the lack of records: the key works often only exist in later medieval copies and their initial composition or translation is difficult to date. The matter is complicated greatly by official disapproval of much of the subject matter, so that those who produced the key works needed at each stage to cover their tracks in a manner even more effective against historians than against inquisitors and magistrates.

What is plain is that by the thirteenth century the new and elaborate form of ceremonial magic had taken root in western Europe, and by the fourteenth the survival of texts becomes good enough to demonstrate that all of the late antique branches of the tradition had been transformed into a Latin Christian guise. Theurgy was present in the shape of spiritual exercises, talismans and prayers designed to ensure ultimate salvation and in the meantime to secure the beatific vision, the view of the supreme deity in all his splendour which was normally only granted to the blessed after death.[80] Overwhelming earthly power was also promised, in the wholly recognisable Graeco-Egyptian manner: one text that offered attainment of the beatific vision also promised to equip its readers to 'conquer the heavenly powers, subjugate those of earth and air together with the infernal; invoke, transmit, conjure, constrain, excite, gather, disperse, bind and restore unharmed'.[81] Another link with the Greek magical papyri is an emphasis upon the acquisition of servitor spirits, while yet another is represented by the use of 'barbarous names' in apparent derivatives of Hebrew, Greek and Babylonian, to which Arabic had now been added, for invocation.[82] The languages concerned do strongly link these later medieval works to those of late antiquity, and suggest the route for transmission of ideas. Knowledge was also power, as before, some texts being filled with rites designed to obtain perfection in every art and science.[83]

One striking feature of this late medieval ritual magic is the emphasis made by much of it on the quartered circle – a circle marked at the four cardinal points of the compass – as the vital unit of sacred space. The four cardinal directions were notable components of Mesopotamian cosmology. Kings in the third millennium BCE designated themselves as rulers 'of the four quarters'. A Muslim source characterised the Harranians as praying to the cardinal points.[84] Far to the west, in Anglo-Saxon England, the same figure was potent in some charms, which were hung around the four sides of a byre or pigsty to protect it or cut on the four sides of a wound or a stick.[85] Likewise the circle was a figure known in ancient and early medieval magic, from one end of the territories covered by the Roman Empire to the other. An Assyrian rite has the magician make a *usurtu*, usually translated as a ring, of sprinkled lime around the images of deities on whom he is going to call. In the Graeco-Egyptian magical papyri a circle was occasionally drawn as a character within which signs could be inscribed; in one case the magician stood inside such a figure. Likewise, it sometimes features in Anglo-Saxon magic, being drawn round wounds or afflicted parts of the body to confine an infection, or dug round plants before culling them, to concentrate the good in them. A Hebrew story from the Roman period features one 'Onias the circle-maker', who ended a drought in Palestine by drawing such a figure and standing inside it to pray to Jehovah for rain.[86] The significant feature of all these references, however, is that they are marginal and incidental to the tradition concerned. The same is true of the rites of the *Ghayat al-Hakim*. By contrast there is no mistaking the central importance of circles and cardinal points in the ritual magic of later medieval Latin Christianity.

Why that importance should have developed is not a question that is answered by the sources assembled for the present study, though it is possible that an expert in Hebrew magic might be able to find a solution. It is present from the earliest references to the appearance of elaborate ritual magic in western Christianity: in the course of his condemnations of that magic, William of Auvergne singled out an operation called 'The Major Circle' that involved summoning spirits from the four quarters.[87] One of the most famous magical texts of the early fourteenth century, variously known as the *Liber Iuratus, Liber Sacer* or *Sworn Book of Honorius*, devotes much space to describing how the circles are to be drawn, and how the ruling entities of the quarters are to be invoked.[88] In the later part of that century, Antonious de Monte Ulmi called the circle the most perfect figure for magical operations and the symbol of the prime mover of the universe, and gave his own instructions for consecrating it.[89] A contemporary of his from the other side of the theological division through the subject was the inquisitor Nicholas Eymeric, who in 1376 published a celebrated handbook for hunters of heresy. He included ritual magic under the latter heading, and described one of its operations as consisting of the invocation of a spirit, using a set text, with a boy as the medium; a practice familiar from the magical papyri. The difference now is that the boy has to stand within a circle drawn on the earth.[90] By the fifteenth century the circle was the key visual element of Christian ritual magic, enclosing the sacred area within which signs and consecrated objects could be placed. The most common width was usually nine feet, and the figure was normally drawn with a consecrated sword or knife.[91]

By the later middle ages, therefore, western Christianity was practising, or at least reading about, a ceremonial magic that placed heavy emphasis on two of the main components of modern Paganism, and especially of Pagan witchcraft: the drawing down of divine power from the heavenly bodies into matter and the working of operations within a consecrated circle with the cardinal points marked. A third major feature of this magic, a sense of the special potency of the five-pointed star or pentagram, had likewise appeared with it in the period around 1200 and was also to be of central importance to modern Pagans; I have dealt with its history elsewhere.[92] All three were rooted in ancient practice, and yet given new prominence in the middle ages. The drawing down of heavenly powers, as suggested, also provided an opportunity for the continued veneration, to varying degrees, of classical pagan deities. The most important of them, in this context, seems to have been Venus, conceived of as a star goddess who also controlled love and generation. In these crucial respects, and from this one refracted perspective, the ritual magic of the later middle ages contained modern Paganism in embryo.

There were, however, other contexts in which places could be found for classical deities within a Christian cosmos. One was provided by scholars who taught at two of the cathedral schools in which the so-called 'Twelfth-Century Renaissance' of western European culture was largely carried on: those at Tours and Chartres in what is now central France. As mentioned, Adelard seems to have studied and worked there, and so did two of the theologians quoted earlier as attributing divinity and effective power to the planets, William of Conches and Bernard Silvester. These schools became associated with a cosmology that attributed a major role to the goddess Natura, whose appearance at the end of antiquity, and acceptance by Christian churchmen, has already been mentioned. Here again, Augustine himself had left the door open, by praising the teachings presented by the natural world, and for a time stating that he thought it to be an animate being. He withdrew that last assertion because he could find no authority for it in the Bible, but did not condemn it.[93] It is not surprising that Natura, and her Greek equivalent Physis, are both still found in literature produced between the fifth and eleventh centuries.[94] None the less, the development of her literary profile at twelfth-century Chartres was still remarkable, and probably due to two cultural forces. The first was the period's recovery and careful perusal of ancient texts. The second was its fervent new discussion of the natural world, from many different points of view.[95] It is possible, however, that Natura would not have been established as a major character in the century's literature had it not been for the particular work of Bernard Silvester.

Brian Stock has teased out the influences that lay behind Silvester's concept of Nature as an allegorical goddess: they consist of Macrobius, Claudian, the Roman astrologer Firmicus Maternus, the earlier Roman natural historian Pliny, the Muslim alchemist Abu Ma'shar, some lesser Roman writers, and one of the most important of the Hermetic texts, the *Asclepius*.[96] It was in the years around 1150 that the clerical scholar combined these into a portrait of Natura as a divinity sprung from the One God and given the task of calling matter into being at the creation of the universe. Thereafter she personified the latter, acting as the engendering force of fertility and procreation.[97] This image was subsequently developed at Chartres in the period between 1160 and 1184 by Alan of Lille (Alanus de Insulis), who made

Natura the agent and representative of the One God in earthly affairs and fashioner of human beings. As such, she was a wholly good entity, and featured in Alan's works as creating a perfect man as her champion against the forces of evil and as denouncing the corruption of the earthly realm by human vice. She is described as a virgin crowned with stars, travelling in a glass coach drawn by peacocks, and attended by a train of virtues. All the cosmos obeys her and is made calm by her.[98] In the 1180s another author operating in the region, Jean de Hauteville, wrote of a youthful hero whose quest, ultimately realised, is to seek out Natura to learn the purpose of life.[99]

None of these works were serious expositions of theology. None recommended rites to honour Natura or suggested how she might fit into the regular framework of Christianity. They were, rather, poetic romances dealing in allegories, and so evaded any risk of ecclesiastical censure. None the less, these Latin compositions had given Natura the status of a powerful symbolic entity, capable of investing the Christian imagination with the concept of a divine feminine presence immediately responsible for the world and in charge of it, and quite detached from biblical tradition. She was sufficiently appealing to be taken up in the vernacular poetry that flourished from the thirteenth century onward. In a section of the major French work, the *Roman de la Rose*, written in the Loire valley, Natura is presented as a being of inexpressible beauty and grace, created by the One God to govern the universe on his behalf. She is at once subordinate to him and the immediate ruler of the cosmos, queen of the world, with a particular interest in love and procreation. Unlike the entity of the twelfth-century writers, she is not concerned with reason, which is the province of God alone, and her natural enemy is chastity.[100] This exalted view of her at last provoked some literary opposition, being attacked in the early fourteenth century by another French poet, who accused her of being the enemy of divine grace.[101] The protest had little apparent effect, for in the latter part of that century she received further reverence from the English poet subsequently celebrated over all others in the middle ages: Geoffrey Chaucer. Her famous appearance in his *Parlement of Foules* is explicitly based on the ideas of Alan of Lille, and she features once more as God's deputy, ruling both the cosmos in general and its particular creatures. Her most important area of responsibility is still fertility and procreation, but she has been restored to her twelfth-century position as sovereign of reason as well.[102] Chaucer's was her last great medieval appearance, but she still featured in passing in works of the early fifteenth century such as a rendering of a French poem into English by Lydgate. There she is represented as maker of a good and beautiful world and exponent of reason.[103]

As a goddess-figure of extraordinary beauty, associated with flowers and having a special responsibility for procreation, Natura had an obvious overlap with an older divine female, Venus. As has been indicated, the latter held her own as a potent being throughout the middle ages in the field of astral magic, and her profile was as high in the realms of poetic and prose romance. As the traditional embodiment of the power of love, she had an obvious purchase on the imagination of a culture in which Christianity had invested divine and human love with a new intensity of significance. Her representation by fifth- and sixth-century episcopal poets has been cited, and in the ninth century a Veronese cleric could still hail a beloved boy as 'thou eidolon of Venus adorable'.[104] The problem with her, of course, was that she was also the traditional patroness of carnal pleasures that represented one highway to the Christian concept of deadly sin. A means of resolving this difficulty had already been provided by Plato: to regard her as two goddesses, concerned with heavenly and earthly love, the one virtuous and benevolent and the other a temptress. By the mid twelfth century this division had become a commonplace , repeated by a string of clerical authors culminating in Bernard Silvester.[105]

As such her former characterisation could be identified with Natura, to whom her latter one could be made to act as a foil. This is how Alan of Lille dealt with her, having Natura enlist the aid of Venus to endow creatures with the gift of procreation. Venus, however, flouts Natura's intentions by engendering appetites for sinful as well as virtuous forms of sexual pleasure. The *Roman de la Rose* has the same plot, Venus subverting Natura's plan for procreative love for purposes of pure self-indulgence. Chaucer follows it as well, but complicates matters by featuring the two aspects of Venus as well as Natura. He begins his *Parlement of Foules* with an invocation of Venus under her classical title of Cytherea, as the powerful star of love and 'blissful lady sweet', acting as intermediary for God's decrees.[106] Later, however, he introduces Venus, under her own name, as the destructive force of romance, responsible for sexual frustration, excessive sensuality and unrequited love.

A similar tension is apparent in other vernacular literature of the later middle ages. By the late fourteenth century Venus had become a very common figure in German romances, represented as the advocate and arbiter of noble and virtuous love, and presiding over a court of appeal to which lovers turn for advice and fair judgement. An Italian work located her court within a mountain in the Appennines.[107] English poetry of the early fifteenth century likewise paid respect to her as a benevolent patroness of true passion, and tamer of haughty young men.[108] It also, however, sometimes referred to her as a temptress, and in German romances of the same period the admirable goddess of the fourteenth century becomes demonised into the embodiment of sensual pleasure, dedicated to leading humans away from salvation. Her court in a hollow mountain, relocated to Germany itself, was turned from a tribunal of divine justice to an earthly paradise of corrupting sensual pleasures, from which the virtuous needed to escape. By the mid fifteenth century this theme had become blended with the figure of the medieval poet Tannhäuser, to produce one of the great German legends.[109]

Even as Venus continued to inspire and disturb the medieval Christian imagination, so did another classical goddess: Diana. Her profile as a figure of allegory, metaphor and romance was nothing like as high, and she was seldom identified with the moon in astral magic as she had been in some Graeco-Roman mythology. None the less, she featured in literature, in two guises: as patroness of chastity, and also of hunting, the main recreation of the aristocracy.[110] It was, however, in what could loosely be called folk tradition that she made her most remarkable appearances. The tradition concerned was one found among common people, and especially women, in wide areas of western and northern Europe, and noted with condemnation by successive churchmen. It was a belief that some of them flew across the land by night – apparently in dream-experiences – in a company led by a divine female figure. The latter was given various names. Some were apparently those of pagan Germanic goddesses or spirits, while she was also called Herodias, after the Hebrew queen who obtained the death of John the Baptist. The most common name for her, found from the ninth to the sixteenth century, was Diana.[111] It is not easy to establish why this should be, as she is known as this in texts that refer to areas in which the classical Diana was never apparently worshipped. Some of the effect may just be created by repetition, especially of one famous text, the so-called 'Canon Episcopi' which first appears in a work from about the year 906. It may also be that the clerical authors of the records substituted the name for others actually used by local people. They may have done so because Diana was the Roman goddess most closely associated with night and with witch-craft, as Hekate was in the Greek-speaking world. Alternatively, she may simply have been the only goddess named in the New Testament, the book best known to Christian Europe, even as Herodias was the wickedest woman found in it. Whatever the reason, the popular tradition of the night rides, and the clerical records of it, kept alive a consciousness of this classical deity as a force in the imagination, of a more dramatic and menacing kind than those found as figures of literary romance.

Latin Christianity, however, represented only half of the medieval Christian world. The other was the province of Greek Orthodoxy, and the Churches descended from it, and this was much more directly and obviously the cultural heir of that Hellenistic world which had produced the developments in religion and magic with which this chapter is concerned. After all, the Roman Empire itself had contracted into the Greek-speaking state of Byzantium, the centre of eastern Christianity, and so it is there that the achievements of earlier Greek culture could be expected to have survived and been developed most clearly. The truth is less straightforward. Because of the eventual obliteration of the Byzantine state by Islam and the resulting eclipse of its culture, less evidence has survived, and what there is has been less studied, than in the Latin-using world. Nor is it apparent that Byzantine scholars showed as much interest in pagan Greek philosophy and spirituality as their Muslim counterparts. None the less, they did make an important contribution to the transmission of both.

There is general agreement that a key part was played in this by Michael Psellus, the central figure of the eleventh-century Byzantine literary revival. John Duffy has hailed Psellus as 'singlehandedly ... responsible for bringing back, almost from the dead, an entire group of occult authors and books whose existence had long been as good as forgotten'.[112] These authors and books consisted of the Hermetic texts, Proclus and the Chaldean Oracles. The extant nature of the sources certainly bears out Duffy's statement, but there is a chance that it merely reflects our lack of knowledge of earlier Byzantine scholarship. It is also possible that the role of Psellus in the recovery of late antique ideas has been inflated. He has been credited, for example, with compiling and ordering what became the standard collection of the religious Hermetic texts, the manuscript from which all later copies were made and from which those texts have passed down to posterity, and which became called the Corpus Hermeticum. Considered more closely, however, it becomes apparent that all that can be said with confidence is that the Corpus could have been put together at any time between the fourth and the fourteenth centuries. It is entirely possible that Psellus played a part in the process, but not demonstrable. The evidence for his involvement boils down to the belief by one later Byzantine copyist that he provided a comment on one of the texts.[113]

What is beyond doubt is that Michael Psellus gave the Chaldean Oracles and later Neoplatonists a prominence greater than that of any known Byzantine scholar before his time; but here other problems of interpretation appear, creating by the subtlety with which Psellus himself operated, and our ignorance of the nature and quality of many of his sources. His consistent attitude to pagan literature was that it could be interpreted in a manner that bolstered the claims of Christianity, and that some of it was inherently valuable. In his own assessment of it he cast his net of research very widely, being interested in 'Chaldean', Egyptian, Greek, Hebrew and Christian texts alike, but praised the Neoplatonists in particular as the ancient Greeks best versed in theology. He accepted the interpretation of pagan mythology as cosmic allegory, and extended it to suggest that much of it anticipated and supported Christian doctrine. He made a particular example of the Chaldean Oracles, compiling a selection of quotations from them and showing how they could be matched with teachings from the Bible.[114]

Psellus was very conscious of the need to distinguish and reject unacceptable components in late antique pagan thought. He condemned alchemy, astrology and ritual magic, and described theurgy as nonsense. Indeed, he turned his scholarly expertise in these fields into a weapon against personal rivals, accusing the patriarch of Constantinople himself, Michael Cerularios, of engaging in such acts in the year 1059. According to Psellus's account, Cerularios had joined with some monks in hiring a female medium who became inspired by singing, monotonous movements and drugs. She then levitated, spoke in trance and summoned apparitions of Christian prophets, martyrs and saints. Georg Luck has commented that these charges show how pagan theurgy had survived in a Christian context.[115] What they certainly demonstrate is how theurgy could be imagined to be transmuted into a Christian form; whether it actually was enacted as described, or whether these scenes were fantasies concocted by the enemies of Cerularios, seems impossible now to determine. It is apparent that theurgy fascinated Psellus, and it is not always easy to reconcile his condemnation of the practice of it with his assertions that the theory behind it contained divine wisdom. Overall, he seems to have used the classical distinction between effects produced by human manipulation, or coercion of supernatural powers, and those produced by divine will. His location of that division, however, differed significantly from that of the later Neoplatonists, for he condemned the ritual use of invocations, incenses, stones and plants to repel or summon spirits or to achieve visions. Instead he praised a contemporary empress of Byzantium, Zoe, for her possession of a religious icon that gave answers to questions by changing colour; this, he felt, was a pious and orthodox means of securing oracles.[116]

It certainly seems that, following his work, Platonism, Neoplatonism and ritual magic had a higher profile among Byzantine intellectuals, although again this pattern may be a result of the survival of evidence. Dealing with them was a tricky business, and not everybody managed the balancing act achieved by Psellus himself. In 1082 the career of his own pupil John Italos was ruined by condemnation for heresy because he was judged to have gone too far in reintepreting Christianity with the use of Platonic concepts.

The story was put about that one of Italos's followers, sentenced to death by drowning in the Bosphorus, called on Poseidon, ancient Greek god of the sea, as he was flung into it. If true, it shows how a study of ancient texts might beget a genuine paganism; but it may be a libel.[117] More fortunate or skilful was Michael Italikos, metropolitan of Philippolis in the mid twelfth century, who pulled off the classic trick of parading his knowledge of magical lore while emphasising his own lack of belief in any of it, or wish to put it into practice. He proclaimed the importance of the Chaldean Oracles and Neoplatonists to learning while steering clear of an endorsement of theurgy, and rated Greek philosophy above the works of 'Chaldeans'.[118]

Swirling around such figures was a medley of occult texts, but it is almost impossible to write the history of their transmission because, while some of those that survive are clearly late antique or early medieval in origin, they exist only in fourteenth or fifteenth-century copies. Many of those used by Psellus are completely lost. Six manuscripts dated from the fifteenth century and later preserve fragments of a Greek work, apparently composed between the seventh and eleventh centuries, that listed the attendant angels and demons of the hours and planets. Other Byzantine codices of the same late date contain parts of a late antique work, the 'Book of Wisdom', which described the angels governing the various divisions of time and gave the secret names of the seasons, sun, moon, heaven, earth, sea and four directions. It recommended the use of prayers to draw their power into physical images. Both texts may have been among the sources of the *Ghayat al-Hakim*.[119] Occult tradition may also, however, have flowed back out of the Islamic world into the Bzyantine one. One of the more influential texts bequeathed by late antiquity to medieval magic was the *Kyranides*, an exposition of the medical properties of birds, fishes, plants and stones and of the means by which they might be locked into healing amulets. It existed in Egypt by the third century at the latest, but was revised by that fourth-century Alexandrian philosopher, Harpokration, from whose name that of the Latin translation of the *Ghaya*, the *Picatrix*, may have been derived. A third revision was made by a Byzantine author before the year 800. What became the standard Latin text of the work, however, was produced from a Greek one that claimed to be a translation from an Arabic version, produced in the 1160s on the orders of the Byzantine emperor Manuel I.[120] This single book illustrates well the complex three-cornered relationship between the Islamic, Byzantine and Latin Christian worlds. Exchanges between the last two are further suggested by the manner in which, during the fourteenth and fifteenth centuries, ritual magic underwent a parallel development in both. Byzantines, like adherents of western Christianity, began to to compile and copy texts that prescribed elaborate ceremonies for the invocation and direction of spirits, and placed particular emphasis on the centrality of the consecrated circle as the working space of a magician.[121]

The Byzantine engagement with late antique paganism and its legacy reached a spectacular climax immediately before the final destruction of the empire, in the work of George Gemistos, commonly nicknamed Pletho or Plethon. He died in 1452, only a year before the fall of the imperial capital to the Turks, having lived out much of his scholarly life at Mistra in the Peloponnese, capital of the last remaining Byzantine province. A miasma of doubt and disputation surrounds the reputation and significance of Pletho, generated by the fact that what was probably his most significant book, the *Nomoi*, was never published, and the manuscript of it was burned as heretical after his death on the orders of the patriarch of Constantinople, George Scholarius. All that we know of it consists of fragments quoted by Scholarius himself, seconded by another of his enemies, George of Trebizond, to justify this condemnation. These extracts can be collated with relevant material from his surviving writings. What is certain is that Pletho was an isolated and highly idiosyncratic thinker, dedicated to restoring the greatness of Greek culture, even as the empire that represented it tottered towards extinction. He aimed to do so by making contemporary Greeks aware of the glories of pagan philosophy, above all that of Plato and the Neoplatonists, although he also used Julian and extracts from the Chaldean Oracles. He represented these late antique texts as the culmination of a tradition that had been founded by Hermes, Orpheus and the Persian Zoroaster.

This programme has, however, been interpreted by modern scholars in two different ways. To some, he was a devout if eccentric Christian, attempting like Psellus to strengthen Greek Orthodoxy with ideas taken from pagan philosophy in order to foster belief in a constantly developing Greek tradition, based on divine revelation and spanning the whole period since the dawn of history. To others, he wished instead to demolish Christianity altogether and substitute a revived pagan religion based on ancient models and featuring a supreme and controlling god, Zeus, from whom all the universe emanated. In this scheme Zeus ruled with the immediate assistance of a god and goddess, Poseidon and Hera, the former occupying much of the role attributed to Jesus in the Christian cosmos, below whom were four descending ranks of lesser divinites. Most prominent among the latter seems to have been Apollo, the power of the sun, with the planetary deities as his companions and ministers. A draft calender and liturgy by him survives, which is Christian with pagan flourishes and connotations. The fragments of his work quoted against him by Scholarius certainly seem to represent a revived paganism, but may have been removed from their true context in order to fabricate a case against him. In a private letter Scholarius himself admitted that he could not really understand Pletho's beliefs; which makes it exceedingly unlikely that we can ever do so.

It can be stated securely that nowhere in any of his extant writings, including those quoted against him by his opponents, did Pletho repudiate Christianity. In none of them, also, did he recommend paganism as such. They make plain that he despised the polytheism of most ancient pagans as much as he deplored what he saw as the superstition of much popular Christianity in his own time. What he was seeking instead were the transcendental principles that he believed to unite both Platonic philosophy and Christianity. How far he compromised the latter in favour of the former, or how far his apparent blueprint for a new paganism was intended as a utopian fantasy or an allegory, rather than a practical proposal, are questions that may be for ever unanswered. The two most recent extended considerations of the subject reach opposite conclusions, with equal confidence.[122]

The French scholar Pierre Chuvin, who has accepted the theory that ancient paganism was preserved far into the middle ages at Harran, has also noted the apparent paganism of Pletho and expressed a feeling that somehow 'the torch was passed' between the two.[123] It would be possible to construct a number of hypothetical routes by which such a transmission might have occurred, but all would run up against some fundamental problems. One is that we have no certain knowledge either of the beliefs of early medieval Harranians or of Pletho. Another is that, whereas Harran certainly sheltered some kind of genuine sectarian tradition, Pletho appears to have been an isolated and original thinker. The third is that one of the most common agreements among medieval Islamic authors, concerning the religion of the Sabians of Harran, is that it contained a prominent component of Hermetism. Pletho disregarded the Hermetic texts even when he cited authorities that admired them. A fourth difficulty is that, in sharp contrast to scholars working within Muslim states, those of Byzantium never seem to have paid attention to Harran, or credited its people as a source of manuscripts or ideas.[124] In addition to all this, it may well be that the notion of torch-bearers is itself misplaced. What seems to have happened instead is that certain texts survived into the middle ages from the ancient world, which at particular moments provoked a flurry of thought among Greek and Latin Christians. How they were transmitted, or even what those thoughts were, is only dimly perceived. The metaphor of torchlight can be reversed, to suggest that much of the history of the subject is in darkness, with a few points and people imperfectly illuminated.

That said, the quantity of illumination increases dramatically from the fifteenth century onward, and the sense of a torch being passed is much more real in the subsequent history of Pletho's thought. He certainly seems to have had at least one pupil to whom he confided his religious beliefs, Demetrius Raoul Kabakes (1397–1487). Kabakes admired his teacher enthusiastically, and devoted his own later years to salvaging what could be retrieved of Pletho's work. He himself admired the writings of Julian, and regarded the sun as the physical embodiment of supreme divinity. He annotated a copy of Julian's hymn to the solar god with the comment that both he and Pletho had venerated the sun, although his master had not actually read this text.[125] Kabakes himself, however, was not an influential thinker, and it was Italians and not Greeks who were to be Pletho's true spiritual heirs. In 1439 Pletho himself served in the Byzantine delegation sent to the council held in Italy to discuss the reunification of the Greek and Roman Churches. The final stages of its meetings were held in Florence, where his lectures on Plato and Platonism caught the attention of some of the city's intellectuals and patrons of learning. Twenty years later the greatest of the latter and the first citizen of Florence, Cosimo de Medici, sponsored the creation of a group of scholars based on the ancient Platonist and Neoplatonist academy of Athens and dedicated to the recovery of Greek learning. This has traditionally been regarded as one of the cultural powerhouses of the Italian Renaissance; such an interpretation is now controversial, but there is no doubt that a network of literary figures operating in and around Florence, partly under Medici patronage, did much to foster Greek studies in Italy. There is no firm evidence that Cosimo was directly inspired to support this movement by having heard Pletho, but there are indications that he had copied a work of Plato from a manuscript brought by the Greek to Florence. At any rate, Florentine scholars later remembered Pletho's visit as having sown the seeds that were eventually to germinate as the project to recover the wisdom of the ancient Greek world.[126]

There is nothing to indicate that the Italians knew anything of the religious ideas that were to earn Pletho his posthumous condemnation; they honoured him for his expertise in ancient Greek philosophy, which was not contentious in itself on either side of the ecclesiastical division. None the less, they were to celebrate his memory in a fashion unknown among the intellectual leadership of his own people. He acquired a particular admirer in one petty prince, Sigismondo Malatesta of Rimini, who had his body exhumed and brought to Italy, for reburial in a sarcophagus of antique style, in the walls of a church rebuilt partly as a shrine to great writers. The remodelling of the building was carried out by the great architect Leon Battista Alberti, and, although still dedicated to Christian worship, it was influenced by the plan of a classical temple. Pope Pius II, in the course of a quarrel with

Sigismondo in which he accused the latter of many crimes including heresy, described the new building as 'full of pagan works, so that it seemed to be a temple of infidels worshipping daemons rather than of Christians'. The pope was at least partially right, for the structure survives, and its rich decorations mix triumphant figures of the planetary deities in their classical forms (Venus being nude) with those of saints, angels and personifications of the sciences and the virtues.[127] It was a resting place for which Pletho himself would probably have been grateful, but we cannot be sure of this. It is at one with the many questions that hang over his career that there is equally little explanation of how the prince came to admire him so much, and what theology actually underpinned the temple or church in which he now lies.

The reception of pagan images and ideas by the Renaissance is a subject for which there is a great deal of good data and which has been well served by scholars. It could be described simplistically as a surge of interest, enthusiasm and reworking caused by the confluence of three streams of material, all of which have been represented in the discussion above. There was the native, Latin Christian, tradition, as it had evolved by the early fifteenth century. There was the Arabic one, represented now most obviously by the wide dissemination of *Picatrix*. Although, as said, the *Ghayat al-Hakim* had been translated into this Latin version, as well as a Spanish one, during the mid twelfth century, for some reason it had failed to make any immediate impact on European scholars in general.[128] Suddenly, in the last three decades of the fifteenth century, knowledge of it spread across western Europe, to make it one of the most renowned, and scandalous, esoteric texts of the next two hundred years. The third stream of tradition and texts was the Greek, and this played the most obvious and celebrated part in the transmission of new material to Latin culture as scholars and manuscripts trickled into Italy from the dying Byzantine realms.

In evaluating the implications of this surge of interest for the reworking of late antique ideas, the shrewdest comment has perhaps been made by the historian of Renaissance Platonism, James Hankins: 'The real contention in Renaissance Italy was not between paganism and Christianity, but rather between competing definitions of what Christianity was and what it meant to be a Christian.'[129] Pletho may have provided the ultimate inspiration for the foundation of the Florentine academy, but the Greek who did most to promote the study of Plato in Italy, and was himself an admirer of Pletho, was of different character and aims. This was Johannes Bessarion, a Byzantine refugee who became a major figure in the Roman Church. He had absorbed the older man's admiration of Platonism as the major ancient

philosophy and his analysis of the decline of Greek culture as the consequence of abandoning ancient wisdom. Bessarion, however, subordinated
Plato's thought firmly to the Bible, believed that it had itself taken concepts
from the Old Testament prophets, and laboured to make it safe for Christians to accept. To do so he employed concepts taken selectively from
Neoplatonism, and especially from Proclus, to reconcile the cosmos of
Platonism with that of Christianity. His teachings became the main channel
by which Platonism, Neoplatonism and the (more respectable) scholarship
of Pletho reached Renaissance Italians.[130]

The acid test of the latter's relationship with images and ideas from
ancient paganism is whether any of them can be proved to have got
sufficiently carried away by these to have revived rites to pagan deities, in
place of the Christian god. The answer seems to be that none ever did. For
a long time scholars entertained the probability that there was an exception
to this rule, in the shape of a group of young intellectuals who gathered
in Rome in the late 1460s. Their mentor was an eccentric aristocrat from
Salerno called Giulo Sanseverino, who advocated the recovery of the city's
imperial heritage by a critical study of texts, coins and monuments. They
held feasts on ancient sites at the dates of pagan holy days, crowning
themselves with laurel wreaths, spoke classical Latin to each other and took
ancient Roman nicknames, Sanseverino himself becoming Pomponius
Laetus. In 1468 the reigning pope, Paul II, arrested the leaders on charges
of sexual immorality, the practice of revived pagan religion, and (last but
not least) conspiring against his own life. For about a century the second
charge, in particular, was believed by historians, but recently expert opinion
has swung sharply against it. It has been noted that no trials seem to have
resulted and that the prisoners were all subsequently released after interrogation. Paul's successor, Sixtus IV, restored the group to favour and
encouraged them to renew their antiquarian activities with direct papal
sponsorship. In 1478 it was formally incorporated as a Christian religious
fraternity dedicated to three saints, and as such flourished to the end of
the century while still continuing its custom of antique names and banquets.
All the evidence suggests that Pope Paul had simply over-reacted, propelled
by unfounded suspicions.[131]

When this has been said, the use of ancient pagan traditions to reinforce
and reinterpret Christianity could itself produce some remarkable blends,
and this is nowhere more obvious, influential and celebrated than in the
work of one of the key figures of the Italian Renaissance, Marsilio Ficino.
He was the leader of Cosimo de Medici's 'academy' at Florence, and the
translator to Latin of the Corpus Hermeticum and some of the Platonist
and Neoplatonist texts. The recovery of the full collection of writings in

the Corpus, with their apparent fervent monotheism, licensed him to ignore the condemnation made by Augustine and subsequent Christian writers of those Hermetic tracts that had survived in the Latin-reading west. In particular, this condemnation had been directed against a passage that endorsed the drawing of divine power into statues after the Egyptian manner. Ficino was now able to appeal to earlier Christian authors, notably Lactantius, who had praised the Hermetic literature as godly, and his defence helped to give its ostensible author, Hermes, the status of a great human prophet. Ficino's readiness to accept magical techniques as a part of both religion and medicine was enhanced by his reading of the Platonists and Neoplatonists. Plato gave him the idea that numbers are the basis of magical harmony, and Plotinus furnished the concept of a World Soul animating the cosmos, reflected in material forms, and capable of being concentrated in special material receptacles such as shrines and statues. Iamblichus taught him that the stars influenced earthly affairs, and Porphyry's writings reinforced the passage from the Hermetic texts that asserted how images could receive invoked divinities. Proclus's little book, *On the Priestly Art*, presented him with a natural, non-demonic magic based on the inherent correspondences between celestial powers and particular plants, stone and incenses. Writings attributed to the medieval scholars Peter of Abano, Albertus Magnus and Thomas Aquinas bolstered his faith in astral magic, and it is possible that he was further influenced by *Picatrix*.[132]

Ficino's three-volume work *Libri de vita*, published in 1489, was the most popular of all his productions, going through more than thirty editions by 1650. It has also often been considered the most significant Renaissance statement on complex ritual magic. Most of it is concerned with the application of the doctrine of occult correspondences to medicine, but it includes a cautious recommendation of the drawing of heavenly powers into talismanic images for healing purposes. Those powers included the ruling spirits of the stars, the signs of the zodiac and its divisions, and (above all) the planets. Most benevolent were the Sun, Jupiter and Venus. He justified the animation of images on the grounds that this was the result of the manipulation of celestial influences and not of the conjuration of demons. The consecrated images were not to be worshipped but used by priests in magical operations, and the whole point of the latter was not to compel spirits but to make the operator and his patients more receptive to the natural influences of heavenly bodies. The talisman that he recommended as most potent was a cross with its arms aligned on the four cardinal points of the compass. This he believed to have been used by the ancient Egyptians, whom he claimed as unwitting prophets of Christianity. For invocations of the three healthful planets, he supplied songs modelled on the late antique Orphic hymns and combining music, specially suited to the character of each, with lyrics reciting their names and attributions.[133] As both D. P. Walker and Frances Yates have pointed out, what Ficino presents here as medicine is a kind of religion.[134]

It was, moreover, a religion embedded in a similarly eclectic cosmology. It depended on the idea that between the World Soul that conveyed divine force from the creator and the World Body composed of matter was a World Spirit, infused through the universe and acting as the medium by which celestial influences could reach humans. Humans could, however, also make a spiritual journey in the other direction, for that reunion with divinity that was the goal of so much late antique writing. Ficino portrayed three classical deities as empowered with the responsibility of assisting them on this journey: Mercury, Apollo and Venus, representing respectively truth and intellect, peace and art, and beauty and love. Mercury was sometimes accorded first place in this triad, as the god who called human minds to higher things and represented the forces of vital curiosity and of reason. In other writings, however, Ficino attributed greatest importance to Venus, as Plato had placed heavy emphasis on love as the power that connected humanity to divinity.[135]

Here he drew on another concept of Plato's that had, as said, already been found useful by medieval Christians: the distinction between a heavenly and an earthly Venus. Ficino, however, made both goddesses equally good, the former representing divine intelligence and the latter the generative power of the World Soul, effectively the role taken earlier by Natura. The former was drawn to contemplate the beauty of the divine, and the latter to create images of divine beauty in an earthly form. Effectively they were the channels by which all creation was invested with the glory of the creator god, and thus earthly and divine love became a single entity and not opposed. Pletho had declared that sexual intercourse was a sacred act; Ficino asserted that contemplation and procreation were both holy and both aspects of the work of the great mediating goddess in her two aspects.[136] In a letter to his pupil Lorenzo di Pierfrancesco he described the special virtues of the planetary deities, the moon aiding the journey of soul and body and the sun representing the One God, Mars giving speed, Saturn tardiness, Jupiter law, Mercury reason and Venus humanity. He then burst into a hymn of rhapsody on the latter, calling her 'a nymph of marvellous loveliness, child of heaven and more than others beloved by God the highest. Her soul and mind are love and charity, her eyes dignity and magnanimity, her hands liberality and magnificence, her feet comeliness and modesty. Her whole then is temperance and honesty, charm and splendour. O what exquisite beauty!'[137] He had made her into the goddess of humanism.

All this, of course, might be taken merely as poetic allegory, and this impression is reinforced by the fact that Ficino was not always consistent or coherent regarding the functions of pagan deities in his Christian Platonism. With Venus he associated those classical demi-goddesses, the Graces, and played with their significance repeatedly, sometimes associating them with procession, rapture and return, sometimes with curiosity, discovery and embellishment, and sometimes with splendour, youth and happiness.[138] He never formed these ideas into a fully-developed theology, nor indicated in detail how these ancient figures related to the Christian Trinity or the processes of sin, salvation, damnation and sainthood, or the structures of Hell, Purgatory and Heaven. It seemed that they represented ideal qualities and forces that might fit humans for salvation, but it was never spelled out exactly how this could actually work. This woolliness, of course, saved Ficino's work from accusations of heresy, but it does not seem that he was being deliberately evasive or that he had any personal tendency to religious unorthodoxy. Unlike Pletho, he himself took holy orders, and his mission seems to have been to reinforce the Christian thought of his age with ancient ideas and images. In his scheme, Christ had revealed the fullness of mysteries previously granted by the One God in part to Moses, Plato and Hermes. None the less, as James Hankins has pointed out, he was attracted to forms of pagan religious belief and practice – Neoplatonism, Hermetism and astrology – that had been developed largely in opposition to late antique and early medieval Christianity [139]

Furthermore, Ficino operated in a network of friends and pupils, and within a cultural context, that shared and reproduced many of his ideas. The most famous of these friendships was with Giovanni Pico della Mirandola, who combined Neoplatonism and the Hermetic texts with the medieval Hebrew cosmological system of Cabbala. For present purposes two aspects of Pico's work are especially important. One is the manner in which he attributed benevolent qualities to the same pagan figures: for him, Venus personified ideal beauty, with the Graces as her attendants, representing different aspects of the beautiful.[140] The second is his endorsement of the art of investing material images and figures with the power of celestial bodies, as something both natural and benevolent. In this respect he anticipated Ficino, advocating these procedures in a pair of works published in 1486 and 1487 and specifying the use of the ancient Orphic hymns to planetary deities to achieve them. Frances Yates has summed up Pico's system as 'an intensely religious and mystical version of conjuring'.[141]

This was precisely how some more orthodox churchmen saw it, and his ideas were condemned by Pope Innocent VIII in 1487 and answered by a Spanish bishop, Pedro Garcia, two years later. It is interesting to note how much ground Garcia actually conceded to astral magic. He agreed that the One God had entrusted the planets and celestial spheres to good spirits, and that the latter controlled earthly phenomena, especially in the spheres of agriculture and medicine. He conceded that humans might work profitably with these and admitted that the use of astral talismans had apparently been endorsed by great medieval thinkers such as Albertus Magnus and Peter of Abano. His only qualification was the one voiced since the time of those earlier scholars: that the invocation of celestial power into material images ran the risk of calling in demons instead. As in the case of Sanseverino and his Romans two decades before, a change of pope meant a change of official attitude. In 1493 a new pontiff, Alexander VI, absolved all Pico's writings, and during the next year Pico himself wrote a further book defending astral magic. The artist Pinturicchio subsequently painted a series of frescoes for Pope Alexander in the Vatican. In one salon the Hebrew prophets and classical sibyls were placed alongside each other, testifying to the coming of Christ, while the ceiling was decorated with images of the planetary deities. In others astrology was given a prominent place among figures of the seven liberal arts and a series of paintings told the story of Isis and Osiris, at once suggesting that the ancient Egyptians had a prophetic vision of the Christian Resurrection and linking the sacred Apis bull of Egypt with the bull that was Alexander's family emblem.[142]

Pico was, moreover, only one of Ficino's acquaintances who shared ideas with him. Lorenzo de Medici, successor to Cosimo as effective ruler of Florence, wrote poetry that hailed Venus as the embodiment of divine beauty. So did Girolamo Benivieni, who added the idea that human souls achieved bliss by ascending to her. Ficino's friend Giovanni Nesi was a poet who described the spheres of heaven as filled with both angels and pagan goddesses and gods. He hailed the planetary deities as expressions of the will of the One God and Venus as the power through which all things are brought into being and preserved. Neri's heaven rang with the songs of the classical Muses.[143] Ficino's pupil Francesco Cattani da Diacceto also identified the planets with their Graeco-Roman deities, and heartily endorsed the manipulation of days, colours, hymns and images magically corresponding to them in order to acquire gifts of mind, body and fortune.[144] The youth to whom Ficino wrote his eulogy on Venus, Lorenzo di Pierfrancesco, was a patron of the artist Botticelli, who probably produced for his villa two of the most famous paintings of the Italian Renaissance, the *Birth of Venus* and the *Primavera*. Historians of art have suggested that both, and the latter in particular, are heavily influenced by Ficino's thought. Frances Yates has gone further, to suggest the the *Primavera* is itself a talisman, designed to draw down the beneficent powers of the deities depicted in it.[145] Nor were such ideas confined to this circle. In 1496 the physician to the queen of Naples published a book defending the making of images of the planetary spirits to utilise their influence.[146]

Interest in these subjects continued at the same pace into the sixteenth century, and began to receive celebrated expression outside Italy. One of the best known of such expressions was in the first full survey of Renaissance magic, the *De occulta philosophia* of the German scholar, physician and adventurer Cornelius Agrippa von Nettesheim. This was published in 1533, but probably written by 1510.[147] It commenced with an exposition of a Neoplatonist concept of the universe, in which the virtue of a single creator god descends through hierarchies of angels and celestial beings to the world of matter. Here Agrippa made clear his literary heroes and influences, praising Hermes, Zoroaster, Orpheus, Pythagoras, Plato and the Neoplatonist philosophers and characterising them as magicians as well as thinkers.[148] He used the doctrine of occult correspondences between celestial and material entities, as Iamblichus, Proclus, *Picatrix* and Ficino had done, to justify the employment of astral magic using incantations, colour and material objects associated with particular planets and other celestial bodies. He boldly asserted the beneficial properties of animated statues, images and talismans, and described the divinities invoked in the celestial bodies as having been established by the One God in the natural order for the wellbeing of humanity. The most potent were those representing the planets, and above all the sun, to whom he referred by their classical pagan names. He also embraced the ancient concept of spiritual reunion found in the ancient Hermetic and Neoplatonist texts, declaring that a good magician had the power to ascend through the spheres of the cosmos to the presence of the One God.[149]

Later in the same work, Agrippa characterised the magician as a holy person, marked out by religious faith and a moral and austere life, and by obvious talents and virtues that commanded the respect of others. He held open the possibility that the vocation might be an initiatory one, a new magus being consecrated like a priest by the laying on of the hands of a veteran. He asserted that Catholic Christianity was the most true of all religions, and that a magician must recognise and honour its One God. He also, however, powerfully diluted this by adding that there was much good in the pagan religions of Babylonia, Egypt, Assyria and Persia, and that much could be learned from them; he was following Graeco-Roman tradition in viewing these eastern cultures as the homelands of magic. He added that the One God rewarded those who practised these older religions. He also qualified his monotheism by emphasising the importance of the three orders of spirits that acted as deputies of the supreme divinity; in descending rank, the supercelestial, the celestial and the elemental. Of these, he stated again the particular importance of the planetary deities, whom he described as secondary divinities whom any successful magician needed to understand and serve, with incantations, talismans, and the offering of incenses.[150]

Despite its emphasis on piety and worthy purposes, this went far beyond anything that orthodox early modern Christians could accept, but the work became an 'underground' classic, copied, printed and translated steadily over the following three centuries. Furthermore, the acceptable limits of its subject matter remained a topic for keen debate among intellectuals of Agrippa's generation. His own friend and mentor Johannes Trithemius, abbot of the German monastery of Sponheim, defended the practice of planetary magic using talismans and invocations. He did so, however, with the amendment, known since the thirteenth century, of declaring that the planets were ruled by angels with Hebrew names, the greatest of a hierarchy that governed the cosmos below heaven itself, and appointed by the One God to respond to human prayers.[151] This stance was also adopted by a Venetian Franciscan, Francesco Giorgi.[152] Other compromises were made. One appeared in the cupola of a chapel of the major church of Santa Maria del Popolo, Rome, which contained the tomb of the banker and patron of artists Agostino Chigi. At some point in the early sixteenth century it was painted with figures representing the planetary divinities, in their classical forms, but with an angel hovering over each to indicate the controlling will of the One God, who himself appears in the centre. The Neapolitan humanist author Pontano wrote an epic on the creation of the cosmos, in which the 'Eternal Father' convenes a group of lesser divinities to aid him. He entrusts the seven planetary Intelligences with the task of completing the work of his creation, by giving form to the terrestrial world and its inhabitants even as he had formed heaven.[153] No popes or Church councils condemned such views, but they still, inevitably, aroused disquiet. The most celebrated scholar of the age, Erasmus, commented that 'if anything is brought from the Chaldeans or Egyptians, merely because of this we intensely desire to know it';[154] a tribute to the contemporary vogue for late antique magic and philosophy. Pico's own nephew, Giovanni Francesco Pico, condemned the views of his uncle and Ficino, especially with regard to talismans and Orphic incantations, and declared that the attempt to find merit in pre-Christian religions was pagan idolatory.[155]

This pattern persisted as the century wore on. Intellectuals still advocated and sometimes practised astral magic involving planetary deities in their Graeco-Roman forms. One was the British scholar John Dee, best known as a mathematician, alchemist and receiver of angelic messages, who wrote to defend the concept that each heavenly body had its own nature, and that skilled people could impress the rays of these bodies on material objects.[156] He left behind a manuscript written in fine Latin script and with elaborate painted illustrations, describing a rite to draw down the power of Venus, conceived of as a classical goddess, by invocations and manipulation of sympathetic substances.[157] Fabio Paolini, a professor of Greek at Venice, added his voice in 1589 to those who argued that the construction of planetary talismans was a legitimate use of the powers of nature, not requiring or risking demonic intervention. In support of this position he marshalled the Neoplatonists, a Hermetic text, Albertus Magnus and Peter of Abano.[158] The existence of such views caused Frances Yates to suggest the presence of such magic in the elaborate court entertainments sponsored by the Queen Mother of France, Catherine de Medici:

> When in the *Ballet comique de la reine* of 1581 ... Catherine saw Jupiter and Mercury descending from heaven in response to the incantatory music and singing, it is doubtful ... whether she saw this as a purely artistic representation. More probably, for her, such a performance was in the nature of an extended and complicated talisman, an arrangement of the planetary gods in a favourable order, invoked by favourable incantations, resulting not only in a marvellous work of art, but in a magical action ... by which the favour of the heavens was actually drawn down in aid of the French monarchy.[159]

This is possible, but unproven, and by Catherine's time official attitudes were hardening against such beliefs and practices in the more restrictive atmosphere of the Counter-Reformation. The Papal Index issued by Pope Paul V in 1559 included works on image-magic and talismans, and Peter of Abano was listed among the authors now forbidden to be read by Catholics. In 1586 Sixtus V prohibited all forms of divination, including astrology.[160] Italian intellectuals who defended astral magic were in for a rougher ride than before. Girolamo Cardano, a teacher at the university of Bologna, temporised by calling the planetary divinities angels, and by suggesting that talismans could be made to draw their power if no incantations were involved. In 1570, however, he was arrested by the local inquisitors, and lost his job, and the following year his books were banned, although he himself was given a papal pension on which to live in retirement.[161] When defending the use of the planetary talismans, Paolini felt obliged to add that the Church, none the less, forbade them and so they could not be used.[162] It was no longer safe to be too enthusiastic about late antique philosophy either. In 1592 Pope Clement VIII was sufficiently impressed by the teachings of a scholar at Ferrara, Francesco Patrizi, to invite him to teach at Rome; Patrizi had called for a revitalisation of Catholicism using the ideas of Plato, Plotinus, Proclus and the Corpus Hermeticum. When he arrived, however, he fell foul of the Roman inquisition, which condemned and suppressed his work.[163] It is not surprising that attacks on astral magic and on talismans by leading theologians, both Catholic and Protestant, increased notably during these decades.[164]

Alongside these controversies, authors continued to employ pagan divinities as allegorical or fictional figures in the medieval manner and, just as in the middle ages, these figures were sometimes given a cosmological significance. The Renaissance's preoccupation with ancient texts and art brought about a reappearance of Pan as the vivifying spirit of the natural world. Natalis Comes could declare that 'truly Pan is nothing other than nature itself', and at the other end of the sixteenth century the evangelical English Protestant Edmund Spenser hailed him in the same fashion. Most writers between tended to treat him in the older and less glorious ancient tradition as a symbol of rural innocence or ignorance, but at times the goat-foot god received still more impressive eulogies. Lorenzo de Medici commissioned a painting from Luca Signorelli, *The School of Pan*, that represented the deity as holding court, apparently as a teacher of the truths of nature, with a heroic dignity. Paulus Marsas identified him with Christ, and Rabelais took up this theme to turn him into a pagan version of the Good Shepherd. This was repeated by subsequent authors, and Pan featured in their work as representative of the redemptive as well as of the generative powers of the natural world; thus prefiguring his major importance in this role during the nineteenth and twentieth centuries.[165] The equivalent female figure, Natura, also made occasional literary reappearances, most notably in Spenser's allegorical epic, *The Faerie Queene*, where she appears as the ancestress of all life, to whom the other pagan deities are as inferior as humans themselves are to deities.[166] The concept of a goddess operating as a great mediatrix between the supreme deity of Christianity and the material world was preserved also in a different form. This was found as an illustration to esoteric writings, by scholars expounding Hermeticist traditions or seeking to reveal divine truths concealed in the remains of ancient civilisations. The first of these is well represented by the work of the English mystic Robert Fludd, the second by that of the Jesuit intellectual Athanasius Kircher. These two very different authors printed in their works an image representing the Platonic World Soul as a nude female, identified with the moon and crowned with stars, and linking heaven and earth, and God and humanity.[167] Both as star-goddess and earth-goddess, therefore, literary tradition maintained some sense of the divine feminine as the immediate power responsible for earthly existence.

The illicit late medieval tradition of elaborate ritual magic to call up spirits, using consecrated circles and cardinal points, special symbolic tools,

sympathetic substances and set invocations, continued to develop luxu-
riantly. Old handbooks were recopied, and new texts – including, apparently,
famous compendia of rites and spells such as the Key of Solomon and the
Goetia – composed. The sixteenth century has left both a larger and a more
varied range of such manuscripts than any before it. At times this tradition
merged with that of astral magic, as illustrated neatly on the title page of
the 1616 edition of the century's most famous dramatic work concerning
ceremonial magic: Christopher Marlowe's *Doctor Faustus*. Its woodcut shows
the magician standing within a circle holding a book of rites and a staff or
wand, and conjuring a demon. The circle is decorated with the symbols of
the seven planets and the signs of the zodiac.

At moments, this tradition made explicit reference to what genuinely seems
to be its source, in late antique Egypt. One sixteenth-century manuscript
contains a charm, 'to see visions and cause dreams', that reads

> Make a drawing of Besa on your left hand, and envelop your hand in a strip of
> black cloth that has been consecrated to Isis, and lie down to sleep without
> speaking a word, even to answer a question. Wind the remainder of the cloth
> around your neck. The ink with which you write must be composed of the blood
> of a cow, the blood of a white dove (fresh), frankincense, myrrh, black ink,
> cinnabar, mulberry juice, rain water, and juices of wormwood and vetch. With
> this write your petition before the setting sun (saying) 'Send the truthful seer
> out of the holy shrine, I beseech thee, Lampsuer, Sumarta, Baribas, Dardalam,
> Iorlex, O Lord, send the sacred deity Anuth Anuth, Salbana, Chambre, Breith,
> now, now, quickly, quickly. Come in this very night.' [168]

Both the deities named (Isis and Bes) are classic Egyptian patrons of magic,
and the whole form of the operation – the actions, ingredients and 'barbarous names' – is one that could have come straight out of the magical
papyri. Whether the spell had actually been transmitted from ancient times,
or whether it was composed by an early modern magician conscious of
Egyptian models, is difficult to say. The lack of direct knowledge of Egypt's
ancient culture that prevailed in sixteenth-century Europe would seem to
favour the former possibility.

In the current historiography of the late sixteenth century, two intellectuals
stand out as illustrating the different conclusions, and fates, to which a love
affair with pagan antiquity could lead in the circumstances of the age. One
is Giordano Bruno, whose role was clarified by the classic study of his career
by Frances Yates. A Neapolitan who had joined and then forsaken the
Dominican order, he attracted the patronage of a liberal Catholic king of
France, Catherine de Medici's son Henri III, while lecturing at Paris in 1581.
The following year he published two books. One declared that the ancient
Egyptian religion, as revealed in the Corpus Hermeticum, had been superior

to the Christianity of his own day. Influenced in part by Agrippa, it included an endorsement of the power of images of the planetary divinities and of those of the zodiac. The other provided incantations to the deities of the seven planets, in their classical forms and referring to them as 'the sacred gods'. Each was accompanied by the use of stones and plants associated with her or him and itself listed all the names and the esoteric material correspondences of the deity. Although based on those provided by Agrippa, they were rewritten with a novel passion and (arguably) beauty.[169]

In 1584 he added two more titles to his publications. The first was a glorification of his perception of the Egyptian magical religion. Here the influence of the Hermetic texts and (perhaps) of Neoplatonism was still clearer. In Bruno's reading, the One God became present in all things, spiritual and material, and the influence of the planetary deities, being his creations and aspects, was likewise resident in the plants, stones and animals especially associated with each. Even as the deities could descend into their statues, so worshippers could use material objects ritually as links to the divinities, and through them as a means of reunion with the One: 'Thus through the light which shines in natural things one mounts up to the life which presides over them.' Within this system, Bruno retained Christ only as an exceptionally powerful and benevolent magician, and he called on the French king to lead a revival of this old and true religion. His second book of the year proclaimed the best philosophy to be that of the Chaldeans, Egyptians, Persians, Orphic writers and Pythagoreans. In it he claimed himself to be the prophet of a new movement, having made a personal spiritual ascent to the heavenly realm and returned.[170]

This was all too much for Bruno's royal patron, and in 1586 the scholar moved on to the German Protestant stronghold of Wittenburg. There he published a new work positing the domination of the universe by a 'supernal triad' of Father, Son and Light, from which the cosmos proceeded in a series of emanations. The latter included a medley of lesser deities drawn from those of the planets, the Graeco-Roman Pantheon and the zodiac. Among them was a triad of goddesses, Minerva, Venus and Thetis, of whom (as an intellectual) he declared the first to be his personal favourite. His last book, never published, provided a similar divine hierarchy in which influence proceeded from the One God to the lesser deities, and so through the heavenly to the earthly realm. A vital link in this, between the stars and the elemental world, was provided by the spirits commonly called demons, and the spiritual ascent of humanity could only be achieved by working with these in ritual, using invocations, incantations and physical objects such as images, seals and characters. In this, as in all his works, Bruno persisted in viewing Christianity as essentially good and wise, and the

Catholic Church in particular as an institution that merely needed reform, rather than destruction, to revive the ancient wisdom. It was this instinctual trust that led him in 1591 to accept an invitation from a Venetian nobleman, who on learning of the extent of his beliefs handed him over to the local inquisition. Under the rules, he was sent on to Rome for final judgement, where, after eight years in which he remained ultimately unwilling to accept that his views constituted heresy, he was burned at the stake.[171] He thus became the only martyr of the Renaissance love affair with antiquity.

The other intellectual whose career typifies the climax of this love affair was a fellow southern Italian, Tommaso Campanella, who has been called the last of the Italian Renaissance philosophers.[172] Like Bruno, he too joined the Dominicans, and recruited heavily among them for a rebellion that he led against Spanish rule over his native province of Calabria. This had its own spiritual aspect, for as part of it he hailed Christianity as a true religion, but one needing reform to refound it more truly on the laws of nature. The failure of the revolt, in 1599, landed Campanella in prison for twenty-seven years, and he seems to have evaded execution only by pretending madness. Once the threat of this had passed, he employed his time in captivity by writing, the first result, in 1602, being a vision of an ideal state based on a City of the Sun. It contained a temple to the solar god himself, and to the other planetary deities and those of the greatest stars, and its religion was directed to achieving a beneficial relationship with these entities, and acting in harmony with their conjunctions. Christ and the apostles were given an honoured place within it, as the greatest of priests and magicians. As Frances Yates has pointed out, the immediate inspiration for this vision was probably a section of *Picatrix*, but the overall model for it is a conception of ancient Egypt, provided by the Corpus Hermeticum. It was presented not as a blueprint, but as an example of a 'natural' religion running parallel to that of Christ, and an encouragment to Christians to incorporate ancient ideas and some taken from study of the cosmos into their own faith. Thus strengthened, Campanella argued, it could convert the world.[173]

This was one of the earliest, and for present purposes the most significant, of a stream of works that he produced in captivity, which eventually convinced the authorities that he was once again both sane and trustworthy. Being released, he soon won favour with the papacy, and in 1628 Urban VIII drew on his reputation as an expert in occult lore for personal benefit. The pontiff had become convinced that he was threatened personally by the presumed malevolent influence of certain eclipses that were about to occur, and engaged Campanella to work a rite of astral magic to avert it. The latter duly obliged, sealing a room from the inside, sprinkling it with rose-water and other aromatics, burning laurel, myrtle, rosemary and cypress, hanging the chamber with white silken clothes, decorating it with branches and lighting it with two lamps and five torches, to represent the sun, the moon and the other planets. He then employed sympathetic magic, represented by a combination of music, stones, plants, odours, colours and flavours (the latter supplied by the drinking of liqueurs distilled at appropriate astrological conjunctions) to draw down the powers of Venus and Jupiter to protect the pope. The latter seems to have been suitably impressed, and grateful.[174]

Campanella's career was now thoroughly refounded, and he completed it by following in the path trod by Bruno decades before, to Paris. There he adapted his imagery of the solar city to suit the new ambitions of the French monarchy, perhaps inspiring some of the symbolism that was to flower so vividly in the next generation at the court of the 'Sun King' Louis XIV. He also published his theory of astral magic there, in 1638, beginning by paying tribute to the intellectual influence of Porphyry, Iamblichus, Proclus, the Corpus Hermeticum and Ficino. He assimilated the planetary divinities to Christian theology by representing them as grander versions of saints or angels. As such, they were beings under the ultimate control of the One God and not to be worshipped as deities themselves, but disposing of great power on which humans could draw for their own benefit, by using the proper procedures. He declared that the respect paid to them had been the noblest and most admirable aspect of ancient pagan religion.[175]

The image of Campanella working his rite to Venus and Jupiter on behalf of a Counter-Reformation pope would be a wonderful one on which to conclude this survey; and indeed Campanella's career has commonly been treated as a terminal point. He was the last of that succession of prominent philosophers and theologians, concerned with reintegrating classical paganism and ritual magic into Christianity, that began with Ficino. In 1614 Isaac Casaubon proved that the Corpus Hermeticum had been composed in the late antique period instead of being, as supposed since the middle ages, a product of the most remote past. This destroyed its credentials as a body of religious literature based on revelation that could take its place beside the Bible as a guide to Christian thought. With this departed much of the basis for the Renaissance attempt to reconcile Christianity with aspects of ancient paganisms; and by the mid seventeenth century Casaubon's revelations had become general knowledge.[176] By that time, also, the tradition of astral magic, seeking to draw down the powers of celestial bodies conceived of as divinities identified with classical goddesses and gods, had ceased to find literary champions. Apart from Campanella himself, the last was probably the Frenchman Jacques Gaffarel, who published in 1629. By contrast, the number of works condemning the tradition increased markedly during the century, and their production was sustained. Significantly, to those that held the practice to be impious was now joined a new category of those who held it to be supersititious and contrary to the laws of astronomy and physics; learned culture was rejecting astral magic and astrology as part of the same mental package.[177]

It could also be argued that the attempt to reconcile Christianity with classical and Graeco-Egyptian paganism had always been as purely an intellectual tradition as was ancient Neoplatonism itself, making no apparent impact on popular belief. Where surveys of the latter are made, they show plenty of concepts that troubled the orthodox of the day, and that drew in some cases on ancient pagan thought, but none that match the notions of the authors and artists studied here. Between 1590 and 1640, for example, evangelical Protestant preachers and writers deplored the tendency of ordinary English people to ascribe the consequences of daily events to a fickle goddess called Fortune, or to the laws of nature, or to the movements of the heavens, rather than to the providential will of the One God as Christian theology directed.[178] None of these traditions, however, included reverence for ancient deities. Likewise, although Agrippa's book and other texts of ritual magic played a large part in the 'cunning craft' of folk magicians in England and Wales until the nineteenth century, they seem to have been used as operative manuals for practical ends, rather than as part of a religion that included a place for the old divinities.[179] There is no sign as yet that things were different elsewhere in Europe.

When these these things have been said, however, it remains possible to argue that the ideas and preoccupations of the Renaissance magi did not completely disappear in the course of the seventeenth century; they just ceased to interest prominent members of the intelligensia. The quantity of publications produced to condemn astral magic and the theories on which it depended suggest that there were still plenty of people around who needed persuasion. In the early eighteenth century it was still believed by some scholars that the planets were animate beings, and a hundred years later doctors could yet be found who were confident that they influenced human health.[180] More texts of ritual magic survive in British archives in seventeenth-century copies than from any other period, and this may be true elsewhere as the copies concerned were often of French or Italian versions. Copying of them continued into the eighteenth century, and one of the most significant works in the tradition, the Book of Abramelin the Mage, exists only in a recension of that date; it may actually have been composed then. When that century's most famous social adventurer,

Casanova, was imprisoned by the inquisition at Venice in 1755, it was for the possession of several such works, including *Picatrix*. He clearly never forgot their contents, because later in his career he worked classic rites of astral magic using talismans and sympathetic metals and jewels to draw on the powers of the planetary divinities.[181] Casanova was a Freemason as well as an occultist, and the mystical societies that burgeoned in the eighteenth century in imitation of Freemasonry included a number with rites based partly on classical pagan models, one at least of which employed Graeco-Egyptian texts.[182] The addiction of the ruling elites of the period to Greek and Roman culture produced a number of half-playful commemorations of its deities, such as the annual procession in honour of Pan organised by a Cotswold squire to entertain his local villagers.[183] A steady stream of connections thus lie between the Renaissance and the occult revival and neo-pagan movements of the nineteenth century.

None the less, the sense of a loss of pace and of reputability for the Renaissance experiment in reconciling Christianity, paganism and ritual magic is very apparent by the mid seventeenth century. Aspects of its preoccupations indeed continued through the next two hundred years, but never united, as between 1460 and 1640, as a grand project. Given this pattern, it can be suggested that there were three great periods in which western Europeans made major and sustained attempts to revivify Christianity, or to compensate for its perceived gaps or failings, by use of ideas and images from pagan antiquity, and from the tradition of ritual magic. Each was propelled by an infusion of new data, partly provided by more rigorous analysis of texts in domestic archives and partly imported from abroad. The first was in the twelfth and thirteenth centuries, when the imported element was represented mainly by Arabic works. The second was in the late fifteenth and the sixteenth centuries, and the foreign element was mainly Byzantine Greek. The third was in the late nineteenth and early twentieth centuries, when archaeology, especially Egyptian, provided the major influx of new material. There were major continuities between the three, each of the last two looking back to the work of the previous one. The first two were both followed by a loss of confidence and energy, induced partly by official repression. The third led on instead to a revival of self-conscious and fully formed pagan religions, the modern Paganism.[184]

In this pattern of events there is nothing to contradict James Hankins's assertion regarding the Italian Renaissance; all the attempts to reconcile Christian and pagan thought made in Europe between 1000 and 1800 were intended to produce a better sort of Christianity rather than to revive paganism as such. In this sense, Ludo Milis's 'pagan middle ages' remain a contradiction in terms, and it can be restated that there were no pagans in Europe after the formal conversion of its respective regions to the Christian faith. What does seem to be apparent is that there were also three major traditions existing within European Christianity that depended directly on ancient pagan models and to some extent worked to supplement or subvert religious orthodoxy. One was that the sun, moon and other planets were themselves divinities, to be identified with the classical pagan deities with whom their names were associated, and that humans might use ritual to draw down their power and infuse it into earthly matter for their own benefit. The second was that between the supreme deity and the earth stood a mediating female figure, with direct responsibility for life. To a great extent this role was taken within mainstream medieval Christianity by the Virgin Mary, but the concern here is with the alternative figures based on pagan models: Natura, Venus or the World Soul. The third tradition was that of complex ritual magic, based on literary texts that were themselves constantly innovative but which also looked back consciously to ancient origins. It depended on the notion of hidden forces within the natural world, sometimes represented by complementary links built into the structure of the cosmos, and sometimes by spirits who could be befriended or commanded. Although the ends of this tradition always consisted of practical benefits to the operator or a client, those benefits could take the form of enhanced knowledge, spiritual power or union with the divine. A combination of these three traditions was to provide the essence of twentieth-century Paganism. Although it was to provide it in a distinctively modern form, and in response to modern needs, all three had ancient roots, all had existed and developed throughout the Christian centuries, and all would not have worked so potently within modernity had it not been for their engagement with medieval and early modern thought. Their survival may well come to be regarded as one of the great themes of western religious culture; but it is a story that has hardly as yet started to be written.

6

A Modest Look at Ritual Nudity

In the spring of 1990 I concluded the writing of my book on what was known of the pagan religions of the ancient British Isles, with a section that drew a series of comparisons and contrasts between those religions and the set which made up modern British Paganism. One of the differences which I suggested specifically concerned the religion of modern Pagan witchcraft, called Wicca: that 'no known cult in the ancient world was carried on by devotees who all worshipped regularly in the nude', as some varieties of Wiccan certainly do.[1] I would not subsequently have used the word 'cult' in this context, for although it was employed here to refer to specific forms of ancient religion for which it might well be valid, it could create confusion by seeming by extension to include Wicca itself. In a later publication I was to look more closely at these formulations and declare that Wicca was more complex than cults, and deserved to be distinguished from them as a full-blown religion.[2] Since 1990, I have also had further opportunity to reflect upon the rest of that statement. On the one hand, the more that I knew of other magico-religious practices, the more convinced I became that my wording had been essentially correct: that Wicca was remarkable in its use of ritual nudity. On the other, it became ever clearer to me that this single sentence represented an entirely inadequate consideration of the subject. The following chapter sets out to substantiate both opinions.

First, it is necessary to look more fully at the place of nudity in Wicca itself. Wiccans themselves have traditionally supplied two justifications for its importance in their workings. One, which has regularly appeared in print for five decades,[3] is that the body naturally releases a field of magical energy which clothes obstruct. The other, which I have often encountered in conversation, is that the nudity of all members of a coven reinforces a feeling of equality and democracy between them. Neither seems particularly satisfying to me. The first may well be a self-fulfilling justification, in that people who are used to being naked to work ritual magic would very probably feel disempowered if made to do it in robes or other dress. It is also true that there seems to be no easy means of evaluating the practical success of groups who practise magic in the nude against those who do not, whether magic is defined as a symbolic system, a means of self-transformation, or a process by which practical results can be achieved by the literal operation of apparently arcane power. What seems disturbing about the concept that clothed magicians are inherently second-rate is that it would consign to this inferior category the most famous and sophisticated societies for the practice of ritual magic which are known to history, including the Golden Dawn, the Stella Matutina, and the Ordo Templi Orientis. Both a sense of justice and common sense should run against such a conclusion. As for the idea that ritual nudity reinforces equality within groups, it encounters the problem that most Wiccan covens are organised according to a hierarchy of training and responsibility, with a single person or couple in clear overall charge. They may operate consensually, but are emphatically not based upon a principle of equality of membership.[4] There may, however, be a symbolic truth in the statement, if a mutual state of nudity reinforces a sense of common purpose and identity among group members.

In a more recent book,[5] I suggested from my personal acquaintance with Wiccans that that there were two practical reasons for the persistence of the custom. One was that it demands a high degree of trust and confidence between members of a coven, and so provides a powerful test for the existence of harmony and unity, without which the rituals cannot be effectively worked. The second was that, in combination with other components normally present, such as candlelight, incense and music, it conveys a very powerful sense that something abnormal is going on; that the participants in the circle have cast off their everyday selves and limitations and entered into a space in which the extraordinary can be achieved. If the experience generates a degree of nervousness – which is initially the case for most people – then this can have the effect of increasing their sensitivity and receptivity and so call forth more powerful ritual performances from them.

None of these considerations, however, explain what ritual nudity is doing in Wicca in the first place. A straightforward answer to this question, which I have sometimes heard, is that it reflects the personal tastes of the individual who was certainly the first great publicist of the religion, and perhaps the main force in its conception: Gerald Gardner. There is no doubt that he was a convinced naturist, with an ardent belief in the physical, moral, and magical benefits of nudity,[6] and left to itself this could indeed make a complete explanation. The latter appears trivial, however, if a step back is taken and this aspect of Wicca is examined in relation to all its other characteristics, as manifested when it first appeared at the end of the 1940s. It gave a particular value and emphasis to precisely those phenomena which western societies had long feared or subordinated, honouring the night above the day, the moon above the sun, the feminine above the masculine, and wild nature above civilisation, presenting itself as a form of paganism which made no compromises with Christianity, and holding up the figure of the witch for admiration and emulation. It was as a part of this package that nudity, traditionally used in those same societies most commonly as a symbol of shame and weakness, was turned into one of confidence and power. Its blatant presence in ritual was just one example of the way in which, during the middle decades of the twentieth century, Wicca crashed the barriers of convention.[7]

All this has made the point, once again, that Wicca is very unusual. The problem now is to settle the question of exactly how unusual it is in the single respect of ritual nudity. There is no doubt that in this respect it was unique in the context of twentieth-century western culture, but did it have ancient prototypes? A scholar moving into this area has few recent signposts. Most of the research into ritual nudity in general, and in ancient Europe and the Near East in particular, was carried out by German academics in the decades around 1900.[8] The main book in the subject, published by J. Heckenbach in 1911, must have been one of the last academic works to have been written entirely in Latin; the learned author was apparently afraid that, if he used any living language, his subject matter might corrupt the unsophisticated and impressionable. These works argued for a large part for ritual nudity in ancient religion, although Heckenbach stretched the definition very widely to encompass (for example) the common notion that sanctuaries should be entered, or magical rites performed, barefoot.

In evaluating the evidence, any historian faces serious problems of interpretation. Some of these concern material remains. On the one hand, it is true that sculptures, vase-paintings, and wall art across the Mediterranean and the Near and Middle East show a lot of naked people. On the other, there is often no apparent means of distinguishing literal from mythological scenes in these works. In Graeco-Roman artistic convention many gods, a few goddesses, many heroes and many nymphs were traditionally portrayed as naked or near-naked. This was one way in which they could be distinguished at a glance from ordinary humans. The occurrence of nudity in some scenes of Middle Eastern art likewise raises questions of metaphor. The rulers of Sumerian city states are sometimes shown kneeling unclad before a deity. This may be a literal scene of worship, but it may be an artistic expression of the comparative lowliness and humility of the human worshipper.[9]

Two particular examples from the Graeco-Roman tradition may serve to point up these difficulties. One consists of the celebrated paintings from the walls of the so-called Villa of the Mysteries at Pompeii, which have been connected, from some of the symbolism incorporated, to the mystery religion of Bacchus or Dionysos. In a central scene a young woman is shown dancing nude. Next to her another is crouched semi-nude over the lap of an older female who is apparently comforting her. She is being scourged by a tall figure, who is aiming blows at her bare back. These reliefs have very commonly been interpreted as successive stages of a rite of initiation into the religion, but there is a glaring problem in doing so; the figure administering the beating has large wings. They may, of course, have been theatrical props donned by a human being for the rite, but they may also indicate that the whole assemblage belongs to the world of dream or myth.[10]

The second example consists of an alabaster bowl of unknown date and provenance, with nude figures of seven males and nine females carved around a winged serpent or dragon in the interior. It also bears an inscription which seems to be a passage from a poem associated with another famous mystery cult, that of Orpheus. In the 1930s it attracted the attention of three scholars working in the German academic tradition, who interpreted the internal scene as the representation of an actual rite of the cult, involving nude worshippers.[11] This reading may be correct, but there are two major difficulties associated with it. The first is that, although the association between the object and the Orphic mysteries is arguable, it is not firmly proven. The second is that, if such a connection exists, the scene may be, once again, a symbolic rather than a literal one. The human figures may exist in the same realm as the serpent or dragon at the centre or the winged cupids carved on the exterior. One of the inscriptions refers to the creation of the world, and it is possible that the scene portrayed is related to that event.

These case-studies typify the problems of using material evidence in this field, and those relating to literary evidence are no simpler. Nobody ever seems to have tried to argue that the celebrants of the public and established religions of ancient Europe, North Africa and the Near East undressed to take part in them. Some misunderstanding can be created by references to specific festivals. For example, the poet Ovid stated that the priests who ran around Rome striking at people with thongs on the feast of the Lupercalia were naked. Other contemporary sources prove that he was speaking economically; they were in fact attired in special girdles or loincloths of goatskin.[12] Another Roman poet, Martial, could challenge his reader with the question 'Who brings clothes to Flora's festival, and permits whores the modesty of a wrap?' The implication, in context, is that such actions are absurd, and so at first sight this strongly suggests that the Floralia, the feast with which the Romans welcomed summer, was celebrated with nude rites. Again, a sufficiency of other testimony proves that Martial was referring not to the religious ceremonies but to the games and entertainments with which the festival had become associated, and which were commonly provided by prostitutes. The younger Cato was so shocked by a striptease act in one of the theatrical performances that he stormed out of the auditorium.[13]

These potentially misleading texts have a significant role in the historiography of the subject. They have taken their place among the pieces of evidence assembled by writers such as Heckenbach for a relatively widespread occurrence of ritual nudity in the ancient world. Furthermore, Ovid attributed the rituals of the Lupercalia to a god whom he equated with the Greek Pan; a guess which has no basis in objective data, which was not made by any other known Roman author, and which is rejected by modern scholars.[14] It is possible, however, that the influence of this famous passage, linking a rite of a horned god to nakedness, may have had some additional bearing on the adoption of the latter tradition by Wicca.

When these distractions are removed from the record, the latter still contains a few references to stark nakedness in the mainstream religions of the European and Near Eastern ancient world; but all seem to be associated with special rites of passage or consecration rather than regular worship. One example is provided by Ibn Fadlan's famous description of the cremation of a Viking chief upon the Volga river in the 920s. The man who lit the funeral pyre had to walk to it, bearing the torch, backwards and completely unclothed.[15] The fact that he reversed the normal direction of movement as well as the normal mode of dress suggests that at that moment he is being set aside from the rest of humanity, and from the general nature of the world, to precipitate the dead man into a different realm. Likewise, the Greek geographer Diodorus Siculus recorded that when a new 'Apis' bull was chosen, to represent divinity in one of the state religions of Hellenistic Egypt, it was kept for forty days at the city of Nicopolis before being taken along the Nile to its shrine at Memphis. During this period it was guarded only by women, who exposed their bodies to it as a religious act.[16] The significance of this was not reported by the ancient author, or not known to him; but if it really happened, then it was presumably linked to concepts of regeneration and fertility. The caution entered against unquestioning acceptance of the report as fact applies even more strongly to the customs reported by Graeco-Roman authors of people whom they regarded as barbarians. Into this category would fall the declaration by Pliny that at festivals of the native British their married women processed naked and were painted black.[17] It may be true, because it seems certain from classical sources that warriors of the tribes of north-western Europe sometimes dyed their bodies and rushed into battle naked. It may also be a titillating fable, brought back to Italy by somebody willing to have fun both at the the expense of the Britons and of a credulous Roman audience. None of these cases approach the Wiccan tradition of regular ritual nudity for all participants, and they seem to provide the closest equivalents to be found in the official and public religions of the ancient world.

It has not been among these religions, however, that modern scholars have found most of their apparent evidence for the custom. The most productive hunting-ground has been among the mystery religions of the Graeco-Roman world, such as those of Dionysos and Orpheus mentioned above. In dealing with these, a cautious investigator faces an obvious problem; that the very nature of closed and secretive bodies of worshippers is to provoke curiosity, gossip, speculation and slander among outsiders, and almost all the relevant sources are represented by writers who were not, or are not known to have been, initiates themselves. In making a link between Orphism and ritual nudity, one of the commentators upon the carved bowl discussed above quoted an early Christian bishop, Epiphanius, who asserted that the Orphic mysteries were particularly worthy of reproach because women were believed to appear in them naked.[18] So indeed they may have done, but the testimony of a fervent protagonist of a rival religion, reporting hearsay while making a catalogue of false beliefs, is not the most reliable form of evidence.

The other two scholars to identify the bowl as an Orphic cult object fell back on Heckenbach for corroboration of an association between Orphism and nude rituals. He provided them with a line from the Athenian playwright Aristophanes: 'it is the custom for novices to enter unclothed'.[19] This throwaway allusion is characteristic of the in-jokes which clutter Greek comedy. We have no certain knowledge of its meaning. It may not refer to mystery religions at all, let alone to Orphism in particular, and if it does, then we have no evidence that Aristophanes was drawing upon accurate information, as opposed to rumour, concerning ritual practices. There is, moreover, a real possibility that it concerns an altogether different custom. One of the signs of the coming of adolescence in a Greek boy was that he was allowed both to put off the clothes of childhood and to strip naked to participate in the adult male world of the gymnasium. In some places the novice youths were called *ekdyomenoi*, 'those who undress'.[20] This could have been Aristophanes's point.

Likewise, the great Graeco-Roman philosopher Plotinus asserted in one of his lectures that 'those who would rise through the degrees of the holy mysteries must cast aside their clothes and go forward naked'.[21] This may be a literal statement, or it may be a metaphor for the need for spiritual purity and candour. Instructive here is a fragment from another celebrated late antique text, likewise derived from Platonism, the Chaldean Oracles: 'For the Divine is acessible not to mortals who think corporeally but to all those who, naked, hasten upward toward the heights'.[22] The devotee here is fairly clearly casting off not just clothes but the world and the flesh, to ascend in spirit. Another example of this sort of difficulty attends the women's mysteries celebrated at the sanctuary of Artemis at Brauron in Greece, which were rites of passage for young women approaching the age of marriage. Vase paintings suggest that for some of the time the girls were naked, but again these scenes may have had a symbolic or mythological significance.[23]

There is, however, good reason for believing that all of these three pieces of evidence may be accepted as references to ritual nudity in religious mysteries, but in a limited and specific capacity: rites of initiation, in which the postulant was completely undressed at the opening and then reclothed at the conclusion. There is a clear metaphor here of rebirth, and also an equally clear cultural context: that, in the ancient Greek and Hellenistic world, the custom of a bath followed by dressing in new robes was not merely the usual purification of somebody about to engage in religious rites, but of anybody about to undergo a rite of passage, such as coming of age or marriage. Some Greek sanctuaries, such as that of Artemis Kranaia, had special bath-tubs for the priests. Before initiation into the Eleusinian mysteries, celebrants all bathed in the sea, although this seems to have taken place after dark and with some modesty; when the courtesan Phryne did so in full view of other participants, proud of her beauty, she got into serious trouble.[24]

There are two very different items of source material which are good evidence for the occurrence of nudity in ancient initiation rites. One consists of a set of wall-paintings at a Mithraeum at Capua in Italy. They show an initiation into this most famous of all the mystery religions of the Roman Empire, that of Mithras, and in every one the postulant is naked and blindfolded, while the person leading and directing him is clothed.[25] The other consists of records of ancient Judaic and Christian baptism. Under the Roman Empire, both Jews and Christians were noted for their dislike of the human body and their aversion to its display unclothed. The Greek gymnasia, in particular, disgusted them. This makes it all the more remarkable that contemporary testimony strongly suggests that converts to Judaism were baptised nude and makes it absolutely certain that Christians were.[26]

Baptism into the early churches was very much a reception into a mystery religion. The posulant had to prepare for two years, and to enter an intensive period of fasting and prayer seven weeks before the event. The actual rite was a private one among a group of initiates, in which the postulant removed all her or his clothes, women loosing their hair as well, and was anointed at several points on the body with holy oil before being immersed in water and dressed anew in white. It was usually directed that, in the case of the baptism of a woman, another female should do the anointing; but if there was no other woman available then the whole process was in the hands of the priest. There is a cautionary tale of a Palestinian monk called Conan, who was asked to baptise a particularly beautiful woman and could not find a female Christian to help him. He fled in panic, only to intercepted by John the Baptist who appeared from heaven to deal with the crisis. John made the sign of the cross three times over Conan's genitals, rendering him permanently incapable of sexual desire; after which everything was fine. It is hard to believe that such a custom would have been incorporated into a religion which loathed and feared nudity as much as early Christianity unless it was regarded as an indispensable, or at least common, part of initiation into mystery faiths.

All this data seems to be tending to a conclusion: that ritual nudity had a place in ancient European religion at certain key moments of transformation, but that any other role for it is unproven and that it vanished from the western religious tradition at the end of antiquity. If this is so, then one significance of its presence in Wicca could be that the latter religion seeks to sustain throughout all its workings the intensity and transformative power of initiatory experiences. This may be correct, but the conclusion would be premature, for it ignores the association between mixed-sex nude rites and Christian heresy. Such rites were a recurrent theme of denunciations by orthodox churchmen of deviant sorts of Christian from the second to the seventeenth centuries. It must be admitted that it was not a very common theme. Heretics were mostly, and persistently, accused of devil-worship, cannibalism, sexual orgies, incest and child sacrifice.[27] It must be thought that in that catalogue nudity would be such a tame or incidental item as to be hardly worth mentioning. This can, none the less, be argued the opposite way; that those few cases where it is included may be the more significant.

The trouble with those cases is that none of them is supported by the two sorts of source material which give real insights into the beliefs of the unorthodox: writings produced by heretics themselves, or confessions provided by them under interrogation and deposited in legal archives. They are found instead in accusations made against aberrant traditions by churchmen determined to blacken their reputations, who may have had no first-hand knowledge of them. This phenomenon, and its attendant difficulties, has already been encountered in the case of Epiphanius and the Orphic mysteries. The same bishop is found again, in a different work, accusing the closed, quasi-Christian sect of the Barbelo Gnostics of enacting certain rites in which the initiates were 'completely nude'.[28] An episcopal colleague of his, Hippolytus, denounced members of another Gnostic sect, the Naasenes, for allegedly holding a nocturnal ceremony by firelight, in which the worshippers, all men, 'must undress and become as bridegrooms' to a female entity representing one form of an indivisible supreme deity.[29] There are also references to the Adamni, a small group of Gnostics who were believed both to live and to worship naked; an ancient naturist club. All these references are from the south-eastern end of the Mediterranean, and there is a single one from the opposite corner: the Synod of Saragossa in 380 condemned the Spanish heresy of Priscillianism because (among other things) its members reputedly read and interpreted the Bible in the nude.[30]

After this clutch of accusations from the world of late antiquity, there is a lapse of almost a thousand years before the charge is heard again, and then it resurfaces in northern Europe. It does so in the case of a fourteenth-century French sect, the Turlupins, who were supposedly given to nakedness and licentiousness. One of them, Jeanne Daubenta, was burned at the stake in 1375.[31] Another group, allegedly calling itself the Men of Intelligence, was denounced by the bishop of Cambrai in the Netherlands during 1411. He accused them of teaching that the Holy Ghost gave inner enlightenment to true believers, who were then released from moral constraints, and its leaders were reported to have confessed to going naked and practising free love as a consequence of this doctrine.[32] There is nothing to determine whether any of this information, ancient or medieval, represents anything more than fantasy.

The most notorious holy naturists of the entire middle ages were the Adamites of Bohemia, who appeared in 1420 as a sect which believed that the religious consecration of wine and bread was unnecessary, and that all that true believers needed was a simple commemorative meal together to represent the Last Supper. Their enemies asserted that some of them, when wandering through hills and forests, threw off their clothes to recapture the primitive innocence of Eden. It must be noted that this is not actually ritual nudity, but it was the detail which subsequently caught the imagination of more orthodox Christians and earned them their name; it is not known what, if anything, they called themselves. That detail may itself have been a libel. We shall never know the truth, because to attack the ceremony of the mass was to play in the first division of medieval heretics, and almost all of them were wiped out within a year by military expeditions.[33]

None the less, for the next four centuries the Adamites were to be the classic naked worshippers in the European imagination, trotted out every time that conservative Christians wanted examples of the dreadful consequences of religious liberty. One of those occasions was during the English Revolution of the 1640s, and references to them surfaced close to the beginning of the events which led up to it, in July 1641. The pamphlet literature of that month turned them briefly into big news, claiming that they had appeared in England and were meeting in the London area, and representing them as the ultimate consequence of separation from the established Church, disowning structure, discipline, order, hierararchy, learning and liturgy, together with clothes. None were actually apprehended, and the interest of pampleteers in them had waned by the end of the year, although they were occasionally mentioned thereafer as a routine entry in catalogues of horrible heresies. David Cressy, who has studied the phenomenon, leaves open the question of whether they ever existed in England outside the realms of fantasy and fiction.[34]

The records for Christian unorthodoxy, therefore, prove that ritual nudity was an occasional charge used by the orthodox against their opponents, but not whether any of those opponents actually practised it. It is not surprising that it became associated at times with the supreme heresy of the later middle ages and early modern period, the newly-identified religion of satanic witchcraft. From the early fifteenth to the early eighteenth centuries some churchmen and lay magistrates made a speciality of describing the characteristics of this religion and trying those accused of adhering to it. For the purposes of the present enquiry, it is remarkable how little attention they paid to the role of nudity in the rites and festivals attributed to witches. Thumbing through the classic texts of demonologists in the period – the fifteenth-century *Formicarius* and *Malleus Maleficarum*, and the later works of Jean Bodin, Martin del Rio, Henri Bouguet, Nicholas Remy and Pierre de Lancre, a historian finds little or no reference to the practice. Nor does it feature much in the confessions extracted from alleged witches. This may, again, be a matter of priority, for the scholars and magistrates were most interested in the more spectacular aspects of the religion which they were attempting to eradicate, which were the familiar litany of accusations made against earlier heretics, of devil-worship, child-sacrifice and sexual orgies, to which was added the making of magic to destroy and injure other humans. It is interesting, however, that when nudity is mentioned, it sometimes echoes the ancient tradition of initiation into mysteries. For example, a woman interrogated in 1480 at Calcinato in northern Italy claimed that, when she made her pact with the Devil, she did so nude and kneeling.[35]

By contrast, the nudity of witches is a very prominent feature of the art of the period, especially that of northern Europe and above all of Germans. From the opening of the sixteenth century, artists regularly portrayed witches attending the sabbat and casting spells as unclad. This may have been a reflection of the fact that most of the alleged practices of the witch religion on which the demonologists concentrated did not lend themselves to re-spectable representation in works of art. To paint or draw witches nude may have been an easy way of representing their essential depravity. It may matter more, however, that to portray witches was one of the very few socially sanctioned ways in which artists in Germany in particular could express the female nude. It must be significant in this context that the first notable artist thought to represent the nude witch, Albrecht Dürer, used poses drawn ultimately from ancient depictions of pagan goddesses. It is not even absolutely certain that he ever depicted witches at all. Of his two works normally placed in this category, one shows four women posed in attitudes taken directly from classical representations of the Graces, and may portray the three goddesses of the Judgement of Paris receiving the apple of discord. The other, showing an old woman riding on a goat or capricorn, echoes a medieval figure commonly used to personify lust, and is taken in turn from an ancient iconic pose of Aphrodite or Venus.[36]

There is no doubt, however, of the identity as witches of some of the women portrayed by two of Dürer's pupils, Albrecht Altdorfer and Hans Baldung Grien, probably inspired by sermons upon the witch religion preached in the city of Strasbourg, where they worked, during the 1500s. Grien in particular made them into one of the main themes of his work, and famously used it to conflate the image of the female body with asso-ciations of sin and menace to turn it into a diabolical vessel in itself. His obsessive treatment of it in this way may have been rooted in his own psyche, but it may also have been provoked by the epidemic of syphilis then sweeping Europe. Whatever the reason, his influence seems to have been decisive in ensuring that, for the rest of the century, the primary concern of artists engaged in portrayals of witchcraft was not the emphasis on the devil as the source of witches' power, made by the literary demon-ologists, but on the moral and sexual disorder represented by the unclad female body.[37] Even when Satan became more prominent in the genre, the convention of nudity remained. When Pierre de Lancre produced his cel-ebrated book on the witch religion in 1611, he placed no emphasis on the state of dress of witches at the sabbat, preferring instead such details as their reversal of social norms by such customs as dancing back to back.

When the second edition appeared, two years later, it was decorated with a very elaborate engraved frontispiece of a sabbat by a Polish artist, Jan Ziarnko, which incorporated all the features described by de Lancre and added nudity for the celebrants.[38] This provided some of the most famous images of witchcraft to emerge from the whole early modern period, and helped to reinforce an artistic tradition of the naked witch which was to continue steadily through the work of major later figures such as Goya, and persists until the present.

The question of whether early modern witches actually worked naked is rendered a non sequitur by the total absence of evidence for any actual witch religion in the period; the satanic cult of the demonologists does seem to have been a complete fantasy. The single emergence into anything like reality seems to be in the Affair of the Poisons in late seventeenth-century France, when one of the mistresses of Louis XIV apparently allowed a Black Mass to be performed over the naked body of a woman with the aim of securing her power over her royal lover.[39] Even this, however, is still a long way from a tradition of ritual nudity among worshippers. The only text before the twentieth century, in fact, which makes it a general rule for witches at their rites is the very late and utterly unique one, Charles Godfrey Leland's purported gospel of witchcraft, Aradia. This states unequivocally, and famously, that 'as the sign that ye are truly free, ye shall be naked in your rites, both men and women also'.[40] It is notoriously hard, however, to determine how far Aradia actually reflects a genuine peasant tradition, let alone a genuine witch religion.[41] As a result, this strange work of the 1890s cannot yet be used as any conclusive evidence for the matter.

There is one slight indication, however, that in the matter of ritual nudity a real popular tradition may underpin both or either the passage in Leland's text and the artistic convention descending from the sixteenth century. This is that the few references to it in the early modern records seem to derive from reports by common people. For example, the famous work of demonology by del Rio contains an anecdote set near Calais in 1587, where two soldiers claimed to have shot a naked woman out of a fast-moving cloud. She turned out to be middle-aged, very fat and very drunk, and only slightly wounded; and refused to answer any questions. They assumed her to have been a witch.[42] Likewise, children who claimed to have attended sabbats during a panic about witchcraft at the German city of Augsburg in 1723 asserted that these meetings were full of naked people.[43] It is possible, of course, that by these dates popular culture had already been influenced by the artistic tradition, mass-marketed through woodcuts. There may also be a functional explanation for the belief; that many people of the time slept naked, and witches were presumed to travel to sabbats direct from their beds. The European material alone provides no resolution of this problem.

Once again, our quarry seems to elude us. It may, however, make the European context plainer to broaden the scope of this study to include examples from the rest of the world. Three areas of it in particular have been identified by travellers and anthropologists as furnishing examples of nudity in a religious context: India, north-west North America and Polynesia. It is worth now examining each in turn. The Indian material is the most enigmatic. Its most celebrated aspect consists of the nakedness of some holy men or fakirs, which sets them apart at a glance from the conventional concerns of humanity. This tradition is especially associated with one sect of the Jains, the *Digambra* or 'sky-clad', whose male ascetics renounce the wearing of clothes as a rejection of worldliness. It is a right which is explicitly denied to women of the same group and might, moreover, be termed symbolic rather than ritual nudity. The standard textbooks on Hinduism, Jainism and Buddhism make no reference to nakedness as an integral part of the worship associated with these religions. The sources which do are concerned, just as in the Graeco-Roman world, with closed mystery cults, and are attended by all the difficulties already noted when dealing with these secretive groups, and a few others of their own. One consists of a summary, by a justly respected writer upon modern Paganism, of a passage in a book by the Englishman Sir John Woodroffe, one of the greatest experts ever to publish upon Indian tantric traditions. It describes a rite in which men and women sat alternately in a circle, presided over by a leader and a beautiful naked priestess representing a goddess. A meal was followed by sexual intercourse as an act of worship. This appears clear enough, but when it is checked against the original text by Woodroffe, on which it is based, a few minor discrepancies appear, one of which is the nudity of the priestess.[44] Another apparent case was provided by reports in Californian works from the late 1980s and 1990s, that police, journalists, and a social reform group in India had all clashed with devotees of the goddess Renuka or Renukamba at a temple dedicated to her at a village beside the River Varda or Varada in the state of Karnataka or Karnatka. The cult allegedly taught that the goddess blessed only those who worshipped her unclothed, but it is unclear from the reports how long it had been established, and indeed very little information was given in them. There is no Indian state of Karnataka, although this seems to be a reference to the southern geographical region of the Carnatic, and standard textbooks on Indian deities contain no reference to Renuka or Renukamba, although this may only signify that hers is a minor and local cult. I have not at the time of writing managed to obtain copies of the original newspaper reports.[45]

The evidence from the other regions is much less problematic. It is plain from nineteenth-century ethnographic reports that a custom formerly obtained among the Mandan tribe of the American Great Plains, and the peoples of the coast of what is now British Columbia, and of the Aleutian Islands strung out from the extremity of Alaska, of naked men personifying spirits at special festivals. The Mandan performer was stripped and painted black, to represent elemental evil. In British Columbia the nude functionaries consecrated rites of human sacrifice, 'making themselves look as unearthly as possible, proceeding in a creeping kind of stoop, and stepping like two proud horses'.[46] During Aleut ceremonies to celebrate the killing of a whale, the celebrants wore large wooden masks to represent the animating powers of sea animals, as their sole attire.[47] In these cases nudity was used to reinforce the identity of these performers as non-human, liminal figures. A different sort of liminality was represented by the Polynesian examples: that of rites of passage. Again, the sources are provided by nineteenth-century European observers. When a Samoan sacred virgin was plighted to marry, she was ceremonially conducted to the village of her intended husband for a public defloration, 'dressed in a fine mat edged with red feathers, her body gleaming with scented oil'. On arrival before him, she threw off this mat and stood naked while he took her virginity with two fingers. When he displayed the blood, 'the female supporters of the bride rushed forward to obtain a portion to smear upon themselves before dancing naked and hitting their heads with stones until their blood ran down in streams, in sympathy with, and honour of, the virgin bride'.[48]

In the Marquesa Islands, female members of the community also danced nude, but the rite involved was one of death. When a chief was buried,

> the women dressed themselves in their finest white tapas, and decorated their heads with splendid feather caps – but ... they were no sooner attired than they mounted a platform in front of the house where the corpse lay, carefully opened their tapas in front and folded them back until their nakedness was fully exposed; then turning their faces to the corpse they danced for some minutes. Then turning to the crowd they continued their shameless dance all day amid shouts of applause. This exposure of their persons they consider the strongest expression of affection they can make to their departed chief.

In the Marquesas, nudity and the sexuality with which it was associated were treated as affirmations of life.[49]

This brief survey seems to indicate that the pattern detected in the ancient European and Near Eastern worlds holds good for other societies around the globe, with a possible exception in India. Ritual nudity features in religious behaviour as a phenomenon of special occasions, to isolate and transform particular people either during unusually important festivals, or at rites of passage such as funerals, weddings, baptisms and initiations.

It might be suggested again, therefore, that Wicca boldly goes where no religions have gone before, either by taking a Christian stereotype of bad behaviour and giving it positive connotations, or by investing the whole of its workings with the intensity and tranformative effect of rites of passage, or by giving all its participants the empowering status normally associated only with liminal figures representing spirits or deities. It might be suggested, but this hypothesis would once again be premature, for there is another dimension to the subject which has hitherto been neglected in this study, and which must be recognised now. It is based upon the fact that in every inhabited continent of the world there are peoples who have believed in the figure to whom the English traditionally give the name of witch. That is, a human being who works secret and malevolent magic against other members of the same community or district, from motives of pure malice, and in a hidden tradition passed on by inheritance, training, or contact with evil powers.[50] All over the world, likewise, peoples who have believed in this figure have also often believed that witches work naked.

This idea was shared by those living in a huge tract of tropical Africa, from Kenya and Uganda in the north to Transvaal and Natal in the south.[51] At times the ethnographers who collected this information suggested practical or functional explanations for it. Thus the Kriges, investigating beliefs in *vuloi* (bad magic) among the Lovedu of northern Transvaal, suggested that the nudity of the alleged practitioners was due to the fact that they were supposed to work at night, leaving their beds in huts where the other inhabitants had been placed in a magical stupor. As the Lovedu slept naked, wrapped in blankets, the Kriges thought that the 'night-witches' had risen straight from their beds without stopping to dress. Likewise, Hugh Stayt, studying the BaVenda, a tribe living in the same region, thought that since their night-witches, called *vhaloi*, were supposed to move about in spirit-form, they had discarded their clothes with their sleeping bodies. Gunter Wagner, working among the Vugusu and Logoli of western Kenya, ascribed the fact that some of the night-witches of these peoples, the *omulogi*, were said to travel around nude, to their desire to move soundlessly[52]

These interpretations miss the point that, in all of these African peoples who ascribed nudity to the witch-figure, it was only part of a package of role-reversals. Across the whole region in which the belief was held, witches were also supposed to go out at night to do their work, among tribes who traditionally feared darkness, and to ride on unclean and untameable beasts, above all hyenas. The *wakindi* or night-witches of the Kaguru of Tanzania were also said to walk on their hands and to smear their black bodies white with ashes. The physical modesty of women among the Gusii of Kenya was especially marked, as well as their horror of the dark; and so, when that people believed that those who became *omorogi* or witches ran out naked at night, these females were breaking all the usual social habits on a grand scale. The night-witches of the Amba of Uganda were also said to stand on their heads or rest hanging upside-down in trees like bats, or to eat salt when thirsty. To this people, as to most of those described, nakedness was seen as something shameless and offensive, so that those who adopted it were proclaiming their exemption from normal controls and conventions. In general, the nudity of the African witch-figure was one aspect of a set of ritual reversals.[53]

Arab peoples likewise believed that witches flew round at night upon sticks, completely unclothed, and haunted cemeteries.[54] In central India they were supposed to ride naked on tigers, crocodiles and other fierce wild animals. A legendary witch of the north-western provinces, Lona, was said to have made rice germinate with extraordinary rapidity by stripping nude and throwing seedlings in the air while uttering spells. In Bengal, a woman who wanted to become a witch (for Bengali witches were stereotypically female), and had no experienced one to teach her, was expected to go to a cremation ground at midnight. There she had to take off all her clothes, sit on the ground, and recite incantations to call spirits to her.[55] The *yoyova* of the Trobriand islanders, off the coast of New Guinea, were women who reputedly flew out in naked spirit-forms at night to cause death to other humans. Among the Chukchi of the north-eastern extremity of Siberia, there was no tradition of a figure approximating to the English witch; instead operative magic was mediated through shamans. None the less, the pattern reappears even here, for a shaman who wanted to utter a curse was expected to perform nude and in the moonlight; a sharp contrast with the healing and divining operations of shamans belonging to this people, which were indoor events requiring special clothing.[56] These African and Asian belief systems are replicated among the Navaho of the south-western United States, to whom witches were people who met at night to plan concerted evil actions, sitting in circles naked except for masks and ornaments.[57]

It can therefore be suggested that the nude witch is a very widespread and powerful cultural stereotype. Whether it was ever translated into practice among these extra-European peoples is a difficult question to answer. Certainly most of the actions of role-reversal ascribed to the witch-figure, such as riding on dangerous wild beasts or flying, were flatly impossible in nature.

It is possible, however, that people sometimes took on other traits of the figure in order to work destructive magic, including nudity. May Edel, working among the Chiga of Uganda, had pointed out to her a woman whom people claimed to have seen abroad naked at night, reports which confirmed her reputation as an *omurogi* or evil magician. Robert LeVine met a Gusii man who recalled how as a child he had once seen a female neighbour hurrying home nude at a dawn, carrying the firepot which was the traditional working tool of an *omorogi*, the local name for the same being.[58] I have a friend whose family came from the Punjab, and whose mother told her of how her own brother, as a young man, came home one night in great fear, claiming to have encountered two wild-looking naked women advancing on him with a malevolent expression; sure signs of witches in that culture. He had the reputation in his family of being a truthful and steady fellow. All of these stories may well be products of fantasy or error; but they need not be. What cannot be doubted is the strength of the stereotypical image.

Once again it seems possible to work towards a conclusion: that one of the more common and widely-dispersed beliefs of the human race is that workers of evil magic operate naked, as part of their general symbolic function of breaking the rules of conventional human behaviour. Again also it seems possible to credit Wiccans with investing that symbolic function with positive qualities, and its worldwide distribution strengthens a characterisation of Wicca as a counter-cultural religion par excellence. Once more, however, a conclusion would be premature, for the most revealing way of putting this image of the witch into perspective is to take a sideways step, into the broader world of operative magic.

Here I am putting my weight once more behind the traditional distinction between religious and magical activities. In acts of magic the human being is believed to possess some measure of operative control over the result, at the least by an arcane understanding of the mechanisms of the natural world, and at most by compelling superhuman entities. Once again I find that this distinction still works well in certain contexts, and one of them happens to be that of ritual nudity. Acts of magic, after all, represent ritual applied to special and extraordinary occasions, requiring a shift of consciousness or a redefinition of being, every bit as much as rites of passage. It should not be a surprise, therefore, to find that nudity plays a prominent part in them.

It features in what is still the best-known text in western culture, the Bible, where Saul 'stripped off his clothes also, and prophesied before Samuel in like manner, and lay down naked all that day and all that night. Wherefore they say, Is Saul also among the prophets?' Here one of the most famous kings of the Hebrews is apparently transforming his status from monarch to prophet, on being possessed by 'the Spirit of God', by the simple act of removing the garments which indicate his familiar status. This interpretation is reinforced by the parallel account of the prophet Isaiah walking 'naked and barefoot three years for a sign', putting off all the clothing which symbolically attached him to the world just as the Jain monks were to do.[59] Such texts had a significant impact upon later, bibliocentric, Christians: there may be no conclusive evidence of nude worship among Christian sects, but it is absolutely certain that in the years 1653–55 at least a dozen of the first English Quaker missionaries preached naked in public places in imitation of Isaiah and as a challenge to worldly and materially-minded attitudes.[60] It may also have been that they believed that the act of undressing would itself facilitate contact with divine revelation, a conclusion which could be drawn from these biblical passages.

The same motif is found in ancient Greek and Roman literature, where certain potent herbs are specified as to be picked by a naked person operating at night, to maximise or supercharge their power.[61] Pliny described a cure for an abcess consisting of a poultice applied by a nude virgin woman speaking a particular charm to Apollo three times.[62] The fact that she had to fast beforehand as well as be naked and virginal suggests that her state of dress was part of a package of purity which set her apart from the corruptions of the world. Nudity also occurs in medieval and early modern European accounts of magic. In particular, it was supposed to be employed by young women in solitary spells and charms by which they sought either to find a husband in general or to win the heart of a particular man. Several appear in collections of sixteenth-century charms. According to one, the practitioner had to undress and run round her neighbourhood unseen, after which she needed to cry three times 'Hecsin, Hecsin, Lauder, Lauder' while touching her breasts and pubes. In another, she had to recite 'Kay o kam, auriagel, kiya mange let bushel' before divesting herself of clothing, and then creep into a room where the man whom she wanted was sleeping, clip a lock of hair from his head and wear it in a bag or ring. Another was to step naked into a lake or river at midnight, and look for the reflection of the face of the future partner on the water. Yet another was to go to a crossroads on St George's Night. There the woman had to undress and comb backwards first the hair upon her head and then that on her body. She was then supposed to prick the little finger of her left hand and let three drops of blood fall to the ground, saying 'I give my blood to my loved one, whom I shall see shall be mine own'. The form of the man would then apparently rise from the blood.[63]

These references make it significant, if not surprising, that when nudity does feature directly in trials for witchcraft and magic in the late medieval and early modern period, it is in descriptions of solitary spell-casting. One of the witnesses against a woman tried for sorcery at Reggio, Italy, in 1375 asserted that the accused had instructed her to go out at night, take off her clothes, kneel down and, looking at the brightest star in the sky, cry out 'I adore thee, O great Devil'. In about the same year a woman was accused at Florence of working a spell which involved placing candles around a dish, taking off her clothes, and standing above the dish making signs with her hands. In 1425 the preacher Bernardino of Siena recounted a folk-tale from Lucca, of how a man asked his godmother, a woman skilled in magic, to help him find a sum of money which he had lost. He spied on her to see how she effected this task, and saw her emerge from her back door at night completely naked and with her hair loose. In this state she conjured up Satan, who told her where the money could be found.[64] One of the women tried for witchcraft at Aberdeen in 1597 was accused by a witness of having been seen on her own farmland in the previous harvest-time, pulling up her clothes about her head to bare her body from the waist down, and walking backwards throwing stones before and behind her.[65] This does sound like a genuine piece of folk-magic, relying on a set of symbolic reversals to drive away harm from the woman's crops.

Parallel operations are recorded in the European folklore collections made in the last two hundred years. Once again, solitary acts of love-magic by young women are prominent. One of the most commonly-quoted at the present day consisted of running naked around the famous prehistoric stone circle of the Rollright Stones, on Midsummer Night, to be granted a vision of a future husband.[66] At the opposite point of the year was another English tradition which stated that a woman who swept her room naked on Midwinter Night would then dream of him.[67] Other female needs than love could be governed by such rites: in southern Sweden it was rumoured that a woman who undressed and trampled the caul of a foal would avoid the pains of childbirth.[68] Sometimes they were collective: a rain-making spell recorded in Romania consisted of the floating of a harrow in water by a group of young women led by an older one. They would all undress completely before the operation, and sit on the floating machine for an hour with a flame burning at each corner.[69]

Finally, such associations are also found in the extra-European world. In many parts of northern India it was believed that drought could be ended if a set of naked women pulled a plough across a field at night, with invocations and pleas directed at the earth or to the god Vishnu. Men were excluded from the vicinity as they worked. Sir James Frazer, who collated the reports of this custom, noted the part played in it, once again, by reversals: Indian women ordinarily never engaged in the work of ploughing, and those who undertook this magical operation were normally from the highest caste, which was completely detached from such menial processes.[70] It may be remembered here that this was a part of the world in which witches were regarded as stereotypically female, and that one of the acts which transformed a woman into one was to undress. This rite directed against the terrible danger of drought was therefore self-evidently an act of good witchcraft; and the same linkage may well exist in several of the European examples given above, as this was another region of the globe where the witch-figure was traditionally a female one. It may now be appreciated why the depiction of the nude witch in early modern European art may reflect an aspect of popular culture.

There are similar male rites recorded elsewhere in the world. In Peru a festival to encourage fruit to ripen took place until suppression by the Spanish in the sixteenth century. It allegedly included a rite in which men and boys assembled stark naked in the orchards and ran to a nearby hill.[71] On the island of Amboyna in the East Indies, a prospective failure in the staple crop, of cloves, was met with one in which men would go nude to the plantations at night, and call on the trees, as if they were women, to produce more.[72] In the parts of Africa in which witches were associated with nudity, the same state was positively recommended at times for ordinary people who wished to work beneficent magic on their own behalf; among the Pondo, of the south-east African coast, it was considered necessary for a spell to protect one's home from lightning.[73]

It may be wise to suppose that different symbolic systems might well be in operation across this range of examples. In some of them, the connotations of reversal are apparently most important in the significance of the nudity, while in others those of sexuality and fertility seem to be paramount, and in still others the state is symbolically one of purity. What appears to link all together, however, is the sense of the empowerment of an ordinary human being by the act of removing the garments by which she or he is usually recognised or familiar. This is not very far from one major function suggested earlier for the practice in Wicca; of separating off the participant from the everyday world. It may, in fact, be identical. In this perspective, therefore, the place of nudity in Wicca is dependent not so much on its character as a counter-cultural religion, apparent though that is, as on its character as a magical religion. As I have argued elsewhere,[74] Wicca self-consciously dissolves the traditional European distinction between religion and magic.

In this perspective, also, it must surely be significant that the only other religion which I have traced in which the whole group of worshippers regularly operated naked is another rare example of one blended in its essence with magical practices. This is voodoo. A detailed account survives of the Midsummer Night rituals held at Bayou St John, Louisiana, in 1872, by the famous voodoo queen Marie Laveau Glapion. After she arrived the crowd sang to her and then built a large fire to heat a cauldron in which water, salt, black pepper, a black snake (cut into three pieces, allegedly to represent the Christian Trinity), a cat, a black rooster and various powders were set to boil. As it heated up, Glapion commanded everybody present to undress, which they did singing a repetitive chorus. At midnight all went swimming in a lake to cool off, and then came out and sang and danced for another hour. Glapion then preached a sermon, and gave celebrants who wished a period of half an hour in which they might make love. After that everybody sang and ate, and then Glapion directed four women to extinguish the fire and pour the contents of the cauldron into a barrel, apparently for use in potions. She then told all present to dress, preached again, and ended the rites as dawn was breaking.[75] This account was published in a local newspaper by a self-claimed eyewitness, and some or all of the details might have been invented. If all were accurately represented, then it is possible that the whole sequence of ritual was of Glapion's own devising, and even that she was influenced by European accounts of witches' sabbats. None the less, the identity of voodoo as a syncretic mixture of religion and magic is not in doubt, and the prominence of nudity in this description, for all celebrants, does not seem coincidental.

Wicca is not then unique in this respect, although it is unusual. In having this particular feature, it does not seem to have been responding to the views of one man, or to certain functional benefits, or even to the impulse to challenge cultural norms in a modern or postmodern context. It is, rather, in a tradition of magical activity which is not merely ancient but virtually worldwide. In reaching this conclusion I have had recourse to a methodology of prising information from context in a wide variety of historical and ethnographic sources, which is regarded with disquiet in related scholarly disciplines and runs counter to prevailing techniques in them. During the past thirty years historians have tended even more than before to specialise in a particular period of time, to understand it as thoroughly as possible, and to learn how its political, social, economic and cultural characteristics interrelated. In the same span of time, anthropologists have generally emphasized the primacy of close and discrete studies of particular societies, and the dangers of attempting to translate concepts between cultures and languages. There is no doubt that these approaches produce excellent results, and that the perils against which they warn, of facile comparisons between decontextualised data, are very real. None the less, it may be suggested that there are some historical and anthropological problems which cannot be adequately treated by a monographic approach alone, and which are best approached by a broad and comparative method. This essay has been offered as an example of that contention.

7

The Inklings and the Gods

Anybody who has heard of C. S. Lewis and J. R. R. Tolkien is likely to know them as two of the world's greatest writers of imaginative literature. Most of those who know them as that are probably also aware that they were personal friends, who taught in the same faculty – that of English Language and Literature – at Oxford University. Both were born in the last decade of the nineteenth century and both published their most popular work in the middle of the twentieth. They were the two most famous members of the 'Inklings', a literary group that gathered around Lewis at Oxford between 1933 and 1947. Those who know all this will also be conscious of one further aspect of their reputation: that they were devout Christians. In one respect, they formed part of that last great wave of Christian creative writers in England that also included G. K. Chesterton, Hilaire Belloc, T. S. Eliot, Grahame Greene and Evelyn Waugh.

The Inklings as a group have been classed as part of this phenomenon. Their fellow Oxonian, Lord David Cecil, subsequently considered Christianity to be 'the most important common factor' to their work.[1] J. S. Ryan, an Australian critic, summed up the products of the group as 'Anglo-Catholic literary apologetics'.[2] Lewis was a celebrated and pugnacious spokesman for the Christian faith, and his most commonly-read works, the seven-book 'Chronicles of Narnia', are often viewed as a subtle means of conveying its tenets to children. He himself wrote of their central character as 'giving an imaginary answer to the question, "What might Christ become like, if there really were a world like Narnia"'.[3] W. H. Auden, one of the earliest and most distinguished critics of Tolkien's great fantasy, *The Lord of the Rings*, declared that 'the unstated presuppositions of the whole work are Christian'.[4] This judgement has been endorsed, in varying degrees, several times since then.[5]

Nobody, in fact, has denied the importance of motifs taken from Christianity to both bodies of work, and it would hardly be possible to do so. What distinguishes some critics of Tolkien is their readiness to emphasise elements that he also appropriated from medieval works representing the pagan past of northern Europe.[6] One, Patrick Curry, has summed up this view with the declaration that '*The Lord of the Rings* transcends any strictly monotheistic reading. Instead, it manifests an extraordinary ethico-religious richness and complexity which derives from the *blending* of Christian, pagan and humanist ingredients'.[7] The contention of the present chapter is that Curry and his colleagues are correct, and that it is possible to go still further, to argue that both Tolkien and Lewis cannot be read and understood properly unless the importance of the pagan elements in their work is appreciated.

The argument is actually easier to make in the case of Lewis, if only because he was a much more simple, transparent and self-expressive sort of person. A major component of his identity as a spokesman for Christianity was that he was himself a convert. Having lapsed in childhood from the largely unthinking faith of his parental background, he was recalled to a fervent belief by a gradual process of conviction that occurred between 1929 and 1931, when he was in his early thirties. This development was partly due to the efforts of Tolkien himself. It is instructive to consider Lewis's literary interests and spiritual inclinations in the period before it occurred. The reading that first inspired him, between the ages of six and eight, was that of the Norse pagan myths. Initially these reached him through the poetry of Longfellow, in which he was smitten with the image of the dying god Balder the Beautiful. This literature remained a passion of his all through adolescence. To it was subsequently added that of ancient Greece and Rome, of which his favourite works were, again, those with a rich religious content: Horace's Odes, the *Aeneid*, Apuleius's *Golden Ass*, and the *Bacchae*. His enthusiasm for Scandinavian and Germanic myth led him to that of pagan Ireland, which likewise caught his imagination. He was also drawn to occultism, and as an undergraduate was thrilled to discover a copy of the most famous work of Renaissance magic, the *Occult Philosophy* of Cornelius Agrippa. The favourite modern authors of his youth were those who drew on ancient or medieval literature, or brewed together magic, paganism and nature-worship: Yeats, Keats, Shelley, Swinburne, William Morris, Algernon Blackwood, James Stephens and Maurice Hewlett. The only explicitly Christian classic to arouse his enthusiasm was the *Morte d'Arthur*, and the only recent writer who relied heavily on Judaeo-Christian tradition to do so was George Macdonald. The work of non-fiction that he remembered as most formative was Sir James Frazer's great compendium of folklore and religion, *The Golden Bough*, one major theme of which was the ubiquity in the ancient world of a belief in a dying and resurrecting god, representing the resurgent forces of nature.[8]

Stray comments on or from his time of childhood and youth testify to the impact of this reading. He recalled later that at the age of eleven he had visualised dwarfs 'so intensely that I came to the very frontiers of hallucination'.[9] The visualisation took long to fade: he was almost sixteen when, seeing a snowy landscape, he commented that 'one almost expects a "march of dwarfs" to come dashing past'.[10] A few months later he was disappointed in a novel by Morris because 'there is nothing supernatural, faery or unearthly in it'.[11] His letters at this period were peppered with casual references to pagan cosmology: in one at the age of sixteen, for example, he assumed that human destinies were determined by 'the Norns or Dana holy mother of them that die not'; a reference that coupled figures from Norse and Irish myth.[12] His attitude became more resolutely sceptical (at seventeen he could declare that 'all religions, that is, all mythologies to give them their proper name are merely man's own invention'),[13] but there is no doubt of the 'mythologies' to which he himself inclined by nature. At the age of twenty-two, he disliked some poetry of Milton because in it 'the Hebrew element finally gets the better of the classical and romantic elements. How can people be attracted to things Hebrew?'[14] Two years later he expressed a yearning for 'a knowledge of the real unhuman life which is in the trees etc'.[15]

Unsurprisingly, his first literary compositions reflected the same tastes. At fifteen he wrote an opera libretto, entitled *Loki Bound*, that expressed the appeal of Norse myth and a contempt for creator deities.[16] A year later he planned an allegorical story based on Irish mythology, in which the Fomor represented the 'stern, ugly, money grubbing spirit, finally conquered by that of art and beauty, as exemplified by the lovely folk of the Shee'.[17] Most revealing is his first published book of poetry, composed in his late adolescence and brought out in 1918. It shocked his stolidly conventional brother in being so openly 'atheist',[18] but at times it breathes a spirit that requires a different name. One poem honours a witch burned in a medieval setting, as the proud and impenitent practitioner of a surviving ancient religion 'at dead of night in worship bent/ At ruined shrines magnificent'.[19] Another boasts of having seen 'the Dadga's throne/ In sunny lands without a tear', and another draws on the same (Irish) mythology to present a passionate vision of the god Angus; 'swift, naked, eager, pitilessly fair/ With a live crown of birds about his head'. Yet another hails the evening star, as a benevolent classical deity.[20] It is escapist romanticism, but of a specifically pagan variety.

In later life, after conversion, Lewis acknowledged this with a characteristic honesty and generosity. He confirmed that the appeal of Norse and Germanic mythology for him was that 'it contained elements which my religion ought to have contained and did not'. He came far nearer to feeling real love for Norse deities 'whom I disbelieved in than I had ever done about the true God while I believed'. When he read the Graeco-Roman classics he discovered that 'Pan and Dionysus lacked the cold, piercing appeal of Odin and Frey. A new quality entered my imagination: something Mediterranean and volcanic, the orgiastic drum beat'. He remembered his mid-adolescence as 'a period of ecstasy ... when the gods and heroes roared through your head, when satyrs danced and Maenads roared on the mountains'. In his twenties, as he began to respond to a longing for spiritual fulfilment, it was the pagan classics that, once again, played a major part in his progress; in particular, a rereading of Euripedes's play *Hippolytus* gave him an overwhelming sense of the presence of divinity in the world.[21]

In this context, it is hard to resist agreement with Humphrey Carpenter's suggestion that he accepted Christianity because it was really the only thing on offer. Virtually all his friends and mentors were devout Christians, and he was existing as a spiritual outsider in the company which he most liked and respected, even while he yearned for a religion. At the moment of conversion he confided to a correspondent that 'the *spontaneous* appeal of the Christian story is so much less to me than that of Paganism'. He never lost his private doubts concerning the faith that he now adopted with such public fervour: over twenty years later he could still wonder in another letter, 'How could I – I of all people – ever have come to believe this cock and bull story?'[22] Lewis knew of no organised pagan religion in Britain at the time, to which he might have turned instead; it is possible that none existed. The nearest known equivalent consisted of the closed societies of ritual magicians, which sometimes did call on pagan deities, but they were few and secretive and he never encountered any active members of them. He admitted later (ungraciously) that they would indeed have held a powerful attraction for him: 'If there had been in the neighbourhood such elder person who dabbled in dirt of the magical kind ... I might now be a Satanist or a maniac.'[23] There was not; and he became a Christian. Most of his skill as an apologist and polemicist for his new-found faith lay in his recognition that it was neither an obvious nor an easy thing to achieve.

In the process, he retained his affection for ancient paganism and preserved a place for it in his theology, as a means by which the Christian god had prepared the way for the coming of Christ. In this manner the history of humanity was made to parallel his own spiritual journey. The ancient myths were turned into 'hints' that were 'fulfilled' in Christianity: as he wrote while in the full flush of conversion, in October 1931, 'the Pagan stories are God expressing Himself through the minds of poets, using such images as He found there, while Christianity is God expressing himself through what we call "real things"'. It seems to have been Tolkien who, at the least, played a major part in putting this idea to him.[24] The problem for Lewis was whether the 'real things' might not be less exciting than the poetry. The year before, he and some friends had planned to celebrate the harvesting of grapes from a vine at their cottage by staging 'a Bacchic festival ... with a Silenus, Corybantes and a Maenad, poetry and dance'. Also in that previous year, he described ancient Roman and Celtic cultures as 'almost one's male and female soul'. In March 1931 he could declare that 'some sensuality one pities: other kinds one admires – full, Pagan magnificence'. In November, during his acceptance of Christ, he repeated his new belief that 'the thrill of the Pagan stories and of romance may be due to the fact that they are mere beginnings ... while Christianity is the thing itself'. He could not help, however, but add wistfully that 'no thing, when you have really started on it, can have for you then and there the same thrill as the first hint'.[25]

This 'thrill' showed very strongly in a narrative poem that he wrote at some point in the early or mid 1930s, and never had published. It was a fantasy in which a queen, escaping from revolution in a Christian state, finds refuge and happiness by passing into fairyland, in the manner depicted in the traditional story of Thomas the Rhymer. Lewis's fairyland, like that in the tale of Thomas (itself ultimately medieval) is a realm detached from the Christian war of heavenly and infernal powers and the material world alike, and outside their concerns: 'untrampled by the warring legions of Heaven and Darkness'. Most strikingly, she obtains entry to the elvish realm by praying to the moon in the names of the pagan goddesses associated with it, Hecate, Diana and Artemis. She offers them her body and soul, and the moonlight seems to fill her as if she had invoked it into herself, purging her of pain and weariness and giving her superhuman strength for her journey.[26]

These were all private revelations; his public attitude to the same concepts were more confident and condescending. In his allegory of conversion, *The Pilgrim's Regress* (1933), he described pagans as 'people who live under the Enemy' (Satan) and are 'corrupt in their imaginations' but are sent 'pictures' by the genuine god, who 'stirs up sweet desire' in them and so prepares them for Christianity. He added that paganism and Judaism were two halves of the truth, united by Christ.[27] One obvious question that remained for him, however, was whether pagan myth and deities had any place in Christianity itself, and in the cosmic order after Christ had arrived in it. He seems to have found an answer in the research for his major scholarly study of medieval literature, *The Allegory of Love*, on which he worked between 1928 and 1936.[28] As part of this, he had to deal with the writings of twelfth-century Christian intellectuals based in the schools of Chartres and Tours, notably Bernard Silvester and Alan of Lille, who reintegrated ancient pagan images into their view of the universe in two different ways. One was to treat the sun, moon and five other visible planets as deities identifiable with the classical gods and goddesses whose names they traditionally bore. In this scheme these deities were appointed by the Christian god to have power over particular aspects of the earthly realm. In the second scheme, the supreme deity had entrusted immediate care for the earth to a mighty female figure, Nature.

Lewis's imaginative assimilation of these concepts was displayed in his first works of popular fiction, the so-called 'cosmic trilogy' of novels that he published between 1938 and 1944. In the first, *Out of the Silent Planet*,[29] he explicitly paid homage to the influence of the twelfth-century thinkers, taking the name for a major character from the work of Bernard Silvester. The story depended on a vision of the solar system that adapted the medieval system to modern astronomy: the galaxy was ruled by a great divinity who had appointed a deity to govern each planet. Here Lewis's essentially pessimistic view of humanity came into play, and appropriated ideas from the older, quasi-Christian tradition of Gnosticism. In his vision, the god given responsibility for the Earth had turned bad, making it the only world to be governed by an evil being.

The second book took the hero (a character partly modelled on Tolkien) to Venus, portrayed as a place of uncorrupted beauty in which the dominant terrestrial beings were a Lady or Queen and a Lord or King. Most of the action concentrates on the Lady, and the battle between the protagonist and a demon sent by the malevolent divinity of planet Earth to destroy her innocence and mar her environment.[30] In one sense, therefore, Venus is shown as Eden and its dominant female as Eve, but, as Lewis himself said, there was more to her than that: 'she's got to be in some ways like a Pagan goddess and in other ways like the Blessed Virgin'.[31] It may be suggested here that, in her green colour, her apparent immortality and her particular affinity with animals, the Lady can be partly identified with the Nature of the twelfth-century authors.

The final novel of the trilogy describes how the hero and his assistants engage in a classic piece of medieval astral magic, to help draw down the other planetary deities to earth so that the latter can employ their full powers to defeat its evil divine overlord. It is furthermore revealed that each planetary divinity has a spirit operating on earth itself to represent it – 'a Cretan Jove as well as an Olympian' – so that they are constant forces within the terrestrial world.[32] It is actually quite hard to see what part Christianity itself plays in the story, although its good characters are repeatedly identified as Christian. The plot occasionally contains allusions to the fact that the Great Spirit ruling the galaxy once manifested as flesh on earth, but this seems to make no difference to the cosmic struggle now in progress. Equally striking is Lewis's insistence that paganism is a spiritual force worthy of respect in its own right. At one point he declares that 'noble thought' can be either Christian or pagan, while at another the hero states that 'there's no niche in the world for people that won't be either Pagan or Christian. Just imagine a man who was too dainty to eat with his fingers and yet wouldn't use forks!'[33] The trilogy closes not on a vision of Jesus, but of Venus.

During the 1940s, as Lewis made a name for himself as an evangelical writer and broadcaster, his theological statements remained true to the position that he had adopted on conversion. In a paper read to Oxford's Socratic Club in 1944, he emphasised that the distinction between pagan and Christian stories 'is not the difference between falsehood and truth. It is the difference between a real event on the one hand and dim dreams and premonitions of that same event on the other.' In a paper entitled 'Religion without Dogma', he identified himself as somebody 'who first approached Christianity from a delighted interest in, and reverence for, the best pagan imagination, who loved Balder before Christ and Plato before St Augustine ... My conversion, very largely, depended on recognising Christianity as the completion, the actualisation, the entelechy, of something which has never been wholly absent from the mind of man.' In a letter to a churchman written in 1949, he reversed the relationship between the two sorts of religion to turn the older one from a preparation for revelation into a residue of it: 'I am inclined to think that Paganism is the primitive revealed truth corrupted by devils.'[34] Less generous as the formula was, it still credited the classical religions with some virtue. His polemic in favour of Christian values, *The Abolition of Man* (1944), praised Plato, Aristotle, Hinduism, Taoism and the nature poetry of Wordsworth, along with Christians and Jews for believing in a divine exemplar for human behaviour. To support Christian morality, he quoted texts from ancient Egypt, Babylonia, Greece and Rome, as well as Old Norse and Chinese literature.[35] A theological tract that he published in 1947 approached the issue again from yet another direction, by claiming that in some respects the ancient pagan deities could be seen as aspects of the Christian one: 'He is Bacchus, Venus, Ceres all rolled into one.'[36]

This was the context for the writing of the Narnian novels for children, between 1949 and 1951.[37] In one sense they were, as acknowledged above, concealed metaphors for Christianity. Since 1939 he had repeatedly propounded the idea that theology could be most successfully conveyed to the majority of people in the guise of romance, the religious message being inherent in the plot, than by blatant proselytising.[38] After the appearance of the last book, in 1956, he admitted that he had hoped that the stories would make elements of his faith more powerfully attractive, 'by representing them in an imaginary world, stripping them of all their stained-glass and Sunday school associations'.[39] Paul Ford's *Companion to Narnia* counts seventy-three phrases or images drawn from the Bible in the seven novels put together, making Scripture the largest single point of direct cultural reference for them. The basic plots of some of the novels can be read as an exposition of Christian concepts.[40] Lewis's imagination, however, ranged far more widely. Writing to a godchild of his own, just before commencing the first Narnian story, he declared that 'I think of myself as having to be two people to you'. The first was 'the Christian godfather', the second 'the fairy godfather'.[41] Both were very much present in the creation of Narnia; the middle-aged Lewis was still seeing dwarfs when the snow fell. This was, indeed, precisely the way in which the chain of stories started:

> All my seven Narnian books, and my three science fiction books, began with seeing pictures in my head. At first they were not a story, just pictures. *The Lion* all began with a picture of a Faun carrying an umbrella and parcels in a snowy wood. This picture had been in my mind since I was about sixteen. At first I had very little idea how the story would go. But then suddenly Aslan came bounding into it. I think that I had been having a good many dreams of lions about that time. Apart from that, I don't know where the Lion came from or why He came.[42]

Lewis added of these images: 'At first there wasn't even anything Christian about them.'[43]

The visions from which Narnia was composed came, therefore, from the rich humus left by Lewis's first and greatest love, his reading into the worlds of classical and northern paganism, of medieval romance and of fairy tale. Ford's *Companion* lists twenty-one individuals or types of being who appear in the books and are taken from pagan mythology, including centaurs, dwarfs, fauns, Fenris the wolf, giants, a kraken, minotaurs, naiads, dryads, nymphs, satyrs, a river god and silvans. The Graeco-Roman figures tend to be in the foreground of events, and benign, while those from northern mythology are more likely to be evil and to lurk in the background.[44] This was despite Lewis's own preference for Norse and Germanic myth, and may simply reflect the actual roles given to these beings in the old tales. A score of seventy-three Christian allusions to twenty-one pagan allusions may sound like a considerable dominance for the former, but the comparison is false. The Bible provided phrases or images, usually as one-offs, while pagan myth supplied Narnia with whole, often recurrent, categories of character. The latter sometimes include pagan deities, operating as forces of benevolence or liberation. Pomona, 'the greatest of the wood people', comes 'to put good spells' on the planting of an orchard in the second book. Later in the same tale, Bacchus, Silenus and the Maenads appear, in wild rout, destroying the more oppressive works of civilization and freeing humans from injustice and sterile conformity.[45] Whether or not Lewis ever got to celebrate a Bacchanalia in reality, as planned in 1930, he did so exuberantly in his fiction.

All these divinities, however, are under the control of the divine lion, Aslan, the dominant being of the Narnian world. If Aslan is Christ, then the pagan deities are firmly subordinated to the Christian Messiah, as in the twelfth-century cosmologies; but *is* he? Lewis certainly, as said, attempted to make him seem so, and at times the parallels are evident, for example in his transformation into a lamb (or Lamb) at one juncture, the capacity of his blood to restore the dead to life, and his increasing tendency to moralize; significantly, these traits belong to the later novels. It must be remembered, however, that the concept of a lion as the central character of the tales came out of Lewis's subconscious, through dreams, and was only subsequently assimilated to Jesus. The identification is far from obvious and certainly not complete. The illustrator of the novels, Pauline Baynes, whose pictures did so much to enhance them for many readers, finished her work on the first book without realising that Aslan was supposed to be a Christian metaphor.[46] It has been pointed out by devout readers that the absence of a proper representation of the Trinity in the books is a 'theological weakness'.[47] The point could be put more bluntly by saying that the Christian god is missing from the stories. Aslan is described as 'son of the great Emperor-beyond-the sea', but this potentate might as well be dead, and the lion has effectively sole responsibility for Narnia from its birth to its death as a world. The essential claim made for Jesus Christ by his followers is that he was not merely the son of a god – as so many pagan heroes were – but the single true deity of the universe, taking on fleshly form for one unique episode. This claim is never advanced for Aslan.

One of the clearest apparent parallels between Aslan and Christ is the emotional centrepiece of the first book, when the lion allows himself to be put to death to redeem a sinner, and returns to life again. Once again, however, it is inexact. Aslan gives his life to save a single human being from execution, not to rescue the entire race from eternal damnation. He returns from death after a few hours, not days, and in fulfilment of an ancient prophecy and in obedience to 'deeper magic from before the dawn of time', not inherent divinity (and he then revenges himself upon the adversary who had put him to death, not with a cosmic sentence, a thunderbolt or a blast of ineffable godhood, but by killing her with teeth and claws, in mid-battle). The concept of a god who dies and resurrects is, after all, very far from unique to Christianity, as Lewis would long have known because of his boyhood reading of *The Golden Bough*. It might be suggested that a direct line ran from his love of the story of Balder the Beautiful, as a young child, to the death of Aslan. There is, however, a stronger association between the lion and the ancient nature gods, and one that points away from Balder to another deity: Aslan's constant identification with the natural world. He himself has an animal's form, and is called 'Lord of the whole wood' and 'King of the Beasts'.[48] Animals almost all recognise and revere him at once, in contrast to humans, and he can reawaken the spirits of trees. In this he follows the prototype of a figure very familiar from Victorian and Edwardian literature, and continuing to feature as a hero of children's fiction in the same decade as that in which Lewis began to write of Narnia.[49] This was the pagan god Pan, seen as benevolent protector of wild nature and the countryside. His most famous twentieth-century appearance in this role was probably in Kenneth Grahame's *The Wind in the Willows*, a classic product of Edwardian literary neo-paganism that would have appealed to every component of Lewis's boyhood tastes. In 1940 he had praised this very work for providing happiness from 'the simplest and most attainable things – even (in a sense) religion'.[50]

If there is a single episode in the later books that approaches the emotional intensity of the death and resurrection of Aslan, it comes in the fourth volume, when the two child protagonists are trapped in an underground world ruled by a wicked sorceress. By a mixture of enchantment and logical argument she attempts to persuade them to abandon belief that a world above ground exists at all. They are saved by their non-human companion, Puddleglum, who staunches the fumes that are aiding her hypnotic spell and declares that even if the sunlit world and its divine ruler, Aslan, are imaginary constructions, they are so fine that he proposes to believe in them anyway. This breaks the spell, and the witch, thwarted, reveals herself as a being of pure evil and is killed. This has often been taken as a parody, and a defiance, of the classic argument of sceptical modernism against Christianity: that its deity and its saviour are both imaginary constructs produced by the emotional needs of humans.[51] Given Lewis's own beliefs, and experiences as an apologist for his faith, this is almost certainly true; but that is not how it reads in the book. Put there, it functions as an argument for humans to be allowed to believe in *anything* that seems symbolically true to themselves and has an inherent goodness and beauty for them. It is as much a plea for fairyland, the old deities, or any imaginative and emotional otherworlds as it is for Christianity. Time and again, passages in the Narnian novels that can, in view of what is known about the author's own beliefs, be interpreted as defences of his own religion can also be read as assertions of the right of individuals to believe in what they wish, especially in circumstances of pressure for social or political uniformity. Whether or not Christ benefits from what happens in Narnia, it is perfectly obvious that talking animals, dryads, fauns and imaginative children do.

The Narnian world in general displays aspects of cosmology which, although they can be reconciled with Christianity, are not inherently part of it. One is animism, the belief that trees and waters are inhabited by sentient and intelligent beings. This is common to many traditional peoples, to the pagan classics and to modern romantic fiction alike, and was certainly absorbed by Lewis. Aslan does not create Narnia, in the sense that the Christian god is said to have created the universe; rather, its beings are called to awake by his summons.[52] Nor does he destroy it, in a great day of wrath, but lets Time extinguish it, when its sun has grown naturally to old age. The other doctrine is Platonism, which Lewis admired both in its original, ancient Greek, form and in the use made of it by medieval poets and theologians. The whole cycle of stories ends with the revelation that Narnia was merely one portion of a classic Platonic universe, in which physical worlds are just shadows or copies of eternal realms: 'the farther up and the farther in you go, the bigger everything gets. The inside is larger than the outside ... world within world ... like an onion, except that as you go in and in, each circle is larger than the rest.' In case the point is missed, one of the wisest human characters adds that 'It's all in Plato'.[53] In Narnia, therefore, Lewis, brought together a very rich and complex intermingling of Christian and pagan themes, characters and motifs. Whether this was, in fact, effective in drawing readers towards Christianity is a moot point. What is undeniable is that it accounted in very large part for the attractiveness of the books as reading.

In the remaining, post-Narnian, phase of his life, Lewis returned repeatedly in his writings to the relationship between pagan and Christian, and stuck by his earlier views of it. He continued to express these in theoretical works. His big scholarly survey of sixteenth-century English literature, published in 1954, declared that 'Paganism is the religion of poetry through which the author can express, at any moment, just so much of his real religion as his art requires'. He added that 'We are all Pagans in Arcadia' (the rural dreamworld of pastoral myth).[54] It was a neat justification of the liberal use of pre-Christian imagery by a Christian author. Four years later, in a theological work, he asserted that Plato had predicted the coming of Christ, and that ancient myths of dying and resurrecting nature-gods had been 'already a likeness permitted by God to that truth on which all depends'.[55]

He sustained the same theme in private writings. To a fellow academic, in 1959, he suggested that 'if every good and perfect gift comes from the Father of Light then all true and edifying writings, whether in Scripture or not, must be in *some sense* inspired'. This, of course, gave his favourite pagan classics something of the status of holy writ. He stated to a churchman that 'the difficulty about Hinduism, and indeed about all the higher Paganisms, seems to me to be our double task of reconciling and converting. The activities are almost opposites, yet must go hand in hand. We have to hurl down false gods, and also elicit the peculiar truth preserved in the worship of each.'[56] He always enjoyed novels which celebrated the mindset of the pagan ancient world, including those of Naomi Mitchison and (towards the end of his life) Mary Renault.[57] In 1956 he produced one of his own, based on the myth of Psyche and set in Asia Minor in the fourth century BCE. It portrayed a world in which the classical deities were both real and essentially good, being manifestations of a greater divinity; after his conversion, Lewis was always still more generous to the old religions in his creative writing than in his theoretical statements.

The latter culminated in a work on literature, published after his death, where he paid tribute once more to the influence of the schoolmen of the middle ages, in justifying his adoption of Christianity without abandoning his love of the pagan past. He declared that the glory of medieval culture was that it had been based on 'Paganism, Judaism, Platonism, Aristotelianism, Stoicism, Primitive Christianity and Patristic', all made to respect one another.[58] In doing so, of course, he was also summing up his own work as the twentieth-century successor to Bernard Silvester and the writers of the twelfth-century Renaissance.

As hinted earlier, Lewis was a much more transparent and accessible personality than Tolkien. If the former was a convert to active faith, who spent much of his life explaining and justifying his beliefs, the latter was brought up a devout Christian by a beloved mother. Tolkien never felt the need to discuss, analyse or defend his religion in print, and was not introspective about it. Indeed, it was different in kind from that of his friend. Lewis was an Anglican. Although he did his best to couch his polemical and theological work in terms designed to appeal to the broadest possible spectrum of Christianities, they had an unmistakably Protestant tinge. Tolkien was a Roman Catholic. For both personal and denominational reasons, his faith was less one of words, texts and disputations and more a combination of instinct, experience, routine and ceremony. The connection between his religion and his creative life must therefore be sought in more implicit sources than the large body of reflections, arguments and proposals left by his friend.

One similarity between them is very clear: the lasting effect on both of childhood and teenage reading. Like Lewis, Tolkien was attracted, powerfully and from an early age, to the old northern literatures. He, however, focused much more tightly on these works, being more or less indifferent to the Greek and Roman classics, and to most writing produced after the year 1400, and considerably less interested in early Welsh and Irish literature. He prized above all those poems and sagas composed by medieval Christian societies that looked backwards proudly to the pagan past: of the Anglo-Saxons (especially *Beowulf*), the Norse (especially the *Elder Edda*), and the Finns (the national epic, *Kalevala*).[59] In one sense there really is no mystery about the relationship between Tolkien's faith and his fantasy world; he reproduced the essential features of those early medieval authors, in being a Christian who wrote heroic stories about a non-Christian or pre-Christian society.[60] This does, however, beg more difficult, and interesting, questions about why he chose to do so, and how this process related to his own religious beliefs.

In providing answers, it is necessary to make extensive use of two bodies of material never published in his lifetime: manuscripts of stories commenced and then abandoned or refashioned, and private letters. The existence of the former makes another contrast with his friend. From the age of thirty-five, Lewis poured out publications almost as easily as he breathed. It seems that nothing that he wrote for print failed to reach it, and he discarded the manuscript versions as worthless. Tolkien found the completion and publication of work ever more difficult, accumulating a mass of reworked and discarded drafts. If the Narnian stories were all composed within forty months, *The Lord of the Rings* took sixteen years from commencement to publication, and the earlier chapters went through repeated revisions. It is possible to gain, from the published works, a completely erroneous sense of how Tolkien's fantasy world evolved. These consist first of a children's story, *The Hobbit* (1937), which told of events in a land that had expanded enormously in size, detail and depth of history by the time that it reappeared in *The Lord of the Rings* (1954–55), and was given a creation story and extensive prehistory in *The Silmarillion* (1977), published only after his death. Since 1983, however, his son Christopher has edited twelve volumes of his manuscripts, which reveal that the process of composition occurred, largely, in the reverse of this pattern: first came the creation myth and the cosmology, which later underpinned the specific tales that saw print in the 1930s and 1950s. This cosmology was already substantially complete by the year 1920, when Tolkien was twenty-eight years old.

He seems to have been initially most interested in fairies, and in a fairyland.[61] This inclination, however, bloomed into a complete universe, produced by a supreme being, Iluvatar, who lives outside all material worlds. This entity sang into being 'the Gods' and they in turn made, under his leadership, the divine music that created the world in which Tolkien's fantasies were to be set. Some of 'the Gods' went to dwell in that creation and to act as stewards of it, and Tolkien distinguished them with the name of Valar. They formed a pantheon of figures perfectly recognisable from several pagan mythologies, extending (curiously in view of Tolkien's northern interests) from Ireland and Scandinavia to Greece and Mesopotamia. This had four leaders, who 'dreamed into being' the four elements respectively. Manwe, the one associated with the air and heavens, was enthroned on a mountain, like the Greek Zeus, with his spouse, Varda or Elbereth, a beautiful star-goddess equatable with ancient figures such as Nuit, Ishtar or Aphrodite Urania. Together they became monarchs of most of the other deities, and of the lesser races of the world. The second most powerful in this group became ruler of the oceans, having the same relationship with Manwe as Poseidon with Zeus. The third was associated with earth and became a divine smith and craftsman, like Hephaestos, Vulcan, Goibhniu, Luchta and Creidhne. The fourth, Melko or Melkor, was deity of fire, and inherently the mightiest of all, but he turned against both Iluvatar and his followers, desiring an independent dominion, and became their adversary, master of the more peripheral and inhospitable regions: he has parallels with Set, Ahriman. Loki and Shamal. Iluvatar himself created two special species, elves and humans. The former were immortal unless killed or wasted away by sorrow, and in such cases underwent reincarnation. The latter were mortal, with short lives, but did 'not perish utterly' on death. The overall form and destiny of the world was therefore a joint product of Iluvatar and the Gods, but both were ultimately decreed by the supreme deity alone.[62]

Shortly after writing this first draft of the story, Tolkien continued and augmented it. He added more figures to his pantheon. Once again, the additions were drawn from recognisable ancient stereotypes, including a fertility goddess associated with nature spirits (like Ceres, Demeter or Freya), a god and goddess of the dead (mirrroring Pluto or Hades and Persephone), a benevolent warrior god (like Mars, Tiw or Marduk), a divine huntsman (like Silvanus or, in modern mythology, Herne), a youthful goddess of the spring (like Flora or Eostre), a young god associated with music (like Apollo, Angus Og or Maponus), and twin deities of discord (probably inspired by Eris and Ares). All these were attended by lesser divinities. Melkor became explicitly the patron of demons and monsters. Tolkien's view of the fate of the human dead was given more detail, again based on ancient Mediterranean mythologies. They were now judged by the goddess of the underworld, who sent the wicked to be tortured by Melkor, kept some in honour at her own court, and set most to wander a dark plain until the end of the world. A few of the best were chosen by the deities to dwell with them in their land of Valinor, around Manwe's mountain seat. A continuation of the story, again probably made before 1920, told of how the deities in Valinor held seasonal feasts to mark the anniversaries of great events in the forming of the world. It represented them as divided in their opinions, given to squabbling, jealousy, duplicity, fear, selfishness, injustice and error, and capable of being deceived, in the manner of the ancient pantheons on which their characters were modelled. Just as in the latter, it is their king, Manwe, who is wisest and most far-sighted. Like those old deities, also, they heard the prayers of mortal beings living in the world outside their divine realm, and sent them dreams to guide them. Yet another link between them and pagan predecessors was that they made sexual unions with each other and bore children. The cycle of stories projected a final end to the world, after the manner of the Norse Ragnarok, in which the heroic son of Manwe would destroy Melkor in a conflict that brought about the ruin of all material things.[63]

There are Christian elements in these stories, of which the most obvious is the rebellion of Melkor. Strife between divine beings is a common theme of pre-Christian traditions, but the pattern here follows the Christian myth of Lucifer more closely than any other: an attempt by a lesser divinity to intervene in the purposes of a supreme one, and the former's relegation to the material world, to function as an adversary of the creator and his adherents. Melkor's fall in turn leads to a second corruption, of mortal beings, although in these tales it is of elves rather than of humans.[64] The character and roles of the Valar, however, are another matter. One scholar of Tolkien, Verlyn Flieger, has pronounced that 'their role in the scheme of things is, from a strictly Christian point of view, eccentric';[65] and that is to put things mildly. Iluvatar is a much more remote and disengaged supreme god than the Christian one, and the Valar resemble pagan deities far more obviously than angels, which is why, of course, Tolkien called them 'the Gods'. The relationship between the two, of a creator emanating a hierarchy of divine beings into existence, some of whom then govern the material world, has been recognised as deriving from Platonism.[66] The identity of those governors, as strongly-marked figures from polytheist pantheons, actually makes Tolkien's system much closer to later Neoplatonism, a cosmology developed partly in opposition to Christianity.[67]

During the three decades following the composition of his first sequence of tales about his fantasy-world. Tolkien's literary imagination expressed itself in three quite different ways. One was simply to augment and elaborate the existing stories, in more manuscripts. In a new version of the creation myth, for example, sketched in the late 1920s, Iluvatar despatched nine Gods to rule the world that he had created, and the theme of the making of it by divine music was omitted.[68] A decade later, in 1936–37, he added a major new component to his cycle, based explicitly on the myth of Atlantis. In this, a third fall from grace was provided, as the best of the human inhabitants of the world were corrupted by Sauron, one of the lesser divinities who had attended Melkor, and rebelled against the Valar. Manwe obtained from Iluvatar the power and the directions for a drastic reshaping of the world to quash the attack, eliminating an entire continent: again, the supreme deity remained in ultimate control, but the action was carried out by the king of the gods on earth.[69]

In the 1930s and 1940s, however, Tolkien also published works, both of scholarship and of fiction, as an explicitly Christian author. In his famous essay on *Beowulf*, issued in 1936, he pointed to a 'theory of courage' as the distinctive contribution of early medieval Norse and Germanic literature to humanity. By this, the authors forsee the ultimate victory of the forces of cosmic evil, but still refuse to take their side, holding that victory and defeat have nothing to do with right and wrong. This heroic pessimism clearly appealed to something in Tolkien, but he was careful to contemplate it from the apparent security of his subsequent conversion to Christianity: to him *Beowulf* 'showed forth the memory of man's struggles in the dark past, man fallen and not yet saved, disgraced but not dethroned'. He also drew attention, with admiration, to the situation of the deities of northern myth, under siege from supernatural adversaries and allied with human heroes against them, which was very much that of the Valar in the developing story of his private fantasy-world.[70] In his essay on fairy stories, written two years later, he both praised the world of Faerie as a means of conveying profound moral, human and cosmological truths, and identified himself as a Christian.[71] At about the same time he wrote an allegorical tale, 'Leaf by Niggle', that was wholly Christian in its trappings and message, proving that he could do so when he wished.[72]

The third of his literary styles consisted of fantasies without divinities present in them. Between 1930 and 1937 he wrote his first bestselling work of fiction, *The Hobbit*, a children's story incorporating many of the figures of northern mythology and romance, including wizards, dwarfs, goblins, a dragon and his own invented race, hobbits themselves.[73] Like the fairy tales to which it bears a strong resemblance, it put no theological structure around the action, the characters operating in a religious vacuum. Other, lighter pieces composed in the 1930s drew likewise on the world of heroic or mock-heroic folk tale and ballad, without recourse to deities.[74]

From 1938 onward he was writing what eventually emerged in the mid 1950s as *The Lord of the Rings*. The religious implications of Tolkien's masterpiece have been discussed many times, and a reasonable degree of consensus now exists over much of the subject. Before providing an outline of this, it is worth emphasising that to a great extent the relevant discussions have been created by an accident of publication. Tolkien had intended the work to be prefaced by the latest versions of his creation myth and the whole cycle of tales now hinging on the cosmic struggles between the Valar and Melkor. This would have put it into a firm theological framework, but no publishing house could be found that was willing to take the other material as well.[75] What was put out, in three successive volumes, was the long and complex epic that Tolkien had composed since 1938.[76] Originally intended as a straighforward sequel to *The Hobbit*, it retained most of the agnostic quality of that book. The 'Middle Earth' in which the action is set is inhabited by a relatively large number of races, societies and polities who universally lack shrines, temples, churches or rites of worship, and are not concerned with the fate of their souls. This has, of course, aided the appeal of the story to a very wide range of readers. It also means that its religious qualities are either inherent or represented by stray sentences and passages.

The consensus that has developed over them can be summarised as follows. There are strong elements that may be persuasively characterised as Christian. Although the story contains martial heroes of the kind familiar from pagan epic, readers identify mainly with, and the victory of the forces of good depends on, characters who are physically small, culturally unsophisticated and politically marginal. It is a drama in which the meek save the earth, even if they do not exactly inherit it. The super-villain, Sauron, is a mighty spirit who was once good in nature and fair of form, but has become corrupted to evil, works through deceit and temptation, is associated with fire and desolation, and has turned physically hideous: another Satan-figure. There are hints throughout the narrative that apparently chance events are devised by a force of destiny that is actually shaping affairs. The structure is that of a quest romance, but one of which the climax is not an act of acquisition and empowerment but of renunciation, set in a wasteland: here there are clear parallels with the myth of the Holy Grail. It is repeatedly emphasised that even characters who are deeply flawed and guilty of crimes may have a potential for good, and should be accorded a chance to redeem themselves. Finally, the quest is undertaken on a date corresponding to Christmas Day and accomplished on 25 March, making the climax of the tale correspond to the feast of Easter.[77] Tom Shippey has neatly summed up this collection of characteristics by stating that '*The Lord of the Rings*, then, contains within it hints of the Christian message but refuses just to repeat it.'[78]

A caution may be entered here against some of these oft-repeated connections. There is nothing specifically Christian about a sense of destiny in
charge of apparently chance events, while Christmas itself corresponds to
the pagan feasts of the winter solstice, traditionally associated with new
beginnings. The 25th of March may have some connection with Easter, but
it was also the official beginning of the pagan Roman year, and in Tolkien's
story its adoption as New Year's Day matches this ancient system. Medieval
Christian epics have warrior heroes of the kind celebrated in their pagan
predecessors, and Tolkien's elevation of the small, homely and humble has
better antecedents, if it is not itself modern, in those folk tales that laud
the triumphs of commoners and underdogs. None the less, all these themes
and motifs may be considered Christian, and those of redemption and
renunciation are much less equivocally so.

In balance to all this, it is generally accepted that the setting, societies
and characters of the story are drawn from the early medieval northern
literatures. There are strong Irish resonances in the references to undying
lands populated by immortal and divinely beautiful races to the west of
Middle Earth. The most sophisticated beings in Middle Earth itself, the high
elves, likewise resemble the fairy races of Celtic mythologies, and the bitter-
sweet nature of their occasional marriages with humans echoes the same
traditions. Most of Middle Earth, however, is resolutely Scandinavian and
Germanic, with huge forests, high mountain ranges, wolves, dwarfs, wood
elves, big rivers, a ring of power, deep caverns, mines, barrow wights, trolls,
goblins and dragons.[79] It might be added here that its cultural as well as
its physical geography reflects that of post-Roman Europe: most of its
western sector is a land of ruins, half-remembered great rulers, economic
contraction and small successor-states; its north-eastern portion populated
by different warlike peoples in a state of constant flux, with vast forests,
subsistence agriculture and wooden trading posts; and its south-eastern
quarter containing Gondor, a centrally-governed, urbanised and literate
remnant of the former imperial state. In true post-Roman manner, the
northern frontier of the latter is guarded by a settled group of barbarian
federates – the people of Rohan – who rule a former province as a separate
kingdom while bound by treaty to aid the remainder of the empire when
required. If Gondor is equivalent to Byzantium in the historical world, it
is no wonder that a north-westerner arriving at the capital city immediately
takes service in the palace guard, like a Viking or Anglo-Saxon arriving at
Constantinople. Like early medieval Europe, also, Tolkien's lands are under
threat of invasion by hordes from the east, and by more cultured adversaries
from the south east who look unmistakably Arab.

If Gondor is Byzantium, then Tolkien's northerners who visit it ought to have the status of pagans arriving at a centre of civilisation which still adheres to the religion that once characterised the now shrunken empire. In Byzantium this was Christianity. In Gondor the parallel holds, for its soldiers are the only people in the whole story who habitually call on divine beings to protect them when in physical danger, and who have something like a religious ritual before partaking of food. The beings whom they honour, however, are the Valar, Tolkien's pagan deities, gathered round their Olympus in Valinor to the west.[80] The even more sophisticated high elves sing hymns to Elbereth, the star goddess and queen of the Valar, whose name has the power to frighten and thwart evil beings in Middle Earth. The most admired of the races of Tolkien's story, therefore, do indeed still adhere in barbaric times to a faith formerly associated with light, imperial monarchy and civilisation: but its true name is Neoplatonism. Just as in Narnia, moreover, animism has its place as well. Tolkien's trees and mountains, if not his rivers, are sometimes sapient and powerful beings, and some represent forces of cosmic malice, independent of the Satan-figure of the story. The natural world, in this imagining, is at once beautiful, alive and, at times, inherently murderous: the Old Forest is a dangerous place to enter.

None of this, however, is presented as a coordinated cosmology, but as fragmentary glimpses of one. It is never explained precisely how the animate trees relate to greater cosmic forces. The Valar remain offstage, and Iluvatar crops up briefly and casually in historical footnotes packed away into appendices to the last volume. It may, of course, be that he is directing the whole story, but in *The Lord of the Rings*, as in 'real' life, it is never demonstrated that events are not merely random after all. Characters in the story, and not the author, suggest the opinion that some design is guiding them, and none of these explicitly credit this guidance to a deity. Some of the handful of apparent religious allusions remain enigmatic. Tom Shippey has drawn attention to the moment near the end of the tale when one of his wisest and most knowledgeable characters, the wizard Gandalf, confronts the acting ruler of Gondor as the latter contemplates suicide in the face of military catastrophe. He rebukes him, declaring that 'only the heathen kings, under the domination of the Dark Power, did thus'. Shippey asks 'Does Gandalf calling somebody a heathen imply that he himself is not one, and if so, what is he? The question as usual is not answered.'[81] If the characterisation of the religion of Gondor made above is correct, then it does not need to be. Gandalf is identifying himself as what he clearly is – and the despairing steward of Gondor should be – a follower of the Valar and through them of Iluvatar. If this is Middle Earth's equivalent to Christianity, then non-believers become 'heathen'. It is true, however, that the point is not made clear.

The religious tension and ambiguity of the work shows most clearly in its approach to the fate of the dead. The essence of Christianity is as a religion of salvation, promising eternal life to its adherents. If the people of Tolkien's Middle Earth are not Christians, was he then, by making an imaginative creation of them, also sentencing them all, good and bad, to eternal damnation? As said above, in his earliest and unpublished work he had dealt with the matter by providing a range of destinations for the dead, based on pagan precedents. His attitude to the ultimate destiny of his characters in *The Lord of the Rings* ranges from the agnostic to the indifferent to the pessimistic. The test case here ought to be the taking of mortality by the (mostly) elven princess, Arwen, to marry the human hero Aragorn. By doing so, she effectively sentences herself to death after what, to elves, is a relatively short span. Tolkien offers virtually no hope to palliate this sacrifice. He says of her farewell to her immortal father, 'bitter was their parting that should endure beyond the ends of the world'.[82] It is not clear whether these 'ends' are geographical or chronological but the finality is absolute.

As Tom Shippey has noted, her second great farewell, to her human husband, is one of the bleakest moments in the whole story. On his deathbed, he appears to offer her theological consolation, however vaguely, telling her that 'In sorrow we must go, but not despair. Behold, we are not bound for ever to the circles of the world, and beyond them is more than memory.' Arwen, however, shows no sign of believing him: she leaves his death-chamber in what looks like despair, and dies herself of what seems to be a broken heart. Tolkien's last comment on her prospects is, as Shippey emphasised, deeply ambiguous; at best it means that she will lie in her grave until the world is changed, at worst that her grave itself will eventually be obliterated, along with all other traces of her world.[83] Christian theologies offered virtuous individuals from a pre-Christian or non-Christian world a spectrum of possibilities, extending from universal damnation at one extreme through limbo (with the prospect of eventual salvation) to heaven on the same terms as Christians. Lewis, faced with the same problem in the world of Narnia, unequivocally awarded good people who worshipped evil deities salvation on just the same terms as those who followed Aslan.[84] Tolkien did not give any such assurance even to the most admired characters of his epic.

We may be expecting too much of him by focusing on such difficulties. In *The Lord of the Rings* he was a compulsive rhetorician, frequently using sonorous and portentous phrases to establish or enhance a mood without troubling to explain what they actually mean. This habit increased as his tale became more grand and solemn. It is possible that he was not pausing to think out all of the implications of his statements, and moments like

Arwen's parting from her father may be of that order. The melancholy of their tone may, however, run deeper, for it was certainly one feature of Tolkien's own character and world-view. As Verlyn Flieger has emphasised, his lifelong commitment to Roman Catholic Christianity masked sharp fluctuations of religious confidence, extending at one extreme to doubt and anxiety regarding the very existence of a deity. This alternation between hope and despair became one of the clearest characteristics of his literary work.[85]

Fortunately, we do not have to rely wholly on analyses of that work for insights into his attitude to such matters, for he wrote quite extensively on them in private correspondence. At least in the form in which it has survived, that correspondence is wholly retrospective: Tolkien was attempting to account for, and sometimes to defend or extenuate, what he had written. He began by explaining to a prospective publisher that his aim had been to create a 'heroic legend' for the English. He rejected the Arthurian cycle as inadequate for that role, principally because 'it is involved in, and explicitly contains, the Christian religion. For reasons which I will not elaborate, that seems to me fatal. Myth and fairy-story must, as in all art, reflect and contain in solution elements of moral and religious truth (or error) but not explicit, not in the known form of the primary "real" world.'[86] Tolkien had thus established a very firm position, but never did 'elaborate' his reasons for it; instead, he continually tried to extenuate the consequences of having adopted it. He repeatedly emphasised, as many of his critics have done, the existence of Christian elements in his story.[87] Conversely, he played down, or explained away, the pagan elements. Iluvatar became 'God' or 'the Creator', the planner of all things that occur in the material world, the sole recipient of divine honours by its good inhabitants, and given to constant intervention in its affairs. The Valar have lost their capital letter as 'Gods' and are compared to angels or saints, attended by lesser angels such as Gandalf. They are there solely to complete the design of the One, and the absence of formal religion in Middle Earth is attributed to the fact that worship is not due to these mere agents of the Almighty. The high elves and the imperial humans whose descendants inhabit Gondor are stated as believing only in Iluvatar.[88] All this adds up to a Christianisation of the figures found in the cycles of stories composed from the 1910s to the 1930s. It is tempting to interpret *The Lord of the Rings* in the light of these subsequent glosses by the author, but there may be real dangers involved in doing so; it is not self-evident that the work was as Christian, either in its inception or its nature, as he later made it out to be.

Two of those glosses, however, reveal different perspectives. One acknowledged that, like Lewis, Tolkien wrote his fantasies instinctually, by the development of images that surfaced from his subconscious: 'The Mines of Moria had been but a mere name: and of Lothlorien no word had reached my mortal ears until I came there. Strider sitting in the corner at the inn was a shock; and I had no more idea who he was than had Frodo ... "seven stars and seven stones and one white tree" had run in my mind long before I knew what the stones and the tree were.' [89] It is not suprising that this way of working left Middle Earth, like Narnia, with various theological ends untied. At times, also, Tolkien was prepared to reassert defiantly that his story was not wholly Christian and need not be. He acknowledged that his myth was different from 'what may perhaps be called Christian mythology' in that the material world in his fiction was created with evil already inherent in it. [90] More generally, and bluntly, he stated that what is 'bad theology' in the 'primary world' is 'a legitimate basis of legends'. In this way he defended to one correspondent his belief that elves should undergo the very unChristian fate of reincarnation. [91]

He did, however, apparently rewrite his creation myth and the subsequent cycle of stories to make them conform more to the Christian reinterpretation put upon them in his letters. The tremendous success of *The Lord of the Rings* made it possible for him to publish them all at last, as he had attempted to do in the early 1950s. Typically, he had not finished the work of adaptation when he died twenty years later, and his son fashioned the manuscripts into a posthumous book, *The Silmarillion*. [92] The Valar had become more dignified, more united and more impressive, better instruments for an active and interventionist supreme deity in governing his creation. It was no longer they who had created the material world, but Iluvatar himself, with a spoken direction, like the God of the Book of Genesis. Like angels, but unlike ancient deities, they now had no children. The knowledge of their king, Manwe, had been curtailed to make him far more obviously just the agent of his creator. They no longer intervened regularly themselves to direct events in Middle Earth, and their feasts were no longer anniversaries of events but offerings of praise to the one true deity. They were 'Gods' no more. Humans now vanished on death to a fate decreed by Iluvatar and not certainly known to the narrator, and the goddess who judged the dead had been replaced by a spirit acting only on the orders of Manwe, who in turn looked to Iluvatar. Tolkien even seems to have changed his mind about the reincarnation of elves: if killed they went into the limbo governed by the spirit who answered to Manwe, to await the end of the world. When all this was accomplished, however, he had still not turned his cosmos into more than a potentially Christian one. It had, after all, taken form not as a realistic prehistory of his own world, nor as an allegory of it, but as a genuine alternative to it, with a different geography, different history, different races, different rules of biology and physics and – therefore not surprisingly – a different religion from his own.

It was said earlier that from one perspective Lewis and Tolkien take their places in the last great generation of authors of Christian creative literature in England. What must now be obvious is that, from a different perspective, they do not: although their personal commitment to that faith is not in doubt, it is reflected in their literary imagination much less straightforwardly than in that of Waugh, Chesterton, Greene and the other writers in that tradition. Far more obviously they belong to a different category, of modern authors who mixed together pagan and Christian motifs to produce a rich cultural matrix within which their tales could be formed. It has been suggested earlier that, although this process was to some extent intrinsic to Christian culture, there were three periods since the end of antiquity when it occurred with especial frequency and vigour.[93] The last was in the late nineteenth and early twentieth centuries, during which it was carried on by, amongst others, Rudyard Kipling in the sphere of the children's story, Rider Haggard in that of the adventure story, W. B. Yeats and George Russell in that of poetry, Algernon Blackwood in that of the short story, and Dion Fortune in that of the occult novel.[94] Tolkien and Lewis occupy the same ground in that of fantasy literature. If their Christianity was more fervent than that of the other authors in this list, it served only to provide a greater creative tension with their attraction to pagan imagery and ideas. In that tension lay much of the success of their work.

8

The New Druidry

'The Gods have returned to Eri and have centred themselves in the sacred mountains and blow the fires through the country. They have been seen by several in vision. They will awaken the magical instinct everywhere and the universal heart of the people will return to the old Druidic beliefs'.[1] So wrote George Russell ('AE'), one of the leading figures of the Anglo-Irish literary revival, to another, W. B. Yeats, in 1896. In one sense his declaration was, and remains, fantastic; the 'universal heart' of any people of the modern British Isles has yet to return to their ancient religions. In another, it was merely premature, for exactly a hundred years after he made it, people calling themselves Druids and inspired in part by what was known of those religions *had* appeared in the archipelago, numerous and dynamic enough to make a significant contribution to its culture. They had not done so, however, in Eri (Ireland), but in the nation which of all those of the isles had the least association with the languages and ethnic identities to which the original Druids had belonged: England.

Nobody has hitherto made a historical analysis of this phenomenon. Three scholarly writers have taken notice of it from other perspectives, and in quite different ways. A Californian literary and cultural critic, Leslie Ellen Jones, added a final section on it to a generally valuable and perceptive book concerned with the changing image of the Druid over the centuries. She commenced by declaring that 'contemporary neo-druidism deserves to be studied in its own right, rather than dismissed as fringe lunacy', and then went on to confine her consideration of it to an analysis of five recent books, by three authors associated with the movement. This consisted wholly of faulting them for failing to conform to her own concepts of what is right and proper, as a modern American woman with a special interest in Welsh literature.[2] The second author was a distinguished British archaeologist, Miranda Green, who likewise took account of contemporary Druidry in a short concluding section to a large-scale work, this time concerned with reconstructing the material and spiritual world of the 'original', Iron Age, Druids. Her representation of it was objective, terse, and carefully devoid of personal comment, concerned with summarising the representations which the new Druids made of themselves through their own statements.[3] The third writer was an expert in religious studies, Graham Harvey, who devoted a chapter to Druids in a survey of modern paganism in Britain. It treated them as essentially a homogenous body, emphasising those chararacteristics which they had in common and explaining their beliefs with profound sympathy and at times positive recommendation.[4]

Here, then, we have three distinctive treatments of the subject, by writers who are as divided in their approaches to it as in their disciplines; it remains to be seen what a historian – or at any rate this historian – can make of it. My own tone will most resemble Harvey's, in that I am setting out to enable readers to understand the phenomenon of the new Druidry by portraying, without criticism and with some personal affection, the thoughts and passions which motivate the people concerned. Like all three of my predecessors, I consider these people to be an interesting modern phenomenon in their own right. Unlike any of them, I am concerned directly with the immediate historical roots of the movement which they represent, with the personalities who have inspired and led it, and with the distinctions between them and the particular forms of new Druidry which they represent. Together, these issues make up a story which has never been told before.

One of its most striking features has been the speed with which it has unfolded. Ever since about 1700 the image of the Druid has been more or less continuously appropriated and reworked in British culture, but in this process the mid twentieth century represented an unusually sluggish point. What Britain possessed then, abundantly, were organisations developed in earlier stages of the reworking. From the Welsh and Cornish cultural revivals had come the respective national Gorseddau of Bards. From the eighteenth-century taste for secret societies, in which the arts of civility might be cultivated within a bonding framework of ritual, had descended the Ancient Order of Druids (AOD) and its offspring, the United Ancient Order of Druids and the Sheffield Equalised Order of Druids. The late Victorian development of esoteric initiatory groups, devoted to the recovery of hidden magical and philosophical wisdom from the world's old civilisations, had bequeathed the Order of the Universal Bond, later commonly known as the Ancient Druid Order (ADO). This was the face of Druidry best known to the general public, for its members were by the 1950s the only remaining Druid body to hold public ceremonies at cardinal points of the year; most celebrated of all was its annual Midsummer rite at Stonehenge. In addition to all these, the mid century gave birth to a small number of new societies in the esoteric tradition of the ADO. By the late 1970s the best known of these was probably Colin Murray's Golden Section Order, which existed until the founder's death in 1986. Murray's profession was architecture, and his instinctual grasp of structure and geometry enabled him to synthesise a system in which images and concepts drawn from prehistoric monuments, numerology, Robert Graves, ogham, ritual magic and many other sources were combined in a design credited to a divine Grand Architect.[5]

In view of what was to come, however, perhaps the most significant single individual in this whole range of organisations was Philip Ross Nichols (1902–1975). He was a leading figure of the academic demi-monde of the capital, being the principal of one of its most celebrated private tuition agencies, Carlisle and Gregson. He was also a poet, an artist and a regular contributor of pieces to periodicals such as the *Occult Observer*. His will illustrates vividly two of his lifelong commitments.[6] One was to the encouragement and education of the young, the other to a range of related early twentieth-century movements for human renewal and improvement. These included naturism (specifically the utopian naturist community at Spielplatz, Hertfordshire), pacifism, and woodcraft societies which provided socialist equivalents to the Boy Scouts. His writings illustrate another, derived from a very Victorian horror at the implications of the theory of the evolution of species. To Nichols it was unbearable to give up the idea that human beings had been accorded some divine faculty or revelation which was not the common property of all creatures. His solution was that provided long before by Theosophy: a belief that humans had experienced a 'transcendental' creation as well as an 'evolutionary' one, the former having been provided by higher beings. At the least, the teachings of these might be pieced together from a close study of all varieties of ancient wisdom; at best, enlightened modern humans might be able to communicate directly with them.[7]

The recovery and synthesis of all human wisdom, to achieve the most perfect possible understanding of the world, was a central aspiration of modern Druidry, since it first sprang from the eighteenth-century Enlightenment. Indeed, that work had been *the* Enlightenment Project, and the appropriation of the image of the Druid had served to place it within a self-consciously home-grown, British, framework. Common to that project also was the notion of a single benevolent divinity, honoured by all major religions and philosophies under different names. This universal divinity had also been a near-essential component of Druid belief, from the Prime Mover of the eighteenth-century Deists to Colin Murray's Grand Architect. To Nichols, the 'One God' was immanent in nature and could manifest in female as well as male forms, so that the Great Mother was as powerful an expression of this entity as the Christian deity.[8] It followed, therefore, that he had no difficulty in remaining a regular attender of Anglican worship while also having membership in more esoteric forms of modern Christianity such as Martinism and the Celtic Church, and friends drawn from both Christian and Pagan strands of British occultism.[9] The same logic made him hail Augustine of Hippo, Pythagoras, William Blake and Sufi mystics impartially as representatives of that wisdom which he termed Druidic.[10]

In 1954 he joined the ADO and ten years later he almost became its chief. His anger at the conduct of the election caused him to secede from the organisation and form one of his own: the Order of Bards, Ovates and Druids, comprising between them the three grades of a practical and intellectual training system which he developed as a spiritual parallel to his professional life as a pedagogue. He led this until his death, and spent his last two years working upon an introduction to his concept of Druidry for general readers.[11] When his death came, however, it was sudden; the manuscript was left unpublished and his order became dormant. To some extent its work was carried on in a different form by the Golden Section Order, and indeed Colin Murray had been his friend.

The main significance of Ross Nichols is that his vision spanned two eras. In large part, as has been indicated, it remained very much that of a western intellectual of the period 1860–1940. His delight in the company of the young, however, enabled him to attract friends and pupils from each new generation. Photographs of ADO ceremonies in which he took part could have represented almost any gathering of that order earlier in the twentieth century; those of his OBOD rituals in the early 1970s look unmistakeably like a convention of Flower Children.[12] Associated with this trait was another; that all through his life he continued to annex fresh concepts to his scheme of mysticism. In his last ten years, the latter absorbed the modern Pagan cycle of eight seasonal festivals, the new interest in megalithic astronomy and geometry, and the new belief in energy-bearing ley-lines which joined sacred sites in the landscape. He contributed to the development of Glastonbury as a major centre of modern mysticism.[13] In this fashion, he anticipated and assisted the assimilation of the image of the Druid to a modern counter-culture.

It is necessary, however, to stress again how little that assimilation had yet occurred by 1975. The older Druid organisations, though stable, had lost dynamism. Those developed in the twentieth century had remained small and usually lapsed with their founders, as OBOD itself had done. None had made any impact on the main cultural developments of the century, including those most closely related to their concerns. The tremendous surge of popular interest in all things to which the label 'Celtic' could be appended passed them by. In the simultaneous growth of modern Paganism, the key figure was not the Druid but the witch. Between 1970 and 1990 the only readily available, popular, book on Druids was by the archaeologist

Stuart Piggott, who represented the modern societies as manifestations of folly, ignorance and deceit.[14]

All this was to change, and the forces which were to achieve this transformation arose from two completely different sources. The first represented, in a way, a further vindication of the prophetic power of George Russell, for it lay in Ireland, in the persons of Olivia and Lawrence Durdin-Robertson. Russell himself would have recognised both, for they belonged to his own Anglo-Irish community, and Olivia was like him a writer in its tradition. Born in 1917, she had in her youth been acquainted with him, and with Yeats, and her person links the two great periods of modern Celtic revivalism. She might have remained a minor, though respected, novelist, illustrator and writer upon Irish life had she not also been a visionary, visited by heavenly beings which from 1946 increasingly took the form of classical goddesses. She eventually reconciled these with her accustomed Anglican faith by recognising them as representing, like Christian angels, intermediaries 'between the incomprehensible Eternal Being we call Absolute Deity and ourselves'.[15] In one sense, this was another formulation of the mystical unitarianism which had been a theme of the past two hundred years, but in another, it reflected a means of reconciling classical paganism and Christianity which had surfaced at points ever since the twelfth century. Such a revelation chimed well with the feelings of her brother Lawrence, a former Anglican rector who had also come to believe in the existence of a single being as the force within all the main religions of the world, but with the significant distinction that to him this entity was specifically female. Like their cousin Robert Graves, he had developed a personal devotion to the figure of the Great Goddess which had been of increasing importance in western culture since the Romantic Movement. In the 1960s the two of them decided to put their insights at the service of the growing quest for alternative spiritualities which marked the decade.[16]

This was much facilitated by the fact that the family home was a castle at Clonegal in County Carlow which formed a perfect base for operations. It began to play the part in the second modern Celtic revival that great houses such as Coole Park and Lissadell had taken in the first. Olivia commenced in 1963 by holding seminars to train people in meditative and trance experience; characteristically, she did not adopt the more fashionable term of workshop, because she had never liked the words 'work' or 'shop'.[17] During the 1970s she and her brother came to realise how much their own spiritual inclinations harmonised with the growing manifestation of feminist spirituality. In 1976 the two of them, with the powerful assistance of Lawrence's wife Pamela, founded the Fellowship of Isis, an organisation intended to provide a network for people from any nation and religion who wished to honour the divine feminine. It began with a manifesto, a newsletter, and a growing body of literature, Lawrence producing historical works intended to facilitate modern practice and Olivia writing sets of rituals.[18] Then it began to ordain members as clergy to focalise local groups of the Fellowship called Iseums, and teaching bodies termed Lyceums. By October 1996 it had 13,399 members, in seventy-three countries.[19]

The Fellowship of Isis is not a Druidic organisation as such. There are (and are) some overlaps – Ross Nichols was a welcome guest at Clonegal, and in 1992 the Druid Clan of Dana was formed within the Fellowship – but it is far too supranational and eclectic to be contained within any one tradition. The country upon which it has made the greatest impact has been Nigeria, while some indication of its multiculturalism is provided by the fact that in 1990 its main Scottish Iseum, dedicated to Brighid, was often represented by the Reverend Swami Prem Sudheer.[20] To Olivia Robertson any benevolent deity and each human spirit is part of the Supreme Deity, and the keynote of her own rituals might be described as Hiberno-Graeco-Egyptian, a mixture which would have been instantly familiar to Yeats and Russell, and proceeded directly from the point where the late Victorian revivals in Celtic cultures and in ritual magic intersected. What the Fellowship did do for Druidry was to set an example of how older forms of spirituality might be conveyed to the contemporary public with dramatic and rapid success. What was needed in addition was a corpus of new material, linked to the traditional associations of Druidry and ideally suited to a contemporary audience. This was now to be provided by Caitlín and John Matthews.

Any analysis of their career (to date) is limited by two factors. The first is that Caitlín has written much more about her formative experiences than John; the second, that both have been relatively reticent about what may have represented a key stage in the formation of their ideas. It is clear that both acquired in childhood a love of early Celtic and medieval Arthurian literature, itself fuelled by the general swell of interest in these subjects from the 1950s. Caitlín also had a different form of propulsion, in that from a very early age she had to come to terms with the experience which had inspired Olivia Robertson, of receiving visits and communications from spiritual beings. Much of her subsequent life has consisted of finding both a context and a purpose for these vivid personal encounters. Both she and John spent brief periods in Pagan witch covens, without satisfaction, while Caitlín had a happier acquaintance with Ross Nichols and later found a congenial ritual environment in the Fellowship of Isis. During the 1970s they began to work together, in London, that seedbed of Druidry ever since the eighteenth century.[21]

It may be suggested, with some temerity, that an especially important influence on their thought was one which occurred at some point between the late 1970s and mid 1980s and is referred to only glancingly in their own publications: when they worked in or with some of the esoteric groups belonging to what has become known as the Western Mysteries Tradition.[22] These groups taught techniques of meditation and guided visualisation which are intended to enable practitioners both to open themselves to contacts from otherworldly beings and to project their own spirit-selves to travel on other planes of existence. Whether or not these higher aims are achieved, such practices usually give those instructed in them an enhanced ability to understand and develop the self. The groups concerned were themselves products of the late Victorian growth in interest in the occult, being decended directly or indirectly from bodies such as the Theosophical Society and the Hermetic Order of the Golden Dawn, to which Russell and Yeats had belonged. During the 1960s and 1970s some of their members formed the opinion that the techniques concerned should be made available, through published manuals, to a wider public. One of the most celebrated of these members took the pen-name of Gareth Knight. In 1985 he wrote a preface to a book which he declared to mark an important new stage in the process by which the knowledge of the traditional societies was offered to the public in a more accessible and contemporary form, intended to enable whomsoever wished it 'to apprehend the forces that form the structure of the "inner worlds"'. The book concerned was the joint work of Caitlín and John, and the first public fruit of their partnership.[23]

It also represented part of another and older process, under way for almost exactly a hundred years, of identifying a distinctive European and Near Eastern mystical tradition to offset the dominance of the Indian, Tibetan and Chinese philosophies which had become established in western esotericism under the influence of Theosophy. Over time the scope of this became ever more closely defined, for whereas earlier participants in the quest, such as Anna Kingsford, William Butler Yeats and Dion Fortune, had looked to the whole of the classical ancient world, the most notable contributor in the mid century, Christine Hartley, had focused her history of the Western Mysteries on the British Isles.[24] The first book by the Matthewses was self-consciously an updating of her work, modernising and enlarging its information to convey a sense of the Otherworld as a constant in human affairs, and provide a history of the interaction between it and the inhabitants of these islands since prehistoric times. It linked ancient religious practices with later hermetic teachings, and proposed that it was time to remodel the latter in a form more attractive to the modern New Age counter-culture; an essential part of the book was the regular inclusion of meditations to enable the reader to make contact with the spirit-world in person, using suggested imagery.[25]

The success of this book launched the couple into a career as professional writers, with a remarkable outpouring of work. They showed exceptional skill in gaining the maximum utility from a quantity of data; thus, in the year 1991 John could issue an historical interpretation of the myth of Taliesin, followed immediately by a collection of narratives based upon that myth and also a practical workbook to enable readers to explore some of the ideas which he had included in the first book. Each came from a different publisher.[26] In this manner Caitlín managed to become the author or co-author of twenty-five books between 1985 and 1995. They balanced these with courses, lectures and workshops, advertised like their writings through their own newsletter; indeed their oral teaching (and, latterly, healing work) has become as important as their literary enterprises. Just as it is not possible to understand the success of the Fellowship of Isis without witnessing the ability of the tiny figure of Olivia Robertson to hold the attention of an audience, so the impact of the Matthewses cannot be comprehended without some sense of Caitlín's skills as a performer. At a workshop held by her and John in August 1991, I watched her move around a company of about twenty people, talking briefly to each. Having completed this circuit she sat down and thought for about ten minutes, and then picked up her harp and told and sang the story of an Irish *immram* or magical voyage. She made vivid mental pictures, each episode based on an early medieval Irish tale, and at the end of the hour-long recital I found that she had woven into them images which answered to the personal emotional needs of each member of her audience. It was an accomplishment of which any medieval bard would have been proud. John's own quieter style of teaching is equally effective, and in addition he proved to be a master of the new information technology.

One aspect of their literary projects has been to introduce newcomers to the world of early Welsh and Irish literature and make personal interpretations of key texts, within the preoccupations manifested in their first book. Another has been to develop the Western Mysteries tradition still further, to meet not only the long-established competition from the orient, but a new one, from the United States. Just as before, the solution consisted of transferring foreign ideas to, or finding parallels for them in, the European past. One such idea was the adaptation of tribal shamanic beliefs concerning soul-flight and soul-retrieval to therapeutic purposes in modern societies: the Matthewses both argued that the same beliefs had been found in ancient Britain and Ireland, and assimilated them to the concepts of inner worlds and other planes found in the esoteric societies. Another was the veneration of the divine feminine embodied in the hold-all notion of The Goddess, of which the Fellowship of Isis was at once a product and a catalyst. Caitlín applied to this the same long-established unitarianism as that continued by Ross Nichols and Olivia Robertson, by declaring that pure Deity was single, imageless and genderless: an energy, power or current. She went further, however, to suggest that it was humans who imposed form and gender on it, by visualisation, and that it was best for the modern world to conceive of it more often as female. This was a distinctively modern, or even post-modern, concept of the divine. John pursued the same sense of essential and enduring continuity in a historical framework, by suggesting that ancient paganism had suffused later Christianity and folk customs to produce a seamless continuity of spirituality rooted in the land since earliest times; again, this had been a major theme of late Victorian scholarship.[27]

The Matthewses earned themselves an immense popularity, treating as they did, in an erudite and accessible form, the four main themes in contemporary 'alternative' spirituality: Celticism, shamanism, The Goddess and King Arthur. They also, however, got caught between the rock of mainstream culture and a number of radical hard places. Their refusal to identify themselves firmly with either Christianity or Paganism, let alone a particular group or denomination within those, left them with no haven in either. Caitlín's writing was both explicitly feminist and explicitly sympathetic to men. Repeatedly, she and John declined to bang a fashionable war-drum – against academe, or patriarchy or the Church. Their scholarship was more rigorous than that of other writers in the counter-culture, but not sufficiently so to be acceptable to most academic experts. It was indeed hardly possible for them to write in the idiom of the latter, for not only did they have different preoccupations but they were constrained by publishers anxious to cash in on the popular (mostly American) New Age market. As a result they became at once much admired and somewhat isolated, providing concepts and practices to people from a great number of creeds and organisations while being themselves firmly identified with none. The fusion of their work with Druidry had to be accomplished in partnership with somebody else.

He proved to be Philip Carr-Gomm, a favourite pupil of Ross Nichols in the latter's last years and the son of one of the tutors at his agency. He was initiated into OBOD as a teenager, in 1969, and made the pilgrimage to Clonegal in the 1970s, but his formal association with Druidry lapsed upon the death of his mentor and the closure of the order. A gentle and cultivated man, educated at Westminster School, he made a successful career as a psychologist interested in contemporary spiritual issues. That interest came dramatically to the fore again in 1984, when Nichols appeared to him during a meditation and told him to revive Druidry in a form which would address one of the main preoccupations of the age: the perceived need to reunite humans with the natural world and their own selves, healing the disorientation implicit for many in an urbanised and industrialised existence. In that moment Philip Carr-Gomm's professional and spiritual concerns fused as a commitment to continue Nichols's life work with the end of helping people to achieve peace: with their own selves, each other and their planet. For four years he brought together the published and manuscript writings of his old teacher, with others bequeathed to the latter from the ADO, and worked the rituals with a group of friends, some of them former colleagues in OBOD. On St Valentine's Day 1988 he and his wife Stephanie refounded the Order of Bards, Ovates and Druids at their home in London. He became chief and she took the post of secretary, while Caitlín and John Matthews were made joint presiders of the order.[28]

The main vehicle of the revived order was one taken over directly from the esoteric societies: a correspondence course. Recipients were also sent a newsletter and could, if they were able, come together to work in local groups. The course led them through the three grades, over as many years, although those who wished could remain in the first or second; which many did. Within the components of it were included teachings of Nichols and the ADO, and the Matthewses made substantial direct contributions of material. The structure, however, was Philip's own, and reflected his skill as a psychologist. It represented an unfolding process of individual self-discovery, linked to concepts drawn from history, poetry, philosophy and the natural world. The identification with Celticity as such was minimal; rather, it continued the long-established tradition of modern Druidry, of uniting images and ideas from many cultures. In the OBOD course, that tradition had been effectively combined with the ideas and aims of the contemporary Human Potential Movement. As part of this process, the course restated the dictum of the ADO and of Nichols, that Druidic teachings should be regarded as an eclectic system of philosophy, open to the practitioners of any religion. In 1990 he and John Matthews edited Nichols's manuscript *Book of Druidry* and got it published at last, and in the following year he summarised some of his own teachings in a book, *Elements of the Druid Tradition*.[29] By the end of 1996, OBOD had over four thousand members. Numbers continued to swell, and to spread geographically, until by 2001 it was, in terms of size and distribution of membership, the greatest Druid order in the contemporary world. Its component groups were found all over North America, Australia, New Zealand and Western Europe, and its English heartland had shrunk to one corner of a supranational organisation.[30]

Inevitably, some of its members subsequently founded their own orders. One, the Cotswold, was distinctively regional, but the other, the British Druid Order, had wider aims and impact. It was the child of Philip Shallcrass, a former Wiccan high priest whose coven had developed rituals based on Welsh mythology during the 1970s. In 1990 he joined OBOD and at the same time began to rework his earlier material to provide a parallel system, which he publicised as the teachings of a separate order two years later. In 1995 he was joined as leader by an OBOD Druid, of powerful personality and beauty, called Emma Restall Orr, and it was the partnership between them which propelled the British Druid Order into becoming an international organisation in its own right by the end of the decade. She invested ritual and meditation with a powerful sensuality missing from earlier Druidic teaching and literature, giving her readers and pupils a startlingly intimate sense of the possibility of personal relationships with the world of nature and of spirits. He shared with her this ability to project experiences of vivid immediacy, and both had that same conviction of reality in encounters with supernatural beings which had inspired Olivia Robertson and Caitlín Matthews. His spirituality drew far more explicitly upon that of the lone tribal shaman of the extra-European world than upon conventional images of the Iron Age Druids. Although belonging recognisably to the same world as that of the Matthewses and of OBOD, their Druidry provided a more sharply-focused, idiomatic and richly-coloured alternative to the comparatively cautious, stately and universalising teachings of their predecessors.[31]

OBOD itself decentralised as it expanded, local groups developing their own style of working with the blessing of the Carr-Gomms. Two general patterns were observable in this process. The first is that, whereas for two centuries women had either been absent from the Druid orders or played a supporting role, they increasingly led the local groups within OBOD. The breakaway Cotswold order was formed by one of these provincial matriarchs and Emma Restall Orr was another of the latter; and many remained within the parent body. The other is that the local components of OBOD have also become much more overtly and self-consciously – though not universally – Pagan. After two centuries, the dream of syncretic unitarianism is breaking down at ground level, to be replaced by a full-blooded commitment to aspects of the old native religions, instinctually linked to the land with which they have been associated. The era of rampant nationalism spawned mystical schemes for unity; that of the Global Village may well prove to be one in which many people yearn for back-garden deities.

That double commitment to the *pagus*, the local unit of land, has also been a feature of the second great source for the revival of Druidry in the 1980s.

Its only ancestral link with the first is a tangential one, through the ADO. As said, by the mid twentieth century this was the sole order to maintain the Edwardian fashion of holding ceremonies at Stonehenge, and in the mid 1970s its annual rite, at midsummer, became accompanied by an unofficial festival which was one of the main gathering-points of the contemporary counter-culture. Some of those who regularly attended the festival found themselves acting as intermediaries to prevent friction between fellow participants and the Druids, and in the process acquired an affection and respect for the latter. One was a young man calling himself Tim Sebastian.[32]

His name was an adopted one, taken from the saint who had been martyred by archers. The experience of being repeatedly pierced by shafts was one with which he identified because of the emotional agony of his boyhood, spent at school in a monastery of the Xavierian Brothers. The hatred which he developed for these, and by extension for the Church of Rome, was to be enduring; yet an ambivalence in it is suggested by the fact that he expressed his pain by taking the name of a man who had died for that Church. On leaving the school, and the faith, he found an alternative in the values of the counter-culture, which seemed to him to preach peace and love as Christians did, but in a libertarian and life-affirming way. Contact with the ADO at Stonehenge revealed to him a means of rooting those values, and himself, in the land and in a historic tradition: as for others, the monument had become for him a national temple bequeathed by a past innocent of Christianity and an exploitative modernity. Although he never joined the ADO, he and his friends came to regard themselves, and the festival, as a lay equivalent to it.[33]

The symbiotic relationship between the two was broken dramatically in 1985 when English Heritage, having ignored the festival for a decade in the hope that it would dissolve, took its celebrated and controversial decision to ban the event and to deny access to Stonehenge to *any* groups at the solstices, including the ADO. This ban was immediately enforced by an enormous police operation, involving what has since officially been recognised as excessive use of force. It soon became obvious that the ADO would only negotiate to regain access for its own members, and so between 1985 and 1988 Tim Sebastian's group crystallised into the Secular Order of Druids, a name chosen to demonstrate that it campaigned for all people who wished to worship and celebrate at Stonehenge, rather than representing a priesthood or esoteric society. He was elected archdruid, to represent it to the public, and the order was henceforth based around his homes in Wiltshire and Somerset.[34]

Sebastian and his companions now trod an ingenious tightrope between the need to be taken seriously by those with whom they negotiated (such as English Heritage), and the need to avoid taking themselves seriously and by this destroying the playful and libertarian atmosphere of the counter-culture which they embodied. With much reluctance, they decided that the first consideration demanded that they adopt the white robes long sported by the older orders. At first they avoided ritual, but Sebastian gradually found himself pushed by the demands of members and friends to perform handfasting (wedding) rites for them. During the early 1990s he and his order reconciled their conflicting impulses in this area by providing ceremonies on stage at the 'rave' gatherings which had become the new festive experience of youth; it was a new and neat way of enabling his form of Druidry to function as the spiritual expression of that culture.[35] Consistently, the order avoided the degrees of initiation associated with the older bodies, demanding instead that new entrants act for a year or two as 'jesters', devising jokes and games to ensure that their self-image and that of their comrades did not slide into pomposity.[36] The tone was set by the very name of the order; it did, as stated above, make a serious point, but it also abbreviated to SOD.

For all this, the nature of the new body was not wholly a secular one. Tim Sebastian himself had, after all, been propelled by a spiritual quest of his own, sublimated at Stonehenge and in the identity of a Druid. His personal allegiance, by the 1980s, was to The Goddess, in her full-blown counter-cultural form as the immanent spirit of the natural world and of the planet, the numinous rallying-point of all enemies of patriarchy, ex-ploitation, repression and pollution. At the same time, he felt an abiding need to reconcile this allegiance with Christianity, not by blending the two but by persuading adherents of each to treat each other with respect. Significantly, the allies whom he found in this work were mainly liberal Roman Catholics, and in 1989 he instituted a five-year series of conferences between Christians and Druid orders – with a monastery hosting the events. Some kind of account was being gracefully settled.[37]

If Stonehenge was one place which had caught the imagination of the counter-culture, then Glastonbury was another, as has been made plain already in the present book. Its modern interpretation as a major prehistoric ritual landscape, benevolently Christianised as a centre of 'the Celtic Church', resonated very well with those of modern Druidry. It has already been mentioned that Ross Nichols held OBOD ceremonies there, and it sub-sequently became the main home of the Golden Section Order outside London. In May 1988 it acquired a Druid body of its own, intended primarily to foster those associations and to enhance the town as a cultural centre. The catalyst for the event was the celebration of the millennium of the abbey's most famous historical head, St Dunstan.[38]

Its archdruid was Rollo Maughfling, another former Wiccan high priest who, like Tim Sebastian, had been part of the counter-culture of the 1960s and 1970s. The two new orders had a great deal in common, and formed an immediate alliance to lobby for the right to celebrate at Stonehenge. Like SOD, the Glastonbury Order of Druids had a jest built into it, for it abbreviated to GOD. It also shared the same spiritual allegiance (to The Goddess), but its tone was rather more serious. Rollo's group was divided like OBOD into Bards, Ovates and Druids, but not as a progressive sequence of training; rather, they were expected to concentrate on different areas of cultural activity. Its rituals had an even 'greener' tinge than those of most modern Druids, reflecting the character of the rich, leafy Somerset country-side. GOD was also distinctive for the creative power of its archdruidesses, most of all the writer Jacki Patterson and the artist Una Woodruff.

The two west country archdruids made a striking and complementary pair. Sebastian was a classic rough diamond, in appearance and speech, while Maughfling, though sporting the long beard and hair of traditional hippiedom, had the voice and accent of Lord Baden-Powell and usually wore a cricketing hat to top off the cloak and robe of his order on ceremonial occasions. Both were soon joined by an even more colourful figure, a Farnborough biker who had experienced vivid dreams and reveries as a boy, 'of leading people into battle, of horses and of wizards'. In 1986 a friend told him that these could have been memories of a past life as King Arthur. He put this notion to the test by going to Stonehenge to ask for a sign. A bird flew out of the centre of the circle, brushing his face with its wings. Taking that for an affirmative, he changed his name (by deed poll) to Arthur Uther Pendragon. A year later he climbed Glastonbury Tor and asked The Goddess that he might find Excalibur again before the next full moon. On the day before the moon reached its fullness he saw a sword, offered for sale in a shop window, which had been made to represent Arthur's sword in a film. He bought it, strapped it on, and vowed to fight for civil liberties and environmental issues.[39] Henceforth he appeared on all public occasions in a surcoat embroidered with a red dragon, the sword hung about him. His powerful build, flowing beard and equally luxuriant greying hair, caught in a head-band, made him an imposingly medieval figure.

In 1990 he was appointed as Pendragon of the Glastonbury Order and Swordbearer of the Secular Order. His particular role in them was to carry out direct action; whereas the archdruids lobbied and negotiated, Arthur took the field. He spent the next winter sleeping in a wood near Stonehenge and devoting each day to urging visitors not to support English Heritage by paying to view it. During 1991 and 1992 he was arrested three times for attempting to enter the monument at solar festivals or for possessing an offensive weapon (the sword). These experiences were to inaugurate a long series of detentions and prosecutions at the hands of the forces of law which were to outlast the decade but to end in dismissal or acquittal each time that a custodial sentence was at stake; Arthur had a talent for impressing judges and juries. By 1992 a group of activists had gathered round him, calling themselves the Loyal Arthurian Warband, and this became recognised as a third west country Druid order. It was divided into three circles of knights, according to degree of commitment and services to the twin causes for which Arthur had vowed to fight.[40] Members swore in public to fight for truth, liberty and justice before being dubbed with Excalibur. Ever since, they have devoted themselves to demonstration and non-violent direct action against a range of government measures and construction projects.

Arthur was certainly a visionary, but not an unworldly one. On one level he was a mystic, and on another an intelligent and adroit operator of political performance art. He activated the myth of the sleeping hero who will awake when his people has need of him, and turned it against an alliance of government and big business which seemed to him to have acquired the status of a menacing and alien power. He transformed a traditional hero of national resistance into one of popular resistance, and caught the attention (and increasingly the sympathy) of the mass media in a way not open to more conventional leaders of protest movements. Nor was his head turned by his role. In August 1995 I watched him make a number of new knights on Solsbury Hill, above Bath, scene of a particularly controversial road-building programme. A crazed admirer knelt before him and asked for leave to worship him. His reply was instant: 'No. I am your brother and your servant, but not your lord and not your deity. In the Warband we aid each other; we don't worship each other.'

It should be clear that these new orders identified with a significantly different image of the ancient Druid than that which had inspired the AOD, ADO, OBOD and BDO. To the latter groups, Druids had been philosophers, healers, priests and peacemakers, arbitrating between tribes. To the former, they were the leaders of opposition to the invading Romans, standard-bearers of liberty against a despotic foreign government which drove highways through the landscape, designed geometrically regular new towns and invented reinforced concrete. Both concepts were securely rooted in Greek and Roman sources. Furthermore, whether or not outsiders may approve of the politics of SOD, GOD and LAW, they had to be taken seriously. Their campaign for access to Stonehenge posed valid questions about the control and representation of the nation's past which eventually provoked a major debate among archaeologists.[41] By 1992, twenty-five of the latter, many of them celebrities, were prepared to write to the *Guardian* newspaper to condemn the policy of English Heritage. At the end of the decade that policy was indeed rejected, in favour of a solution advocated by the West Country orders and (so far) a considerable success: free entry to Stonehenge for all comers on the night of the summer solstice. The attitude of these new Druids to the rural landscape, as a common inheritance to be defended against destructive development, was no mere bucolic sentimentality but part of a major parallel debate which developed in the 1980s over the ownership and use of the countryside.[42]

In one sense the attitudes and actions of these new orders were part of a new sort of hands-on politics which developed world wide in the late twentieth century, based on the intersection of human rights, local empowerment and ecological concern. In another, they had distinctively English resonances. England is probably the only state in the contemporary western world which has no formal point of origin; it has developed steadily since before records begin. The sense of an organic relationship between nation, people and land, present throughout the new Druidry and the writings of mentors such as Nichols and the Matthewses, has some foundation in historical experience. Furthermore, England is unusual among democracies in that its inhabitants have traditionally conceived of the bedrock of their liberties as consisting not of representative institutions but of a common law, descending from time immemorial and binding upon all rulers. Echoes of this belief, however distant and incoherent in many cases, informed the protests against a new set of measures which the reigning government enacted in the early and mid 1990s to extend police powers and enlarge the definition of trespass, most notably the Criminal Justice Act. Such statutes were in part designed specifically to combat activities such as those of Arthur and his comrades. The resulting contest was more than one between authority and subversion; it was also between two different concepts of legality. It was not for nothing that the name of Arthur's order abbreviated to LAW.

In this context it is worth noting again that both Tim Sebastian and Arthur had taken assumed names and identities, and adding that Rollo Maughfling at times claimed to be the hereditary heir of Merlin. In part this reflected the creative play already noted as a characteristic of the counter-culture from which they all came, and in part it helped them to undertake the daunting task of standing up to major structures of established power. In another sense, however, it placed them in a long succession of leaders of popular British resistance movements who had assumed charismatic names and theatrical trappings, such as Captain Pouch, Lady Skimmington, Captain Swing and Rebecca's Daughters. The three Druid chiefs had, again, drawn on themes embedded in national folk-memory.

An increasing cooperation between them and the other orders turned the first half of the 1990s into boom years for the new Druidry. In 1989 a Council of British Druid Orders was set up to coordinate activity at a national level, most obviously over such issues as access to Stonehenge. A link with the Golden Section Order was provided by the figure of Colin Murray's widow Liz, in the chair, and it brought together GOD, SOD and OBOD with the venerable AOD. Also represented was one of the small mid century esoteric societies, the Universal Druid Order, which was revived in 1986 as the London Druid Group, and some Welsh organisations. The most conspicuous absentee was, ironically, the order which had acted most as a progenitor of the new bodies, the ADO. It had never forgiven OBOD for Ross Nichols's secession, nor the Stonehenge festival for having provoked the English Heritage ban.

Another leap forward was taken at midsummer 1992, on the bicentenary of one of the key events in the origin of modern Druidry, Iolo Morgannwg's proclamation of the Gorsedd of the Bards of Britain on Primrose Hill, London. OBOD acted as hosts of a ceremony there which included all the recently-founded English orders. Sebastian and Maughfling were made honoured guests together with representatives of Welsh, French and Breton groups, and Caitlín Matthews harped and sang. The occasion also witnessed the launching of two periodicals, the *Druid's Voice*, representing the national council and edited by Philip Shallcrass, and *Aisling*, produced by the Druid Clan of Dana, the group just founded out of the Fellowship of Isis.[43] One leader of the latter, the well-known London occultist Steve Wilson, subsequently furnished the Council with a press officer, with the necessary skills to defend both Druidry and modern Paganism on television chat-shows and to journalists. Over the following couple of years new orders and groups were established and received into the Council at virtually every one of its quarterly meetings, and this process was maintained at a slower pace until the time of writing.[44]

From 1994 onward, Philip Shallcrass also represented Druidry at a series of academic conferences called to discus modern Paganism, which was now receiving international attention. He brought to this task a knowledge of the medieval Welsh and Irish texts rivalled in the Druid world only by the Matthewses, and a style of speaking marked by a charm and candour which easily won sympathy. For some of his performances he wore the cream-coloured woollen robe that he donned for ritual, with a magnificent wolfskin cloak which rescued his appearance from conforming perfectly to the standard children's book image of Jesus Christ.

He made another prominent contribution to the movement, by writing a set of rituals for an occasion which in the mid 1990s became its central event. From the beginning of the decade Tim Sebastian had taken to holding SOD rituals at the other major prehistoric monument of Wiltshire, the stone circles and surrounding earthworks at Avebury. In 1993 he hosted a conference there which grew into a regular gathering for rites and exchanges of news, held at each of the eight modern Pagan seasonal festivals. Stonehenge remained closed at these times, and the Criminal Justice Act frightened the local authority into banning conventions on Primrose Hill. Avebury, in the tolerant if nervous hands of the National Trust, represented a spectacular setting at a natural route centre, and by 1996 the 'Gorsedd of the Bards of Caer Abiri' numbered hundreds. Those focalising the rites, who tended increasingly to be Philip Shallcrass and his joint-chief Emma Restall Orr, found themselves coping with a new phenomenon: the appearance of numbers of 'folk pagans', not themselves attached to any specific group but wanting to be handfasted to each other or have their children blessed by those who were. Caer Abiri was putting Druids, by slow stages, into the role of clergy ministering to Pagan congregations. From 1995 the BDO also organised camps on a commercial site near Avebury, to synchronise with the summer Gorseddau, welcoming leaders and members of the other orders and providing discussion of a succession of themes related to Druidry. Since 1992, also, the Council had discussed a parallel development, of establishing bardic chairs at sites of historic interest and natural beauty, to be competed for by local artists and performers and so foster creativity within regional communities.

After all this expansion and optimism, the middle of the decade ushered in a period of apparent division and contraction, and of disappointed hopes. None of the projected bardic contests were actually held up till then; instead individual Druid chiefs treated the local 'chairs' as titles of honour to be claimed by themselves or awarded to friends as part of a patronage system. In 1996 the AOD withdrew from the Council of British Druid Orders, for reasons which remain disputed, and so did OBOD and the BDO, for reasons which are all too clear. Members of various orders foresook the Gorsedd at Avebury, and the series of accompanying camps came to an end. Attempts were made to found a national 'Druid Forum' from which SOD, GOD and LAW were excluded – in one incident, directly.

In part the troubles were the almost inevitable consequence of the speed and ambition with which the new Druidry had expanded. In part, also, they resulted from personality clashes and tactical errors. There was in addition an element of territoriality, for the west country archdruids regarded Avebury and Stonehenge both as national centres and as their own local shrines, at which they would always expected to be treated as hosts by other Druids; and this was ceasing to happen. Fundamentally, however, the gulf which opened ran along the fault-line which had always existed between the two different points of origin of the new Druidry: the esoteric orders and the free festivals. There was no simple cultural division, for members of OBOD were found living in tree-houses in the path of controversial road-construction projects as well as the Loyal Arthurian Warband, and Philip Shallcrass was as self-conscious a product of the late 1960s counter-culture as Tim Sebastian or Rollo Maughfling. Every leading Druid, by definition, has powerful spiritual values, and Arthur had (and has) as close a relationship with the Otherworld as Caitlín Matthews. When all this is said, however, a distinction of experience and instinct was still present. There was no obvious compatibility between Philip Carr-Gomm's image of the Druid as bringer of peace and Arthur's role as a warrior. Political issues which were central to one tradition were marginal to the other. When tempers flared between them, caricaturing became an easy matter: one could be abused as 'New Age' or 'weekend' Druids, timid bourgeoisie enjoying fancy dress, while the other could be dismissed as hooligans. Each could accuse the other of betraying the 'true' spirit of Druidry.

It is a testimony to the vigour and dynamism of the movement which they all represented that the latter reacted to this period of crisis like a well-pruned rose bush. Schism did not destroy the Avebury gatherings, but split them into two groups meeting on different days; and the numbers attending each in the later 1990s were often as large as those represented at the original Gorsedd in the middle of the decade. The British Druid Order began to hold summer camps again, for its own members alone, and these flourished. OBOD had provided such events since 1994, and by 1996 these had become not annual but quarterly, and remain so till the present. The west country orders revived the scheme for regional competitions for bardic chairs, and that at Bath, hosted by the Secular Order, had turned by 1998 into a three-week series of cultural events which attracted much notice and support from a local community already unusually well supplied with such entertainments. The Council of British Druid Orders, although now bereft of some of the most important of these organisations, remained numerically as large because the spaces were soon filled up with newly-founded groups; and it preserved the same level of activity. What had seemed like a potential collapse in the middle of the century's last decade had turned into a second rapid phase of expansion by its conclusion.

It is time to take stock. In doing so it is important to emphasise that this has been a consideration of an international phenomenon, and that in the past twenty years groups using the name of Druid have also appeared or multiplied in several nations of continental Europe, North America and Australasia, as well as in the Irish Republic. I would argue, however, that

those in England have made the greatest impact on national culture and
the public imagination. In 1996 I made a personal computation of total
membership of Druid orders in the country, based on the precise data kept
by organisations such as OBOD and the BDO, and the more impressionistic
but still plausible computations made by the west country groups. I came
to a rough figure of six thousand, two-thirds of whom were in OBOD.
Since then it is certain that most of the orders which were operating at
that date have continued to grow, and others have appeared. Between them,
these societies have made a distinctive contribution to the history of religious
and magical culture in England, and another to the history of popular
politics. It is an impressive dual achievement, in such a few years, for
movements which so clearly address issues specific to modernity, yet do so
in terms of images drawn from the remote past.

I shall close with a portrait of a single incident, minor in the catalogue
of recent Druid activity but sufficient to have passed, if briefly, into local
legend. In 1996 a new quarry was opened in the hills near Bristol, scarring
an area which was both picturesque and of botanic importance. The development unsurprisingly provoked some local opposition, and three young
women from OBOD decided to join a demonstration against it, dressed in
their Druid robes. Owing to a misunderstanding, one of them, who had
never been involved in such action before, became separated from her
friends and suddenly found herself alone, at the entrance to the quarry
itself while digging was in progress. Feeling that duty propelled her to take
some action, she walked into the site and addressed the work-force upon
the issues raised by their project and her objection to it. As far as she was
concerned, she was merely 'a little, red-faced stammering thing'. To many
of those listening she was an extraordinary apparition, who seized their
attention so dramatically that they downed tools and listened, with the
exception of the foreman who was making a panic-stricken telephone call
to the manager to report what was happening. When she had concluded,
she turned and vanished into the neighbouring woods, leaving behind her
some doubt, some division, some curiosity – and much admiration. She
was a modern woman, addressing an matter of specifically contemporary
concern, and yet in her way she had made a perfect equivalent to figures
such as Fedelm and Veleda in the tales of old. Like the image of the Druid
itself, she had become in that moment a being both inside and outside of
historical time.

9

Living with Witchcraft

Two concepts which have recently become very prominent in the social sciences are reactivity and reflexivity. Reactivity is the effect produced on a social group by the scholar who is studying it. In the course of the twentieth century it has become very obvious how much the process of making such a study can alter, significantly and permanently, the people who are being studied. Reflexivity is the readiness of scholars to be openly aware of the prejudices, preoccupations, instincts, emotions and personal traits which they bring to their studies, and the way in which these can influence the latter. It can also include the impact of the process of study itself upon the personality and attitudes of the scholar.[1] Neither concept has so far made much impact upon the professional writing of history. Reactivity is naturally barely relevant to the latter, for the obvious reason that in most cases the people being studied are dead and therefore presumably beyond the reach of any influence exerted upon their beliefs and lifestyles by academics. Reflexivity should have a much more obvious application to the work of historians of all kinds, but they have as yet hardly begun to recognise the need for it. Where it is assayed among them, it is still liable to be termed 'self-indulgence'. Both, however, became issues of quite acute importance to me when I was engaged in the writing, and observing the reception, of the book to which I gave the title of *The Triumph of the Moon: A History of Modern Pagan Witchcraft*.

When I wrote the last part of that book, in October 1998, I intended to include a relatively long section reflecting on those issues. I drafted this, and then, after some thought, excised it. As I stated in the introduction, I found much of what I had to write too painful and personal for publication. At the same time I left open the possibility that the pages concerned might be published in separate form at a later date, when I was more distanced from the experiences concerned. When I wrote those words I had no idea whether they would attract much attention or interest. Since the book appeared, I have repeatedly been made aware, both in reviews and in private conversation, that they have provoked a great deal of both. In some cases this was the result of pure curiosity, but in most it very clearly proceeded from a belief that the missing section would have aired important issues concerning the conduct and implications of academic research. I am still not altogether sure that this is correct, but enough time has passed to make me willing to consider, in a public setting, the matters which were originally designed to be discussed in the missing part of the book's conclusion. One very obvious reason for doing so is that some commentators have formed their own notions as to what the deleted section would have contained; and have been completely wrong.

The reason why the book raised these matters for me in such an acute form must be obvious enough. I was attempting to become the first person to write the history of one of the most sensational and radically counter-cultural of the world's mystery religions, which had taken to itself the glamour and fear associated with the traditional stereotype of the witch. My reasons for undertaking this work were fully expressed in the book's preface, and were largely based on a wholly conventional set of scholarly instincts and ambitions. During the course of writing my three previous major works, one on the pagan religions of the ancient British Isles and two on the history of the ritual year in Britain, I had become aware of how much the existing scholarship in both fields had been conditioned by the ways in which paganism and magic in general had been discussed in Britain since 1800. I wanted to write a study of attitudes to both phenomena during that period, and to use the history of modern Pagan witchcraft as a micro-history of them. The project presented me with two obvious challenges. The first was that it automatically turned me into a pioneer, undertaking the history of a subject which had never been attempted in depth before, at least by an academic scholar. The other was that it involved trying to reconstruct the story of the origins and development of a mystery religion, relying in large part on records in private hands which the custodians were committed by tradition to keeping secret. I could not write about Pagan witchcraft unless I possessed the confidence and support of Pagan witches. In attempting to justify this, I had to reckon with a legacy of distrust created by my own professional world. In part this derived from a general problem: that the traditional history of Pagan witchcraft, in which many of its adherents had believed, had diverged sharply over the previous couple of decades from that taught and written within the academy. In part, it derived from a specific difficulty: the impact of Tanya Luhrmann.

The latter had been an American postgraduate student based at Cambridge University in the mid 1980s, who had written a doctoral thesis on the practice and ideology of witchcraft and ritual magic as carried on at the time in London and the surrounding counties. This was published in 1989, as a book which made a considerable impact on both the academy and the world of Paganism and magic in which she had moved.[2] Her aim had been to explain, as a professional anthropologist, how it was that beliefs long rejected by mainstream western culture as fantasy or superstition could retain a hold upon a relatively large number of apparently sane and reasonable people living within the same culture. To solve this problem, she won the confidence of a number of covens, and of circles or lodges of magicians, and worked with some of them, as a full member, for a couple of years. She was clearly a person of considerable intelligence and charm, and became for a time a trusted friend of some of the leading figures in these traditions. When her research was complete and her thesis passed, she returned to the United States to take up the tenured academic career which her labours had earned her. Although still working within the field of the anthropological study of religion, she has since shown no obvious interest in Paganism or magic.

This pattern of behaviour was in itself enough to induce feelings of betrayal among many of the British witches and magicians among whom she had worked, and those feelings were considerably reinforced when her book was published and the same people found their beliefs and activities analysed in print. They were not universal, some leading figures among occultists feeling that Luhrmann had acted in a manner of which she had always given due warning, and that her portrayal of their thought world had some objective merit. She was remembered by a few prominent individuals with enduring affection, and they believed both that she had brought the ritual magic of the modern world to the attention of an international intellectual establishment that would otherwise have ignored it, and that she had inspired magicians themselves to take a more rigorous and analytical attitude to their work. More common, however, was the enduring impression of her as an academic outsider who had been welcomed and taken into confidence, only to use those who had trusted her as a means to further her professional career, and discard and deride them when their utility was ended. Those who held these beliefs were not disposed to repeat the welcome to another academic. Working alongside of me in the mid 1990s was a younger scholar called Joanne Pearson, who was producing a doctoral thesis on the spirituality of contemporary British Wicca, the main and longest-established of the various traditions of modern Pagan witchcraft. This naturally involved her in considerable fieldwork, and repeatedly she found herself hampered by the impression of perfidy which Luhrmann had left behind her. Like me, she had to devote much of her initial energy to rebuilding the trust which our predecessor had shattered. The problem was summed up for her in the immediate question put by one witch priestess: 'You're not going to do another Tanya on us, are you?'[3]

This was therefore one of the clearest possible examples of negative reactivity in research. There was no doubt that the manner in which Lurhmann had carried out her pioneering work had made the task of any successors in the same field considerably harder. What was less obvious, at least to me, was whether she had acted unethically, and whether it would have been possible for her, given her position, to have behaved in any other way. There was no doubt that her book had been a considerable professional success and, as a member of her profession, I respected it as being a well-written study which made many valuable points about a hitherto neglected subject. I also thought it to be remarkably honest. Its main theme was to explain the manner in which modern magicians came to believe in magic by a process which Luhrmann termed 'interpretive drift', an accumulation of selective perception and recollection which induced an acceptance of conclusions which were not self-evident from the apparent data. It was this suggestion that they were essentially the victims of self-delusion which made many of the people with whom she had worked feel betrayed and belittled. What was truly remarkable about the book, however, was the way in which it made clear at one point (although only at one point, and then implicitly) that 'interpretive drift' could actually work the other way round. In two pages she described personal experiences which, had she chosen to treat them as such, could have provided for her objective reasons to accept the literal existence of physical reactions caused by human will-power or emotion alone, and of a spiritual otherworld with which humans could cooperate.

What had prevented her from making that acceptance, as she made equally plain, had not been any objective consideration, but her practical need to interpret such phenomena in the manner demanded by the hegemonic, rationalist ideology of her society, to ensure that she obtained an academic post:

> the only reason I continued to think of myself as an anthropologist, rather than as a witch, was that I had a strong disincentive against asserting that rituals had an effect on the material world. The anthropologist is meant to become involved, but not native. The very purpose of my involvement – to write an observer's text – would have been undermined by my assent to the truth of magical ideas ... I stood to gain nothing by belief in power which I was told that I could exercise unconsciously even if I made no explicit acceptance, but I stood to lose credibility and career by adherence. Throughout my time in magic, whenever I felt magical power inside the circle or wanted to say that a ritual had 'worked', I chalked up the event as an insight into the field. In other words, the process of becoming involved in magic makes the magic believable, and makes explicit belief in magical theory quite tempting unless there is a strong disincentive against it.[4]

In other parts of her book, Luhrmann trod the same careful line between appearing to endorse and share the beliefs of the people whom she had studied and overtly rejecting them as fallacious. At its opening she declared that

> neither here nor elsewhere in the book shall I consider the question of whether the rituals might work, and whether the strange forces and abilities spoken of in magic might actually exist. Magical ideas are not incontestably true; neither are they incontestably false, just as libertarianism and Christianity are not necessarily true.[5]

To appear to give a faith in magic precisely the same status as those two great western belief systems was a bold step indeed towards relativism and tolerance. The trouble was that Luhrmann's stance could not be genuinely independent. As she explained, professional considerations forced her to interpret her fieldwork in one way rather than another, and they also caused her to distance herself much more obviously from the people whom she had studied than from rationalist intellectuals. On the very next page after that on which she had proclaimed the possible truth of magic, she found it necessary to state that 'I am no witch, no wizard, although I have been initiated as though I were'.[6]

That sentence was the nub of the problem: the first half a reassurance to at least some academics, the latter part a betrayal to at least some witches. She preceded it with the admission that 'I was honest about my enterprise, but my intention was to fit in, to dispel outsider status, and I was rather relieved when people forgot what I had so carefully told them'.[7] What to her appeared to be forgetfulness on the part of others appeared to many of those people – as I was made aware by them – to be a genuine change of heart on her own part. A crucial misunderstanding was thus made possible: what to her was at best a sin of omission (allowing others to forget that she was distancing herself mentally from their views), was to them one of commission (causing them to believe, wrongly, that she had come to accept those views). It was not only magicians and witches who found this situation disturbing; another American anthropologist, Katherine Ewing, commented that Luhrmann's distancing strategies made 'her claims of respect for the people she worked with sound somewhat hollow'.[8]

A case could be made on her behalf which does not depend upon acceptance of the traditional strictures against 'going native'; and it may be noted that Luhrmann herself did not positively endorse those strictures even though she bowed to their pressure. It is very likely that had Luhrmann dared to declare at least a provisional acceptance of the efficacy of operative magic or the existence of a spirit-world, then she would have encountered hostile prejudices within the academy strong enough to deny her the doctorate, the publishing contract and the tenured post which all followed her fieldwork. As things stood, she managed to disarm those prejudices sufficiently to achieve all these targets, while providing the sole account of British occultism and paganism to be published until that time by an academic scholar which was well-informed and relatively sympathetic. I myself find that the ethical issues surrounding her tactics of investigation, interpretation and publication are so complex that they deter me from making any unequivocal judgement. What is perfectly certain is that no scholar who followed her would have a realistic option of 'doing another Tanya'. Any future person carrying out research among British witches and ritual magicians would have to persuade them that she or he would treat them in a different manner, in order to obtain any access to the data required. Having given such an undertaking, both personal and professional honour would demand that it had to be kept.

In approaching this problem, I possessed certain advantages and disadvantages which set me apart from specialists in anthropology, sociology, theology and religious studies.[9] The chief of the former was that I was setting out to write the history of modern Pagan witchcraft rather than to inform the public of what present-day witches actually did and believed, and why. There was no absolute reason why I needed to engage with the problem which had so vexed Luhrmann, of whether contemporary witches literally believed in witchcraft, and if so, how they could do this. Because my main concern was with the past of a movement, even if this included the recent past, I was not putting its current practitioners under study in the manner of a social scientist. On the other hand, I was interacting with those practitioners as a person already clearly committed to an adversarial relationship with their traditions. When I began to work on the book, my existing publications had identified me as somebody who rejected the claim made by many Pagan witches over the previous four decades (and based firmly on earlier academic scholarship) that their religion was that which had been persecuted under the name of witchcraft in the early modern period, had survived in Britain continuously since antiquity, and had persisted in secret during the past few centuries before surfacing in the 1950s. In this I was simply accepting and reinforcing the findings of mainstream historical scholarship, but, as the only professional historian whom most witches had personally encountered, I often had to bear the brunt of their reactions to those findings. Furthermore, it was obvious to me that I could not carry out my research effectively if I sealed off the practices and beliefs of Pagan witches at the present from those in the past. In order to understand the history of the religion, I had to understand the significance of its tenets and rites, and could only do so by having interacted with its practitioners. It all added up to a considerable challenge, but for me that only augmented the excitement which I felt at entering a field in which no professional historian had trod before. Furthermore, I enjoyed one strength which had been denied to Tanya Luhrmann, and the other young scholars who subsequently undertook the study of pagan witchcraft and magic as contemporary belief-systems, such as Joanne Pearson: my career was not at stake. When I committed myself fully to this research project I had long held a tenured academic post, and my reputation was firmly established within my profession. I could afford to take a risk.

As things turned out, the concept of myself as an academic outsider, pitting my strength against the foundation myths and legendary history of the movement which I was studying, was wholly erroneous. I was, rather, an ally enlisted on one side of a division which had already opened within Pagan witchcraft. The crucial event in this relationship was a seminar held at King's College of the University of London on 15 December 1990, under the auspices of the recently-established Institute for the Study of New Religions. It was the brainchild of another American scholar studying in England, though this time one who has settled down here for at least part of the year: Michael York. His purpose was to bring together academic experts and Pagans to discuss 'New Age Dimensions of Goddess Spirituality', and the Pagans invited consisted almost wholly of leading British representatives of Pagan witchcraft. I was present on the strength of my work on ancient paganism, but it is significant that I was asked to attend by one of the witches rather than by the academic organisers. In the course of the day I heard the spokespeople for witchcraft declare, one by one, that its traditional historiography should be regarded as myth and metaphor rather than as literal history. This removed at a stroke any inherent tension between their attitudes and mine, and left all of us with a common interest and purpose, of recovering – as so far as it could be done – their real history. I was aware that the foundation myth was still taken literally by a great many witches in Britain, let alone abroad, but those who had now relegated it to mythology were the figures who dominated the religion in the nation.

My position within the world of modern Pagan witchcraft was made still easier in the following year, when an American, Aidan Kelly, published a book about the origins of that witchcraft.[10] Kelly was a prominent member of the Pagan community in the United States, and his book represented a powerful and bitter attack on its creation myths. He concentrated upon Wicca, the witch religion which had generally been regarded as the template for modern Pagan witchcraft in general, and which had been revealed to the world in Britain by a retired colonial civil servant, Gerald Gardner, in 1951. In Kelly's reading, Wicca had actually been created by Gardner in the

1940s, to suit his own spiritual and practical needs, and passed off by him as a surviving ancient tradition, the Old Religion of Europe. To me, this work provided two considerable services. First, it drew attention to the importance of a set of papers which had belonged to Gerald Gardner and was now kept in Toronto, and in particular to a single manuscript among them, 'Ye Bok of ye Art Magical', which represented the earliest known version of the Wiccan liturgy. Second, it meant that the world of Pagan witchcraft had now itself produced the two extreme and opposed examples of possible attitudes to the puzzle of its development. On the one side was the claim of an enduring ancient religion, as made by Gardner, and on the other Kelly's assertion of a modern tradition created by Gardner himself. Moreover, Kelly had made that assertion in the strongest and most rancorous possible terms, reflecting ideological divisions within American Wicca. By establishing the position of ultimate revisionism, he had ensured that my own work was likely to appear moderate and polite by comparison. Rather than representing an attack from the outside upon much that Pagan witchcraft cherished and held to be self-evident, my research now represented a contribution to a major historiographical debate already under way among Pagan witches, and conducted in terms of evidence entirely customary and intelligible to a professional.

In Aidan Kelly's case, however, that evidence came to pose problems which are not usually found among professionals. The trouble did not derive from the fact that the conclusions which he drew could not be securely proven from the sources which he cited; that is a very common situation among historians, and it is quite sufficient, and respectable, to make a possible set of inferences from the material and to argue those as a preferred interpretation. The crucial difficulty was that the sources which he provided – and much of his book consisted of a detailed edition of key documents – were contaminated by inaccuracy. Anybody who compares the original texts with the version printed by him soon notices discrepancies, in some cases considerable. I was initially inclined to ascribe these entirely to bizarre accidents at the point of publication, especially as Kelly, in a brief but very courteous and helpful private exchange, supplied me with a copy of a revised manuscript version of the book. This contained a full critical commentary and carefully arranged transcripts of the sources, both missing from the printed edition which had been put out by a populist publisher. I was accordingly able, in my own subsequent book, to point out the difficulties with the latter while recommending the manuscript, calling for a repaired published version and attempting to rescue Kelly's reputation as a scholar.[11] The problems of the new information technology, however, meant that I was initially unable to read all of the manuscript, and when at last I could make a full copy of it, I found that some inaccuracies, although many fewer, were still present in texts quoted there.

None of this represented a real problem, let alone a serious one, for me. No more than seven pages of the 486 in the book which I eventually wrote took account of Aidan Kelly, and I based none of my own work upon his, carrying out in every case the essential duty of consulting the original sources myself and drawing my own conclusions. My debt of honour and gratitude to him for locating and identifying the texts concerned remains undiminished. I have not yet been persuaded that the inaccuracies in his printed and manuscript transcriptions are the result of a systematic attempt to falsify the evidence in order to bear out his arguments.[12] None the less, it was a matter of some concern to me as I worked, and as I monitored the reactions to the publications which I based upon my initial research in the field, that the polemical case for the creation of Wicca by Gardner rested upon foundations which were not merely flawed but justifiably controversial. A set of positions which had seemed to be neatly staked out had proved on closer inspection to be based at both ends, the traditional and the revisionist, on questionable material.

It was of some comfort to me, while operating within this situation, that the negative part of my work had been carried out right at the beginning. In my book *The Pagan Religions of the Ancient British Isles*, published in 1991,[13] I had briefly considered the claims of Pagan witchcraft to be a continuously descending survival of those religions, and declared my opposition to them. Having thus already expressed my disbelief in its traditional history, I was now provided with the much more positive task of trying to uncover its genuine origins. In the process, I felt committed to a particular very important responsibility. It was very easy for some minds, at least, to form the opinion that by playing my part in attacking the foundation myths of a belief system I was attacking the system itself and appearing to suggest that it was not viable for its adherents or worthy of respect by outsiders. This seemed to me to be an unproductive attitude to religious experience in general, and certainly in a multicultural and polyvocal society such as my own. I therefore felt it necessary at the same time to explore the way in which the foundation myths had grown up, to seek to discover the true story of the development of Pagan witchcraft, and to emphasise at every point that I considered it to be a fully legitimate religion of real value to its practitioners.

It was an additional comfort that I was simultaneously employing two different and complementary approaches to my research. One was the methodology used by Aidan Kelly, and of predecessors of his within Wicca such as Janet and Stewart Farrar, and Doreen Valiente, who had made the first tentative but crucial steps to find a history for their tradition. It consisted of attempting to work from the inside out, by tracing Wiccan documents and lineages back as far as could be done, reviewing the historical claims made by other and possibly separate strands of modern witchcraft, interviewing survivors from the earliest known period of each, and seeing how much this process of internal reconstruction and recovery could achieve. I naturally had to engage in this process myself, and to profit as far as I could from the insights of those who had undertaken it before me, but I also needed to work from the outside in. This entailed scanning British society since 1800 for beliefs, symbols and practices which were subsequently to become prominent in Wicca, and seeking to explain how they had developed within the wider culture of my nation and of those with which it interacted.

Compared with the first approach, this one was both easy and rapid, and achieved remarkable results. My expectation that I would reap particular rewards by being first in the field was amply borne out, as I found myself making connections between modern Paganism and earlier developments in different areas of society which had not been related to them before, and finding new importance in certain activities of well-known figures that had previously been considered marginal or baffling. My central argument which resulted was that modern Pagan witchcraft represented not a marginal, isolated and thoroughly eccentric creed, arguably produced by one rather odd ex-colonial, but an extreme distillation and combination of important cultural currents within mainstream British society which had developed or been imported during the previous two hundred years. These were: a concept of ancient paganism as a happy life-affirming religion with a love of humanity and the natural world; a literary cult of nature, sometimes personified as the god Pan or as a Great Goddess; a tradition of initiation into secret societies which claimed continuous descent from antiquity and an immemorial wisdom; a revival of interest in ritual magic; a notion of early modern witchcraft as an enduring pagan religion; and a yearning for a female face to divinity. Before I commenced my research I had been aware of Rider Haggard as a novelist, imperialist and Norfolk squire; I had not thought of him as somebody who habitually bowed to the moon as the image of the goddess Isis and honoured Thor and Odin. To me Kenneth Grahame had been the author of *The Wind in The Willows*. I had always recognised that this latter work contained one of the most striking manifestations of Pan in English literature, but had not known that Grahame's first book had been called *Pagan Papers*, and that on the morning of their wedding his wife Elspeth rolled in dew and wove herself a chain of flowers to symbolise the closeness of her relationship with the natural world. Yeats was of course familiar as a poet, and also as somebody with a personal mysticism rich in occult symbolism. I had not realised that at one point of his life he had hailed the return of the pagan deities to Ireland.[14]

It follows from all this that the question of reactivity, when applied to my researches in this area, must either be declared inapplicable or else be resolved by finding me as guilty as it is possible to be. It seemed very likely that my work would have some impact on the self-image of Pagan witches. What left my conscience completely clear upon the issue was, of course, that I was not breaking into a traditional thought-world which might have persisted longer unchanged without my intervention. In a double sense I was part of that world already. On the one hand, I was contributing to a historiographical debate which had already commenced among Pagan witches. The welcome that I received from many of them, and which contributed tremendously to my ability to write the book, was dependent largely on my willingness to communicate to them recent academic research and opinion, and historical texts, relevant to their beliefs and interests. I did so freely, and received goodwill and assistance in return. On the other hand, these witches were sophisticated and highly literate members of my own society, engaging with it in every respect and constantly developing their own ideas. Viewed from a professional perspective, they were one part of the tax-paying public to whom academics have repeatedly been told in recent years to regard themselves as accountable.

What, then, of reflexivity? It may be remembered that the concept embodied two different meanings, the first being the need of scholars to be openly aware of the prejudices, personal characteristics and other conditioning factors which they brought to their researches. On the positive side of this balance, I brought certain advantages and areas of competence to this particular study. The simplest and most fundamental was that I had myself been brought up as a Pagan. The form concerned was not that of Pagan witchcraft, but had much common ground – in parallel terms about the same that is shared between Anglican and Pentacostalist Christianity (Wicca representing the latter end of the spectrum). Aided by this, I had been personally acquainted with Pagan witches since my adolescence. This background meant that I would never have the classic experience of the anthropologist, of entering a society or sub-culture from the outside and having to familiarise myself with its ways. Nor would I ever have the shock or thrill of a religious conversion experience, or have to struggle with the reputed problem of how far to 'go native'; I had grown up native. That did not mean, of course, that I had necessarily remained very interested in religion, but the terrain on which I would have to operate, and explore further, was already in a literal sense home ground.

I had in fact only ever undergone one great process of personal transformation, and only one experience of induction into, and the giving of heartfelt loyalty to, a spiritual tradition to which I had hitherto been an outsider. That commenced when I entered higher education. It is with only a limited measure of irony that I regard the academy as the greatest mystery religion of the modern western world, with its imposing shrines, its three degrees of initiation (bachelor, master, doctor) with their gorgeous robes, its long, hidden processes of training, and its claim to place its initiates to some measure in contact with the truths of the universe. I honour, extol and attempt to augment its achievements, and my acute sense of its limitations and errors has only sharpened my tendency to praise what it does do well. This may have supplied the one large and distorting prejudice that I brought to my work. It is possible that I consistently overestimated the importance of academic publication to the history of modern Pagan witchcraft, and overvalued written or printed records preserved from the past in relation to remembered tradition. It is also possible that I did not do so, and that dominant norms of the treatment of evidence in any case left me little choice; but the danger remains. More generally, I entered upon the research with a natural gratitude to Pagans who valued academic scholarship and a proportionate antipathy to those who rejected or derided it.

This, then, was the prior intellectual and emotional equipment which I brought to the work, the acknowledgement of which corresponds to one half of the process of reflexivity. What of the other half, a recognition of the impact of the study upon my own attitudes? Here there is no doubt that I found the experience of dealing with witches, and in particular with Wiccans, very much easier and more pleasant than I might have expected it to be. The great majority responded to my researches with a remarkable warmth, generosity and fair-mindedness, including those – again the bulk – with whom I had had no previous acquaintance. Many accepted me as a bringer of information which, if not always palatable, was worth having. More still exploited me joyfully as a source of raw historical data from which invocations and other ritual motifs could be fashioned. As said, on entering the field I was automatically adopted as an ally by one tendency within Pagan witchcraft, but even those who opposed the latter generally accorded me a hearing, treated me with courtesy and debated according to the empirical rules of evidence. I soon became aware that Pagan witchcraft encourages qualities of loyalty, dedication, comradeship and trustworthiness which endow many of its adherents with a gift for friendship. It was soon equally obvious to me that it attracts personalities who tend to be independent, self-confident, enquiring, creative, dynamic, argumentative and highly literary: for an academic, the mind-set associated with ideal students and colleagues. The only determined and embittered hostility which I met with directly was from non-initiatory Pagans who treated the label of Paganism largely as a garnish for radical politics rather than as an expression of religiosity. Even this was small in quantity and decreased over time.

In understanding my reactions to the experience of what witches actually do, it is important to appreciate a point which I emphasised in the book: that modern Pagan witchcraft is not a religion of faith, or of salvation, or of doctrine, or of evangelism, and so the whole language of conversion experience, applied to religious traditions which have those characteristics, is irrelevant to it. What it does do, as I tried to make equally clear in my book, is provide a set of ritual practices intended to induce personal transformations and the sensation of contact with divine forces. The question of what is actually happening in those experiences, and of the literal existence of spirits or divinities, is generally left up to the individual to determine, or to leave open. Among witches I encountered reactions to it from all parts of a spectrum extending from complete personal belief in particular deities and devotion to them, to a conception of divine powers as human constructions, symbols or projections. What I did gain unequivocally from participation in these rites was a powerfully reinforced sense of the latent powers within human beings. I was repeatedly provided with examples, to a greater extent than ever before, of the majesty, wisdom, eloquence and creative power of otherwise ordinary people, and the capacity of religious ritual and ritual magic to exert powerful transformative effects upon them. Having carried out research into the history and nature of modern Pagan witchcraft, I felt better able to understand at least some aspects of religious experience in general, and in doing so perhaps became more effective both as a member of the present world and as a historian.

When considering the second aspect of reflexivity, therefore, the balance-sheet of my experiences with witches was overwhelmingly positive. The subject itself proved to be so interesting and so revealing of many broader aspects of culture, and the company of the people connected to it was so pleasant and supportive, that had I only needed to deal with them alone, I would gladly have remained in the field longer and perhaps made an enduring speciality of it. I had reckoned, however, without the rest of society.

In dealing with the wider framework of my research into pagan witchcraft, it must be emphasised that all the usual structures of academic support were placed at my disposal and maintained with perfect consistency until the work was complete. My faculty research fund provided the money for my single overseas expedition, to read the documents located by Aidan

Kelly in Toronto, in full and without question. Between 1990 and 1994 I taught a final-year seminar-based course unit upon the pagan religions of the ancient British Isles, which allowed participants the option of devoting a tenth of their studies to considering the relationship between ancient paganism and modern Paganism in Britain. Between 1998 and 2001 I taught a course-unit for a larger group which considered more narrowly what could be known of pagan beliefs and practices in Britain since the opening of history, and the ways in which images of that ancient past had been reworked in subsequent periods. This increased the proportion of time which could be devoted to modern Paganism to a quarter. In both cases the units were heavily subscribed and the participants achieved excellent results. In each, a few of them took a particular interest in the modern dimensions of the subject. Only once, at the beginning of the whole sequence of teaching, did a colleague of mine make a disparaging remark about the subject-matter, and that was intended to be humorous. My own career continued its upward trajectory throughout the time in which I worked on Pagan witchcraft, and in 1996 I was promoted to a professorial chair, the apex of the academic profession in Britain.

In the wider world of the academy I found support and admiration for my research subject. Pagans were starting to attract the attention of specialists in religious studies, anthropology and sociology, and as the only British historian currently working in the field I was treated as a useful ally to these disciplines. In 1994 Graham Harvey and Charlotte Hardman hosted the first full-scale academic conference upon Paganism in contemporary Britain at the Department of Religious Studies in the University of Newcastle, and invited me to deliver the keynote address. This was followed by the much bigger international conference on nature religion organised by Joanne Pearson at Lancaster in 1996, and a successor provided by Graham Harvey at King Alfred's College, Winchester, in 1997. I was given a prominent place at the former and the opening address at the latter. Over the same period, student societies dedicated to an interest in Paganism, at the universities of Exeter, Nottingham and Dundee, and the university colleges of Wales at Swansea, Cardiff and Lampeter, asked me to speak upon my research and gave me fine entertainment and many exciting questions. My proposal for the book which became *The Triumph of the Moon*, submitted to Oxford University Press as my first choice, was accepted with more speed, and with readers' reports of less qualified approval, than any of those which I had sent to publishers previously in what by then was a long and happy experience of such dealings.

Nor at any point of my research did I suffer from attacks or interference from the two forces which Pagan witches regarded (with some reason) as their worst enemies: fundamentalist religious sects and the tabloid press. Indeed, my relationships with both Christian Churches and the mass media were, in general, improved by the process. As my work became better known in the Pagan communities, I was with increasing frequency invited to speak as a historian at conferences and gatherings concerned with the nature of modern spirituality. There I made the acquaintance of a number of clergy from the established Christian denominations, mostly Anglican and Roman Catholic, who discussed with me the differences and similarities of Pagan and Christian religious experience. They did so with intelligence, sympathy, modesty and insight, and reinforced the better understanding of religion which I was already starting to acquire by studying Pagans consistently. As for the mass media, producers and researchers for documentary programmes on radio and television soon identified me as one of the very few academic experts on Paganism in Britain. I was repeatedly involved in the making of those programmes, as consultant and interviewee, and learned a great deal and enjoyed myself in the process.

In all these respects the experience of this research project was actually better than that associated with the books which I had written before. In others, it was not. One of the simplest, most understated and most consistent of the special difficulties of this one was loneliness. This is a very common sensation for scholars in arts subjects, where the sources are generally written texts which must be studied alone, and in which the individual viewpoint of each specialist is the basic working tool. It is just as common for such scholars to feel isolated within their university departments, where they are likely to be the only expert in their particular area. What accentuated these feelings in my case was, of course, my otherwise exciting and liberating position as the only academic historian currently working in this area. The very few other scholars moving into it were based in different disciplines as well as other universities, and had separate preoccupations. Although, as said, I was given prominent billing at the three major conferences concerning Paganism to be held in Britain, and was welcomed to student societies, I was never once invited to deliver a paper to a research seminar, the basic unit in which academics hear and debate current work for mutual benefit. My work just did not fit into any of the research clusters and chronological divisions into which the academy had been organised.

There was more to my isolation, however, than functional considerations; reactions to the news of my research project from fellow academics were often accompanied by a greater than usual sensation of distancing, disapproval or derision. Although some of the incidents concerned were colourful, I feel that they were too petty and personal to be worth recounting in detail, even if the other participants were rendered anonymous, and might well justify a charge of self-indulgence. They were, however, both common and continuous enough to have a cumulative effect of discouraging me from discussing my research project on Pagan witchcraft with most of my fellows in the academy. This discouragement, and the attitudes which fostered it, were a more general experience within the society which surrounded and included my academic companions. If I considered that one part of my relationship with Pagan witches was that I was honour-bound to supply them with news of relevant professional research and historical data when required, so in non-Pagan company I considered myself equally bound by honour to supply objective information about modern witches when invited, and to try to dispel prejudice and misunderstanding. By both undertakings I felt that I was providing a service for a public in the manner proper for a professional partly dependent on public money. Furthermore, taken together, they represented the main portion of my basic ethical strategy: to conduct my research in a way which would serve my own purposes and still be of genuine benefit to the people whose history I was studying. This was the main response to my commitment to avoid being perceived to 'do another Tanya'. In the process of speaking informally about witches to non-Pagans, I gained some unexpected insights into the nature of British society in a post-Christian age.

One concerned the sheer scale of the ignorance concerning Paganism, and the wildness of the hostile assumptions readily made about it, even among highly-educated, sophisticated, influential and generally well-informed individuals. The dominant tone of the social world in which I tended naturally to move was liberal, humanist, agnostic and tolerant. Virtually none of its non-Pagan members had any prior accurate knowledge of Pagan witchcraft at all, despite the large number of publications which its practitioners had produced since the 1950s and the growing number of profiles of them featured in newspapers and in broadcast documentaries. Where they had made any assumptions about them at all, they associated them vaguely with blood sacrifice, child abuse and sexual orgies, following a general stereotype of antisocial behaviour which had prevailed in Europe since the beginning of history and become linked to witches by early modern demonologists.[15] Interestingly, none of them ever evoked the more positive fictional image of medieval witchcraft as a liberal resistance movement produced by nineteenth-century Romantics. Where any of them knew of the former academic association of witchcraft with ancient paganism, which had grown out of that image, they rightly regarded it as discredited, and then made the conceptual leap to asserting that this therefore discredited modern witchcraft altogether.

Two examples of the prevalent ignorance may stand, at their opposite social extremes, as representative of its spectrum of colourful manifestations. One was produced for me in a restaurant in 1994, by a prominent figure in the international academic community, a deeply respected scholar who was then the director of a major research institution. When the subject of my prospective research was raised, this person turned out to have the impression that the mass-suicides of small Christian sects which had taken place during the early 1990s in Texas, Switzerland and Canada had all been of Pagan groups. The person concerned had no religious beliefs which would instil any prejudice, and ample access to mass-media reports of the events concerned; and yet had jumped to this wholly erroneous interpretation of them as the obvious and natural one. We were accompanied at our restaurant table by another distinguished (and agnostic) historian, who added the information that Pagan witches sacrificed babies and cited a report in a high-quality national newspaper as the evidence. On this occasion I needed to say nothing, for the fourth person present was a noted theologian and leading figure in the contemporary Church of England. It was he who intervened to provide the correct information upon the sectarian suicides and to establish that the newspaper report had in fact debunked the assertion concerning child sacrifice. I subsequently thanked him and asked him if he had ever been tempted to conduct research into Paganism himself. 'Oh no,' he replied, 'I find Anglicanism so much less demanding.' The other example further proves his point, and reveals a parallel to this sort of conceptual linkage at a different social and spatial level during that same year of 1994. It was provided by a journalist in a small Somerset seaside town, who telephoned me to explain that a couple of black cats had gone missing there at about the same time, and that a rumour had immediately swept it that these animals had been stolen for sacrifice by devil-worshipping witches. He wanted to know whether, as a 'known expert' on the subject, I could provide any comment. I could only reply that none of the witches whom I had encountered or of whom I had heard either worshipped devils or sacrificed cats; and, as no more animals disappeared, the rumour subsequently died out. I wish that both these cases could be regarded as exceptional, but they are not; over the course of the decade I encountered scores of them.

A second shocking relevation produced by reactions to my research project was the quantity of rank superstition which persisted in British society at the end of the twentieth century, even in ostensibly the most respectable and worldly of company. I had expected to meet with difficult experiences in my encounters with some witches, but it had never occurred to me that the process would have any occult terrors. As I indicated at the end of one chapter of *Triumph*, I was surprised by the fact that by far the most common question asked of me about witchcraft by highly-educated non-witches was not of a sociological or theological nature, but whether its spells really worked.[16] More surprising and interesting was the revelation that the majority of those who posed that question were already predisposed to believe that they did. Many of them were quite prepared to make the progression from that belief to one that its practitioners should therefore be prevented from operating. None of them had actually met a Pagan witch – at least to their knowledge – but their view of the cosmos and its workings was sufficiently insecure for them both to credit the real efficacy of magic and to feel genuine fear and awe of those who might be able to operate it. It was entirely logical that most of the people who had this reaction shared many of the interests and instincts of witches themselves: a belief in alternative medicine, or earth energies, or divination, or extrasensory perception. The difference was that the witches whom I met, and whom I observed, had rationalised these beliefs into a framework which gave them a sense of situation and confidence within it. The others had not, and their degree of confusion, and anxiety, and incipient suspicion and hatred of humans who might understand and operate arcane phenomena more effectively, was proportionately increased.

My own segregation from those feelings was assisted by a personal trait: my lack of any vivid personal sense of a spirit-world. In this I was comfortably at home with most people in my society, but my research brought home to me the fact that there was a large minority of its members who regularly saw apparitions or heard voices not apparently attached to any physical forms. Some of them I met among witches, but the overwhelming majority were friends or acquaintances without any personal involvement in witchcraft or the occult, who now confided in me because my research seemed to indicate that I would treat them with an unusual insight and sympathy; in which they were correct. Some indication of the extent of the phenomenon is provided by a small number of statistical surveys. In 1894 the Society for Psychical Research distributed forms for a 'census of hallucinations' to over 17,000 individuals throughout Britain. Of the replies, about 10 per cent admitted to having seen or heard extraordinary phenomena while wide awake, 5 per cent had seen a realistic apparition, and 3 per cent had seen one of a recognised person. In 1948 a Cambridge University professor, Donald J. West, got 1519 responses to a similar questionnaire, of which 14 per cent were affirmative. In 1975 the parapsychologist Erlendur Haraldsson conducted a national survey of Iceland asking if anybody had seen or felt the presence of a deceased person, and 31 per cent of replies were affirmative; it is not clear whether cultural or geographical factors account for the higher proportion than in Britain.[17] I considered this pattern in a section of my book,[18] and one aspect of it which I found especially significant was that modern western society is apparently unique in the human record in its utter lack of provision of any generally or officially accepted frame of reference for such experiences and any system of explanation within which they may be rendered familiar and harmless, or else effectively countered.[19] Instead, the public response of our society is simply to pretend that they do not happen. To a relatively large number of people they certainly do, and the resulting sense of confusion and vulnerability among many of these is one aspect of a situation in which people retain the same sensations when considering witchcraft and magic. In this context, it was again striking that Pagan witches tended to find paranormal phenomena not only much less threatening but much less interesting than non-witches. Very few of them were much bothered about ghosts or poltergeists, or concerned with conversing with the dead, or drawn to forms of mediation with a spirit-world such as ouija boards. They possessed a cosmological framework, and set of practices, which made them at ease with spirits and divinities and neutralised the anxieties which seemed to beset others.

The phenomenon of ignorance was wholly compatible with that of fear, and often intrinsic to it, but it was also associated with a quite different reaction to the topic of Pagan witchcraft in non-Pagan society. This was embodied by people who, on learning of my research project, immediately blasted the whole concept of modern Paganism with mockery, the simplest and most effective discursive strategy for attempting both to damn something and to remove it from the sphere of rational debate. It was the most common reaction which I encountered among intellectuals, both within and outside the academy. It united both some people who still professed a Christian faith and many who were overtly irreligious; though both types articulated this reaction within the context of a post-Christian culture. Those who still actively adhered to Christianity now saw themselves as a minority within a mainly secular society. They were prepared on the whole to accept this position, and also to accord respect to religions or spiritualities of comparable historic importance and longevity associated with other cultures, such as Buddhism. What moved them to scathing ridicule was the notion that a newly-appeared or revived religion (even one drawing on ancient ideas) should bid for equal respect within the apparently shrinking compass of committed religious identity. The sceptics, agnostics and atheists who made up the majority of my accustomed social world were likewise ready to pay courtesy to members of familiar and established religions, though often with the presumption that they represented inhabitants of a disappearing world. What inspired them to often vehement scorn was the possibility that other forms of religious belief might be accepted as having similar rights.

After a few years of such experiences I began to avoid mentioning my study of Pagan witchcraft in the social occasions of non-witches. What I found most interesting about them was that they completely violated the norms of the liberal humanist discourse which prevailed in the social groups among which I generally moved. It was significant that newly-appeared British religions could be treated by those groups with the sort of dismissive facetiousness with which they no longer deemed it acceptable to turn upon people of a different race or gender, or indeed religious systems associated with other ethnicities. Within the academy I often found myself dealing with historians who (according to their subject) studied human beings in the past who married their siblings, or attempted to call up demons, or burnt people at the stake, disembowelled them for treason, fed them to sacred crocodiles, cut out their hearts on altars or shipped them across oceans into slavery. These colleagues insisted that we had no right to mock or dismiss such dead cultures out of hand but should attempt instead to explore and understand the internal logic of their thought-worlds. I wholly agreed, and yet observed that the same academics seemed instinctually to deny this treatment to the people whose history I was studying, and who were members of their own nation whose behaviour was a good deal less offensive in terms of prevailing social norms.

There were also some specific experiences which deepened my sense of unease. Most would fall into the category of the petty and personal which I defined earlier as unworthy of repetition, but three may illustrate the range of discomforts involved. In late 1994 I addressed a national Pagan conference upon a topic of ancient history, and was congratulated afterwards by a courteous and effusive stranger who asked me details about my professional position. I did not realise – and could not know – that he was actually a member of the evangelical wing of the Church of England, who was attending the event, without disclosing his identity, to gather information on modern Paganism in order to combat it. Two months later he denounced me to a convention of churchmen, using my presence at the Pagan conference as an example of the support which Paganism was gaining and of its growing menace to the Church and to society. His comments were reported in a national newspaper, causing the head of my university department (for once) to express concern to me about the direction in which my research was moving. The second incident came when a new junior colleague was recruited to the department in 1997, and admitted to me that, as the candidates for the post were gathered for interview, the main item of conversation among them was that a witch was reputed to be a member of the staff. This was one of a number of occurrences which made me wish that if fellow scholars would only show to my face a tithe of the excitement about my work which they manifested behind my back, then research would have been considerably less lonely. The third incident came in 1998, when the student newspaper of my university asked me for an interview, claiming that it wanted to publish a profile of my forthcoming book; instead it printed a spoof on me as a witch. Such experiences drove home the point that modern Pagan witchcraft was not just another topic, and that to study it entailed certain risks.

It is important not to overstate these; at no time of my engagement with the subject did I feel that I had suffered from what I would regard as actual persecution. In all essentials, the academy bore out my high opinion of it as a place of remarkable cultural tolerance, personal generosity and professional rigour. None the less, it did seem at times as if by undertaking this particular study I had entered a crazy, comic-grotesque, carnival world of role-reversal. It had been the Pagans who had turned out to play by the rules which I had been trained to respect as an academic. They had taken my work seriously, and while I had sometimes encountered hostility among them – amounting on rare occasions to outright abuse – it had never focused on my personal characteristics and never included ridicule or denigration. Rather, my Pagan critics had regarded the issues in contention as matters which rested on empirical evidence and could be resolved by discussion of it. They treated me in the same manner whether speaking to my face or behind my back, and none ever pretended to identities or motivations which they did not possess. All the experiences which I had encountered during my work that violated the traditional norms of professional scholarship – of gross superstitition, irresponsible anti-rationalism, intellectual discourtesy, duplicity, prejudice and sensationalist gossip – had occurred within the non-Pagan world. My research had revealed to me at least as much about the latter as it had about modern witches.

The book appeared in November 1999, and with it I was able at last to lay my whole programme of work before the public. Like the research on which it was based, the finished product very clearly mirrored certain of my own interests, characteristics and predispositions. One of the most important of these was that I am a British subject, based in England and concerned mainly with the history of England, Britain and the British Isles, in descending order of importance and expertise. This doubtless had much to do with my characterisation of Wicca, and the other forms of Pagan witchcraft inspired by or related to it, as a specially English form of religion; in many respects the only full-formed religion which England can be said to have given the world. This was not my own unique perspective – a common American term for the Wiccan family of practices is 'British Traditional' – but I gave it an increased emphasis. My stress upon England was largely a way of separating Wicca from other forms of Paganism, such as some kinds of Druidry, which were based much more firmly on cultural associations from other parts of Britain and drew on movements which had arisen in part as a counterweight to English hegemony. I recognised explicitly that in another perspective Pagan witchcraft drew on themes, practices and ideas which had been developing steadily in European culture since a genesis in the Hellenistic Near East, and that in another it represented a distillation of relatively cultural motifs with their roots outside Britain, above all in German Romanticism. My emphasis, however, was on the fact that the matrix which was required to produce it came together in England between 1800 and 1940.

This emphasis was linked to another, which has been discussed earlier: my insistence that rather than representing a bizarre, isolated and wholly counter-cultural phenomenon, Pagan witchcraft was just an unusually concentrated expression of various long-term developments within mainstream British (and, again, more particularly English) culture. This seemed to me simply to be one of the most obvious readings of the data, but it also fitted well with my own position as a mediator and interpreter between witches and mainstream society. The second half of the book was devoted mainly to the internal history of the movement, and here the chapters tended to be longer, more complex, and less conclusive as I struggled with the opacity of the documentary evidence, the contradictions of the memories provided by surviving witnesses, and the lack of any objective data to substantiate most retrospective claims made by members of the different traditions. There were essentially two different but interlinked issues: whether Wicca had existed, in anything like its later form, before Gerald Gardner encountered or developed it, and whether there were any forms of Pagan witchcraft which were older than Gardnerian Wicca and in some kind of parental or sibling relationship with it. To both of these, after much sifting of detailed source material, the book returned no definite answer. There was a complete lack of decisive evidence to substantiate the existence of Pagan witchcraft before Gardner and his companions began to work it in the North London area during the late 1940s, but neither could its origins be proved to lie with those people and at that place and time. The data could be plausibly interpreted to argue a range of different possibilities.

This meant, of course, that the book itself could be made to serve an equal number of different polemical purposes. Among Pagan witches, in the United Kingdom, North America and Australia, the public response was overwhelmingly favourable to the book. Several reviewers writing in Pagan magazines used it as a weapon with which to berate witches who still adhered to the origin myth of their religion as the ancient one of the British Isles and of western Europe, and represented it as essentially a work of iconoclasm and demolition, although in some cases they also praised it for providing a better-substantiated alternative account of its beginnings. Others preferred to emphasise the open-ended nature of its conclusions regarding the immediate origins of Wicca.[20] Some of these reviewers, and editors of the journals in which they appeared, assumed that I would cause considerable anger and hostility among witches with a devotion to traditional beliefs, and some of the editors encouraged readers to submit their responses to what was clearly expected to be a considerable controversy. At the time of writing, however, no such debate has ensued in any of these magazines, and if the hostile reaction among witches has been as widespread and vehement as was expected, then so far (to September 2002) it has been not been made public. Instead, those who preserve a traditional view of the origins of their religion have tended to ignore my work completely and to carry on writing as though it had never appeared, as successive articles in recent issues of magazines such as the *Cauldron* evince. I am personally entirely happy with this situation, as I had never regarded myself as taking the part of a historiographical evangelist to witches; my concerns had always been primarily with situating modern witchcraft within its parent society.

My greatest pleasure in observing the impact of my book on Pagans themselves was to perceive how it had served to foster and accelerate research into their history by scholars from within their own community. In this respect it has reinforced the work of Aidan Kelly, without so far having had its provocative and divisive quality. Some of these have already taken our knowledge of the context and personalities of the early story of Wicca beyond that which I have achieved: I think particularly of Philip Heselton, Gareth Medway and Roger Dearnaley.[21] How far any of them will succeed in solving the major puzzles of the subject, and how far they will respectively feel able to publish their research to audiences drawn from outside the compass of what is still, for many practitioners, the private world of a mystery religion, remains to be seen. Collectively, however, we have made a good beginning.

It is significant that at least two out of the three scholars named above have manifested a predisposition to disprove the hard-line Kelly version of Wiccan revisionism and show that the roots of the religion itself are longer and more complex than a simple composition by Gerald Gardner. All are individuals of such probity, as well as such talent in research, that this predisposition must be accepted as a healthy stimulant to their work rather than a danger to its quality. As my own reading of the problem in my book was so complex and so open-ended, it may be helpful to set down here, with the maximum concision, my opinion of what the possible solutions to it may be. In my formulation, five exist:

1. Gardner was initiated into a surviving coven of the Old Religion of western Europe, which had been driven underground under the name of witchcraft by the persecutions of the early modern period.

2. Gardner was initiated into a group practising another sort of pagan religion which had survived in secret since antiquity.

3. Gardner was initiated into a group practising a modern pagan religion which had been developed in the early twentieth century or, at furthest remove and with much less plausibility, in the nineteenth.

4. Wicca was created by a group of people in the 1940s, among whom Gardner was a key figure, perhaps the leading personality and certainly the only one who wanted to perpetuate the religion by revealing it to the public.

5. Gardner created Wicca himself, composing all its early rites.

Of the above, I currently find the first unbelievable, in the light of what we now know of medieval and early modern history, and the second and fifth both strain credulity almost to the same extent. The second encounters most of the problems of the first, while the fifth is at variance with the manner in which Gardner himself worked.[22] This was generally to produce texts in partnership with others, or to encourage those of his initiates with special creative talents to generate new rituals for particular occasions; indeed he placed high value on individual creativity in general. This makes it unlikely that he produced the central corpus of Wiccan material single-handed and without collaboration and negotiation. He certainly had such potential partners, assistants or amanuenses before Wicca emerged into firmly recorded history; the witch known as Dafo, who featured prominently in my own book, is one of them. I therefore tend to accept the third and fourth propositions as most likely, or perhaps a mixture of the two, with some present tendency towards the fourth which could easily be reversed in the face of better evidence. This is the balance of probability presented in my book.

If the reactions of Pagans to the book were on the same lines as those which they had displayed to my research for it, those of non-Pagans were also of a piece: mainly favourable and supportive, but also more complex and problematic. Not enough time has passed for its impact on the academy to become apparent, but it has clearly been read and regarded as significant by large numbers of people. A signal demonstration of the changes in attitude which it is producing was made a few months after its publication by the editors of the *New Dictionary of National Biography*, the nation's pantheon of individuals who are regarded as having made significant contributions to its history. Following the arguments made in *The Triumph of the Moon*, they decided to include in the dictionary for the first time three people whose claim to fame rests wholly upon their work in promoting Pagan witchcraft and on their identity as modern witches: Gerald Gardner, Alex Sanders and Doreen Valiente. I was invited to write their entries and did so with enormous pleasure. The book was also a critical success. Very few notices have as yet been published in academic journals, which are usually both the last to appear and the least generous, but the expected time-lag before they are due is not yet expired, and it may well be that I have missed some in periodicals associated with disciplines which are not my own. The book has, however, been very kindly treated in newspapers, from the *Shrewsbury Chronicle* to the main national dailies and their supplements, and in magazines, and most of the reviewers were distinguished authors, mainly academic.[23]

One in particular seemed highly significant to me, for reasons that must be obvious: Tanya Luhrmann. Her notice took up the whole back page of an issue of the *Times Literary Supplement*, a prime position for anybody who wanted work read and discussed by the maximum number of academics.[24] She praised the book itself almost as lavishly as it was possible to do, being especially generous in providing the sort of punch-line that makes authors glow and furnishes publishers with perfect blurb-bites for back covers of second editions. What was especially revealing, and startling, however, was her retrospective attitude to witchcraft and magic. It was made the more poignant by an apparent misprint, whereby she stated that her membership of a London coven had been during the early 1990s, making it appear more or less contemporary with my own research, instead of in the early 1980s as was actually the case. She summed up my work as 'a history of a small and in some ways irrelevant practice – that of perhaps 1000 or more English people'. Here again there seemed to be a curious typographical error, for my book had calculated the probable number of initiated pagan witches in the United Kingdom at 10,000, but I had also made clear that there were probably another 100,000 people in my nation who regarded themselves as Pagans in a form heavily influenced by Wicca, and that the number of pagan witches in the USA was much greater. Taken in the same sentence as her characterisation of their religion as 'small and in some ways irrelevant' (to what or whom?), this gave an overwhelming impression that she was literally belittling the people who had welcomed her in the 1980s and on whom, in large part, she had built her career. Furthermore, as the whole thrust of my book itself had been to show how their practices actually did relate to mainstream British society and culture, it represented an attempt to consign them to the margins and to mystification once more in the face of all my efforts to the contrary.

This impression was reinforced by further remarks. In the face of my careful and ambivalent consideration of the evidence, she summed up Gerald Gardner as 'the somewhat eccentric man who founded modern witchcraft'. She went on to comment upon my apparent failure to perceive both the 'edgy sexuality' which was in her opinion intrinsic to Wiccan sensibility, and the Wiccan emphasis upon the dark and destructive aspects of divinity. It may well be that the difference in our perceptions was a result of the different periods in which we conducted our research, or of the fact that as a woman certain things would have been apparent to her which were not to me. Having said that, it is striking that she emphasised neither point in the very substantial book in which she published her research back in 1989, and in which both would surely have had a place if they had seemed so important in the immediate aftermath of her actual fieldwork. A dozen years had passed since she achieved her tenured post, in which Pagan witchcraft had become much more prominent in the western consciousness and the academic prejudices to which she had (explicitly) bowed had become much weaker – as I am about to make clear. These changes might have allowed her to attempt a still more multivalent and sympathetic portrait of witchcraft and magic, but the reverse had occurred. Her inclination to distance herself from them had increased to the point at which it was tantamount virtually to dismissal, and the feelings of betrayal and exploitation articulated towards her by many British witches had obtained a further measure of justification. I was left both very grateful to her for her kindness to me and saddened that she seemed to have slighted the subject that might, at last, have brought the two of us together.

Her words prompted me to further thoughts about the different contexts and dilemmas of research that we had faced, and the means by which we had coped with them. Ironically, in my own discipline of history, as in theology, the question of a scholar's ideological position or personal relationship with the subject-matter has not seemed to be particularly problematic. In the recent historiography of the English Reformation, for example, the undoubted facts that Jack Scarisbrick and Eamon Duffy are devout Roman Catholics, that Geoffrey Dickens had as patent an Anglican

Protestant faith, and that Patrick Collinson came from a background in Protestant dissent and Diarmaid MacCulloch from one in Anglicanism, have never been regarded as a matter for concern. It is blatantly clear in every case that these personal beliefs or spiritual inheritances have conditioned the attitudes of the historian concerned to the data, but such differing perspectives are regarded as providing the most useful possible range of approaches and intepretations. The difference with Wicca, of course, is two-fold. It is virtually impossible to obtain contrasting perspectives upon the latter from informed observers, because only somebody who has got inside it can write about it with authority; and to many people it is not regarded as a 'legitimate' religion in the manner of denominations of Christianity.

The relationship of anthropology with the same issues has been much more complex. It would be completely false to suggest that its practitioners observe the activities of the people whom they study but do not participate in them. This has not been true since the 1930s at the latest, when a pioneer like Evans-Pritchard could, famously, settle down to study the cattle-rearing Nuer of the Sudan by getting himself a herd of cattle. The crucial distinction was that, although anthropologists could behave like natives, they were not supposed to think like them, but to interpret their thought and behaviour in terms of western knowledge and concepts, which were automatically supposed to be superior. As the colonial empires gave way to independent states, and as western societies themselves became more multiethnic and culturally diverse, so attitudes began to soften and blur. From the 1960s a new emphasis was placed upon the ability of the anthropologist to immerse herself or himself so completely in the culture or subculture under study that it became possible to understand its deepest instincts and reflexes. In 1967 George Devereux could already confront the professional demand for 'objectivity' with the assertion that 'informed subjectivity ... is the royal road to an authentic, rather than fictitious, objectivity'.[25] Eleven years later, Benetta Jules-Rosette spoke of social science as a 'journey towards becoming the phenomenon', in which the practitioner 'attempts to assume the competence of the subject studied.'[26]

By the early 1980s this approach was producing some notable successes. David Hayano, writing about poker players in American society, recorded that 'after several years I had virtually become one of the people I wanted to study'.[27] Liza Dalby, examining the culture of the geishas of Japan, worked as one herself until she learned how to behave and think automatically as they did.[28] The most relevant work of this sort for scholars of witchcraft was Jeanne Favret-Saada's account of traditional beliefs concerning bewitchment in the countryside around Mayenne in western France, published in

French in 1978 and translated into English in 1980. She stated roundly that in the nexus of witchcraft beliefs 'there is no room for uninvolved observers'. In order to understand them properly, she had to engage in them, by being taken for and behaving like a bewitched person herself, befriending those who thought themselves similarly afflicted and seeking relief from local 'unwitchers'. In 1990 Favret-Saada reconsidered the implications of her research and reinforced them, with the declaration that ' "participant observation" is an oxymoron'. 'If I tried to "observe", that is is to keep my distance, there would be nothing left for me to observe.'[29] The new orthodoxy declared in all this work was that the anthropologist had to 'go native', in action and thought; but not to *stay* native. Dalby did not remain a geisha, while Favret-Saada never took up the work of an unwitcher herself and never adopted a literal and personal belief in witchcraft. The ideal was now that the anthropologist should assume a cultural role like an actor taking on a part, and then shed it when the work was done and the time came to write up the study. It was this ideal to which Tanya Luhrmann felt obliged to adhere; her study was in that sense a classic product of 1980s anthropology.

Even during that decade, however, it was already obvious that this template of behaviour had serious drawbacks. It was designed, like its more overtly imperialist and conformist predecessor, for scholars from 'developed' societies studying more traditional peoples. It was not easily applied by academically trained writers from non-western societies who were studying their own people, and these were starting to appear in significant numbers during the 1980s. It was particularly ill-suited to female, and even less so to feminist, anthropologists who were seeking to express the experiences of women in such cultures.[30] By the end of the decade some practitioners were starting to realise that it had weaknesses which made it questionable in virtually any conditions. One was that it retained the assumption that the beliefs and attitudes of the people studied were valueless in themselves, and that the anthropologist would accordingly suffer no loss in shaking them off at the end of the project. The second was that it turned the researcher into a form of impostor, an undercover agent for a different culture who acted out membership of a group before leaving it and throwing off the disguise. This aspect of Luhrmann's own work was, it may be remembered, criticised explicitly by a professional colleague, Katherine Ewing, in 1994. Ewing included this specific expression of doubt in a general attack on the philosophy of research which underpinned Luhrmann's approach: 'By creating a blind spot, by placing a taboo around the possibility of belief, anthropologists have prevented themselves from transcending the contradictions embedded in a situation in which the imposition of one's own mode of discourse interferes with the project of representation.' More bluntly, she declared that 'the taboo against "going native" results from a refusal to acknowledge that the subjects of one's research might actually know something about the human condition that is personally valid for the anthropologist: it is a refusal to believe'. She was able to cite by that date four colleagues who had already published their acceptance that they had learned something valuable from the peoples whom they had studied.[31] Three years beforehand, another American, Philip Peek, had edited a collection of essays on native African divination systems by a dozen contributors, presented as a concerted attempt 'to understand their sources of knowledge'. This was, significantly, offered as an explicit breach with British anthropologists, 'who treated divination with great derision'.[32]

The key text in this movement was probably another American collection which appeared in 1994, and represented ten anthropologists who all believed that westerners needed to give serious attention to non-western beliefs concerning the spirit-world. All, to some extent, had been altered in their own attitudes by studying those of other cultures with regard to meaningful dreams, visions and other 'extraordinary experiences' for which their own society had no explanation and which indeed it refused to recognise: a problem to which I referred earlier. The editors began with the declaration that 'because of the fear of ostracism, an entire segment of cross-cultural experience common to many investigators, is not available for discussion and scientific investigation'. They went on 'to entertain the notion that what is at first seen as an "extraordinary experience" is in fact the normal outcome of genuine participation in social and ritual performances through which social realities are generated and constituted'.[33] This was Tanya Luhrmann's 'interpretive drift', but reformulated in such a way as to suggest that by drifting away from the interpretations made by mainstream rationalist western culture, scholars could learn something genuinely valid and useful about the nature of the world. In practice, the contributors to the volume differed widely as to the meaning of the phenomena concerned, on a spectrum ranging from Charles Laughlin, who thought that they could be satisfactorily explained by neurology, to Edith Turner, who accepted the literal existence of spirits. In fact, being convinced that she herself had seen a spirit-form emerge from the back of a patient during a healing rite in Zambia in 1985, she had gone on to make a literal acceptance of what westerners commonly call magic. In a separate publication, she declared her certainty that trance-states could give humans access to 'non-empirical healing, clairvoyance and accurate divination'. She went on to call for a new anthropological methodology of 'radical participation'.[34] Such a methodology had already been developed by feminist anthropologists and those native to the cultures under study, who could hardly avoid applying it and who produced a notable body of important work in the course of the 1990s [35]

Over the same period parallel developments were occurring in a different discipline, of religious studies. This discipline consists, essentially, of the application of techniques drawn from the social sciences to the study of religions, involving participation by the scholar in groups practising the beliefs concerned, 'without prejudice and with sympathetic understanding'. It was not considered necessary, or even desirable, for the scholar actually to embrace the religion under study with full personal commitment: instead the duty of the researcher was to seek to suspend personal judgements, and to represent as faithfully as possible what the members of the religion believed, how they expressed these beliefs and (as far as possible) why they held them. [36] By the 1990s this model was running into trouble, for much the same reasons that it was being questioned in anthropology. David Hufford could complain that 'disinterest is urged on scholars of religion, but disinterest is impossible in religious issues'. [37] Two different initiatives developed in response to this dilemma. The first was an increasing tendency to credit members of a religion who happened to have academic training and affiliations with at least as much ability to speak of it in scholarly terms as non-believers: a privilege, of course, which had always been extended to practitioners of faiths which western intellectuals regarded with respect, such as established Christianities, Judaism, Islam and Buddhism. By 1997 Elizabeth Puttick, considering new religious movements in the west, could observe that the 'insider as researcher' position was becoming increasingly common in the discipline. [38] The other initiative was to urge non-believers who chose to carry out participant observation within religious groups to do so with still greater tact and willingness to suspend personal opinion. Jone Salomonsen, a Norwegian studying pagan witches in California, coined the expression 'compassionate anthropology' to describe the study of such groups 'from the inside of lived reality'. She expected anthropologists henceforth to share in their religious life not simply behaviourally, or even emotionally, but cognitively; to seek to share what the other members of the group were experiencing, as far as it was personally possible to do so. [39]

My own investigation of the history of Pagan witchcraft was undertaken alongside the work of no less than five scholars based in university departments of anthropology, archaeology or religious studies, who were working in the same or related fields according to these two new models for research. All took their projects to successful conclusion. One was Amy Simes, who produced a doctoral thesis on Paganism in the north-east midlands in a fashion which was a direct practical anticipation of Salomonsen's 'compassionate anthropology'. [40] Another was Joanne Pearson, who has already been mentioned as studying Wicca itself and running up against just that legacy of distrust and suspicion left by Tanya Luhrmann which I noted myself. Her position was explicitly that of an 'insider' to the religion and challenged the whole prejudice against 'going native' by suggesting that a privileged position for research was available to one who was a 'native' already.[41] The third was Susan Greenwood, whose subject consisted of pagan witchcraft and ritual magic in the London area, ten years after Luhrmann's work there. She was also, inevitably, obliged to contend with the results of that work, and did so by establishing the theoretical position that concepts of scientific truth and academic objectivity should no longer be set up in opposition to the insights gained by full participant observation: rather, that spiritual experience should be accepted as a source of knowledge in its own right.[42] The fourth was Robert Wallis, who looked at shamanism among modern western pagans, and its relationship with archaeology. He endorsed the concept that beliefs are best studied by holding them sincerely, and condemned the traditional concept of scholarly objectivity as itself a dogmatic intellectual position based on outmoded colonialist and monocultural attitudes.[43] The fifth scholar was Graham Harvey, who published a general survey of paganisms in contemporary Britain, mentioned in the previous chapter in this book. It was characterised by a constant sympathetic representation, which amounted at moments to a warm endorsement of the ideals of the people under study.[44]

The only professional historian in Britain who worked on anything like a related field during the time of my own research was one who only intermittently operated within the academy. This was the expert on early modern and modern astrology, Patrick Curry, who wrote that it was impossible to produce an 'impartial' history of the subject. Ever since the eighteenth century, its practitioners had been undermined, marginalised and silenced by mainstream scholarship, and so to seek to understand them – to show the consistency and integrity of their beliefs as well as those of their critics – was to affirm the legitimate consideration of more than one version of the truth. This automatically conflicted with the hitherto dominant mixture of Christian monotheism and universalist secular humanism which had characterised western intellectuals and so represented an engagement in a debate between two opposed views of reality which was still under way.[45]

It must be obvious from the above that my own research had been undertaken within a context of rapidly developing theory and practice in all the disciplines related to it: history, anthropology and religious studies. In producing it I did not depart as far from traditional scholarly constraints as many of the anthropologists cited above. I did not affirm the reality of spirits, or even insist that the 'extraordinary experiences' associated with ritual magic, divinatory systems or the reception of visions might tell us something valuable about the cosmos. This was not just because the 'reality' of witchcraft was not part of my concern, but because I simply did not have extraordinary experiences of that kind. My interpretation of the history of Pagan witchcraft was wholly compatible with a rationalist and humanist view of the world, although it did not depend on such a view and left open the possibility of others. I did not recommend Pagan witchcraft as a system of practice and belief, being content to explain and explode traditional misrepresentations of it which have circulated in society at large and to explain why its practitioners found it attractive and (to some extent) what they were like. These targets released me from the need to describe and analyse its actual rites in detail, and that release enabled me to keep faith with members of what is, after all, a mystery religion, by leaving them some privacy after writing so much about them in other respects.

Things were, however, not that simple. My work was not equivalent to that of the anthropologists, sociologists and specialists in religious studies who had considered forms of Paganism; I was leaning in the opposite direction to them. As their starting-point was to portray the nature of the religions considered, from what was at least some form of participant observation, they had to signal very firmly what it was that gave their work some academic quality; in other words, what distinguished it from that of the 'natives' in general. Each did so by using a framework of analysis and a set of methods which were intelligible to fellow scholars and provided insights into the religions concerned which neither outsiders nor most or all of the practitioners would have spotted, left to themselves. My starting-point needed no such distinction. I was already well known for having rejected the traditional historiography of Pagan witchcraft, and I was at best enlisted as an ally in a division of opinion which had already taken place within it. My task, as said, was to write a history of that witchcraft which was as accurate as possible while still leaving it dignity as a religion, and which could not be used as a weapon by those determined to deny it any such status. Whereas other scholars needed to distinguish themselves in some fashion from other members of the groups and traditions under study, I was striving to ensure that my work had any value for the latter.

Furthermore, Patrick Curry was right; it is impossible to write sympathetically about subjects such as divination, magic and witchcraft in modern history without automatically taking sides in at least one major, and often bitter, cultural debate. When I characterised the recent models of 'radical participation' and 'insider position' as the cutting-edge methods of anthropology and religious studies, I neglected to make clear how much their proponents have felt themselves to be opposed to ingrained prejudice and hostility within their own disciplines. It must be admitted that no body of literature has yet appeared to articulate that opposition, in sharp contrast to the outpouring of works which propound the new approaches, but the assumption of controversy and hostility is still significant. When Jone Salomonsen defined 'compassionate anthropology', she insisted that its practitioners, however seriously they took the beliefs of the people under their study, should never become 'scholarly converts and proselytisers'.[46] The trouble with this superficially impeccable distinction is that, in the eyes of a hostile critic any sympathy and compassion may be be condemned as conversion and proselytisation. There *was* an evangelical ideology embedded in my book, which extended, by implication, to proselytisation. It was an assumption that the best condition for a future Britain would be as a formally secular state in which its members are free to follow an effectively infinite range of religious traditions, or none, according to their own spiritual inclinations and needs. Each of these religions, old or new, should be regarded with equal respect and tolerance by those who do not belong to it, only providing that it does no clear and obvious harm to its own members and to others. The last clause, of course, leaves room for plenty of accusation and disputation in itself; but even to articulate that basic liberal and humanist position is to pit oneself against the beliefs of a great many people in contemporary British society. My book was not intended to be a propaganda piece for witchcraft, but it embodied a sociopolitical ideal of religious tolerance and equality which itself could be regarded as polemic.

On some issues, moreover, the book remained reticent, as has this essay. The latter commenced by speaking of reflexivity, and yet has failed to respond to the challenge of the latter concept in a major way: at no point have I ever discussed in print my own attitudes to Wicca and its sister traditions, or my personal experiences of them and reactions to them as religions and how (if at all) these may have changed over time. The true reason for that is simple: that at no point have I been given any practical incentive to do so, while on the contrary I have been provided with a number of disincentives. My own lack of any impulse to characterise my life in terms of religion, the absence of any generally recognised need for a historian to discuss personal belief, and the unpleasantness with which my research was sometimes treated, represented three of the less important of these. The most important, however, was that virtually everybody who was seriously interested in my work in the field had important reasons for wanting me to erase the autobiographical aspects of it. These were apparent from the beginning, but intensified once the appearance of the book established me as (literally) an academic authority in the field. Many Pagans, and especially witches, faced with a potential loss of homes, jobs or custody of children because of prejudices against their religion, called on me as somebody holding a respected public position who seemed apparently well qualified to speak on the matter. More often, however, the call came from the other side, from members of the police forces, the caring services, the prison service, the hospital service, local government bodies, head teachers, school governors or the legal profession, and employers and landlords or landladies. These people had Pagan witches either in their care or employment or otherwise vulnerable to them, and likewise wanted some well-supported information on their beliefs and practices that would determine how they should be treated. In most of these cases I was the only academic specialist – indeed the only expert witness of any sort – to whom they could turn in a hurry.

I always responded to these approaches, by providing the necessary data as fully as I could, supporting it with specific evidence, pointing out areas in which I was better informed than others and emphasising the need for further research independent of my own. In general terms, I could be perfectly confident that what I was saying was correct, and in many cases the prejudices that I was being invited to dispel, and the anxieties that I was asked to allay, were so ill-founded and so dangerous that the value of the exercise seemed beyond doubt. Throughout, the role defined for me was that of a person defined by a specialist training in techniques of investigation and analysis that could now be placed at the service of the public. The fact that my professional observations had to be conditioned by my own experiences, personality, instincts and conceptual assumptions – as obvious to any thinking person as to an academic sensitised to the issue by the recent concentration on it – was disregarded as an inconvenience. I was viewed as somebody with professional qualifications who had succeeded in making available data for anybody who sought it in an area where little or none had seemed to exist before, and which could immediately be put to use. In an academic system that depended largely on public funding, this looked like value for money. Given this context, for me to concentrate on my own subjective attitudes and experiences could indeed be made to look self-indulgent. I was never asked for them, and on many occasions hints were dropped – and in some direct injunctions issued – that they would be unwelcome. In this respect, reflexivity looks like a luxury that my society cannot yet afford.

In the process of such a work of mediation, two aspects of the process became very obvious to me. One was that makers of television and radio documentaries are a different sort of person from investigative journalists and feature-writers. Whatever the theory of the matter, in practice it is very clear that the former are mostly concerned with educating as well as entertaining the public, while the latter are primarily interested only in selling stories. Two examples may serve to exemplify my experiences, the first being propelled by a man who telephoned me in early 2000 claiming to work for one of Scotland's most reputable newspapers, the *Scotsman*. He had become interested in witchcraft because of a conference on the early modern trials due to be held at Edinburgh, at which I was a speaker. When he contacted the organisers and expressed an interest in modern witches, they referred him to me and I summarised some of the data in my book. The result was that a set of different local Scottish newspapers published a story sold on to them by him, in which he attributed to me either a misheard or an invented statement condemning the Church of Scotland. This ran exactly counter to my own views, and earned me a string of angry and distressed responses from pious Scots, to whom I had to explain that we had both been gulled.

Much worse was the result of the genuine approach which I received from an equally respected English national Sunday newspaper, hitherto generally admired by liberals, to give an interview to a feature-writer who wanted to produce a piece based on my book. I agreed, and during the conversation I was asked how the paper might meet any witches. I recommended that it contact the main national body which represents Britain's Pagans, the Pagan Federation. It did, and duly interviewed, among others, its youth officer, the person responsible for formulating policy towards approaches from young people and monitoring the place of Paganism in school courses on religious studies. He happened to be a schoolteacher himself, and here the paper spotted an angle for a eye-catching story. Contrary to the promises made by its journalist, it published a piece which named him and included a photograph of him, to 'alert' the nation to the plans of witches to put their message across to young people. It was careful to contact two hostile clergyman and the local Conservative MP, and to enter their warnings and expressions of outrage beneath the report; and the teacher was suspended pending a disciplinary hearing. I am pleased to say that I was subsequently able to play some part in providing the evidence which got him reinstated.

The other factor that my mediating role brought home to me more vividly than before is the emotive power of language, and in particular of the process of labelling. In this case the significant words were 'Pagan' and, above all, 'witch'. In the period since completing the book, I have worked (among other projects) on the historical associations of two other traditions within the constellation which make up Paganism: shamanism and Druidry. Both have beliefs and practices which overlap with those of Pagan witchcraft, while modern Druidry in particular has absorbed a number from it. Both can likewise be characterised as counter-cultural forms of religious or spiritual behaviour. I have found, however, that neither word triggers reactions of alarm, hostility, prurient curiosity or savage derision among people who do not belong to the traditions concerned. On the whole, 'shaman' has connotations of tribal spirituality (generally neutral, and often positive), while 'Druid' now has associations of homegrown amiable eccentricity, at least when it is made clear that the modern manifestations of the image are under discussion. There seems to be little doubt that a researcher working on either has a much easier time than one concerned with Pagan witchcraft. Since I moved out of the latter field, my professional life has undoubtedly become a more pleasant one.

In writing *The Triumph of the Moon*, I found myself attempting to fulfil responsibilities to three different groups and constituencies. One consisted of the academy and my colleagues in it, for whom I was trying to produce work that seemed to represent original research making significant points about the nature of the past and present. Another comprised Pagans, and Pagan witches in particular, whose history I was hoping to write without doing anything that might provide ammunition to those prejudiced against them, and without gratuitously undermining their claims to represent a valid religion. A third consisted of the non-Pagan public, and in particular those parts of it concerned with witches in a capacity that gave them some inherent power over the latter, and who needed more substantial information to condition the way in which Pagan witches ought to be treated. All the signs to date have been that my book has, to a very great extent, managed to satisfy all the three groups; but somehow, in the process, reflexivity got lost. It seems to have done so because nobody really wanted it to be there in the first place. With that uneasy observation, I am content now to let my own work in the field itself dissolve into history.

Notes

Notes to Chapter 1: How Myths Are Made

1. Nigel Barley, *The Innocent Anthropologist* (London: British Museum Publications, 1983), p. 83.
2. Alan Houghton Brodrick, *The Abbé Breuil: Prehistorian* (London: Hutchinson, 1963).
3. Pre-eminent is probably Benedict Anderson, *Imagined Communities: Reflections on the Origin and Spread of Nationalism* (London: Verso, 1983). For another famed example, see Peter Sahlins, *Boundaries: The Making of France and Spain in the Pyrenees* (Berkeley: University of California Press, 1989).
4. Hugh Trevor-Roper, 'The Invention of Tradition: The Highland Tradition of Scotland', in Eric Hobsbawm and Terence Ranger (ed.), *The Invention of Tradition* (Cambridge: Cambridge University Press, 1983), pp. 21–40.
5. Alfred Fell, *The Early Iron Industry of Furness and District* (Ulverston, 1908), pp. 346–89: Arthur Raistrick, *Quakers in Science and Industry* (London: Bannisdale, 1950), pp. 95–107; *The Edinburgh Magazine*, 1 (22 March 1786), p. 235.
6. *Dictionary of National Biography*, s.n. Stewart, David (1772–1829); David Stewart, *Sketches of the Character, Manners and Present State of the Highlands of Scotland* (Edinburgh, 1822), 2 vols; John Telfar Dunbar, *History of the Highland Dress* (Edinburgh: Oliver and Boyd, 1962), p. 11; quotation taken from this.
7. Stewart, *Sketches*, i, p. 76; Dunbar, *History of the Highland Dress*, pp. 70–147; Trevor-Roper, 'Invention', pp. 31–40.
8. P. Berresford Ellis, *The Cornish Language and its Literature* (London: Routledge, 1974), p. 151.
9. Prys Morgan, 'From a Death to a View: The Hunt for the Welsh Past in the Romantic Period', in Hobsbawm and Ranger (ed.), *The Invention of Tradition*, pp. 48–60.
10. Ibid., pp. 77–81; twelve articles on Benjamin and Augusta Hall by Maxwell Fraser in *the National Library of Wales Journal*, 11 (1959–60), 12 (1961–62), 13 (1963–64), 14 (1965–66), and 16 (1969–70); F. G. Payne, 'Welsh Peasant Costume', *Folk Life*, 2 (1964), pp. 42–57; *Dictionary of Welsh Biography*, s.n. Hall, Benjamin; Marion Wynne-Davies, *Women and Arthurian Literature* (London: Macmillian, 1996), pp. 107–26.
11. D. George Boyce, *Nationalism in Ireland* (London: Routledge, 3rd edn, 1995), pp. 384–85.

12. Hiram Morgan, *Tyrone's Rebellion* (Woodbridge: Doydell, 1993), passim.

13. Ronald Hutton, *The British Republic, 1649–1660* (London: Macmillan, 1990), pp. 44–49; Toby Barnard, 'Irish Images of Cromwell', in R. C. Richardson (ed.) *Images of Oliver Cromwell* (Manchester University Press, 1993), ch. 11; Tom Reilly, Cromwell: *An Honourable Enemy* (Dingle: Brandon, 1999).

14. Sean O'Faolain, *The Irish* (London: Pelican, 1947), pp. 9, 91–93; Marianne Elliott, *Wolfe Tone* (New Haven: Yale University Press, 1989), passim; Boyce, *Nationalism in Ireland*, pp. 162–208.

15. F. S. Lyons, *Culture and Anarchy in Ireland, 1890–1939* (Oxford: Oxford University Press, 1979), pp. 32–82; Boyce, *Nationalism in Ireland*, pp. 154–58; O'Faolain, *The Irish*, pp. 127–46.

16. Biographies in the Irish Lives series published by Gill in Dublin include Leon O Broin's *Michael Collins* (1980), T. Ryle Dwyer's *Eamon De Valera* (1980), and Ruth Dudley-Edwards's *James Connolly* (1981). For other material, see Declan Kiberd, 'Romantic Ireland', *Times Literary Suplement*, 31 July 1998, p. 26; Richard English, *Ernie O'Malley* (Oxford: Clarendon Press, 1998); Ruth Dudley-Edwards, *Patrick Pearse* (London: Gollancz, 1977).

17. Berresford Ellis, *Cornish Language*, pp. 147–62; Brian Murdoch, *Cornish Literature* (Woodbridge: Brewer, 1993), p. 144.

18. Lewis Mumford, *Herman Melville* (London: Secker and Warburg, 1929), pp. 24–46; Newton Arvin, *Herman Melville* (New York: Viking, 1950), pp. 50–61; T. Walter Herbert, *Marquesan Encounters* (Cambridge, Massachusetts: Harvard University Press, 1980), pp. 149–91; Jan Leyda, The *Melville Log* (New York: Harcourt, 1951), pp. 129–39; see p. 129 for the entry to the bay; Charles Stewart, *A Voyage to the South Seas* (New York, 1831), i, pp. 226–31.

19. Mumford, *Melville*, p. 43; Jack London, *The Cruise of the Snark* (London: Merlin edition, 1971), pp. 154–77; Gavin Young, *Slow Boats Home* (London: Penguin, 1986), pp. 273–96; Paul Theroux, *The Happy Isles of Oceania* (London: Hamilton, 1992), pp. 398–400; Greg Dening, *Islands and Beaches: Discourse on a Silent Land* (Honolulu: University of Hawaii Press, 1980), passim.

20. *Dictionary of National Biography*, s.n. Jones alias Moetheu, Thomas; Samuel Rush Meyrick, *The History and Antiquites of the County of Cardigan* (1810): repr. Brecon, 1907), pp. 240–41; Patricia Shore Turner, 'Thomas Jones of Tregaron', in Robert Turner (ed.), *Elizabethan Magic* (Shaftesbury: Element, 1989), pp. 111–28.

21. *Dictionary of Welsh Biography*, s.n. Prichard, Thomas Jeffrey Llewelyn: *Dictionary of National Biograph*, s.n. Deacon, William Frederick; W. F. Deacon, *The Inn-Keeper's Album* (London, 1823), pp. 258–320; T. J. Llewelyn Prichard, *The Adventures and Vagaries of Twm Sion Catti* (Aberystwyth, 1828); Morgan, 'From a Death to a View', pp. 85–86.

22. Clare A. Simmons, *Reversing the Conquest: History and Myth in Nineteenth-Century British Literature* (New Brunswick: Rutgers University Press, 1990), chs 3–4.

23. The story of Alfred and the cakes is one of a set of legends about the king's stay at Athelney, found in sources from the twelfth century onward: William

of Malmesbury and the *Lives* of St Neot and St Cuthbert. In his actual stay at Athelney Alfred was never a solitary refugee but accompanied by a retinue and war-band. The remark attributed to Marie-Antoinette was actually given to a princess in Rousseau's *Confessions*, published before Marie-Antoinette's own reign: only writers in English seem to have taken it seriously. The words credited to Chief Seattle were invented by a scriptwriter called Ted Perry in the early 1970s: Peter Coates, *Nature: Western Attitudes since Ancient Times* (Cambridge: Polity Press, 1998), p. 92. The story about Raleigh is first found in a mid seventeenth-century text, Thomas Fuller's *The Worthies of England*. For the developing story of Drake and the bowls, see James A. Williamson, *Sir Francis Drake* (London: Collins, 1951), 114.

24. William Alexander Clouston, *Popular Tales and Fictions* (Edinburgh, 1887); D. E. Jenkins, *Bedd Gelert: Its Facts, Fairies and Folklore* (Portmadoc, 1899), pp. 56–73; Morgan, 'From a Death to a View', p. 87; Lord Raglan, *The Hero: A Study in Tradition, Myth and Drama* (New York: Vintage, 1956), p. 39.

25. Kenneth Hurlstone Jackson, *The International Popular Tale and Early Welsh Tradition* (Cardiff: Cardiff University Press, 1961).

26. Kenneth Hurlstone Jackson, *The Oldest Irish Tradition* (Cambridge: Cambridge University Press, 1964), pp. 37–38; Nicholas B. Aitchison, 'The Ulster Cycle', *Journal of Medieval History*, 13 (1987), pp. 87–116.

27. Michael J. O. Kelly, *Early Ireland* (Cambridge: Cambridge University Press, 1989), pp. 254–55; David Greene, 'The Chariot as Described in Irish Literature', in Charles Thomas (ed.), *The Iron Age in the Irish Sea Province* (London: Council for British Archaeology Reports 9, 1972), pp. 59–73; Stuart Piggott, *The Earliest Wheeled Transport* (London: Thames and Hudson, 1983), pp. 235–38.

28. E. G. Stanley, *The Search for Anglo-Saxon Paganism* (Cambridge: Brewer, 1975), pp. 83–96, 122; William A. Chaney, 'Paganism to Christianity in Anglo-Saxon England', *Harvard Theological Review*, 53 (1960), p. 203.

29. Glynn Custred, 'Magic, Sorcery and Witchcraft: An Anthropological Perspective' (lecture given at the University of California, Berkeley, 23 June 1983).

30. Aubrey Burl, *Rites of the Gods* (London: Batsford, 1981), pp. 13–14.

31. Leslie Grinsell, 'Barrow Treasure in Fact, Tradition, and Legislation', *Folklore*, 78 (1967), pp. 1–38.

32. Raglan, *The Hero*, p. 28; Jack Goody and Ian Watt, 'The Consequences of Literacy', in Jack Goody (ed.), *Literacy in Traditional Societies* (Cambridge: Cambridge University Press, 1968), pp. 32–33.

33. Goody and Watts, 'The Consequences of Literacy', pp. 32–34; Jan Vansina, *Oral Tradition as History* (London: 2nd edn, Routledge, 1985), esp. pp. 184–200; Joseph C. Miller (ed.), *The African Past Speaks* (Folkestone: Dawson, 1980); David P. Henige, *The Chronology of Oral Tradition* (Oxford: Oxford University Press, 1974).

34. Rosalind Thomas, *Oral Tradition and Written Record in Classical Athens* (Cambridge: Cambridge University Press, 1989).

35. Raglan, *The Hero*, p. 36.

36. Mark Whittow, *The Making of Orthodox Byzantium, 600–1025* (London: Macmillan, 1996), pp. 83–84.

37. L. R. Sullivan, *Marquesan Somatology* (Honololu: Bishop Museum Memoirs, 9.2, 1923); E. S. C. Handy, *The Native Culture in the Marquesas* (Honolulu: Bishop Museum Bulletin, 9, 1923); *Polynesian Religion* (Honolulu: Bishop Museum Bulletin, 34, 1927), and *Marquesan Legends* (Honolulu: Bishop Museum Bulletin, 69, 1930); Thor Heyerdahl, *The Kon-Tiki Expedition* (London: Allen and Unwin, 1950), *American Indians in the Pacific* (London: Allen and Unwin, 1952), and *Fatu-Hiva: Back to Nature* (London: Allen and Unwin, 1974); Robert Carl Suggs, *The Archaeology of Nuku Hiva* (New York: Anthropological Papers of the American Museum of Natural History, 49.1, 1961); *The Prehistory of Polynesia*, ed. J. D. Jennings (Canberra: University of Australia Press, 1979); Dening, *Islands and Beaches*, passim; Nicholas Thomas, *Marquesan Societies* (Oxford: Oxford University Press, 1990).

38. W. S. Lack-Szyrma, 'Folklore Traditions of Historical Events', *Folklore Record*, 3 (1881), pp. 157–68. My knowledge of modern Cornish nationalist lore is based on my experience as the honorary Reader in History at Cornwall College between 1985 and 1994.

39. L. V. Grinsell, 'A Century of the Study of Folklore of Archaeological Sites, and Prospects for the Future', in Venetia Newall (ed.), *Folklore Studies in the Twentieth Century* (Woodbridge: Brewer, 1980), pp. 213–17.

40. Leslie V. Grinsell, *Folklore of Prehistoric Sites in Britain* (Newton Abbot: David and Charles, 1976), p. 245.

41. Jeremy Harte, 'Folk Memory', *3rd Stone*, 31 (1998), p. 5.

42. Ellis Davies, *The Prehistoric and Roman Remains of Flintshire* (Cardiff: Lewis, 1949), pp. 256–63.

43. John and T. W. Webb, *Memorials of the Civil War ... As It Affected Herefordshire* (London, 1879), ii, p. 37; C. A. H. Burne, 'Examples of Folk Memory from Staffordshire', *Folk-Lore*, 27 (1914), pp. 247–48.

44. A. L. Le Quesne, *After Kilvert* (Oxford: Clarendon Press, 1978), p. 69.

45. Ronald Hutton, *The Royalist War Effort, 1642–1646* (London: Longman, 1981), p. 199.

46. Alan Smith, 'The Image of Cromwell in Folklore and Tradition', *Folklore*, 79 (1968), pp. 23–31; H. R. Ellis Davidson, 'Folklore and History', *Folklore*, 85 (1974), p. 81; Wendy Boase, *The Folklore of Hampshire and the Isle of Wight* (London: Batsford, 1976), pp. 53, 98.

47. Davidson, 'Folklore and History', p. 81.

48. Burne, 'Examples of Folk Memory', pp. 240–41.

49. Kate Lee, 'History and Tradition', *Folklore*, 14 (1903), pp. 178–79.

50. Boase, *Folklore of Hampshire*, p. 54; Roy Palmer, *The Folklore of Warwickshire* (London: Batsford, 1976), p. 20; Jacqueline Simpson, *The Folklore of the Welsh Border* (London: Batsford, 1976), pp. 37–38.

51. Palmer, *Folklore of Warwickshire*, p. 23; *A True Relation of the Inhuman Cruelties Exercised by the Cavaliers at Birmingham* (London, 1643); *Prince Rupert's Burning Love for England* (London, 1643).

52. *A Military Memoir of Colonel John Birch*, ed. by T. W. Webb (Camden Society, 1873); Webb and Webb, *Memorials of the Civil War*, passim; Ella Mary Leather, *The Folk-Lore of Herefordshire* (Hereford, 1912), p. 36.

53. Raglan, *The Hero*, pp. 31–32.

54. *The Journal of William Schellinks' Travels in England*, ed. by Maurice Exwood and H. L. Lehmann (Camden Society, 1993), pp. 43, 95.

55. Barley, *The Innocent Anthropologist*, p. 95; E. H. Stenning, *Portrait of the Isle of Man* (London: Hale, 1958), pp. 111, 123.

56. Simpson, *Folklore of the Welsh Border*, pp. 109.

57. John Kenyon, *The Popish Plot* (London: Heinemann, 1972), pp. 100–2, and sources listed at nn. 48–49.

58. Bernard Newman and I. O. Evans (ed.), *Anthology of Armageddon* (London: Greenhill, 1989), pp. 39–40.

59. It was Wolfgang Behringer who teased out the story of the origin and development of the figure, in 'Neun Millionen Hexen', *Geschichte in Wissenschaft und Unterricht*, November 1998, pp. 664–85. I am grateful to James Sharpe for this reference. The story of its later use is told in chapters 8 and 18 of Ronald Hutton, *The Triumph of the Moon: A History of Modern Pagan Witchcraft* (Oxford: Oxford University Press, 1999). In 1991 I proposed an overall estimate of about 40,000 executions in Europe between 1400 and 1800: Ronald Hutton, *The Pagan Religions of the Ancient British Isles* (Oxford: Blackwell, 1991), pp. 306, 370. Five years later Robin Briggs proposed 'something between 40,000 and 50,000': *Witches and Neighbours* (London: HarperCollins, 1996), p. 8. In 2001 Geoffrey Scarre and John Callow declared that experts considered a 'maximum figure of 40,000' to be reasonable: *Witchcraft and Magic in Sixteenth- and Seventeenth-Century Europe* (2nd edn, Basingstoke: Palgrave, 2001), p. 21. In the same year one of those experts, James Sharpe, pronounced that a consensus now existed on the figure of 40,000: *Witchcraft in Early Modern England* (Harlow: Pearson, 2001), p. 6. A rival estimate of 100,000 was produced in Anne Llewellyn Barstow, *Witchcraze* (San Francisco: Pandora, 1994), pp. 179–81. I formerly intended to publish a criticism of her methodology in reaching this total, but the work has now been done by Jenny Gibbons: a summary of it is found in her article, 'Recent Developments in the Study of the Great European Witch Hunt', *The Pomegranate*, 5 (1998), pp. 15–16.

60. Derek Freeman, *Margaret Mead and Samoa: The Making and Unmaking of an Anthropological Myth* (Cambridge, Massachusetts: Harvard University Press, 1983).

61. Reviews of Freeman by Lowell D. Holmes in *The Sciences*, 33 (1983), pp. 14–18; Robert I. Levy in *Science*, 220 (1983), pp. 829–32; George F. Marcus in *New York Times Book Review* (27 March 1983), pp. 3, 22, 24; and David M. Schneider in *Natural History*, (June 1983), pp. 4–10; debate edited by Ian Brady in *American Anthropologist*, 85 (1983), pp. 908–47; Allen Abramson, 'Beyond the Samoan Controversy in Anthropology', in Pat Caplan (ed.), *The Cultural Construction of Sexuality* (London: Routledge, 1987), pp. 193–216.

62. Brodrick, *Abbé Breuil*, pp. 94–108.

63. Henri Bégouen, 'La magie aux temps prehistoriques', *Mémoires de l'Académie des Sciences, Inscriptions et Belles-Lettres* (1924), ii, pp. 417–32; 'The Magic Origin of Prehistoric Art', *Antiquity*, 3 (1929), pp. 5–19; 'Les bases magiques de l'art prehistorique', *Scientia*, fourth series, 33 (1939), pp. 202–16.

64. Margaret Murray, *The God of the Witches* (London: Sampson Low, 1931), pp. 23–24; Henri Breuil, *Four Hundred Centuries of Cave Art* (Montignac: Centre d'Etudes et de Documentation Prehistoriques, 1952), p. 170; and *The Men of the Stone Age* (London: Harrap, 1959; 2nd edn 1965), pp. 255–56.

65. Breuil, *Four Hundred Centuries*, fig. 130 and p. 170.

66. Peter J. Ucko and Andree Rosenfeld, *Palaeolithic Cave Art* (London: Weidenfeld, 1967), fig. 89 and p. 206.

67. E.g. Jean Clottes and David Lewis-Williams, *The Shamans of Prehistory* (New York: Abrams, 1998), p. 69.

68. Breuil, *Four Hundred Centuries*, p. 170.

69. Elizabeth Shee Twohig, 'A "Mother Goddess" in Ancient Europe, *c.* 4200–2500 BC?', in Lucy Goodison and Christine Morris (ed.), *Ancient Goddesses: The Myths and the Evidence* (London: British Museum Press, 1998), pp. 165–67.

Notes to Chapter 2: Arthur and the Academics

1. In fact, the only recent discussion of which I know is in N. J. Higham, *King Arthur: Myth-Making and History* (London: Routledge, 2002), pp. 10–37; it makes a significant contrast with my own interpretation, provided here.

2. This is all discussed extensively in the literature below, but of special relevance to the characterisation here are Kenneth Jackson, 'On the Northern British Section in Nennius', in Jackson et al., *Celt and Saxon* (Cambridge: Cambridge University Press, 1963), pp. 20–62; David N. Dumville, 'Some Aspects of the Chronology of the *Historia Brittonum*', *Bulletin of the Board of Celtic Studies*, 25 (1972–74), pp. 439–45; '"Nennius" and *Historia Brittonum*', *Studia Celtica*, 10 (1975), pp. 78–95; and 'On the North British Section of the *Historia Brittonum*', *Welsh History Review*, 8 (1976–77), pp. 345–54; Higham, *King Arthur*, pp. 116–69.

3. Again, there is much debate in the works cited below, but see especially Kathleen Hughes, 'The Welsh Latin Chronicles', *Proceedings of the British Academy*, 59 (1973), pp. 233–58; and Higham, *King Arthur*, pp. 170–217.

4. In addition to the works below, see David N. Dumville, 'Palaeographical Considerations in the Dating of Early Welsh Verse', *Bulletin of the Board of Celtic Studies*, 28 (1977), 246–51; Leslie Alcock, 'Gwyr y Gogledd: An Archaeological Appraisal', *Archaeologia Cambrensis*, 132 (1983), pp. 1–18; T. M. Charles-Edwards, 'The Authenticity of the *Gododdin*', in Rachel Bromwich and R. Brinley Jones (ed.), *Astudiaethau ar yr Hengerdd* (Cardiff: University of Wales Press, 1978), pp. 44–71; Higham, *King Arthur*, pp. 180–85.

5. In addition to works below, see M. Miller, 'Bede's Use of Gildas', *English*

Historical Review, 90 (1975), pp. 241–61; Michael Lapidge and David Dumville (ed.), *Gildas: New Approaches* (Cambridge: Boydell, 1984); Higham, *King Arthur*, pp. 38–97.

6. All these points figure in the literature discussed below.

7. Perfectly true, as Gildas, Bede and the *Historia Brittonum* all refer to it; for an extended discussion, see Peter Hunter Blair, 'The Origins of Northumbria', *Archaeologia Aeliana*, fourth series 25 (1947), pp. 1–51.

8. E. K. Chambers, *Arthur of Britain* (London, 1927), ch. 1; Gilbert Sheldon, *The Transition from Roman Britain to Christian England* (London, 1932), passim; W. G. Collingwood, 'Arthur's Battles', *Antiquity*, 3 (1929), pp. 292–98; O. G. S. Crawford, 'Arthur and his Battles', *Antiquity*, 9 (1935), pp. 277–91.

9. R. G. Collingwood and J. N. L. Myres, *Roman Britain and the English Settlements* (Oxford, 1936), pp. 321–24.

10. Such as the bestsellers by Alfred Duggan, Henry Treece and Rosemary Sutcliff.

11. For example Trelawney Dayrell Read, *The Battle for Britain in the Fifth Century* (London, 1944); and Jack Lindsay, *Arthur and his Times* (London: Muller, 1958), both considered worthy of purchase by university libraries.

12. The one imposed on me in the mid 1960s not only presented Collingwood's theory as established fact but included a lively drawing of an Arthurian cavalryman equipped for action. I regret that I cannot remember author or illustrator.

13. Rachel Bromwich, 'The Character of the Early Welsh Tradition', in H. M. Chadwick et al., *Studies in Early British History* (Cambridge: Cambridge University Press, 1954), pp. 83–186.

14. Nora K. Chadwick, *Celtic Britain* (London: Thames and Hudson, 1963), 46–48.

15. Kenneth Hurlstone Jackson, 'The Arthur of History', in Roger Sherman Loomis (ed.), *Arthurian Literature in the Middle Ages* (Oxford: Oxford University Press, 1959), pp. 1–11.

16. Quoted in Helen Hill Miller, *The Realms of Arthur* (London: Davies, 1969), p. 84.

17. C. A. Ralegh Radford, 'Tintagel: The Castle and Celtic Monastery', *Antiquaries Journal*, 15 (1935), pp. 401–19; 'Tintagel in History and Legend', *Journal of the Royal Institution of Cornwall*, 86 (1942), appendix, pp. 25–41; and 'The Celtic Monastery in Britain', *Archaeologia Cambrensis*, 111 (1962), pp. 7–16.

18. R. A. S. Macalister, *Corpus inscriptionum insularum Celticarum* (Dublin: Stationary Office, 1945), i, pp. 465–67.

19. C. A. Ralegh Radford, 'Report on the Excavations at Castle Dore', *Journal of the Royal Instition of Cornwall*, new series 1 (1951), appendix, pp. 1–119.

20. Rachel Bromwich, 'Some Remarks upon the Celtic Sources of "Tristan"', *Transactions of the Honourable Society of Cymmrodorion* (1953), pp. 32–60.

21. Charles Thomas, 'Imported Pottery in Dark-Age Western Britain', *Medieval Archaeology*, 3 (1959), pp. 89–111.

22. Stated in the preface to the 1973 edition.

23. C. A. Ralegh Radford, 'The Church in Somerset Down to 1100' *Proceedings of the Somerset Archaeological and Natural History Society*, 106 (1962), pp. 28–35.

24. Different aspects of his earlier work are well represented by *Dinas Powys*

(Cardiff: University of Wales Press, 1963), and 'Pottery and Settlements in Wales and the March, AD 400–700', in I. L. Foster and L. Alcock (ed.), *Culture and the Environment* (London: Routledge, 1963), pp. 281–303.

25. Geoffrey Ashe, *King Arthur in Fact and Legend* (London: Allen, 1963).

26. Leslie Alcock, *Arthur's Britain* (London: Allen Lane, 1971). p. xv.

27. Leslie Alcock, *By South Cadbury is that Camelot ...* (London: Thames and Hudson, 1972).

28. D. J. V. Fisher, *The Anglo-Saxon Age* (London: Longman, 1973), pp. 9–10.

29. Miller, *Realms of Arthur*; Christopher Hibbert, *The Search for King Arthur* (London: Cassell, 1969); Peter Davies, *The Realms of Arthur* (London, 1970).

30. See his *Avalonian Quest* (London: Methuen, 1982).

31. 'Are These The Walls of Camelot?', *Antiquity*, 43 (1969), pp. 27–30.

32. It was finally published in 1992: Philip Rahtz et al., *Cadbury Congresbury, 1968–73* (British Archaeological Reports, British Series 223). Five seasons had been needed to dig a total of 5 per cent of the site, at a cost of £5000. Another £11,000 was spent on analysing the finds and preparing the report for publication. The conclusion was that 'we still do not know what it was or is that we excavated' (p. i). The episode is an exemplar of conscientious archaeology.

33. 'Somerset, AD 400–700', in P. J. Fowler (ed.), *Archaeology and the Landscape* (London: Baker, 1972), pp. 206–10; review of Alcock in *History*, 58 (1973), p. 423; and 'Castle Dore: A Reappraisal of the Post-Roman Structures', *Cornish Archaeology*, 10 (1971, pp. 49–54.

34. Rachel Bromwich, 'Concepts of Arthur', *Studia Celtica*, 11 (1975–76), pp. 163–64; Hughes, 'Latin Welsh Chronicles'.

35. Hence J. N. L. Myres, in the *English Historical Review*, 90 (1975), pp. 113–16; and D. P. Kirby and J. E. Caerwyn Williams, in *Studia Celtica*, 11 (1976), pp. 454–86.

36. David N. Dumville, 'Sub-Roman Britain: History and Legend', *History*, 62 (1977), pp. 173–92.

37. Thus Susan Pearce, *The Kingdom of Dumnonia* (Padstow: Lodenek, 1978), p. 155; Wendy Davies, *Wales in the Early Middle Ages* (Leicester: Leicester University Press, 1982), passim; Charles Thomas, *Celtic Britain* (London: Thames and Hudson, 1986), pp. 1–48; Malcolm Todd, *The South-West to AD 1000* (London: Longman, 1987), passim; and the works cited in this context below.

38. Thomas Charles-Edwards, 'The Arthur of History', in Rachel Bromwich, A. O. H. Jarman and Brynley F. Roberts (ed.), *The Arthur of the Welsh* (Cardiff: University of Wales Press, 1991), ch. 1.

39. Leslie Alcock, 'Cadbury-Camelot: A Fifteen-Year Perspective', *Proceedings of the British Academy*, 68 (1982), pp. 355–88.

40. Geoffrey Ashe, *Avalonian Quest*; preface to edition of *King Arthur's Avalon* by Barnes and Noble, New York, 1990.

41. Geoffrey Ashe, '"A Certain Very Ancient Book": Traces of an Arthurian Source in Geoffrey of Monmouth's "History"', *Speculum*, 56 (1981), pp. 301–23.

42. As well as *Avalonian Quest* and the reissued *King Arthur's Avalon*, I have been

able to trace *The Landscape of King Arthur* (Exeter: Webb and Bower, 1987), and *The Arthurian Handbook* (New York: Garland, 1988).

43. Charles Thomas, 'St Patrick and Fifth-Century Britain', in P. J. Casey (ed.) *The End of Roman Britain* (British Archaeological Reports British Series 71, 1979), pp. 81–101.

44. J. W. L. Myres, *The English Settlements* (Oxford: Oxford University Press, 1986), pp. 13–16.

45. C. J. Arnold, *Roman Britain to Saxon England* (London: Croom Helm, 1984); Michael Wood, *Domesday* (London: London Book Club Associates, 1987), which synthesises various monographs; A. S. Esmonde Cleary, *The Ending of Roman Britain* (London: Batsford, 1989).

46. O. J. Padel, 'Some South-Western Sites with Arthurian Associations', in Bromwich, Jarman and Roberts (eds), *The Arthur of the Welsh*, ch. 11.

47. I. C. G. Burrow, 'Tintagel: Some Problems', *Scottish Archaeological Forum*, 5 (1973–74), pp. 99–103; Charles Thomas, *A Provisional List of Imported Pottery in Post-Roman Western Britain and Ireland* (Institute of Cornish Studies Special Report, 7, 1981), pp. 28–29, and 'East and West', in Susan M. Pearce (ed.) *The Early Church in Western Britain and Ireland* (British Archaeological Reports British Series 102, 1982), pp. 17–34; O. J. Padel, 'The Cornish Background to the Tristan Stories', *Cambridge Medieval Celtic Studies*, 1 (1981), pp. 53–82.

48. Leslie Alcock, *Cadbury Castle, Somerset: The Early Medieval Archaeology* (Cardiff: University of Wales Press, 1995); Michael Costen, *The Origins of Somerset* (Manchester: Manchester University Press, 1992), p. 70; N. J. Higham, *The English Conquest* (Manchester: Manchester University Press, 1994), p. 211; and *King Arthur*; O. J. Padel, 'The Nature of Arthur', *Cambrian Medieval Celtic Studies*, 27 (1994), pp. 1–31; Edward James, *Britain in the First Millennium* (London: Arnold, 2001), p. 101.

49. Charles Thomas, *English Heritage Book of Tintagel* (London: Batsford, 1993); C. D. Morris and Rachel Harvey, 'Excavations on the Lower Terrace, Site C, Tintagel Island, 1990–94', *Antiquaries Journal*, 77 (1997), pp. 1–44; Christopher Morris, 'Tintagel', *Current Archaeology*, 159 (1998), pp. 84–88.

Although all information in this chapter is based either on publications or on my own eye-witness experience, I am very grateful to Geoffrey Ashe, Philip Rahtz and David Dumville for conversations which, as well as being a joy in themselves, served to clarify their intentions in some of their writings.

Notes to Chapter 3: Glastonbury: Alternative Histories

1. All of the above is based upon James P. Carley, *Glastonbury Abbey* (London: Guild, 1988), and Philip Rahtz, *English Heritage Book of Glastonbury* (London: Batsford, 1993), with additional material from the *Verse Lyfe of Joseph*, ed. Walter W. Skeat (Early English Text Society, 44, 1871), pp. 35–52, and Leland's notes in *The Famous History of Chinon of England*, ed. W. E. Mead (Early English Text Society, 165, 1925), p. 76.

2. Carley, *Glastonbury Abbey*, pp. 173–74.

3. Ibid., 181–83.

4. Ibid., 174.

5. Rahtz, *Glastonbury*, p. 65; C. A. Ralegh Radford, 'Glastonbury Abbey before 1184', in Nichola Coldstream and Peter Draper (ed.), *Medieval Art and Architecture at Wells and Glastonbury* (British Archaeological Conference Transactions, 4, 1981), pp. 110–34.

6. G. W. Wright, 'The Chalice Well, or Blood Spring, and its Traditions', *Proceedings of the Glastonbury Antiquarian Society*, 1 (1886), pp. 20–36.

7. 'Preface', *Proceedings of the Glastonbury Antiquarian Society*, 1 (1886).

8. Arthur Bulleid, *The Lake Villages of Somerset* (Glastonbury Antiquarian Society: 6th edn, 1968); John Coles, Armynell Goodall and Stephen Minnitt, *Arthur Bulleid and the Glastonbury Lake Villages* (Somerset Levels Project, 1992).

9. Margaret Deansley, *The Pre-Conquest Church in England* (London: Black, 1961), pp. 12–13; quotation on p. 12.

10. Patrick Benham, *The Avalonians* (Glastonbury: Gothic Image, 1993), passim; Michael Hurd, *Immortal Hour: The Life and Period of Rutland Boughton* (London: Routledge, 1962), passim.

11. Albany F. Major, 'Somerset Folklore', *Folk-Lore*, 22 (1911), p. 495.

12. Benham, *Avalonians*, pp. 192–226; Frederick Bligh Bond, *The Gate of Remembrance* (1918: repr. Wellingborough: Thorsons, 1978); William W. Kenawell, *The Quest at Glastonbury* (New York: Garret, 1965); John Michell, *The View over Atlantis* (1969: revised edn, London: Garnstone, 1975), pp. 131–45. For hostile views see H. J. Wilkins, *False Psychic Claims in 'The Gate of Remembrance'* (Bristol, 1923), and Marshall McKusick, 'Psychic Archaeology: Theory, Method, and Mythology', *Journal of Field Archaeology*, 9 (1982), pp. 101–6.

13. Ronald Hutton, *The Triumph of the Moon: A History of Modern Pagan Witchcraft* (Oxford: Oxford University Press, 1999), pp. 112–31.

14. Benham, *Avalonians*, pp. 37–39; quotation on p. 39.

15. Hurd, *Immortal Hour*, p. 72.

16. John Cowper Powys, *A Glastonbury Romance* (London, 1933), pp. 70, 113.

17. Dion Fortune, *Avalon of the Heart* (London, 1934), pp. 10, 58.

18. Benham, *Avalonians*, pp. 266–67.

19. Richard Deacon, *John Dee* (London: Muller, 1968), pp. 82, 131–32. I wish heartily that this text provided a reference to the original source, so that Dee's words could be checked in context.

20. K. E. Maltwood, *A Guide to Glastonbury's Temple of the Stars* (1929: repr. London: Clarke, 1964).

21. Benham, *Avalonians*, p. 169.

22. C. A. Ralegh Radford, 'Glastonbury Abbey', in Geoffrey Ashe et al., *The Quest for Arthur's Britain* (London: Pall Mall, 1968), pp. 119–38; quotations on pp. 128–29.

23. Geoffrey Russell, 'The Service of the Grail', in Mary Williams (ed.), *Glastonbury and Britain: A Study in Patterns* (Orpington: Research into Lost Knowledge Organisation, 1990), pp. 27–30.

24. Michell, *View Over Atlantis*, pp. 56–64, 131–45.

25. Mary Caine, *The Glastonbury Zodiac: Key to the Mysteries of Britain* (Torquay: Grael Communications, 1978); Elizabeth Leader, 'The Somerset Zodiac', in Williams (ed.) *Glastonbury and Britain*, pp. 8–12; Janet Roberts, 'Somerset Legendary Geomancy', in Anthony Roberts (ed.), *Glastonbury: Ancient Avalon, New Jerusalem* (Tiptree: Rider, 1977), pp. 63–77.

26. Geoffrey Ashe, *The Finger and the Moon* (London: Heinemann, 1973), pp. 172–74.

27. Kathy Jones, *The Goddess in Glastonbury* (Glastonbury: Ariadne Publications, 1990).

28. Anthony Roberts, 'Glastonbury: The Ancient Avalon', in Roberts (ed.), *Glastonbury*, pp. 10–25; quotation on p. 17.

29. The basic texts are J. Armitage Robinson, *Two Glastonbury Legends* (Cambridge: Cambridge University Press, 1926), pp. 1–27; R. F. Treharne, *The Glastonbury Legends* (London: Cresset, 1926), pp. 40–104; and Antonia Gransden, 'The Growth of the Glastonbury Traditions and Legends in the Twelfth Century', *Journal of Ecclesiastical History*, 27 (1976), pp. 337–58.

30. Treharne, *Glastonbury Legends*, p. 104; S. C. Morland, 'King Arthur's Leaden Cross', *Somerset and Dorset Notes and Queries*, 31 (1984), pp. 366–67.

31. Richard Barber, 'Was Mordred Buried at Glastonbury?', *Arthurian Literature*, 4 (1985), pp. 31–69; and *King Arthur: Hero and Legend* (Woodbridge: Boydell, 3rd edn, 1986), pp. 131–35.

32. Robinson, *Two Glastonbury Legends*, pp. 28–50; Treharne, *Glastonbury Legends*, pp. 1–40, 110–21; Carley, *Glastonbury Abbey*, pp. 53–57, 69–70, 87–90; Valerie M. Lagorio, 'The Evolving Legend of St Joseph of Glastonbury', *Speculum*, 46 (1971), pp. 209–31.

33. Carley, *Glastonbury Abbey*, p. 147; and 'A Grave Event', in Martin B. Shichtman and James P. Carley (ed.), *Culture and the King: The Social Implications of the Arthurian Legend* (Albany: State University of New York Press, 1994), pp. 129–48.

34. Deborah K. E. Crawford, 'St Joseph in Britain: Reconsidering the Legends', *Folklore*, 104 (1993), pp. 86–98, and 105 (1994), pp. 51–59; 'Addendum', *Folklore*, 106 (1995), pp. 92–93; and 'The Ghost of Criticism Past', *Folklore*, 107 (1996), pp. 98–101; quotation on p. 98 of latter.

35. Elissa R. Henken, *Traditions of the Welsh Saints* (Cambridge: Brewer, 1987), pp. 221–26.

36. Gransden, 'Growth of the Glastonbury Traditions', p. 346.

37. Henken, *Traditions of the Welsh Saints*, pp. 221–26.

38. Ceridwen Lloyd-Morgan, 'From Ynys Widrin to Glasybri', in Lesley Abrams and James P. Carley (ed.), *The Archaeology and History of Glastonbury Abbey* (Woodbridge: Boydell, 1991), pp. 301–15.

39. The text is fully discussed in Treharne, *Glastonbury Legends*, pp. 30–35.

40. H. P. R. Finberg, *West Country Historical Studies* (Newton Abbot: David and Charles, 1969), p. 82; Carley, *Glastonbury Abbey*, pp. 105–7.

41. Finberg, *West Country Historical Studies*, pp. 84–85; Carley, *Glastonbury Abbey*,

pp. 107–9; Michael Lapidge, 'The Cult of St Indract at Glastonbury', in Dorothy Whitlock, Rosamund McKitterick and David Dumville (ed.), *Ireland in Medieval Europe* (Cambridge: Cambridge University Press, 1982), pp. 179–212.

42. *The Works of St Patrick*, ed. by Ludwig Bieler (Westminster, Maryland, 1953), p. 35.

43. Finberg, *West Country Historical Studies*, pp. 78–80.

44. Ibid., pp. 74–77.

45. Ibid., pp. 79, 83–85.

46. Carley, *Glastonbury Abbey*, p. 2; Lesely Abrams, *Anglo-Saxon Glastonbury: Church and Endowment* (Woodbridge: Boydell Studies in Anglo-Saxon History, 1996), p. 5. One spurious Anglo-Saxon source sometimes cited is a letter from St Augustine to Pope Gregory, a transcript of which was owned by an early twentieth-century vicar of Glastonbury and printed in C. C. Dobson, *Did Our Lord Visit Britain as They Say in Cornwall and Somerset?* (Glastonbury, 3rd edn, 1938), p. 24. It speaks of a church built by Christ himself on 'a certain royal island' in 'the western confines of Britain'. On face value this appears to be a major piece of evidence for Glastonbury's existing sanctity and antiquity by the end of the sixth century. As Dobson noted, however, it was taken from a thirteenth-century recension of William of Malmesbury's history of the abbey. This does not credit it to Augustine, but to a 'historian of the Britons' whose work existed in copies at Bury St Edmund's and St Augustine's Abbey, Canterbury: William of Malmesbury, *De antiquitate Glastonie Ecclesie*, ed. John Scott (Woodbridge: Boydell, 1981), pp. 44–47. It is thus one of the later interpolations into William's history, apparently drawing on one of the later recensions of the *Historia Brittonum*, and as such has no value for the early middle ages. Dobson did not check his source, and nor did Gordon Strachan, who has repeated the error in *Jesus the Master Builder: Druid Mysteries and the Dawn of Christianity* (Edinburgh: Floris, 1998), pp. 45–47, a work which, like Dobson's, may be considered a contribution to the twentieth-century Christian mythology of Glastonbury. Bewilderingly, Strachan also refers to a seventeenth-century Latin work by Sir Henry Spelman, in which the correct text by William is given.

47. Sarah Foot, 'Glastonbury's Early Abbots', in Abrams and Carley (ed.), *Glastonbury Abbey*, pp. 163–89; Lesley Abrams, *Anglo-Saxon Glastonbury*, pp. 5–6.

48. Michael Aston and Roger Leech, *Historic Towns in Somerset: Archaeology and Planning* (Somerset County Council, 1977), pp. 57–59.

49. Philip Rahtz, 'Glastonbury Tor', in Ashe et al., *Quest for Arthur's Britain*, pp. 139–40; Radford, 'Glastonbury Abbey', in Coldstream and Draper (ed.), *Medieval Art and Architecture*, p. 114; Peter Ellis, 'Excavations at Silver Street, Glastonbury, 1978', *Somerset Archaeology and Natural History*, 126 (1982), pp. 17–38; Abrams, *Anglo-Saxon Glastonbury*, pp. 2–3; Charles and Mary Hollinrake, 'The Abbey Enclosure Ditch and a Late-Saxon Canal', *Somerset Archaeology and Natural History*, 136 (1992), pp. 73–94.

50. Rahtz, *Glastonbury*, pp. 118–27.

51. Ibid., pp. 106–7.

52. Ibid., p. 129; Richard Warner, *A History of the Abbey of Glaston* (Bath: Cruttwell, 1826) p. lxx; Wright, 'The Chalice Well', pp. 30–34.

53. Benham, *Avalonians*, pp. 158–59.

54. Rahtz, *Glastonbury*, pp. 23–28; and 'Glastonbury Tor', p. 153; Radford, 'Glastonbury Abbey', p. 115.

55. Rahtz, *Glastonbury*, p. 28; Carley, *Glastonbury Abbey*, pp. 27–42.

56. Rahtz, 'Glastonbury Tor', pp. 146–48; and *Glastonbury*, pp. 51–65.

57. Philip Rahtz, 'Irish Settlements in Somerset', *Proceedings of the Royal Irish Academy*, 76. C (1976), pp. 223–30.

58. A Somerset origin for Patrick was mooted by R. P. L. Hanson, *St Patrick: His Origins and Career* (Oxford: Oxford University Press, 1968), pp. 113–16. The fullest recent discussion is in Henry Jelley, *St Patrick's Somerset Birthplace* (Cary Valley Historical Publications, 1998).

59. Keith Branigan, 'The End of Roman West', *Transactions of the Bristol and Gloucestershire Archaeological Society*, 91 (1972), pp. 117–28.

60. For a survey of research into European mazes, see W. H. Matthews, *Mazes and Labyrinths* (London, 1922). My information upon medieval land hunger in Somerset is based on a personal communication from my Bristol colleague Michael Costen, 15 March 2000; Michael Costen is the author of *The Origins of Somerset* (Manchester: Manchester University Press, 1992). My thoughts on the status of the Tor features were worked out in a series of exchanges with Philip Rahtz between November 1999 and March 2000. His latest view of them is now published, as 'Glastonbury Tor: A Modified Landscape', *Landscapes*, 3.1 (2002), pp. 4–18.

61. Geoffrey Ashe, *The Landscape of King Arthur* (Exeter: Webb and Bower, 1987), p. 19; Michell, *View over Atlantis*, p. 17.

62. Compare, for example, Maltwood, *Guide to Glastonbury's Temple of the Stars*, and Caine, *Glastonbury Zodiac*. Cf. the comment in Benham, *Avalonians*, p. 271.

63. Michell, *View over Atlantis*, pp. 17, 19.

64. David Clarke, 'A Provisional Model of an Iron Age Society and its Settlement System', in David L. Clarke (ed.), *Models in Archaeology* (London: Methuen, 1972), pp. 801–70; Bryony and John Coles, *Sweet Track to Glastonbury: The Somerset Levels in Prehistory* (London: Thames and Hudson, 1986), pp. 168–83; Stephen Minnitt and John Coles, *The Lake Villages of Somerset* (Somerset Levels Project, 1996).

65. E.g. Rahtz, *Glastonbury*, p. 107.

66. Radford, 'Glastonbury Abbey', p. 111.

67. Peter Leach, 'The Roman Pottery', and Warwick Rodwell, 'Comment', in Peter Ellis (ed.), *Excavations in Silver Street, Glastonbury* (Taunton: Somerset County Council, 1978), pp. 22–24, 35–37; Rahtz, *Glastonbury*, p. 99.

68. Philip Rahtz, personal communications., 24 November 1999 and 15 March 2000.

69. Roberts, 'Glastonbury', pp. 12, 17.

70. William Stukeley, *Itinerarium curiosum* (London, 1724), i, pp. 143–46.

71. Aldhelm, *Carmen ecclesiasticum III*.

72. Benham, *Avalonians*, pp. 158–59, 195.
73. Ashe, *Landscape of King Arthur*, pp. 7–9.
74. Carley, *Glastonbury Abbey*, pp. vii, ix.
75. Crawford, 'The Ghost of Criticism Past', p. 98.

Notes to Chapter 4: The New Old Paganism

1. Ronald Hutton, *The Pagan Religions of the Ancient British Isles* (Oxford: Blackwell, 1991), pp. 335–37.
2. The catalyst of this work was provided in 1995 by the visit to Bristol of Jan Bremmer, to deliver the Read-Tuckwell lecture series of that year, which he later published as *The Rise and Fall of the Afterlife* (London: Routledge, 2002). Conversations with him and with his host, my colleague Richard Buxton, convinced me of the importance of late antique Hellenism as a model for modern Paganism and of my need to deal with it. I first published my recognition of this need, and some of my initial research in response to it, in an article, 'Paganism and Polemic: The Debate over the Origins of Modern Pagan Witchcraft', *Folklore* 111 (2000), pp. 103–9. That essay was intended as a reply to an American writer, Donald H. Frew, who had emphasised the same connection without substantive supporting argument, in 'Methodological Flaws in Recent Studies of Historical and Modern Witchcraft', *Ethnologies*, 1 (1998), pp. 33–65. I subsequently had a brief but hectic exchange of correspondence with Mr Frew, in which he greatly encouraged my own work without disclosing either his own arguments or his primary source material. When his research reaches completion, it will be interesting to see whether (and if so, how) it differs from my own.
3. Ramsay MacMullen, *Paganism in the Roman Empire* (New Haven: Yale University Press, 1981), pp. 2–5. This justly admired general survey made a great impact on my impression of the general European context of my researches into the British Isles, as published in *Pagan Religions*.
4. Ken Dowden, *European Paganism: The Realities of Cult from Antiquity to the Middle Ages* (London: Routledge, 2000).
5. Garth Fowden, 'Constantine's Porphyry Column', *Journal of Roman Studies* 81 (1991), p. 119n., and 'Polytheist Religion and Philosophy', in Averil Cameron and Peter Garnsey (ed.), *The Cambridge Ancient History*, 13 (Cambridge; Cambridge University Press, 1998), pp. 538–60. The same terminology crept into the work of Peter Brown by the end of the decade: 'Christianization and Religious Conflict', in ibid., pp. 632–65.
6. John Peter Kennedy, 'Monotheistic and Polytheistic Elements in Classical Mediterranean Spirituality', in A. H. Armstrong (ed.), *Classical Mediterranean Spirituality* (London: Routledge, 1986), pp. 270–71.
7. Polymnia Athanassiadi and Michael Frede (ed.), *Pagan Monotheism in Late Antiquity* (Oxford: Oxford University Press, 1999).
8. Ibid., pp. 1–20, 190.

9. Julian, *Letter to Themistius* (pp. 266–67 in the Heinemann edition of 1913); Themistius, *Speeches*, no. 5, ed. H. Schenkl et al. (Leipzig: Teubner, 1974), pp. 68–69; Sallustius (sic), *Concerning the Gods and the Universe*, ed. A. D. Nock (Cambridge University Press, 1926), ch. 2; Symmachus, *Memoranda*, ed. O. Seeck (Monumenta Germaniae Historica, Auctores Antiquissimi, 6, Berlin, 1883), sections 3.8–10. The author of *Concerning the Gods* was called Sallustius in the early twentieth century, but has since then been identified as Salutius; both names, inevitably, appear in the present work according to the context in which they are used.

10. Gaston H. Halsberghe, *The Cult of Sol Invictus* (Leiden: Brill, 1972); Polymnia Athanassiadi-Fowden, *Julian and Hellenism* (Oxford: Oxford University Press, 1981), pp. 113–24; Julian, *Oration IV: Hymn to King Helios*, i, pp. 353–435, in the Loeb Classics Library edition of his works.

11. Bremmer, *Rise and Fall of the Afterlife*, pp. 54–55.

12. G. W. Bowersock, *Hellenism in Late Antiquity* (Cambridge: Cambridge University Press, 1990), pp. 17–26.

13. Clifford Ando, 'Pagan Apologetics and Christian Intolerance in the Age of Themistius and Augustine', *Journal of Early Christian Studies*, 4 (1996), pp. 171–207.

14. M. L. West, 'Towards Monotheism', in Athanassiadi and Frede (ed.), *Pagan Monotheism*, pp. 21–40; Michael Frede, 'Monotheism and Pagan Philosophy in Later Antiquity', in ibid., pp. 41–67; Javier Texidor, *The Pagan God: Popular Religion in the Graeco-Roman Near East* (Princeton: Princeton University Press, 1977), pp. 3–16; Geraldine Pinch, *Magic in Ancient Egypt* (London: British Museum, 1994), pp. 23–24; Jan Assmann, 'Magic and Theology in Ancient Egypt', in Peter Scafer and Hans G. Kippenberg (ed.), *Envisioning Magic* (Leiden: Brill, 1997), pp. 1–18.

15. A. H, Armstrong, 'Plotinus', in A. H. Armstrong (ed.), *The Cambridge History of Later Greek and Early Medieval Philosophy* (Cambridge: Cambridge University Press, 1967), pp. 195–60; A. C. Lloyd, 'The Later Neoplatonists', in ibid., pp. 161–277; R. T. Wallis, *Neo-Platonism* (London: Duckworth, 1972), pp. 2–106; Pierre Hadot, 'Neoplatonist Spirituality, 1, Plotinus and Porphyry', in A. H. Armstrong (ed.), *Classical Mediterranean Spirituality* (London: Routledge, 1986), pp. 230–49; Pierre Hadot, *Plotinus* (Chicago: University of Chicago Press, 1993); Dominic O'Meara, *Plotinus* (Oxford: Oxford University Press, 1993).

16. Lloyd, 'The Later Neoplatonists'; Wallis, *Neo-Platonism*, pp. 118–37; Dominic O'Meara, *Pythagoras Revived: Mathematics and Philosophy in Late Antiquity* (Oxford: Oxford University Press, 1989), passim; Giovanni Reale, *The Schools of the Imperial Age*, ed. and trans. John R. Catan (Albany: State University of New York Press, 1990), pp. 411–17.

17. Julian; *Orations IV-V* and *Against The Galilaeans* (I have used the Loeb edition of his works); Polymnia Athanassiadi, 'A Contribution to Mithraic Theology', *Journal of Theological Studies*, new series, 28 (1977), pp. 360–71; Athanassiadi-Fowden, *Julian and Hellenism*; Rowland Smith, *Julian's Gods* (London: Routledge, 1995), esp. pp. 139–78.

18. Wallis, *Neo-Platonism*, pp. 138–57; H. D. Saffrey, 'Neoplatonist Spirituality, 2, From Iamblichus to Proclus and Damascius', in Armstrong (ed.), *Classical Mediterranean Spirituality*, pp. 250–65, quotation from p. 263; L. J. Rosan, *The Philosophy of Proclus* (New York: Cosmos, 1949); Lucas Siorvanes, *Proclus: Neo-Platonic Philosophy and Science* (Edinburgh: Edinburgh University Press, 1996); Sarah Rappe, *Reading Neoplatonism* (Cambridge: Cambridge University Press, 2000), pp. 143–96; Garth Fowden, 'The Pagan Holy Man in Late Antique Society', *Journal of Hellenic Studies*, 102 (1982), pp. 33–38; Polymnia Athanassiadi, 'Persecution and Response in Late Paganism', *Journal of Hellenic Studies*, 113 (1993), pp. 3–18.

19. On which, for example, see Peter Kingsley, 'From Pythagoras to the *Turba Philosophorum*: Egypt and the Pythagorean Tradition', *Journal of the Warburg and Courtauld Institutes*, 56 (1994), pp. 1–13.

20. Eunapius, *Lives of the Philosophers*, section 455. I have used the Loeb Classics Library edition of 1922.

21. Marinus, *Life of Proclus*, ch. 7. See note 144.

22. Halsberghe, *Cult of Sol Invictus*, pp. 26–71.

23. Especially in his work *Philosophy from Oracles*; see Johannes Geffcken, *The Last Days of Greco-Roman Paganism* (1920: repr. Amsterdam: North Holland Publishing Co., 1978), p. 59.

24. Athanassiadi, 'Persecution and Response in Late Paganism', p. 3.

25. MacMullen, *Paganism in the Roman Empire*, pp. 68, 77, 87.

26. Fowden, 'The Pagan Holy Man', 33–59.

27. Polymnia Athanassiadi, 'The Chaldean Oracles', in Athanassiadi and Frede (ed.), *Pagan Monotheism*, p. 178; Athanassiadi and Frede, *Introduction*, in ibid., pp. 1–2.

28. Hutton, *Pagan Religions*, pp. 205–46.

29. Eunapius, *Lives*, section 455.

30. Macrobius, *The Saturnalia*, ed. by Percival Vaughan Davies (New York: Columbia, 1969); Alan Cameron, 'The Date and Identity of Macrobius', *Journal of Roman Studies*, 56 (1966), pp. 25–38; Wolf Liebeschuetz, 'The Significance of the Speech of Praetextatus', in Athanassiadi and Frede (ed.), *Pagan Monotheism*, pp. 185–205.

31. Bowersock, *Hellenism in Late Antiquity*, pp. 41–44, 65; Pierre Chuvin, *A Chronicle of the Last Pagans*, trans. by B. A. Archer (Cambridge, Massachusetts: Harvard University Press, 1990), p. 118.

32. Alan Cameron, 'The Latin Revival of the Fourth Century', in Warren Treadgold (ed.), *Renaissances Before The Renaissance* (Stanford, California: Stanford University Press, 1984), pp. 42–58.

33. Bowersock, *Hellenism in Late Antiquity*, pp. 41–53; Betz, *The Greek Magical Papyri*, p. xlvii; Fowden, *The Egyptian Hermes*, p. 29; C. S. Lewis, *The Allegory of Love* (Oxford, 1936), pp. 66–77.

34. Bowersock, *Hellenism in Late Antiquity*, pp. 41–53; Fowden, *The Egyptian Hermes*, p. 29.

35. Patricia Merivale, *Pan the Goat-God: His Myth in Modern Times* (Cambridge,

Massachusetts: Harvard University Press, 1969), pp. 1–11; quotation on p. 1; John Boardman, *The Great God Pan: The Survival of an Image* (London: Thames and Hudson, 1997), pp. 26–40.

36. Errnst Robert Curtius, *European Literature and the Latin Middle Ages* (London: Routledge, 1953), pp. 106–27; Lewis, *The Allegory of Love*, pp. 54–74; George D. Economou, *The Goddess Natura in Medieval Literature* (Cambridge, Massachusetts: Harvard University Press, 1972), pp. 4–57; Damasius, *In Parmenidem*, ed. by C. A. Ruelle (Paris, 1889), p. 157.

37. Lewis, *Allegory of Love*, pp. 76–77; Sidonius, *Carmina* XI, lines 14–16, the edition used was the Loeb Classics Library one of 1936; Ennodius, *Carmina*, book 1, no. 4, lines 29–52, the edition used being that in the Monumenta Germaniae Historica series, Berlin, 1885.

38. Prudence Jones, 'The Three Goddesses', *Pagan Dawn*, 136 (2000), pp. 26–28; quotation on p. 26; Sarah Iles Johnston, *Hekate Soteira* (Atlanta, Georgia: Scholars Press, 1990), pp. 23–42; J. E. Lowe, 'Magical Hekate', in Stephen Ronan (ed.), *The Goddess Hekate* (Hastings: Chthonios, 1992), pp. 11–15; L. R. Farnell, 'Hekate's Cult', in ibid., pp. 17–35; L. R. Farnell, 'Hekate in Art', in ibid., pp. 36–50.

39. Ruth Benedict, 'Magic', in *Encyclopedia of the Social Sciences*, 10 (1933), pp. 39–41, and 'Religion' in Franz Boas (ed.), *General Anthropology* (Boston: Heath, 1938), pp. 64–67; William J. Goode, 'Magic and Religion', *Ethnos*, 14 (1949), pp. 172–82, and *Religion among the Primitives* (Glencoe: Freepress, 1951), pp. 52–55.

40. E. E. Evans-Pritchard, *Theories of Primitive Religion* (Oxford: Oxford University Press, 1965), pp. 33, 110–11; Murray and Rosalie Wax, 'The Notion of Magic', *Current Anthropology*, 4 (1963), pp. 495–503; Dorothy Hammond, 'Magic: A Problem in Semantics', *American Anthropologist*, 72 (1970), pp. 1349–56; quotations from p. 1355.

41. K. E. Rosengren, 'Malinowski's Magic', *Current Anthropology*, 17 (1976), pp. 667–85; and see the works listed and discussed in Malcom B. Hamilton, *The Sociology of Religion: Theoretical and Comparative Perspectives* (London: Routledge, 1995), pp. 34–41.

42. Much of the literature is summarised in Hamilton, *Sociology of Religion*, pp. 21–64.

43. David E. Aune, 'Magic in Early Christianity', *Aufsteig und Niedergang der Römischen Welt*, II.23.2 (1980), pp. 1507–10; H. S. Versnel, 'Some Reflections on the Relationship Magic-Religion', *Numen*, 38 (1991), p. 181.

44. E.g. Robert Browning, *The Emperor Julian* (London: Weidenfeld, 1975), p. 40; John M. Hull, *Hellenistic Magic and the Synoptic Tradition* (London: SCM Press, 1974), p. 27.

45. Ramsay MacMullen, *Paganism in the Roman Empire*, p. 70, and *Christianity and Paganism in the Fourth to Eighth Centuries* (New Haven, Connecticut: Yale University Press, 1997), pp. 143–44. As I pointed out in 'Paganism and Polemic', p. 105, MacMullen cited ten works in a footnote intended to make his case. Of these, only one supported his statement unequivocally. The others

either retained some sense of distinction between religion and magic or else argued that a strict boundary between the two could not be found, rather than that they could not be distinguished at all.

46. Apart from MacMullen himself, this was true of C. R. Phillips III, 'Nullum Crimen sine Lege: Socioreligious Sanctions on Magic', in Christopher A. Faraone and Dirk Obbink (ed.), *Magika Hiera: Ancient Greek Magic and Religion* (Oxford: Oxford University Press, 1991), p. 262; David E. Aune, 'Magic in Early Christianity', *Aufsteig und Niedergang der Römischen Welt* II.23.2 (1980), pp. 1507–10; Richard Kieckhefer, *Magic in the Middle Ages* (Cambridge: Cambridge University Press, 1989), pp. 14–15; Marvin Meyer and Richard ·Smith (ed.), *Ancient Christian Magic: Coptic Texts of Ritual Power* (Princeton, New Jersey: Princeton University Press, 1999), pp. 1–6.

47. Christopher A. Faraone and Dirk Obbink, 'Introduction', in Faraone and Obbink (ed.), *Magika Hiera*, p. vi; Fritz Graf, 'Prayer in Magical and Religious Ritual', in ibid., p. 188.

48. Versnel, 'Some Reflections', pp. 177–98; Hugh Parry, *Thelxis: Magic and Imagination in Greek Myth and Poetry* (New York: University Press of America, 1992), pp. 1–7.

49. Bengt Ankarloo and Stuart Clark (ed.), *Witchcraft and Magic in Europe*, ii, *Ancient Greece and Rome* (London: Athlone, 1999): the contributors were, in order of discussion, Daniel Ogden, Richard Gordon, Georg Luck and Valerie Flint; quotation from p. 286.

50. David R. Jordan (ed.), *The World of Ancient Magic* (Bergen: Norwegian Institute at Athens, 1999): the contributors were, respectively, Jens Braarvig, Einar Thomassen and Emmanuel Voutiras; quotations from pp. 51 and 65.

51. Richard Kieckhefer, *Magic in the Middle Ages* (Cambridge: Cambridge University Press, 1989), pp. 14–15; Valerie J. Flint, *The Rise of Magic in Early Medieval Europe* (Oxford: Oxford University Press, 1991), pp. 3–8; Clare Fanger (ed.), *Conjuring Spirits: Texts and Traditions of Medieval Ritual Magic* (Stroud: Sutton, 1998).

52. Peter Green, 'The Methods of Ancient Magic', *Times Literary Supplement*, 19 April 2002, pp. 5–6. It neatly illustrates the current diversity – or polarisation – of views that he was reviewing three works that both rejected the traditional distinction and assumed that to do so is now orthodoxy: Sulochana R. Asirvathani et al. (ed.), *Between Magic and Religion* (Lanham, Maryland: Rowman and Littlefield, 2001), p. xiv; Daniel Ogden, *Greek and Roman Necromancy* (Princeton: Princeton University Press, 2001), pp, xviii–xix; and Matthew W. Dickie, *Magic and Magicians in the Greco-Roman World* (London: Routledge, 2001), pp. 18–20. It is notable that in the last, the most detailed and comprehensive of these studies, the author begins by denying the existence of an essential concept of magic, but by the last third of the book is using the word consistently and in a traditional fashion, without treating it as problematic.

53. E.g. Christopher A. Faraone, 'The Agonistic Context of Early Greek Binding Spells', in Faraone and Obbink (ed.), *Magika Hiera*, pp. 3–32; Roy Kotansky,

'Incantations and Prayers for Salvation on Inscribed Greek Amulets', in ibid., pp. 107–37; Fritz Graf, 'Prayer in Magic and Religious Ritual', in ibid., pp. 188–213; Hans Dieter Betz, 'Magic and Mystery in the Greek Magical Papyri', in ibid., pp. 244–59; Alan F. Segal, 'Hellenistic Magic: Some Questions of Definition', in R. van den Broek and M. J. Vermaseren (ed.), *Studies in Gnosticism and Hellenistic Religions* (Leiden: Brill, 1981), pp. 349–75; Daniel Ogden, 'Binding Spells: Curse Tablets and Voodoo Dolls in the Greek and Roman Worlds', in Ankarloo and Clark (ed.), *Witchcraft and Magic in Europe*, ii, pp. 38–86; John Gager, 'Introduction', in John Gager (ed.), *Curse Tablets and Binding Spells from the Ancient World* (Oxford: Oxford University Press, 1992), p. 12.

54. Graf, 'Prayer in Magic and Religious Ritual'; Fritz Graf, *Magic in the Ancient World* (1994: English trans. Cambridge, Massachusetts: Harvard University Press, 1997), pp. 222–29.

55. Peter Kingsley, *Ancient Philosophy, Mystery and Magic* (Oxford: Oxford University Press, 1995), p. 306.

56. Aune, 'Magic in Early Christianity', pp. 1507–10, 1518.

57. Einar Thomassen, 'Is Magic a Subclass of Ritual?', in Jordan et al. (ed.), *The World of Ancient Magic*, p. 55.

58. Richard Gordon, 'Reporting the Marvellous: Private Divination in the Greek Magical Papyri', in Peter Schafer and Hans G. Kippenberg (ed.), *Envisioning Magic* (Leiden: Brill, 1997), p. 66. In the same year one of the leading critics of the traditional formulation, Charistopher Faraone, published a book, *Ancient Greek Love Magic* (Cambridge, Massachusetts: Harvard University Press, 1999), in which he repeated confidently that to divide 'magic' from 'religion' or 'science' was not appropriate in studies of ancient Greece (p. 17). On the previous page he described magic as 'a set of practical devices and rituals used by the Greeks in their day-to-day lives to control or otherwise influence supernaturally the forces of nature, animals or other human beings'. This is just the classic definition, and the one used traditionally to distinguish 'magic' from 'religion' or 'science'.

59. Meyer and Smith (ed.), *Ancient Christian Magic: Coptic Texts of Ritual Power*, pp. 1–6; quotation on p. 5.

60. Mary Beard, John North and Simon Price, *Religions of Rome*, i, *A History* (Cambridge: Cambridge University Press, 1998), p. 219; Segal, 'Hellenistic Magic', pp. 350–52; Richard Gordon, 'Imagining Greek and Roman Magic', in Ankarloo and Clark (ed.), *Witchcraft and Magic in Europe*, ii, pp. 162–62; Gager, 'Introduction', in Gager (ed.), *Curse Tablets and Binding Spells*, pp. 24–25; Ogden, *Greek and Roman Necromancy*, pp. xix–xx; Dickie, *Magic and Magicians*, pp. 19–27.

61. This pedigree was neatly charted out by Aune, 'Magic in Early Christianity', pp. 1512–16.

62. Segal, 'Hellenistic Magic', pp. 367–70; J. A. North, 'Novelty and Choice in Roman Religion', *Journal of Roman Studies*, 70 (1980), pp. 186–91; Hans G. Kippenberg, 'Magic in Roman Civil Discourse', in Schafer and Klippenberg (ed.),

Envisioning Magic, pp. 137–63; C. R. Philips III, 'The Sociology of Religious Knowledge in the Roman Empire to AD 284', *Aufsteig und Neidergang der Römischen Welt*, II.16.3 (1986), pp. 2677–2773; and 'Nullum Crimen sine Lege', in Faraone and Obbink (ed.), *Magika Hiera*, pp. 260–76; Jonathan Z. Smith, 'Trading Places', in Marvin Meyer and Paul Mirecki (ed.), *Ancient Magic and Ritual Power* (Leiden: Brill, 1995), pp. 13–27; Stephen D. Ricks, 'The Magician as Outsider in the Hebrew Bible and New Testament', in ibid., pp. 131–43.

63. My reasons for adopting it are stated in Ronald Hutton, *The Triumph of the Moon: A History of Modern Pagan Witchcraft* (Oxford: Oxford University Press, 1999), pp. 3–4.

64. Lewis provides an excellent miniature illustration of the distinction in his children's story *The Silver Chair* (1953: edition used Collins, 1980), p. 17.

65. Philostratus, *Life of Apollonius*, lines 8.7.9–10, edition used being that of the Loeb Classics Library, 1912; Apuleius, *Apologia*, section 26.6, edition used being that of H. Butler and A. Owen, in 1914; Iamblichus, *De mysteriis*, ed. Edouard des Places (Paris 1971), lines 40.19, 161.10–16; Pliny, *Natural History*, section 30.1–18, edition used being that of the Loeb Classics Library, 1962; Seneca, *Oepidus*, lines 561–63, edition used being that of the Loeb Classics Library, 1979; Plotinus, *Enneads*, lines 2.9.14.1–8.

66. Graf, *Magic in the Ancient World*, pp. 21–29.

67. Plato, *Laws*, section 10.909B, edition used being that of the Loeb Classics Library, 1926.

68. The importance of this work in the present context was noted by Versnel, 'Some Reflections on the Relationship Magic-Religion', p. 191; and Braarvig, 'Magic: Reconsidering the Grand Dichotomy', pp. 37–40. It is included in W. H. S. Jones's edition of Greek medical texts, *Hippocrates* (London, 1923–31), iii, 140–51.

69. On which see Graf, *Magic in the Ancient World*, pp. 27–29, and Dickie, *Magic and Magicians*, pp. 22–45.

70. Faraone, 'The Agonistic Context of Early Greek Binding Spells', pp. 17–20; H. S. Versnel, 'Beyond Cursing: The Appeal to Justice in Judicial Prayers', in Faraone and Obbink (ed.), *Magika Hiera*, pp. 60–106; Gager, 'Introduction', in Gager (ed.), *Curse Tablets and Binding Spells*, pp. 12–25; Daniel Ogden, 'Binding Spells: Curse Tablets and Voodoo Dolls in the Greek and Roman Worlds', in Ankarloo and Clark (ed.), *Witchcraft and Magic in Europe*, ii, pp. 38–86; Dickie, *Magic and Magicians*, pp. 50–60.

71. Dickie, *Magic and Magicians*, pp. 50–52.

72. Robert Kriech Ritner, *The Mechanics of Ancient Egyptian Magical Practice* (Chicago: Oriental Institute of University of Chicago Studies in Ancient Oriental Civilization, 54, 1993), pp. 1–72, 220–47; Jan Assmann, 'Magic and Theology in Ancient Egypt', in Schafer and Kippenberg (ed.), *Envisioning Magic*, pp. 1–18; David Frankfurter, 'Ritual Expertise in Roman Egypt and the Problem of the Category "Magician"', in ibid., pp. 115–35; Dominic Montserrat, *Ancient Egypt: Digging for Dreams* (Glasgow: Glasgow City Council, 2000), pp. 22–23; Pinch,

Magic in Ancient Egypt, pp. 47–60, 73–74; Joris F. Borghouts (ed.), *Ancient Egyptian Magical Texts*) Leiden: Brill, 1978), passim.

73. Gager, 'Introduction', in Gager (ed.), *Curse Tablets and Binding Spells*, pp. 23–24; Gordon, 'Imagining Greek and Roman Magic', pp. 254–55.

74. Ritner, *Mechanics of Ancient Egyptian Magical Practices*, pp. 57–67; Pinch, *Magic in Ancient Egypt*, pp. 46, 60–64, 70–72, 76–79, 100.

75. Pinch, *Magic in Ancient Egypt*, p. 47; Graf, *Magic in the Ancient World*, pp. 89–90; Matthew W. Dickie, 'The Learned Magician and the Collection and Transmission of Magical Lore', in Jordan et al. (ed.), *World of Ancient Magic*, pp. 163–93.

76. Ritner, *Mechanics of Ancient Egyptian Magical Practice*, p. 237; Montserrat, *Ancient Egypt*, p. 23; Pinch, *Magic in Ancient Egypt*, p. 72. In another publication, 'Egyptian Magical Practice under the Roman Empire', *Aufstieg und Niedergang der Romischen Welt* II.18.5 (1995), p. 3353, Ritner declared that the Egyptian material illustrates 'the inherent inadequacy of all supposed "universal" definitions of magic'. The supposed definition that he holds to be invalidated, however, is that of magic as antisocial or foreign religious behaviour, which is not the one applied here.

77. Frederick H. Cryer, 'Magic in Ancient Syria-Palestine – and in the Old Testament', in Marie-Louise Thomsen and Frederick H. Cryer, *The Athlone History of Witchcraft and Magic in Europe*, i, *Biblical and Pagan Societies* (London: Athlone, 2001), pp. 114–22; Valerie Flint, 'The Demonisation of Magic and Sorcery in Late Antiquity', in Ankarloo and Clark (ed), *Witchcraft and Magic in Europe*, ii, pp. 295–97.

78. Marie-Louise Thomsen, 'Witchcraft and Magic in Ancient Mesopotamia', in Thomsen and Cryer, *Athlone History of Witchcraft and Magic in Europe*, pp. 13–56, 88–93; R. Campbell Thompson, *The Devils and Evil Spirits of Babylonia* (London, 1903), passim.

79. For overviews, see Roelof Van Den Broek, 'Gnosticism and Hermetism in Antiquity', in Roelof Van Den Broek and Wouter J. Hanegraaf (ed.), *Gnosis and Hermeticism from Antiquity to Modern Times* (Albany, New York: State University of New York Press, 1998), pp. 1–20; *The Way of Hermes*, translated by Clement Salaman et al. (London: Duckworth, 1999) (I am very grateful to Nicholas Spicer for the gift of this text); Walter Scott (ed.), *Hermetica*, vol. i (Oxford: Oxford University Press, 1924); Giovanni Reale, *The Schools of the Imperial Age*, edited and translated by John R. Catan (Albany, New York: State University of New York Press, 1990), pp. 276–81; Garth Fowden, *The Egyptian Hermes* (Cambridge: Cambridge University Press, 1986).

80. Hans Dieter Betz (ed.), *The Greek Magical Papyri in Translation* (Chicago: University of Chicago Press, 1986). Although the original ordering of the texts was made by Karl Preisendanz, all references here are to this edition.

81. E.g. Papyrus III, lines 494–501, Papyrus IV, lines 930–1114; Papyrus XIa, lines 1–40.

82. E.g. Papyrus IV, lines 850–929; Papyrus V, lines 1–53; Papyrus VII, lines 540–78; Papyrus XIV, lines 1–92, 150–231.

83. Papyrus IV, lines 850–929.
84. The usual explanation of these so-called 'barbarous names' is that they were intended to impress by virtue of their inherent mystery and auditory impact. When they seemed to refer to any genuine language it was commonly a foreign one to Egypt such as Hebrew or Babylonian, to increase the sense of the exotic. Joscelyn Godwin, however, has argued that their vowel sounds actually embody a system related to the spheres and planets, expounded by some Neoplatonist, Gnostic and Neopythagorean writers, something on which I am not qualified to pronounce: *The Mystery of the Seven Vowels in Theory and Practice* (Grand Rapids, Michigan: Phanes, 1991). I am grateful to Donald Frew for this reference.
85. E.g. Papyrus V, lines 146–50.
86. Papyrus III, lines 211–29; Papyrus XIII, lines 335–39.
87. Graf, *Magic in the Ancient World*, pp. 5–6, 118–74.
88. Jonathan Z. Smith, 'The Temple and the Magician', in Jacob Jervell and Wayne A. Meeks (ed.), *God's Christ and his People* (Oslo: Universitetsforlaget, 1977), pp. 233–48; and 'Trading Places', pp. 23–26; Gordon, 'Reporting the Marvellous', pp. 67–92; Pinch, *Magic in Ancient Egypt*, p. 59; Hans Dieter Betz, 'The Formation of Authoritative Tradition in the Greek Magical Papyri', in Ben F. Meyer and E. P. Sanders (ed.), *Jewish and Christian Self-Definition*, iii, *Self Definition in the Graeco-Roman World* (London: SCM Press, 1982), pp. 161–70; Ritner, 'Egyptian Magical Practice under the Roman Empire', pp. 3345–58.
89. E.g. Papyri XII, lines 92–94, and IV, lines 475–77.
90. Betz, 'The Formation of Authoritative Tradition', 161–70; Betz (ed.), *The Greek Magical Papyri*, p. xlvi; Fowden, *The Egyptian Hermes*, pp. 82–85; Segal, 'Hellenistic Magic', p. 373; Graf, *Magic in the Ancient World*, pp. 97–116.
91. Papyrus I, lines 53, 127, 191.
92. Papyri LXX, lines 5–16, and III, lines 559–610.
93. Papyrus IV, lines 164–221.
94. Papyrus IV, lines 475–750.
95. Segal, 'Hellenistic Magic', 373;
96. Graf, 'Prayer in Magic and Religious Ritual', pp. 188–213; Thomassen, 'Is Magic a Subclass of Ritual?', pp. 57–58; Hans Dieter Betz, 'Magic and Mystery in the Greek Magical Papyri', in Faraone and Obbink (ed.), *Magika Hiera*, pp. 244–59; quotation on p. 254.
97. Lucan, *Pharsalia*, Book VI, lines 415–830; the edition used being the Loeb one of 1911.
98. Apuleius, *Apologia*, sections 35–43.
99. Wallis, *Neo-Platonism*, p. 106; Johnston, *Hekate Soteira*, p. 87; Rowland Smith, *Julian's Gods* (London: Routledge, 1995), p. 101.
100. E. R. Dodds, 'Theurgy and its Relationship to Neoplatonism', *Journal of Roman Studies*, 37 (1947), pp. 55–69, an essay given much wider circulation by its reprinting in his bestseller, *The Greeks and the Irrational* (Berkeley: University of California Press, 1951), pp. 283–97. For Dodds's personal interests, see

Gregory Shaw, 'Theurgy: Rituals of Unification in the Neoplatonism of Iamblichus', *Traditio*, 41 (1985), pp. 1–2.

101. Dodds, *Greeks and the Irrational*, p. 291; Wallis, *Neo-Platonism*, p. 3; Polymnia Athanassiadi, 'Dreams, Theurgy and Freelance Divination', *Journal of Roman Studies*, 83 (1993), p. 116; Segal, 'Hellenistic Magic', p. 364; Johnston, *Hekate Soteira*, pp. 76–77, and 'Rising to the Occasion: Theurgic Ascent in its Cultural Milieu', in Schafer and Klippenberg (ed.), *Envisioning Magic*, p. 165; Gregory Shaw, 'Eros and Arithmos', *Ancient Philosophy*, 19 (1999), p. 121; Georg Luck, *Ancient Pathways and Hidden Pursuits* (Ann Arbor: University of Michigan Press, 2000), pp. 110; 118; Smith, *Julian's Gods*, p. 103; Dickie, *Magic and Magicians*, p. 206.

102. The fragments were first assembled, edited and numbered by Wilhelm Kroll, *De oraculis Chaldaicis* (Breslau, 1894). A second edition was made by Edouard des Places, *Oracles Chaldaiques* (Paris, 1971), and an English translation by Ruth Majercik, *The Chaldean Oracles* (Leiden: Brill, 1989). The standard numbering of the fragments, used here, is that of des Places. For acerbic comments on editions, see Michel Tardieu, 'La Gnose Valentinienne et les Oracles Chaldaiques', in Bentley Layton (ed.), *The Rediscovery of Gnosticism*, i, *The School of Valentinus* (Brill: Leiden, 1980), pp. 194–96. For complaints about Kroll's arbitrary ordering of the material, see Polymnia Athanassiadi, 'The Chaldean Oracles', in Athanassiadi and Frede (ed.), *Pagan Monotheism*, p. 158.

103. Johnston, *Hekate Soteira*, p. 2; Smith, *Julian's Gods*, p. 93; Athanssiadi, 'The Chaldean Oracles', pp. 153–55.

104. Kroll, *De oraculis Chaldaicis*; Lynn Thorndike, *A History of Magic and Experimental Science*, i (London: Macmillan, 1923), p. 308; Tardieu, 'La Gnose Valentienne', pp. 194–239; Philip Merlan, 'Religion and Philosophy from Plato's *Phaedo* to the Chaldean Oracles', *Journal of the History of Philosophy*, 1 (1963), pp. 163–71; Kingsley, *Ancient Philosophy, Mystery and Magic*, p. 304; Smith, *Julian's Gods*, p. 95; Johnston, 'Rising to the Occasion', pp. 169–70; Stephen Ronan, 'Chaldean Hekate', in Ronan (ed.), *The Goddess Hekate*, pp. 80, 118–26; Majercik, *The Chaldean Oracles*, pp. 5–9; Reale, *The Schools of the Imperial Age*, p. 285.

105. Fragments 50 and 74.

106. Hans Lewy, *Chaldean Oracles and Theurgy*, ed. by Michel Tardieu (Paris: Etudes Augustiniennes, 1978), pp. 12–105; Johnston, *Hekate Soteira*, pp. 49–74; Smith, *Julian's Gods*, pp. 98–101; Majercik, *Chaldean Oracles*, pp. 1–9; Ronan, 'Chaldean Hekate', pp. 80–89.

107. Fragments 7 and 9.

108. Fragment 115.

109. Georg Luck, 'Theurgy and Forms of Worship in Neoplatonism', in Jacob Neusner et al. (ed.), *Religion, Science and Magic* (Oxford: Oxford University Press, 1989), pp. 187–88, 192; quotation on p. 192.

110. These are discussed by Johnston, *Hekate Soteira*, pp. 90–98; Majercik, *Chaldean Oracles*, pp. 9–10; Stephen Ronan, 'Hekate's Iynx', *Alexandria*, 1 (1991), pp. 321–35.

111. Fragments 2, 109, 132–33, 135, 150.

112. Fragments 146–48.

113. Fragment 149.

114. Fragments 219, 221, 223–25.

115. Majercik, *Chaldean Oracles*, pp. 23, 27.

116. Ibid, pp. 9–44; Johnston, *Hekate Soteira*, pp. 76–133, and 'Rising to the Occasion', pp. 174–89; Luck, 'Theurgy and Forms of Worship', pp. 189–200; Smith, *Julian's Gods*, pp. 98–102.

117. The edition I have used is that by Thomas Taylor, published as a preface to his translation of Iamblichus, *On the Mysteries* (in the reprint made by Bertram Dobell in 1895).

118. These issues are debated, with full references, in Andrew Smith, *Porphyry's Place in the Neoplatonic Tradition* (The Hague: Martinus Nijhoff, 1974), pp. 103–39; Johnston, *Hekate Soteira*, p. 79; Wallis, *Neo-Platonism*, pp. 2–3, 105–6; Luck, 'Theurgy and Forms of Worship', p. 196, and *Ancient Pathways and Hidden Pursuits* (Ann Arbor: University of Michigan Press, 2000), p. 141; Smith, *Julian's Gods*, p. 105.

119. I have used the standard edition by Edouard des Places, published in Paris in 1966.

120. For an ancient opinion, by an admirer, see Eunapius, *Lives of the Philosophers*, section 458. For a modern one, see Polymnia Athanassiadi, 'Dreams, Theurgy and Freelance Divination', *Journal of Roman Studies*, 83 (1993), pp. 128, and 'The Oecumenism of Iamblichus', *Journal of Roman Studies*, 85 (1995), p. 244.

121. *De mysteriis*, lines 96.13–97.8.

122. Ibid., lines 5.22–23, 233.7–16.

123. Matthew W. Dickie, 'The Learned Magician and the Collection and Transmission of Magical Lore', in Jordan et al. (ed.), *The World of Ancient Magic*, pp. 163–93; Peter Kingsley, 'From Pythagoras to the "Turba Philosophorum"', *Journal of the Warburg and Courtauld Institutes*, 57 (1994), pp. 1–13; Dickie, *Magic and Magicians*, pp. 117–23.

124. *De mysteriis*, lines 264.14–265.6.

125. *De mysteriis*, lines 197.12–199.5.

126. *De mysteriis*, lines 233.11–16, 218.5–10.

127. Ibid., lines 161.10–16; cf. Athanassiadi, 'Dreams, Theurgy and Freelance Divination', pp. 117–23.

128. *De mysteriis*, lines 83.9–86.4, 175.15–180.4.

129. Ibid., lines 176.13–177.26.

130. Ibid., lines 227.1–230.16.

131. Ibid., lines 132.3–134.20.

132. Ibid., lines 41.4–11.

133. Ibid., lines 184.7–8.

134. Ibid., lines 92.8, 96.13–97.9, 221.5–230.18, 237.8–240.18.

135. Ibid., lines 112.10–12, 267.6–12.

136. For various recent considerations of the subject see Athanassiadi, 'Dreams,

Theurgy and Freelance Divination', pp. 115–30, and 'The Oecumenism of Iamblichus', pp. 255–50; A. H. Armstrong, *Hellenic and Christian Studies* (Aldershot: Variorum, 1990), pp. 179–88; Gregory Shaw, 'Theurgy: Rituals of Unification in the Neoplatonism of Iamblichus', *Traditio*, 41 (1985), pp. 1–28; 'Theurgy as Demiurgy', *Dionysius*, 12 (1988), pp. 37–59; 'Embodying the Stars', *Alexandria*, 1 (1991), pp. 97–103; 'Eros and Arithmos', *Ancient Philosophy*, 19 (1999), pp. 121–44;

137. Eunapius, *Lives of the Philosophers*, sections 459–60.

138. Not the same person as the near-contemporary Christian author.

139. Eunapius, *Lives of the Philosophers*, sections 474–80; quotations from section 474–75.

140. Smith, *Julian's Gods*, pp. 111–13.

141. Proclus, *Theologia Platonica*, ed. by H. D. Saffrey and L. G. Westerlinck (6 vols, Paris, 1968–97), esp. line 1.26.63 (the quotation) and section 4.16. For discussions of this text, see Rappe, *Reading Neoplatonism*, pp. 167–96; and Luck, 'Theurgy and Forms of Worship in Neoplatonism', pp. 205–11.

142. Translated by Brian Copenhaver, 'Hermes Trismegistus, Proclus and the Question of a Philosophy of Magic in the Renaissance', in Ingrid Merkel and Allen G. Debus (ed.), *Hermeticism and the Renaissance* (Washington: Folger Shakespeare Library, 1988), pp. 103–5.

143. Dodds, *Greeks and the Irrational*, p. 296.

144. Proclus, *In Platonis Timaeum Commentari*, line 3.41.3 (ed. by E. Diehl, Leipzig, 1903–6).

145. Dickie, *Magic and Magicians*, pp. 317–18.

146. Marinus, *Life of Proclus*, chs 26–28. I have used the translation by K. S. Guthrie (New York: Platonist Press, 1925; reprinted by Phanes Press, 1986), and am very grateful to Colin Irving for the loan of this work. Whereas Guthrie does not find any specific rite for the rainmaking in the text, L. J. Rosan translates it as saying that it was achieved by moving a magical wheel, apparently the same tool as the top: Rosan, *The Philosophy of Proclus* (New York: Cosmos, 1949), pp. 28–29.

147. Johnston, *Hekate Soteira*, p. 90; Ronan, 'Hekate's Iynx', p. 326.

148. *Life of Proclus*, chapter 29.

149. Anne Sheppard, 'Proclus's Attitude to Theurgy', *Classical Quarterly*, new series 32 (1982), pp. 212–24; Wallis, *Neo-Platonism*, pp. 153–54; Siorvanes, *Proclus*, pp. 191–99.

150. Damascius, *The Philosophical History*, translated by Polymnia Athanassiadi (Athens: Apamea Cultural Association, 1999), section 4A.

151. Ibid., sections 9, 22, 34D, 46D-E, 72, 80, 85, 97.

152. The relevant extracts from his work are printed by des Places in his edition of the Chaldean Oracles, pp. 70, 187–219. See commentaries by Dodds, *Greeks and the Irrational*, pp. 291–92, 297; Smith, *Julian's Gods*, p. 101; Ronan, 'Hekate's Iynx', pp. 322; and 'Chaldean Hekate', pp. 87–103; Luck, 'Theurgy and Forms of Worship', pp. 212–13; Lewy, *Chaldean Oracles*, p. 230.

153. A few scholars have read the texts (mainly the Chaldean Oracles) as indicating

that theurgy was practised by small groups: notably Luck, 'Theurgy and Forms of Worship in Neoplatonism'; and Johnston, 'Rising to the Occasion', pp. 174–78. I find the evidence inconclusive.

154. Fragments 153–54.

155. *De mysteriis*, lines 218.5–10, 219–14, 220.6–9, 225.1–5, 230.18, 233.11–16.

156. Julian, *Orationes*, no. 5, section 172.

157. She first presented these ideas in Anna B. Kingsford and Edward Maitland, *The Perfect Way* (London, 1882), and they feature also in her posthumously published works, *Clothed with the Sun* (London, 1889), and *The Credo of Christendom* (London 1916).

158. R. A. Gilbert, *The Magical Mason* (Wellingborough: Aquarian, 1983), passim.

159. Ellic Howe, *The Magicians of the Golden Dawn* (London: Routledge, 1972), pp. ix–xxv; Charles Wycliffe Goodwin, *Fragment of a Graeco-Egyptian Work upon Magic* (Cambridge: Cambridge Antiquarian Society, 1852).

160. Hutton, *Triumph of the Moon*, pp. 80–81; Frederick Lees, 'Conversations with the Hierophant Rameses and the High Priestess Anasi', *The Humanitarian*, 16.2 (New York, February 1900), reprinted on www.tarot.nv/gd/isis.htm. I am grateful to Alison Butler for this reference.

161. Florence Farr, *Egyptian Magic* (reprinted by Kessinger, in Kila, Montana, n.d.). I am very grateful to Alison Butler for lending me a copy of this work.

162. Cited in Shaw, 'Theurgy', p. 1.

163. Dolores Ashcroft-Nowicki, *The Forgotten Mage* (London: Aquarian, 1986), pp. 22–186; quotation on p. 68.

164. Hutton, *Triumph*, pp. 180–88.

165. Gerald Gardner, *Witchcraft Today* (London: Rider, 1954), pp. 91–92. I am grateful to Donald Frew for drawing my attention to these references.

166. Gerald Gardner, *The Meaning of Witchcraft* (London: Aquarian, 1959), pp. 186–89.

167. Doreen Valiente, *The Rebirth of Witchcraft* (Custer, Washington: Phoenix, 1989), pp. 60–63; Janet and Stewart Farrar, *Eight Sabbats for Witches* (London: Hale, 1981), pp. 35–47.

168. It does not feature in any surviving Wiccan work of which I am aware, dating from before 1964. In her first autobiography, *Witch Blood!* (New York: House of Collectibles, 1974), pp. 39–40, Patricia Crowther quotes it as used at her initiation by Gardner. The latter event is now firmly dated to 6 June 1960, in Patricia Crowther, *One Witch's World* (London: Hale, 1998), pp. 30, 40. In the text of the initiation rite given in *Witch Blood!*, however, the Dryghtyn Prayer is substituted for the ritual purification that was an essential component of Gardner's first-degree initiation ceremony. This raises the probability that it was interpolated for the purposes of publication in 1974; now confirmed by Patricia Crowther in *Pagan Dawn*, 145 (2002), p. 23.

169. Gardner, *Meaning of Witchcraft*, pp. 26–27, 260.

170. Vivianne Crowley, *Wicca: The Old Religion in the New Age* (London: Aquarian, 1989), pp. 154–58; quotation on p. 158.

171. Starhawk, *Truth or Dare* (San Francisco: HarperSanFrancisco, 1987), p. 7.

172. Van den Broek, 'Gnosticism and Hermetism in Antiquity', pp. 8–20; Scott (ed.), *Hermetica*, passim.

173. Armstrong, 'Plotinus', pp. 223–56.

174. On which see Smith, *Julian's Gods*, pp. 100–1.

175. Iamblichus, *De mysteriis*, lines 199.6–240.19. Cf. Shaw, 'Theurgy as Demiurgy', pp. 41–48.

176. Robert Browning, *The Emperor Julian* (London: Weidenfeld, 1975), p. 157.

177. Marinus, *Life of Proclus*, chs 12–19; Athanassiadi, 'Persecution and Response in Late Paganism', p. 10; Fowden, 'The Pagan Holy Man', p. 47; Saffrey, 'Neoplatonist Spirituality, 2', p. 264.

178. Sallustius, *Concerning the Gods*, chs 14, 19.

179. Gardner, *Meaning of Witchcraft*, pp. 26, 260.

180. Iamblichus, *De mysteriis*, lines 200.1–219.19; Sallustius, *Concerning the Gods*, ch. 16.

181. Fowden, *The Egyptian Hermes*, p. 66.

Notes to Chapter 5: Paganism in the Missing Centuries

1. Ludo J. R. Milis, *The Pagan Middle Ages* (English translation, Woodbridge: Boydell, 1998).

2. Ronald Hutton, *The Triumph of the Moon* (Oxford: Oxford University Press, 1999), pp. 132–50, 272–86, 377–80.

3. Michel Tardieu, 'Sabiens Coraniques et "Sabiens" de Harran', *Journal Asiatique*, 274 (1986), pp. 1–44; and 'Les calendriers en usage à Harran d'après les sources arabes et le commentaire de Simplicius a la *Physique* d'Aristotle', in Ilstraut Hadot (ed.), *Simplicius* (Peripatoi, 15, Berlin 1987), pp. 40–57.

4. Ilstraut Hadot, 'La vie et l'oeuvre de Simplicius d'après des Sources Grecques et Arabes', in Hadot (ed.), *Simplicius*, pp. 3–33; Pierre Chuvin, *A Chronicle of the Last Pagans*, translated by B. A. Archer (Cambridge, Massachusetts: Harvard University Press, 1990), pp. 149–50; Polymnia Athanassiadi, 'Persecution and Response in Late Paganism', *Journal of Hellenic Studies*, 113 (1993), pp. 25–29; Garth Fowden, *Empire to Commonwealth* (Princeton: Princeton University Press, 1993), pp. 62–65.

5. Paul Foulkes, 'Where was Simplicius', *Journal of Hellenic Studies*, 112 (1992), p. 143; Averil Cameron, *The Mediterranean World in Late Antiquity* (London: Routledge, 1993), pp. 76–77; H. J. Blumenthal, *Aristotle and Neoplatonism in Late Antiquity* (London: Duckworth, 1996), pp. 44–46; Anne Sheppard, 'Philosophy and Philosophical Schools', in Averil Cameron et al. (ed.), *The Cambridge Ancient History*, xiv, *Late Antiquity* (Cambridge: Cambridge University Press, 2000), pp. 841–42; N. G. Wilson, *Scholars of Byzantium* (London: Duckworth, 1983), p. 41.

6. Polymnia Athanassiadi, *Damascius: The Philosophical History* (Athens: Apamea Cultural Association, 1999), pp. 51–53.

7. Bardaisan of Edessa, *The Book of the Laws of Countries*, ed. and translated by J. W. Drijvers (Assen: Studia Semitica Neerlandica, 1965); J. W. Drijvers, *Bardaisan of Edessa* (Assen: Studia Semitica Neerlandica, 1966), 'Bardaisan of Edessa and the Hermetic', *Jaarbericht van het Vooraziatisch-Egyptisch Genootschap "Ex Oriente Lux"*, 21 (1969–70), pp. 190–210, and *Cults and Beliefs at Edessa* (Leiden: Brill, 1980), pp. 61–62, 154–222; Tamara M. Green, *City of the Moon God: Religious Traditions of Harran* (Leiden: Brill, 1992), pp. 1–93; Steven K. Ross, *Roman Edessa* (London: Routledge, 2001), pp. 87, 119–27.

8. Sebastian P. Brock, 'A Syriac Collection of Prophecies of the Pagan Philosophers', *Orientalia Lovaniensia Periodica*, 14 (1983), pp. 203–46.

9. Sinasi Gunduz, *The Knowledge of Life: The Origins and Early History of the Mandaeans and their Relation to the Sabians of the Qur'an and to the Harranians* (Oxford: Oxford University Press, 1994), pp. 131–32; Green, *City of the Moon God*, p. 94.

10. Bar Hebraeus, *The Chronology*, ed. and translated by E. A. Wallis Budge (Oxford: Oxford University Press, 1932), p. 110.

11. F. Rosenthal, 'The Prophecies of Baba the Harranian', in W. B. Henning and E. Yarshalter (ed.), *A Locust's Leg: Studies in Honour of S. H. Taqizadeh* (London: Lund, Humphries and Co., 1962), pp. 220–32; Sebastian P. Brock, 'Some Syriac Excerpts from Greek Collections of Pagan Prophecies', *Vigiliae Christianae*, 38 (1984), pp. 77–90, and 'A Syriac Collection of Prophecies'.

12. G. W. Bowersock, *Hellenism in Late Antiquity* (Cambridge: Cambridge University Press, 1990), pp. 78–79.

13. Dimitri Gutas, *Greek Thought, Arab Culture* (London: Routledge, 1998), p. 190; J. B. Segal, 'The Sabian Mysteries', in Edward Bacon (ed.), *Vanished Civilizations* (London: Thames and Hudson, 1963), p. 212; Green, *City of the Moon God*, pp. 94–95; Gunduz, *The Knowledge of Life*, pp. 131–33; R. T. Wallis, *Neo-Platonism* (London: Duckworth, 1972), p. 163.

14. For a summary, see Gunduz, *The Knowledge of Life*, pp. 22–49; Green, *City of the Moon God*, pp. 6, 101–20.

15. Gunduz, *The Knowledge of Life*, pp. 32–37; Green, *City of the Moon God*, p. 4, 120.

16. Seyyed Hossein Nasr, *Islamic Life and Thought* (London: Allen and Unwin, 1981), p. 108; Gunduz, *The Knowledge of Life*, pp. 30–31; Green, *City of the Moon God*, pp. 121–22; D. S. Rice, 'Medieval Harran', *Anatolian Studies*, 2 (1952), pp. 36–84.

17. Steven Runciman, *A History of the Crusades* (Cambridge; Cambridge University Press, 3 vols, 195–54), passim; *The Travels of Ibn Jubayr*, translated by Roland J. C. Broadhurst (London: Cape, 1952), pp. 153–57; Rice, 'Medieval Harran', pp. 36–82.

18. *The Fihrist of Al-Nadim*, ed. and translated by Bayard Dodge (New York: Columbia University Press, 1970), pp. 745–73.

19. E.g. R. Campbell Thompson, *The Devils and Evil Spirits of Babylonia* (London, 1903), pp. xlii–xliii. In the calendars to be discussed below, 'the Seven' are clearly distinguished at times from the planetary divinities.

20. Detailed comparisons are made by Gunduz, *The Knowledge of Life*, pp. 143–83; and Green, *City of the Moon God*, pp. 145–60. The latter (p. 145) aptly says that they 'present innumerable difficulties of interpretation'.

21. A. J. Arberry, *Revelation and Reason in Islam* (London: Allen and Unwin, 1957), pp. 34–35; Gutas, *Greek Thought, Arab Culture*, p. 145; Nasr, *Islamic Life and Thought*, pp. 63–64; Charles Genequand, 'Platonism and Hermetism in Al-Kindi's *Fi al-Nafs*', *Zeitschrift fur Geschichte des Arabisch-Islamischen Wissenschaften*, 4 (1987–88), pp. 1–18. Genequand's stress on the Hermetic-Gnostic elements may, however, be contrasted with Ian Richard Netton, *Allah Transcendent* (Richmond: Curzon, 1994), pp. 45–98, who emphasises the influence of Aristotle, and C. A. Qadir, *Philosophy and Science in the Islamic World* (London: Croom Helm, 1988), p. 39, who cries up that of Stoicism.

22. Al-Kindi, *De radiis*, ed. by M. T. D'Alverny and F. Hudry, *Archives d'Histoire Doctrinale et Littéraire du Moyen Age*, 41 (1974), pp. 139–260.

23. Joel L. Kramer, *Philosophy in the Renaissance of Islam* (Brill: Leiden, 1986), pp. 20–21; Francis E. Peters, 'Hermes and Harran', in Michael M. Mazzaoui and Vera B. Moreen (ed.), *Intellectual Studies on Islam* (Salt Lake City: University of Utah Press, 1990), pp. 203–5; Bar Hebraeus, *The Chronology*, p. 152–53; Seyyed Hossein Nasr, *Science and Civilization in Islam* (Cambridge, Massachusetts: Harvard University Press, 1968), p. 44–45, 149, 170, 195.

24. Bar Hebraeus, *The Chronology*, p. 153; Walter Scott (ed.), *Hermetica* (Oxford: Oxford University Press, 1936), i, p. 105; Green, *City of the Moon God*, p. 114.

25. Frank Carmody (ed.), *The Astronomical Works of Thabit b. Qurra* (Berkeley: University of California Press, 1960), passim; quotation on p. 167.

26. Joel L. Kramer, *Humanism in the Renaissance of Islam* (Leiden: Brill, 1986), pp. 84–85.

27. D. Chwolsohn, *Die Sabier und der Sabismus* (St Petersburg: Imperial Academy, 1856), ii, 366–79; Gunduz, *The Knowledge of Life*, p. 31; Hadot, 'The Life and Work of Simplicius', pp. 280–300; Scott (ed.), *Hermetica*, iv, pp. 253–55.

28. Chwolsohn, *Die Sabier*, ii, p. 367.

29. Ibid., ii, pp. 381–83.

30. Ian Richard Netton, *Muslim Neoplatonists* (Edinburgh: Edinburgh University Press, 1991), passim; Henry Corbin, 'Ritual Sabeen et Exégèse Ismaelienne du Rituel', *Eranos Jahrbuch*, 19 (1950), pp. 181–246; Yves Marquet, 'Sabeens et Ihwan Al-Safa', *Studia Islamica* 24 (1966), pp. 35–80, and 25 (1966), pp. 77–109; Green, *City of the Moon God*, pp. 181–86, 207–10; George Widegren, 'The Pure Brethren and the Philosophical Basis of their System', in Alford T. Welch, *Islam: Past Influence and Present Challenge* (Albany: State University of New York Press, 1979), pp. 57–69; Seyyed Hossein Nasr, *An Introduction to Islamic Cosmological Doctrines* (Albany: State University of New York Press, 1993), pp. 25–104.

31. Chwolsohn, *Die Sabier*, ii, passim; Scott (ed.), *Hermetica*, iv, pp. 256–74; Gunduz, *The Knowledge of Life*, pp. 38–49.

32. E.g. Segal, 'The Sabian Mysteries'; and Bayard Dodge, 'The Sabians of Harran',

in Fuad Sarruf and Suha Tamim (ed.), *American University of Beirut Festival Book* (Beirut: American University, 1967), pp. 59–85.

33. Henry Corbin, *Temple and Contemplation* (London: KPI, 1986), pp. 132–82; Gunduz, *The Knowledge of Life*, pp. 135–213; Green, *City of the Moon God*, pp. 122–215.

34. Scott (ed.), *Hermetica*, i, p. 100; Athanassiadi, 'Persecution and Response in Late Paganism', pp. 25–29; Garth Fowden, 'Polytheist Religion and Philosophy', in Averil Cameron and Peter Garnsey (ed.), *The Cambridge Ancient History*, xiii (Cambridge: Cambridge University Press, 1998), pp. 554–55; Arberry, *Revelation and Reason in Islam*, p. 38; Kramer, *Humanism in the Renaissance of Islam*, pp. 84–85; Peters, 'Hermes and Harran', pp. 199–200; David Pingree, 'Some of the Sources of the *Ghayat al-Hakim*', *Journal of the Warburg and Courtauld Institutes*, 43 (1980), pp. 2–5; and 'Indian Planetary Images and the Tradition of Astral Magic', ibid., 52 (1989), pp. 8–11; Hildegard Levy, 'Points of Comparison between Zoroastrianism and the Moon-Cult of Harran', in Henning and Yarshalter (ed.), *A Locust's Leg*, pp. 139–61; H. E. Stapleton, 'The Antiquity of Alchemy', *Ambix*, 5 (1953), pp. 1–43; A. E. Affifi, 'The Influence of Hermetic Literature on Moslem Thought', *Bulletin of the School of Oriental Studies, London*, 13 (1949–50), p. 842; S. M. Stern, 'Abd al-Jabbar's Account of How Christ's Religion was Falsified by the Adoption of Roman Customs', *Journal of Theological Studies*, new series, 19 (1968), p. 160; and authors cited at nn. 32–33.

35. Peters, 'Hermes and Harran', p. 206.

36. For the Mandaeans, and their relationship to Sabianism, see, most recently, Gunduz, *The Knowledge of Life*, pp. 1–130, 133.

37. Green, *City of the Moon God*, pp. 6, 101, 124, 144–55, 160–62, 173–74, 215, 217.

38. Seton Lloyd and William Brice, 'Harran', *Anatolian Studies*, 1 (1951), pp. 77–111; Rice, 'Medieval Harran', pp. 36–84; Kay Prag, 'The 1959 Deep Sounding at Harran', *Levant*, 2 (1970), pp. 63–94; Nurrettin Yardmici, 'Excavations, Surveys and Restoration Works at Harran', in M. Frangipane et al. (ed.), *Between the Rivers and Over the Mountains* (Rome: University of Rome Press, 1993), pp. 439–49.

39. This was inspired by an article by Donald H. Frew, 'Harran: Last Refuge of Classical Paganism', *The Pomegranate*, 9 (1999), pp. 4–17, which apparently earned offers of money that have held out hope for a survey and excavation project: letter from Donald Frew, *The Pomegranate*, 11 (2000), p. 55.

40. J. B. Segal, 'Pagan Syriac Monuments in the Vilayet of Urfa', *Anatolian Studies*, 3 (1953), pp. 97–120; and 'Some Syriac Inscriptions of the 2nd–3rd Century AD', *Bulletin of the School of Oriental and African Studies*, 16 (1954), pp. 13–36; H. J. W. Drijvers, 'Some New Syriac Inscriptions and Archaeological Finds from Edessa and Sumatar Harabesi', ibid., 36 (1973), pp. 1–14. Gunduz, *The Knowledge of Life*, pp. 198–200; Green, *City of the Moon God*, pp. 71–72.

41. Kramer, *Humanism in the Renaissance of Islam*, pp. xix–xxiv, 76; Gutas, *Greek Thought, Arabic Culture*, pp. 1–14; Margaret Smith, *Studies in Early Mysticism in the Near and Middle East* (London: Sheldon, 1931), pp. 253–54; De Lacy

O'Leary, *Arab Thought and its Place in History* (London: Kegan Paul, 1922), pp. 1–55; Peters, 'Hermes and Harran', pp. 192–93.

42. Netton, *Allah Transcendent*, pp. 7–16.

43. Qadir, *Philosophy and Science in the Islamic World*, pp. 1–39.

44. Gerhard Bowering, *The Mystical Vision of Existence in Classical Islam* (Berlin: De Gruyter, 1980), pp. 50–58; Smith, *Studies in Early Mysticism*, pp. 191–97; Georges C. Anawati, 'Philosophy, Theology and Mysticism; in Joseph Schacht and C. E. Bosworth (ed.), *The Legacy of Islam* (Oxford: Oxford University Press, 2nd edn, 1979), pp. 371–76; Peter Kingsley, *Ancient Philosophy, Mystery and Magic* (Oxford: Oxford University Press, 1995), pp. 389–90.

45. Newton, *Allah Transcendent*, p. 7.

46. On this, see in particular Newton, *Allah Transcendent* and *Muslim Neoplatonists*; but also Kramer, *Philosophy in the Renaissance of Islam*; Smith, *Studies in Early Mysticism*; Nasr, *Islamic Life and Thought*; Parviz Morewedge (ed.), *Neoplatonism and Islamic Thought* (Albany: State University of New York Press, 1992); Affifi, 'Influence of Hermetic Literature'; and Paul E. Walker, *Early Philosophical Shiism* (Cambridge: Cambridge University Press, 1993).

47. For a classic mixture of formal condemnation mixed with obvious familiarity with the main literary works in question, see Ibn Khaldun, *The Muqaddimah*, translated by Franz Rosenthal (London: Routledge, 1958), iii, pp. 151–62.

48. A list of works attributed to ibn Wahshiyya is provided in the entry on him by Toufic Fahd in B. Lewis et al. (ed.), *The Encyclopaedia of Islam* (Leiden: Brill, new edition, 1971), iii, p. 963–65. Those available in translation are the *Kitab al-Filaha al-nabatiyya*, translated as *L'agriculture Nabateene* by Toufic Fahd (Damascus: Institute Français de Damas, 1993); the *Kitab al-Sumum*, translated as *Medieval Arabic Toxicology* by Martin Levy (Philadelphia: American Philosophical Society, 1966); and the *Kitab Shawk al-mustaham fi ma'rifat rumuz al-aklam*, translated as *Ancient Alphabets and Hieroglyphic Characters Explained* by Joseph von Hammer-Purgstall (London, 1806).

49. The debates are summarised in Seyyed Hossein Nasr, *Islamic Science* (Westerham, Kent: World of Islam Festival Publishing Company, 1976), pp. 56, 221; Peters, 'Hermes and Harran', p. 194; Manfred Ullmann, *Die Natur- und Geliemwissenschaften im Islam* (Leiden: Brill, 1972), pp. 440–42; M. Th. Houtsma et al. (ed.), *Encyclopaedia of Islam* (Brill: Leiden, 1913), ii., p. 427; Toufic Fahd, 'Retour à Ibn Wahshiyya', *Arabica*, 16 (1969), pp. 83–88, and in the introductions to the editions by Fahd and Levy, cited above, which have of course been those used for the present work. One of the puzzles thrown up by the texts credited to ibn Wahshiyya concerns a figure used to represent the secret of the world's nature, in the (completely bogus) list of translations of the Egyptian hieroglyphs given in his book on alphabets. It is labelled 'Bahumed', apparently the name of the important spirit indicated by the figure. It is well known that, at their trial in the early fourteenth century, the Knights Templar were accused of worshipping a demon called Baphomet. There is an agreement among current experts both that the Templars were innocent and the charges

against them fantasies, and that 'Baphomet' is merely an Old French corruption of Muhammed: a Provençal troubadour song of the 1260s gives the form 'Bafometz' for the prophet. Thus Peter Partner, *The Murdered Magicians: The Templars and their Myth* (Oxford: Oxford University Press, 1981), pp. 34, 138; and Malcolm Barber, *The New Knighthood: A History of the Order of the Temple* (Cambridge: Cambridge University Press, 1994), p. 321. Is there any connection between Bahumed and Baphomet? And if so, on which does it reflect most seriously: the opinions of experts on the Templars, or the authenticity of the text attributed to ibn Wahshiyya?

50. The text was only rediscovered by modern scholars in about 1920: Willy Harner, 'Notes on Picatrix', *Isis*, 56 (1965), pp. 438–51. It was translated into German as *Picatrix: Das Ziel des Wiesen von Pseudo-Magriti*, by Hellmut Ritter and Martin Plessner (London: Warburg Institute, 1962).

51. Pingree, 'Some of the Sources of the *Ghayat al-Hakim*', and 'Indian Planetary Images and the Tradition of Astral Magic', *Journal of the Warburg and Court-auld Institutes*, 52 (1989), pp. 1–13.

52. Chwolsohn, *Die Sabier*, ii, pp. 380–414.

53. Ritter and Plessner (ed.), *Picatrix*, book 3, ch. 7.

54. Ibid., book 2, ch. 12, and book 3, ch. 7. These accounts are discussed and compared with others in Gunduz, *The Knowledge of Life*, pp. 174, 212; and Green, *City of the Moon God*, pp. 179–80, 213–14.

55. All this is based on the work of my late colleague at Bristol, Jim Tester: S. J. Tester, *A History of Western Astrology* (Woodbridge: Boydell, 1987), pp. 11–29.

56. And others, such as an Arabic text transcribed in a fifteenth-century Italian manuscript and attributed to a tenth- century Spanish Muslim, which describes talismans particular to each planet: Kristen Lippincott and David Pingree, 'Ibn al-Haytim on the Talismans of the Lunar Mansions', *Journal of the Warburg and Courtauld Institutes*, 50 (1987), pp. 57–81.

57. IV.2891–2942 and VII.795–845. I have used the edition by Hans Dieter Betz, *The Greek Magical Papyri in Translation* (Chicago: University of Chicago Press, 1986). These texts are noted by Pingree, 'Some of the Sources of the *Ghayat al-Hakim*', p. 11.

58. Corpus Hermeticum II and XVI, and Asclepius I, ch. 3. I have used the edition by Walter Scott, *Hermetica* (Oxford: Oxford University Press, 1924).

59. Pingree, 'Some of the Sources of the *Ghayat al-Hakim*', pp. 5–6; Frances A. Yates, *Giordano Bruno and the Hermetic Tradition* (London: Routledge, 1964), pp. 47–49; Henry and Renee Kahane and Angelina Pietrangeli, 'Picatrix and the Talismans', *Romance Philology*, 19 (1966), pp. 574–93; Lynn Thorndike, *A History of Magic and Experimental Science*, i (London: Macmillan, 1923), pp. 582–87.

60. Hartner, 'Notes on Picatrix', p. 441.

61. Aristotle's view is in his *Metaphysics*, book 12, Cicero's in *On the Nature of the Gods*, book 2, section 15.

62. *De errore profanarum religionum*, edited by K. Ziegler (Leipzig, 1907).

63. *Mathesis*, edited by W. Kroll and F. Skutsch (Leipzig, 1896).
64. Thorndike, *History of Magic and Experimental Science*, i, p. 689; Tester, *History of Western Astrology*, pp. 132–42.
65. Lynn Thorndike, *A History of Magic and Experimental Science*, i (London: Macmillan, 1923), pp. 5–6.
66. Peter Brown, *Authority and the Sacred* (Cambridge: Cambridge University Press, 1995), p. 15.
67. Thorndike, *History of Magic and Experimental Science*, ii, pp. 5–6, 56–57, 103–104; Bernard Silvester, *De mundi universtate sive Megacosmus et Microcosmus*, edited in Bibliotheca Philosophorum Mediae Aetatis, 1 (Innsbruck, 1876), lines 1.36–7, 1.3.33, 2.4.49–50, 2.6.47.
68. Charles Burnett, *The Introduction of Arabic Learning into England* (London: British Library, 1997), pp. 2–39; Adelard of Bath, *Conversations with his Nephew*, edited and translated by Charles Burnett (Cambridge: Cambridge University Press, 1998), pp. xi–xix.
69. This is to accept the argument of Kahane and Pietrangeli, 'Picatrix and the Talismans'. The translation history of the text is anlaysed by David Pingree, 'Between the *Ghaya* and *Picatrix*, 1, The Spanish Verson', *Journal of the Warburg and Courtauld Institutes*, 44 (1981), pp. 27–56. David Pingree has also edited it: *Picatrix: The Latin Version of the Ghayat al-Hakim* (London: Warburg Institute, 1986).
70. Thorndike, *History of Magic and Experimental Science*, ii, pp. 323, 393, 445, 628–29.
71. William of Auvergne, *Opera omnia*, edited by Damian Zenaro (Venice, 1591), p. 895.
72. David Pingree, 'The Diffusion of Arabic Magical Texts in Western Europe', in *La diffusione delle scienze islamiche nel medio evo Europeo* (Rome: Accademia Nazionale dei Lincei, 1987), pp. 76–77.
73. William of Auvergne, *Opera*, pp. 64–82.
74. Pingree, 'Diffusion of Arabic Magical Texts', pp. 75–76.
75. Thorndike, *History of Magic and Experimental Science*, ii, pp. 588, 671–73, 697–98, 849–54, 900–1, 948–68.
76. Bibliothèque Nationale, MS 7337, pp. 1–9, 26.
77. Lynn Thorndike, *A History of Magic and Experimental Science*, iv (New York: Columbia University Press, 1934), pp. 117–23.
78. Kenneth Clark, *The Nude: A Study of Ideal Art* (London: Murray, 1956), p. 91.
79. For England alone, see G. Storms, *Anglo-Saxon Magic* (The Hague, 1948); British Library, Harleian MS 585; T. O. Cockayne, *Leechdoms, Wortcunning and Starcraft of Early England*, 3 volumes, Rolls Series (London, 1864–66); J. H. G. Grattan and C. Singer, *Anglo-Saxon Magic and Medicine* (Oxford: Oxford University Press, 1952); N. F. Barley, 'Anglo-Saxon Magico-Medicine', *Journal of the Anthropological Society of Oxford*, 3 (1972), pp. 67–77; Karen Louise Jolly, *Popular Religion in Late Saxon England* (Chapel Hill: University of North Carolina Press, 1996).

80. Robert Mathiesen, 'A Thirteenth-Century Ritual to Attain the Beatific Vision from the *Sworn Book* of Honorius of Thebes', in Claire Fanger (ed.), *Conjuring Spirits: Texts and Traditions of Medieval Magic* (Stroud: Sutton, 1998), pp. 143–62; Richard Kieckhefer, 'The Devil's Contemplatives: The *Liber Iuratus*, the *Liber Visionum* and Christian Appropriation of Jewish Occultism', in ibid., pp. 250–65;

81. British Library, Sloane MS 3854, fol. 129v (the manuscript concerned is one set of extracts from the *Liber Iuratus* or *Sworn Book* of Honorius).

82. Ibid., passim; Mathiesen, 'Thirteenth-Century Ritual', Claire Fanger, 'Plundering the Egyptian Treasure', in Fanger (ed.), *Conjuring Spirits*, pp. 216–49.

83. Nicholas Watson, 'John the Monk's *Book of Visions of the Blessed and Undefiled Virgin Mary, Mother of God*', in Fanger (ed.), *Conjuring Spirits*, pp. 163–215; Fanger, 'Plundering the Egyptian Treasure', pp. 216–49; Thorndike, *History of Magic and Experimental Science*, ii, pp. 281–83; Frank Klaassen, 'English Manuscripts of Magic, 1300–1500: A Preliminary Survey', in Fanger (ed.), *Conjuring Spirits*, pp. 14–19.

84. Nicholas Campion, *The Great Year* (London: Penguin, 1994), pp. 87–94; Al-Nadim, *The Fihrist*, edited and translated by Bayard Dodge (New York: Columbia, 1970), pp. 746–47.

85. Storms, *Anglo-Saxon Magic*, pp. 87–88.

86. Betz, *The Greek Magical Papyri in Translation*, papyrus iv, lines 2006–25; and vii, lines 846–61; Storms, *Anglo-Saxon Magic*, pp. 86–87; C. K. Barrett, *The New Testament Background: Selected Documents* (revised edn: London: SPCK, 1987), pp. 191–92; C. J. S. Thompson, *The Mysteries and Secrets of Magic* (London: Bodley Head, 1927), pp. 157–58.

87. William of Auvergne, *Opera omnia*, pp. 64–82.

88. This is to accept the argument for dating in Kieckhefer, 'The Devil's Contemplatives', pp. 253–54; and Norman Cohn, *Europe's Inner Demons* (Falmer: University of Sussex Press, 1975), p. 178. The copy that I know best is British Library, Sloane MS 3854, in which fos 127–32 are especially relevant here.

89. Bibliothèque Nationale, MS 7337, pp. 3–9.

90. Nicholas Eymeric, *Directorium inquisitorum*, edited by F. Pena (Rome, 1587), p. 338.

91. Richard Kieckhefer, *Magic in the Middle Ages* (Cambridge: Cambridge University Press, 1989), pp. 159–61; Thompson, *The Mysteries and Secrets of Magic*, pp. 157–64.

92. Ronald Hutton, *The Triumph of the Moon: A History of Modern Pagan Witchcraft* (Oxford: Oxford University Press, 1999), pp. 67–68.

93. Thorndike, *History of Magic and Experimental Science*, ii, pp. 5–6.

94. Ernst Robert Curtius, *European Literature and the Latin Middle Ages* (London: Routledge, 1953). p. 107; George D. Economou, *The Goddess Natura in Medieval Literature* (Cambridge, Massachusetts: Harvard University Press, 1972), pp. 28–52.

95. Ibid., pp. 53–58; Brian Stock, *Myth and Science in the Twelfth Century: A Study of Bernard Silvester* (Princeton: Princeton University Press, 1972), pp. 63–64.

96. Ibid., pp. 44–102.

97. Bernard Silvester, *De mundi universitate*; C. S. Lewis, *The Allegory of Love* (Oxford: Oxford University Press, 1936), pp. 90–97; Economou, *The Goddess Natura*, pp. 53–103; Stock, *Myth and Science in the Twelfth Century*, pp. 63–77.

98. Lewis, *Allegory of Love*, pp. 98–102; Economou, *The Goddess Natura*, pp. 53–103.

99. Lewis, *Allegory of Love*, pp. 109–111; Economou, *The Goddess Natura*, p. 103.

100. Jean de Meun, *Roman de la Rose*, edited by Ernest Langlois (Paris: Société des Anciens Textes Français 71, 1921–24), esp. lines 16233–44; Lewis, *Allegory of Love*, pp. 139, 149–50; Economou, *The Goddess Natura*, pp. 104–24.

101. Lewis, *Allegory of Love*, pp. 266–67.

102. Geoffrey Chaucer, *The Parlement of Briddes*, or *The Assembly of Foules*, ii, lines 295–308; J. A. W. Bennett, *The Parlement of Foules* (Oxford: Oxford University Press, 1957), passim; Economou, *The Goddess Natura*, pp. 125–50.

103. Lewis, *Allegory of Love*, pp. 271–75.

104. Curtius, *European Literature and the Latin Middle Ages*, p. 114.

105. Economou, *The Goddess Natura*, pp. 85–86.

106. In lines 113–19.

107. J. M. Clifton-Everest, *The Tragedy of Knighthood: Origins of the Tannhäuser Legend* (Oxford: Society for the Study of Medieval Languages and Literature, 1979), pp. v, 123–24.

108. Lewis, *Allegory of Love*, p. 121.

109. Clifton-Everest, *Tragedy of Knighthood*, pp. 1–16, 98, 123–27.

110. For Chaucer's treatment of her, see the lines listed under her entry in Eric Smith, *A Dictionary of Classical Reference in English Poetry* (Cambridge: Brewer, 1984).

111. The best overall summary of the tradition in English is probably still Carlo Ginzburg, *Ecstasies: Deciphering the the Witches' Sabbath* (English translation: Harmondsworth: Penguin, 1992), pp. 6–14, 90–138. For a sixteenth-century reference, see P. G. Maxwell-Stuart, *Witchcraft in Europe and the New World 1400–1800* (Basingstoke: Palgrave, 2001), p. 21.

112. John Duffy, 'Reactions of Two Byzantine Intellectuals to the Theory and Practice of Magic', in Henry Maguire (ed.), *Byzantine Magic* (Washington DC: Dumbarton Oaks Research Library, 1995), p. 83.

113. Nobody seems to have got past the analysis of this problem made by Walter Scott (ed.), *Hermetica* (Oxford: Oxford University Press, 1924), i, pp. 25–30.

114. Duffy, 'Reactions of Two Byzantine Intellectuals', pp. 83–92; Wilson, *Scholars of Byzantium*, pp. 153–66.

115. Georg Luck, 'Theurgy and Forms of Worship in Neoplatonism', in Jacob Neusner et al. (ed.), *Religion, Science and Magic* (Oxford: Oxford University Press, 1989), pp. 203–4.

116. Duffy, 'Reactions of two Byzantine Intellectuals', pp. 84–92.

117. Wilson, *Scholars of Byzantium*, pp. 161–66; C. M. Woodhouse, *George Gemistos Plethon: Last of the Hellenes* (Oxford: Oxford University Press, 1986), p. 70.

118. Duffy, 'Reactions of Two Byzantine Intellectuals', pp. 93–97.

119. Pingree, 'Some Sources of the *Ghayat al-Hakim*', pp. 9–10.

120. Kahane and Pietrangeli, 'Picatrix and the Talismans', pp. 574–89; Thorndike, *A History of Magic and Experimental Science*, ii, pp. 229–31.

121. Richard P. H. Greenfield, 'A Contribution to the Study of Palaeologan Magic', in Maguire (ed.), *Byzantine Magic*, pp. 117–53; and *Traditions of Belief in Late Byzantine Demonology* (Amsterdam: Hakkert, 1988), pp. 157–63, 220–33, 286–87.

122. The two recent considerations are Woodhouse, *George Gemistos Plethon*; and James Hankins, *Plato in the Italian Renaissance* (Leiden: Brill, 1990), i, pp. 197–206. A good listing of the various former authorities in the debate is provided in the latter book, in the notes to p. 197. Those employed here are Plethon, *Traité des Lois*, edited by G. Alexandre (Paris, 1858); Nesca A. Robb, *Neoplatonism of the Italian Renaissance* (London: Allen and Unwin, 1935), pp. 47–48; Milton V. Anastos, 'Pletho's Calendar and Liturgy', *Dumbarton Oaks Papers*, 4 (1948), pp. 185–305; I. Masai, *Plethon et le Platonisme de Mistra* (Paris: Belles Lettres, 1956); Eugenio Garin, *Astrology in the Renaissance*, translated by C. Jackson and J. Allen (London: Routledge, 1983), pp. 58–61; Ihor Sevcanko, 'The Palaeologian Renaissance', in Warren Treadgold (ed.), *Renaissances before The Renaissance* (Stanford, California: Stanford University Press, 1984), pp. 144–72.

123. Chuvin, *Chronicle of the Last Pagans*, pp. 149–50.

124. Scott (ed), *Hermetica*, i, p. 108, suggests that the Corpus Hermeticum might have been brought to the Byzantines by one of the Sabian community at Baghdad, fleeing the climate of persecution endured by his people both there and at their native Harran in the eleventh century. That the Hermetic texts were important to the Sabians seems virtually beyond doubt, and it is entirely possible that the Corpus came to the attention of Psellus and his fellow Greek scholars by this route. On the other hand, Scott himself describes this idea as 'an unproved hypothesis', without any actual evidence behind it, and it is at least as likely that Hermetic texts had survived in the Byzantine Empire itself, ignored or undervalued, until the literary revival of which Psellus was the greatest figure.

125. Woodhouse, *George Gemistos Plethon*, pp. 34–35.

126. Robb, *Neoplatonism of the Italian Renaissance*, pp. 47–58; James Hawkins, 'Cosimo de Medici and the 'Platonic Academy', *Journal of the Warburg and Courtauld Institutes*, 53 (1990), pp. 144–62.

127. Sevcanko, 'The Palaeologan Renaissance', pp. 170–71; Woodhouse, *George Gemistos Plethon*, p. 160; quotation on latter. For a detailed study of the 'Tempio dei Malatesta', see Adrian Stokes, *The Stones of Rimini* (London, 1934), pp. 169–256: I am grateful to A. V. Antonovics for this reference.

128. Thorndike, *History of Magic and Experimental Science*, ii, pp. 813–14.

129. Hankins, *Plato in the Italian Renaissance*, i, p. 206.

130. Ibid., i, pp. 207–62.

131. A. J. Dunston, 'Pope Paul and the Humanists', *Journal of Religious History*, 7 (1973), pp. 287–306; Richard J. Pallermino, 'The Roman Academy, the Catacombs and the Conspiracy of 1468', *Archivium Historiae Pontificiae*, 18 (1980), pp. 117–55; Harold B. Segel, *Renaissance Culture in Poland* (Ithaca, New York:

Cornell University Press, 1989), pp. 38–43; Hankins, *Plato in the Italian Renaissance*, i, pp. 211–13; Kate Lowe, 'The Political Crime of Conspiracy in Fifteenth- and Sixteenth-Century Rome', in Trevor Dean and K. J. P. Lowe (ed.), *Crime, Society and the Law in Renaissance Italy* (Cambridge: Cambridge University Press, 1994), pp. 184–203; Ingrid D. Rowland, *The Culture of the High Renaissance* (Cambridge: Cambridge University Press, 1998), pp. 10–17. I am very grateful to my colleague at Bristol, A. V. Antonovics, for most of these references, and the loan of one of the works.

132. This is based on the well-known analyses of D. P. Walker, *Spiritual and Demonic Magic from Ficino to Campanella* (London: Warburg Institute, 1958), pp. 35–51; Frances A. Yates, *Giordano Bruno and the Hermetic Tradition* (London: Routledge, 1964), pp. 56–67; and Brian Copenhaver, 'Hermes Trismegistus, Proclus, and the Question of a Philosophy of Magic in the Renaissance', in Ingrid Merkel and Allen G. Debus (ed.), *Hermeticism and the Renaissance* (Washington DC: Folger Shakespeare Library, 1988), pp. 79–110.

133. Marsilio Ficino, *Opera omnia* (2nd edn, Basle, 1576), pp. 532–72.

134. Walker, *Spiritual and Demonic Magic*, pp. 32–33; Yates, *Giordano Bruno*, p. 82.

135. This is based on the views of Edgar Wind, *Pagan Mysteries in the Renaissance* (London: Faber, 2nd edn, 1967), pp. 36, 81–123; Yates, *Giordano Bruno*, pp. 68–69; and Robb, *Neoplatonism of the Italian Renaissance*, pp. 79–104.

136. Ficino, *Opera omnia*, pp. 1326–27.

137. Ibid., p. 805.

138. Wind, *Pagan Mysteries in the Renaissance*, pp. 26–52; E. H. Gombrich, 'Botticelli's Mythologies', *Journal of the Warburg and Courtauld Institutes*, 8 (1945), pp. 34–36.

139. Hankins, *Plato in the Italian Renaissance*, i, 282.

140. Gombrich, 'Botticelli's Mythologies', p. 33; Wind, *Pagan Mysteries*, pp. 36–52.

141. Yates, *Giordano Bruno*, pp. 84–107; quotation on p. 107.

142. Ibid., pp. 112–15; Thorndike, *History of Magic and Experimental Science*, iv, pp. 501–4. For a detailed discussion of the paintings of the Borgia Apartment, in the Vatican, see F. Saxl, *Lectures* (London: Warburg Institute, 1957), pp. 174–88: I am grateful to A. V. Antonovics for this reference.

143. Robb, *Neoplatonism of the Italian Renaissance*, pp. 104–55.

144. Walker, *Spiritual and Demonic Magic*, pp. 30–33.

145. Gombrich, 'Botticelli's Mythologies', pp. 7–60; Yates, *Giordano Bruno*, p. 77; for a different view, still recognising the importance of Ficino, see Charles Dempsey, *The Portrayal of Love* (Princeton: Princeton University Press, 1992), esp. pp. 160–62. I am grateful to A. V. Antonovics for this latter reference.

146. Girolamo Torrella, *Opus praeclarum de imaginibus astrologicis* (Valencia, 1496).

147. The edition that I have used is the translation by James Freake, edited by Donald Tyson (St Paul, Minnesota: Llewellyn, 2000).

148. Ibid., pp. 4–7.

149. Ibid., pp. 8–430.

150. Ibid., pp. 441–677.

151. Johannes Trithemius, *Steganographia* (Frankfurt, 1606), pp. 162–77.

152. Walker, *Spiritual and Demonic Magic*, pp. 112–19.

153. Seznec, *The Survival of the Pagan Gods*, pp. 80–83.

154. Quoted in Yates, *Giordano Bruno*, p. 165.

155. Ibid., pp. 157–59.

156. Lynn Thorndike, *A History of Magic and Experimental Science*, vi (New York: Columbia University Press, 1941), p. 392.

157. Warburg Institute, London, 'Tuba Veneris'.

158. Fabio Paolini, *Hebdomades* (Venice, 1589), pp. 207–9.

159. Yates, *Giordano Bruno*, p. 176.

160. Thorndike, *History of Magic and Experimental Science*, vi, pp. 147, 156.

161. Lynn Thorndike, *A History of Magic and Experimental Science*, v (New York: Columbia University Press, 1970), pp. 569–73; and vi, pp. 152–53.

162. Paolini, *Hebdomades*, p. 209.

163. Yates, *Giordano Bruno*, pp. 181–84.

164. Ibid., pp. 158–59; Thorndike, *History of Magic and Experimental Science*, vi, pp. 304–24; Walker, *Spiritual and Demonic Magic*, pp. 152–85.

165. Patricia Merivale, *Pan the Goat-God: His Myth in Modern Times* (Cambridge, Massachusetts: Harvard University Press, 1969), pp. 11–24; John Boardman, *The Great God Pan: The Survival of an Image* (London: Thames and Hudson, 1997), p. 9. For Pan's nineteenth-century literary career, see Ronald Hutton, *The Triumph of the Moon: A History of Modern Pagan Witchcraft* (Oxford: Oxford University Press, 1999), pp. 43–51.

166. Edmund Spenser, *The Faerie Queen*, book 8, lines 8–15.

167. See the frontispieces to Robert Fludd, *Utriusque cosmi historia* (Oppenheim, 1617), and Athanasius Kircher, *Ars magna lucis et umbrae* (Rome, 1646).

168. This is quoted in C. J. S. Thompson, *The Mysteries and Secrets of Magic* (London, 1927), p. 58, as taken from a sixteenth-century manuscript in the British Library. Thompson gives no exact reference for it, any more than for any other parts of the book, but he accurately lists in a bibliography the full collection of early modern manuscripts of magical rites and recipes held in that library by his time. I have not systematically worked through them, and have not come across the original of this spell, but wherever I have read particular items in the pursuit of other enquiries, I have found Thompson's quotations to be accurate; so I take the risk of citing this one here.

169. Yates, *Giordano Bruno*, pp. 190–202. The books concerned were *De umbris idearum* and *Cantus circaeus*.

170. Yates, *Giordano Bruno*, pp. 211–60. The books concerned were *Spaccio della bestia trionfante* and *Cena de le ceneri*; quotation on p. 212.

171. Yates, *Giordano Bruno*, pp. 264–355. The manuscript works concerned were *Lampas triginta statuarum* and *De Magia*.

172. The view of Walker, *Spiritual and Demonic Magic*, pp. 224–25; and Yates, *Giordano Bruno*, p. 360.

173. Yates, *Giordano Bruno*, pp. 360–73.

174. Walker, *Spiritual and Demonic Magic*, pp. 207–13.

175. Ibid., pp. 207–36; Yates, *Giordano Bruno*, pp. 374–75.

176. Yates, *Giordano Bruno*, pp. 398–405.

177. Lynn Thorndike, *A History of Magic and Experimental Science*, vii (New York: Columbia University Press, 1958), passim; Gaffarel on pp. 304–5.

178. For this, see Alexandra Walsham, *Providence in Early Modern England* (Oxford: Oxford University Press, 1999), pp. 21–25.

179. On which see Hutton, *Triumph of the Moon*, pp. 84–111.

180. E.g. David Boyd Haycock, *William Stukeley* (Woodbridge: Boydell, 2002), pp. 57, 97–98.

181. S. Guy Endore, *Casanova: His Known and Unknown Life* (London: Routledge, 1930), pp. 78, 119–25, 208–19, where the accounts in the *Memoirs* are checked against contemporary records.

182. *Krata Repoa* (Berlin, 1782).

183. Timothy Mowl, 'In the Realm of the Great God Pan', *Country Life*, 17 October 1996, pp. 54–59.

184. A story sketched out provisionally in Hutton, *Triumph*.

Notes to Chapter 6: A Modest Look at Ritual Nudity

1. Ronald Hutton, *The Pagan Religions of the Ancient British Isles* (Oxford: Blackwell, 1991), p. 337.

2. Ronald Hutton, *The Triumph of the Moon: A History of Modern Pagan Witchcraft* (Oxford: Oxford University Press, 1999), p. 410.

3. Gerald Gardner, *Witchcraft Today* (London: Rider, 1954), pp. 19–24; Justine Glass, *Witchcraft: The Sixth Sense – and Us* (London: Spearman, 1965), p. 101; Patricia and Arnold Crowther, *The Witches Speak* (Douglas: Athol, 1965), p. 148; Doreen Valiente, *Witchcraft for Tomorrow* (London: Hale, 1978), pp. 98–99; Starhawk, *The Spiral Dance* (San Francisco: Harper and Row, 1979), p. 60; Janet and Stewart Farrar, *The Life and Times of a Modern Witch* (London: Piatkus, 1987), pp. 85–92; Vivianne Crowley, *Wicca: The Old Religion in the New Age* (London: Aquarian, 1989), pp. 59–60.

4. Hutton, *Triumph of the Moon*, p. 407.

5. Ibid., p. 399.

6. Plain in his ghosted autobiography, Jack Bracelin, *Gerald Gardner: Witch* (London: Octagon, 1960).

7. Hutton, *Triumph of the Moon*, pp. 205–40.

8. K. Weinhold, 'Zur Geschichte des Heidnischen Ritus', *Abhandlungen d. Kon. Akad. D. Wissenschaften zu Berlin 1896* (philo-hist. Kl.), no. 1, pp. 1–50; J. Heckenbach, *De nuditate sacrisque vinculis* (Giessen, 1911), pp. 1–63.

9. Cf. H. W. F. Saggs, *The Greatness That Was Babylon* (London: Sidgwick and Jackson, 1962), pp. 28, 182.

10. A recent summary of the utter lack of expert agreement on the meaning of the paintings may be found in Mary Beard, John North and Simon Price,

Religions of Rome, i, *A History* (Cambridge: Cambridge University Press, 1998), pp. 162–64.

11. R. Delbruek and W. Vollgraff, 'An Orphic Bowl', *Journal of Hellenic Studies*, 54 (1934), pp. 129–39; Hans Leisgang, 'The Mystery of the Serpent' (1939), repr. in Joseph Campbell (ed.), *The Mysteries: Papers from the Eranos Yearbooks* (Princeton University Press: Bollingen Yearbooks 30, no. 2, 1955), pp. 194–260.

12. H. H. Scullard, *Festivals and Ceremonies of the Roman Republic* (London: Thames and Hudson, 1981), pp. 76–78. Ovid's account is in his *Fasti*, ii, lines 267–440.

13. Scullard, *Festivals and Ceremonies*, pp. 110–11. Martial's comment is in his *Epigrams*, i.35.8.

14. Such as Scullard, at n. 11 above.

15. The passage is translated in G. Jones, *A History of the Vikings* (Oxford: Oxford University Press, 1968), pp. 425–30.

16. Diodorus Siculus, *Library of History*, i.85.3. By contrast, the description by Herodotus, of a similar gesture employed by women en route to the religious festival at Bubastis in the Nile delta, seems to belong to a different category. In his account, they formed part of groups of revellers travelling to the festivities by boat along the river and making merry as they went. When they passed a riverside town, some of the women exposed their genitals to the inhabitants as one of a number of gestures which also included the shouting of mockery at local females. The context seems therefore to be one of ribaldry and playful insult rather than of piety; the equivalent of the modern 'flashing' or 'mooning'. The festival at Bubastis was both the biggest in Egypt at that time and particularly associated with drunkenness: Herodotus, *Histories*, book 2, ch. 60, line 20. All classical references are to Loeb Classics Library editions, unless otherwise stated.

17. Pliny, *Natural History*, book 32, ch. 2.

18. Leisgang, 'The Mystery of the Serpent', p. 254: the quotation is from Epiphanius, *Catholicae et Apostolicae Ecclesiae Fidei expositio*, ch. 10.

19. Delbruek and Vollgraaf, 'An Orphic Bowl', p. 132; Heckenbach, *De nuditate*, p. 13; Aristophanes, *The Clouds*, line 498.

20. Walter Burkert, *Structure and History in Greek Mythology and Ritual* (Berkeley: University of California Press, 1979), p. 29, and *Greek Religion: Archaic and Classical* (Oxford: Blackwell, 1985), p. 261.

21. Plotinus, *Enneads*, book 1, ch. 6, line 7.

22. *The Chaldean Oracles*, ed. Ruth Majercik (Leiden: Brill, 1989), p. 93.

23. Burkert, *Greek Religion*, p. 263.

24. Ibid., p. 78. For Phryne's famous adventures and misadventures, see Athenaeus, *The Deipnosophists*, book 13, sections 590–91.

25. M. J. Vermaseren, *Mithras: The Secret God* (London: Chatto and Windus, 1963), pp. 131–33.

26. This and what follows is based on Jonathan Z. Smith, 'The Garments of Shame', *History of Religions*, 5 (1965–66), pp. 217–38; and Margaret A. Miles, *Carnal*

Knowing: Female Nakedness and Religious Meaning in the Christian West (Boston: Beacon, 1989), pp. 37–49.

27. For which see Norman Cohn, *Europe's Inner Demons* (Falmer: Sussex University Press, 1975), pp. 1–125, and sources cited there.

28. Epiphanius, *Panarion*, book 26, section 5. The edition used was that of the Akademie Verlag, Berlin, 1985.

29. Hippolytus, *Elenchos*, book 5, ch. 8, lines 41–43. The edition used was that of De Gruyter, 1986.

30. David Cressy, *Travesties and Transgressions in Tudor and Stuart England* (Oxford: Oxford University Press, 1999), pp. 257–58.

31. Ibid., p. 258.

32. Jeffrey Burton Russell, *Witchcraft in the Middle Ages* (Ithaca, New York: Cornell University Press, 1972), p. 224.

33. Howard Kaminsky, *A History of the Hussite Revolution* (Berkeley: University of California Press, 1967), pp. 422–32.

34. Cressy, *Travesties and Transgressions*, pp. 259–69.

35. Russell, *Witchcraft in the Middle Ages*, p. 260.

36. Peter Streider, *Dürer: Paintings, Prints, Drawings* (London: Muller, 1982), pp. 182–84; Kenneth Clark, *The Nude: A Study of Ideal Art* (London: Murray, 1956), pp. 315–16; Charles Zika, 'Dürer's Witch, Riding Women and Moral Order', in Dagmar Eichberger and Charles Zika (ed.), *Dürer and his Culture* (Cambridge: Cambridge University Press, 1998), pp. 118–40.

37. Zika, 'Dürer's Witch', pp. 131–40; Charles Zika, 'She-Man: Visual Representations of Witchcraft and Sexuality in Sixteenth-Century Europe', in Andrew Lynch and Philippa Maddern (ed.), *Venus and Mars* (Perth: University of Western Australia Press, 1995), pp. 147–90; Joseph Leo Koerner, *The Moment of Self-Portraiture in German Renaissance Art* (Chicago: University of Chicago Press, 1993), pp. 323–35; Miles, *Carnal Knowing*, pp. 125–39.

38. Pierre de Lancre, *Tableau de l'inconstance des mauvais anges* (2nd edn, Paris, 1611).

39. François Ravaisson, *Archives de la Bastille* (Paris, 1873), pp. 333–36.

40. Charles Godfrey Leland, *Aradia: Gospel of the Witches* (1990 reprint: Phoenix, Washington: Custer, 1990), p. 7.

41. Hutton, *Triumph of the Moon*, pp. 141–48; Leland, *Aradia*, trans. Mario and Dina Pazzaglini (London: Hale, 1998).

42. Martin del Rio, *Investigations into Magic*, ed. P. G. Maxwell-Stuart (Manchester: Manchester University Press, 2000), p. 197. See also p. 97 for a general comment that people were sometimes sighted abroad without clothes and assumed to be travelling to or from the sabbat.

43. Lyndal Roper, 'Evil Imaginings and Fantasies: Child-Witches and the End of the Witch Craze', *Past and Present*, 167 (May 2000), pp. 107–39.

44. Doreen Valiente, *Witchcraft for Tomorrow* (London: Hale, 1978), pp. 136; Sir John Woodroffe, *S'akti and S'akta* (Madras: Ganesh, 3rd edn, 1927), pp. 388–90.

45. The reports are in *Green Egg*, 87 (1989), p. 9, and Cec Cinder, *The Nudist Idea* (Riverside, California: Ultraviolet, 1998), p. xv. The works which I have

consulted for goddesses are Osborn Martin, *The Gods of India* (Delhi: Ideological Book House, 1972); and David Kinsley, *Hindu Goddesses* (Berkeley: University of California Press, 1986).

46. George Caitlin, *Letters and Notes on the Manners, Customs and Conditions of the North American Indians* (New York, 1841), i, p. 166; R. C. Mayne, *Four Years in British Columbia and Vancouver Island* (London, 1862), pp. 284–88.

47. Waldemar Jochelson, *The Koryak* (Leiden, 1908), p. 66.

48. John Williams, quoted in Derek Freeman, *Margaret Mead and Samoa* (Cambridge, Massachussets: Harvard University Press, 1983), pp. 230–31.

49. William Alexander, quoted in T. Walter Herbert Jnr, *Marquesan Encounters* (Cambridge, Massachusetts: Harvard University Press, 1980), p. 42.

50. For a full development of this perception, see Ronald Hutton, 'The Global Context of the Scottish Witch-Hunt', in Julian Goodare (ed.), *The Scottish Witch-Hunt in Context* (forthcoming from Edinburgh University Press).

51. John Beattie, 'Sorcery in Bunyoro', in John Middleton and E. H. Winter (ed.), *Witchcraft and Sorcery in East Africa* (London: Routledge, 1963), pp. 27–55; T. O. Beidelman, 'Witchcraft in Ukaguru', in ibid., pp. 57–98; Robert F. Gray, 'Some Structural Aspects of Mbugwe Witchcraft', in ibid., pp. 143–73; Robert A. LeVine, 'Witchcraft and Sorcery in a Gusii Community', in ibid., pp. 221–55; E. H. Winter, 'The Enemy Within: Amba Witchcraft and Sociological Theory', in ibid., pp. 277–99; R. G. Willis, 'Kamcape: An Anti-Sorcery Movement in South-West Tanzania', *Africa* 38 (1968), pp. 3–4; J. R. Crawford, *Witchcraft and Sorcery in Rhodesia* (Oxford: Oxford University Press, 1967), pp. 26, 121; E. Jensen Krige and J. D. Krige, *The Realm of a Rain-Queen* (Oxford, 1943), p. 251; Hugh A. Stayt, *The BaVenda* (Oxford, 1931), pp. 273–74; Harriet Ngubane, 'Aspects of Zulu Treatment', in J. B. Loudon (ed.), *Social Anthropology and Medicine* (London: Academic Press, 1976), p. 328; Gunter Wagner, *The Bantu of Western Kenya* (Oxford: Oxford University Press, 1970), p. 113; May Mandelbaum Edel, *The Chiga of Western Uganda* (Oxford: Oxford University Press, 1957), p. 165; Isak A. Niehaus, 'Witch-Hunting and Political Legitimacy: Continuity and Change in Green Valley, Lebowa, 1930–91', *Africa*, 63 (1993), p. 503; Suzette Heald, 'Witches and Thieves: Deviant Motivations in Gisu Society', *Man*, new series, 21 (1986), p. 74.

52. Krige and Krige, *Realm of a Rain-Queen*, p. 251; Stayt, *The BaVenda*, p. 274; Wagner, *Bantu of Western Kenya*, p. 113.

53. Beidelman, 'Witchcraft in Ukaguru', pp. 57–98; LeVine, 'Witchcraft and Sorcery in a Gusii Community', pp. 221–55; Winter, 'The Enemy Within', pp. 277–99.

54. Julius Wellhausen, *Reste Arabischen Heidenthums* (Berlin, 1897), p. 159.

55. W. Crooke, *An Introduction to the Popular Religion and Folklore of Northern India* (Allahabad, 1894), pp. 352–56, 366–67.

56. Bronislaw Malinowski, *Argonauts of the Western Pacific* (London: Routledge, 1922), p. 242; Waldemar Bogoras, *The Chukchee* (Brill, 1909), pp. 448–49.

57. Clyde Kluckhorn, *Navaho Witchcraft* (Cambridge, Massachusetts: Peabody Museum, 1944), ch. 2, section 3.

58. Edel, *The Chiga*, p. 165; LeVine, 'Witchcraft and Sorcery', p. 232.

59. I Samuel 19.24; Isaiah 20.2–3.

60. Cressy, *Travesties and Transgressions*, pp. 277–78.

61. Anne-Marie Tupet, *La magie dans la poèsie latine* (Paris: Société d'Edition "Les Belles Lettres", 1976), vol. 1, p. 60.

62. Pliny, *Natural History*, book 2, section 60. The famous passage in the same work at book 8, section 23, lines 77–78, describing how women who walked naked around a cornfield were believed to destroy insect pests in it, has no place in the present study. That whole section of Pliny is devoted to the dangerous properties of menstrual blood, and the central point of the belief cited above is that the women concerned were menstruating, and their flows overcame the pests; their nudity was just a practical aid to the loosing of the allegedly baneful power of the blood.

63. These spells are collected in Peter Haining, *The Warlock's Book* (London: W. H. Allen, 1972), pp. 61–62, and taken from manuscripts in the British Library. Mr Haining never gives any precise references for these, but as I have come across other passages which he quotes from documents in the same collection in the originals, and found his transcription to be accurate, I accept these.

64. Russell, *Witchcraft in the Middle Ages*, pp. 209–10; Franco Mormando, *The Preacher's Demons: Bernardino of Siena and the Social Underworld of Early Renaissance Italy* (Chicago: University of Chicago Press, 1999), pp. 77–80.

65. Margaret Alice Murray, *The Witch-Cult in Western Europe* (Oxford: Oxford University Press, 1921), p. 173.

66. Roy Palmer, *The Folklore of Warwickshire* (London: Batsford, 1976), pp. 85–86; Aubrey Burl, *Great Stone Circles* (New Haven: Yale University Press, 1999), p. 23.

67. Violet Alford, *Sword Dance and Drama* (London: Merlin, 1962), p. 209.

68. Carlo Ginzburg, *Ecstasies: Deciphering the Witches' s Sabbath* (Harmondsworth: Penguin, 1989), pp. 264–65.

69. J. G. Frazer, *The Magic Art and the Evolution of Kings* (London, 1911), i, p. 282.

70. Ibid., pp. 282–84.

71. P. J. de Arriaga, *Extirpacion de la idolatria del Piru* (Lima, 1621), pp. 36–40.

72. Frazer, *The Magic Art*, ii, p. 100.

73. Monica Hunter, *Reaction to Conquest* (Oxford: Oxford University Press, 1961), pp. 298–99.

74. Hutton, *Triumph of the Moon*, pp. 394–97.

75. Rosemary Ellen Guiley, *The Encyclopedia of Witches and Witchcraft* (2nd edn, NewYork: Checkmark, 1999), p. 197. I am very grateful to the author for the gift of this work.

Notes to Chapter 7: The Inklings and the Gods

General note: Lewis made the plural of dwarf into 'dwarfs', Tolkien into 'dwarves'. Both are philologically quite permissable, and I have used the former simply because I discuss Lewis first.

1. David Cecil, 'Is there an Oxford 'School' of Writing?', *The Twentieth Century*, 67 (1955), p. 562.

2. J. S. Ryan, *Tolkien: Cult or Culture?* (Armidale, Australia: University of New England, 1969), p. 33.

3. W. H. Lewis (ed.), *Letters of C. S. Lewis* (London: Geoffrey Bles, 1966), p. 283. I am very grateful to Ana Adnan for the loan of this work.

4. Quoted in Willis B. Glover, 'The Christian Character of Tolkien's Invented World', *Mythlore*, 10 (1975), p. 3.

5. E.g., by ibid., pp. 3–8; C. S. Kilby, 'The Christian Interpretation of Tolkien', *Mythlore*, 1.1 (1969), pp. 27–29; Mary Carman Rose, 'The Christian Neoplatonism of C. S. Lewis, J. R. R. Tolkien and Charles Williams', in Dominic J. O'Meara (ed.), *Neoplatonism and Christian Thought* (Albany State University of New York Press, 1982), pp. 203–4; Colin Duriez, 'Sub-Creation and Tolkien's Theology of Story', in K. J. Battarbee (ed.), *Scholarship and Fantasy: Proceedings of the Tolkien Phenomenon* (Turku, Finland: University of Turku, Anglicana Turkuensia, 12, 1993), p. 146; Joseph Pearce, *Tolkien: Man and Myth* (London: HarperCollins, 1998), pp. 83–125.

6. Of these the earliest was probably Ryan, *Tolkien*, pp. 132–35, 155–59; the most erudite probably T. A. Shippey, *The Road to Middle Earth* (London: Grafton, 1992), and *J. R. R. Tolkien: Author of the Century* (London: HarperCollins, 2000); the most forceful probably Patrick Curry, *Defending Middle Earth* (London: Floris, 1997).

7. Ibid., p. 117.

8. C. S. Lewis, *Surprised By Joy: The Shape of My Early Life* (London: Bles, 1955), pp. 23, 62–64, 74, 111–15, 164–69; Lewis (ed.), *Letters*, pp. 110–11; George Sayer, *Jack: A Life of C. S. Lewis* (London: Hodder and Stoughton, 1988), pp. 86, 98–109 (I am very grateful to Ana Adnan for the gift of this book); Walter Hooper (ed.), *They Stand Together: The Letters of C. S. Lewis to Arthur Greeves, 1914–1963* (London: Collins, 1979), pp. 59–192.

9. Lewis, *Surprised By Joy*, p. 57.

10. Hooper (ed.), *They Stand Together*, p. 62.

11. Ibid., p. 72.

12. Ibid., p. 77.

13. Ibid., p. 135.

14. Lewis (ed.), *Letters of C. S. Lewis*, p. 64.

15. Ibid., p. 89.

16. Sayer, *Jack*, p. 86; Humphrey Carpenter, *The Inklings* (London: Allen and Unwin, 1978), p. 7.

17. Hooper (ed.), *They Stand Together*, pp. 56–57.

18. C. S. Lewis, *Spirits in Bondage*, ed. by Walter Hooper (San Diego: Jovanovich, 1984), p. xxxvii.

19. Ibid., p. 23.

20. Ibid., pp. 53, 61–62.

21. Lewis, *Surprised By Joy*, pp. 77–78, 111, 115, 205.

22. Carpenter, *The Inklings*, pp. 40–41, 46–47; quotations on last two pages.

23. Lewis, *Surprised By Joy*, p. 166. By 1926 he had already turned against ritual magic, with a loathing that was to last for the the remainder of his life and manifest in the Narnia novels. He ascribed this change to the madness and death of a friend, which he blamed on Spiritualism (a movement that is, in fact, not at all the same thing as ceremonial magic): C. S. Lewis, Preface to the 1950 edition of *Dymer*, reprinted in C. S. Lewis, *Narrative Poems*, ed. by Walter Hooper (London: Bles, 1969); p. 5 in the 1994 Fount Paperback edition. I am very grateful to Ana Adnan for the loan of this work.

24. Ibid., p. 221; Hopper (ed.), *They Stand Together*, p. 427. For Tolkien's role, see Carpenter, *The Inklings*, pp. 43–44.

25. Hooper (ed.), *They Stand Together*, pp. 367, 374, 411, 430.

26. Lewis, *Narrative Poems*, pp. 168–73.

27. C. S. Lewis, *The Pilgrim's Regress* (London: Bles, 1933), pp. 151–55.

28. C. S. Lewis, *The Allegory of Love* (Oxford: Oxford University Press, 1936). For the length of time spent on it, Lewis (ed.), *Letters of C. S. Lewis*, pp. 20, 127.

29. London: Bodley Head, 1938.

30. *Perelandra* (London: Bodley Head, 1943).

31. Lewis (ed.), *Letters of C. S. Lewis*, p. 195.

32. C. S. Lewis, *That Hideous Strength* (London: Bodley Head, 1944); p. 681 in the Pan Books 1989 reprint of the trilogy.

33. Lewis, *That Hideous Strength*, pp. 540, 679 in the Pan edition.

34. Walter Hooper, *C. S. Lewis: A Companion and Guide* (London: HarperCollins, 1996), pp. 585, 598, 672.

35. C. S. Lewis, *The Abolition of Man* (Oxford: Oxford University Press, 1944), pp. 9–11, 41–48.

36. C. S. Lewis, *Miracles* (London: Collins, 1947), p. 115.

37. Carpenter, *The Inklings*, p. 227. Publication was more carefully staggered, between 1950 and 1956.

38. Sayer, *Jack*, p. 255.

39. C. S. Lewis, 'Sometimes Fairy Stories May Say Best What's to be Said', reprinted in C. S. Lewis, *Of This and Other Worlds*, ed. by Walter Hooper (London: Collins, 1982), p. 73. I am very grateful to Ana Adnan for the loan of this work.

40. Paul Ford, *Companion to Narnia* (San Francisco: Harper and Row, 1980), pp. 51–56. See also Walter Hooper, *Past Watchful Dragons: The Narnian Chronicles of C. S. Lewis* (London: Collier Macmillan, 1979), pp. 94–118; and T. A. Shippey, 'The Chronicles of Narnia', in Frank N. Magill (ed.), *Survey of Modern Fantasy Literature* (Englewood Cliffs, New Jersey: Salem, 1983), pp. 248–55, for different evaluations of the Christian element in the books, which both agree to be very strong but Tom Shippey sees as more complex and problematic. His reading of them should be set against my own, as examples of difference of vision and emphasis.

41. Lewis (ed.), *Letters of C. S. Lewis*, p. 215.

42. C. S. Lewis, 'It All Began With A Picture ...', in Lewis, *Of This and Other Worlds*, p. 79.

43. Lewis, 'Sometimes Fairy Stories May Say Best What's to be Said', p. 72.

44. Ford, *Companion to Narnia*, p. 206.

45. C. S. Lewis, *Prince Caspian* (London: Bles, 1951), pp. 24, 135–38 in the Puffin edition of 1962.

46. Hooper, *Past Watchful Dragons*, p. 107.

47. Hooper, *C. S. Lewis: A Companion*, p. 438. There is apparently a reference to the doctrine in the fifth book, *The Horse and His Boy*, when Aslan, asked who he is, replies 'Myself' three times. If so, the point is made with a subtlety likely to cause it to slip past most adult readers, let alone the children at whom the works were primarily aimed; p. 139 in the 1965 Puffin edition.

48. C. S. Lewis, *The Lion, The Witch and the Wardrobe* (London: Bles, 1950); p. 74 in the 1962 Puffin edition.

49. 'B. B.', *The Little Grey Men* (London, 1942).

50. C. S. Lewis, 'On Stories', in Lewis, *Of This and Other Worlds*, p. 38. For the place of Grahame's work in neo-paganism, see Ronald Hutton, *The Triumph of the Moon* (Oxford: Oxford University Press, 1999), pp. 28, 44–45, 118, 154–55.

51. For an especially effective version of this argument, setting it in the context of the book as a whole, see Shippey, 'The Chronicles of Narnia', pp. 253–54.

52. Ford, *Companion to Narnia*, p. 206.

53. C. S. Lewis, *The Last Battle* (London: Bodley Head, 1956); pp. 152–63 in the 1964 Puffin edition; quotation on p. 154. Cf. Rose, 'The Christian Platonism of C. S. Lewis', p. 204.

54. C. S. Lewis, *English Literature in the Sixteenth Century* (Oxford: Oxford University Press, 1954), p. 342.

55. C. S. Lewis, *Reflections on the Psalms* (London: Bles, 1958), pp. 99–108; quotation on p. 105.

56. Lewis (ed.), *Letters of C. S. Lewis*, pp. 286, 300.

57. Roger Lancelyn Green and Walter Hooper, *C. S. Lewis: A Biography* (London: Collins, 1974), pp. 294–95.

58. C. S. Lewis, *The Discarded Image: An Introduction to Medieval and Renaissance Literature* (Cambridge: Cambridge University Press, 1964), p. 11.

59. On which see Carpenter, *J. R. R. Tolkien*, pp. 22–106; and Shippey, *J. R. R. Tolkien*, pp. 1–50.

60. Suggested by Ryan, *Tolkien*, pp. 132–40; Randel Helms, *Tolkien's World* (London: Thames and Hudson, 1974), p. 15; Shippey, *Tolkien*, passim but esp. pp. 179, 259–62; George Clark, 'J. R. R. Tolkien and the True Hero', in George Clark and Daniel Timmons (ed.), *J. R. R. Tolkien and his Literary Resonances* (Westport, Connecticut: Greenwood, 2000), p. 39; Douglass Parker, 'Hwaet We Holbylta', *Hudson Review*, 9 (Winter, 1956–67), pp. 598–609.

61. J. R. R. Tolkien, *The Book of Lost Tales*, ed. by Christopher Tolkien (London: Allen and Unwin, 1983), i, pp. 13–44.

62. Ibid., i, pp. 45–63.

63. Ibid., i, pp. 45–245; ii, pp. 1–143.

64. Shippey, *The Road to Middle Earth*, pp. 209–13; and *J. R. R. Tolkien*, p. 238; Pearce, *Tolkien*, pp. 83–99.

65. Verlyn Flieger, *Splintered Light: Logos and Language in Tolkien's World* (Grand Rapids, Michigan: Eerdmanns, 1983), p. 53.

66. Ibid., p. 54; and Rose, 'Christian Platonism', pp. 205–6.

67. For which, of course, see ch. 4 of the present work.

68. J. R. R. Tolkien, *The Shaping of Middle Earth*, ed. by Christopher Tolkien (London: Allen and Unwin, 1986), pp. 11–75.

69. J. R. R. Tolkien, *The Lost Road and Other Writings*, ed. by Christopher Tolkien (London: Unwin Hyman, 1987), pp. 7–35.

70. J. R. R. Tolkien, 'Beowulf: The Monsters and the Critics', *Proceedings of the British Academy*, 22 (1936), pp, 245–95. Compare Tolkien, *Shaping of Middle Earth*, pp. 76–218, and *The Lost Road*, pp. 7–35.

71. J. R. R. Tolkien, 'On Fairy Stories', reprinted in J. R. R. Tolkien, *Tree and Leaf* (London: HarperCollins, 2001), pp. 1–50. I am very grateful to Ana Adnan for the loan of this work.

72. J. R. R. Tolkien, 'Leaf by Niggle', *Dublin Review* (January 1945), pp. 46–61.

73. J. R. R. Tolkien, *The Hobbit* (London: Allen and Unwin, 1937).

74. J. R. R. Tolkien, *Farmer Giles of Ham* (London: Allen and Unwin, 1949), and *The Adventures of Tom Bombadil* (London: Allen and Unwin, 1962). Both these works were rewritten and (in the case of the latter) augmented before publication, but their genesis was in the 1930s.

75. Carpenter, *J. R. R. Tolkien*, pp. 201–30.

76. J. R. R. Tolkien, *The Fellowship of the Ring* (London: Allen and Unwin, 1954); *The Two Towers* (London: Allen and Unwin, 1954); *The Return of the King* (London: Allen and Unwin, 1955). I have used the second edition, of 1966.

77. Ryan, *Tolkien*, pp. 167, 178–88; Helms, *Tolkien's World*, pp. 74–77; Shippey, *J. R. R. Tolkien*, pp. 208–10; Duriez, 'Sub-Creation and Tolkien's Theology', pp. 145–46; Pearce, *Tolkien*, pp. 100–25; Kilby, 'Christian Interpretation of Tolkien', pp. 27–29; Glover, 'Christian Character of Tolkien's Invented World', pp. 3–8; Edmund Fuller, 'The Lord of the Hobbits', in Neil D. Isaacs and Rose A. Zimbardo (ed.), *Tolkien and the Critics* (Notre Dame, Indiana: University of Notre Dame Press, 1969), pp. 29–35; Patricia Meyer Spacks, 'Power and Meaning in *The Lord of the Rings*', in ibid., pp. 82–92; R. J. Reilly, 'Tolkien and the Fairy Story, in ibid., pp. 129–50; Paul Kocher, *Master of Middle Earth* (London: Thames and Hudson, 1972), pp. 36–84.

78. Shippey, *J. R. R. Tolkien*, p. 210.

79. Ryan, *Tolkien*, pp. 132–34; Kocher, *Master of Middle Earth*, pp. 12–13.

80. Tolkien, *The Two Towers*, pp. 269, 284–85.

81. Shippey, *J. R. R. Tolkien*, p. 177.

82. Tolkien, *The Return of the King*, p. 256.

83. Ibid., p. 344; Shippey, *J. R. R. Tolkien*, pp. 177–78.

84. Lewis, *The Last Battle*, pp. 146–50 in the 1964 Puffin edition. The case concerned is that of an inhabitant of Calormen, a southern land with a culture very clearly that of a medieval Muslim state. Its god is a demon, Tash, whose theological relationship with Aslan and whose place in the destiny of his cosmos is never explained. Given the cultural associations of Calormen, Tash would be Allah, but his worship, with temples, altars, images and rites of blood sacrifice, sounds far more like the 'wrong' sort of paganism. I am very grateful to Tom Shippey for focusing my attention on these issues in a personal discussion, including his copying to me of Alcuin's celebrated diatribe on the damnation of all pagans, with which Tolkien would have been very familiar.

85. Flieger, *Splintered Light*, pp. 1–5.

86. Humphrey Carpenter (ed.), *The Letters of J. R. R. Tolkien* (Boston: Houghton Mifflin, 1981), p. 144. I am very grateful to Ana Adnan for the loan of this work.

87. Ibid., pp. 145–47, 221, 237, 243, 252, 255, 326–27.

88. Ibid., pp. 146–47, 193–94, 202–6, 235–37, 243, 259–60, 284–86.

89. Ibid., p. 216.

90. Ibid., p. 286.

91. Ibid., p. 189.

92. J. R. R. Tolkien, *The Silmarillion*, ed. by Christopher Tolkien (London: Allen and Unwin, 1977).

93. See ch. 5.

94. Hutton, *Triumph of the Moon*, pp. 151–88.

Notes to Chapter 8: The New Druidry

Much of this essay has been based on first-hand observation of the Order of Bards, Ovates and Druids, the British Druid Order, the Loyal Arthurian Warband, the Gorsedd of the Bards of Caer Abiri, the Council of British Druid Orders and the workshops of Caitlín and John Matthews. Where no reference is given for a statement, it may be taken to have been based on eyewitness experience. The abbreviations which I have used for names of Druid orders have been based on the conventions which they themselves habitually use, even when they lack complete logic or consistency: thus, the Order of Bards, Ovates and Druids is always known as 'OBOD', without a definite article, while the British Druid Order is always *the* BDO.

1. Richard Ellmann, *Yeats: The Man and the Masks* (London: Faber, 1949), p. 123.

2. Leslie Ellen Jones, *Druid, Shaman, Priest: Metaphors of Celtic Paganism* (Enfield: Hisarlik, 1998), pp. 229–40.

3. Miranda J. Green, *Exploring the World of the Druids* (London: Thames and Hudson, 1997), pp. 158–79.

4. Graham Harvey, *Listening People, Speaking Earth: Contemporary Paganism* (London: Hurst, 1997), pp. 17–34.

5. A former member donated a full set of the training papers for the Order to my own archive.

6. Preserved at Somerset House.

7. Ross Nichols, *The Book of Druidry*, ed. by John Matthews and Philip Carr-Gomm (London: Aquarian, 1990), p. 19, and 'Essentials of Druidry', *The Druid's Voice*, 4 (1994), pp. 10–11.

8. Nichols, *Book of Druidry*, passim, but esp. pp. 119–23; Philip Carr-Gomm, *The Elements of the Druid Tradition* (Shaftesbury: Element, 1991), pp. 66–67.

9. Nichols, *Book of Druidry*, p. 15; Carr-Gomm, *Elements of the Druid Tradition*, p. 33.

10. Nichols, *Book of Druidry*, p. 19.

11. Ibid., pp. 9–10, 16–17.

12. I am very grateful to Marian Green and Philip Carr-Gomm for showing me the photographs in their respective collections.

13. Nichols, *Book of Druidry*, passim.

14. Stuart Piggott, *The Druids* (London: Thames and Hudson, 1968).

15. Olivia Robertson, 'The Rebirth of the Goddess', in Caitlín Matthews (ed.), *Voices of the Goddess* (Wellingborough: Aquarian, 1990), pp. 30–33.

16. Olivia Robertson, *The Call of Isis* (Clonegal, Eire: Cesara, 1975), passim; and 'Rebirth of the Goddess', pp. 36–37.

17. Robertson, 'Rebirth of the Goddess', p. 37.

18. Robertson, *Call of Isis*, passim; *Dea: Rites and Mysteries of the Goddess* (Clonegal: Cesara, 1983); *Sophie: Cosmic Consciousness of the Goddess* (Clonegal: Cesara, 1986); *Pantheia: Initiations and Festivals of the Goddess* (Clonegal: Cesara, 1988); *Sybil: Oracles of the Goddess* (Clonegal: Cesara, 1989); Lawrence Durdin-Robertson, *Priestesses* (Clonegal: Cesara, 1976); *Juno Clovella: Perpetual Calendar of the Fellowship of Isis* (Clonegal: Cesara, 1982); *The Year of the Goddess: A Perpetual Calendar of Festivals* (Clonegal: Cesara, 1990).

19. Robertson, 'Rebirth of the Goddess', pp. 38–42; *Isian News*, 82 (1996), p. 15.

20. Robertson, 'Rebirth of the Goddess', pp. 41–42.

21. Caitlín Matthews, The Testament of Rhiannon', in Matthews (ed.), *Voices of the Goddess*, pp. 87–97; and 'Following the Awen', in Philip Carr-Gomm (ed.), *The Druid Renaissance* (London: Thorson, 1996), pp. 224–26; John Matthews, 'Breaking the Circle', in Prudence Jones and Caitlín Matthews (ed.), *Voices from the Circle* (Wellingborough: Aquarian, 1990), pp. 127–36.

22. Matthews, 'The Testament of Rhiannon', p. 98; cf. Tanya Luhrmann, *Persuasions of the Witch's Craft* (Oxford: Blackwell, 1989), p. 256 and n. 55.

23. Caitlín and John Matthews, *The Western Way: A Practical Guide to the Western Mystery Tradition* (London: Arkana, 2 vols, 1985); quotation by Knight on i, p. xi.

24. Christine Hartley, *The Western Mysteries Tradition* (London: Aquarian, 1968).

25. Matthews and Matthews, *The Western Way*, passim but esp. pp. 1–21.

26. John Matthews, *Taliesin: Shamanism and the Bardic Mysteries in Britain and Ireland* (London: Aquarian, 1991); *The Song of Taliesin* (London: Unwin Hyman, 1991); *The Celtic Shaman: A Handbook* (Shaftesbury: Element, 1991).

27. Sources cited at nn. 24 and 26, plus Caitlín Matthews, *Mabon and the Mysteries of Britain* (London: Arkana, 1987); *Arthur and the Sovereignty of Britain* (London: Arkana, 1989); *The Elements of the Celtic Tradition* (Shaftesbury: Element, 1989); *The Elements of the Goddess* (Shatesbury: Element, 1989); *Sophie: Goddess of Wisdom* (London: Unwin and Hyman, 1990); *Singing the Soul Back Home* (Shaftesbury: Element, 1995); Caitlín and John Matthews, *The Aquarian Guide to British and Irish Mythology* (Wellingborough: Aquarian, 1988); *The Arthurian Book of Days* (London: Sidgwick and Jackson, 1990); *The Arthurian Tarot* (Wellingborough: Aquarian, 1990); *Hallowquest: Tarot Magic and the Arthurian Mysteries* (Wellingborough: Aquarian, 1990); John Matthews, *The Elements of the Arthurian Tradition* (Shaftesbury: Element, 1988); *The Elements of the Grail Tradition* (Shaftesbury: Element, 1989); *Gawain: Knight of the Goddess* (Wellingborough: Aquarian, 1990); *The Celtic Shaman's Pack* (Shaftesbury: Element, 1995); *King Arthur and the Grail Quest* (London: Cassell, 1995). For the late Victorian interest in continuities, see Ronald Hutton, *The Triumph of the Moon: A History of Modern Pagan Witchcraft* (Oxford: Oxford University Press, 1999), pp. 112–31.

28. Carr-Gomm, *Elements of the Druid Tradition*, pp. 58–59; Nichols, *Book of Druidry*, pp. 9–13.

29. Full details of both given at nn. 7–8.

30. This information is based on successive personal communications from Philip Carr-Gomm and the supporting evidence of the order's monthly magazine, *Touchstone*.

31. Emma Restall Orr, *Spirits of the Sacred Grove* (London: Thorsons, 1998); *Principles of Druidry* (London: Thorsons, 1998); *Ritual* (London: Thorsons, 2000); Philip Shallcrass, *The Passing of the Year* (St Leonards: British Druid Order, 1997); *Druidry* (London: Piatkus, 2000). In addition to these works, I have drawn information and opinions from the order's magazine, *Tooth and Claw*, and many conversations with its two chiefs.

32. Tim's name is given as 'Sebastian' in the 1990s and 'Sebastion' at times since then. As my references here are to his work before the end of the twentieth century, I have held to the earlier version in this essay, to avoid clashes with citations of it in sources from that period.

33. Tim Sebastian, 'Triad: The Druid Knowledge of Stonehenge', in Christopher Chippindale (ed.), *Who Owns Stonehenge?* (London: Batsford, 1990), pp. 88, 106–9; Mary Newberry, 'The Ancient Druids in Celtic Society and their Role in the New Age', *The Druid's Voice*, 1 (1992), p. 13; Elen Evert Hopman, 'Interview with Tim Sebastian', *Keltria*, 31 (1996), pp. 20–23.

34. Hopman, 'Interview', p. 21.

35. Conversation with Tim Sebastian, Bath, 26 August 1995.

36. Hopman, 'Interview', p. 23.

37. Ibid, p. 21; Nichols, *Book of Druidry*, p. 14.

38. Conversation with Rollo Maughfling, 25 February 1997.

39. All information above taken from an interview with Arthur in *The Big Issue*, 132 (29 May 1995).

40. Manifesto of Loyal Arthurian Warband, *The Druid's Voice*, 2 (1992), p. 17.

41. Chippindale, *Who Own's Stonehenge?*, passim.

42. E.g. Marion Shoard, *The Theft of the Countryside* (London: Temple Smith, 1980); *This Land is Our Land* (London: Paladin, 1987); Richard Mabey, *The Common Ground* (London: Hutchinson, 1980); Charlie Pye-Smith and Chris Rose, *Crisis and Conservation* (Harmondsworth: Penguin, 1980); Philip Lowe, *Countryside Conflicts* (Aldershot: Gower, 1986); Howard Newby, *The Countryside in Question* (London; Hutchinson, 1988).

43. 'Alban Heruin', *The Druid's Voice*, 2 (1992), pp. 32–35.

44. I possess a largely complete set of the Council's minutes and working papers generated between 1992 and 1996, and a complete one since 1997.

Notes to Chapter 9: Living with Witchcraft

1. These concepts have been especially prominent in recent American scholarship, and have tended to filter through to British academics from that source. Notable works in the genre have been Jay Ruby, *A Crack in the Mirror: Reflexive Perspectives in Anthropology* (Philadelphia: University of Pennsylvania Press, 1982); James Clifford and George E. Marcus (ed.), *Writing Culture: The Poetics and Politics of Ethnography* (Berkeley: University of California Press, 1986); Victor W. Turner and Edward M. Bruner (ed.), *The Anthropology of Experience* (Urbana: University of Illinois Press, 1986); and Renato Rosaldo, *Culture and Truth: The Remaking of Social Analysis* (London: Routledge, 1989). I am very grateful to Sabina Magliocco for recommending these titles.

2. Tanya Luhrmann, *Persuasions of the Witch's Craft* (Oxford: Blackwell, 1989).

3. Joanne Pearson, 'Religion and the Return of Magic: Wicca as Esoteric Spirituality' (unpublished Ph.D. thesis, Lancaster University, 2000), pp. 90–93; quotation on p. 92. And see Joanne Pearson, '"Going Native in Reverse"': The Insider as Researcher in British Wicca', forthcoming in *Nova Religio*.

4. Luhrmann, *Persuasions of the Witch's Craft*, pp. 318–20; quotation on p. 320.

5. Ibid., p. 16.

6. Ibid., p. 18.

7. Ibid., p. 17.

8. Katherine P. Ewing, 'Dreams from a Saint: Anthropological Atheism and the Temptation to Believe', *American Anthropologist*, 96 (1994), p. 573.

9. To see how experts in religious studies coped with the same challenge, see Pearson, 'Religion and the Return of Magic', esp. pp. 90–94 (this thesis is now due for publication as a book); and the results of another postdoctoral thesis completed over the same period: Susan Greenwood, *Magic, Witchcraft and the Otherworld: An Anthropology* (Oxford: Berg, 2000). Her engagements with Tanya Luhrmann are on pp. 40–49, 141, 180–81.

10. Aidan Kelly, *Crafting the Art of Magic* (St Paul, Minnesota: Llewellyn, 1991).

11. For which see Ronald Hutton, *The Triumph of the Moon: A History of Modern Pagan Witchcraft* (Oxford: Oxford University Press, 1999), pp. 207, 228, 233–35,

449; 'Paganism and Polemic: The Debate over the Origins of Modern Pagan Witchcraft', *Folklore*, 111 (2000), pp. 112–13.

12. Though this charge has been made: see Donald H. Frew, 'Methodological Flaws in Recent Studies of Historical and Modern Witchcraft', *Ethnologies*, 1 (1998), pp. 33–37. I am grateful to Donald Frew and Allyn Wolfe for clarifying the issues for me in private exchanges.

13. By Blackwell, in Oxford.

14. The themes can be found treated in the first eight chapters of *Triumph*; the three authors are found on pp. 151–58.

15. The classic study of this is Norman Cohn, *Europe's Inner Demons* (Falmer: Sussex University Press, 1975). I included an analysis of its modern application to pagan witchcraft in Hutton, *Triumph*, pp. 253–71.

16. Hutton, *Triumph*, p. 271.

17. The results are collated in Melvyn J. Willin, 'Paramusicology: An Investigation of Music and Paranormal Phenomena' (unpublished Ph.D. thesis, Sheffield University, 1999), pp. 138–39. I am very grateful to the author for the loan of a copy of this work.

18. Hutton, *Triumph*, pp. 269–70.

19. I have returned to this theme in Ronald Hutton, *Shamans: Siberian Spirituality and the Western Imagination* (London: London and Hambledon, 2001).

20. Thus Gareth Medway in *Fortean Times* (January, 2000), n.p.; Michael Howard in the *Cauldron*, 95 (February, 2000), pp. 35–36; Chris Wood in *Quest*, 121 (March 2000), pp. 35–37; Damh in *Touchstone* (March 2000), p. 15; Lou Hart in *Wood and Water*, 70 (2000), pp. 9–13; Tony Geraghty and then John Macintyre in *Pagan Dawn* (Beltane 2000), pp. 37–40; unsigned in *Pagan Times* (Australian Spring Equinox 2000), p. 8; Gina O'Connor and then Sarah Whedon in *The Pomegranate*, 14 (Autumn 2000), pp. 48–51; Ashleen O'Gaea in *Circle Magazine* (Summer 2001), pp. 34–40. Margot Adler and Judy Harrow kindly forwarded to me copies of reviews which they had written for journals in the USA.

21. These are the practitioners in the field with whom I am myself best acquainted, and whose work I have read in a well-developed form. There may, however, be others, and I think especially in this context of the Californians Donald H. Frew, Allyn Wolfe and Anna Korn. Only Philip Heselton has as yet published any of his research in a format accessible to the general public: *Wiccan Roots* (Chievely: Capal Bann, 2000).

22. As decribed in print by Doreen Valiente, in her own book, *The Rebirth of Witchcraft* (Custer, Washington: Phoenix, 1989), pp. 40–63, and Janet and Stewart Farrar, *Eight Sabbats for Witches* (London: Hale, 1981), pp. 45, 148. Her impression of his methods has been confirmed to me by others who worked with him regularly, especially Frederic Lamond and Lois Bourne.

23. Apart from that discussed below, they included Owen Davies in *History Today* (March 2000), p. 60; Robert Irwin in the *Independent on Sunday* (11 December 1999), n.p.; Kevin Sharpe in the *Sunday Times* (11 December 1999), pp. 40–41;

Jeremy Harte in *3rd Stone*, 38 (2000), p. 45; Simon Coleman in the *Times Higher Education Supplement* (in 2000, but I regret that my cutting does not have the date). The least sympathetic was Marina Warner, in the *Times* (25 November 1999), p. 46, but then she was also the least expert: she evaluated the book by the simple technique of praising it for scholarly rigour every time that it was critical of modern witches or their traditions, and accusing it of partiality every time that it said something nice about them.

24. T. M. Luhrmann, 'Hello Corn Dolly', *Times Literary Supplement* (19 May 2000), p. 36.
25. George Devereux, *From Anxiety to Method in the Behavioural Sciences* (The Hague: Mouton, 1967), pp. xvi–xvii.
26. Benetta Jules-Rosette, 'The Veil of Objectivity', *American Anthropologist*, 80 (1978), pp. 549–70; quotation on p. 550.
27. David Hayano, *Poker Faces* (Berkeley: University of California Press, 1982), p. 149.
28. Liza C. Dalby, *Geisha* (Berkeley: University of California Press, 1983), passim.
29. Jeanne Favret-Saada, *Deadly Words: Witchcraft in the Bocage* (Cambridge: Cambridge University Press, 1980), pp. 10, 12; 'About Participation', *Culture, Medicine and Psychiatry*, 14 (1990), pp. 190, 192.
30. Classics of this genre are Lila Abu-Lughod, *Veiled Sentiments: Honour and Poetry in a Bedouin Society* (Berkeley: University of California Press, 1986); and Kirin Narayan, *Storyteller, Saints and Scoundrels: Folk Narrative in Hindu Religious Teaching* (Philadelphia: University of Pennsylvania Press, 1989). I am grateful to Sabina Magliocco for these references.
31. Ewing, 'Dreams from a Saint', pp. 571–72.
32. Philip M. Peek (ed.), *African Divination Systems: Ways of Knowing* (Bloomington: University of Indiana Press, 1991); quotation on p. 9.
33. David E. Young and Jean-Guy Goulet (ed.), *Being Changed by Cross-Cultural Encounters: The Anthropology of Extraordinary Experience* (Peterborough, Ontario: Broadview Press, 1994); quotations from pp. 8–9.
34. Edith Turner, 'The Reality of Spirits', *Revision*, 15.1 (1992), pp. 28–32; quotation from p. 28.
35. E.g. Kirin Narayan, *Mondays on the Dark of the Moon: Himalayan Foothill Tales* (Oxford: Oxford University Press, 1997); Ruth Behar, *The Vulnerable Observer: Anthropology Which Breaks Your Heart* (Boston Beacon, 1996); Ruth Behar and Deborah Gordon (ed.), *Women Writing Culture* (Berkeley: University of California Press, 1995); Lila Abu-Lughod, *Writing Women's Worlds: Bedouin Stories* (Berkeley: University of California Press, 1993). I am very grateful to Sabina Magliocco for supplying these references.
36. This is taken from one of the foundation-texts of the discipline, Ninian Smart, *The Religious Experience of Mankind* (London: Collins, 1981); quotation on p. 12.
37. David J. Hufford, 'The Scholarly Voice and the Personal Voice', *Western Folklore*, 54 (1995), pp. 57–76; quotation on p. 60.
38. Elizabeth Puttick, *Women in New Religions* (London: Macmillan, 1997), p. 6.

39. Jone Salomonsen, 'Methods of Compassion or Pretension?', *The Pomegranate*, 8 (1999), pp. 4–13.

40. Amy Caroline Simes, 'Contemporary Paganism in the East Midlands' (unpublished Ph.D. thesis, Nottingham University, 1995); 'Mercian Movements', in Graham Harvey and Charlotte Hardman (ed.), *Paganism Today* (London: Thorson, 1996), pp. 169–90.

41. Pearson, 'Religion and the Return of Magic', pp. 90–94; 'Going Native in Reverse', passim.

42. Greenwood, *Magic, Witchcraft and the Otherworld*, passim.

43. Robert J. Wallis, 'Autoarchaeology and Neo-Shamanism' (unpublished Ph.D. thesis, Southampton University, 2000), esp. pp. 1–11.

44. Graham Harvey, *Listening People, Speaking Earth: Contemporary Paganism* (London: Hurst, 1997).

45. Patrick Curry, 'Astrology on Trial, and its Historians', *Culture and Cosmos*, 4 (2000), pp. 47–56.

46. Salomonsen, 'Methods of Compassion or Pretension?', p. 10.

Index

Abelard, Pierre 159
Abraham 140, 145
Abrams, Lesley 74, 75, 84
academic scholarship 36, 54
Adamites of Bohemia (holy naturists) 201, 202
Adelard of Bath 160, 162, 166
ADO *see* Ancient Druid Order
Aelius Aristides 88
Affair of the Poisons, France 204
Africa 19, 196, 207–9, 212
Agathodaimon (philosopher) 147–48
Alan of Lille (Alanus de Insulis) 166, 167, 168, 219
Alberti, Leon Battista 175
Alcock, Leslie 47–54, 56, 57
Aldhelm, St 83
Alexander VI, Pope 181
Alexandria 141, 146, 152
Alfonsi, Petrus 160
Alfred, the Great, King of Wessex 15, 73
Allah 153
Allen, Ian and Charles Hay 4, 5
Altdorfer, Albrecht 203
Alton, Hampshire 24
Ambrosius Aurelianus 41, 42, 44
America 84, 247, 248, 266
    and Druidry 246, 257
    Pagan communities in 265
    and ritual nudity 205, 206, 208
    and voodoo 213
    Wicca 266
Ancient Druid Order (ADO) 240, 242, 250, 253, 255
ancient monuments 22, 45, 62, 82
    The Tristan Stone 48, 51

Ancient Order of Druids (AOD) 240, 253, 255, 256
ancient Paganism 87, 90, 138, 174, 177
    in Harran 149–50
    and Islam 158
    see also Paganism
Ando, Clifford 90
Anglo-Saxons 40, 46, 146
animism 225, 233
Annales Cambriae 40–41, 49, 51
anthropology 19, 104, 285–91
AOD (Ancient Order of Druids) 240, 253, 255, 256
Apollonius of Tyana (holy man) 108, 115
Apuleius Lucius 88, 89, 108, 110, 117
Aquinas, Thomas 178
Arabia 152
arcane correspondences 114
archaeology 55, 75, 151
Aristophanes 198
Aristotle 144, 159
Arnald of Villanova 162
Artemis Kranaia sanctuary 199
Arthur of the Britons (TV series) 50
Arthur, King of the Britons (semi-legendary) 39–58, 68–69
    legends *see* Arthurian legend
    tomb 60, 68, 70
Arthur, philology of the name 42, 43, 44, 52, 54, 58
Arthur Uther Pendragon 252–53
Arthurian legend 39, 44, 56, 57, 62
    academic rejection of 56, 57
Asclepiodotus (writer) 127
Asclepius, Hermetic text 166

Ashe, Geoffrey 48, 80, 84
  and Camelot 46–47, 49, 50
  King Arthur's Avalon 46, 66
Asia Minor 117, 124
Assyria 112, 182
astral magic 157–58, 163, 181–86, 190, 191
  Campanella and Pope Urban VIII 188
  Campanella's theory of 189
  Christianity and 159
  and Ficino 178
  Muslims and 159
  text translated 160
astrology 157, 159, 181, 184, 190, 289
  translated texts on 160
astronomy 163
Athanassiadi, Polymnia 93, 118, 139
Athens 20
Athens academy 91–92, 125, 134, 138, 175
  members settle in Harran (disputed) 139
Auden, W. H. 215
Augustine, St, 'Augustine of Hippo' 90, 97, 107, 159, 166
Aune, David 103
Aurelian, Emperor 89, 92
Austen, Jane 12
Australasia 248, 257
Avebury 256

Baba (Harranian prophet) 140
Babylonia 182
Bacon, Roger 162
Badon Hill, siege of 41–42
Baghdad 145, 151
Baker, Samuel 19
Bannventa Berniae/Banwell (putative family home of St Patrick) 78
baptism 199–200
barbarous names 114–15, 120, 121, 164, 316(n)
Barber, Richard 84

Bardaisan(philosopher) 139
Barley, Nigel 1, 27
Barnard, Toby 10
Barthomley church, Cheshire 23
Bath 76, 257
Baynes, Pauline 223
BDO (British Druid Order) 249, 253, 256, 257, 258
Beard, Mary 104
Beckery, Isle of Avalon 61, 76
Bede, the Venerable, St 71–72
Beere, Richard, Abbot of Glastonbury 61
Bégouen, Count Henri Napoléon 33
Belloc, Hilaire 215
Benedict, Ruth 10, 99, 106
Benen, St 72
Benignus/Beonna, St 60, 72
Benivieni, Girolamo 181
Bernardino (preacher) 211
Bessarion, Johannes 176, 177
Betz, Hans Dietar 116, 117
Bible 209
Birch, Alice 26
Birch, John 26
Birmingham 25, 26
al-Biruni, Abu al-Rayhan Muhammed ibn Ahmad 143
Black Watch regiment 3
Blackwood, Algernon 216, 237
Bodin, Jean 202
Boethius 18
Bohemia 201
Bold Fact, and myth 29–36
Bolus of Mendes (writer) 123
Bond, Frederick Bligh 64, 80, 84
Book of Abramelin the Mage 190
Boorman, John 53
Bouguet, Henri 202
Bowersock, G. W. 89
Bradley, Marion Zimmer 53
Brean Down Pagan temple 82
Bremmer, Jan 89
Brent Knoll, Somerset 78, 82

Brent Marsh 77
Breuil, Abbé Henri 33, 34, 35
Bridget, St 61, 72, 73, 74
Bristol 50, 57, 81
Britain 93, 133, 197, 246, 291
  Irish raids on 78
British Academy 47
British Columbia 206
British Druid Order (BDO) 249, 253,
  256, 257, 258
British society 274–75, 277–79
Brittany 5
Bromwich, Rachel 44, 45, 51, 52, 56
Broughton, Rutland (composer) 63–64
Bruno, Giordano 186–88
Bryn yr Ellyllon, Wales 22, 23
Buckton, Alice 63, 76, 84
Bucratis (author) 160
Buddhism 205, 288
Burke, Edmund 10
Butt, Isaac 10
Byzantium 170, 173, 174

Cadbury Castle, Bristol 50
Camelot 46–47, 48, 49, 50, 78
Camelot (musical) 47
Camelot Research Committee 46, 47,
  50, 58
Cameron, Alan 95
Camlann/Camlaun, strife of 40–41
Campanella, Tommaso 188–89
Cannington, Somerset 82
'Canon Episcopi' text 169
Canterbury, Kent 27
Cantimpre, Thomas de 161
Caradoc of Llancarfan 70
Cardano, Girolamo 184
cardinal points 165, 178, 185
Carley, James 70, 84
Carlyle, Thomas 15
Carpenter, Humphrey 218
Carr-Gomm, Philip 247, 248, 249, 257
Carr-Gomm, Stephanie 248, 249
Carrawburgh, Northumberland 76

Carrhae, Turkey (modern) see Harran
Carver, Martin 57
Casanova, Giovanni Giacomo 191
Casaubon, Isaac 189
Castle Dore, Cornwall 45, 48, 51, 55
Castle Guinnion, battle of 40
Catholicism 22, 62, 182, 184, 188
  and Druids 251
  Irish 8, 9, 10
Catterick/Catraeth, Yorkshire 41
Cau-Durban, Abbé 1
Cecil, Lord David 215
Celidon Wood, Scotland (modern) 43
Celsus (author) 88
Centwine, King of Wessex 83
ceramics see pottery
ceremonial magic 164, 165, 186
Cerularios, Michael 171
Chadwick, Nora 44, 51
Chaldean Oracles 98, 118–21, 127, 128,
  134
  and Psellus 170, 171
  on ritual nudity 199
Chaldeans 113, 119
Chalice Well, Glastonbury Tor 60, 61,
  63, 76, 251
Chalice Well Trust 66, 76
Chambers, Sir Edmund 43
Chancellor, Matthew 76
Charles I, King of Great Britain and
  Ireland 23, 24
Charles II, King of England and
  Scotland 24
Charles-Edwards, Thomas 52
Chartres, France 166
Chaucer, Geoffrey 167, 168
Chesterton, G. K. 215, 237
Chigi, Agostino 183
China 17, 245
Christianity 93, 113, 135, 141, 288
  and astral magic 159
  baptism 199
  Bruno on 187–88
  and ceremonial magic 165

and Druids 251
in Europe 192
and Platonism 171, 174
and Pletho 174
and reconciliation with Paganism 189, 190, 191, 243
and theurgy 171
and Venus 168
and Wicca 285
Christianity and Paganism 177
in literature 225, 237
Chrysostom, John 135
Churchill, Sir Winston 44
Chuvin, Pierre 139, 174
Cicero 159
circles 164, 165, 173, 185
Civil War, English 15, 23–24, 26, 52
Claudian (poet) 95, 97, 166
Clement VIII, Pope 184
Clifford, Charles 26
Coffin Texts 110
collective memory 18–26
Collen, St 61, 71
Collingwood, W. G. 43, 44
Collins, Michael 11
Collinson, Patrick 285
Combe Manor, Berkshire 25
Comes, Natalis 185
Commissioner of Works 45
common law 254
'compassionate anthropology' 288, 291
Conan (Palestinian monk) 200
Congresbury, Somerset 82
Connolly, James 11
Constantine I (the Great), Emperor 89
Coote, Sir Charles 9
Corbin, Henry 148
Cornish Gorsedd (Gorseth) 12
Cornish Tourist Board 48
Cornutus (Stoic philosopher) 96
Cornwall 5, 12, 45, 46, 56
literary fiction 18
rebellions 22, 62
Tristan legend 56

Corpus Hermeticum 170, 189
cosmology 14, 164, 166, 178, 179
Costen, Michael 57
Cotswold Order of Druids 249
Council of British Druid Orders 255, 256, 257
counter-culture 50, 251, 254, 260, 294
and Druidry 245
and Sebastian 251
Crawford, Deborah 70, 84
Crawford, O. G. S. 43, 44
Cressy, David 202
Criminal Justice Act 254, 256
Cromwell, Oliver 9, 10, 24, 27
Crowley, Vivianne 133
Cryer, Frederick 112
Cuneglasus, King 42
Cunomorus, King 45
Curry, Patrick 215, 216, 289, 290
curse-tablets 109
Cyril of Panopolis (author) 95

Dafo (witch) 282
Dalby, Liz 285, 286
Dalriada, Scotland 78
Daly, Mary 31
Damascius (author) 97, 126, 127, 131, 138
Dana, Druid Clan of 244, 255
Dark, K. R. 57
d'Ascoli, Cecco 162
Daubenta, Jeanne 201
Davis, Thomas 10
De gestis regum Angliae (William of Malmesbury) 71
De imaginibus (Thabit) 162
De occulta philosophia (Nettesheim) 182
De Valera, Eamon 11
Dearnaley, Roger 281
Dee, John 65, 183–84
Demotic papyri 114, 115, 116, 117
Dening, Greg 22
Devereux, George 285

Devon 46, 62
Diacceto, Francesco Cattani da 181
Diana (goddess) 98, 169
Dickens, Charles 15
Dickens, Geoffrey 284
Dickie, Matthew 104, 109, 118, 126
al-Dimashqi, Shams al-Din
  Muhammed 156
divinity/divinities 95–98, 117, 241
Dodds, E. H. 118, 125
Dostoyevsky, Fyodor 15
Dowayo tribe, Cameroon 1, 27
Dowden, Ken 88
Drake, Sir Francis 15
Drogheda, Cromwell's conquest of 9
Druidry (new Druidry) 64, 239–58
  membership 258
Dryghton Prayer 132
Duddon, Cheshire 25
Dudley Castle 23
Duffy, Eamon 284
Dumville, David 52, 54, 55, 56, 74
Dunstan, St 73, 251
Durdin-Robertson, Olivia and
  Lawrence 243, 244
Durdin-Robertson, Pamela 243
Dürer, Albrecht 203
Durham 29
Durkheim, Emile 105
Durston Pagan temple 82
Dworkin, Andrea 31
Dyfed, Wales 78

East Indies 212
Edel, May 209
Edessa (under Roman rule) 139
Egypt 89, 90, 92, 110–13, 152
  and astral magic 158, 163
  and astrology 157
  and Greek magical papyri 121
  and magic 117, 120, 128, 130, 187
  and myth 17
  and Paganism 87, 182
  and ritual nudity 197

eisteddfod 5–6
Elizabeth I, Queen of England and
  Ireland 9, 14
Ely, Cambridgeshire 24
England 14–15, 18, 20–21, 207, 248
  and Druidry 239, 254, 258
  and ritual nudity 202, 211
  Wicca as a religion in 279–80
English Civil War 15, 23–24, 26, 52
English Heritage 250, 254, 255
English Reformation 284
Enlightenment, The 241
Ennodius (poet) 97
Epiphanius, Bishop 198, 201
Erasmus 183
Eunapius (philosopher) 94, 124
Europe 88, 137, 203, 211, 248
  and Christianity 192
  and Druidry 257
  and nudity in art 196, 198, 200–202,
    212
  religions 88, 137
Eusebius (author) 121, 124
Evans-Pritchard, E. E. 99, 104, 285
evil 134
Ewing, Katherine 263, 286–87
excavations 82, 140
  at Beckery 61, 76
  at Glastonbury Abbey 63, 66, 75
  at Glastonbury (Isle of Avalon) 63,
    64, 75, 76
  at Glastonbury Tor 77, 79, 81
  at Harran 151
  Syria 140
Eymeric, Nicholas 165

Fairfax, Lady 26
Faithful Companions (Ikhwan al-Safa)
  147
fantasy novels 56–57
Faraone, Christopher 109
Faris village, Jordan 21
Farleigh Wick, Somerset 24
Farr, Florence 130

Farrar, Janet and Stewart 267
Favret-Saada, Jeanne 285–86
Fellowship of Isis 243, 244, 246, 247, 255
feminism 31, 53, 54
Ficino, Marsilio 177–81
Fihrist el-Ulum (al-Nadim) 142–44
Finberg, H. P. R. 73, 84
Fionn Mac Cumhail (Fionn) 57
Fitzgerald family 8, 10
Flieger, Verlyn 229, 235
Florence, Italy 175, 177
Flower, Robin 11
Fludd, Robert 185
'folk pagans' 256
folk-lore 13, 14, 15, 211
folk-magic 211
folk-medicine 28
folk-memory 18–26
folk-wisdom 27–28
Foot, Sarah 74, 75, 84
Ford, Paul 222
Fortune, Dion 65, 66, 131, 237, 245
Fowden, Garth 88, 93, 139
Fowler, Peter 51, 57
France 33, 34, 166, 204
    and myth 17, 54
Fraternity of the Inner Light 131
Frazer, Sir James 99, 106, 107, 211, 216
Frede, Michael 93
Freeman, Derek 32, 33
Freemasonry 129, 130, 191
French Revolution 15

Gaffarel, Jacques 190
Gage, Matilda Joslyn 31, 33, 34, 35
Gager, John 104, 109
Garcia, Pedro, Bishop 180, 181
Gardner, Gerald 31, 131–34, 194, 265–67, 281–82
    Luhrmann on 284
    in *New Dictionary of National Biography* 283

Gaul 93
gematria (holy numbers) 64, 80
Gemistos, George (Pletho) 173–76, 179, 180
Geoffrey of Monmmouth 68
George IV, King of Great Britain 3, 4
George of Trebizond 173
Germany 30, 168, 187, 203, 204
Gerson, Jean 163
Ghana 19
Ghayat al-hakim 154–58, 160, 165, 172, 176
Gildas, St 41–42, 55, 56, 61, 70
Giorgi, Francesco 183
Glapion, Marie Laveau (voodoo queen) 213
Glastonbury Abbey 48, 50, 60, 61
    charters 74, 75, 83
    excavations 63, 66, 75
    foundation 60, 74, 75, 83
    history 71, 72
    legendary tomb of King Arthur and Guinevere 60, 68, 70
    Radford on 48, 53, 75
Glastonbury Antiquarian Society 63
Glastonbury (Isle of Avalon) 20, 46, 56, 69, 80
    described 66
    excavations at 63, 64, 75, 76
    King Arthur's Avalon (Ashe) 46, 48
    lake villages of 63, 64, 80
    philology of 71
Glastonbury Order of Druids (GOD) 252, 253, 255, 256
Glastonbury Tor 53, 59, 61, 63, 77–79
    Chalice Well 60, 61, 63, 76, 251
    excavations on 77, 79, 81
    leys 67, 80
    pottery at 48
    processional way 65, 66
    spiral maze 79
Glastonbury town 59, 80, 82
Glastonbury Zodiac 65, 67, 79–80
Gnosticism 13, 113, 114, 133–35, 201

GOD (Glastonbury Order of Druids) 252, 253, 255, 256
Goetia rites 186
Golden Dawn, Hermetic Order of the (founded 1880) 129–30, 194, 245
Golden Section Order (founded c. 1970) 240, 242, 251
Gondeshapur, Iraq 152
Goodchild, John 64
Goode, William J. 99
Goodrich Castle, Herefordshire 26
Goody, William 106
Gordon, Richard 103, 104
Gorsedd of the Bards of Britain 255
Gorsedd of the Bards of Caer Abiri 256
Gorsey Bigbury circle 82
Goya, Francisco 204
Graeco-Egyptian magical papyri 164
Graeco-Romans, and ritual nudity 195, 198
Graf, Fritz 103, 108, 116
Graham, Sir Richard 24
Grahame, Kenneth 224, 268
Gransden, Antonia 70, 84
Grattan, Henry 10
Graves, Robert 241, 243
Greece 102, 109, 110, 157, 199
Greek magical papyri 114–21, 128–30, 135, 158, 164
and the *Ghaya* 155
Greeks 90, 154
Green, Miranda 239
Green, Peter 102
Green, Tamara 149, 150–51
Greene, Graham 215, 237
Greenwood, Susan 289
Grien, Hans Baldung 203
Grimm, Jakob 30
Grinsell, Leslie 22
Grosseteste, Robert 161
Guest, Lady Charlotte 7, 17
Guest, Sir Josiah 7
Guild of Glastonbury theatre troupe 63

Guinevere, Queen (legendary) 48
tomb (Glastonbury Abbey) 60, 68, 70
Gwyn ap Nudd (mythical lord of the Underworld) 61

Hadot, Ilstraut 139
Haemgils, Abbot of Glastonbury 74, 75
Haggard, Rider 237, 268
Hall, Augusta (née Waddington) 6, 7
Hall, Benjamin (Baron Llanover) 6, 7
Hammond, Dorothy 100
Hankins, James 176, 191
Hankins, John 180
Haraldsson, Erlendur 276
Hardman, Charlotte 272
Harpokration (philosopher) 160, 172
Harran 138–40, 145–50, 152, 164, 174
excavations at 151
feasts 143, 144
and religion 151
see also Sabians of Harran
Harte, Jeremy 23
Hartley, Christine 245
Harvey, Graham 240, 272, 289
Hauteville, Jean de 167
hawthorne 61, 62, 69
Hayano, David 285
Heckenbach, J. 195, 197, 198
Henley Wood Pagan temple 82
Henri III, King of France 186
Henry II, King of England 68
Henry V, King of England 70
Henry VIII, King of England 61
heresy 200, 201, 202
Hermetic Order of the Golden Dawn (founded 1880) 129–30, 194, 245
Hermetism 113–14, 134, 135, 145, 152
al-Misri's adaptation of 153
and astral magic 158
and Islam 152
texts 170, 178
Hermopolis city 152
Herodotus (historian) 17
Heselton, Philip 281

Heyerdahl, Thor 21
Higgins, Godfrey 65
Higham, N. J. 57
Hinduism 205, 226
Hippolytus, St (antipope) 201
Historia Brittonum (reputedly Nennius)
  39–40, 52
historians 19, 55
history, discipline of 36–37
Holy Grail 63
Homer 17, 18, 90, 147–48
Hopton, Sir Ralph 24–25
Hufford, David 288
Hughes, Kathleen 51
Hutton, Ronald 267, 276, 279
  background 269, 270
  career 272
  as a critic of Kelly 266–67
  as a mediator 292
  Triumph of the Moon, The: A History
    of Modern Pagan Witchcraft see
    Triumph of the Moon, The: A
    History of Modern Pagan Witchcraft
Hyde, Douglas 10

Iamblichus (author) 91–92, 108,
  122–34 *passim*, 178, 189
ibn Fadlan 197
ibn Jubayr (Spanish Muslim) 141
ibn Wahshiyyah al-Nabati, abu Bakr
  Ahmed 153
Iceland 276
Ikhwan al-Safe ('The Pure Brethren')
  147, 148
Ilchester, Somerset 82
India 154, 156, 212, 245
  Pancha Tantra 16
  and ritual nudity 205, 207, 209, 211
Indracht, St 66, 72
Indrechtach, Abbot of Iona 72
Industrial Revolution 52
'Inklings' literary group, Oxford 215,
  237
Innocent VIII, Pope 180

Institute for the Study of New
  Religions, University of London 265
'interpretive drift' 262, 287
Iran 152
Iraq 152
Ireland 5, 8–12, 17, 18, 40
  and Druidry 243, 246, 255
  raids on Britain 78
Ireton, Henry 10, 25
Irish Republic 257
Irish Tourist Board 9
Islam 140, 141, 152, 158, 288
  and Harran 140, 149–50, 151
  and magic 153
Isle of Man 27
Italian Renaissance 191
Italikos, Michael 172
Italos, John 171
Italy 159, 168, 175, 177
  and ritual nudity 198, 199, 203, 211

Jackson, Kenneth Hurlstone 16, 17, 44,
  51, 52
Jainism 205, 210
James, Edward 58
Jenner, Henry 12
Jesus Christ 140, 162
John the Baptist 169, 200
John, Eric 58
Johnston, Sarah Iles 118, 119, 121
Jones, John (Welsh cleric) 7
Jones, Kathy 67, 80
Jones, Leslie Ellen 239
Jones, Prudence 98
Joseph of Arimathea 60, 61, 62, 63, 83
  investigation of legend 68, 69
Jovian, Emperor 89
Joyce, James 10, 11
Judaeo-Christian tradition 101
Judaism 141, 152, 199, 288
Jules-Rosette, Benetta 285
Julian, Emperor 89, 91, 134
Julius Firmicus Maternus 159, 166
Justinian, Emperor 138, 147

Kabakes, Demetrius Raoul 175
Kelly, Aidan 265, 266, 267, 281
Kennedy, John P. 88
Kent 24, 55
Kenya 208
Key of Solomon rites 186
al-Kindi 142, 144, 146
  and the cosmos 144
Kingsford, Anna 129, 245
Kingsley, Peter 103
Kipling, Rudyard 237
Kircher, Athanasius 185
Knight, Gareth (pseud.) 245
Knights of the Round Table 47
Kollman, Anton Jacob 30
Kyranides medical text 172

Lack-Szyrma, W. S. 22
Lactanius (author) 97, 178
lake villages of Glastonbury 63, 64, 80
Lamyatt Beacon Pagan temple 82
Lancre, Pierre de 202, 203–4
Laud, William 27
Laughlin, Charles 287
LAW (Loyal Arthurian Warband) 253, 256
leaden cross of King Arthur 68, 69
Lecky, W. E. H. 30
lector-priests 115
Leland, Charles Godfrey 204
Levant 113
Leveson, Thomas 23
LeVine, Robert 209
Lewis, C. S. 107, 215, 216, 218, 237
  reading 216, 218, 222, 224, 226
  works 216–21 passim, 225, 226
    Narnian novels 221, 222, 223, 224, 225, 236
Lewy, Hans 119
Lincolnshire 24
literary fiction 12–18, 167–69
  see also national myths and symbols
Livingstone, Ken 31
Lloyd-Morgan, Ceridwen 71, 84

London 244, 255, 265
London Druid Group 255
Lord of the Rings, The (Tolkien) 215
Louis XIV, King of France 189
Loyal Athurian Warband (LAW) 253, 256
Lucan (poet) 117
Lucius, King 60, 72
Luck, Georg 118, 120, 121, 171
Luhrmann, Tanya 260–64, 283, 284, 289
  methodology 286

Mabinogion, The 8
Macaulay, Thomas, 1st Baron 15
MacCulloch, Diarmaid 285
MacDonagh, Thomas 12
Macdonald, George 216
Macdonnell, Ian 2
Mackay, Charles 30
MacMullen, Ramsey 88, 93, 94, 101
Macrobius (author) 94, 95, 96, 166
Macwilliam family 8
magic 98–105 passim, 126, 131, 211, 260
  in Al-Hatifi 142
  ceremonial magic 164, 165, 186
  in de imaginibus 145
  and Egypt 117, 120, 128, 130, 187
  in the Ghaya 155
  of Harran 149, 164
  and Islam 153
  and Roman Empire 117
  see also astral magic; planetary magic; ritual magic
magic and religion 98–112, 116–18, 170, 209
Magnus, Albertus 162, 178, 181, 184
Majercik, Ruth 119, 121
Malatesta, Prince Sigismondo 175
Malinowski, Bronislaw 99
Maltwood, Katherine 65, 67, 79, 84
Ma'mun, Caliph 141
Manuel I (Byzantine Emperor) 172
Marie Antoinette, Josephe Jeanne, Queen of France 15

Marinus 126, 127, 128
Mark, King (legendary) 45, 55
Marlowe, Christopher 186
Marquesa Islands 13, 21, 22, 206
Marquet, Yves 148
Marsas, Paulus 185
Martial (Roman poet) 196, 197
Marwan II, Caliph 140
Maryatt, Frederick 15
Ma'shar, Abu (alchemist) 166
mass hallucination 28–29
al-Mas'udi, Abu al-Hasan ibn Husayn 146–47, 148, 150, 156
Mathers, Moina 130
Mathers, Samuel Liddell 130
Matthews, Caitlín 249, 255
Matthews, Caitlín and John 244–48, 254, 255, 257
Maughfling, Rollo 252, 254, 255, 257
Maurice, Emperor 139, 147
Mauss, Marcel 105
Maximus of Madaura 88, 90
Maximus of Tyre 88
Mead, Margaret 31, 32, 35
Meare (putative village) 81
media 273, 292–93
Medici, Catherine de 184
Medici, Cosimo de 175
Medici, Lorenzo de 181, 185
Medway, Gareth 281
Melville, Herman 13
Melwas, King of Somerset 48, 61
memorial stones 42
Men of Intelligence (sect) 201
Merivale, Patricia 96
Merlin (myth.) 44
Mesopotamia 90, 92, 112, 113, 155
   and astral magic 157, 158
   Chaldean Oracles 119
   cosmology 164
   and Hermetism 152
   magical tradition 143
methodology 36
Meyer, Marvin 104

Michael of Amesbury 77
Michelet, Jules 15
Michell, John 67, 80
Milis, Ludo 137, 191
Milton, John 39, 217
Mirandola, Giovanni Pico della (Pico) 180, 181
al-Misri, Dhu al-Nun Abu'l-Faid Tauban ibn Ibrahim 152, 153
Mitchison, Naomi 226
Mithraism 113, 116, 143
modern Pagan witchcraft 260, 265, 268
modern Paganism 87, 129, 165, 191, 255
   growth of 242
   in three traditions 192
   see also Paganism
Mongols 151
monotheism 88–95 passim, 140, 147, 152
   and Harran 147
   of Islam 140
Montserrat, Dominic 112
monuments, ancient 22, 45, 62, 82
   The Tristan Stone 48, 51
Moore, George 10, 11
Morgannwg, Iolo 65, 255
Morland, S. C. 84
Morris, Christopher 58
Morris, John 49, 50, 51, 53
Morris, William 216, 217
Muhammed (Mohammed) 141, 153
Murray, Colin 240–41, 242
Murray, Liz 255
Murray, Margaret 33, 34
Muslim 144, 150, 153, 159
Myres, J. N. L. 55
myth 1–37, 54, 265
myth-busting 36, 37

Nabataean Agriculture (Wahshiyyah) 154, 157
al-Nabati, Abu Bakr Ahmed ibn Wahshiyya (Wahshiyyah) 153

al-Nadim, Muhammed ibn Isaq ibn
142, 143, 144, 148
Fihrist el-Ulum 142, 143, 144
Nance, Robert Morton 12
national myths and symbols 2, 4
Cornwall 12
Ireland 8–12
Scotland 2–5
see also literary fiction
National Trust 256
Natura (Nature) 96–97, 166–68, 179,
185, 192
Needwood forest, Staffordshire 24
Nennius/Nemnius (author) 39
Neoplatonism 91–95, 113, 121, 134, 136
and Bessarion 177
and Islam 152
and Psellus 171
Nesi/Neri, Giovanni 181
Netherlands 201
Nettesheim, Cornelius Agrippa von
(Agrippa) 182, 183, 187
new Druidry 239–58
New Guinea 208
New Testament 169
New Zealand 248
Newbury, Berkshire 25
newspapers 47, 273, 275, 278, 293
Nichols, Philip Ross 20, 241–42, 244,
247, 248, 255
Nigeria 244
Ninnius (author) 39
Nonnus of Panopolis (poet) 95
North Africa *see* Africa
North America *see* America
North, John 104, 105
Norton Conyers, Yorkshire 24
Nuky-Hiva island, Polynesia 12–13

objectivity 36, 285, 289
OBOD (Order of Bards, Ovates and
Druids) 242, 248, 253, 255–58 *passim*
O'Brien, Murrough (Murrough of the
Burnings) 8, 9

Observer newspaper 47, 48
occult studies 162
occult texts 172
Ogden, Daniel 104, 109
O'Grady, Standish 10
O'Malley, Ernie 11
O'Neill, Hugh 8, 9
oral history 19, 23
oral tradition 19–23, 26, 42, 70
Orczy, Baroness Emmuska 15
Order of Bards, Ovates and Druids
(OBOD) 242, 248, 253, 255–58
passim
Order of the Universal Bond *see*
Ancient Druid Order
Ordnance Survey 47, 65
Ordo Templi Orientis ritual magic 194
Orphic bowl 196, 198
Orphic mysteries 196, 198, 201
Orr, Emma Restall 249
Ovid (poet) 196, 197
Owain, and Arthurian legend 44
Oxford University Press 43

Packwood House, Warwickshire 25
Padel, Oliver 55, 56, 57
Pagan Federation 293
Pagan witchcraft 270, 278, 290
Hutton's study of 288
research into development of 267,
271
Paganism
and Christianity 177, 225, 237
conferences 272, 273, 278
development of 128–29
Egypt and 87, 182
and magic 260
membership 283
and Pletho 174
and reconciliation with Christianity
189, 190, 191, 243
in Tolkien 216
see also ancient Paganism; modern
Paganism

Pagans Hill Pagan temple 82
pagus 249
Palaeolithic cave art 1, 33, 34
Palestine 112
Palmer, Roy 25
Paolini, Fabio 184
Papal Index 184
paranormal phenomena 64, 277
Paris, France 162, 189
Parnell, Charles Stewart 10
Patrick, St 55, 66, 72, 73
    birthplace 74, 78
    burial 74
    confusion with other names 72, 73, 74
    relics 72, 74
    shrine (Glastonbury Abbey) 60
Patrizi, Francesco 184–85
Patterson, Jacki 252
Paul II, Pope 177
Paul V, Pope 184
Pearse, Patrick 11
Pearson, Joanne 261, 265, 272, 288
Peek, Philip 287
Pendragon, Arthur Uther 252–53, 254,
    257
Pendragon Society 47
pentagram 165
perceived orthodoxy 30
Peredur, and Arthurian legend 44
Persia 113, 138, 152, 182
Peru 212
Peter of Abano 162, 178, 181, 184
Peters, Francis 150
Petroc, St 74
Philip the apostle 60
Philips, Charles Robert 105
Philosophical Christianity 130
philosophy, in Byzantium 170
philosophy, Pagan 173
Phryne (courtesan) 199
Physis (Greek) *see* Natura
Picatrix (*Ghaya*) 160, 172, 176, 178, 191
Pico della Mirandola, Giovanni 180, 181
Pico, Giovanni Francesco 183

Pierfrancesco, Lorenzo di 179, 181
Piggott, Stuart 243
Pilgrimage of Grace 61–62
Pinch, Geraldine 112
Pingree, David 155, 156, 157, 158
Pinturicchio (artist) 181
Pius II, Pope 175
planetary magic 162–63, 178, 182–84,
    187, 190
Plato 91–92, 108, 126, 175
    and astrology 157
    and heavenly bodies 159
    magical numbers 178
    quotation from 146
    on Venus 168, 179
Platonism 145, 171, 174, 177
    in Narnian novels 225
    in Tolkien 229
Pletho (Plethon, Georgio Gemistos)
    173–76, 179, 180
Pliny ('the elder') 108, 166, 197, 210
Plotinus 91, 94, 108, 121, 134
    concept of World Soul 178
    on ritual nudity 198
Poe, Edgar Allen 15
Polynesia 12–13, 21, 31
    and ritual nudity 205, 206
polytheism 88, 89, 90, 92, 94
    and Harran 147
    and Islam 140
    and Pletho 174
Pontano (author) 183
Pontefract, Yorkshire 24
Ponter's Ball earthworks 66, 76–77, 79
Popish Plot 28
popular memory 18–26
popular tradition 27
Porphyry (philosopher) 91, 92, 98,
    121–22, 178
pottery 45, 46
    at Glastonbury Tor 48
    at Ponter's Ball earthwork 76
    at South Cadbury 46
    at Tintagel 46

Powys, John Cowper 65
Price, Simon 104
Prichard, Thomas Jeffrey Llewelyn 6–7, 14
Priddy circle 82
Pritchard, David 16
Proclus (philosopher) 92, 93, 125–27, 144, 189
  his biographer 128
  On Priestly Art 178
  studies on 131
Prophecies of Baba the Harranian 140
Protestantism 8, 9, 10, 22, 62
Prudentius (author) 97
Psellus, Michael 127, 131, 170–72
Ptolemy *Opus imaginum* 162
Punk culture 52, 53
Pure Brethren (Ikhwan al-Safa) 147
Puttick, Elizabeth 288
Pyramid Texts 110
Pythagoras 147, 242

Quakers 210
Quedlinburg, Germany 30

Radford, C. A. Ralegh 45, 53, 72, 75, 81
  excavates Abbey precinct 66
  forms Camelot Research Committee 46
  on Glastonbury Abbey 48, 53, 75
  on Ponter's Ball 77
  on Tintagel and Castle Dore 48, 55
'radical participation' 287, 290
Raglan Castle, Monmouthshire 26
Rahtz, Philip 47, 48, 50, 51, 55
  70th birthday 57
  excavation of Chalice Well 76
  excavation of the Tor 79
  on Glastonbury 84
  on Ponter's Ball 77
Raleigh, Sir Walter 15, 39
Ravenna, Italy 159
Rawlinson, Colonel (royalist) 25
Rawlinson, Thomas (Quaker) 2

reactivity 259, 262, 269
Red Book of Hergest 7
reflexivity 259, 269, 271, 291, 294
Regardie, Irael 131
religion
  conversion to Christianity 137
  and cosmology 179
  of Harran 151
  in Ikhwan al-Safa writings 147
  Mithras 143
  of the Roman Empire 88
  of the Sabians 141, 174
  and satanic witchcraft 202
  in Somerset 62
  and voodoo 213
  Wicca in England 279
  and witchcraft 264
religion and magic 98–112, 116–18, 170, 209
religious studies 288, 289, 290
Remy, Nicholas 202
Renault, Mary 226
research 32, 36, 267–74 *passim*, 289
  among British witches 264
  Camelot Research Committee 46–47
  dilemmas 284
  objectivity in 285
  reactivity in 262
  Society for Psychical Research 276
'revisionism,' 51
Richard I, Coeur de Lion, King of England 68
Ricks, Stephen 105
Rimini, Italy 175
Rio, Martin del 202, 204
rites of passage 199, 206, 207
Ritner, Robert 111
ritual magic 164, 165, 178, 185, 192
  developments in 172
  and nudity 194
  and Psellus 171
  surviving copies of 190
ritual nudity 193–214
Roberts, Anthony 67–68

Robertson, Olivia 246, 247, 249
Roman Empire 93, 95, 98, 113, 117
    creation of 89
    disintegration of 94
    religions 88
Romania 211
Rome 102, 110, 196
    Santa Maria del Popolo church 183
Ronan, Stephen 119
Rosenfeld, André 34
Roskoff, Gustav 30
Rupert, Prince 25–26
Russell, Geoffrey 66
Russell, George 10, 11, 237, 239, 243
    member of Golden Dawn 245
Ryan, J. S. 215

Sabianism 141, 142, 150, 157
Sabians of Harran 141, 145, 146, 147,
    157
    in *Fihrist el-Ulum* 142
    and Hermetism 174
    and magical lore 154
    religion of 141, 174
    rites of 156
    Tamara Green on 150
    see also Harran
sacrifice ritual 135
St Alban's Abbey, Hertfordshire 60
St Joseph's Well, Glastonbury 76
Salmon of Wisdom legend 64
Salomensen, Jone 288, 291
Salutius/Sallustius (philosopher) 89,
    131, 132, 134
Samoa, Polynesia 31, 32, 206
Sanders, Alex 283
Sanserverino, Giulo 177, 181
al-Sarakhsi, Ahmad ibn al-Tayyib 142,
    148
Satanism 131
Saul, King of the Hebrews 209–10
Scandinavia 137
Scarisbrick, Jack 284
Schellinks, William 27

Scheltema, Jacobus 30
schism within Druids 257
Schliemann, Heinrich 47, 49
Scholarius, George 173
scientific truth concept 289
Scot, Michael 161
Scotland 2–5, 43, 78, 211
Scott, Sir Walter 3, 14–15
Scropton, Staffordshire 24
Seattle, Chief 15
Sebastian, Tim 250–57 *passim*
Second Romantic Movement 50, 51,
    56
Secular Order of Druids (SOD) 250,
    251, 253, 255, 256
Sedgemoor, battle of 62
Segal, Alan 16, 104, 105, 118
Seneca (philosopher) 108
Servius (author) 96, 98
Seymour, Charles 131
Shallcrass, Philip 249, 255, 256, 257
shamanism 289, 294
shamans 208, 246, 249
Sharp, William 64
Shaw, Gregory 118
Sheffield Equalised Order of Druids 240
Sheldon, Gilbert 43
Sheppard, Anne 126
Shepton Mallet, Somerset 82
Sherborne, Somerset 83
Shippey, Tom 231, 233, 234
Siberia 208
Siculus, Diodorus 197
Sidonius Apollinaris (poet) 97
Signorelli, Luca 185
Silvester, Bernard 159, 166, 168, 219,
    226
Simes, Amy 288
Simplicius (Greek commentator) 139
Simpson, Jacqueline 25, 28
Siorvanes, Lucas 127
Sixtus V, Pope 184
Sixtus VI, Pope 177
Smith, A. S. D. 12

Smith, Jonathan Z. 105
Smith, Richard 104
Smith, Rowland 118, 119, 121
social mobility 160
Society for Psychical Research 276
SOD (Secular Order of Druids) 250, 251, 253, 255, 256
Somerset 24, 46, 62, 82, 83
  South Cadbury hill-fort 46–51, 53, 57, 78
Somerset Archaeolgical Society 63
Somerton, Somerset 83
Sorcerer of Trois-Frères 33, 34
South Cadbury hill-fort, Somerset 46–51, 53, 57, 78
Spain 93
Spanish Armada 22
Spanish Inquisition 15
Spenser, Edmund 185
Stanton Drew stone circle 82
Starhawk (witch) 133
Stayt, Hugh 207
Steeple Gidding, Huntingdonshire 24
Stella Matutina ritual magic 194
Stewart, Charles *A Visit to the South Seas* 13
Stewart, David 3–4
Stock, Brian 166
Stoicism 157
Stone Age art 33
Stonehenge, Wiltshire 80, 240, 251, 252, 256
  access to 253, 255
  midsummer festival 250
Stukely, William 82
Sudheer, Revd Swami Prem 244
Sufism 152, 242
Sumaria 195
Sumatar Harabesi (archaeological site) 151
sun-worship 89, 91, 92
Sweden 211
symbolism 2, 3, 5
Symmachus (senator) 89, 90, 92

Synge, John Millington 10, 11
Syria 89, 92, 117, 124, 152
  Qasr al-'Amra excavations 140
Syrian texts 93

al-Tabari 156
Taipi–vai valley, Nuku-Hiva 13
Tannhäuser 169
Tanzania 208
Tardieu, Michel 138
tartan kilts 2–5
Taunton, Somerset 83
Thabit (Abu al-Hasan Tabith ibn Qurrah) 145, 146, 158, 162
The Reformation 51–52
'The Sorcerer' (Palaeolithic cave art) 33, 34, 35
Themistius (orator) 89, 90, 92
Theosophical Society 245
Theosophy 241, 245
theurgy 117–18, 120, 122–29, 131, 164
  and Christianity 171
Thierry, Augustin 15
Thomas, Charles 50, 54, 56, 57, 58
Thomassen, Einar 116
Tibet 245
Tintagel Castle, Cornwall 45, 46, 55, 56, 58
Tintagel library 56
Tolkien, Christopher 227
Tolkien, J. R. R. 215, 235, 237
  Paganism in 216
  reading 226–27
  religion 226, 235
  works 227, 228, 229, 230, 231, 232, 233, 234, 235
    The Hobbit 227, 230, 231
    The Lord of the Rings 227, 230, 231, 232, 233, 234, 235, 236
    The Silmarillion 227, 236
Tone, Wolfe 10
Tours, France 166
traditional belief 28
transubstantiation 159

tree of the holy thorn (*Cratagus Oxyacantha Praecox*) 69
Treharne, R. F. 84
trespass laws 254
Trevor-Roper, Hugh 2
Trigg, Grace 25
trinities 91, 179, 187, 223
  pagan 89, 213
Tristan, and Arthurian legend 44, 45, 48, 56
Trithemius, Johannes 183
Triumph of the Moon, The: A History of Modern Pagan Witchcraft (Hutton) 259, 260, 272, 280, 294
  published 279
  reactions to 282–83
  reviews 281, 283–84
Trois-Frères cave, France 33, 34
Turlupins (French sect) 201
Turner, Edith 287
Tutbury Castle, Staffordshire 24
Twm Sion Cati (poet and genealogist) 13–14
Tylor, Sir Edward 106, 107

Ucko, Peter 34
Uganda 209
Ulmi, Antonious de Monte 163, 165
Umar II, Caliph 141
Umayyad Caliphs 147
United Ancient Order of Druids 240
United Irishmen 10
United States of America *see* America
universal divinity (Prime Mover, Grand Architect) 241
Universal Druid Order 255
Urban VIII, Pope 188

Vale of Taunton Deane 79
Valiente, Doreen 132, 267, 283
Vansina, Jan 70
Venus (goddess) 97, 166, 168–69, 179, 180
Versnel, H. S. 101, 109

Vikings 22
Villa of the Mysteries of Pompeii 196
Virgin Mary 192
Voltair, François Marie 30
voodoo 213

Waddington, Mr (merchant) 6
Wagner, Gunter 207
Wales 5–8, 22–23, 40, 78, 246
  folklore 13–14
  literary fiction 15, 16, 17
  medieval texts 255
  pottery finds 46
Walker, D. P. 179
wall-paintings 196, 199
Waller, Sir William 25
Wallis, Robert 289
Wallis, R. T. 118, 126
Wansdyke (defensive earthwork) 55
Waugh, Evelyn 215, 237
Wax, Murray and Rosalie 99–100
Welsh Manuscripts Society 7
Westcott, William Wynn 130
Western Mysteries Tradition 245, 246
Wexford, Eire 9
Wheeler, Sir Mortimer 47, 49, 50
Whitby, Yorkshire 28, 79
Whiting, Richard, Abbot 61
Wicca 129, 131–35 *passim*, 193–200 *passim*, 279–80
  in America 266
  and Christianity 285
  contemporary 261
  development of 26, 282
  liturgy 266
  research on 267, 268
  and ritual nudity 209, 212, 213
  stereotypes 207
William of Auvergne 161, 162, 165
William of Conches 159, 166
William of Malmesbury 71
William of Newburgh 39
Williams, Edward (Iolo Morganwg) 6, 12

Wilson, Steve 255
Wirrall Hill, Glastonbury 62, 82
witch trials 30, 31
witchcraft 110, 130, 132, 135, 165
    artists' portrayals of 203
    enemies 273
    foundation myth 265
    histiography of 265
    images of 204
    persecution 264
    and ritual nudity 211
    satanic 202
    spells 276
    stereotypes 207, 208, 209, 212, 260
women 31, 212, 249, 286
Woodroffe, Sir John 205
Woodruff, Una 252

Wordsworth, William 12
World Soul 178, 179, 192
Wynne-Davis, Marion 7

Y Gododdin (poem), and Arthurian
    legend 41, 44
Yates, Frances 179, 180, 181, 184, 186,
    188
Yeats, William Butler 10, 11, 237, 239,
    268–69
    member of Golden Dawn 245
York, Michael 265
Yorkshire 24, 28, 41, 79

Zambia 287
Ziarnko, Jan 204
Zoe, Empress of Byzantium 171